David
Na
Kalamaz

THE
STRUGGLE FOR
EQUALITY

ABOLITIONISTS AND THE NEGRO
IN THE CIVIL WAR
AND RECONSTRUCTION

THE STRUGGLE FOR EQUALITY

ABOLITIONISTS AND THE NEGRO
IN THE CIVIL WAR
AND RECONSTRUCTION

———

BY JAMES M. MC PHERSON

PRINCETON, NEW JERSEY
PRINCETON UNIVERSITY PRESS

THIS BOOK IS DEDICATED
TO ALL THOSE
WHO ARE WORKING TO ACHIEVE
THE ABOLITIONIST GOAL
OF EQUAL RIGHTS FOR ALL MEN

PREFACE

MOST historians have paid little attention to the abolitionist movement after 1860. Yet it was in the 1860's that the abolitionist crusade reached the height of its power and saw the achievement of most of its objectives. After the outbreak of the Civil War, abolitionists were transformed almost overnight from despised fanatics to influential and respected spokesmen for the radical wing of the Republican party. Early in the war, abolitionists outlined a broad program of emancipation, employment of Negro soldiers in the Union Army, creation of a Freedmen's Bureau, government assistance for the education of the freedmen, civil and political equality for all black men, and grants of confiscated land to the freed slaves. Under the military pressures of war and the political pressures of reconstruction, the Republican party adopted all of these policies except the wholesale confiscation of southern plantations. True, the North retreated from radicalism after 1870 and failed to enforce the provisions of Reconstruction after 1877, but the equalitarian achievements of the Civil War and Reconstruction remained in the Constitution and the statute books, where they constitute today the legal basis for the "Second Reconstruction" of the South.

Despite the prominence of abolitionists during the war and reconstruction years, standard historical treatments of the antislavery movement virtually ignore the period after 1860. The implicit assumption is that abolitionism merged itself with the Republican party during the war and therefore no longer possessed a separate identity or purpose. Garrison's willingness to cease publication of his *Liberator* and to dissolve the antislavery societies in 1865 is deemed proof that abolitionists considered the Thirteenth Amendment the consummation of their crusade and were little concerned with the Negro after emancipation. Nothing could be more misleading. It is true that for the first time in their lives, abolitionists marched in step with a major political party after 1861. But they marched far in advance of the Republican party, and frequently the party refused to follow them as fast as they desired. At such times they would chastise the Republicans with old-time vigor and abandon. Throughout the 1860's most abolitionists preserved their separate identity, and cooperated with the Republican party only when that party was marching in the direction they wanted to go. Abolitionists showed a greater concern for the plight of the Negro after 1865 than anyone else except the Negro himself. The American Anti-Slavery Society and its auxiliaries remained in existence after the war to wage battle for the full civil and political equality of the Negro. Even Garrison, despite his withdrawal from the antislavery societies in 1865, did not consider his crusade ended when the slave was freed. Along with many other abolitionists, he was active in the movement to educate the freedmen, and his denunciations of racial discrimination were no less militant after 1865 than before.

This book is an effort to trace the history of the abolitionist movement during the Civil War and Reconstructon, to evaluate the contribution of abolitionists to the efforts to solve the race problem in those years, and to view America's greatest social and political revolution through the eyes of the nation's foremost equalitarians. No claim will be made that the abolitionists were primarily responsible for the gains of the Negro in the war and reconstruction. Abolitionists did not forge or control events; but neither was their influence negligible. In many respects the abolitionists served as the conscience of the radical Republicans. They provided an idealistic-moral-humanitarian justification for the policies of the Republican party—policies which were undertaken primarily for military or political reasons. The ideas, activities, and responses of abolitionists during a period when their movement reached its climax are not without historical interest.

I am indebted to the following library staffs: the American Antiquarian Society, Worcester, Massachusetts; the Boston Public Library; the Columbia University Library; the Concord Public Library, Concord, Massachusetts; the Cornell University Library; the Frederick Douglass Memorial Home, Anacostia Heights, Washington, D.C.; the Essex Institute Library, Salem, Massachusetts; the Houghton Library, Harvard University; the Johns Hopkins University Library, especially the interlibrary loan division; the Library of Congress; the Massachusetts Historical Society; the New York Historical Society; the New York Public Library; the Pierpont Morgan Library, New York City; the Radcliffe Women's Archives, Radcliffe College; the Rochester

University Library; the Smith College Library; the Syracuse University Library; the Vermont Historical Society, Montpelier, Vermont; the Wayland Historical Society, Wayland, Massachusetts; and the Worcester Historical Society, Worcester, Massachusetts. They were very kind and I wish to thank them for assistance in locating materials and for permission to quote from manuscripts in their possession.

I owe a special debt of gratitude to Professor C. Vann Woodward, whose advice and counsel proved valuable at every stage of this work. I wish also to thank Professor David Donald, Professor Martin Duberman, and Mrs. Willie Rose, all of whom read the entire manuscript and made helpful suggestions. The encouragement and assistance of my wife, Patricia McPherson, has been inestimable from the first conception of this project to its final completion.

James M. McPherson

Department of History
Princeton University
Princeton, New Jersey

CONTENTS

Preface   vii

Key to Abbreviations   xii

Introduction   3

I.   The Election of 1860   9

II.   Secession and the Coming of War   29

III.   The Emancipation Issue: 1861   52

IV.   Emancipation and Public Opinion:
        1861-1862   75

V.   The Emancipation Proclamation and the
        Thirteenth Amendment   99

VI.   The Negro: Innately Inferior or Equal?   134

VII.   Freedmen's Education: 1861-1865   154

VIII.   The Creation of the Freedmen's Bureau   178

IX.   *Men of Color, to Arms!*   192

X.   The Quest for Equal Rights in the North   221

XI.   The Ballot and Land for the Freedmen:
        1861-1865   238

XII.   The Reelection of Lincoln   260

XIII.   Schism in the Ranks: 1864-1865   287

XIV.   Andrew Johnson and Reconstruction: 1865   308

XV.   The Fourteenth Amendment and the
        Election of 1866   341

XVI.   Military Reconstruction and Impeachment   367

XVII.   Education and Confiscation: 1865-1870   386

XVIII. The Climax of the Crusade: the Fifteenth
        Amendment   417

Bibliographical Essay   433

Index   451

KEY TO ABBREVIATIONS

The following symbols are used in the footnotes to designate repositories of manuscript collections:

AAS . . . . . American Antiquarian Society, Worcester, Massachusetts

BPL . . . . . Boston Public Library

CU . . . . . Columbia University Library

Cornell . . . Cornell University Library

HU . . . . . Houghton Library, Harvard University

LC . . . . . Library of Congress

MHS . . . . Massachusetts Historical Society

NYHS . . . . New York Historical Society

NYPL . . . . New York Public Library

PML . . . . Pierpont Morgan Library, New York City

RU . . . . . Rochester University Library

SC . . . . . Smith College Library

SU . . . . . Syracuse University Library

VHS . . . . . Vermont Historical Society, Montpelier

The following abbreviation is used in the footnotes to designate the *National Anti-Slavery Standard*, organ of the American Anti-Slavery Society: *N.A.S. Standard*.

THE
STRUGGLE FOR
EQUALITY

ABOLITIONISTS AND THE NEGRO
IN THE CIVIL WAR
AND RECONSTRUCTION

INTRODUCTION

IN this study the term "abolitionist" will be applied to those Americans who before the Civil War had agitated for immediate, unconditional, and universal abolition of slavery in the United States. Contemporaries of the antislavery movement and later historians have sometimes mistakenly used the word "abolitionist" to describe adherents of the whole spectrum of antislavery sentiment. Members of the Free Soil and Republican parties have often been called abolitionists, even though these parties were pledged officially before 1861 only to the limitation of slavery, not to its extirpation. It is a moot question whether such radical antislavery leaders as Charles Sumner, John Andrew, George Julian, Thaddeus Stevens, or Owen Lovejoy were genuine "abolitionists." In their hearts they probably desired an immediate end to slavery as fervently as did William Lloyd Garrison. But they were committed publicly by political affiliation and party responsibility to a set of principles that fell short of genuine abolitionism. The names of Sumner, Julian, and other radical Republicans will crop up frequently in this book, for they were closely connected with the activities of abolitionists during the Civil War and Reconstruction. No attempt will be made, however, to settle the question whether Sumner, for example, was an authentic abolitionist. The focus of this study will be upon those men and women who made no apologies for their radicalism and who crusaded militantly for immediate, unconditional, and universal emancipation.

In 1860 there were three loosely defined and somewhat interrelated abolitionist groups in the North. First and most prominent in the eyes of the public were the Garrisonians—the members of the American Anti-Slavery Society and its auxiliaries. The Garrisonians had a more cohesive and active organization than any of the other genuine abolitionist groups, and many of the ablest writers and speakers in the movement were affiliated with them. William Lloyd Garrison was widely regarded as the pioneer and leader of the militant abolitionist crusade. Wendell Phillips was universally acknowledged to be one of the finest platform speakers in the nation. In addition the American Anti-Slavery Society

3

contained a host of lesser luminaries who were fairly well known to the antislavery public: Lydia Maria Child, Theodore Tilton, Edmund Quincy, Parker Pillsbury, Oliver Johnson, Abby and Stephen S. Foster, Elizabeth Cady Stanton, Susan B. Anthony, Sydney Howard Gay, James and Lucretia Mott, Samuel J. May, Robert Purvis, James Miller McKim, and many others.

The Garrisonians were small in number, but their influence and their impact on public opinion cannot be measured by size alone. The radicalism of their doctrines, the vehemence of their language, and the prominence of their leaders gave them an audience and a notoriety far out of proportion to their numbers. This small army of talented and articulate reformers was active primarily in the eastern states. New England, of course, was the center of Garrisonian abolitionism. The *Liberator* was published in Boston. Eleven of the twelve members of the American Anti-Slavery Society's executive committee were from New England (the twelfth was from New York). The Massachusetts Anti-Slavery Society was the most vigorous auxiliary of the national organization. But there were pockets of Garrisonian strength elsewhere. Oliver Johnson, Theodore Tilton, and Sydney Howard Gay formed the core of a small group of Garrisonians in New York City. Johnson edited there the *National Anti-Slavery Standard*, organ of the American Anti-Slavery Society. In Philadelphia there were two Garrisonian organizations: the Pennsylvania Anti-Slavery Society, led by J. Miller McKim, James and Lucretia Mott, and Robert Purvis; and the Philadelphia Female Anti-Slavery Society, dominated by Mary Grew and Sarah Pugh. Scattered through parts of upstate New York were several active Garrisonians who constituted the leadership of the New York Anti-Slavery Society: Samuel J. May, Aaron M. Powell, Elizabeth Cady Stanton, and Susan B. Anthony. Finally, in the Western Reserve of Ohio there existed another outpost of Garrisonianism: Marius Robinson edited there the *Anti-Slavery Bugle*, organ of the near-moribund Western Anti-Slavery Society, and Giles B. Stebbins and Josephine S. Griffing headed the lecture corps of these western Garrisonians.

The second group of abolitionists active in 1860 is more difficult to delineate. Roughly it consisted of those who, for one reason or another, had broken with Garrison in 1840, but who had

nevertheless refused to submerge their abolitionist identity in the
Free Soil or Republican parties. Of the men who had founded
the Liberty party in 1840, some had died and many had been
absorbed by the Republican party, but an indomitable remnant
of political abolitionists had refused to adulterate their beliefs
with the pale antislavery doctrines of the Republican party, and
had kept the Liberty party alive through the 1850's. In 1860
they called their organization the Radical Abolitionist party.
They proclaimed the constitutional right and duty of the
federal government to abolish slavery in the states. Leaders of
this party were Gerrit Smith, William Goodell, and Frederick
Douglass. The center of their strength was in upstate New York,
and the party organ, the *Principia*, was edited in New York City
by Goodell.

Closely allied with the Radical Abolitionists was the Church
Anti-Slavery Society, successor of Lewis Tappan's American and
Foreign Anti-Slavery Society which had died a quiet death in the
1850's. The Church Anti-Slavery Society was founded in 1859
by a Connecticut Congregationalist minister, Henry Cheever, and
his more famous brother, George Cheever, pastor of the Church of
the Puritans in New York City. The Cheever brothers hoped to
convert the northern Protestant clergy to the doctrine of immediate and unconditional emancipation, but the radicalism of
the Society, and its insistence that slaveholding as well as slavery
was a sin, alienated most of the northern clergy. No more than a
few hundred members, mostly Congregational and Presbyterian
ministers in New England, New York, and the upper tier of
western states, ever belonged to the Society, and its influence
was limited. Many members of the Society were also adherents of
the Radical Abolitionist party, and Goodell's *Principia* doubled
as an unofficial organ of the Church Anti-Slavery Society.

Another abolitionist-controlled organization, informally associated with the Radical Abolitionist party and the Church Anti-
Slavery Society, was the American Missionary Association. Organized by Lewis Tappan, George Whipple, and Simeon S.
Jocelyn in 1846, the A.M.A. was ostensibly nonsectarian, but in
reality it was dominated by Congregationalists. It organized anti-
slavery churches in the West and in Kentucky, carried on mission
work in Africa, and in 1855 founded Berea College in Kentucky.

In 1860 the A.M.A. was small, with its major work of freedmen's education still in the future.

The third major grouping of abolitionists is almost impossible to define precisely. Speaking broadly, one might say that it consisted of all those who advocated the immediate, unconditional, and universal abolition of slavery, but who did not belong to any of the formal abolitionist organizations described in the preceding paragraphs. This included a majority of the old Liberty party stalwarts who had followed Henry B. Stanton, Joshua Leavitt, and Elizur Wright into the Free Soil party in 1848 and ultimately into the Republican party. Most of the western political abolitionists had pursued this course and had almost completely submerged their abolitionist identity in the weaker antislavery principles of the Republican party. Yet they remained militant and uncompromising in their basic abolitionist beliefs.

A subgrouping of abolitionists who do not fall readily within any organizational framework were the supporters of John Brown. The most famous members of this group were the "Secret Six" who had subsidized Brown's campaigns in Kansas and his abortive invasion of Virginia. Of these six, Theodore Parker had died and Gerrit Smith has been classified with another group, but the other four remained very much alive and were destined to play important roles in the drama of the Civil War: George L. Stearns, wealthy Boston lead-pipe manufacturer; Samuel Gridley Howe, world-famous for his work with the blind; and the young, romantic intellectuals, Thomas Wentworth Higginson and Frank Sanborn. All four were from Massachusetts. James Redpath and Richard J. Hinton, British-born radicals who had known John Brown in Kansas and who later published biographies of Old Ossawatomie, also lived in the Bay State.

In fact, Massachusetts was by far the most radical antislavery state in the Union. In addition to being the center of Garrisonian activity, Massachusetts was the home of many of the prominent non-Garrisonian abolitionists, and the state boasted two of the strongest antislavery senators in Congress, Charles Sumner and Henry Wilson. The center of this antislavery political power was a small, informal organization known as the Bird Club. The Bird Club originated about 1850 when a group of radical leaders of the Massachusetts Free Soil party began meeting together in

Boston on Saturday afternoons for dinner and long, confidential political discussions. Host on these occasions was Frank Bird, an East Walpole paper manufacturer and radical Free Soiler. Sumner, Wilson, and John Andrew, the famous war governor of Massachusetts, were members of this club, and as the decade progressed it became more and more powerful until by 1860 it virtually controlled the state's Republican party. For the next twelve years the Bird Club ruled Massachusetts politics. A majority of the men in the Club were probably not abolitionists according to the definition of that term used in this study, but a number of genuine abolitionists *did* belong to the Club. Stearns, Howe, Sanborn, Charles W. Slack, and other abolitionists were members, and exerted a strong influence on the Club's policies. Frank Bird himself presided over a disunion convention in 1857 organized by Garrisonians. Elizur Wright, who had served as secretary of the American Anti-Slavery Society in the 1830's and had helped found the Liberty party in 1840, was a member of the Bird Club. The line between abolitionist and Free Soiler was often blurred and indistinct in Massachusetts. If the Bird Club was not a formal abolitionist organization, it was the next thing to it.

There were also many abolitionists who did not belong to any definite antislavery organization, but who were nevertheless well known and influential in their communities and states: Dr. Henry I. Bowditch, Boston physician; James Freeman Clarke, Boston Unitarian minister; Levi Coffin, the Quaker "President" of the Underground Railroad in Cincinnati; Octavius B. Frothingham, liberal Unitarian minister and Transcendentalist intellectual of New York City; Gilbert Haven, a Massachusetts Methodist preacher and militant abolitionist; John Jay, wealthy grandson of the first chief justice; Samuel Sewall, Boston lawyer; John G. Whittier, beloved Quaker poet of Amesbury, Massachusetts; and Samuel Johnson of Lynn, Massachusetts, Unitarian minister and expert on Oriental religions. These were only a few of the scores of prominent men throughout the North who refused to identify themselves formally with any antislavery society, but who frequently appeared on abolitionist platforms and bore powerful testimony for freedom in their daily callings.

These various groups of abolitionists often differed on points of procedure or emphasis, but on the main objectives of the abolitionist crusade they were united. The crisis of the Civil War obscured most of their old academic disputes and caused them to close ranks, at least for a time, in the struggle for the freedom and equality of the Negro. The chapters that follow are the story of that struggle.

HE election of 1860 confronted Garrisonian abolitionists with a dilemma. For the first time an avowedly antislavery party had an excellent chance of winning the presidency. This intoxicating prospect was too much for some Garrisonians, especially those of the younger generation, who forsook the antipolitical traditions of the movement and gave positive support to Abraham Lincoln. A majority of Garrisonians, however, remained true to their principles, refused to give an explicit endorsement to the Republican party (though hoping for its victory), and criticized the party sharply for its antislavery shortcomings.

Garrisonians had always taken an ambivalent attitude toward antislavery political parties. In the 1840's Garrison and Phillips were not entirely displeased by the growth of the free soil coalition. "We look upon the Free Soil movement as the unavoidable result of our principles and agitation," declared Phillips in 1849, "and hail it so far as its formation gives proof of a wider spread of a degree of antislavery feeling in the community." But it remained nevertheless a *free soil* and not an abolitionist party, unworthy of genuine abolitionist support because it was not "pledged to trample underfoot the compromises of the Constitution."[1]

In 1856 many Garrisonians expressed sympathy for the Republican party and its dashing presidential candidate, John C. Frémont. From 1856 to 1860 there was a growing debate within the American Anti-Slavery Society over the attitude abolitionists should take toward the Republican party. Some Garrisonians became outright Republicans. Most of them, however, continued to shun politics, watching the course of the Republicans critically but sympathetically. In 1859 Garrison accused the Republican party of being a "timeserving, a temporizing, a cowardly party," but found some hope in the fact that it possessed "materials for growth."[2]

[1] *Liberator*, Feb. 2, 1849. See also William Lloyd Garrison to Henry Wilson, May 2, 1872, Garrison Papers, BPL.

[2] *Liberator*, Feb. 4, 1859. For a discussion of Garrison's attitude toward the rise of antislavery political parties, see John L. Thomas, *The Liberator: William Lloyd Garrison* (Boston, 1963), 325-26, 342-43, 388-89; and Walter M. Merrill, *Against Wind and Tide: A Biography of William Lloyd Garrison* (Cambridge, Mass., 1963), 212-14, 273-74.

In the left wing of the Society there was a group of contentious radicals, led by Parker Pillsbury, Stephen S. Foster, and his wife Abby Kelley Foster, who insisted on condemning the Republican party as no better than any other party. They considered Republicans "the greatest obstacles to the spread of anti-slavery" because the party stood for little more than the exclusion of slavery from the sparsely populated territories. Pillsbury charged that the weak-kneed policy of the party made it "*really* more dangerous to the cause of liberty . . . than any other party ever formed since the foundations of government were laid."[3]

Garrisonians carried their love-hate complex toward the Republican party into the 1860 presidential campaign. Prior to the Chicago convention it appeared that 1860 might be a year of abolitionist-Republican cooperation. William H. Seward seemed to have the nomination in hand, and for a decade Seward had been one of the brightest stars on the antislavery political horizon. A

Masthead of the *Liberator*.

week before the Republican convention Wendell Phillips declared that "the Republican party, so far as it has a heart, means to grapple slavery, and to strangle it. . . . When William H. Seward enters the Presidential chair, he means that his portrait . . . shall be painted with one hand upon the American eagle, and the other on the jugular vein of the slave system."[4]

[3] *Liberator*, Mar. 28, 1856, June 5, 1857. See also Abby K. Foster to Wendell Phillips, June 24, 1859, Foster Papers, AAS; and Maria W. Chapman to Sydney H. Gay, n.d., but probably written sometime in 1859, Sydney H. Gay Papers, CU.
[4] *Liberator*, May 18, 1860.

But to the surprise and disappointment of most eastern anti-slavery men, Seward was shunted aside for a relatively obscure politician from the Illinois prairies. Eastern abolitionists knew little about Lincoln, and as they searched his record they found little to commend. In his 1854 speech at Peoria, Lincoln had made a revealing statement on the subject of slavery: "If all earthly power were given me, I should not know what to do, as to the existing institution. My first impulse would be to free all the slaves, and send them to Liberia,—to their own native land. But . . . [this] is impossible. . . . What then? Free them, and make them politically and socially, our equals? My own feelings will not admit of this; and if mine would, we well know that those of the great mass of white people will not." In his debates with Stephen Douglas in 1858, Lincoln proclaimed that "I have no purpose directly or indirectly to interfere with the institution of slavery in the States where it exists. I believe I have no lawful right to do so, and I have no inclination to do so." He reasserted his opposition to the unconditional repeal of the fugitive slave law and to immediate and unconditional emancipation in the District of Columbia.[5]

Such sentiments could hardly endear Lincoln to abolitionists. But antislavery Republicans could also point to statements by Lincoln revealing a deep-rooted moral abhorrence of slavery. In 1858 he had branded the institution as "a moral, social and political wrong . . . an unqualified evil to the negro, to the white man, to the soil, and to the State." In his famous "House Divided" speech Lincoln expressed the belief that "this Government cannot endure, permanently half *slave* and half *free*." He hoped that "the *opponents* of slavery, will arrest the further spread of it, and place it where the public mind shall rest in the belief that it is in the course of ultimate extinction."[6]

Abolitionists were understandably perplexed about this man Lincoln. He was plainly *against* slavery, but he was just as plainly not *for* its immediate and total abolition. The *Annual Report* of the American Anti-Slavery Society considered Lincoln "a good enough Republican for the party's purposes, but far from being

<hr>

[5] Roy P. Basler, ed., *The Collected Works of Abraham Lincoln* (9 vols., New Brunswick, N.J., 1955), II, 255-56, III, 16, 41-42.
[6] *ibid.*, III, 92, II, 461.

the man for the country's need." He was "a sort of bland, respectable middle-man, between a very modest Right and the most arrogant and exacting Wrong; a convenient hook whereon to hang appeals at once to a *moderate* anti-slavery feeling and to a timid conservatism."[7]

"Who is this huckster in politics?" asked Wendell Phillips a few days after Lincoln's nomination. "Who is this county court advocate? Who is this who does not know whether he has got any opinions?" The *National Anti-Slavery Standard*, official organ of the American Anti-Slavery Society, warned abolitionists that they could not "without utter self-stultification, vote for a man who is opposed to allowing the negro the rights of citizenship . . . and opposed to the unqualified abolition of Slavery in the District of Columbia." Edmund Quincy, the urbane, witty associate editor of the *Standard*, remarked acidly in June 1860, that for the next few months the country would be flooded with political oratory, mass meetings, tons of campaign pamphlets, and when it was all over the result would be "the election of a new administration pledged to the support of slavery in our Southern States, and this equally, whether success be to the Democrats or the Republicans."[8]

The Republican party made careful efforts to dissociate itself from public identification with the abolitionists and their doctrines. During the campaign Republicans frequently declared themselves the true "white man's party." Horace Greeley proclaimed that the Republican party "contemplates PRIMARILY the interest of Free White Labor, for which it struggles to secure the unoccupied territory of the Union." Democratic orators charged that Republicans intended to abolish slavery as soon as they had a chance. "That is not so," roared Greeley. "Never on earth did the Republican Party propose to abolish Slavery. . . . Its object with respect to Slavery is simply, nakedly, avowedly, its restriction to the existing states."[9]

Little wonder that abolitionists were sometimes disgusted with Republicans. "The Republican party means to do nothing, can

[7] *Twenty-Eighth Annual Report of the American Anti-Slavery Society, for the Year Ending May 1, 1861* (New York, 1861), 30-31.

[8] *Liberator*, June 8, 1860; *N.A.S. Standard*, June 2, 1860.

[9] *Liberator*, Oct. 5, 1860; *New York Tribune*, Sept. 7, 1860. See also Emerson D. Fite, *The Presidential Campaign of 1860* (New York, 1911), 124-25.

do nothing, for the abolition of slavery in the slave states," said Garrison. "The Republican party stands on a level with the Fugitive Slave law." Josephine Griffing complained that Republican leaders were covertly trying to discourage abolitionists from holding meetings during the campaign, for they feared such meetings might jeopardize Republican success. "Their great effort," wrote Mrs. Griffing, "is to convince the public mind that they are not Abolitionists, and the Abolitionists, that they *hate* slavery as much as they do. 'For by their sorceries were all nations deceived.' "[10]

The Pillsbury-Foster faction, traditionally hostile to Republicanism, attacked the party even more aggressively than did Garrison and Phillips. Under Pillsbury's influence the Western Anti-Slavery Society, meeting at Salem, Ohio, in late September, resolved that the Republicans were "committed to every constitutional compromise for slavery ever claimed by Calhoun or conceded by Webster . . . they are [unfit] to be entrusted with the interests of humanity and liberty."[11] In his attacks on Republicans, Pillsbury reasserted the conventional Garrisonian disunion views, but Stephen S. Foster went further and tried to organize an out-and-out abolitionist political party. Gadfly of the Garrisonians, Foster had for several years considered the disunion doctrine barren of promise for the slave. In 1860 Foster and John Pierpont, a Liberty party veteran, issued a call for a political abolitionist convention in Worcester, Massachusetts, in mid-September. The convention organized a new party to be known as "The Union Democratic Party" and adopted resolutions affirming that the Constitution, fairly interpreted, prohibited slavery in the *states* and gave the federal government ample power for its abolition therein. The new party made no nominations, but at Frederick Douglass' suggestion it extended "earnest sympathy and hearty Godspeed" to the Radical Abolitionist party and its presidential candidate, Gerrit Smith.[12]

10 *Liberator*, July 20, 1860; Josephine S. Griffing to Parker Pillsbury, Aug. 22, 1860, published in *Liberator*, Aug. 31. See also the resolutions adopted by the Vermont Anti-Slavery Society at its convention of October 17, 1860, in *Liberator*, Nov. 2, 1860.

11 *N.A.S. Standard*, Oct. 13, 20, 1860.

12 Stephen S. Foster to Elizabeth Cady Stanton, Aug. 21, 1860, E. C. Stanton Papers, LC; *Liberator*, Aug. 31, Sept. 28, Oct. 5, 1860.

Rejecting both the nonpolitical stance of Garrison and the political abolitionism of Foster, a number of Garrisonians actively campaigned and voted for Lincoln in 1860. These Republican Garrisonians included some of the ablest men in the Society: Theodore Tilton, vice president of the New York City Anti-Slavery Society and member of the editorial staff of the *New York Independent*; Sydney Howard Gay, the only non-Massachusetts member of the American Anti-Slavery Society's executive committee and editorial writer for the *New York Tribune*; David Lee Child, husband of Lydia Maria Child and an expert on the legal aspects of slavery; and Moncure D. Conway, Virginia-born abolitionist who in 1860 held a Unitarian pastorate in Cincinnati and edited a Unitarian-Transcendentalist magazine, *The Dial*. These four and several other prominent Garrisonians voted for Lincoln in 1860 on the ground that a Republican triumph would be indirectly a victory for the abolitionist cause.[13]

In Massachusetts, the Republican party gave abolitionists something to cheer about by nominating John A. Andrew for governor. Andrew was one of the most steadfast antislavery men in politics. He had helped raise money for John Brown's legal defense, and at a meeting in Boston a month after the Harper's Ferry raid, Andrew had said that he did not know whether John Brown's enterprise in Virginia was wise or foolish, right or wrong; "I only know that . . . JOHN BROWN HIMSELF IS RIGHT. (Applause) I sympathize with the man, I sympathize with the idea, because I sympathize with and believe in the eternal right."[14] Conservative Republicans in Massachusetts were opposed to Andrew, but the powerful Bird Club secured his nomination. Samuel Bowles, editor of the conservative *Springfield Republican*, groaned at the news of Andrew's nomination. "His John Brown sympathies and speeches, his Garrisonian affiliations, his negro-training predilections and all that sort of extreme anti-slaveryism, with which his record abounds, will be trumpeted far and wide in the state

---

[13] Theodore Tilton to William H. Seward, Oct. 10, 1860, Seward Papers, RU; *New York Tribune*, Oct. 30, 1860; Oliver Johnson to Samuel May, Jr., Aug. 18, 1860, Samuel May, Jr. Papers, BPL; David Lee Child to Gerrit Smith, July 23, 1864, Smith Papers, SU; Mary E. Burtis, *Moncure Conway* (New Brunswick, N.J., 1952), 76.

[14] *Liberator*, Sept. 21, 1860; Henry G. Pearson, *The Life of John A. Andrew* (2 vols., Boston, 1904), I, 100-101.

to injure him, [and] out of it to harm Lincoln," wrote Bowles.[15]

Andrew toned down his antislavery utterances during the campaign to make them conform with the Republican platform, but Garrisonians were nevertheless delighted by his nomination. Garrison declared that Andrew "represents the highest phase of political anti-slavery feeling as yet developed." One Massachusetts Republican appealed directly to Samuel May, Jr., general agent of the American Anti-Slavery Society, for Garrisonian support of Andrew. Abolitionists should vote for Andrew, he wrote, because many conservative Republicans would not, and it would look bad if Andrew ran behind Lincoln in Massachusetts. "If the Anti Slavery men of Mass. do not do this, they will surely lose all the sympathy they had outside of their immediate body, which I assure you is no small am[oun]t. Andrew has done everything he could for them, & the cause of John Brown, and they will be the most ungrateful of men" if they do not give him hearty support at the polls. May responded enthusiastically, and it is probable that many Garrisonians voted for Andrew.[16]

As the campaign progressed the Garrisonians' critical attitude toward Lincoln and the Republicans seemed to soften. In August, Garrison had written privately that "the election of Lincoln seems more and more probable. He will do nothing to offend the South." Seven weeks later, however, Garrison declared in the *Liberator* that because the Republican party stood for the exclusion of slavery from the territories, "it will do no slight service to the cause of freedom; and to that extent, and for that reason, it has our sympathies and best wishes." The *Annual Report* of the American Anti-Slavery Society was severe in its strictures of Republican shortcomings, but pointed out the other side of the coin as well. "It would be injustice to the party not to say," commented the *Report*, "that all through the campaign its presses and its speakers uttered many noble sentiments; exposed, with many words of earnest reprobation, the folly and the wrong of slavery. . . . So that, with all its serious defects, the canvass hardly can have failed to do good service to the cause of freedom."[17]

15 *Springfield Republican*, Aug. 30, 1860.

16 *Liberator*, Sept. 7, 1860; W. G. Weld to Samuel May, Jr., Oct. 24, 1860, May to Richard Webb, Nov. 6, 1860, Samuel May, Jr. Papers, BPL. Andrew ran about one thousand votes behind Lincoln in Massachusetts.

17 Garrison to Oliver Johnson, Aug. 9, 1860, Garrison Papers, BPL; *Liberator*,

The attitude of moderate Garrisonians toward the election was best illustrated by Oliver Johnson, editor of the *Anti-Slavery Standard*. Johnson thought that the Western Anti-Slavery Society had been crippled by Parker Pillsbury's fulminations against all Republicans. "Instead of allowing a fair margin for honest differences of opinion, and thus keeping on good terms with the better portion of the Republicans," wrote Johnson, the Western Society "has selected for special denunciation such men as Sumner, and thereby reduced itself needlessly & recklessly to a small faction of growlers." Despite the deficiencies of the Republican party, Johnson regarded its success "as the beginning of a new and better era. Let Stephen Foster and his sympathizers say what they will, to me it seems utterly preposterous to deny that Lincoln's election will indicate growth in the right direction."[18]

✦

Hostility toward the Republicans was greater within the Radical Abolitionist party than among Garrisonians. When invited in 1855 to join the antislavery coalition that was soon to blossom into the Republican party, Gerrit Smith scornfully replied: "I wish to have nothing to do with such trash as an anti-Nebraska party. If a disease is raging at my vitals I'd not wish a physician called to attend to a scratch on my little finger."[19] In 1856 the Radical Abolitionists nominated Smith for president on a platform calling for abolition of slavery in the states. Politically it was a forlorn gesture: Smith polled only 165 votes in the entire state of New York. But the Radical Abolitionists did not expect to win elections; they nominated candidates in order to keep their organization alive and to spread knowledge of their principles.[20]

One of the most prominent Radical Abolitionists was Frederick Douglass. In 1856, however, Douglass had dismayed his fellow party members by coming out publicly for Frémont. In 1860 there was little point in nominating Radical Abolitionist candidates unless Douglass could be persuaded to endorse the ticket, for without the support of New York's Negro voters the Radical

---

Sept. 28, 1860; *Twenty-Eighth Annual Report of the American Anti-Slavery Society*, 33-34.

[18] Johnson to J. Miller McKim, Nov. 8, Oct. 11, 1860, McKim Papers, Cornell.
[19] Gerrit Smith to W. D. Phillips, Mar. 23, 1855, Gerrit Smith Papers, NYHS.
[20] Benjamin Quarles, *Frederick Douglass* (Washington, 1948), 159-63.

Abolitionist party would amount to almost nothing. Gerrit Smith, William Goodell, and other white Radical Abolitionists watched anxiously for Douglass' reaction to Lincoln's nomination. Initially that reaction was favorable. A week after the nomination Douglass described Lincoln as "a man of unblemished private character; . . . one of the most frank, honest men in political life." Douglass would have liked the Republican party to inscribe upon its banners "Death to Slavery" instead of "No more Slave States." But "in the absence of all hope of rearing up the standard of such a party for the coming campaign, we can but desire the success of the Republican candidates."[21]

William Goodell immediately mounted an attack on the Republican party in the columns of the *Principia*, the official organ of the Radical Abolitionist party. Goodell summarized Lincoln's policy statements on slavery and the Negro, and commented: "If any abolitionist or free-soiler, professing to remain such," could read these statements "and then give his vote for Mr. Lincoln, we can only say that we know not how to vindicate the sincerity of his professions, except by entertaining a less elevated conception of his intelligence." A prominent Ohio Radical Abolitionist declared that Lincoln "ignores all the principles of humanity in the colored race, both free and slave; and as abolitionists claim the right to freedom of the one class, and political equality to the other, how can they be consistent, to say nothing of honest, in supporting such a man?"[22]

Such criticism from his associates caused Douglass to moderate his enthusiasm for the Republican party, and he asked his friend Gerrit Smith for advice on the duty of abolitionists in the election. "I cannot support Lincoln," wrote Douglass, "but whether there is life enough in the Abolitionists to name a candidate, I cannot say: I shall look to your letter for light on the pathway of duty." Smith replied in a letter that was published as a broadside and circulated widely among political abolitionists. He asserted that abolitionists should vote only for those candidates who favored the entire abolition of slavery. The "low condition of the anti-slavery cause," wrote Smith, had been caused by the exodus of Liberty

---

[21] *Douglass' Monthly*, June 1860.
[22] *Principia*, June 2, 1860; W. A. Hunter to William Goodell, June 13, 1860, published in *Principia*, July 21, 1860.

party men into the Republican party. "The mass of those who were once intent on abolishing slavery every where, do not go now for its abolition any where. The calculating policy of non-extension has taken the place of the uncompromising principle of abolition."[23]

Two weeks after publication of this letter Douglass assailed the Republican party for its timidity. In a speech on August 1, he charged that by taking a limited defensive position against slavery the Republicans had allowed their opponents to choose the battleground. "Instead of basing ourselves firmly and immovably on the principle of immediate, unconditional emancipation . . . and being the aggressors, we have been defending outposts and allowing [the South] to be the aggressors. . . . The whole abolition . . . *train* . . . has been switched off the abolition track to that of non-extension." Douglass censured the old Liberty party men for allowing themselves to be weakened and absorbed by the Free Soil party. From 1848 to 1860 the antislavery element in the Free Soil and Republican parties had been diluted to the point where Douglass was hard put "to find *even a fibre*, to say nothing of a plank of abolition in the platform adopted at Chicago." Douglass declared his intention to act with the Radical Abolitionist party in the 1860 election.[24]

In a bellicose mood, Radical Abolitionists gathered in Syracuse on August 29 for a combined national and New York state convention. Gerrit Smith was nominated for president and William Goodell for governor of New York. The convention resolved that "the sole legitimate end of all true government is the protection of human rights, the execution of equal and exact justice between a man and his neighbor," and denounced all the major political parties for their eagerness "to assure slaveholders, who trample on all human rights, that they will protect them in so doing."[25]

Garrison expressed his respect for "the motives and aims" of the Radical Abolitionists, but pronounced "the act of making the nominations aforesaid extremely farcical." The Republican press paid little attention to the Radical Abolitionist convention. The

[23] Douglass to Smith, July 2, 1860, Smith Papers, su; *Gerrit Smith to Frederick Douglass*, July 13, 1860 (Peterboro, 1860).

[24] *Douglass' Monthly*, Sept. 1860.

[25] *Principia*, Sept. 8, 15, 1860.

New York Tribune ridiculed the whole affair. Frederick Douglass countered with an attack on the Republican party. "It is simply opposed to allowing slavery to go where it is not at all likely to go," he wrote angrily. "It promises to be about as good a Southern party as either wing of the old Democratic party." Douglass declared that ten thousand votes for Gerrit Smith would do more for the abolition of slavery than two million for Lincoln "or any man who stands pledged before the world against all interference with slavery in the slave states and who is not opposed to making free states a hunting ground for men under the Fugitive Slave Law."[26]

In spite of Douglass' outburst, many political abolitionists voted for Lincoln. Their reasons for doing so were probably similar to those of Edward Gilbert, a New York lawyer and member of the Church Anti-Slavery Society. In June, Gilbert had complained: "How heretical our Republican Party is getting! Every where political leaders teach the people that it is for *white* men and *free soil*. . . . What political Atheism, what infidelity is this!" By October, however, Gilbert was hoping for Republican victory. He wrote to an abolitionist friend: "I quite agree with you as to the Republican party, though I ardently hope that Lincoln will be elected. He will disappoint us no doubt with a conservative administration, yet it will be *one step* and one which will place the hand of Freedom on the jugular & carotid of the slave oligarchy. . . . I am laboring with the Republicans. . . . There is a pulse in the rank and file of the party not to be controlled by the Chicago platform, a pulse impelled by the spirit of God's truth."[27]

Gerrit Smith did not take his own candidacy very seriously. In a letter accepting the nomination he wrote that the purpose of his party was not to win a victory at the polls, but to give abolitionists who believed in the duty of voting an opportunity to vote for a

26 *Liberator*, Sept. 7, 1860; *New York Tribune*, Oct. 2, 1860; *Douglass' Monthly*, Oct. 1860.
27 Edward Gilbert to Charles Sumner, June 9, 1860, Sumner Papers, HU; Gilbert to George Cheever, Oct. 17, 1860, Cheever Papers, AAS. Henry Cheever, Lewis Tappan, and Simeon S. Jocelyn were tempted to vote for Lincoln, but they rejected the temptation and voted for Smith instead. See William Goodell to George Cheever, Oct. 13, 1860, Cheever Papers, AAS; and Beriah Green to Gerrit Smith, Mar. 20, 1861, Smith Papers, SU.

genuine abolitionist candidate.[28] There is no record of the number of votes cast for Smith in 1860, but it seems unlikely that it was greater than two or three thousand, and it may have been less.

✦

Members of the third major group of abolitionists—those unaffiliated with any formal abolitionist organization—nearly all voted for Lincoln in 1860. Many of them contributed importantly to the Republican effort. Richard Hinton, for example, wrote the first campaign biography of Lincoln. He published it anonymously, for his connection with John Brown made it necessary to conceal his authorship if the book was to help Lincoln. In the biography Hinton went to great lengths to emphasize Lincoln's antislavery sentiments. In actual fact, however, Hinton was not very enthusiastically in favor of Lincoln because he considered him too conservative on the slavery question. Hinton had supported Seward for the nomination. Antislavery Republicans were so confident of Seward's nomination that Hinton had actually written a campaign biography of the New York senator prior to the convention. In any event, Hinton's hastily prepared biography of Lincoln did good service during the campaign. Ten thousand copies were sold inside of two weeks, and the book went through three editions in all.[29]

Two other abolitionists performed an important service for the Republicans by publishing collections of campaign songs. Ever since the famous Harrison-Van Buren campaign of 1840, songs had been a vital part of every presidential election. In 1860 the huge Republican rallies and spectacular "Wide-Awake" parades demanded more songs than ever before, and John Wallace Hutchinson and William H. Burleigh supplied them. John Hutchinson was a member of the famous singing Hutchinson family, the most popular singing group in the North. The whole family were abolitionists, sturdy products of the New Hampshire hills. They provided the music for abolitionist conventions, and they had sung for the antislavery political parties in every election since the Free Soil campaign of 1848.[30]

[28] *Liberator,* Sept. 28, 1860.
[29] C. Carroll Hollis, "R. J. Hinton, Lincoln's Reluctant Biographer," *The Centennial Review of Arts & Science,* v (Winter 1961), 72-75.
[30] Carol Brink, *Harps in the Wind, The Story of the Singing Hutchinsons* (New York, 1947), passim.

In the summer of 1860, John Hutchinson published a little book of fifty-one campaign songs, many of them written by members of the Hutchinson family. Most of the songs stayed within the free-soil bounds of the Republican platform, but some of them were out-and-out abolitionist songs. For example, these two stanzas from "Jordan":

> Slavery and Freedom, they both had a fight,
>   And the whole North came up behind 'em,
> Hit Slavery a few knocks, with a free ballot box,
>   Sent it staggering to the other side of Jordan.
>
> If I was the Legislature of these United States,
>   I'd settle this great question accordin';
> I'd let every slave go free, over land and on sea,
>   Let 'em have a little hope this side of Jordan.
>   Then rouse up, ye freemen, the sword unsheath,
>   Freedom's the best road to travel, I believe.[31]

William H. Burleigh also published a *Republican Campaign Songster* in 1860; he was the brother of Garrisonian abolitionist Charles C. Burleigh and had been a lecturer for the American Anti-Slavery Society in the 1830's. For a time he turned to the quiet life of a poet, but in 1860 he returned to the political fray and edited a little monthly campaign tract, *The Republican Pocket Pistol*, and published his *Songster*. Most of the songs carried a free soil and "Hurrah for Lincoln" message but a few were of a distinctly abolitionist nature, for example, "The Banner of Freedom":

> And the hour hastens on when the Right shall prevail,
> And the banner of Freedom triumphantly wave
> O'er the land of the free and the home of the brave! . . .
>
> Then a shout for our banner, a shout for our cause,
>   'Tis the noblest on earth, and our watch-word shall be,
> "The whole Constitution, the Union and Laws,
> And freedom to all that by nature are free."[32]

---

[31] John W. Hutchinson, ed., *Hutchinson's Republican Songster, for the Campaign of 1860* (New York, 1860), 25-26.
[32] William H. Burleigh, *Poems by W. H. Burleigh, with a Sketch of his Life*

Another veteran abolitionist, Henry B. Stanton, served the Republican party effectively as a stump speaker in 1860. Stanton had been one of the most forceful lecturers in the American Anti-Slavery Society in the 1830's, but he broke with Garrison in 1840, helped organize the Liberty party, and in 1848 led a majority of Liberty party men into the Free Soil party. In 1860 he stumped New York state for Lincoln. Stanton was as much an abolitionist at heart as ever, but he had lost some of his crusading zeal since the early days when he had been mobbed more than two hundred times, and in 1860 he confined himself to proclaiming the conventional nonextension Republican policy on slavery.[33]

These four and many other Republican abolitionists played active roles in the 1860 campaign. Occasionally they had qualms of conscience about supporting a party whose leaders repeatedly proclaimed that their accession to power would pose no danger to slavery in the states. One abolitionist, Elizur Wright, worked out a careful justification of his support for Lincoln, and his explanation is representative of the feelings of other abolitionists who voted Republican in 1860. Some of Wright's friends charged him with inconsistency in supporting the nonabolitionist Lincoln for president. Replied Wright to one of these critics: "Accepting facts as facts and treating them as facts, I know my vote isn't going to make you or Gerrit Smith or Wm. Goodell president. . . . In the Republican platform . . . are some just and right things. . . . I believe the average sentiment of the party is more anti-slavery than the platform, and the sentiment of the most active & efficient leaders still more so."[34]

Another conscientious Republican abolitionist was John Jay, grandson of the first chief justice of the Supreme Court, and son of William Jay, one of the most faithful of the early abolitionists.

by *Celia Burleigh* (New York, 1871), v-xvii; William H. Burleigh, ed., *The Republican Campaign Songster for 1860* (New York, 1860), 28.

[33] Louis Filler, *The Crusade Against Slavery, 1830-1860* (New York, 1960), 72, 134, 189; Henry B. Stanton, *Random Recollections* (3rd ed., New York, 1887), 50, 213; Henry B. Stanton to Salmon P. Chase, July 10, 1860, Chase Papers, LC; *New York Tribune*, Sept. 12, 1860.

[34] Wright to unknown, Oct. 8, 1860, Wright Papers, LC.

Jay explained the reasons for his support of Lincoln in a long speech to his Westchester County neighbors on the eve of the election. The history of the Republican party showed that "it is the embodiment of the Anti-Slavery sentiment of the country," he said. "I do not intend to intimate that all the Anti-Slavery sentiment of the country is represented in that party, or that all the members of that party sympathize with the Abolitionists." Nevertheless, the inauguration of Lincoln would inaugurate "the beginning of the end of American Slavery." Jay predicted that when the Republicans gained a majority in Congress they would outlaw slavery in the territories, abolish slavery in the District of Columbia, prohibit the foreign and internal slave trade, and so constrict slavery as to put it on the road to imminent extinction. Oliver Johnson printed this speech as a supplement to the *Anti-Slavery Standard*, with an explanation that Jay's views, "in some important respects, differ from ours, but we are glad of the opportunity to lay before our readers a Republican speech so thoroughly imbued with the spirit of abolition that it is not likely to gain admission to any of the leading presses of the party."[35]

Jay, Wright, Stanton, Burleigh, the Hutchinsons, Thomas Wentworth Higginson, George L. Stearns, and the other Republican abolitionists who voted for Lincoln in 1860 did so because they hoped that somehow his election would prove to be the first step toward the eventual abolition of slavery.

✦

Republican indifference and even hostility to equal citizenship for free Negroes was an important reason for the coolness of many abolitionists toward the party. Democratic efforts to pin the Negro equality label on the Republican party usually produced vigorous Republican denials. In his fourth debate with Stephen Douglas in 1858 Lincoln stated with painful clarity:

"I will say then that I am not, nor ever have been in favor of bringing about in any way the social and political equality of the white and black races, (applause)—that I am not nor ever have been in favor of making voters or jurors of negroes, nor of qualifying them to hold office, nor to intermarry with white

---

[35] *N.A.S. Standard*, Nov. 24, 1860.

people; and I will say in addition to this that there is a physical difference between the white and black races which I believe will for ever forbid the two races living together on terms of social and political equality. And inasmuch as they cannot so live, while they do remain together there must be the position of superior and inferior, and I as much as any other man am in favor of having the superior position assigned to the white race."[36]

"The 'negro question,' as we understand it," wrote an Ohio Republican, "is a *white man's question*, the question of the right of free white laborers to the soil of the territories. It is not to be crushed or retarded by shouting 'Sambo' at us. We have no Sambo in our platform. . . . We object to Sambo. We don't want him about." In the 1860 campaign, Senator Seward explained that "the motive of those who have protested against the extension of slavery" had "always really been concern for the welfare of the white man," and not, as some erroneously assumed, an "unnatural sympathy with the negro."[37]

Republican declarations of white supremacy infuriated many abolitionists. The elevation of free Negroes to civil and political equality was an essential corollary of the abolitionist belief in the right of all men to equal freedom. The Western Anti-Slavery Society denounced the Republican party for its racism, noting that "Ohio, under Republican rule, ostracizes the colored man, refuses his ballot, denies him equal educational rights, and shuts him out of the jury-box, and even out of the county poorhouse." In Massachusetts, the Essex County Anti-Slavery Society resolved that "inasmuch as Abraham Lincoln denies the equality of all men, as taught in the Declaration of American Independence, . . . he is, therefore, unworthy of the votes of all those who love freedom and regard justice." Several other county antislavery societies in New England passed similar resolutions.[38] Gerrit Smith wrote a public letter in October 1860, warning abolitionists not to vote for Lincoln because he "is for a white man's party [and] is opposed to extending equal political rights to the black

[36] Basler, ed., *Collected Works of Lincoln*, III, 145-46.

[37] Ohio Republican quoted in Leon F. Litwack, *North of Slavery* (Chicago, 1961), 270; Seward quoted in the *Twenty-Eighth Annual Report of the American Anti-Slavery Society*, 32.

[38] *N.A.S. Standard*, Oct. 13, 1860; *Liberator*, Aug. 31, Sept. 21, Nov. 9, 23, 1860.

man." Among the banners borne by enthusiastic Republicans at a mass meeting in Lincoln's home town of Springfield was one which read: "NO NEGRO EQUALITY IN THE NORTH." The *Anti-Slavery Bugle* commented dryly: "We hope those colored men who are bawling themselves hoarse for Lincoln and Hamlin, will have a good time."[39]

Many northern Negroes did support Lincoln in 1860 for the same reason that many white abolitionists supported him: whatever its shortcomings, the Republican party embodied the anti-slavery sentiment of the North. Several Negro abolitionists, however, sharply criticized the Republican party: H. Ford Douglass, a colored leader from Illinois, declared that Lincoln's nomination held out little hope for the Negro, and noted that Lincoln had once refused to sign a petition requesting repeal of an Illinois law barring Negro testimony in court cases involving whites. If Negroes tried to send their children to public schools in Illinois, charged Douglass, "Abraham Lincoln would kick them out, in the name of Republicanism and anti-slavery! . . . I care nothing about that anti-slavery which wants to make the Territories free, while it is unwilling to extend to me, as a man, in the free States, all the rights of a man."[40]

Frederick Douglass, who early in the campaign had praised Lincoln and his party, was later angered by Republican declarations of white supremacy. In 1860 there was a proposal on the New York state ballot to abolish the $250 property qualification for Negro voters and to admit Negroes to the polls on equal terms with whites. Douglass stumped upstate New York for this proposition, distributing 25 thousand pamphlets published by the New York City and County Suffrage Committee of Colored Citizens. The suffrage amendment had been passed by a Republican legislature and enjoyed the support of a number of Republican newspapers including the powerful *New York Tribune*, but during the campaign most Republican newspapers and stump orators ignored it or manifested only half-hearted support for it. On November 6, Lincoln carried New York by 50 thousand votes, but the Negro suffrage amendment was defeated by nearly a two to one margin.

[39] Gerrit Smith's letter was published in the *Principia*, Oct. 27, 1860; the comment of the *Anti-Slavery Bugle* was quoted in the *Principia*, Sept. 8, 1860.
[40] *Liberator*, July 13, 1860.

Scores of thousands of Republicans had voted against the amendment. "The black baby of Negro Suffrage was thought too ugly to
exhibit on so grand an occasion," wrote Douglass bitterly. "The
negro was stowed away like some people put out of sight their
deformed children when company comes."[41]

✦

On the morrow of the election there was general rejoicing
among abolitionists—including some who had sharply rebuked
the Republicans during the campaign—over the result. There
were still some dissenting voices, to be sure. "I do not expect that
Lincoln will take high and brave ground against slavery," wrote
Gerrit Smith. "I think that their policy will be a very conservative
one." George Thompson, noted British abolitionist and close
friend of Garrison, warned American abolitionists that Lincoln's
victory placed their cause in "a new, a critical and a trying position. . . . You have now to grapple with the new doctrine of
Republican *conservatism*. You have now to make genuine converts
of those who have as yet only been baptized into the faith of non-
extension, and whose zeal in that direction is mere *white-man-
ism*."[42]

But the voices of doubt and dissent were few. Joshua Leavitt
expressed the feelings of most Republican abolitionists when he
exulted that Lincoln's election was the victorious culmination of
the battle begun by the Liberty party in 1840. "Thank God!
Lincoln is chosen!" wrote Leavitt. "What a growth since 1840.
. . . It is a joy to have lived to this day." Whittier rejoiced in
Lincoln's victory as "the triumph of our principles—so long
delayed." Henry Cheever wrote four days after the election that
"since the Republican triumph, even though Lincoln should prove
another John Tyler, I think abolitionism will be able to show a
bolder hand."[43] Even Frederick Douglass had a good word for

[41] Quarles, *Douglass*, 166-67; *Douglass' Monthly*, Aug., Dec. 1860. See also
Principia, Oct. 13, 1860; *New York Tribune*, Sept. 17, Nov. 3, 1860; *Liberator*,
Nov. 2, 1860; and *Twenty-Eighth Annual Report of the American Anti-Slavery
Society*, 114-15. The *Anti-Slavery Standard*, Nov. 17, 1860, commented that the
defeat of the Negro suffrage amendment was proof that the Republican party
could not be trusted.

[42] Smith to Charles B. Sedgwick, Nov. 15, 1860, quoted in Ralph Volney Harlow,
Gerrit Smith: Philanthropist and Reformer (New York, 1939), 428; George
Thompson to Garrison, Nov. 23, 1860, published in *Liberator*, Dec. 14, 1860.

[43] Leavitt to Salmon P. Chase, Nov. 7, 1860, Whittier to Chase, Nov. 9, 1860,
Chase Papers, LC; Henry Cheever to Garrison, Nov. 10, 1860, Garrison Papers, BPL.

the Republican victory. No longer, he said, would the slave power rule the nation: "Lincoln's election has vitiated their authority, and broken their power. . . . More important still, it has demonstrated the possibility of electing, if not an Abolitionist, at least an *anti-slavery reputation* to the Presidency."[44]

Edmund Quincy expressed the views of most Garrisonians in a postelection editorial in the *Anti-Slavery Standard*. "Our readers know that we expect little or no Anti-Slavery help from Mr. Lincoln," wrote Quincy, "but we none the less recognize his election as an Anti-Slavery triumph and the result of long Anti-Slavery labors. It is not the harvest, but it is the green blade that must go before it." Samuel May, Jr. was more enthusiastic. "Is not the result *wonderful?*" he exclaimed. "Not that L. & his administration will be likely to do anything antislavery, but in view of the fact that *the North* has stood fast, and, in face of all the Southern threats & bombast & defiance, chosen the candidate which the South had denounced."[45]

In June, Wendell Phillips had called Abraham Lincoln "The Slave-Hound of Illinois." A brilliant, incisive, intuitive thinker, Phillips believed with Emerson that "a foolish consistency is the hobgoblin of little minds." On the day after the election Phillips stood before a packed auditorium in Boston's Tremont Temple and with prophetic vision told the cheering audience:

"If the telegraph speaks truth, for the first time in our history the *slave* has chosen a President of the United States. (Cheers.) We have passed the Rubicon. . . . It is the moral effect of this victory, not anything which his administration can or will do, that gives value to this success. Not an Abolitionist, hardly an antislavery man, Mr. Lincoln consents to represent an antislavery idea. A pawn on the political chessboard, his value is in his position; with fair effort, we may soon change him for knight, bishop, or queen, and sweep the board. (Applause) . . .The Republican party have undertaken a problem, the solution of which will force them to our position. . . . Not Mr. Seward's 'Union and Liberty,' which he stole and poisoned from Webster's 'Liberty and Union.'

[44] *Douglass' Monthly*, Dec. 1860.
[45] *N.A.S. Standard*, Nov. 24, 1860; Samuel May, Jr. to Samuel J. May, Nov. 11, 1860, Samuel J. May Papers, BPL.

No: their motto will soon be 'Liberty first,' (a long pause) 'Union afterwards.' " (Applause and a solitary hiss)[46]

That solitary hiss perhaps expressed the sentiments of South Carolina, for a member of the Palmetto State's legislature quoted Phillips' speech as one justification for his state's secession from the Union.[47]

[46] Wendell Phillips, *Speeches, Lectures, and Letters,* 1st Series (Boston, 1863), 294, 314.
[47] *Twenty-Eighth Annual Report of the American Anti-Slavery Society,* 44.

"WE appear to be on the eve of the oddest Revolution that History has yet seen," wrote Edmund Quincy as the cotton states prepared to leave the Union. "A Revolution for the greater security of Injustice, and the firmer establishment of Tyranny!"[1] The South did indeed launch a revolution in the winter of 1860-1861, but its final outcome was rather different from what the revolutionists hoped.

Even before South Carolina seceded on December 20, 1860, pressure began to build up in the North for concessions and conciliation to save the Union. Dozens of compromise proposals were introduced into Congress. These plans included: repeal of northern personal liberty laws; admission of New Mexico as a slave state; disfranchisement and colonization of free Negroes; and perpetual guaranties of slavery in the states where it already existed, in the District of Columbia, and in all territories lying south of the line 36° 30'. Most antislavery Republicans stood firm against any compromise on the issue of slavery in the territories. In the end the only measures adopted were the repeal or modification of personal liberty laws in three states and congressional passage of a constitutional amendment guaranteeing slavery in the states against federal interference.[2]

For several months during the winter of 1860-1861, however, the various plans to conciliate the South were seriously debated in Congress. Abolitionists did not agree among themselves on the best method of dealing with the secession crisis, but they presented a united front against compromise. The *Anti-Slavery Standard* denounced "Doughface Republicans" who offered "base and humiliating concessions" to the South. William S. Robinson, a member of the Bird Club in Massachusetts, was disgusted with all compromisers. "How many skulking, compromis-

---

[1] *N.A.S. Standard*, Dec. 1, 1860.

[2] The best studies of the North during the secession winter are David M. Potter, *Lincoln and His Party in the Secession Crisis* (New Haven, 1942); and Kenneth M. Stampp, *And the War Came: The North and the Secession Crisis, 1860-61* (Baton Rouge, 1950).

ing creatures there are!" he wrote in his weekly column in the *Springfield Republican*. "For a truce, for a little ease, a chance to live three or four years longer in peace, men are willing to entail on their children a severer struggle than this, or, on their remotest posterity, all the evils of a slaveholding despotism."[3]

The most comprehensive Union-saving measure was popularly known as the "Crittenden Compromise," named for its sponsor, Senator John Crittenden of Kentucky. Crittenden's compromise consisted of a series of constitutional amendments to protect slavery in the states and in the District of Columbia, to exclude slavery north of the line 36° 30' and guarantee it south of that line in all territories now held "or hereafter acquired," and to provide for the disfranchisement and colonization abroad of free Negroes. These amendments were to be perpetually binding; that is, they could never be repealed.[4] Abolitionists excoriated the Crittenden plan in the strongest language they could command. "This so called Crittenden compromise . . . *nails* Slavery into the Constitution," wrote the Reverend R. C. Waterston, a Massachusetts abolitionist. "To me it seems infamous. This question between Slavery & Freedom may as well be met now, as at any other time. Better now than after the rivets have been made more secure."[5]

Abolitionists were confident that radical Republicans would not betray the antislavery cause by accepting a compromise, but they had less faith in the moderate Republicans and in the northern people generally. "My trust, just now, is in the South rather than the North," wrote Mary Grew in January 1861. "I am not sure the North will not make disgraceful concessions of principles, but I am tolerably confident that the South will not accept them." Lydia Maria Child was bitter toward Republicans who were willing to compromise their principles to prevent secession: "If all this excitement does not settle down into a miserable mush of concession, leaving the country in a worse state than it found it,

[3] *N.A.S. Standard*, Dec. 15, 22, 1860; *Springfield Republican*, Jan. 19, 1861.

[4] *Cong. Globe*, 36 Cong., 2 Sess., 112-14, 237, 1093-94, 1259-61, 1368, 1405.

[5] R. C. Waterston to Charles Sumner, Feb. 11, 1861, Sumner Papers, HU. For other examples of abolitionist denunciation of the Crittenden plan, see Samuel May, Jr. to Garrison, Jan. 11, 1861, Garrison Papers, BPL; Milton Sutliff to Salmon P. Chase, Feb. 14, 1861, Chase Papers, LC; and *Liberator*, Feb. 1, Mar. 15, 1861.

we shall owe it less to the steadfastness of Republican leaders, than to the utter impossibility of satisfying the demands of the South, however patiently we may crawl in the dust, or whatsoever quantity of dirt we may consent to eat."[6]

Abolitionists were apprehensive about Lincoln's attitude during the secession crisis. The president-elect maintained a public silence from the time of his election until his departure for Washington in February. Privately, however, he made known his opposition to any concession on the issue of slavery in the territories, and it was due more to his influence than to any other factor that most moderate Republicans voted against compromise when the showdown came.[7] Abolitionists were apprised of Lincoln's position by his law partner, William Herndon. "Mr. Lincoln yet remains firm as a rock," Herndon informed Massachusetts abolitionists in February. "He has told me, not only once, but often & often, that rather than concede to traitors, his soul might go back to God from the wings of the Capitol. . . . Say to the Mass[achusetts] boys 'Stand firm—keep your convictions true to your soul.' " Abolitionists appreciated Lincoln's role in preventing compromise. "It is much to the credit of Mr. Lincoln," wrote Garrison, "that he has maintained his dignity and self-respect intact, and gives no countenance to any of the compromises."[8]

✦

Opposition to compromise was essentially a negative policy. What positive solution of the secession crisis could abolitionists offer? For most Garrisonians the answer was easy: let the South go. For nearly twenty years they had been urging the secession of free states from the slaveholding Union. When secession finally came, it was the South that broke away from the North, but this made little difference to Garrisonians—the end result was the same.

The basic Garrisonian argument for disunion was a simple one.

6 Mary Grew to Garrison, Jan. 15, 1861, Garrison Papers, BPL; L. M. Child to Sumner, Jan. 28, 1861, Sumner Papers, HU.

7 Potter, *Secession Crisis*, 133-70, 176-87.

8 Wm. Herndon to Samuel Sewall, Feb. 1, 1861, Garrison Papers, BPL; *Liberator*, Feb. 15, 1861. Some abolitionists, however, were bitter toward Lincoln because of his approval of the proposed constitutional amendment to guarantee slavery in the states forever against congressional interference. *Principia*, Mar. 9, 16, 23, 1861.

Under the Constitution the national government was pledged to protect slavery. The number of southern slave states had increased from six to fifteen during the existence of the Union. Since the adoption of the Constitution, the slave power had marched on from one victory to another until in 1857 a southern-dominated Supreme Court had declared that Negroes were not citizens of the United States. The national government had failed to suppress the African slave trade. Under the aegis of the Union, Florida and Texas were acquired for slavery. The federal government was pledged to return fugitives into bondage. The national army and the militias of free states could be called upon to crush any slave uprising in the South. "We have a right to call on you to give your blood to maintain the slaves of the South in bondage," taunted Robert Toombs of Georgia in a speech Garrisonians were fond of quoting. "Gentlemen, deceive not yourselves; you cannot deceive others. This is a pro-slavery government. Slavery is stamped on its heart—the Constitution."[9]

Disunion, argued Garrisonians, would relieve the North of responsibility for the sin of slavery. It would remove the powerful protective shield of the United States army from slavery, thus allowing slave insurrections a better chance of success. It would end the North's obligation to enforce the fugitive slave law, and encourage a greater exodus of fugitive slaves from the South. Disunion would isolate the South and hold up its peculiar institution to the moral condemnation of the world. Disunion grew out of American principles. The Declaration of Independence stated that any government which undermined natural and God-given rights should be destroyed and a new one formed. Garrisonians maintained that they were fulfilling the revolutionary tradition of the founding fathers by attacking the proslavery Constitution and Union.[10]

[9] The Toombs statement is quoted in Ralph Korngold, *Two Friends of Man* (Boston, 1950), 164-65.

[10] For an excellent discussion of Garrisonian disunionism see Irving H. Bartlett, *Wendell Phillips: Brahmin Radical* (Boston, 1961), 114-37. Some Negro abolitionists were even more strongly disunionist than Garrison. Philadelphian Robert Purvis denounced the Union as "one of the basest, meanest, most atrocious despotisms that ever saw the face of the sun," and said that any man with decent self-respect would look upon it with *"contempt, loathing,* and *unutterable abhorrence!"* H. Ford Douglass asserted that "I can hate this Government without being disloyal, because it has stricken down my manhood, and treated me as a saleable commodity." Leon F. Litwack, *North of Slavery* (Chicago, 1961), 265-66.

This was the Garrisonian case for disunion prior to 1860. During the secession winter the argument was refined and amplified in an effort to convince the North to let the slave states depart in peace. At first some Garrisonians feared that the South would not carry out its secession threats. "What a stir at the South!" exclaimed William Fish of New York on November 21, "& what a matter of rejoicing it would be to us, if all the Southern States *would* secede! No such encouraging result, I fear." Even after South Carolina had gone, Marius Robinson of Ohio could not persuade himself that "it is anything more than a magnificent game of bluff, & that she will win thereby such compromises as she wants. The only hope is in her madness & insolence."[11]

Most abolitionists, however, believed in the implacable determination of secessionist leaders to carry their states out of the Union. Edmund Quincy was confident that "the abolition of slavery will be hastened by this Disunion movement, whatever shape it may finally take."[12] Most Garrisonians agreed with Quincy. Samuel May, Jr., rejoiced in the secession movement. "I say, with you, Let the South go—put not a *straw* in her way—interpose not even an objection or a regret; let her go." Bankruptcy and ruin or European dependence awaited her, and the North could form its own Union without slavery. Mattie Griffith, a young Kentucky-born woman who had emancipated her inherited slaves and impoverished herself to help them get a new start in life, and had come North herself to join the Garrisonian crusade, believed that "a calm and peaceable dissolution of the Union would be a splendid point in the history of the country, and surely the most signal blow the 'peculiar institution' has ever received."[13]

At the beginning of the new year Garrison pronounced all Union-saving efforts "simply idiotic." He said, "At last 'the covenant with death' is annulled, and 'the agreement with hell' broken. The people of the North should recognize the fact that THE UNION IS DISSOLVED, and act accordingly." The North would then be free indeed, and the South left with all her dread responsibilities resting on her own head. "In that case, she cannot

11 Wm. Fish to Samuel May, Jr., Nov. 21, 1860, Garrison Papers, BPL; Marius Robinson to May, Dec. 21, 1860, Samuel May, Jr. Papers, BPL.

12 *N.A.S. Standard*, Jan. 12, 1861.

13 May to Samuel J. May, Dec. 9, 1860, Samuel J. May Papers, BPL; Mattie Griffith to S. H. Gay, Dec. 28, 1860, Gay Papers, CU.

long uphold her tottering slave system—speedy emancipation will follow—and the final result will be the formation of a Union stretching from the Atlantic to the Pacific, one in spirit, in purpose, in glorious freedom, the bitter past forgotten, and the future full of richest promise!"[14]

Wendell Phillips fervently welcomed secession. "All my grown-up years," he told a New Haven audience, "have been devoted to creating just such a crisis as that which is now upon us." During the secession winter he lectured widely on behalf of disunion, advocating the South's revolutionary right of secession: "Standing with the principles of '76 behind us, who can deny them the right?"[15] Phillips considered disunion the first step toward emancipation. "What supports slavery?" he asked. "Northern bayonets, calming the masters' fear. . . . Disunion leaves God's natural laws to work their good results. . . . Under God's law, insurrection is the tyrant's check. Let us stand out of the path, and allow the Divine law to have free course." Rather than make concessions to keep the slave states in the Union, Phillips would "build a bridge of gold, and pay their toll over it,—accompany them out with glad noise of trumpets. . . . But let the world distinctly understand why they go,—to save slavery; and why we rejoice in their departure,—because we know their declaration of independence is the jubilee of the Slave."[16]

The Garrisonians' implied endorsement of slave insurrections troubled some observers. The pre-Civil War generation could remember the senseless butchery of Nat Turner's uprising, and all Americans had heard blood-curdling stories about the massacre of Haitian whites by Negroes in 1804. The constitution and "Declaration of Sentiments" of the American Anti-Slavery Society, moreover, explicitly disavowed insurrection as a means of abolishing slavery, and some of the Garrisonians, including Garrison himself, were avowed pacifists. How, then, could they sanction insurrection? Garrison declared in December 1860, that if the patriots of 1776 were justified in their resort to arms against Britain, the slaves were justified a thousand times over in rising

[14] *Liberator*, Jan. 4, Feb. 15, Mar. 8, 1861.

[15] *ibid.*, Mar. 22, 1861; George L. Austin, *The Life and Times of Wendell Phillips* (2nd ed., Boston, 1901), 206.

[16] Wendell Phillips, *Speeches, Lectures, and Letters*, 1st Series (Boston, 1863), 350-62.

against their oppressors. "Brand the man as a hypocrite," he wrote, "who, in one breath, exults in the deeds of Washington and Warren, and in the next, denounces Nat Turner as a monster for refusing longer to wear the yoke and be driven under the lash." Garrison personally believed in nonresistance, but most of his countrymen did not, and he measured them by their own standard. "If the doctrine of non-resistance ought to be spurned for oppressed white men, it is equally to be spurned for oppressed black men. . . . I test the nation by its own revolutionary standard, taking Bunker Hill monument for my measuring line."[17]

Phillips was no pacifist, and he had less difficulty than Garrison in justifying his endorsement of insurrection. "The reason why I have advised the slave to be guided by a policy of peace is because he has had, hitherto, no chance," said Phillips in February 1861. In a southern Confederacy, however, his chances for successful insurrection would be much better: "I acknowledge the right of two million and a half of white people in the seven seceding States to organize their government as they choose. Just as freely I acknowledge the right of four million of black people to organize *their* government, and to vindicate that right by arms." The South had never known real peace. "Slavery is a form of perpetual war. . . . I hesitate not to say, that I prefer an insurrection which frees the slave in ten years to slavery for a century. . . . Where is the battle-field, however ghastly, that is not white,— white as an angel's wing,—compared with the blackness of that darkness which has brooded over the Carolinas for two hundred years?"[18]

Garrisonians sincerely believed that disunion would destroy slavery. They overestimated the readiness of slaves to rise in revolt, and they underestimated the potential military strength of the white South, but these were mistakes of judgment committed by most northerners. Indeed, the Garrisonian thesis that disunion meant emancipation found a great deal of support among non-Garrisonians and nonabolitionists. "Phillips' last speech rings gold-like—has the chime of true metal in it," exclaimed William Herndon on February 1, 1861. "I do not agree with Phillips about

[17] *Liberator*, Dec. 7, 1860. See also John L. Thomas, *The Liberator: William Lloyd Garrison* (Boston, 1963), 135-36, 382, 397-98.

[18] Phillips, *Speeches, Lectures, and Letters*, 1st Series, 383-85.

Disunion, though I see that Disunion is liberty to the Slave, and God speed that day." A Republican editor in Indianapolis stated flatly that "the dissolution of the American Union seals the doom of American slavery." A southern Confederacy would be a foreign nation, continued the editor, "No more protection then, no more fugitive slave laws, no more surpressing [sic] of slave insurrections by Federal troops. . . . How long would the abnormal institution of slavery . . . live when brought under the crushing effects of these great influences?" A Des Moines paper declared that "the most effectual way to bring about the enfranchisement of every slave on this continent, is to dissolve this Union." And Samuel Bowles, no sympathizer with abolitionists, affirmed that outside of the Union, slavery "will be pretty certain to come to a violent and bloody death."[19]

When nonabolitionists could argue thus, it is not surprising that William Lloyd Garrison, Jr., could write in February 1861, that "From the standpoint of the Abolitionists never have events looked so propitious for the jubilee of the slave"; or that the *Anti-Slavery Standard* could congratulate abolitionists upon having never "had more abundant reason for satisfaction as to the past and hope as to the future than they have now."[20] Despite this optimism, however, and despite a widespread feeling that secession would spell the doom of slavery, it seems likely that in the short run peaceful disunion would have strengthened rather than weakened slavery, at least in the deep South. If the North had followed the advice of Garrisonians in 1861, the peculiar institution, in all probability, would not have come to an end as soon as it did.

✦

Many non-Garrisonian abolitionists also avowed a willingness to let the South secede peaceably in 1860-1861. Four of the five living members of the "Secret Six"—that group of abolitionists who had helped finance John Brown's exploits in Kansas and

[19] Herndon to Samuel Sewall, Feb. 1, 1861, Garrison Papers, BPL; *Indianapolis Daily Journal*, Dec. 14, 1860; *Des Moines Iowa State Register*, Jan. 23, 1861, quoted in Howard C. Perkins, *Northern Editorials on Secession* (2 vols., New York, 1942), 117-118, 440; *Springfield Republican*, Dec. 22, 1860.

[20] William L. Garrison, Jr., to Samuel Johnson, Feb. 9, 1861, Samuel Johnson Papers, Essex Institute; *N.A.S. Standard*, Mar. 2, 1861.

Virginia—favored disunion rather than concession. Dr. Samuel Gridley Howe opposed any efforts to preserve the Union with the "cancerous excrescences which shoot out from its southern extremities." Thomas Wentworth Higginson said that if the crisis "simply ends in Disunion, even with a state of temporary war, I should be glad—for I think that is a mere question of time & it may as well come now." Frank Sanborn observed in January that "the present condition of National affairs gives me much hope for the Slave. Whatever may be the issue—and I think it will be *real* disunion—Slavery will be greatly weakened."[21] Two days before South Carolina adopted her secession ordinance, Gerrit Smith wrote that it would be "infinitely better" for the Union to be "broken asunder" than to be "recemented by concessions to Slavery." Three months later Smith said: "I insist that the Nation has the right and is therefore bound to abolish Slavery. But if it will not do so, then let there be Disunion & Abolition will follow."[22]

In December 1860, Frederick Douglass declared that "if the Union can only be maintained by new concessions to the slaveholders; if it can only be stuck together and held together by a new drain on the negro's blood . . . then will every right-minded man and woman in the land say, let the Union perish, and perish forever." John Pierpont of Massachusetts, an aged Liberty party veteran, affirmed that secession "would abolish the fugitive slave act and bring the Canada line several degrees of latitude further south."[23] John Jay fervently declared that "if we cannot have liberty & union in any new readjustment, I go for liberty without union." Edward Gilbert reported that "all the Abolitionists I know would hail disunion with delight and hope. We all feel that any further compromise with slavery would render the country unfit for honest men to live in." John G. Whittier summed up the abolitionist position in a poem entitled "A Word for the Hour":

[21] Harold Schwartz, *Samuel Gridley Howe: Social Reformer* (Cambridge, Mass., 1956), 249; Higginson to Louisa Higginson, Nov. 23, 1860, Higginson Papers, HU; Frank Sanborn to Gerrit Smith, Jan. 27, 1861, Smith Papers, SU.

[22] Gerrit Smith to S. P. Chase, Dec. 18, 1860, Smith Papers, SU; Gerrit Smith to Frank Sanborn, Mar. 20, 1861, Sanborn Papers, LC.

[23] *Douglass' Monthly*, Jan. 1861; Pierpont to Charles Sumner, Dec. 10, 1860, Sumner Papers, HU.

They break the links of Union: shall we light
The fires of hell to weld anew the chain
On that red anvil where each blow is pain?
Draw we not even now a freer breath,
As from our shoulders falls a load of death? . . .
Pity, forgive, but urge them back no more
Who, drunk with passion, flaunt disunion's rag
With its vile reptile-blazon. Let us press
The golden cluster on our brave old flag
In closer union, and, if numbering less,
Brighter shall shine the stars which still remain.[24]

✦

Most abolitionists were prepared to acquiesce in peaceable secession. To some, however, this seemed a renunciation of their duty
to the slave. Stephen S. Foster, for example, could not see "how
the slaves could possibly be benefited by a political separation
from the North, where most of their active friends now reside."
He was aware that disunion was sometimes "demanded of the
North as a matter of consistency, to free herself from the responsibility of slavery." But this would leave the slaves "unprotected
in the hands of their plunderers—a deliberate refusal to employ
in their behalf the potent agencies on which we depend for the
maintenance of our own freedom." Foster thought the federal
government had the power under the Constitution to abolish
slavery, and during the secession crisis he asserted that by preserv-

[24] Jay to Sumner, Feb. 4, 1861, Sumner Papers, HU; Gilbert to George Cheever,
Jan. 17, 1861, Cheever Papers, AAS; John G. Whittier, *Songs of Labor and Reform*
(vol. III of his *Poetical Works*, Riverside Edition, Boston, 1888), 218-19. Two
non-Garrisonian abolitionists wrote lengthy pamphlets supporting peaceful secession in 1861. In the first, James Freeman Clarke asserted that concessions
would be far worse than disunion. "The Union is a means to an end," he wrote.
"Give up the end in order to preserve the means, and both become worthless.
. . . The end of the Union is to secure prosperity, peace, justice, equal rights,
and liberty. It is evident, therefore, that these are not to be sacrificed, even to
preserve the Union." Clarke, *Secession, Concession, or Self-Possession: Which?*
(Boston, 1861), 13. A second disunionist pamphlet, by George Bassett of Illinois,
proclaimed that "the tendency of secession will be to terminate . . . American
slavery. Separate the slave States from the others, and slavery must stand on
its own merits. . . . It is . . . well known that the general government is pledged
against any effective measures to bring slavery to a speedy end. In theory and
practice, it is the bulwark of chattel slavery." Bassett, *A Northern Plea for the
Right of Secession* (Ottawa, Ill., 1861), 22-23.

ing the Union "and enforcing an anti-slavery construction of the constitution, slavery could ere long be wiped out."[25]

William Goodell, who also believed in the right of the government to abolish slavery in the states, could not countenance disunion in any form. The disunionist abolitionist, wrote Goodell, "feels an uncomfortable weight of responsibility for slavery. . . . But he overlooks the still more crushing responsibility of giving over the struggle, and giving up the slaves to the tender mercies of the slaveholders." Abolitionists had "no moral or political right to allow [the slaves] to be kidnapped out of the Union, when it is the religious and constitutional duty of the Union to set them free."[26]

Goodell realized that few persons agreed with his antislavery interpretation of the Constitution, and in January he switched to an argument that was to become familiar to millions in subsequent years: the right of the government to abolish slavery under the war power. Goodell contended that the Republican party was absolved of its pledge of noninterference with slavery in the states by the acts of the seceding states themselves. By seizing United States property, he argued, the South had levied war on the United States and made herself liable to the usages and fortunes of war. "If the . . . rebellion cannot be put down otherwise than by liberating all the slaves of all the slave States, what consideration should hinder its being done?" Meeting in New York City, the Church Anti-Slavery Society adopted Goodell's argument and resolved that the secession crisis gave the government, "by the express provision of the constitution in case of rebellion or insurrection, the right to suppress rebellion and to abolish slavery, the cause of it."[27]

"Instead of looking around for means of reconciling freedom and slavery," declared Frederick Douglass in January 1861, "how immeasurably better would it be if, in our national councils, some Wilberforce or a Buxton could arise, and . . . propose a plan for the complete abolition of slavery." There was no Wilberforce or Buxton in Washington, but here and there in the North a few

[25] *N.A.S. Standard*, Dec. 1, 1860; *Worcester* (Mass.) *Spy*, Feb. 11, 1861. See also Samuel May, Jr., to Garrison, Feb. 17, 1861, Garrison Papers, BPL.
[26] *Principia*, Nov. 24, Dec. 8, 1860.
[27] *ibid.*, Jan. 12, Feb. 2, 1861; *New York Evening Post*, Jan. 24, 1861.

Republican newspapers tentatively suggested plans of compensated emancipation in the border states. In an editorial entitled "The Only Possible Compromise," the *New York Tribune* proposed that the federal government appropriate $240,000,000 over the next fifteen years to purchase and liberate the slaves in Delaware, Maryland, Missouri, Arkansas, Texas, and Louisiana at an average price of $400 per slave.[28] The *Boston Advertiser* suggested an annual appropriation of $50,000,000 or more to compensate slaveholders who wished to participate in a nationwide program of compensated emancipation. This suggestion was advanced as a means of breaking the secession impasse. It would not bring back the Gulf states, but it might hold the border states and inaugurate the abolition of slavery therein at the same time.[29]

Abolitionists had traditionally opposed the idea of compensated emancipation because indemnification implied recognition of the right of property in man. But during the secession winter several abolitionists endorsed the suggestion of compensated emancipation. A convention of Garrisonians in Syracuse, for example, adopted resolutions written by Samuel J. May affirming that "the dissolution of the Union, even, may not relieve us; for if slavery still remains in the land, it will be a perpetual trouble to the inhabitants thereof, whether they be separate or whether they be united." Inasmuch as the North was equally guilty with the South of the sin of slavery, "our wealth, and the wealth of the nation ought to be put in requisition to relieve those who may impoverish themselves by setting their captives free."[30] None of the plans for compensated emancipation got beyond the drawing-board stage, however, and they had little or no effect in stemming the tide of secession.

✦

While abolitionists were thundering against compromise from the platform, pulpit, and press, the compromisers took more direct action against abolitionists, inaugurating a season of mob violence unparalleled since the early years of the antislavery movement. The northern mobs of 1860-1861 were composed of

[28] *Douglass' Monthly*, Feb. 1861; *New York Tribune*, Jan. 19, 1861.
[29] Elizabeth Peabody to Gerrit Smith, Jan. 25, 1861, Smith Papers, sv.
[30] Samuel J. May, *Some Recollections of Our Anti-Slavery Conflict* (Boston, 1869), 388-94; *N.A.S. Standard*, Feb. 9, 1861.

two elements: "gentlemen of property and standing" who feared the loss of millions of dollars by secession and blamed the abolitionists for the nation's troubles; and urban workingmen, whose virulent anti-Negro and proslavery prejudices were deeply rooted.

During the secession winter, the Democratic and conservative press was filled with incendiary attacks on abolitionists. "The Anti-Slavery agitation is the true and only cause of all our woes and trouble," proclaimed the *Chicago Times and Herald*. The paper urged concessions to the South, hoping that "this negro question will be again settled, and settled in a manner never again to disturb railroad stocks in this world." The *Cincinnati Daily Enquirer* asserted that the crisis of the Union "was created by crack-brained fanatics, ignorant or careless of their duty to the Government as citizens of the Union. . . . The people of the North must put down this party in their midst, whose only basis is hostility to the institutions of half of the States of this Union." The *Chicago Times* published the following advice to the nation:

"Evil, and nothing but evil, has ever followed in the track of this hideous monster, Abolition. . . . Will you allow the brightest American hopes and prospects to be dashed to earth by this vile struggle . . . to degrade the white man to the negro's level? . . . Let the South have her negroes to her heart's content, and in her own way—and let us go on getting rich and powerful by feeding and clothing them. Let the negroes *alone*!—let them ALONE! . . . Kill the vile cause of disunion, and disunion itself will perish for *lack of food*. ABOLITION IS DISUNION. It is the 'vile cause and most cursed effect.' It is the Alpha and Omega of our National woes. STRANGLE IT!"[31]

With feeling running so high, the desire for compromise with the South was bound sooner or later to manifest itself in mob violence against abolitionists and Negroes. On December 3, a group of Boston abolitionists who believed in John Brown's method of attacking slavery held a meeting in Tremont Temple to discuss the question, "How Can American Slavery be

[31] *Chicago Daily Times and Herald*, Nov. 21, 1860; *Cincinnati Daily Enquirer*, Dec. 6, 1860; *Chicago Times*, Dec. 7, 1860. All these editorials are printed in Perkins, *Northern Editorials on Secession*, 94-97, 140-41, and 429-31.

Abolished?" No sooner had James Redpath called the meeting to order than the hall was invaded by a group of "North end Roughs and Beacon Street Aristocrats" led by lawyers and merchants, "nearly all of whom have uncollected debts [in the South] and many of them mortgages on slaves."[32] They began to shout and stamp their feet, making it impossible for Redpath and his followers to carry on. A few of the "Broadcloth rowdies" marched to the platform, forcibly ejected the astonished Redpath, took over the meeting, and passed resolutions urging concessions to the South "in the interests of commerce, manufactures, and agriculture." The abolitionists organized a counterattack, and a general scuffling broke out. Finally the police, who sympathized with the mob and had refused to protect the abolitionists, dispersed the meeting and ordered everybody home.[33]

The abolitionists decided to continue their meeting in the Negro Baptist church on Joy Street. That night the church was crowded with abolitionists and Negroes, while several hundred "Union men" gathered outside in an ugly mood. Wendell Phillips gave the main speech of the evening, a scorching attack on the Boston authorities for failing to protect free speech. After the meeting the mob assaulted colored people with stones and clubs as they emerged from the church. Phillips was saved from a similar fate by a tight-lipped cordon of friends who escorted him home through the mob. The frustrated rioters retired to the Negro section and expressed their Union-saving sentiments by smashing the windows of several houses.[34]

On four Sundays during the secession winter, Phillips spoke to large crowds in Boston's huge, barn-like Music Hall, and each

[32] This description of the mob is taken from the accounts by William S. Robinson in the *New York Tribune*, Dec. 5, 7, 1860. The leader of this mob was Richard Fay, a wealthy Boston lawyer. Many of his confederates were also prominent lawyers, merchants, or brokers: Rufus Choate, Jr., John Bell, B. F. Russell, Oliver Stevens, Thomas L. Parkins, John C. Boyd, William C. Rogers, T. J. Coolidge, Jr., William Aspinwall, and Amos A. Lawrence. For a discussion of the Boston antiabolitionist mobs of 1860-61, see Edith Ellen Ware, *Political Opinion in Massachusetts during the Civil War and Reconstruction* (New York, 1916), 85-90.

[33] This account of the meeting is drawn from descriptions in the *New York Tribune*, Dec. 7, 1860; *Boston Courier*, Dec. 4, 1860; *Worcester Spy*, Dec. 4, 1860; and *Liberator*, Dec. 7, 14, 1860.

[34] *New York Tribune*, Dec. 7, 1860; *Liberator*, Dec. 7, 14, 21, 1860; *Twenty-Eighth Annual Report of the American Anti-Slavery Society*, 177.

time but the first the hall was surrounded by hundreds of clerks, lawyers, merchants, and common laborers who thought they saw their livelihoods threatened by the breakup of the Union. Their feelings toward Phillips were expressed by one well-dressed young businessman: "Damn him! He has depreciated stocks $3,000,000 by his slang." Alarmed for Phillips' safety, his friends organized a company of about forty men, who stationed themselves in strategic parts of the hall to prevent any attack on Phillips. When Phillips finished speaking his men would form a circle around him and escort him home through the jeering, cursing mobs. Two or three close friends stayed with Phillips several nights, sleeping in the next room with their revolvers near at hand. Phillips himself was a good shot with a revolver, and carried one with him whenever he ventured onto the streets of Boston during the winter.[35]

The convention of the Massachusetts Anti-Slavery Society in Tremont Temple on January 24 erupted into pandemonium. Merchants and shopkeepers gave their employees the day off to attend the meeting, and two or three hundred young clerks and rowdies crowded into the galleries. They heckled and shouted at every speaker, but reserved their greatest fire for Phillips. As he tried to speak they shouted, sang, and threw seat cushions at the platform. "Such yelling, screeching, stamping, and bellowing I never heard," wrote Lydia Maria Child, who was present at the meeting. "It was a full realization of the old phrase, 'All hell broke loose.'" After trying unsuccessfully to make himself heard above the uproar, Phillips suddenly leaned forward and began talking quietly to reporters in the front row. "Abolitionists! Look here!" he said. "These pencils [pointing to the reporters] will do more to create opinion than a hundred thousand mobs. While I speak to these pencils, I speak to a million of men. . . . We have got the press of the country in our hands. Whether they like us or not, they know that our speeches sell their papers. (Applause and laughter) With five newspapers we may defy five hundred boys." The hecklers yelled to Phillips: "Speak louder. We want to hear what you're saying," and having gained their attention Phillips

[35] Thomas W. Higginson, *Cheerful Yesterdays* (Boston, 1898), 240-44; George W. Smalley, *Anglo-American Memories,* 1st Series (London, 1911), 91-99; Bartlett, *Phillips,* 225-31; *Liberator,* Dec. 21, 1860, Jan. 25, 1861; Higginson to Louisa Higginson, Jan. 21, 1861, Higginson Papers, HU.

spoke for half an hour without interruption. When he sat down, however, the mob renewed its clamor, drowning out most of the other speakers. Finally the police cleared the galleries, but when the abolitionists returned for their evening meeting they found themselves locked out by order of the mayor, a Democrat.[36] The mob had won this round, and at least one southern newspaper rejoiced. "A John Brown meeting cannot be held in Boston now," wrote a correspondent to an Atlanta newspaper. "We have got a most powerful organization here that will be heard from in due time. . . . Tell the people of Georgia not to be too rash. Tell them to bear with us a little longer and all will be well."[37]

Boston was not the only place where abolitionists were shouted down. In nearly every city where they tried to speak they were greeted by mobs. Susan B. Anthony arranged a series of abolitionist meetings in upstate New York during January and February. In Buffalo a riotous assemblage led by ex-Governor Horatio Seymour hooted down the abolitionists, drove them from the platform, organized the meeting themselves, and adopted Union-saving resolutions denouncing "the wild theories of fanatical abolitionists." At Rochester, Rome, and Auburn abolitionist speakers were howled down. The Utica city council denied them the use of any public hall. In Syracuse the abolitionists were met by a drunken rabble armed with pistols, knives, and rotten eggs. The mob dragged effigies of Susan B. Anthony and Samuel J. May through the streets and burned them in the city square. Only in Albany was free speech vindicated. The Democratic mayor of that city stationed a heavy guard of police around the hall and sat on the platform himself with a revolver in his lap to make sure the meeting was not disturbed.[38]

William H. Furness, abolitionist pastor of a Unitarian Church in Philadelphia, feared mob violence against his church, and members of his congregation came armed to Sunday services from December 1860, until the following April. A gang of young toughs attacked Charles C. Burleigh as he was attempting to lecture in

[36] *Liberator*, Feb. 1, 1861; Lydia Maria Child to Sarah B. Shaw, Jan. ?, 1861, in Harriet W. Sewall, ed., *Letters of Lydia Maria Child* (Boston, 1883), 148; Frank Sanborn to Gerrit Smith, Jan. 27, 1861, Smith Papers, su.

[37] The Atlanta newspaper was quoted in the *Liberator*, Feb. 8, 1861.

[38] *N.A.S. Standard*, Jan. 19, 26, Feb. 2, 9, 16, 1861; *Twenty-Eighth Annual Report of the American Anti-Slavery Society*, 182-88.

the schoolhouse at Westfield, Massachusetts. In the ensuing struggle the rioters knocked over the stove and burned down the building. Some of the most vicious mobs were encountered by Parker Pillsbury, Josephine Griffing, and Giles B. Stebbins in Ohio and Michigan. At Ann Arbor a group of university students and local hangers-on assaulted abolitionists with wooden benches, clubs, and broken glass, injuring several persons and demolishing the inside of the meeting-hall.[39]

Abolitionists believed that the purpose of these mobs was "to conciliate the plotters of treason at the South, to stay the progress of secession, and lure back seceders and armed rebels, by creating an impression that the North is ready to adopt the cowardly policy of concession."[40] Garrison was discouraged by the virulent anti-abolitionist spirit abroad in the land. "I fervently trust this pro-slavery Union is broken beyond the possibility of restoration by Northern compromise," he wrote, "yet, when I see our meetings everywhere mobbed down . . . I am not sure but the whole country is to come under the bloody sway of the Slave Power."[41]

In the final analysis, however, the mobs probably helped the abolitionists by attracting public attention and sympathy to them. "Every sentence that Mr. Phillips utters is read as never before," wrote William Lloyd Garrison, Jr. "The *Tribune* scatters his speeches broadcast thru the North, & the *Herald* prints them likewise to send South."[42] Their enemies could denounce, deride, and mob the abolitionists, but they could not prevent abolitionist words and ideas from being heard and read throughout the land.

✦

To most Americans during the winter of 1860-1861, war was but a dimly glimpsed possibility. The only alternatives seemed to be disunion, concession, or a long period of waiting until south-

[39] Elizabeth M. Geffen, "William Henry Furness, Philadelphia Antislavery Preacher," *Pennsylvania Magazine of History & Biography*, LXXXII (July 1958), 290; Wm. L. Garrison, Jr., to Samuel Johnson, Feb. 9, 1861, Johnson Papers, Essex Institute; Parker Pillsbury to C. K. Whipple, Jan. 30, 1861, Garrison Papers, BPL; *Twenty-Eighth Annual Report of the American Anti-Slavery Society*, 180-81, 188-90.

[40] *ibid.*, 190.

[41] Garrison to Oliver Johnson, Jan. 19, 1861, Garrison Papers, BPL.

[42] Wm. L. Garrison, Jr., to Samuel Johnson, Feb. 9, 1861, Johnson Papers, Essex Institute.

ern Unionists brought their states back into the Union voluntarily. Some abolitionists foresaw war; few desired it.

In spite of their hopes for peace, several abolitionists feared that war would be the outcome of the secession struggle. "I am here at the center of political commotion," wrote Henry B. Stanton from Washington in January, "& I assure you this Union is going to destruction as fast as it can. . . . Civil War is close upon us." A month later Lydia Maria Child observed: "if the Republicans do *not* yield up all they have gained, I suppose the alternative is civil war. It is a horrid alternative. . . . But here lies the alarming fact; we must *always* keep on compromising our principles, or else civil war will be threatened. . . . Freedom must come up manfully to the struggle, or die by a slow but certain poison. Therefore, much as I deprecate civil war, I deliberately say even *that* is better than compromises of principles, at this momentous crisis."[43]

Even as late as the first part of April, however, most abolitionists did not anticipate war. Frederick Douglass believed the North too cowardly and proslavery to fight. "All talk about putting down treason and rebellion by force," he wrote, "are as impotent and worthless as the words of a drunken woman in a ditch. Slavery has touched our government, and the cirute has gone out of its arms." In a speech at New Bedford on April 9, Wendell Phillips alluded to telegraphic reports (false, of course) that Fort Sumter was already under attack. Let South Carolina have the fort, said Phillips—he wanted no war with her. Phillips had as low an estimate of northern courage and patriotism as Douglass: "You cannot go through Massachusetts, and recruit men to bombard Charleston or New Orleans. The Northern mind will not bear it: you can never make such a war popular. . . . Instead of conquering Charleston, you create a Charleston in New England, you stir up sympathy for the South."[44]

Three days after this speech the shore batteries in Charleston opened fire on Fort Sumter in earnest. Contrary to the expectations of abolitionists, the North was galvanized into a frenzy of patriotism by the event. Political differences were temporarily

[43] H. B. Stanton to E. C. Stanton, Jan. 12, 1861, Stanton Papers, LC; L. M. Child to Henrietta Sargent, Feb. 9, 1861, Child Papers, Cornell.

[44] *Douglass' Monthly*, April 1861; George L. Austin, *The Life and Times of Wendell Phillips* (2nd ed., Boston, 1901), 206-09.

forgotten. Every northern hamlet held its war meeting. Abolitionists were astounded by the northern reaction to Sumter. For thirty years the North had tamely submitted to the demands of the slave power, but in 1861 the free states decided to submit no more. Dr. Henry Bowditch, a Boston abolitionist, wrote: "Ye gods, what a change has come over the spirit of our people since that occurrence [the firing on Sumter]. We had been lying as in a state of apparent listlessness. . . . Now . . . the whole North is a unit. . . . Young and old, men and women, boys and girls, have caught the sacred enthusiasm. . . . The times are ripening for a march of a liberating army into the Confederate States. If slavery is to be the cornerstone of treason, slavery will, must be, undermined."[45]

"You have no idea how the war fever rages here," wrote Oliver Johnson from New York. "There was never anything like it." After attending a mass war meeting in Worcester, Higginson wrote: "Tonight we have more than enthusiasm, we have unanimity. . . . Never before since I lived here (or anywhere else) has there been [such] absolute unanimity on a single subject." Samuel May, Jr. rejoiced, "These are very hopeful times indeed. There is a North at last, and the Southern people are absolutely confounded at the sight." Frederick Douglass was compelled by the mass enthusiasm to change his mind about northern courage and patriotism. "What a change now greets us!" he wrote two weeks after Sumter. "The Government is aroused, the dead North is alive, and its divided people united. . . . The cry now is for war, vigorous war, war to the bitter end."[46]

Opposed to war before the firing on Sumter, most abolitionists did an about-face when war finally came, for they saw in the conflict the imminent destruction of slavery. When he heard the news of Sumter's bombardment, Samuel Gridley Howe seized a pen and wrote: "Since they will have it so,—in the name of God, —Amen! Now let the Governors and Chief men of the people see

[45] Vincent Y. Bowditch, *Life and Correspondence of Henry Ingersoll Bowditch* (2 vols., Boston, 1902), II, 2-4. The northern reaction to the firing on Sumter is described in Stampp, *And the War Came*, 288-89.

[46] Oliver Johnson to Samuel May, Jr., Apr. 15, 1861, Johnson Papers, VHS; Higginson to Louisa Higginson, Apr. 17, 1861, Higginson Papers, HU; Samuel May, Jr., to C. C. Burleigh, Apr. 25, 1861, Samuel May, Jr., Papers, BPL; *Douglass' Monthly*, May 1861.

to it that war shall not cease until Emancipation is secure." Henry B. Stanton wrote from Washington a few days after Sumter: "I hear Old John Brown knocking on the lid of his coffin & shouting 'Let me out,' 'let me out!' The doom of slavery is at hand. It is to be wiped out in blood. Amen!"[47]

Some abolitionists voiced tentative doubts about the value of war to the antislavery cause. William Goodell noted sourly that the speakers at a huge Union meeting in New York disavowed any intention to interfere with slavery and proclaimed the sole purpose of the war to be restoration of the Union.[48] Lydia Maria Child thought there was little "of either right principle, or good feeling, at the foundation of this unanimous Union sentiment." She pointed out that within two weeks of the firing on Sumter the federal forces at Fort Pickens had returned thirty fugitive slaves to their masters, and General Benjamin Butler had offered to use his Massachusetts troops to suppress any slave uprising in Maryland. "I want to love and honor the flag of my country," wrote Mrs. Child, "but how can I, when it is used for such purposes?" Her husband David had attended a Union meeting in Wayland, Massachusetts, and was almost mobbed when he said something about the duty of the government to slaves who came within Union lines. He was told in no uncertain terms that the war had "nothing to do with the damned niggers." "In view of these things," lamented Mrs. Child, "the Union-shouts, and hurrahs for the U.S. flag, sound like fiendish mockery in my ears."[49]

Few abolitionists, however, could share this pessimism in the ebullient days after Sumter. They realized perfectly well that the official war aim was Union rather than emancipation, but foresaw that some measure of abolition was inevitable before the war ended. "It matters little, comparatively, that the rallying cry is 'the Union and the Constitution,' " said Oliver Johnson. "We all know that, in spite of every effort to control and qualify it, the war must be, essentially, a war of freedom against slavery." J. Miller McKim boldly declared: "This is to be an abolition war. The South has elected to give it this character. . . . The North has not been

[47] Howe to John Andrew, Apr. 13, 1861, Andrew Papers, MHS; H. B. Stanton to E. C. Stanton, Apr. ?, 1861, E. C. Stanton Papers, LC.
[48] *Principia*, Apr. 27, 1861.
[49] L. M. Child to Lucy Osgood, Apr. 26, May 7, 1861, Child Papers, Cornell.

and is not yet prepared for final action on this question; but she has no alternative." The *Anti-Slavery Standard* said, "This outburst of spirit and enthusiasm at the North may spring chiefly from indignation at the wrongs of the white man, but it will none the less finally right those of the black man."[50]

One of the biggest questions of the day for abolitionists, and for many who were not abolitionists, was the attitude of Wendell Phillips toward the war. "It will be a pity if Wendell Phillips continues to claim for the secessionists that they are only carrying out the doctrine of State Rights," remarked Oliver Johnson. A young abolitionist in New York reported that his friends were asking where Phillips stood. "I replied that I did not know, but if he did not now enlist under the stars & stripes, I was no longer under him."[51]

Phillips passed through an agony of indecision during the first days after Sumter. For twenty years he had urged disunion; could he now renounce his past just because of the loss of one fort? Phillips came into the law office of his young friend George Smalley in Boston one day, looking tired and uneasy. He discussed his problem with Smalley, who told him: "I don't think it matters much what you sacrifice—consistency, principles, or anything. They belong to the past. They have nothing to do with to-day. The war is upon us. You must either support it or oppose it. If you oppose it, you fling away your position and all your influence. You will never be listened to again." As a clinching argument Smalley said: "I will tell you what I once heard a negro say: 'When my massa and somebody else quarrel I'm on the somebody else's side.' Don't you think the negro knows? Do you really doubt that a war between the Slave Power and the North, be the result what it may, must end in Freedom?" Phillips left after a few more words, but when Smalley saw him again that evening Phillips announced his intention to speak in the Music Hall next Sunday, April 21, on the subject of the war.[52]

The word spread rapidly through Boston. Newspapers pre-

[50] Oliver Johnson to J. M. McKim, Apr. 18, 1861, McKim Papers, Cornell; *N.A.S. Standard*, Apr. 20, 27, 1861. McKim's statement is from his weekly column in the *N.A.S. Standard*, Apr. 20, 1861.

[51] O. Johnson to J. M. McKim, Apr. 18, 1861, McKim Papers, Cornell; Edward Bunker, Jr., to W. L. Garrison, Jr., Apr. 25, 1861, Garrison Papers, sc.

[52] Smalley, *Anglo-American Memories*, 1st Series, 108-10.

dicted that Phillips would come out for the Union and the war. Four thousand people jammed into the Music Hall on Sunday. The first thing that greeted their eyes was the platform decked with American flags. Phillips came forward and began speaking in his quiet, melodious voice:

"Many times this winter, here and elsewhere, I have counselled peace,—urged, as well as I knew how, the expediency of acknowledging a Southern Confederacy, and the peaceful separation of these thirty-four States. One of the journals announces to you that I come here this morning to retract those opinions. No, not one of them! (Applause) I need them all,—every word I have spoken this winter,—every act of twenty-five years of my life, to make the welcome I give this war hearty and hot. . . . I rejoice . . . that now, for the first tme in my antislavery life, I speak under the stars and stripes, and welcome the tread of Massachusetts men marshalled for war."

At these words the audience sprang to its feet, and four thousand throats made the rafters echo with cheer after cheer. When calm returned, Phillips continued:

"No matter what the past has been or said; to-day the slave asks God for a sight of this banner, and counts it the pledge of his redemption. (Applause) Hitherto it may have meant what you thought, or what I did; to-day it represents sovereignty and justice. (Renewed applause) The only mistake that I have made, was in supposing Massachusetts wholly choked with cotton-dust and cankered with gold. (Loud cheering) The South thought her patience and generous willingness for peace were cowardice; to-day shows the mistake. She has been sleeping on her arms since '83, and the first canon-shot brings her to her feet with the war-cry of the Revolution on her lips." (Loud cheers)

Phillips admitted that Union war aims at this time did not include emancipation, but John Quincy Adams had long ago affirmed the right of the nation in time of war to abolish slavery, and "when the South cannonaded Fort Sumter the bones of Adams stirred in his coffin. (Cheers) And you might have heard him, from that granite grave at Quincy, proclaim to the nation: 'the hour has struck! Seize the thunderbolt God has forged for you, and annihilate the system which has troubled your peace for seventy years!' (Cheers)" Phillips concluded, "I believe in the possibility of justice, in the certainty of union. Years hence, when the smoke of this conflict clears away, the world will see under our banner all tongues, all creeds, all races,—one brotherhood,—and on the banks of the Potomac, the Genius of Liberty, robed in light, four and thirty stars for her diadem, broken chains under her feet, and an olive-branch in her right hand. (Great applause)"[53]

It was the greatest speech of his life. Five years before, when young Richard Hinton was leaving for bleeding Kansas, Phillips had asked what he planned to accomplish there. Hinton replied that he hoped freedom in Kansas would open the road to freedom in South Carolina. Hinton was in the audience on this memorable April 21, 1861, and as the hall rang with cheers at the end of the speech Phillips leaned over and shouted in his ear, "Well, Hinton, we've reached South Carolina at last!"[54]

As Phillips left the hall he met a mob of people milling around outside, but this time the crowd cheered him every step of the way home instead of threatening his life. The *Liberator* published an extra containing Phillips' speech, and newsboys sold sixteen thousand copies on the streets—the largest edition of the *Liberator* ever printed. The *Anti-Slavery Standard* and *Anglo-African* published several thousand copies of the speech and sold them on the streets in New York. Metropolitan papers in several cities printed the address, and more than 200,000 copies were sold in all.[55]

"Wendell's speech is magnificent; I read it with moist cheeks and a throbbing heart," wrote Oliver Johnson from New York. "What a speech!" cried young William Bunker, a friend of the Garrisons, as he rushed off to enlist. The high priest of disunion had taken up the cudgels for Union and liberty, and abolitionists everywhere enthusiastically closed ranks behind him.[56]

[53] The speech was published by many northern newspapers, including the *Boston Advertiser*, Apr. 22, 1861, and the *New York Sunday Times*, Apr. 28, 1861. It is most readily accessible in Phillips, *Speeches, Lectures, and Letters*, 1st Series, 396-414. George Smalley, *Anglo-American Memories*, 1st Series, 110-12, and Charles W. Slack, in Austin, *Phillips*, 217-18, describe the scene at the Music Hall during and after the speech.
[54] C. Carroll Hollis, "R. J. Hinton, Lincoln's Reluctant Biographer," *The Centennial Review of Arts & Sciences*, v (Winter 1961), 75.
[55] *Liberator*, May 10, 1861; O. Johnson to J. M. McKim, Apr. 29, 1861, McKim Papers, Cornell; Austin, *Phillips*, 218.
[56] O. Johnson to McKim, Apr. 25, 1861, McKim Papers, Cornell; Edward Bunker, Jr., to W. L. Garrison, Jr., Apr. 25, 1861, Garrison Papers, sc.

HIS war plays the deuce with peace principles," declared pacifist William Furness three weeks after the firing on Sumter. Another peace-minded abolitionist, Samuel J. May, confessed at the outbreak of war that "the conduct of the rebels and the impending fate of our country has shaken my confidence in the *extreme* principles of the non-resistants."[1] The coming of a war which they hoped would destroy slavery posed a serious moral dilemma for pacifist abolitionists. Only a small number of abolitionists were actual nonresistants, but nearly all nineteenth-century reformers professed peace sentiments to some degree. The constitutions of most antislavery societies pledged their members to advocate only peaceful means for the overthrow of slavery. When confronted by a choice between a (potentially) antislavery war and a proslavery peace, however, most abolitionists did not hesitate to choose war. Much as they loved peace, they hated slavery more.

After Lincoln's call for troops Garrison announced that "all my sympathies and wishes are with the government, because it is entirely in the right, and acting strictly in self-defence and for self-preservation." The war would be horrible, as all wars were horrible, "but if it shall end in the speedy and total abolition of slavery, the fountain-source of all our national difficulties, it will bring with it inconceivable blessings." Garrison's son and namesake wrote: "As a non-resistant, believing all war to be wicked & unchristian, I can yet delight that this conflict is upon us." Why? The nonresistant favored a peace based on love and compassion for humanity. "But, peace which is the result of cowardice is despicable. Well, the North for the past twenty years has suffered every indignity, submitted to every degradation which the South could inflict." There was cause for rejoicing in the North's awakening from its moral stupor: "Instead of the utter subjection to slavery which we had feared, a regeneration has taken place, & the tyrant now reads in an aroused North, the handwriting on the wall prophecying his destruction. So I hail with acclamation

[1] Furness to Moncure Conway, May 7, 1861, Conway Papers, cu; G. B. Emerson, S. May, and T. J. Mumford, *Memoir of Samuel Joseph May* (New York, 1871), 226.

every man who shoulders a musket for the purpose of getting a shot at the slave-power."[2]

The elder Garrison denied that support of the war involved any compromise of his pacifist principles. He would not take up arms himself, but would judge by their own standards "those who, rejecting the doctrine of non-resistance, profess to believe in the right and duty of maintaining their freedom by the sword. The worst thing they can do is to be recreant to their own convictions in such a crisis as this. I thank God when men who believe in the right and duty of wielding carnal weapons, are so far advanced

"Emancipation." Nast in *Harper's Weekly*

that they will take those weapons out of the scale of despotism and throw them into the scale of freedom."[3]

Gerrit Smith, a member of the American Peace Society, rationalized his support for the war on the ground that the government was merely defending itself against "traitors and pirates who are at work to overthrow it. If there are principles of the Society forbidding this, I am not aware of them." Another abolitionist member of the Peace Society said that its meetings had become war meetings and that he found himself praying that the sword would not be sheathed until there was no longer a slave in the land.[4] The Peace Society made an official distinction between international wars, which it opposed, and the suppression of domestic rebellion, which it approved.

A few abolitionist-pacifists refused to accept this reasoning. Elihu Burritt, one of the foremost proponents of universal peace, lamented "the insidious drifting that has carried nearly all our peace friends into the wake of this war." Burritt ridiculed the Peace Society's position "that this terrible conflict, in which each party is arraying 500,000 armed men against the other, is not *war* but quelling a mob on the part of the Federal Government. . . . I feel that this sophistry and position have shorn the locks of the Society of all the strength of principle; and I have been saddened to silence."[5]

British pacifists sharply rebuked Garrison for his prowar stand. Garrison's friends replied angrily. "If the editor of the London Herald of Peace does not understand that Slavery is war," cried James Redpath, "and that, therefore, the putting down of Slavery is the true peace policy, . . . Mr. Garrison does, and every other man of good judgment here does." Did Britons think that non-resistant abolitionists should require the government to "sit still, and have the handcuffs applied, the gag forced into their mouth, and consent to be driven out of the seat of government, and allow the slaveholders to walk in & occupy?" asked Samuel May, Jr. "It is plain to me that the non-resistants would have been nothing less than the allies of the slaveholders, to have taken any such ground."[6]

Prowar abolitionists developed the argument that slavery itself was the worst form of war imaginable, and that a civil war, however terrible, was worth the cost if it held out a chance of abolishing slavery. "Tho' a peace man, and a lover of peace, I regard slavery perpetuated as much more deplorable than a . . . bloody war

[4] *Gerrit Smith to George C. Becksmith, May 18, 1861* (printed letter, Peterboro, 1861); *Principia*, June 8, 1861.

[5] Elihu Burritt to Henry Richard, May 26, 1861, in Merle Curti, ed., *The Learned Blacksmith: Letters and Journals of Elihu Burritt* (New York, 1937), 138-39. The Peace Society suspended its activities for the duration of the war, and soon disintegrated.

[6] *The Pine and Palm*, Sept. 7, 1861; Samuel May, Jr., to Richard Webb, Dec. 24, 1861, Samuel May, Jr., Papers, BPL.

that may overthrow it," declared an Iowa abolitionist. Moncure Conway, the Virginia-born abolitionist who grew up on a slave plantation, wrote in 1862 that "Slavery is perpetual war. . . . A single day of Slavery and its rule in this country witnessed more wrong, violence, corruption, more actual war, than all that civil war even could bring." Wendell Phillips exclaimed, "In my view, the bloodiest war ever waged is infinitely better than the happiest slavery which ever fattened men into obedience. And yet I love peace. But it is real peace; not peace such as we have had; not peace that meant lynch-law in the Carolinas and mob-law in New York, . . . a gag on the lips of statesmen, and the slave sobbing himself to sleep in curses. No more such peace for me."[7]

✦

At the height of war enthusiasm in the North following the firing on Sumter, Garrison urged abolitionists to " 'stand still, and see the salvation of God' rather than attempt to add anything to the general commotion." This glorious hour was "no time for minute criticism of Lincoln, Republicanism, or even the other parties, now that they are fusing for a death-grapple with the Southern slave-oligarchy."[8]

Similar advice poured into abolitionist headquarters from prominent Garrisonians in Boston, New York, Philadelphia, and elsewhere. The pressure for quiet and conformity became so strong that the executive committees of the American and New England Anti-Slavery Societies took the unprecedented step of canceling the annual conventions of these societies.[9] In an editorial explaining the reason for this cancellation, the *Anti-Slavery Standard* conceded that criticism and agitation had always been the duty of abolitionists, "But, in a crisis like this, criticism may suspend its judgment for awhile and watch the sequence of events." Abolitionists should do nothing to endanger "the storm of Northern in-

[7] Joseph Dugdale to J. Miller McKim, June 27, 1861, McKim Papers, Cornell; Moncure Conway, *The Golden Hour* (Boston, 1862), 12, 33; Wendell Phillips, *Speeches, Lectures, and Letters*, 1st Series (Boston, 1863), 419.

[8] Garrison to Oliver Johnson, Apr. 19, 1861, Garrison Papers, BPL.

[9] J. M. McKim to Garrison, Apr. 20, 1861, O. Johnson to Garrison, Apr. 22, 1861, Garrison to O. Johnson, Apr. 23, 1861, J. S. Gibbons to Garrison, Apr. 25, 1861, Garrison Papers, BPL; John Jay to Charles Sumner, Apr. 18, 1861, Sumner Papers, HU; Edmund Quincy to Sydney Howard Gay, Apr. 19, 1861, Gay Papers, CU; Records of the Board of Managers of the Massachusetts Anti-Slavery Society, p. 118 (in possession of the BPL).

dignation against the South which is now beating against the outworks of slavery. Should it slacken, or turn its force backward on its own region, the time of criticism and censure will have come again."[10]

This action brought protests from some who thought that abolitionists should remain vigilant and active. After all, they argued, there were few signs of an antislavery purpose on the part of the North. In his proclamation of April 15 calling for 75,000 troops to suppress rebellion, Lincoln promised "to avoid any destruction of, or interference with, property," that is, slavery. General Benjamin Butler offered in April to use his Massachusetts troops to put down a rumored slave insurrection in Maryland, and in subsequent months several other northern generals made similar offers to border-state slaveholders.[11] On April 22 Secretary of State Seward officially instructed the American minister in Paris that "the condition of slavery in the several states will remain just the same whether [the rebellion] shall succeed or shall fail."[12] The *New York Times*, rapidly becoming the most accurate journalistic spokesman for administration policy, editorially stated that "it is a great mistake to suppose that the war . . . is a war . . . against Southern institutions." Even the *New York Tribune* declared a month after the surrender of Sumter that "this War is in truth a War for the preservation of the Union, not for the destruction of Slavery; and it would alienate many ardent Unionists to pervert it into a War against Slavery. . . . We believe that Slavery has nothing to fear from a Union triumph."[13]

Pointing to statements such as these, several abolitionists deplored the cancellation of the annual meetings. Parker Pillsbury and Aaron M. Powell thought abolitionists should "reserve and exercise the right of *criticism*." Susan B. Anthony could not see "*one good* reason for the abandonment of all our meetings."[14]

[10] *N.A.S. Standard*, Apr. 27, 1861.

[11] Roy P. Basler, ed., *The Collected Works of Abraham Lincoln* (9 vols., New Brunswick, N.J., 1955), IV, 332; *The War of the Rebellion: A Compilation of the Official Records of the Union and Confederate Armies* (128 vols., Washington, 1880-1901), Series 1, vol. II, 593, 47-49, 662, vol. III, 373. (Hereafter cited as *O.R.*)

[12] Edward L. Pierce, *Memoir and Letters of Charles Sumner* (4 vols., Boston, 1877-94), IV, 39.

[13] *New York Times*, May 10, 1861; *New York Tribune*, May 14, 1861.

[14] *N.A.S. Standard*, May 11, 1861; Pillsbury to Wm. Lloyd Garrison, Jr., May 28, 1861, Pillsbury Papers, SC; A. M. Powell to Wm. L. Garrison, May 8, 1861,

From Illinois George Bassett expressed his disgust for the "universal infatuation" of abolitionists who gave unqualified support to the war. "It is not a war for Negro Liberty, but for national despotism. It is a tariff war, an aristocratic war, a *pro-slavery* war." A Garrisonian at Yale College found it "singular" that "Abolitionists and Disunionists of thirty years' standing should now be found lending pen and voice to uphold and urge on a war waged solely and avowedly to preserve and perpetuate the Union." This was no antislavery conflict: "Is any one so blind as to fancy that the capitalists, who last winter were mobbing Mr. Phillips, have now struck hands with him for a crusade against slavery? . . . Point me to a single word or whisper of love or regard for the rights of the slave, in all this disgusting and senseless vaporing about the flag, and the Union, and the dignity of the Government."[15]

Garrison tried to answer these criticisms in a long *Liberator* editorial on May 10. He admitted that the war, at least on the surface, was not an abolitionist war. Garrison considered this, however, "a verbal and technical view of the case." He asserted that "the one great cause of all our national troubles and divisions is SLAVERY: the removal of it, therefore, is essential to our national existence. What can be plainer than this?" It was so plain, he thought, that the North would soon realize it and take steps to remove this pernicious cause of all its troubles. For abolitionists to persist in the old policy of disunion and excoriation of the national government would be a blind and obstinate consistency; abolitionists must be flexible and adjust themselves to the changed situation.

As the weeks passed, however, the war settled into a conservative pattern—a pattern that soon discouraged many abolitionists. Republican newspapers made it painfully clear that, unless unforeseen obstacles arose, it would not be an antislavery war. Said the widely respected *Springfield Republican*: "If there is one point of honor upon which more than another this administration

Garrison Papers, BPL; Susan B. Anthony to Martha Wright, May 28, 1861, Anthony Papers, SC.

15 Bassett to Gerrit Smith, May 9, 1861, Smith Papers, SU; *Liberator*, May 10, 1861. See also George W. Bassett, *A Discourse on the Wickedness and Folly of the Present War, delivered in the Court House, Ottawa, Ill., August 11, 1861* (Ottawa, 1861).

will stick, it is its pledge not to interfere with slavery in the states."
Governor Andrew of Massachusetts, seeking advice from Washington on the tone he should take toward national affairs in his message
to a special session of the legislature, was bluntly told by Montgomery Blair to "drop the nigger." Even Henry Ward Beecher,
a strong antislavery man, trimmed to the conservative breeze of
public opinion. "Some people ask if this is to be a crusade of
emancipation," noted Beecher in a sermon on June 23. "No, it
is not. I hate slavery intensely. . . . Liberty is the birthright of
every man, yet ours is not an army of liberation. Why? Because
the fifteen States of the South are guaranteed security in their
property, and we have no right by force to dispossess them of
that property."[16]

Under such circumstances some abolitionists who had interpreted
the northern war fever after Sumter as an incipient revolution
against slavery began to have second thoughts. "I am beginning
to have some fears that this uprising is a sham & that the slave
may not be free," wrote Edward M. Davis of Philadelphia on May
30. James Redpath was one of those who had welcomed the outbreak of war as the impending doom of slavery. But six weeks later
he was no longer so sure. "The signs of the times have not and
do not now indicate to our mind any such hopeful result," he
wrote. "On the contrary, the drift of public sentiment appears, day
by day, to be steadily setting against even the recognition of the
slave in this contest." Especially disheartening were the frequent
reports of the return to their masters of fugitive slaves who had
sought refuge within Union lines. Lydia Maria Child said that
"Every instance of sending back poor fugitive slaves has cut into
my heart like the stab of a bowie-knife, and made me dejected for
days."[17]

When the Garrisonian abolitionists of New England gathered
for their annual Fourth of July picnic at Framingham, Massachusetts, there was a vocal element of opposition to the Garrison-
Phillips policy of supporting the Union war effort. Stephen S.
Foster brought this discontent to a head by introducing a resolu-

[16] *Springfield Republican*, June 8, 1861; Henry G. Pearson, *The Life of John
A. Andrew* (2 vols., Boston, 1904), I, 248-49; *New York World*, June 24, 1861.
[17] E. M. Davis to S. H. Gay, May 30, 1861, Gay Papers, CU; *Pine and Palm*,
June 1, 1861; L. M. Child to Henrietta Sargent, July 26, 1861, in Harriet W. Sewall,
ed., *Letters of Lydia Maria Child* (Boston, 1883), 154.

tion which affirmed that until the government proclaimed emancipation, abolitionists could "give it no support or countenance
in its effort to maintain its authority over the seceded States."
Passage of this resolution would have virtually committed abolitionists to disloyalty, and Garrison, Phillips and others hastened
to speak out against it. "I cannot say that I do not sympathize
with the Government, as against Jefferson Davis and his piratical
associates," declared Garrison, and he continued, "There is not
a drop of blood in my veins, both as an abolitionist and a peace
man, that does not flow with the Northern tide of sentiment." If
the government should try to conclude a peace on the basis of
the Union with slavery as secure as ever, "then will be the time
for me to open all the guns that I can bring to bear on it. But,
blessed be God, that 'covenant with death' has been annulled, and
that 'agreement with hell' no longer stands. I joyfully accept the
fact, and leave all verbal criticism until a more suitable opportunity."

Phillips thought that despite appearances, "there is a prevailing and unconscious, perhaps, but assured sentiment and purpose
at the North, that the Union either does or shall mean liberty in
the end." Phillips had been criticized for discarding his disunionism and coming out for the war. He replied to his critics that "no
man should flatter himself he can mould the world exactly in
his method. . . . I have advocated Disunion for fifteen years, because I thought it a practicable and peaceable method of freeing
the North from the guilt of slavery, and of planting at the South
the seeds of early and entire emancipation. But it has pleased the
Nation to seek that result in a different way." Abolitionists should
not renounce the Lincoln administration, said Phillips. They
should try to influence public opinion in favor of emancipation,
and bring that opinion to bear on the government. Several other
speakers supported the position of Garrison and Phillips. When
the vote was taken, Foster's antigovernment resolution was defeated by a large margin.[18]

This did not end the matter, however. At the annual celebration
of West Indian emancipation on August 1 at Abington, Massachusetts, Parker Pillsbury introduced another resolution denouncing the Lincoln administration. "I have no higher opinion of

[18] *Liberator*, July 12, 1861.

Abraham Lincoln, and his Cabinet . . . than I have of the President and Cabinet . . . of the Confederate States," said Pillsbury in a biting speech. Pillsbury's resolution was also defeated, but in subsequent weeks criticism of the Garrison-Phillips position increased. James McCune Smith, Negro abolitionist and editor of the *Anglo-African* in New York City, wrote a letter to his friend Gerrit Smith rebuking the progovernment stand of Smith and the Garrisonians. "Because the South chose to storm Sumter and rave generally," complained McCune Smith, "you lent the sanction of your great name to the support of an Administration which, with trembling knees and in the face of the enemy endeavored to pacify the South by returning fugitive slaves!"[19] Pillsbury indignantly announced that he was going to the West for a lecture tour "in the hope that all the old Life Guard of Freedom at the West will still be found, as in the past, at their posts. No party, no Administration, no army as yet, has shown itself worthy to be entrusted with the hallowed interests of liberty and humanity."[20]

This kind of criticism was not without effect on progovernment abolitionists. "The situation of persons like ourselves is far from pleasant," Gerrit Smith told Garrison and continued, "While we condemn the Cause of the South, we cannot advocate the Cause of the North. Nevertheless we are filled with the hope that the Cause of the North will become the Cause of Truth." In reply to criticism by British abolitionists, Samuel May, Jr., wrote: "I do not disguise nor apologize for the follies & mistakes of our own Government, but speak of them plainly. But, so far as the Govt. is right, it deserves to be sustained, & we do cheerfully sustain it to that degree."[21]

But by September 1861, the truce that had prevailed between most abolitionists and the Lincoln administration was beginning to wear thin. The fond hopes for a short war and a quick end to slavery had proven illusory; the North had measured the strength of the Confederacy and found that it was in for a long, hard war. Abolitionists began to organize more actively and thoroughly to

[19] *ibid.*, Aug. 16, 1861; James McCune Smith to Gerrit Smith, Aug. 22, 1861, Smith Papers, su.
[20] *N.A.S. Standard*, Aug. 24, 1861.
[21] Smith to Garrison, Sept. 2, 1861, Garrison Papers, bpl; May to Richard Webb, Dec. 24, 1861, Samuel May, Jr., Papers, bpl.

bring pressure on the government to adopt an emancipation policy. There had never actually been a lack of such pressure. From the beginning of the conflict abolitionists had individually and collectively called for emancipation as a war policy. At first they made little impression on public opinion, but as the strife grew hotter, the iron necessities of war began to convince more and more northerners that emancipation was the only road to victory.

One of the first tasks of antislavery propaganda was to persuade a skeptical North that Negro slavery was the fundamental cause and basic issue of the war. Most northerners at first were inclined to agree with Stephen Douglas, who said in an Illinois speech early in the war: "The issue is not the negro; this question is above all the negroes in Christendom; it involves the freedom and independence of the ten millions, soon to be a hundred millions, of free white men in this valley."[22] Elizur Wright retorted that a war merely for Union, "tho' not on a false, is on a superficial issue. The war at its foundation is all about the black man, . . . and before the war is through the black man is almost certain to be fighting for himself on one side or the other." "If the slavery question is ignored," warned John Jay, "& the people are taught to look upon it as a mere sectional struggle for power, it will sink to a mere political question in which they will take but little interest."[23]

Abolitionists pointed out that the Confederates did not consider the Negro question insignificant in this war. In an address at Savannah on March 21 Alexander Stephens, vice president of the Confederacy, criticized Thomas Jefferson and the founding fathers for their erroneous belief that all men were created equal and that slavery was wrong. The statesmen of the Confederacy would not repeat this error. "Our new Government," said Stephens, "is founded upon exactly the opposite ideas; its foundations are laid, its corner stone rests upon the great truth that the negro is not equal to the white man; that slavery, subordination to the superior race, is his natural and normal condition. This, our new Government, is the first in the history of the world, based upon this great physical, philosophical, and moral truth."[24]

[22] *Liberator*, May 3, 1861.

[23] Wright to S. P. Chase, May 4, 1861, Jay to Chase, June 4, 1861, Chase Papers, LC.

[24] *Liberator*, July 5, 1861. Edward McPherson, *The Political History of the United States of America during the Great Rebellion* (Washington, 1865), 103-04, also prints this speech.

This and similar statements by other Confederate leaders caused Thomas Wentworth Higginson to write: "It is impossible to blink the fact that Slavery is the root of the rebellion. . . . Either slavery is essential to a community or it must be fatal to it,—there is no middle ground; and the Secessionists have taken one horn of the dilemma with so delightful a frankness as to leave us no possible escape from taking the other. Never, in modern days, has there been a conflict in which the contending principles were so clearly antagonistic. The most bigoted royal house in Europe never dreamed of throwing down the gauntlet for the actual ownership of man by man." Frederick Douglass declared that "the American people and the Government at Washington may refuse to recognize it for a time; but the 'inexorable logic of events' will force it upon them in the end; that the war now being waged in this land is a war for and against slavery."[25]

Early in the war abolitionists developed the argument that slavery was both a source of strength and weakness to the Confederacy. It was a source of strength because, as Douglass quoted from the *Savannah Republican*, "the labor of the South is not, as elsewhere, the fighting element of the State." The *Montgomery Advertiser* proclaimed that slavery was a "tower of strength to the Confederacy." Ten per cent of the total white population was required to fill the ranks of the army. "In any other country than our own, such a draft could not be met," said the *Advertiser*, "but the Southern States can furnish that number of men and still not leave the material interests of the country in a suffering condition. . . . The institution of slavery in the South alone, enables her to place in the field a force so much larger in proportion to her white population than the North."[26]

Frederick Douglass wholeheartedly agreed that slavery was "a tower of strength" to the Confederacy, and urged the North to convert it into an element of weakness by proclaiming emancipation. "Why? Oh! why, in the name of all that is national, does our Government allow its enemies this powerful advantage?" asked Douglass. "The very stomach of this rebellion is the negro in the

25 T. W. Higginson, "The Ordeal by Battle," *Atlantic Monthly*, viii (July 1861), 94, 89; *Douglass' Monthly*, May 1861.
26 *Savannah Republican*, quoted in *Douglass' Monthly*, July 1861; *Montgomery Advertiser*, Nov. 6, 1861, quoted in *Principia*, Nov. 16.

condition of a slave. Arrest that hoe in the hands of the negro, and you smite the rebellion in the very seat of its life." There were thousands of slaves doing the heavy physical labor of the southern army—digging trenches, building fortifications, serving as teamsters, drivers, etc.—allowing soldiers to conserve their strength for the actual fighting. Douglass said, "The negro is the key of the situation—the pivot upon which the whole rebellion turns. . . . To fight against slaveholders, without fighting against slavery, is but a half-hearted business, and paralyzes the hands engaged in it."[27] Abolition of slavery, then, became a "military necessity" for victory in the war for the Union. That phrase, "military necessity," became the watchword of abolitionists in subsequent months; and "military necessity" was eventually cited by Lincoln as the main reason for his Emancipation Proclamation.

William Goodell urged abolitionists to keep the following facts before the people: the war was costing a million dollars a day; it could not be terminated without emancipation; every day's delay in proclaiming emancipation would cost the nation another million dollars; liberation of the slaves would transfer more than 500,000 able-bodied men from the Confederate to the Union side; the rebellion was a slaveholder's rebellion, and could not be put down without destroying slavery; and a compromise peace, leaving slavery intact, would fail to remove the cause of the strife and doom the nation to future discord and conflict. The *Anti-Slavery Standard* neatly summed up the abolitionist argument: "Success in the War, without Emancipation, is a Military Impossibility, and a Reunion with Slavery a political one."[28]

Abolitionists argued that emancipation was not only a military necessity, but also a moral necessity if the North hoped to justify the war to itself and to the world. In a popular book, *The Rejected Stone*, which went through three editions in 1861-62, Moncure Conway contended that the war had revealed the nation's fatal weakness. When the founding fathers constructed the edifice of the Union they cast aside one essential foundation stone, and Americans of 1861 were reaping the consequences of this folly. "That stone is, essentially, JUSTICE. The form in which it stands for

[27] *Douglass' Monthly*, July, Aug., Sept. 1861.
[28] *Principia*, Aug. 17, 1861; *N.A.S. Standard*, Dec. 7, 1861. In 1861 the American Anti-Slavery Society issued a pamphlet entitled *The War and Slavery: or Victory only through Emancipation* (Boston, 1861).

us is THE AFRICAN SLAVE." Napoleon once said that God was on the side of the strongest battalions. He found time to ponder his error in the solitude of St. Helena. The northern defeat at Bull Run, asserted Conway, proved that *"God is NOT on the side of the strongest battalions."* An army fights much better when it has a noble cause for which to fight, and the rebels were *"fighting for their liberty.* True, it was their liberty; the liberty of Wrong, the free course of Anarchy, the untrammelled rule of Passion, the uncurbed privilege of trampling the most sacred rights and hopes of mankind." Nevertheless, they believed they were fighting and dying for a sacred cause. "Now, North-men," asked Conway, "with what do you confront this? Have you any Freedom-frenzy, with its superhuman strength? Do you worship Liberty with a passion?" Until the North acquired such a passion it would not be able to match the South's fighting spirit. When the North began to fight for the liberty of all races, it would learn that God was not on the side of the strongest battalions, but "The strongest battalions are those on the side of God."[29]

Abolitionists argued that England and Europe could have little sympathy for the North so long as it fought merely for political dominion. "Great Britain can see no principle of freedom in the war, as regards the enslaved, no intention of justice or of mercy toward them," wrote George Cheever from England, where he spent the first four months of the war. Zebina Eastman, Illinois abolitionist, served as American consul in Bristol during the war, and continually bombarded Washington with pleas for an emancipation policy. He reported that he was doing his best to foster pro-Union sentiment among the British people, but found it difficult in 1861-1862 because they viewed the war as a mere contest for power, with moral superiority on the side of the South, which was fighting for its own freedom. Once the North proclaimed emancipation, argued Eastman, it would win the powerful hosts of British middle- and lower-class opinion to its side.[30]

Whittier summed up the abolitionist wartime indictment of

[29] Moncure D. Conway, *The Rejected Stone: or Insurrection vs. Resurrection in America* (Boston, 1861), 23-24, 68-73.

[30] George Cheever, Diary, entry of June 12, 1861, in Cheever Papers, AAS; Zebina Eastman to S. P. Chase, Jan. 8, 1862, Chase Papers, LC; Eastman to Seward, Sept. 11, 1862, Seward Papers, RU.

slavery in a widely quoted poem, "Hymn of Liberty," intended
to be sung to the tune of Luther's hymn, "A Mighty Fortress Is
Our God."

> What gives the wheat-field blades of steel?
> What points the rebel cannon?
> What sets the roaring rabble's heel
>   On the old star-spangled pennon?
>   What breaks the oath
>   Of the men o' the South?
>   What whets the knife
>   For the Union's life?—
> Hark to the answer: Slavery!
>
> Then waste no blows on lesser foes
>   In strife unworthy freemen.
> God lifts to-day the veil, and shows
>   The features of the demon!
>   O North and South,
>   Its victims both,
>   Can ye not cry,
>   'Let slavery die!'
> And Union find in freedom?[31]

✦

In many ways the Civil War was a revolutionary conflict. The
grant of freedom to four million slaves constituted the greatest
social and economic revolution in American history. From the
beginning of the war, abolitionists hoped for such an outcome and
called on their fellow Americans to take up the revolutionary
crusade for freedom. In an editorial entitled "The Second American Revolution," written less than three weeks after the fall of
Sumter, William Goodell solemnly proclaimed: "It has begun.
It is in progress. . . . The Revolution must go on, to its completion
—*a National Abolition of Slavery*. . . . What but the insanity of
moral blindness can long delay the proclamation, inviting [the
slaves] to a share in *the glorious second American Revolution*."[32]

The South tried to justify its secession by appealing to the tra-

[31] John G. Whittier, *Anti-Slavery Poems: Songs of Labor and Reform* (vol. iii
of his *Poetical Works*, Riverside Ed., Boston, 1888), 220.
[32] *Principia*, May 4, 1861.

ditions of '76. Moncure Conway, however, refused to recognize the southern rebellion as a revolution: "Revolution depends for its dignity and heroism purely upon the worth and justice of its cause. Had our American Revolution been for the purpose of forming our Colonies into a band of robbers and pirates" it would not have been a revolution. The South was fighting for slavery, "therefore it is wrongly called Revolution." It was the North that must fight a revolution of freedom. "The revolution is on our side, and as soon as the nation feels that, and acts upon it, the strength of the South is gone. . . . WE ARE THE REVOLUTIONISTS."[33]

It was all very well for abolitionists to urge the North forward on a revolutionary crusade for freedom, but a generation of Americans nurtured in a tradition of veneration for the Constitution could not be moved by such appeals alone. The constitutional inviolability of slavery in the states was held as an article of faith by most Americans. If abolitionists wished to see their dream of universal emancipation come true during the war, they would have to find some constitutional sanction for such a radical measure. They lost no time in doing so. Fortunately for them, there was a ready-made doctrine at hand for just such an emergency—the principle of the war power of the national government over slavery, developed and elaborated by John Quincy Adams twenty years earlier. During the Civil War the "war power" phrase became a companion to "military necessity" as the rallying cries under which wartime emancipationists drove the nation forward to total abolition of slavery.

On the day after the surrender of Fort Sumter, abolitionists began urging Lincoln and Congress to proclaim emancipation under the war power. They circulated petitions, wrote letters, made speeches, or talked personally with their congressmen. "That the President is authorized to liberate the slaves is as clear as that he may, when judging there is military necessity for it, order the destruction of all the rail roads in the Slave States," proclaimed Gerrit Smith on July 12 and continued, "In making war upon us the South has authorized us to cripple her in all the ways we

[33] Conway, *Rejected Stone*, 75-80, 110. For a similar appeal to the North to make the war a revolution for freedom, see [Elizur Wright], *The Programme of Peace, by a Democrat of the Old School* (Boston, 1862), 3-5.

66

can." The American Anti-Slavery Society published a pamphlet entitled *The Abolition of Slavery the Right of the Government under the War Power*. The pamphlet quoted extensively from John Quincy Adams, and included statements from Joshua Giddings, Orestes Brownson, and several other prominent Americans. It was published anonymously and cleverly edited: none of the articles or statements in it were by abolitionists, yet every one of them asserted the necessity or right of emancipation under the war power. Presumably such arguments would make a deeper impression on conservatives if they were known not to come from "fanatical" abolitionists.[34]

It took more than quotations from Adams and Giddings, however, to convert conservatives. As the emancipation pressure from abolitionists and radical Republicans mounted, the Democratic and conservative press countered with daily assertions that emancipation by the federal government, even under the war power, was manifestly unconstitutional. Clearly the abolitionists would have to wheel forth their heaviest legal artillery to prove the constitutionality of wartime emancipation. Two of the most learned lawyers in the abolitionist camp undertook the task. In the late summer of 1861 the American Anti-Slavery Society published a long pamphlet by David Lee Child entitled *The Rights and Duties of the United States Relative to Slavery under the Laws of War*. Under the United States Constitution slaves were regarded as both persons and property. Whether considered as persons *or* property, asserted Child, the federal government had the right to free them under the laws of war. He wrote: "As 'persons,' slaves stand in the same relation to an enemy conquering and occupying the country of their residence, as their masters do. Here is a principle of the laws of war, perfectly settled and unquestioned: Conquerors have the right, to the extent of their conquests, to establish such government and laws as they see fit. . . . They may dissolve the system of society which they find, and substitute any other which they deem more conducive to the improvement and happiness of the vanquished, and the peace and safety of the conquering na-

[34] *Gerrit Smith to Owen Lovejoy, July 12, 1861* (published letter, Peterboro, 1861), printed in broadside form and in the *New York Tribune*, July 28; *The Abolition of Slavery the Right of the Government under the War Power* (Boston, 1861), passim.

tion." If slaves were considered merely as property, the nation still had every right to emancipate them: "By the laws of war, the victors in a just cause may seize, appropriate to the uses of the war, carry off, confiscate, distribute or destroy every species of property, public or private, belonging to their enemies." As persons *or* property, therefore, slaves could be confiscated "to weaken our enemies, strengthen ourselves, and hasten the achievement of a beneficial and permanent peace."[35]

Another and even more thorough dissertation on the war power was published in the spring of 1862 by William Whiting of Concord, Massachusetts. Whiting was one of the ablest lawyers in New England, and was considered by his colleagues to be the foremost patent lawyer in the country. He was an abolitionist and served as a vice president of the Massachusetts Anti-Slavery Society. His father had been one of Garrison's earliest supporters, and his wife was a leading spirit in the Concord Anti-Slavery Society. The Whitings and the Garrisons were personal friends.[36] In his treatise Whiting pointed out that the Constitution had been adopted to "form a more perfect Union, establish Justice, insure domestic Tranquility, provide for the common defence, promote the general Welfare, and secure the Blessings of Liberty." But what had happened? "A handful of slave-masters have broken up that Union, have overthrown justice, and have destroyed domestic tranquility." Slavery had become irreconcilable with republican institutions, and must be destroyed. In time of war, under martial law, military officers had the undisputed right to seize private property for military purposes. Article I, Section 8 of the Constitution gave Congress the power to provide for the common defense and general welfare of the nation, including the right to abolish slavery should this prove necessary. "This right of seizure and condemnation is harsh," concluded Whiting, "as all the proceedings of war are harsh, in the extreme, but it is nevertheless lawful."[37]

[35] David Lee Child, *Rights and Duties of the United States Relative to Slavery under the Laws of War* (Boston, 1861), 5-6, 11, 24.

[36] Mrs. S. Barker to M. W. Chapman, Jan. 13, 1860, Chapman Papers, BPL; *Liberator*, July 12, 1861; *N.A.S. Standard*, Feb. 1, 1862; Frank Sanborn to unknown, Dec. 28, 1862, Sanborn Papers, Concord Public Library; Garrison to Helen Garrison, June 11, 1864, Mrs. Wm. Whiting to Garrison, Dec. 11, 1864, Garrison Papers, BPL.

[37] William Whiting, *The War Powers of the President, and the Legislative*

Whiting's book enjoyed an amazing popularity. In little more than a year it went through seven editions. In subsequent years chapters on military arrests, reconstruction, military government, and war claims were added, and in 1871 the expanded book of 695 pages was still in such demand as to require the printing of a forty-third edition. On the strength of the original treatise, Whiting was appointed solicitor of the War Department in December 1862, where he gained the friendship of Lincoln and Secretary of War Stanton.[38]

✦

When General Butler put his Massachusetts troops at the disposal of Maryland's Governor Thomas Hicks for the suppression of potential slave insurrections, there was a loud outcry from the Republicans and abolitionists in the Bay State. Governor Andrew curtly informed Butler that "the matter of servile insurrection among the community in arms against the Federal Union is no longer to be regarded by our troops in a political, but solely in a military point of view, and is to be contemplated as one of the inherent weaknesses of the enemy."[39] The chameleon-like Butler quickly discerned the drift of public opinion in Massachusetts. When three fugitive slaves came into his lines at Fortress Monroe in Virginia on May 23, he promptly labeled them contraband of war, refused to return them to their masters, and put them to work

---

Powers of Congress in Relation to Rebellion, Treason, and Slavery (7th ed., Boston, 1863), 3, 26-28, 46-48, 52, 54-55, 58. It should be noted that not all authorities on international and constitutional law were in agreement on the belligerent right of confiscation. The United States Supreme Court, however, later upheld the confiscation measures passed by Congress during the war. For a discussion of this question, see James G. Randall, *Constitutional Problems under Lincoln* (New York, 1926), 294-302, 312-15, 343-51, 373-85.

[38] The 8th edition in 1864 was published under the title *The War Powers of the President, Military Arrests, and Reconstruction of the Union*; the 10th edition in 1864 was published under the title *War Powers under the Constitution of the United States*; the 43rd edition was published in 1871 under the title *War Powers under the Constitution of the United States. Military Arrests, Reconstruction and Military Government*. For Whiting's appointment as War Department solicitor and his friendship with Lincoln, see Frank Sanborn to unknown, Dec. 28, 1862, Sanborn Papers, Concord Public Library; and Basler, ed., *Collected Works of Lincoln*, VIII, 373.

[39] Lewis Tappan to Andrew, Apr. 29, 1861, Andrew to Tappan, Apr. 30, 1861, published letters, clippings in Tappan Papers, LC; Andrew to Butler, Apr. 25, 1861, in Jesse A. Marshall, ed., *Private and Official Correspondence of Gen. Benjamin F. Butler during the Period of the Civil War* (5 vols., Norwood, Mass., 1917), I, 37-38.

constructing a new bake-house. Thenceforth the word "contra-band," which technically applied to military goods sold to an enemy nation by a neutral, acquired a new meaning in the United States. By July 30 the number of contrabands behind Butler's lines had reached nine hundred. Their exact status was indefinite and they were by no means yet free, but their presence within Union lines helped partially to offset abolitionist bitterness over the continued return of fugitive slaves to their masters by other Union generals.[40]

Abolitionists were disheartened by Lincoln's renewed pledge in a July 4th message to Congress not to interfere with slavery in the states. They were slightly encouraged a few days later by House passage of Owen Lovejoy's resolution affirming that "it is no part of the duty of the soldiers of the United States to capture and return fugitive slaves." But this resolution was merely an expression of opinion by one branch of Congress and had little effect on army officers who continued to return fugitives. Near-unanimous passage by the House on July 22 and by the Senate three days later of the Crittenden and Johnson resolutions stating that "this war is not waged upon our part . . . for any purpose . . . of overthrowing or interfering with the rights or established institutions of . . . southern States" plunged the abolitionists into deeper gloom.[41]

Little public attention was focused on these resolutions when they were passed because they came immediately after the Union had suffered its setback at Bull Run. While most of the North reacted with despair and dejection, abolitionists took on new hope from the defeat. They foresaw that it would compel the northern people, most of whom had expected a short and easy war, to reassess their war policy and to reflect more seriously on the slavery issue. Many northerners began tentatively to agree with the abolitionists

[40] Edward L. Pierce, "The Contrabands at Fortress Monroe," *Atlantic Monthly,* VIII (Nov. 1861), 627-30. Several Union commanders imitated Butler's example and admitted fugitives to their lines. There was no uniform national policy on this subject in 1861, and each commanding general was allowed to do pretty much as he pleased regarding fugitive slaves.

[41] Basler, *Collected Works of Lincoln*, IV, 439; *Cong. Globe*, 37 Cong., 1 Sess., 32, 222-23, 258-60; Wendell Phillips to Charles Sumner, July 15, 1861, Sumner Papers, HU; *Douglass' Monthly*, Aug., Sept. 1861.

after Bull Run that the Union should convert slavery from a source of Confederate strength to a source of weakness by initiating an emancipation policy.

"The result of the battle was a fearful blow," wrote Moncure Conway two days after Bull Run, but "I think it may prove the means of rousing this stupid country to the extent & difficulty of the work it has to do." Wendell Phillips thought that Bull Run was "just what we wanted, and was perhaps the best thing that could have happened."[42] George L. Stearns considered it "the first step toward emancipation. If we had won a decisive victory, in less than six months the rebellious states would be back in the Union, the government would be out-voted in Congress, and we should have all our work to do over again." David Child believed that "A dozen victories would not have done so much to bring us to the right path as that disgraceful rout. We needed it." The moderate Charles Francis Adams, Jr., feared that "this defeat tends more and more to throw the war into the hands of the radicals, and if it lasts a year, it will be a war of abolition."[43]

In the weeks following Bull Run there was a marked increase of emancipationist feeling among the people of the North. "Public sentiment is changing almost as rapidly since that great disaster as it did after the fall of Fort Sumter," reported veteran Free Soiler Amasa Walker on August 8. "There is less noise made on the subject, but the current is strong and deep." Henry Cheever related the story of a Democrat who told his neighbor: "I went out to Bull's Run battlefield a Breckinridge Democrat, coming home I turned into a fighting Abolitionist."[44] Frederick Douglass thought that the defeat "has much changed the tone of Northern sentiment as to the proper mode of prosecuting the war, in reference to slavery, the cause of the war. . . . A cry has gone forth for the abolition of slavery." The *New York Tribune* began cautiously to hint at an emancipation policy. Even the *New York Times*,

---

[42] Moncure Conway to Ellen Conway, July 23, 1861, Conway Papers, cu; Phillips' remark is quoted in Sarah Forbes Hughes, ed., *Letters and Recollections of John Murray Forbes* (2 vols., Boston, 1899), I, 227.

[43] Frank P. Stearns, *The Life and Public Services of George Luther Stearns* (Philadelphia, 1907), 254; D. L. Child to Garrison, July 29, 1861, Garrison Papers, BPL; C. F. Adams, Jr., to C. F. Adams, July 23, 1861, in Worthington C. Ford, ed., *A Cycle of Adams Letters, 1861-65* (2 vols., Boston, 1920), I, 23.

[44] *Independent*, Aug. 8, 1861; *N.A.S. Standard*, Aug. 10, 1861.

which had previously tried to stifle any mention of the Negro in connection with the war, proclaimed four days after Bull Run that "there is one thing, and only one, at the bottom of this fight—and that is the *negro*."[45]

Partly in response to the growing public desire for action against slavery, Congress passed on August 6 a confiscation act providing for the seizure of all property used "in aid of the rebellion," including slaves. This bill applied only to slaves who had actually worked on Confederate military fortifications, naval vessels, and so on, and did not specifically *emancipate* such slaves, but it was nevertheless a significant step in the direction of emancipation. Thomas Wentworth Higginson wrote on August 23: "I am satisfied that we are gravitating towards a bolder anti-slavery policy. The desideratum is to approach a policy of emancipation by stages so clear & irresistible as to retain for that end an united public sentiment."[46]

On August 30, General John C. Frémont, commander of the Western Department, electrified the country with a bold and dramatic proclamation instituting martial law in Missouri and freeing the slaves of every rebel in the state. Frémont had taken this step with the advice and consultation of a quartermaster on his staff, Captain Edward M. Davis, a Philadelphia abolitionist and personal friend of the general. Davis telegraphed the first news of the proclamation to his fellow abolitionist, Sydney Howard Gay of the *New York Tribune*, who published Davis' dispatch in the issue of August 31, scoring a tremendous beat for the *Tribune* over its rivals.[47]

Abolitionists applauded Frémont's proclamation. Garrison hailed it as "the beginning of the end"; Gerrit Smith informed Lincoln in a public letter that "this step of General Frémont is the

[45] *Douglass' Monthly*, Aug. 1861; *New York Tribune*, Aug. 6, 12, 1861; *New York Times*, July 25, 1861. See also *New York Times*, July 29. The *Principia*, Sept. 21, 1861, quoted articles and editorials from a large number of northern newspapers in the weeks after Bull Run calling for some degree of emancipation.

[46] McPherson, *Political History of the Great Rebellion*, 195-96; Higginson to Louisa Higginson, Aug. 23, 1861, Higginson Papers, HU.

[47] E. M. Davis to S. H. Gay, May 22, Aug. 27, Sept. 1, 1861, Gay Papers, CU; Allan Nevins, *Frémont: Pathmarker of the West* (New York, 1955), 500, 503. The text of Frémont's proclamation is in *O. R.*, Ser. 1, vol. III, 466-67. See also E. M. Davis to J. M. McKim, Sept. 19, 1861, McKim Papers, Cornell; and Edmund Quincy to Richard Webb, Oct. 25, 1861, Quincy-Webb Correspondence, BPL.

first unqualifiedly and purely right one, in regard to our colored population, which has taken place during the war." Governor Andrew declared that Frémont's order gave "an impetus of the grandest character to the whole cause."[48] From Maine to Missouri the Republican press and a surprising number of conservative and Democratic papers expressed approval of the measure.[49] Lincoln, however, was afraid it would "alarm our Southern Union friends and turn them against us; perhaps ruin our rather fair prospect for Kentucky." On September 11, the president modified the proclamation to make it conform with the Confiscation Act of August 6, which confiscated only those slaves who had directly aided the Confederate military forces.[50]

Many Republicans could scarcely believe the news that Lincoln had revoked Frémont's order. Abolitionists were appalled. Garrison charged Lincoln with a "serious dereliction of duty." His annulment of Frémont's order was "timid, depressing, suicidal." In private Garrison fumed bitterly that even if Lincoln was "six feet four inches high, he is only a dwarf in mind." Edmund Quincy thought that revocation of the order "was one of those blunders which are worse than crimes." Frederick Douglass was disgusted by Lincoln's deference to the wishes of Kentuckians. "What is the friendship of these so-called loyal slaveholders worth?" asked Douglass. "The open hostility of these so-called loyal slaveholders is incomparably to be preferred to their friendship. They are far more easily dealt with and disposed of as enemies than as allies. From the beginning, these Border Slave States have been the mill-stone about the neck of the Government."[51]

From all over the North, abolitionists and antislavery Republicans reported popular opposition to Lincoln's action. "I cannot convey to you the burning sense of wrong which is filling the

[48] *Liberator*, Sept. 6, 1861; *Gerrit Smith to President Lincoln, Aug. 31, 1861* (Peterboro, 1861), published as a broadside and in the *New York Tribune*, Sept. 9; Pearson, *Andrew*, I, 249.

[49] *New York Times*, Sept. 2, 1861; *New York Herald*, Sept. 3, 1861; *Worcester Spy*, Sept. 2, 1861; *Springfield Republican*, Sept. 17, 1861. The *Principia*, Nov. 23, 1861, quoted statements from several dozen northern newspapers, including most of the great metropolitan dailies, endorsing Frémont's proclamation.

[50] Basler, *Collected Works of Lincoln*, IV, 506-07, 517-18.

[51] *Liberator*, Sept. 20, 1861; Garrison to Oliver Johnson, Oct. 7, 1861, Garrison Papers, BPL; *N.A.S. Standard*, Sept. 28, 1861; *Douglass' Monthly*, Oct. 1861.

breasts of our people here, as they gradually come to see that there is no President of the United States—only a President of Kentucky," wrote Moncure Conway from Cincinnati. B. Rush Plumly, Philadelphia Quaker abolitionist who was on duty in St. Louis as a special agent of the Treasury Department, wrote to his chief, Salmon P. Chase: "I wish you were here at this hour to see and feel the effect of the 'President's Order' in respect of Genl. Frémont's Proclamation. If the President had emptied the Arsenals of the Government into the Camps of the Rebels, he could not have so effectually strengthened them. . . . Better lose Kentucky, than keep her, at such a price." Plumly came East soon after this, had a talk with Lincoln in Washington, and later vented his wrath privately at the president's "pigheaded stupidity."[52]

Lincoln's revocation of Frémont's proclamation ended the five-months' armistice between abolitionists and the administration. Gone were the fond hopes that the president would quickly perceive the need to strike at slavery in order to win the war. Sharp criticism of Lincoln began to appear more frequently in abolitionist writings; it was not a time for pulling punches or speaking softly. There was a moral and political conflict in the North between conservatives and radicals over the question of human freedom. Abolitionists enlisted wholeheartedly for the duration of this struggle, determined that it should end in nothing less than universal emancipation.

[52] Moncure Conway to Charles Sumner, Sept. 17, 1861, Sumner Papers, HU; B. Rush Plumly to Chase, Sept. 15, Oct. 19, 1861, Chase Papers, LC. See also Henry Wright to Garrison, Sept. 16, 23, 1861, Garrison Papers, BPL; and *Principia*, Nov. 23, 1861.

ISSATISFIED with the progress of the antislavery cause, Gerrit Smith and Henry Cheever wanted to hold a national convention of abolitionists in Washington or Philadelphia on September 24 to publicize the demand for emancipation. All branches of the abolitionist movement would be represented at the proposed convention. Cheever consulted Garrison, who threw cold water on the project. "Such a Convention, called by the parties and persons suggested by you, 'pronounced abolitionists,' would be more likely to excite popular prejudice at this crisis, and thus to damage a movement for the abolition of slavery under the war power, than to do good," argued Garrison. As long as the government was fighting a deadly battle with the slave power, "it seems to us the part of wisdom to avoid conspicuity as radical abolitionists in convention assembled, and to merge ourselves, as far as we can without a compromise of principle, in the onward sweeping current of Northern sentiment." Garrison hinted mysteriously at the emergence of a new antislavery organization in Boston, composed of abolitionists and antislavery Republicans alike, whose purpose would be to promote emancipation by means of newspaper articles, lectures, and petitions.[1]

Garrison was referring to a group of prominent Massachusetts abolitionists, including himself, Phillips, Frank Sanborn, George Stearns, William Henry Channing, Edmund Quincy, and Frank Bird, who were invited by Dr. Samuel Gridley Howe to meet at his Boston office on September 5 to discuss ways and means of channeling public opinion toward emancipation. A second meeting took place on September 10.[2] These gatherings became the subject of considerable hush-hush comment among abolitionists. Lydia Maria Child informed Whittier that "the warmest of the Republicans, and the most unprejudiced of the Abolitionists, are laying their

---

[1] Henry Cheever to Gerrit Smith, Aug. 20, Sept. 13, 1861, Smith Papers, su; Garrison to Henry Cheever, Sept. 9, 1861, Cheever Papers, aas.

[2] Frank B. Sanborn, *Dr. Samuel Gridley Howe: Philanthropist* (New York, 1891), 284; Laura E. Richards, *Letters and Journals of Samuel Gridley Howe: The Servant of Humanity* (Boston, 1909), 499-500; Frank P. Stearns, *The Life and Public Services of George Luther Stearns* (Philadelphia, 1907), 256-57.

heads together, with no more *publicity* than is necessary, to influence popular opinion, through the press, and help on the turning-tide in the right direction." Stearns told J. Miller McKim about the group, warning him to keep the information quiet, for "we do not as yet wish the movement to be made public."[3]

At the second meeting in Howe's office an executive committee was appointed to formulate plans of action. The committee decided that their primary objective should be to educate the public to understand "much better than it now does, the magnitude of the war in which the country is involved, and the bearing of slavery upon its continuance and final issue." They planned to solicit emancipation articles and editorials from prominent abolitionists to be sent out on printed slips to small-town newspapers all over the North. The articles would be anonymous "so that the truths they present may have their due weight, without prejudice." The group tentatively called itself the Boston Emancipation League, and decided to work under cover for the time being because of the prevailing popular prejudice against abolitionists.[4]

The decision of the Emancipation League to inaugurate a propaganda campaign was partly spurred by Lincoln's revocation of Frémont's Missouri proclamation. A large section of the northern press which had welcomed Frémont's order when it appeared now followed Lincoln and condemned Frémont for having gone too far. Emancipationist feeling in the North was fickle and ill-formed at best; a massive program of popular education would be necessary to create a public opinion that would eventually compel the abolition of slavery.[5]

The opening gun in this battle of words was fired by Charles Sumner in his address to the Massachusetts state Republican convention in Worcester on October 1. Sumner was on terms of friendship with most of the founders of the Emancipation League and was well aware of their activities. In his October 1 speech he de-

[3] L. M. Child to Whittier, Sept. 10, 1861, Child-Whittier Correspondence, LC; Stearns to J. M. McKim, Oct. 1, 1861, McKim Papers, Cornell.

[4] Stearns to McKim, Oct. 1, 1861, McKim Papers, Cornell; James M. Stone to Gerrit Smith, Oct. 10, 1861, Smith Papers, SU.

[5] L. M. Child to Whittier, Sept. 22, 1861, Child-Whittier Correspondence, LC; *Principia*, Oct. 26, 1861; *N.A.S. Standard*, Nov. 2, 1861; *Independent*, Nov. 7, 1861; *New York Times*, Dec. 5, 1861.

clared that "Slavery is our Catiline. . . . It is often said that the war will make an end of slavery. This is probable; but it is surer still that the overthrow of slavery will make an end of the war. It is not necessary even . . . to carry the war into Africa; it will be enough if we carry Africa into the war." James Freeman Clarke, a member of the executive committee of the Emancipation League and a delegate to the convention, introduced resolutions from the floor affirming that Massachusetts would "welcome any act under the war power which should declare all slaves within the lines of our armies free . . . compensating all loyal owners." A majority of delegates probably favored such a statement, but fearing that it might be interpreted as a rebuke to Lincoln for his recent modification of Frémont's order, the convention tabled Clarke's resolution.[6]

Sumner's abolitionist friends praised his speech, while Boston conservatives glowered and growled.[7] "Mr. Sumner's speech has created a great sensation," reported a Boston friend of the senator. "The elements of Hunkerism have boiled over. Yet he is hardly in advance of the times more than six months."[8] The *New York Tribune* published the speech in its weekly edition, assuring it a potential reading audience of nearly a million persons. The Emancipation League sent copies of the speech to editors of northern newspapers, to every clergyman and country storekeeper in Massachusetts, and to every member of the Massachusetts legislature.[9]

Abolitionist strategy during October and November 1861, was to remain in the background of the growing emancipation movement, letting others less burdened with the odium of a lifetime of devotion to freedom take the lead. "I have discouraged any distinct antislavery movement by the old abolitionists in New York," reported John Jay in October, "from the belief that such action would rather retard than advance the conversion of the Democratic masses." Lewis Tappan tried to imitate Boston's example and form an Emancipation League in New York, but Jay and other leading Republicans defeated the attempt. "Abolition will

6 *Boston Advertiser*, Oct. 2, 1861. Sumner's speech is printed in his *Works*, vi, 1-29.

7 There are about a dozen letters from abolitionists praising Sumner's speech, in the Sumner Papers, HU.

8 James W. Stone to S. P. Chase, Oct. 5, 1861, Chase Papers, LC.

9 James M. Stone to Sumner, Dec. 18, 1861, Sumner Papers, HU.

come as a military necessity as our army advances," argued Jay, and "its advocacy at this moment by those who have always opposed [slavery] on moral grounds is calculated rather to divide the North."[10]

Jay was in touch with leading "War Democrats" in New York, trying quietly to persuade them to come out for emancipation as a military necessity. Maria Weston Chapman was also a firm advocate of this approach. "Start the thing by others & then fall in, is our best plan," she wrote. "I have been long in correspondence with leading N.Y. Merchants—Our friend John Jay is doing the same work with the Butler & Dickinson people,—the fire is lighting at every corner." In November this method began to pay off. Daniel S. Dickinson, Colonel John Cochrane, George Bancroft, Benjamin Hallett—all of them prominent Democrats or conservatives before the war—began to deliver emancipation speeches. Cochrane and Secretary of War Simon Cameron made several joint appearances in the Northeast, calling for emancipation and the arming of Negro soldiers as a military necessity. The *New York Tribune* was delighted with these developments. "We now see men like Daniel S. Dickinson and Gerrit Smith," said the *Tribune*, "who have heretofore stood at the antipodes of this controversy, and classes like Hard-Shell Democrats and Garrisonian Abolitionists, who have represented the most antagonistic opinions in regard to it, taking substantially the same view of the part which Slavery ought to play in this sanguinary drama."[11]

On November 27, Sumner spoke for emancipation before a huge audience in New York's Cooper Union. Sitting on the platform next to prominent Republicans were Oliver Johnson, George Cheever, Octavius B. Frothingham, Dexter Fairbanks, William Goodell, Edgar Ketchum, Henry B. Stanton, Theodore Tilton, and Edward Gilbert, all of them veteran abolitionists. Commented Goodell afterwards: "To ourselves and a remnant of our old associates, on the platform and in the meeting, who remembered the scenes of [anti-abolitionist] mob violence in this city, . . . the

[10] John Jay to Sumner, Oct. 16, Nov. 8, 1861, Henry Hartt to Sumner, Oct. 18, 1861, Sumner Papers, HU; Lewis Tappan, Journal, entry of Sept. 12, 1861, Tappan Papers, LC; *Principia*, Oct. 26, 1861.

[11] M. W. Chapman to J. M. McKim, Oct. ?, 1861, Garrison Papers, BPL; *New York Times*, Nov. 14, 1861; *New York Tribune*, Nov. 12, 14, 20, 1861. Cochrane was Gerrit Smith's nephew.

contrast was most striking and cheering. To any of our Radical friends in the country who may be surprised at seeing the names of Oliver Johnson, William Goodell, &c. on the list of Vice-Presidents of a meeting invited by a Young Men's *Republican* Association, we may say that our own surprise is equal to theirs. Let them not however infer that we have backslidden from our Radical Abolition faith. The speech and the responses show that our fellow citizens, not ourselves, are changing."[12]

With the growing popularity of emancipation and the consequent increase in the prestige of abolitionists, the founders of the Emancipation League decided to bring their organization into the open. They held a formal inauguration meeting in Boston on December 16, with Samuel Gridley Howe in the chair. George S. Boutwell, onetime Democratic governor of Massachusetts and now a Republican, gave the main address, flanked on the platform by the elite of Massachusetts abolitionism and Republicanism. "The Emancipation League is now in full blast," screamed the hostile *Boston Herald*, "the furnace is heated ten times hotter than ever, and the whole pack of Anti-Slavery, Abolition devils are at work to make Bedlam appear lovely and inviting."[13] The League ignored such outbursts and formally elected its officers on January 27, 1862, choosing Samuel Sewall, one of the original abolitionists, as president. The executive committee was dominated by abolitionists, and George L. Stearns served as treasurer. The League recruited a fairly large dues-paying membership among Massachusetts abolitionists and Republicans, but a large part of the organization's funds were contributed by the wealthy Stearns. During the first year of its existence, the League sponsored nine lectures and six free-discussion sessions, published and circulated nearly 100,000 pamphlets, and supplied scores of northern newspapers with emancipation editorials and articles. During 1862 Stearns kept one clerk busy full time sending out documents, pamphlets, and speeches. In August 1862, a weekly newspaper, the *Boston Commonwealth*, was founded under the auspices of the League.[14]

---

[12] *Principia*, Dec. 7, 1861.

[13] *Liberator*, Dec. 20, 27, 1861; *Boston Herald*, quoted by *Liberator*, Dec. 27, 1861.

[14] Stearns, *Stearns*, 258-59; *Boston Commonwealth*, Jan. 24, May 29, 1863; George Stearns to Frank Sanborn, Apr. 30, 1862, Sanborn Papers, Concord Public Library. The membership book of the Emancipation League is in the Rare Book Department, BPL.

In the winter and spring of 1861-62 the number of emancipation organizations and lecture associations proliferated rapidly. William Goodell and J. Walden, publisher of Goodell's *Principia*, organized a "National Emancipation Association" in New York City on November 6, 1861. The Association served as a clearing-house for emancipation petitions sent to the president and Congress during the 1861-1862 congressional session. In Boston, Charles W. Slack, chairman of Theodore Parker's old Twenty-Eighth Congregational Society, organized a course of emancipation lectures. Susan B. Anthony arranged a similar lecture series in Rochester, which featured several prominent abolitionist speakers. New York City abolitionists formed an Emancipation League, similar to the Boston organization, in June 1862 and sponsored a course of popular lectures.[15]

One of the most effective emancipation organizations was formed in the national capital. In November 1861, a group of young antislavery officeholders decided to organize a lecture association to bring outstanding antislavery speakers to Washington. One of these young men later told the following story: "About nine o'clock there was a knock at the door and it was opened to admit a venerable man with long flowing white hair and a beard like Raphael's Saint Jerome, a quick, nervous manner, a glowing pink face and vivacious and merry blue eyes. He paused, leaned against the door, and said, 'Gentlemen, I saw an advertisement summoning young men to come here to consult to-night, and here I am!'" The "young" patriarch was John Pierpont, seventy-six years old and a battle-scarred veteran of the abolitionist crusade, who now held a job in the Treasury Department. The younger antislavery clerks were so charmed by Pierpont's enthusiasm that "without much discussion, or even consideration, we elected this 'young man' to be our president, organizing as the Washington Lecture Association."[16]

15 *Principia*, Nov. 9, 30, 1861, June 12, 26, 1862; Stearns, *Stearns*, 260-61; Ida H. Harper, *The Life and Work of Susan B. Anthony* (3 vols., Indianapolis, 1898-1908), I, 217; S. B. Anthony to George Cheever, Mar. 6, 1862, Parker Pillsbury to Cheever, Mar. 11, 1862, Cheever Papers, AAS; S. B. Anthony to Theodore Tilton, Mar. ?, 1862, Apr. 14, 1862, Anthony Papers, NYHS; *New York Tribune*, June 13, 1862.
16 Wm. A. Croffut, *An American Procession, 1855-1914* (Boston, 1930), 56-57. See also Abe C. Ravitz, "John Pierpont: Portrait of a Nineteenth Century Re-

The Association sponsored a course of more than twenty lectures in the hall of the Smithsonian Institution during the winter. Some of the foremost abolitionists and Republicans in the nation were featured in the series. The lectures were an overwhelming success. Lincoln attended several of them, and leading members of Congress were in the audience at every lecture.[17] Pierpont marveled that the series had "been more entirely and triumphantly successful, than the most sanguine of us dared to hope." It did his heart good "to hear the emphatic applause with which the radicalisms of the lectures are received—the more radical the more rapturous —and this in Washington, where nothing of the kind has ever been attempted before."[18] Kentucky's proslavery Senator Garrett Davis was greatly disturbed by the popularity of the lectures. "The utterances they have dared to put forth in this city have desecrated the Smithsonian Institution," he fumed, and continued, "What will you do with these monsters? I will tell you what I would do with them and with the horrible monster Greeley, as they come sneaking around here, like hungry wolves, after the destruction of Slavery. If I had the power, I would take them and the worst Seceshers and hang them in pairs."[19]

✦

William Goodell wrote in December 1861: "Never has there been a time when Abolitionists were as much respected, as at present. Never has there been a time in which their strongest and most radical utterances . . . were as readily received by the people, as at present. . . . Announce the presence of a competent abolition lecturer and the house is crammed."[20]

What had happened in the space of a few short months to change the abolitionists from a set of despised fanatics to a group of reformers whose advice was eagerly sought and listened to? The answer lies, partially at least, in the swelling tide of emanci-

former," Ph.D. dissertation, New York University, 1955, 301-02; and W. A. Croffut to George Cheever, Nov. 25, 1861, Cheever Papers, AAS.

[17] Croffut, *American Procession*, 57-74; Ravitz, "Pierpont," 305; T. W. Higginson to Louisa Higginson, Dec. 7, 1861, Higginson Papers, HU; *New York Tribune*, Jan. 15, 1862; *Independent*, Jan. 16, 1862; W. A. Croffut to George Cheever, Mar. 5, 1862, Cheever Papers, AAS.

[18] Pierpont to Wm. Cullen Bryant, Jan. 12, 1862, Pierpont Papers, PML.

[19] *New York Tribune*, Jan. 25, 1862.

[20] *Principia*, Dec. 21, 1861.

pationist opinion in the North. The hard, inescapable necessities of war were pushing the North, slowly and reluctantly, to the extremist position of the abolitionists. Victor Hugo once said that "There is no greater power on earth than an idea whose time has come." By December 1861, the powerful idea of universal freedom was taking deep root in America. As lifelong champions of this idea, abolitionists began to reap the benefits of its growing popularity. For thirty years they had been crying in the wilderness, telling the people that slavery was destroying the moral and political fabric of the nation. The mass of the people paid little attention except to denounce the abolitionists as troublesome fanatics. When the Union broke apart and war erupted, many persons began to regard the abolitionists in a new light. They no longer appeared as zealous crackpots, but as prophets who had tried to save their country before it was too late.[21]

The evidence of the new-found popularity, prestige, and influence of abolitionists in 1861-1862 is overwhelming. In the last two months of 1861, Frederick Douglass and several other abolitionist speakers were welcomed enthusiastically when they spoke in Syracuse, a city that had mobbed them ten months before. A nonpartisan literary journal in New York observed that "one of our most ably edited and uniformly well written journals is the New York Anti-Slavery Standard. Before the great rebellion, the Standard was a tabooed paper, except in exclusively 'abolition' circles; but now the Standard may be read and quoted by anybody without loss of character or business."[22] When Wendell Phillips spoke in New York on December 19, the street in front of Cooper Union was filled with a crowd an hour before the doors opened. The audience packed every corner of the hall and nearly a thousand people were turned away for lack of room. The listeners applauded Phillips' most radical utterances, and afterwards voted unanimously to invite Garrison to speak.[23]

[21] Richard Hofstadter has perceptively analyzed the role of the radical reformer in a time of crisis in his "Wendell Phillips: The Patrician as Agitator," in *The American Political Tradition and the Men Who Made It* (New York, Vintage Books, 1958), 139.

[22] *Douglass' Monthly*, Dec. 1861; *New York Courier*, quoted in *N.A.S. Standard*, Nov. 16, 1861.

[23] *New York Tribune*, Dec. 20, 1861; *N.A.S. Standard*, Dec. 28, 1861; Oliver Johnson to Garrison, Dec. 20, 31, 1861, Theodore Tilton to Garrison, Jan. 1, 1862, Garrison Papers, BPL.

The newborn prominence and prestige of abolitionists was graphically portrayed by a correspondent of the *New York Times* (a paper hostile to abolitionism) who reported the annual meeting of the Massachusetts Anti-Slavery Society in January 1862. The *Times* reporter wrote: "In years heretofore a great deal has been said and much fun has been made of the promiscuous and somewhat peculiar features of these gatherings. The facts that black and white met socially here, and that with equal freedom men and women addressed the conglomerate audience, have furnished themes for humorous reporters and facetious editors; but no such motive has drawn here the representatives of fifteen of the most widely circulated journals of the North." Abolitionist meetings were now notable political events. "Peculiar circumstances have given to this, the oldest Anti-Slavery Society in the country, and to similar organizations elsewhere, an importance which hitherto has not been theirs, and which justifies the most wide circulation of their sayings, doings, prophecies and lamentations."[24]

A small group of Republican congressmen invited George Cheever to preach an antislavery sermon in the House of Representatives on Sunday, January 12. Cheever accepted, and his sermon produced such a powerful effect that forty-three congressmen and senators invited him to preach another one on January 26.[25] These two sermons and Cheever's lecture at the Smithsonian Institution were the talk of Washington for several days. A private in a regiment stationed near the capital heard Cheever's first sermon and wrote to him afterwards: "Previous to this war, I hated the name of an abolitionist. But within the last nine months I have seen enough of the beauties of slavery to turn me right about. And I agree with you that the salvation of the country depends on the adoption by the government of a sweeping emancipation policy." Another Washington observer wrote:

"I have rarely seen an audience more completely magnetized by a speaker than the crowded assembly in the Smithsonian were, last Friday, by Cheever. Almost every sentence elicited applause, and several times the heartiest cheers broke forth irrepressibly. Yester-

[24] *New York Times,* Jan. 25, 1862.
[25] Committee of twelve Republican congressmen to Cheever, Jan. 9, 1862, Committee of forty-three Republican congressmen and senators to Cheever, Jan. 14, 1862, Cheever Papers, AAS.

day, also, he preached to an assembly of two thousand and upwards in the Hall of Representatives, thrilling his auditors with his trumpet calls to action. . . . And when, at the close, the Hutchinsons sang the plaintive Prayer of the Fugitive Slave, and the vast multitude burst out in one tumultuous acclamation, it was startling to think of the utter transformation wrought by one year's tremendous experience."[26]

More than twenty years later a Republican congressman still remembered Cheever's sermons as "the most terrific arraignment of slavery I ever listened to." Invitations to speak showered upon Cheever from all over the Northeast, and he accepted as many of them as he could, including a request to address a joint session of the Pennsylvania legislature.[27]

Other abolitionists who lectured in Washington during the winter made almost as great an impression as Cheever. Gerrit Smith spoke in the capital on March 1, and remarked afterwards: "A great change has taken place in that City. The most radical Abolitionist is now applauded by a Washington audience for his most radical utterances." William Goodell was encouraged by his reception in the capital. "In and out of Congress . . . radical views, in Washington City, . . . are on the advance. To this improved condition of things, the lectures in the Smithsonian Institute, this season, have greatly contributed."[28] Goodell, Moncure Conway, and William Henry Channing had personal interviews with Lincoln while they were in the capital. Conway was impressed by Lincoln, probably because the president complimented his

[26] John B. Geyser to Cheever, Jan. 15, 1862, Cheever Papers, AAS; O. B. Frothingham, *Memoir of William Henry Channing* (Boston, 1886), 323-24. A captain in the Sickles Brigade, stationed in Charles County, Maryland, wrote in a private letter December 15, 1861, that "the more our officers and soldiers see of the institution of slavery the more they detest it. Five months ago, ninety out of every hundred of the Sickles Brigade would have been delighted to mob an abolitionist—now they want to abolish slavery, root and branch." Quoted in the *Anglo-African*, Dec. 28, 1861.

[27] George Julian, *Political Recollections, 1840 to 1872* (Chicago, 1884), 370; Committee of twenty-one members of the Pennsylvania legislature to Cheever, Jan. 17, 1862, Gordon S. Berry (clerk of the Pennsylvania legislature) to Cheever, Jan. 25, 1862, Cheever Papers, AAS.

[28] Gerrit Smith to Richard Webb, Mar. 15, 1862, Smith to Garrison, Mar. 17, 1862, Garrison Papers, BPL; *Principia*, Apr. 10, 17, 1862.

book, *The Rejected Stone*. Lincoln was "astonished to learn that its author was really a native of Virginia."[29]

The greatest triumph for the abolitionists was Wendell Phillips' visit to Washington in March. "A year ago Wendell Phillips would have been sacrificed to the Devil of Slavery anywhere on Pennsylvania Avenue," wrote the Washington correspondent of the *New York Tribune*, but "To-day he was introduced by Mr. Sumner on to the floor of the Senate. The Vice-President left his seat and greeted him with marked respect. The attentions of Senators to the apostle of Abolition were of the most flattering character." Phillips lectured three times to enthusiastic audiences at the Smithsonian Institution; he was guest of honor at a dinner party given by Speaker of the House Galusha Grow; and he had a private interview with Lincoln, from which he emerged with a more favorable impression of the president than he had previously held. The *New York Tribune* drew a significant moral from Phillips' welcome in the capital. It had been little more than a year since he was mobbed in Boston for expressing the same sentiments he now uttered in Washington. "Both then and now he is a representative man," observed the *Tribune* editorially, "and the fierce anger that then sought his death, and the deference and respect now paid to him by men in the highest places of the nation, are tributes to the idea of which he, more than any other one man, is a popular exponent. It is not often that history presents such violent contrasts in such rapid succession."[30]

Phillips had been lecturing in the Northeast most of the winter, and when he left Washington he headed west for a brief tour. In Cincinnati he was greeted by rock- and egg-throwing toughs from Kentucky. It was the first and last occurrence of antiabolitionist mob violence during the war. It helped rather than harmed

---

[29] Moncure Conway to Ralph Waldo Emerson, Jan. 22, 1862, Conway to Ellen Conway, Mar. 17, 1862, Conway Papers, cu.

[30] *New York Tribune*, Mar. 15, 18, 19, 1862. The Washington correspondent of the *Boston Journal* reported that "the matchless oratory of Wendell Phillips has taken the town by storm." The correspondent of the *Springfield Republican* stated that Phillips had "uttered the most ultra sentiments without the slightest interruption or censure. This is in itself almost a miracle, and will be set down as an 'event' when the history of these times comes to be written. . . . Phillips was a real lion while here. . . . It was the complete triumph of free speech on slave soil." Quoted in the *N.A.S. Standard*, Mar. 29, 1862.

Phillips. Editors throughout the North denounced the Kentucky rioters, and lecture invitations poured in on Phillips at a redoubled rate. He wrote to a Boston friend, "You have no idea how the disturbance has stirred the West. I draw immense houses, and could stay here two months, talking every night." The *New York Tribune* estimated that during the winter and spring of 1861-1862 no less than 5 million people heard or read Phillips' antislavery discourses.[31]

In 1862, Charles A. Dana neared the completion of fifteen years as managing editor of the *New York Tribune*, but he was finding it increasingly difficult to get along with Greeley and in March 1862, Dana resigned. His successor was Sydney Howard Gay, the mild-mannered, intellectual, hard-working Garrisonian abolitionist who had been a member of the *Tribune* staff since 1857. Before that he had edited the *Anti-Slavery Standard* for fourteen years. Greeley had been impressed by the quality of Gay's work on the *Standard* and had personally offered him a position with the *Tribune*. Life on the *Tribune* staff was not always easy for a Garrisonian abolitionist from 1857 to 1861. Greeley was no abolitionist; he was erratic in his devotion to the antislavery cause. Dana, Gay, and other members of the editorial corps worked hard to keep the paper consistently antislavery in spite of Greeley's deviations. When war came in 1861 the *Tribune* did not immediately call for emancipation. Not until after Bull Run did Greeley begin to hint cautiously at abolition, and it was not until the late months of 1861 that the *Tribune* became known as a consistent and thoroughgoing champion of emancipation.[32]

In his five years with the *Tribune*, Gay had proved himself the most valuable member of the editorial staff and he was a natural choice to succeed Dana. Abolitionists were delighted with the news that one of their own had become managing editor of America's most powerful newspaper at a time of America's greatest crisis. Oliver Johnson, a personal friend of both Greeley and Gay, told Garrison that Gay's accession was "a most important change,

[31] *Liberator*, Mar. 21, Apr. 11, 25, 1862; *New York Tribune*, Apr. 4, 1862.

[32] Louis M. Starr, *The Bohemian Brigade: Civil War Newsmen in Action* (New York, 1954), 18-19, 98-99; Horace Greeley to S. H. Gay, Aug. 18, 1861, Gay to Wendell Phillips, Oct. 28, 1861, Parker Pillsbury to Gay, Nov. 21, 1861, J. G. Whittier to Gay, Nov. 14, 1861, Gay Papers, cu.

and one that will improve the tone of the paper. This *inter nos*."[33]

As managing editor, Gay soon showed himself a more efficient administrator and harder worker than his predecessor. He was in the office from noon until 3 a.m., six days a week. He wrote editorials, supervised the makeup of the paper, and directed the far-flung corps of *Tribune* war correspondents. As the war progressed, Greeley spent more and more time on his voluminous private correspondence, his lecture tours, and his political activities in Washington and New York. Gay took on a growing amount of responsibility for the paper. Greeley determined the general editorial policy and usually wrote the leading editorial each day when he was in town, but Gay superintended the day-to-day policy of the *Tribune* and gradually acquired a greater power over editorial strategy than even Dana had exercised. Gay soon earned a reputation of excellence among his fellow journalists. Edward Dicey of the *London Spectator*, one of the best foreign correspondents in the United States during the war, considered the *Tribune* under Gay's management "better printed, more thoughtfully written, and more carefully got up than any of its contemporaries." And Charles Congdon, the brilliant, acid-tongued editorial writer for the *Tribune* and a good friend of Dana's, paid Gay a supreme compliment: "You must know that the *Tribune* in my opinion never was a better paper. It is due to you to say this."[34]

A second journalistic event of great importance for abolitionists in 1861-1862 was the change in editorship of the *New York Independent*, the largest and most influential political-religious weekly newspaper in the country. The *Independent* had been founded in 1848 as a Congregational antislavery journal by Henry C. Bowen,

[33] Oliver Johnson to Garrison, Mar. 31, 1862, Garrison Papers, BPL. See also Pillsbury to Gay, Apr. 2, 1862, Gay Papers, CU; and O. Johnson to J. M. McKim, Dec. 29, 1862, McKim Papers, NYPL.

[34] Starr, *Bohemian Brigade*, 98-99, 116-24, 133-34; Elizabeth N. Gay to Sarah M. Gay, Apr. 1, 12, 1862, Gay Papers, CU; S. H. Gay to Garrison, Nov. 1, 1862, Garrison Papers, BPL. The quoted tributes to Gay from Dicey and Congdon are in Starr, *Bohemian Brigade*, 133-34. James R. Gilmore, a friend of Greeley and Gay, wrote in his memoirs that Gay "had more influence with [Greeley] than any other person." Gilmore asserted that "from the resignation of Charles A. Dana, early in 1862, until the close of the war, Mr. Gay controlled the course of the *Tribune*, and in all that time he did what no other man—except Mr. Dana—ever did or could do,—he held Mr. Greeley's great powers to the steady support of the Union." James R. Gilmore, *Personal Recollections of Abraham Lincoln and the Civil War* (Boston, 1898), 81, 94.

New York silk merchant and son-in-law of Lewis Tappan. For thirteen years it was edited by three Congregational clergymen: Leonard Bacon, Joseph Thompson, and Richard S. Storrs. During this period the *Independent* pursued a conservative antislavery course, attacking slaveholders and abolitionists with about the same spirit. In 1861 the three clergymen editors hesitated, vacillated, and refused to declare openly for an emancipation policy. Meanwhile the war had forced Bowen's silk business into bankruptcy, and to save the *Independent* he turned it over temporarily to Tappan in December 1861 without consulting the three editors. The three clergymen resigned, and Tappan persuaded Henry Ward Beecher to become the new editor-in-chief of the *Independent.* [35]

Abolitionists rejoiced at the change. Beecher did not quite measure up to radical antislavery standards, but he was an improvement over his predecessors; abolitionists also knew that Beecher's editorship would be little more than nominal. The real source of the *Independent's* editorial policy after December 1861, was Theodore Tilton, the brilliant young abolitionist who had been on the *Independent* staff since 1856. With his busy schedule, Beecher scarcely had time to write more than one editorial a week. Tilton took over most of the editorial work, and in less than a year his journalistic genius and Beecher's name more than doubled the *Independent's* circulation, bringing it to the amazing total (for a religious journal) of 70 thousand. In the spring of 1863, Beecher resigned and went to England on a lecture tour to win British support for the Union cause. Tilton became editor-in-chief of the *Independent.* Under his editorship it became less a religious journal and more a radical, crusading political weekly. Tilton frequently consulted his friends Garrison and Oliver Johnson about editorial policy, and for all practical purposes the powerful *Independent* became an abolitionist organ.[36]

[35] Frank Luther Mott, *A History of American Magazines* (3 vols., New York and Cambridge, 1930-38), II, 367-71; Louis Filler, "Liberalism, Anti-Slavery, and the Founders of the *Independent*," *New England Quarterly,* XXVII (Sept. 1954), 291-306; Edward Gilbert to George Cheever, Nov. 27, 1860, Cheever Papers, AAS; Lewis Tappan, Journal, 1861, entry of Dec. 7, 1861; Tappan, "Resumé of my Life," 1861, Tappan Papers, LC; *Independent,* Dec. 19, 1861. Tappan relinquished the proprietorship of the *Independent* to Bowen after the latter had gotten his business back on its feet in the early months of 1862.

[36] Mott, *American Magazines,* II, 371-73; *N.A.S. Standard,* Dec. 21, 1861,

The increasing influence of abolitionists was reflected in the exasperation of their opponents. A writer in the conservative *Boston Courier* denounced Phillips as a treasonable fanatic: "It will not do to represent this torch of incendiarism as a person of no influence or consideration, for the contrary is notoriously the fact. . . . There is not at this moment in Massachusetts a person of more wide influence over the general heart and mind than he is. As a public lecturer, he is by far the most popular man in the State." After Phillips had lectured in Washington, Kentucky's Senator Garrett Davis lamented that the abolitionists "have such skillful and dexterous and able and unscrupulous leaders here that they can cajole the simple, moderate, conservative, constitutional Republicans to their extreme measures." Davis thought Phillips should be "manacled and confined at Fort Warren or Fort Hamilton." Acidulous old James Gordon Bennett of the *New York Herald* demanded that "the Government send these ranters to Fort Lafayette a while, to be seasoned, and then string them up with the rebels, like dried haddock, at the end of the war. Thus the country will be saved, and his Satanic Majesty be enabled to settle his accounts with Phillips very speedily."[37]

Abolitionists themselves never ceased to marvel at their new-found popularity. "It is hard to realize the wondrous change which has befallen us abolitionists," wrote Mary Grew early in 1862. "After thirty years of persecution . . . abolitionists read with wonder, in prominent journals of this city [Philadelphia], . . . respectful tributes to men whose names had hitherto been used as a cry wherewith to rally a mob; and see with joy their own arguments and phraseology adopted by those journals."[38] Another Philadelphian was amazed that she could now make a profit on an

---

Feb. 1, 1862; S. B. Anthony to Tilton, Mar. ?, 1862, Anthony Papers, NYHS; Oliver Johnson to Garrison, May 28, July 25, 1862, Tilton to Garrison, May 27, June 11, 1863, Garrison Papers, BPL; Garrison to Tilton, June 5, 1863, Garrison Papers, NYHS; Frederick Douglass to Tilton, Oct. 21, 1862, Douglass Papers, Misc. MS, NYHS; Tilton to Douglass, Apr. 30, Oct. 22, 1862, Douglass Papers, Anacostia; Amasa Walker to Tilton, July 22, 1864, Tilton Papers, NYHS. On Jan. 1, 1863, the *Independent* claimed twice the circulation of any other weekly religious newspaper in the world.

[37] The statements of the *Courier*, Davis, and Bennett were quoted in the *Liberator*, Feb. 7, May 9, 16, 1862.

[38] Mary Grew to Wendell P. Garrison, Jan. 9, 1862, Garrison Papers, RU; *Twenty-Eighth Annual Report of the Philadelphia Female Anti-Slavery Society* (Phila., 1862), 10.

abolitionist lecture instead of losing money: "To think that the day has come to supply our Treasury instead of emptying it on such an occasion. What next?" Phillips noted that "Lyceums which could not formerly endure an Abolitionist on any topic, now invite them, stipulating that they shall talk on slavery." Henry Ward Beecher thought it "a great day that we have lived to see, when Mr. Garrison is petted, and patted, and invited, and praised by Governors, and judges, and expectants of political preferment. What is the world coming to?"[39]

What indeed? Abolitionists had never known the exhilaration of such power and prestige. Their speakers were in great demand all over the North. Their ranks contained some of the most popular and effective platform lecturers in the country. One of their number was managing editor of the most powerful newspaper in the nation; another was the editor of the largest political-religious weekly journal in the world. Abolitionism was no longer at a discount; abolitionists no longer went begging for listeners. Men who had felt obliged to work under cover to promote emancipation in October 1861, were wined and dined in the nation's capital five months later. Abolitionism had arrived.

✦

There were some abolitionists, however, who wondered whether their newfound popularity had been purchased too dearly. One fact greatly disturbed them: this growing northern zeal for emancipation was not based upon concern for the rights of the Negro as a *person*, but upon the argument of "military necessity" to save the Union. There was no question of Charles Sumner's genuine compassion for the slave, but he refused to express that compassion in his early wartime emancipation arguments. "You will observe that I propose no crusade for abolition, . . . making it a war of abolition instead of a war for preservation of the Union," he wrote on November 3, 1861. He argued instead that the Union could be saved only by striking at slavery. "In short, abolition is not to be the object of the war, but simply one of its agencies." A week later Sumner told John Jay that emancipation "is to be presented strictly as a measure of military necessity, and the argu-

[39] Sarah Pugh to Elizabeth N. Gay, Apr. 6, 1862, Gay Papers, CU; *Liberator*, Jan. 31, Mar. 21, 1862.

90

ment is to be thus supported rather than on grounds of philan-thropy."[40]

Some abolitionists strongly questioned these tactics. "This doctrine of the abolition of slavery at last, as *'a military necessity,'* is the rock on which we are in more danger of splitting than perhaps any other," cried Parker Pillsbury. "It is, to me, the most God-insulting doctrine ever proclaimed." The pleas of military necessity reminded Pillsbury of the deathbed conversion of a sinner. Emancipation would be worth very little, he thought, unless it proceeded from a conviction of justice and right. Lydia Maria Child was also discouraged by the military necessity argu-ment: "This entire absence of a moral sense on the subject, has disheartened me more than anything else. Even should they be emancipated, merely as a 'war necessity,' everything *must* go wrong, if there is no heart or conscience on the subject. . . . It is evident that a great moral work still needs to be done."[41]

In January 1862, James R. Gilmore and Robert J. Walker launched a new emancipation journal called the *Continental Monthly*. Neither of these men was an abolitionist: Gilmore was a New York businessman and cotton trader; Walker was a former governor of Kansas territory and a friend of Lincoln. Gilmore selected Charles G. Leland as editor of his new journal. In the first two issues of the *Monthly*, Leland and Gilmore frankly stated their indifference to the moral issue of slavery. "This is not now a question of the right to hold slaves, or the wrong of so doing," declared Leland. "All of that old abolition jargon went out and died with the present aspect of the war. So far as nine-tenths of the North ever cared, or do now care, slaves might have hoed away down in Dixie" forever, if their masters had not re-

[40] Sumner to R. Schleiden, Nov. 3, 1861, Sumner to John Jay, Nov. 10, 1861, quoted in Edward L. Pierce, *Memoir and Letters of Charles Sumner* (4 vols., Boston, 1877-94), IV, 49. In 1864 Jay told Sumner that "my own view of the most expedient manner of proceeding against slavery in all its phases, has been as you are aware from the commencement of the war, so far at least as the old aboli-tionists are concerned, in favour of grounding our action on military necessity, & the national safety, & leaving the moral argument which we have used for the last thirty years to be monopolized for the present by the new converts to aboli-tion by whom they can be wielded with the masses with ten-fold effect." Jay to Sumner, Mar. 8, 1864, Sumner Papers, HU.

[41] Pillsbury's statement was quoted by the *N.A.S. Standard*, Nov. 23, 1861; for Mrs. Child, see *Liberator*, Jan. 17, 1862, and L. M. Child to Gerrit Smith, Jan. 7, 1862, Smith Papers, SU.

belled and sought to destroy the Union. Leland continued: "Now let every friend of the Union boldly assume that, so far as the settlement of this question is concerned, he does not care one straw for the Negro. Men have tried for thirty years to appeal to humanity without success, for the Negro, and now let us try some other expedient. Let us regard him not as a man and a brother, but as 'a miserable nigger,' if you please, and a nuisance. But whatever he be, if the effect of owning such creatures is to make the owner an intolerable fellow, seditious and insolent, it becomes pretty clear that such ownership should be put an end to."[42]

Gilmore, Leland, and Walker coined the word "emancipationist" to distinguish themselves from the abolitionists and their disreputable humanitarian motives. Abolitionists were shocked and saddened by the attitude of these "emancipationists." Charles K. Whipple, Garrison's editorial assistant on the *Liberator*, admired the energy of the men who were backing the *Continental Monthly*, but "it is unspeakably saddening to see . . . men so intelligent and sagacious in worldly wisdom . . . deliberately repudiating a higher motive and adopting a lower one." No doubt they would gain more support for emancipation by adopting this course, "for it is a sad fact that most Northerners are afflicted by intense colorphobia." But they could not remain indifferent to human rights with impunity. "It is God's law that injustice shall not prosper," proclaimed Whipple. "Why not have done with oppression? Why not choose justice, and adhere to its dictates?"[43]

A young abolitionist in the army reported to Garrison that many of his fellow soldiers had become "emancipationists" only because they wanted to end the war and go home. They still disliked the Negro as much as ever: "Though these men wish to abolish slavery, it is not from any motive outside of their own selfishness; and is there not a possibility that at some not very distant day, these old rank prejudices, that are now lulled to sleep by selfish motives, may again possess these men and work evil?" Frederick Douglass felt the same fear and expressed it in a speech at Cooper Union: "Much as I value the present apparent

---

[42] Gilmore, *Personal Recollections*, 39-56, 66-70; *Continental Monthly*, I (Jan. 1862), 97-98, and (Feb. 1862), 113-17.
[43] *Liberator*, Feb. 14, 1862.

hostility to Slavery at the North, I plainly see that it is less the outgrowth of high and intelligent moral conviction against Slavery, as such, than because of the trouble its friends have brought upon the country. I would have Slavery hated for that and more. A man that hates Slavery for what it does to the white man, stands ready to embrace it the moment its injuries are confined to the black man, and he ceases to feel those injuries in his own person."[44]

✦

Nearly every abolitionist shared this fear that the North might discard the Negro as soon as he ceased to be a "military necessity," but in the rush of events and hard work during 1861 and 1862 there was little time to stop and brood about the problem. In the fall and winter abolitionists spent a great deal of time circulating emancipation petitions. Garrison wrote the most widely circulated petition, which urged Congress to decree "the total abolition of slavery throughout the country" under the war power, giving fair compensation to *loyal* masters "as a conciliatory measure, and to facilitate an amicable adjustment of difficulties." Abolitionists had been traditionally hostile to the idea of compensation and there was some opposition to the inclusion of compensation to loyal owners in Garrison's petition, but most abolitionists waived their theoretical objections in this case and signed the petition. For those who refused, William Goodell's National Emancipation Association circulated a petition that did not call for compensation.[45]

Abolitionists worked to obtain signatures to these petitions with a will and energy unknown since the great petition campaigns of 1836 to 1844. They found many people eager to sign. One abolitionist who obtained twenty-five signatures wrote that "not four of these men would have signed this petition previous to the bombardment of Sumpter [sic]."[46] Memorials bearing thousands of signatures began piling up on congressional desks. In January, the Washington correspondent of the *New York Tribune* reported

---

[44] Jacob Allen to Garrison, Oct. 23, 1862, Garrison Papers, BPL; Speech of Frederick Douglass at Cooper Union, Feb. 6, 1863, published in the *New York Tribune*, Feb. 7.

[45] *Liberator*, Sept. 27, 1861; M. W. Chapman to J. M. McKim, Oct. 7, 1861, Garrison Papers, BPL; *Principia*, Nov. 16, Dec. 28, 1861.

[46] *Principia*, Dec. 28, 1861.

(with some exaggeration) that "the petitions for universal emancipation to the present Congress have been more numerous and respectably signed than were those presented to the Parliament which abolished West Indian Slavery, at its opening."[47]

Lincoln's annual message to Congress on December 3, 1861, threw a dash of cold water on abolitionist hopes. His only reference to emancipation was a recommendation that the United States acquire territory in which to colonize slaves freed by the Confiscation Act of August 6. Otherwise he reiterated earlier assurances that he had no intention of interfering with the domestic institutions of the South. We should be "anxious and careful," said the president, that the war did not "degenerate into a violent and remorseless revolutionary struggle."[48]

Abolitionists were appalled. A revolutionary struggle for freedom was precisely what they wanted. Gerrit Smith publicly assailed the message as "twattle and trash" and complained that Lincoln was "bound hand and foot by that Pro-Slavery regard for the Constitution in which he was educated."[49] In the *Liberator* Garrison characterized the message as "feeble and rambling," and complained privately: "What a wishy-washy message from the President! . . . He has evidently not a drop of anti-slavery blood in his veins. . . . If there be not soon an 'irrepressible conflict' in the Republican ranks, in regard to his course of policy, I shall almost despair of the country. A curse on that Southern 'loyalty' which is retained only by allowing it to control the policy of the Administration!" Garrison concluded sorrowfully that Lincoln was "a man of very small calibre, and had better be at his old business of splitting rails than at the head of a government like ours, especially in such a crisis."[50]

[47] *New York Tribune*, quoted in *Principia*, Jan. 30, 1862. See also *Principia*, Jan. 23, 1862; *N.A.S. Standard*, Dec. 21, 1861, Jan. 11, 1862; *Liberator*, Feb. 21, May 9, July 4, 1862; S. B. Anthony to Matilda J. Gage, Feb. 27, 1862, Gage Papers, Radcliffe Women's Archives; Samuel May, Jr. to J. M. McKim, Oct. 9, 1861, McKim Papers, Cornell; Samuel May, Jr., Day Book, entries of Mar. 6, 11, 1862, May Papers, BPL.

[48] Roy P. Basler, ed., *The Collected Works of Abraham Lincoln* (9 vols., New Brunswick, N.J., 1955), v, 48-49.

[49] *Gerrit Smith to Thaddeus Stevens*, Dec. 6, 1861 (published letter, Peterboro, 1861); *Gerrit Smith to George Thompson*, Jan. 25, 1862 (published letter, Peterboro, 1862).

[50] *Liberator*, Dec. 6, 1861; Garrison to Oliver Johnson, Dec. 6, 1861, Garrison Papers, BPL.

Some abolitionists found consolation in the belief that Congress and public opinion were in advance of the president. "Foolishly as the President acts," observed Oliver Johnson, "there is much in the aspect of things at Washington and in the state of public opinion to encourage us."[51] Abolitionist confidence in Congress was not misplaced. In an implied repudiation of Lincoln's annual message, the House on December 4 refused to reaffirm the Critten-den resolution. The next day, Senator Trumbull introduced a far-reaching confiscation bill and Thaddeus Stevens offered a resolution urging emancipation under the war power. Owen Lovejoy introduced a bill making it a penal offense "for any officer or private of the Army or Navy to capture or return, or aid in the capture or return, of fugitive slaves." Emancipation petitions continued to pour in on Congress. On one day alone, January 6, 1862, ten such petitions bearing thousands of signatures were presented in the Senate. A week later no less than seven different bills dealing with emancipation and confiscation of rebel property were reported out of congressional committees.[52]

As Congress laboriously debated a variety of emancipation proposals, the mood of abolitionists fluctuated between hope and despair. "Never, since I became an Abolitionist, have I seen such hopeful times as these . . . never a time when the minds & hearts of the people were so receptive of light touching Slavery," wrote Samuel May, Jr., on November 26. Less than two months later, however, Lydia Maria Child confessed that "My courage flags a little, and hope grows faint. The *people* head in the right direction; but we are unfortunate in the men we have placed in power. Lincoln is narrow-minded, short-sighted, and obstinate. . . . Gerrit Smith writes me that his friends Thaddeus Stevens and Gen. Frémont almost despair of the ship of state."[53]

The antislavery cause began to brighten a bit as the spring of 1862 approached. The *New York Tribune* stepped up its demands

[51] Johnson to Garrison, Dec. 5, 1861, Garrison Papers, BPL.
[52] *Cong. Globe*, 37 Cong., 2 Sess., 6, 15-16, 18-19, 33-34, 57-60, 185, 327-32, 334, 497. Republican Congressman George Julian kept the abolitionists well informed on the progress of the antislavery cause in Congress during the 1861-62 session. See the dozens of letters exchanged between Julian and leading abolitionists in the Giddings-Julian Correspondence (LC), Gerrit Smith Papers (SU), Cheever Papers (AAS), and Garrison Papers (BPL).
[53] May to Richard Webb, Nov. 26, 1861, Samuel May, Jr., Papers BPL; L. M. Child to Whittier, Jan. 21, 1862, Child-Whittier Correspondence, LC.

for emancipation. "It is time for us to cease this idle babble about the constitutional guaranties for a vicious system of society which the Constitution nowhere mentions by name," thundered Sydney Gay in the *Tribune* of February 5. He continued, "It is time for us to consider how much longer we can afford to follow the modern device of holding slavery sacred above all other things. . . . As our armies go forward let them find only two classes in the revolted States—Union men and rebels, let their color be what it may."[54] In early March the leading Republicans and abolitionists of New York City organized a huge emancipation rally at Cooper Union —a rally which attracted national attention.[55]

Lincoln could hardly ignore the buildup of emancipation pressure. On March 6, he sent a message to Congress recommending passage of a joint resolution offering federal compensation to any state "which may adopt gradual abolishment of slavery."[56] It was Lincoln's first specific recommendation on the subject of slavery and it touched off a great deal of discussion. Abolitionist reaction to the president's message was generally favorable, with some exceptions. Moncure Conway likened the proposal to "the insertion of a wedge so neatly as to do credit to the President's knowledge of rail-splitting," but he disliked the word "gradual"; emancipation was "one of the Commander-in-Chief's guns; and to make it gradual would be like firing off a gun a little at a time." Maria Weston Chapman was also sorry for the word "gradual" in the message, but supposed it "to be only a make-weight, like the word compensation: a couple of sops thrown to two heads of slaveholders. Meanwhile, events are compelling immediatism." Wendell Phillips welcomed the message as "one more sign of promise. . . . If the President has not entered Canaan, he has turned his face Zionward."[57]

There were some dissenting voices, however. "Multitudes of petitions from all the free states signed by tens of thousands of estimable citizens, are before Congress, asking for the immediate

[54] *New York Tribune*, Feb. 5, 1862; J. M. McKim to S. H. Gay, Feb. 8, 1862, Gay Papers, cu.

[55] *Liberator*, Mar. 7, 14, 1862.

[56] Basler, *Collected Works of Lincoln*, v, 144-46.

[57] Moncure Conway to Ellen Conway, Mar. 8, 1862, Conway Papers, cu; Conway, *Golden Hour*, 52; M. W. Chapman to Mary Estlin, Mar. 18, 1862, Estlin Papers, bpl; Phillips' speech published in *Liberator*, Mar. 14, 1862.

abolition of slavery," declared Garrison, and he then asked, "Are these to be satisfied by proposing such a will-of-the-wisp as a substitute?" Privately, Garrison expressed fear that "the President's message will prove 'a decoy duck' or 'a red herring,' so as to postpone that decisive action by Congress which we are desirous of seeing." And George Cheever wrote: "How pitiable the attitude of President Lincoln, beseeching rebel States to do what God, justice, humanity and our Constitution require *him* to do."[58] Congress passed Lincoln's resolution on April 10, but a majority of border-state representatives refused to consider any plan of voluntary emancipation.

Congress enacted several antislavery measures in the spring of 1862. On March 10, the Senate passed (the House had previously acted) a new article of war prohibiting army officers from returning fugitive slaves. On April 16, President Lincoln signed into law a measure for compensated emancipation of all slaves in the District of Columbia. In June, Congress prohibited slavery in all the territories of the United States. Legislation was also enacted providing for the more effectual suppression of the African slave trade and for the education of colored children in the District of Columbia.[59] Abolitionists were pleased by passage of these measures, especially by emancipation in the District of Columbia. "Well, it is something to get slavery abolished in ten miles square, after thirty years of arguing, remonstrating, and petitioning," wrote Lydia Maria Child. "The effect it will produce is of more importance than the act itself. I am inclined to think that 'old Abe' *means* about right, only he has a hide-bound soul." Garrison considered abolition of slavery in the capital "an event of far-reaching importance." Congressman George W. Julian thought Garrison right "in regarding abolition here as a great triumph. We are gaining ground. The current is setting in the right direction." Samuel May, Jr., observed that "Our govt. moves very cautiously, very slowly, and their steps are not strides. But it does seem to me that all these steps are *forward*—none backward."

[58] *Liberator*, Mar. 14, 1862; Garrison to Oliver Johnson, Mar. 18, 1862, Garrison Papers, BPL; George Cheever to Charles Sumner, Mar. 22, 1862, Sumner Papers, HU.
[59] *Cong. Globe*, 37 Cong., 2 Sess., 1,446-51, 1,526, 1,629-31, 1,640-49, 2,041-64; *U.S. Statutes at Large*, XII, 354, 376-78; Wendell P. Garrison and Francis J. Garrison, *William Lloyd Garrison* (4 vols., Boston, 1885-89), IV, 49-50.

The *Anti-Slavery Standard* regarded emancipation in the District of Columbia as "the Beginning of the End of Slavery."[60]

During the spring of 1862, abolitionists bubbled over with optimism. "I trust I am not dreaming but the events taking place seem like a dream," wrote Frederick Douglass happily. Theodore Tilton joyfully observed that "the cause is striding forward with seven-league boots. If you do not hurry and grow old," he jokingly told Garrison, "you may see Slavery abolished before you have a gray hair on the top of your head!" Mary Grew was delighted by the progress of the antislavery cause, but she knew that politicians had not suddenly become saints: "such things are not expected by sane reformers. It is enough to elicit our deep thanksgiving that, by events over which the govt. has or has not control; from motives pure, selfish, or commingled, the abolition of slavery is at hand." And Wendell Phillips declared on May 6 that slavery was doomed to utter extinction. "Abraham Lincoln may not wish it; he cannot prevent it; the nation may not will it, but the nation can never prevent it," said Phillips, and continued, "I do not care what men want or wish; the negro is the pebble in the cog-wheel, and the machine cannot go on until you get him out. . . . Abraham Lincoln simply rules; John C. Frémont governs."[61]

[60] L. M. Child to Robert Wallcutt, Apr. 20, 1862, Garrison Papers, BPL; Garrison to Julian, Apr. 13, 1862, Giddings-Julian Correspondence, LC; Julian to Garrison, Apr. 16, 1862, Garrison Papers, BPL; Samuel May, Jr., to Samuel J. May, Apr. 14, 1862, S. J. May Papers, BPL; *N.A.S. Standard*, Apr. 26, 1862.

[61] Douglass to Sumner, Apr. 7, 1862, Sumner Papers, HU; Tilton to Garrison, Apr. 3, 1862, Mary Grew to Helen Garrison, June 20, 1862, Garrison Papers, BPL; Phillips' speech published in *Liberator*, May 16, 1862.

V ✦ THE EMANCIPATION PROCLAMA-
TION AND THE THIRTEENTH
AMENDMENT

A sharp contest still raged within the ranks of the abolitionists between those who supported the government in its war against rebellion and those who refused to support any government that was not thoroughly abolitionist. W. O. Duvall, who belonged to the latter group, criticized Gerrit Smith for his support of the Union. "Of what use, for Heaven's sake, has this government ever been to you or me?" asked Duvall. "It was never anything but a gigantic swindler and robber; and yet you argue that there is no sacrifice too great for its continuance." Duvall also had some harsh words for the Garrisonians: "Edward Everett and Wendell Phillips sitting side by side! The Liberator puffing D. S. Dickinson's blarney!! How has the fine gold become dim! Prophets become partisans! Truly, these are the days of small things." Stephen S. Foster agreed with Duvall and said in January 1862: "There has never been an Administration so thoroughly devoted to slavery as the present. No other ever returned so many fugitive slaves, nor did so much to propitiate the Slave Power. Under these circumstances, is there any sufficient reason for us to . . . give our sanction and support to the Government?"[1]

Phillips and Garrison responded to these criticisms in well-publicized speeches at Cooper Union. In December 1861, Phillips insisted that only emancipation could end the irrepressible conflict and bind the Union together with hooks of steel. He continued: "People may say this is a strange language for me,—a Disunionist. Well, I was a Disunionist, sincerely, for twenty years. I did hate the Union, when the Union meant lies in the pulpit and mobs in the street, when Union meant making white men hypocrites and black men slaves. (Cheers) . . . But now, when I see what the Union must mean in order to last, when I see that you cannot have union without meaning justice, . . . why should I object to it?

[1] Duvall to Gerrit Smith, Dec. 15, 1861, Smith Papers, NYPL; Foster's statement quoted in *Liberator*, Jan. 31, 1862.

. . . Do you suppose I am not Yankee enough to buy union when I can have it at a fair price?" A month later Garrison came before a similar New York audience and reaffirmed all of his abolitionist principles. But he no longer wished to stand apart from the rest of the antislavery North. "What are all your paltry distinctions worth?" he asked. "You are not Abolitionists. Oh, no. You are only anti-slavery." In the eyes of the South, however, there was no real difference. An antislavery man would be hanged in Charleston as soon as an abolitionist: "Why, the President of the United States . . . is an outlaw in nearly every slave State in this Union. . . . I think it is time, under these circumstances, that we should all hang together." Garrison had been charged with inconsistency because he now supported the Union, and he replied, "Well, ladies and gentlemen, when I said I would not sustain the Constitution, because it was a 'covenant with death, and an agreement with hell,' I had no idea that I would live to see death and hell secede. (Prolonged applause and laughter) Hence it is that I am now with the Government to enable it to constitutionally stop the further ravages of death, and to extinguish the flames of hell forever. (Renewed applause)"[2]

Over the objections of Stephen S. Foster, Garrison steered a resolution through the annual convention of the Massachusetts Anti-Slavery Society in January affirming that "this Society regards the Government as wholly in the right, and the Secessionists wholly and atrociously in the wrong, on the issues presented." Two weeks later Garrison submitted the same resolution to the annual meeting of the New York Anti-Slavery Society in Albany. Parker Pillsbury immediately jumped up and offered another set of resolutions denouncing the Lincoln administration's failure to take effective action against slavery. If the war should end in some form of compromise with slavery, said Pillsbury, "the Abolitionists will have more to answer for than any other class of people." The government had no intention "to interfere with

[2] Wendell Phillips, *Speeches, Lectures, and Letters*, 1st Series (Boston, 1863), 440; William Lloyd Garrison, *The Abolitionists, and Their Relation to the War* (*Pulpit and Rostrum*, numbers 26 and 27, New York, 1862), 31, 28, 46. On December 13, 1861, Garrison removed the maxim, "The United States Constitution is a covenant with death and an agreement with Hell" from the head of the first page of the *Liberator* and replaced it with the command, "Proclaim Liberty throughout all the land, to all the inhabitants thereof."

the condition of a single slave in the land. . . . I do not wish this government prolonged another day in its present form." In reply, Garrison pointed to several antislavery acts by the government: the Confiscation Act, Butler's contraband policy, and Union protection of more than 8 thousand fugitive slaves on the South Carolina sea islands. The exchange became heated. Finally Aaron M. Powell stepped in to try to smooth things over, and suggested that both sets of resolutions—Garrison's and Pillsbury's— be adopted. This was done, and the convention adjourned in a spirit of apparent harmony, but beneath the surface the gulf between the Garrison and Pillsbury factions was wider than ever.[3]

The growing division between the two groups was revealed in their private correspondence. Most abolitionists, especially those in Boston, New York, and Philadelphia, supported Garrison's point of view. Pillsbury's following was small, recruited mainly from rural New England and New York, and from some of the western states. Stephen S. Foster was Pillsbury's most faithful ally. In private Foster shook his head sadly over Garrison's course: "How lamentable it is that those who have stood for so many years with their feet firmly planted on the rock of truth should falter in this hour of our nation's greatest peril, & . . . virtually make over our cause & themselves to the government." Pillsbury said privately, "I dare not yet trust the interests of the Anti-Slavery cause in the hands of the present, any more than in any former, Presidential administration. Nor do I see how we can any more change our mottoes, and our glorious old battle cry, 'No Union with Slaveholders,' than we might have done at the election of General Taylor."[4]

Supporters of Garrison considered Pillsbury slightly unbalanced. When slavery was abolished in the District of Columbia, Oliver Johnson asked: "Will not even the croakers now be willing to confess that our cause has made progress? . . . Will not our friend Pillsbury be able to discern a ray of light stealing over the dark picture that seems to be always hanging before his mind's eye?" Pillsbury was evidently not cheered by emancipation in the

[3] *Liberator*, Jan. 31, 1862; *N.A.S. Standard*, Feb. 15, 1862. See also S. B. Anthony to E. C. Stanton, Feb. 9, 1862, Stanton Papers, LC.

[4] S. S. Foster to George Thompson, Mar. 16, 1862, Foster Papers, AAS; Pillsbury to Elizabeth B. Chace, Mar. 24, 1862, in Lillie C. Wyman and Arthur C. Wyman, *Elizabeth Buffum Chace* (2 vols., Boston, 1914), I, 229.

nation's capital. "P. P. is . . . not in a quite healthy state of mind," commented Samuel May, Jr. "When he heard of the President's signing the Bill for Abolition in the District of Columbia, he said he dreaded to give way to any rejoicing, for he had noticed that any *good* thing in the Government was quite sure to be followed by some extraordinary baseness!"[5]

Oliver Johnson feared that the abolitionists' intramural squabbles would be revealed to public view at the annual convention of the American Anti-Slavery Society in May. He urged Garrison to prepare careful resolutions for the meeting with a mind to bridging the gap between the two wings of the Society. "You know just how far it will do for us to go in the direction that P. P. would lead us," wrote Johnson, "and if you will put in proper shape the *needed criticism* of the government, not sparing censure where it is deserved, but showing proper discrimination, we shall have no difficulty in carrying with us the common sense of the Society."[6] Garrison prepared and introduced resolutions urging the government to adopt universal emancipation, criticizing Lincoln and Congress for their slowness, but nevertheless supporting the government in its efforts against rebellion. Stephen S. Foster offered another resolution affirming that although the government "from purely selfish motives" had "done many acts favorable to the freedom of the slaves, it has in no instance evinced a genuine regard for their rights as citizens." Foster noted that the administration still enforced the fugitive slave law in the District of Columbia, and in other ways observed the proslavery compromises of the Constitution. Garrison's resolutions were passed and Foster's was laid on the table because of "lack of time" to discuss it.[7]

In the three weeks between the convention of the American Anti-Slavery Society and the meeting of the New England Anti-Slavery Society at the end of May, many other abolitionists began to have doubts about the wisdom of Garrison's course. During these three weeks several events occurred which undermined the confidence and optimism prevailing earlier in the spring: Lincoln

[5] Oliver Johnson to Garrison, Apr. 18, 1862, Garrison Papers, BPL; Samuel May, Jr., to E. B. Chace, Apr. 22, 1862, in Wyman and Wyman, *Chace*, I, 236.

[6] Johnson to Garrison, Apr. 10, 1862, Garrison Papers, BPL.

[7] *Liberator*, May 16, 1862.

revoked General David Hunter's military order proclaiming emancipation in South Carolina, Georgia, and Florida; the administration continued to enforce the fugitive slave law in the District of Columbia; and the House narrowly defeated a confiscation bill emancipating all the slaves of rebels. At the New England meeting there was a great deal of oratory denouncing these actions, and Foster introduced resolutions affirming that abolitionists could give no more support to the Union than to the Confederate government. "Abraham Lincoln is as truly a slaveholder as Jefferson Davis," said Foster. "He cannot even contemplate emancipation without colonization." Many of the speakers supported Foster's side of the argument, but Wendell Phillips, who had earlier in the meeting denounced Lincoln in the strongest terms, nevertheless could not agree that Lincoln was as bad as Jefferson Davis. Foster and Pillsbury were trying to create the impression that the Society had abandoned its principles by supporting the government, said Phillips. "No such body has proposed to support the Government *as it is*. It *advises*, not supports the Government." Phillips declared that he had "supported it by trying to force it on to a better position." This expressed the will of a majority of the delegates, and Foster's resolutions were defeated by a vote of nearly two to one.[8]

The meeting left a bitter taste in the mouths of many abolitionists. "There was . . . some unpleasant feeling caused, by Pillsbury's pretty openly charging, & Powell's (& others) *insinuating* . . . that the Anti-Slavery Societies & their Committees had lowered their moral standard," reported Samuel May, Jr., to a friend. May agreed completely with Garrison's position: "We hold the Government, the parties, the churches,—as ever,—to their highest duty. But we hope not to part with our common sense." This was precisely what May thought Pillsbury had done in suggesting that "the present administration is the worst one we ever had" and that "Jeff. Davis would be preferable as a President to Abraham Lincoln." "These and kindred positions," concluded May, "seem to us to be really and truly characterized by fanaticism."[9] The truth was that Pillsbury and Foster were

[8] *Liberator*, June 6, 1862.

[9] Samuel May, Jr., to Richard Webb, June 30, 1862, Samuel May, Jr. Papers, BPL.

temperamentally incapable of supporting any government. They had been oppositionists and "come-outers" so long that their hostility to authority was ingrained, no matter what the authority stood for. Their inflexible opposition to the Union cause during the first year of the war brought into the open the growing schism in the American Anti-Slavery Society.

Even as the Society seemed to be splitting into two factions, however, there was on another plane a trend toward reconciliation of those abolitionists who had been bitterly opposed to each other since the schism of 1840. The war rendered academic all the old constitutional and methodological disputes among the various schools of abolitionism. James Redpath recognized this in November 1861, when he proclaimed that "the policies both of the Gerrit Smith and the Garrisonian school of abolitionists have been practically suspended. Events have so changed the position of affairs that their old-time policies are no longer applicable." An old abolitionist who had broken with the Garrisonians in 1840 and had gone into the Liberty party, wrote to Garrison in February, 1862: "There never was any but an imaginary chasm between us, and the providential events of the last few months have bridged it all over."[10] Early in 1862 Garrison invited Gerrit Smith to attend the Garrisonian antislavery meetings of that year. Smith could not come, but he responded handsomely with praise of the Garrisonians and their work, an acknowledgment that there was no longer any reason for differences among abolitionists, and a check for $50 for the American Anti-Slavery Society.[11]

An article by Frederick Douglass in his *Monthly* of March 1862, strikingly illustrated the progress of reconciliation among old abolitionist enemies. For years there had been bitterness between Douglass and Garrison, dating from the early 1850's when Douglass had repudiated Garrisonian disunionism. But in 1862 Douglass was ready to bury their differences. "Every man who is ready to work for the overthrow of slavery, whether a voter or non-voter, a Garrisonian or a Gerrit Smith man, black or white, is both clansman and kinsman of ours," he wrote. "Whatever polit-

---

[10] *The Pine and Palm*, Nov. 23, 1861; Charles W. Denison to Garrison, Feb. 24, 1862, Garrison Papers, BPL.

[11] Gerrit Smith to Wendell P. Garrison, Jan. 16, 1862, Garrison Papers, RU; Gerrit Smith to Wm. Lloyd Garrison, Apr. 16, 1862, Garrison Papers, BPL; *Liberator*, May 9, 1862.

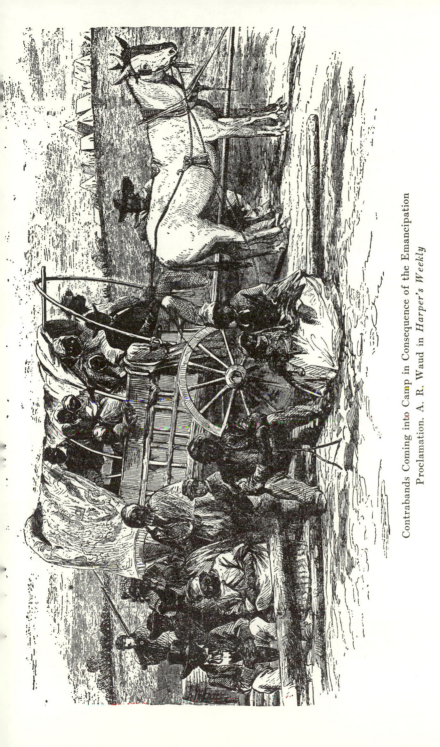

Contrabands Coming into Camp in Consequence of the Emancipation Proclamation. A. R. Waud in *Harper's Weekly*

ical or personal differences, which have in other days divided and distracted us, a common object and a common emergency makes us for the time at least, forget those differences." Douglass praised the work of Garrisonians during the war. "No class of men are doing more according to their numbers, to conduct this great war to the Emancipation of the slaves than Mr. Garrison and the American Anti-Slavery Society."[12] Garrisonians responded heartily to Douglass' magnificent gesture, and Douglass once again became a featured speaker at Garrisonian antislavery meetings.

There were many other examples of wartime cooperation among old abolitionist rivals. The American Anti-Slavery Society used George Cheever's Church of the Puritans in New York for its business meetings, and a bond of friendship grew up between Garrisonians and members of Cheever's Church Anti-Slavery Society. Garrisonians and John Brown men worked together in the Boston Emancipation League. It was Garrison who arranged Theodore Weld's return to the antislavery lecture platform during the war, and brought Weld once again to meetings of the American Anti-Slavery Society.[13]

Some breaches, of course, were too wide and too personal to be healed even by the wartime emergency. The gulf between Garrison on the one hand, and Lewis Tappan and Joshua Leavitt on the other, had been too wide to be easily bridged. But on the whole, while a rift was developing within the American Anti-Slavery Society during the war, Garrisonians as a group were closing ranks with the rest of the abolitionist movement to fight a common battle against slavery and rebellion.

✦

Most abolitionists were riding the crest of a wave of optimism in the early spring of 1862, but far back in their minds was a nagging doubt about the basis for this confident outlook. What if the rebellion should suddenly collapse? Would not the old devil of compromise enter into the peace settlement, leaving slavery essentially intact?

[12] *Douglass' Monthly,* Mar. 1862.
[13] Oliver Johnson to Samuel May, Jr., July 31, 1861, Johnson Papers, vhs; Frank Preston Stearns, *The Life and Public Services of George Luther Stearns* (Philadelphia, 1907), 274; Oliver Johnson and Theodore Tilton to Garrison, Sept. 25, 1862, Weld to Garrison, Oct. 8, 31, 1862, Johnson to Garrison, Apr. 9, 1863, Garrison Papers, bpl; Garrison to Weld, Apr. 6, 1863, Weld Papers, lc.

In February 1862, Union arms won a series of victories climaxed by the capture of Fort Donelson. The North was exultant; editors assured their readers that "the rebellion is crumbling" and "the end is approaching."[14] Higginson noted in his diary that "there is such a glare of victory that we only count the months or perhaps weeks until Richmond and New Orleans shall have submitted." But he discerned danger in this development. "The less success on our part, the more likelihood of an emancipatory policy —& so the other way." Charles Sumner stated privately that "these victories have a good side and a bad side. They will set us up in Europe, but I fear they will put back our ideas at home." George Cheever was not happy with the turn of events, "for our victories, if continued, will just result in bringing back those States as slaveholding States again in the Union."[15]

In April 1862, abolitionists put these fears out of mind while they rejoiced over the abolition of slavery in the District of Columbia, but three events in the second half of May brought back all their doubts and apprehensions stronger than ever. On April 25, General David Hunter, commander of the Union forces occupying the islands and coastline of South Carolina, Georgia, and Florida, had proclaimed martial law in the "Department of the South," comprising all of these three states. On May 9, he issued a second order stating that "Slavery and martial law in a free country are altogether incompatible" and declaring all slaves in the three states "forever free." The edict was published in northern newspapers on May 16. It was immediately acclaimed by abolitionists, who assumed that Lincoln had authorized it. "Has not the President used a very sharp knife, in Genl. Hunter's hands, to cut the knot?" exclaimed Francis George Shaw joyfully.[16]

But Lincoln had not authorized Hunter's action; he did not even know of the order until he read it in the newspapers. The conservative and Democratic press demanded that Lincoln re-

[14] For examples of northern editorial assurances that the rebellion was crumbling, see the *Springfield Republican*, Feb. 2, 8, 27, 1862, and the *New York Tribune*, Feb. 5, 1862.

[15] Higginson, Diary, entry of Feb. ?, 1862, Higginson to Louisa Higginson, Feb. 21, 1862, Higginson Papers, HU; Charles Sumner to S. H. Gay, Feb. 18, 1862, Gay Papers, CU; George Cheever to Elizabeth C. Washburn, Apr. 4, 1862, Cheever Papers, AAS.

[16] Shaw to Garrison, May 16, 1862, Garrison Papers, BPL.

scind the order. Secretaries Chase and Stanton, on the other hand, assured President Lincoln that nine-tenths of the Republicans approved of Hunter's proclamation, and urged him to let it stand. The president deferred to the wishes of conservatives and border state Unionists, however, and revoked Hunter's order on May 19. Lincoln renewed his plea to the border states to take advantage of his offer of compensated emancipation, and hinted ominously that should they not do so he might find it necessary eventually to proclaim military emancipation.[17]

Abolitionists were deeply disappointed by Lincoln's action. William Goodell wrote, "He has grieved and weakened his best friends. He has gladdened and strengthened his worst enemies— the worst enemies of the country." "Shame and confusion to the President for his halting, shuffling, backward policy!" cried Garrison.[18] Anna Dickinson, a rising young abolitionist orator, denounced the president as "not so far from . . . a slave-catcher after all," and privately wrote that Lincoln was "an Ass . . . for the Slave Power to ride."[19]

Some abolitionists, however, found grounds for hope in Lincoln's reiteration of the offer of compensated emancipation and his implied warning of possible future military emancipation. Samuel May, Jr., observed that the president had "again sadly disappointed the Anti-Slavery portion of the country & the army,— which now has grown to be a very large portion," by annulling Hunter's proclamation. But May thought Lincoln sincere in his wish to abolish slavery through a program of voluntary, compensated emancipation: "Slow, timid, altogether too patient with & too trustful of the Slaveholders, as he is, I do think his appeal a very solemn one to those States."[20]

In the last week of May, the northern press was full of the shocking story that open season on fugitive slaves had been declared in Washington. Slave catchers from neighboring states were invading the District, seizing Negroes on the streets and claiming

[17] T. Harry Williams, *Lincoln and the Radicals* (Madison, Wisc., 1941), 137-38; Roy P. Basler, ed., *The Collected Works of Abraham Lincoln* (9 vols., New Brunswick, N.J., 1955), v, 222-23.

[18] *Principia*, May 22, 1862; *Liberator*, May 23, 1862.

[19] *Liberator*, June 6, 1862; Anna Dickinson to Susan Dickinson, May 27, 1862, Dickinson Papers, LC.

[20] May to Richard Webb, May 27, 1862, Samuel May, Jr., Papers, BPL; see also *Independent*, May 22, 1862.

them as fugitives. One report told of a fugitive who ran up the steps of the Capitol with heavy chains on his legs in a frantic effort to escape his pursuers. "Is it possible that such a deed can be perpetrated by the Government and not be branded by the nation as a disgrace?" asked Theodore Tilton in the *Independent*. The New England Anti-Slavery Society angrily condemned the Lincoln administration for allowing the national capital to be turned into a slave pen.[21]

On May 26, the House of Representatives defeated by four votes a bill for the confiscation and emancipation of all slaves belonging to rebel masters. Five congressmen from Massachusetts voted against the bill, providing the narrow margin of defeat. The New England Anti-Slavery Society denounced the House for its "astounding infatuation" and "utter moral cowardice." The Society passed a resolution urging Massachusetts voters to send the five recusant congressmen into a "dishonored retirement at the next election." George Cheever was profoundly depressed by the defeat of this bill. "The first time, the very first time in all our history that the possibility of emancipation has been distinctly presented . . . it is decided in the negative—by the votes from Massachusetts!" he lamented. "Which *now* is the most guilty, the North or the South? And what reason has England to sympathize with the North rather than the South?"[22]

The events of May plunged abolitionists from the pinnacle of confidence to the depths of despair. For more than two months following his interview with Lincoln in March, Wendell Phillips had praised the president's virtues and predicted an early end to slavery. By June, however, Phillips' patience was wearing dangerously thin. He began to doubt his policy of supporting the administration. "This cabinet *fears opposition* more than it *values support*," he told Charles Sumner. "Let them feel that *we* can *criticize* & *demand* as well as the Border States & Conservative Side." Phillips urged congressional Republicans to get tough and threaten to withhold supplies unless the administration adopted a more radical policy. "Lincoln is doing twice as much to-day to break this Union as Davis is," he charged. "We are paying thou-

[21] *Independent*, May 29, 1862; *Liberator*, June 6, 1862.
[22] *Cong. Globe*, 37 Cong., 2 Sess., 2,363; *Liberator*, June 6, 1862; Cheever to Elizabeth C. Washburn, June 3, 1862, Cheever Papers, AAS.

sands of lives & millions of dollars as penalty for having a *timid* & *ignorant* President, all the more injurious because *honest*."[23]

As the summer progressed and McClellan's army mired itself in the mud flats of the Chickahominy, the pressure for emancipation mounted ever higher. On June 20, a delegation from the Society of Progressive Friends, a small liberal Quaker association dominated by Garrisonian abolitionists, presented to Lincoln a memorial urging emancipation under the war power. The memorial had been written by Garrison and was read to the president by Oliver Johnson. Lincoln replied politely to the delegation, agreeing with them that slavery was wrong, but questioning whether a proclamation of emancipation would have any effect in the South when he could not even enforce the Constitution there. Johnson replied briefly, conceding that "the Constitution cannot now be enforced at the South, but you do not on that account intermit the effort to enforce it, and the memorialists are solemnly convinced that the abolition of Slavery is indispensable to your success." Lincoln made no promises, but intimated that he would take action against slavery when he thought, under God's guidance, that such action would be helpful and effective.[24]

In July, John Jay organized an emancipation meeting of prominent conservative New Yorkers at Cooper Union. "Our old Conservative solid men are ready for the most radical measures," Jay informed Sumner, "& we can speak in their names in such a way as to give voice to the whole country and demand not for the blacks but for ourselves & for the Union as our only hope an emancipation policy."[25] In the same month the *Independent* began publishing a series of widely quoted editorials by Beecher and Tilton militantly calling for the abolition of slavery.[26] Susan B. Anthony started on a whirlwind speaking tour through the smaller towns of upstate New York. In New Jersey, Angelina Grimké Weld published a petition entitled "A Declaration of War on Slavery" and circulated it herself in the Perth Amboy neighborhood, obtaining hundreds of signatures even in that Democratic

[23] Phillips to Sumner, June 7, 29, 1862, Sumner Papers, HU.
[24] Garrison to Helen Garrison, June 9, 1862, Garrison Papers, BPL; *New York Tribune*, June 21, 1862; Basler, ed., *Collected Works of Lincoln*, v, 278-79.
[25] Jay to Sumner, July 4, 16, 1862, Sumner Papers, HU; Jay to S. P. Chase, July 3, 1862, Chase Papers, LC.
[26] *Independent*, July 10, 24, 31, Aug. 14, 1862.

stronghold.[27] Throughout the North abolitionists and Republicans were engaging in similar activities, while the Republican press became increasingly bold in calling for emancipation.

"The great phenomenon of the year," observed the conservative Republican *Boston Advertiser* in August 1862, "is the terrible intensity which this [emancipation] resolution has acquired. A year ago men might have faltered at the thought of proceeding to this extremity in any event. The majority do not now seek it, but, we say advisedly, they are in great measure prepared for it." Senator John Sherman wrote from Ohio to his brother, General Sherman: "You can form no conception of the change of opinion here as to the Negro Question. . . . I am prepared for one to meet the broad issue of universal emancipation." Oliver Johnson thought "the slowness and the stupidity of the President are very trying, but the constantly improving state of the public mind gives me hope, or at least keeps me from despair."[28]

Lincoln felt the pressure. On July 12 he summoned the congressmen and senators from the border slave states to the White House and pleaded with them to accept his offer of compensated emancipation. If they delayed much longer "the institution in your states will be extinguished by mere friction and abrasion." When he repudiated General Hunter's proclamation, Lincoln continued, "I gave dissatisfaction, if not offence, to many whose support the country can not afford to lose. And this is not the end of it. The pressure, in this direction is still upon me, and is increasing. By conceding what I now ask, you can relieve me." The border state representatives thought it over for two days, and on July 14 a majority of them sent a reply rejecting Lincoln's appeal. Eight days later the president submitted the first draft of an emancipation proclamation to his cabinet, but was persuaded by Seward to withhold it until Union arms won a victory.[29]

Congress felt the pressure too, and on July 17 it passed the

27 Alma Lutz, *Susan B. Anthony, Rebel, Crusader, Humanitarian* (Boston, 1959), 95-96; Catherine H. Birney, *The Grimké Sisters: Sarah and Angelina Grimké, The First American Women Advocates of Abolition and Women's Rights* (Boston and New York, 1885), 285.

28 *Boston Advertiser*, Aug. 20, 1862; John Sherman to William T. Sherman, Aug. 24, 1862, in Rachel S. Thorndike, ed., *The Sherman Letters, Correspondence between General and Senator Sherman from 1837 to 1891* (London, 1894), 156-57; Oliver Johnson to Samuel May, Jr., July 25, 1862, Garrison Papers, BPL.

29 Basler, ed., *Collected Works of Lincoln*, v, 317-19, 336-37.

second Confiscation Act, declaring all slaves of rebel masters "forever free" as soon as they came within Union lines. But abolitionists no longer considered a confiscation act sufficient. In the first place the emancipation clause of the act was buried in the middle of several paragraphs of dry legal language. Secondly, the law freed only one, a dozen, or a hundred slaves at a time, as they came within Union lines. Abolitionists desired a bold and sweeping edict declaring all slaves immediately free and proclaiming to the world that the North was fighting for universal freedom. Finally, abolitionists realized that lengthy litigation would be necessary to determine whether each individual slaveowner had been engaged in rebellion under the terms of the law, and whether, therefore, his slaves were actually freed by the act. Maria Weston Chapman expressed the opinion of most abolitionists when she called the Confiscation Act "an Emancipation bill with clogs on."[30]

Moreover, to the public eye it appeared that Lincoln had no intention of enforcing the act. Abolitionists pointed out that the law would remain a dead letter unless antislavery generals were appointed to important commands. Lincoln appointed few antislavery generals to important commands; instead on July 11 he named General Henry Halleck, who had tried to exclude fugitive slaves from his lines while in command of the Department of the West, as general in chief of the United States Army. After passage of the Confiscation Act, abolitionists hoped for a ringing proclamation from the president ordering his generals to put the law into effect.[31] But nothing of the kind was forthcoming. The administration "is blind as a bat to its true line of policy," cried Garrison in despair. "Stumbling, halting, prevaricating, irresolute, weak, besotted," were the only words he could find to describe Lincoln's course.[32]

In a speech at Abington, Massachusetts, on August 1 Wendell Phillips released his pent-up frustration in a savage attack on the

[30] U.S. Statutes at Large, XII, 589-92; M. W. Chapman to Anne G. Chapman, July 20, 1862, Weston Papers, BPL. For a discussion of the meaning of the Second Confiscation Act as it applied to slavery, see James G. Randall, Constitutional Problems under Lincoln (New York, 1926), 358-63.
[31] Williams, Lincoln and the Radicals, 148-49; New York Tribune, Aug. 6, 13, 1862; N.A.S. Standard, July 26, 1862.
[32] Liberator, July 25, 1862.

administration. "I do not believe in the government," he said. "I do not believe this government has got either vigor or a purpose. It drifts with events." Phillips dismissed Lincoln as "a first-rate *second-rate* man. . . . He has not uttered a word which gives even a twilight glimpse of any antislavery purpose. He may be honest, —nobody cares whether the tortoise is honest or not; he has neither insight, nor prevision, nor decision." McClellan and his proslavery ideas were ruining the country. "I do not say that McClellan is a traitor," declared Phillips, "but I say this, that if he had been a traitor from the crown of his head to the sole of his foot, he could not have served the South better than he has done since he was commander-in-chief (applause); . . . and almost the same thing may be said of Mr. Lincoln."[33]

The speech was denounced by the northern press. "WENDELL PHILLIPS SPOUTING FOUL TREASON," screamed the *New York Herald*. One editor claimed that imprisonment of Phillips would be worth 100,000 men to the Union cause. The *Philadelphia Press* proclaimed that "Wendell Phillips is a traitor in his soul. He differs from Jefferson Davis in this only, that Davis has drawn the sword, while Phillips is effective without it."[34] George Livermore, Massachusetts Republican, wrote to Sumner on August 10: "Cannot you have influence with some of Wendell Phillips' friends and have him sent to a madhouse before he is arrested as a traitor? . . . If he is sane, the prison is too good for him; if crazy, have him gently treated but not suffered to go at large." Most abolitionists sprang to Phillips' defense. But some of them regretted the severity of the speech. "I disapprove & regret [the course] of W. Phillips," wrote John Jay. "The President is to be sustained by us as far as possible, & we are not to throw away our influence over him & give him up to our opponents."[35]

Phillips came to his own defense in a letter to the *New York Tribune*. He denied that he was disloyal or that he was still a disunionist at heart. He fervently believed in the Union *with freedom*. "But government and the Union are one thing. This *administra-*

[33] Excerpts of the speech were published in many northern newspapers. It is published in full in Phillips, *Speeches, Lectures, and Letters*, 1st Series, 448-63.
[34] Press reaction to the speech was quoted in the *Liberator*, Aug. 15, 22, 1862; *Philadelphia Press*, Aug. 11, 1862.
[35] Livermore to Sumner, Aug. 10, 1862, Jay to Sumner, Aug. 7, 1862, Sumner Papers, HU.

tion is quite another. Whether the administration will ever pilot us through our troubles, I have serious doubts: that it never will, unless it changes its present policy, I am quite certain." Phillips believed that he must "educate, arouse, and mature a public opinion . . . by frankly and candidly criticizing [the administration's] present policy. . . . Such criticism is always every thinking man's duty. War excuses no man from this duty: least of all now, when a change of public sentiment to lead the administration to and support it in a new policy, is our only hope of saving the Union." If he were in the Senate, said Phillips, he would refuse to vote the administration a dollar until it proclaimed emancipation. "My criticism is not, like that of *The Boston Courier* and its kindred, meant to paralyze the Administration, but to goad it to more activity and vigor."[36] Phillips' letter seemed to achieve its desired effect. At any rate the Republican press ceased to assail him and resumed its demand for an emancipation policy—the same demand Phillips was making.

Sydney Gay was not having an easy time as managing editor of the *Tribune* in the summer of 1862. His boss, Greeley, was prone to sudden whims and was becoming increasingly impatient with Lincoln and talking of issuing some kind of public ultimatum for emancipation. Gay desired emancipation as much or more than Greeley, but wanted to keep the *Tribune* an administration paper and avoid extreme anti-Lincoln criticism. Letters from impatient Republicans denouncing Lincoln were coming into the *Tribune* every day, and on July 30 Gay sent a private note to the president, enclosing a typical letter. These letters evinced "a deep-seated anxiety on the part of the people," Gay told Lincoln. "I do not publish them because I know they would exercise a most serious influence on the public mind. I cannot, however, justify it to myself that . . . [you should be] left in ignorance of that which so many thousands of people desire [you to] hear. Taking a middle course, therefore, I send you one letter as a specimen of all the rest." The letter was from George Rathbun, a prominent Republican and former congressman from upstate New York, who charged that "the President . . . hangs back, hesitates, & leaves the country to drift. . . . The people are uneasy, anxious, and

---

[36] Phillips to the editor of the *New York Tribune*, Aug. 16, 1862, in the *Tribune*, Aug. 20.

suspicious. They begin to fear . . . that we are trifled with, that there is not & never has been any serious determination to put down the rebels."[37]

Upon reading these letters Lincoln immediately telegraphed Gay an invitation to the White House, asking that he bring Rathbun with him. Gay replied that a death in the family would prevent him from coming at once, but promised to come as soon as possible. When he had heard nothing from Gay for eight days, Lincoln telegraphed him again, asking imploringly "When will you come?"[38] Gay turned up in Washington the next day, without Rathbun, who had declined to come. Gay had a long and pleasant conversation with the president, and presented the argument for emancipation calmly and firmly. Lincoln regaled the editor with apt anecdotes, but made no promises. Gay left the interview with a favorable impression of the president; Lincoln later told a friend that he considered Gay "a truly good man & a wise man."[39]

Lincoln hoped the interview would mollify the *Tribune* and silence Greeley's criticisms—he once said that having Greeley "firmly behind me will be as helpful to me as an army of one hundred thousand men"—but from this standpoint his meeting with Gay was a failure. Greeley was not in a mood to be mollified. On August 7 he wrote to Sumner: "Do you remember that old theological book containing this: 'Chapter One—Hell; Chapter Two—Hell Continued.' Well, that gives a hint of the way Old Abe *ought to be* talked to in this crisis."[40] Gay tried unsuccessfully to calm his irate colleague. James R. Gilmore, a friend of both Lincoln and Greeley, reported the editor's intractability to the president, who reluctantly authorized Gilmore to inform Greeley of the draft emancipation proclamation reposing in a White House desk drawer. Gilmore rushed back to New York, but arrived just hours

[37] Gay to Lincoln, July 30, 1862, Lincoln Papers, LC, copy also in Gay Papers, CU; George Rathbun to the editor of the *New York Tribune*, July 28, 1862, Gay Papers, CU.

[38] Lincoln to Gay, Aug. 1, 9, in Basler, ed., *Collected Works of Lincoln*, V, 353, 364; Gay to Lincoln, Aug. 1, 1862, Lincoln Papers, LC.

[39] Louis M. Starr, *Bohemian Brigade: Civil War Newsmen in Action* (New York, 1954), 126-27; Lincoln's statement quoted in H. L. Stevens to Gay, Sept. 7, 1862, Gay Papers, CU.

[40] William H. Hale, *Horace Greeley, Voice of the People* (Collier Books edition; New York, 1961), 268-69.

too late; Greeley's famous "Prayer of Twenty Millions," demanding of the government an emancipation policy, had already gone to press.[41]

Wendell Phillips thought Greeley's Prayer "superb, terrific. If I could rouse myself to envy anybody I could almost envy G. for the power to do it. . . . Just the man. Just the act."[42] Many abolitionists agreed with Phillips, although some, like Gay, probably regretted the timing of the "Prayer." Lincoln took the unusual step of replying publicly to Greeley's manifesto. "My paramount object in this struggle *is* to save the Union, and is *not* either to save or to destroy slavery," wrote the president. "If I could save the Union without freeing *any* slave I would do it, and if I could save it by freeing *all* the slaves I would do it; and if I could save it by freeing some and leaving others alone I would also do that."[43]

Abolitionist reaction to Lincoln's reply was mixed. Edmund Quincy wrote that the president's position was "what we had always believed that it must be." Abolitionists had never expected Lincoln to interfere with slavery in the states except as a military necessity to preserve the Union. "A President of the United States, under an oath to support the Constitution, is not to be expected to act upon motives of mere morality and humanity," wrote Quincy with perhaps a trace of irony. Abolitionists, however, believed that Lincoln had been too slow to recognize the military necessity that now urgently demanded an emancipation policy. "The President has tried 'to save the Union without freeing any slave,' and has failed; is it not time to see what effect 'freeing some,' if not 'all,' would have?"[44]

Most abolitionists probably agreed with Quincy. Gay told Lincoln that "your letter to Mr. Greeley has infused new hope among us. . . . I think the general impression is that . . . you mean presently to announce that the destruction of Slavery is the price of our salvation. The loyal North longs to hear that word from you." Phillips, however, did not agree. Lincoln "won't be flattered," thought Phillips; "he can only be frightened and bullied

[41] Starr, *Bohemian Brigade*, 127-28; James R. Gilmore, *Personal Recollections of Abraham Lincoln and the Civil War* (Boston, 1898), 76-84.
[42] Phillips to Gay, Sept. 2, 1862, Gay Papers, cu.
[43] Lincoln to Greeley, Aug. 22, 1862, published in *New York Tribune*, Aug. 25.
[44] *N.A.S. Standard*, Aug. 30, 1862.

into the right policy." Admitting that most Boston abolitionists concurred with Gay, Phillips nevertheless considered Lincoln's reply to Greeley "the most disgraceful document that ever came from the head of a free people." A Vermont abolitionist thought the reply proved that Lincoln regarded the slavery question as "one of mere policy." "Was ever a more heartless policy announced? . . . With the President public policy is *everything*, humanity and justice nothing."[45] But the very nature of the presidency compelled Lincoln to proceed more cautiously than radicals desired. The multitude of conflicting pressures on the president and the crushing responsibilities of the war forced him to base his actions primarily on "public policy."

In the early days of September a sense of despondency settled heavily upon the northern people. General Pope's loss of the second Battle of Bull Run was a fearful blow. "The war is upon us like a dead weight," wrote Robert Collyer, a Unitarian minister and abolitionist from Chicago. "Surely we cannot go much longer as we are—God help us." Lincoln seemed to be further away from emancipation than ever. On September 13 he told a delegation of Chicago clergymen that an emancipation proclamation would do no more good than "the Pope's bull against the comet."[46] "I am growing more and more skeptical as to the 'honesty' of Lincoln," wrote Garrison. "He is nothing better than a wet rag." Frederick Douglass expressed his "ineffable disgust" with the president's conduct. Gerrit Smith could only lament: "Our poor, guilty, wretched, wicked nation! Very faint is my hope that it will be restored."[47]

From depths of despondency the abolitionist mood was suddenly catapulted to heights of joy by Lincoln's unexpected issuance of a preliminary Emancipation Proclamation on September 22. On September 17 McClellan had turned back Lee's invasion of Maryland at Sharpsburg, and seizing upon this as the victory

[45] Gay to Lincoln, undated, but probably about Aug. 26, 1862, Lincoln Papers, LC; Phillips to Gay, Sept. 2, 1862, Gay Papers, CU; "J. S." to Garrison, Sept. 1, 1862, in *Liberator*, Sept. 5.

[46] John H. Holmes, *The Life and Letters of Robert Collyer* (2 vols., New York, 1917), I, 288; Basler, ed., *Collected Works of Lincoln*, V, 420.

[47] Garrison to Oliver Johnson, Sept. 9, 1862, Garrison Papers, BPL; Frederick Douglass to Gerrit Smith, Sept. 8, 1862, Smith Papers, SU; Smith to Garrison, Sept. 20, 1862, Garrison Papers, BPL.

for which he had waited, the president issued his Proclamation five days later. On January 1, 1863, all slaves in rebellious states would be declared "forever free"; loyal slave states and any rebellious states which returned to the Union before that time would be exempt from the terms of the edict. Lincoln also promised to present to Congress in December a plan for the gradual, compensated abolition of slavery in loyal states.[48]

"I have been in a bewilderment of joy ever since yesterday morning," Theodore Tilton informed Garrison on the day after publication of the Proclamation. "I am half crazy with enthusiasm! I would like to have seen whether *you* laughed or cried on reading it: *I* did both." Frederick Douglass happily declared, "We shout for joy that we live to record this righteous decree. Border State influence, and the influence of half-loyal men, have been exerted and have done their worst. The end of these two influences is implied in this proclamation." Both Gerrit Smith and Moncure Conway cried, "God Bless Abraham Lincoln!" And Wendell Phillips echoed dryly, "How decent Abe grows."[49]

A few abolitionists were disappointed by the conservative, conditional nature of the Proclamation. "How cold the President's Proclamation is!" shivered Sallie Holley of Rochester. George Cheever denounced it as "nothing but a bribe to win back the slaveholding states to loyalty by giving and confirming to them the privilege of tyrannizing over millions of their fellow creatures in perpetual slavery." Garrison's first reaction upon reading the Proclamation was one of disappointment. He had hoped that an emancipation edict, when forthcoming, would be immediate and complete; instead Lincoln had confined it to rebellious states, given them one hundred days of grace, and coupled it with his favorite scheme of gradual, compensated emancipation. "The President can do nothing for *freedom* in a direct manner, but only by circumlocution and delay," complained Garrison. "How prompt was his action against Frémont and Hunter!"[50]

[48] Basler, ed., *Collected Works of Lincoln*, v, 433-36.

[49] Tilton to Garrison, Sept. 24, 1862, Garrison Papers, BPL; *Douglass' Monthly*, Oct. 1862; Gerrit Smith to Lincoln, Oct. 9, 1862, Lincoln Papers, LC; Conway in *Commonwealth*, Sept. 27, 1862; Phillips to Elizabeth Gay, Sept. 23, 1862, Gay Papers, CU.

[50] Sallie Holley to A. K. Foster, Sept. 30, 1862, Foster Papers, Worcester Historical Society; George Cheever to Elizabeth C. Washburn, Sept. 29, 1862,

Nevertheless Garrison publicly rejoiced in the Proclamation as "an important step in the right direction, and an act of immense historic consequence." Governor John Andrew declared, "It is a poor *document*, but a mighty *act*." Samuel May, Jr., would not "stop to criticize now, & say this freedom ought (as indeed it ought) to have been made immediate, that it ought to have been proclaimed (as it ought) seventeen months ago. . . . I cannot stop to dwell on these. Joy, gratitude, thanksgiving, renewed hope and courage fill my soul."[51]

The principal worry of abolitionists between September and January was whether Lincoln could withstand the strong conservative pressure for modification or revocation of the Proclamation. The Democratic press unleashed a savage attack on the edict, calling it unconstitutional, dictatorial, and ruinous. Democrats made opposition to emancipation one of their main issues in the 1862 congressional elections, appealing to northern race prejudice and to the white workingman's fear of low-wage competition from free Negroes.[52]

Abolitionists were distressed by Democratic electoral victories in several key states, but were encouraged by Lincoln's removal of the conservative McClellan from command of the Army of the Potomac on November 7. "The removal of McClellan lights up the whole horizon," wrote Oliver Johnson. "From all that I can learn, the President is not contemplating any change of policy, so far as emancipation is concerned, in consequence of the result of the recent election. The removal of McClellan tends to show that . . . he is satisfied, at last, that all attempts to conciliate the pro-slavery Democracy are vain."[53]

But Lincoln's annual message to Congress on December 1 dealt a sharp blow to abolitionist confidence. The president urged adoption of a constitutional amendment granting compensation to

---

Cheever Papers, aas; Garrison to Fanny Garrison, Sept. 25, 1862, Garrison Papers, bpl.

[51] *Liberator*, Sept. 26, 1862; John Andrew to Albert G. Browne, Sept. 23, 1862, in Henry G. Pearson, *The Life of John A. Andrew* (2 vols., Boston, 1904), ii, 51; May to Richard Webb, Sept. 23, 1862, Samuel May, Jr., Papers, bpl.

[52] William G. Cochrane, "Freedom without Equality: A Study of Northern Opinion and the Negro Issue, 1861-1870," Ph.D. dissertation, University of Minnesota, 1957, 46-49. See also *New York World*, Sept. 24, 1862; and John Jay to S. P. Chase, Sept. 27, 1862, Chase Papers, lc.

[53] Johnson to Garrison, Nov. 10, 1862, Garrison Papers, bpl.

any state that undertook to abolish slavery by 1900. Slaves freed "by the chances of the war" would remain "forever free"; but all others would remain slaves until they were gradually emancipated by the respective states or individual owners.[54]

Abolitionists were astounded by this proposal. "We cannot refrain from expressing our astonishment at the folly and infatuation evinced in his plan for buying up Southern treason 'in lots to suit purchasers,' " declared Garrison in the *Liberator*. Did this message mean that Lincoln had decided against issuing his emancipation proclamation on January 1 after all? The *New York World* and *Herald* gleefully said that it meant just that, and many abolitionists feared they were right. "If the President means to carry out his edict of freedom on the New Year," asked Moncure Conway, editor of the newly established *Boston Commonwealth*, "what is all this stuff about gradual emancipation?"[55]

As the decisive New Year's Day drew near, abolitionists grew tense and anxious. They asked each other apprehensively whether Lincoln would remain true to his promise. They wrote to friends in Washington for information on the president's intentions.[56] Oliver Johnson did not doubt that Lincoln would "fulfill the promise of Sept. 22, but I presume he will do it in such a cold, formal, uninspiring way, that we shall feel ourselves under a wet blanket. . . . 'Old Abe' seems utterly incapable of a really grand action." Garrison observed on December 26 that "it seems to be the general conviction" that Lincoln would stand by his Proclamation, "though we shall not be greatly surprised if he substitute some other project for it. A man so manifestly without moral vision . . . cannot be safely relied upon in any emergency." After a talk with Lincoln, Charles Sumner assured his abolitionist friends that "the Presdt. is firm. He says that he would not stop the Procltn. if he could, & he could not if he would."[57]

On New Year's Day 1863, Boston's Negro and white abolitionists crowded into Tremont Temple to celebrate the expected proc-

[54] Basler, ed., *Collected Works of Lincoln*, v, 529-37.

[55] *Liberator*, Dec. 5, 1862; *Commonwealth*, Dec. 6, 1862.

[56] Gerrit Smith to Garrison, Dec. 13, 1862, Garrison Papers, BPL; William Goodell to Sumner, Dec. 24, 1862, S. E. Sewall to Sumner, Dec. 28, 1862, Sumner Papers, HU; *N.A.S. Standard*, Dec. 27, 1862; *Principia*, Jan. 1, 1863.

[57] Johnson to Garrison, Dec. 27, 1862, Garrison Papers, BPL; *Liberator*, Dec. 26, 1862; Charles Sumner to S. G. Howe, Dec. 28, 1862, Sumner-Howe Correspondence, HU.

lamation of freedom. The festivities began gaily enough, but as speech followed speech and no news of the Proclamation came over the telegraph wires, doubt began to gnaw at the hearts of the assembled crusaders. Perhaps Sumner had been misinformed; perhaps Lincoln would not issue the great edict of freedom after all! In the evening several speakers, climaxed by Frederick Douglass, tried to entertain and distract the audience while they waited for the Proclamation. But a general restlessness, a mood almost of despair, began to pervade the hall. Just as Douglass himself was about to succumb to despondency a messenger ran through the door shouting "It is coming! It is on the wires." "A thrill shot through the crowd; the enthusiasm was intense," wrote an eyewitness the next day. When the complete Proclamation was received, Charles Wesley Slack (a young white abolitionist who had led the fight in the Massachusetts legislature to abolish segregated schools) read it aloud to the crowd. As he finished, the cheers, applause, and yells erupted into pandemonium for several minutes. "The people seemed almost wild with delight," wrote the eyewitness. "It is the dawning of a New Day!"[58]

All over the North, and in Union-occupied portions of the South, similar jubilee meetings took place. It was a day of joy and thanksgiving, the climax of the first phase of the abolitionist movement. In the first flush of enthusiasm, abolitionists lavished lofty praise on Lincoln and his Proclamation. "This is a great Era! A sublime period in History! The Proclamation is grand. The President has done nobly," exclaimed the Reverend R. C. Waterston, a Massachusetts abolitionist and official of the Church Anti-Slavery Society. "Hurrah! Hosanna! Hallelujah! Laudamus! Nunc dimittis! Jubilate! Amen!" cried the usually restrained Maria Weston Chapman. Garrison hailed the Proclamation as "a great historic event, sublime in its magnitude, momentous and beneficent in its far-reaching consequences."[59]

As they studied the Proclamation more closely, however, abolitionists found one important shortcoming: it applied only to the

[58] *Liberator*, Jan. 9, 16, 1863; *N.A.S. Standard*, Jan. 10, 1863; eyewitness account quoted from R. C. Waterston to Charles Sumner, Jan. 2, 1863, Sumner Papers, HU.

[59] Waterston to Sumner, Jan. 2, 1863, Sumner Papers, HU; M. W. Chapman to A. H. Gibbons, Jan. 5, 1863, in Sarah H. Emerson, *Life of Abby Hopper Gibbons* (2 vols., New York, 1896-97), I, 384; *Liberator*, Jan. 2, 1863.

Confederate states, and of these Tennessee and parts of Louisiana and Virginia were exempted "for the present." The executive committee of the American Anti-Slavery Society accused Lincoln of being "derelict in his duty in exempting any part of the slave states, or any portion of the slave population." Most abolitionists, however, were inclined to be lenient on this point; they noted that Lincoln had exempted certain portions of the Confederacy only "for the present," and that slavery was doomed in the border states anyway. "I regret, of course, that the Act was not universal," wrote Tilton. "But Providence means to supplement it *de facto*, by adding the omitted states in good time."[60]

Some nonabolitionist critics laughed at the Proclamation as a *brutum fulmen*, a harmless threat. They pointed out that it "emancipated" only those slaves beyond the power of the federal government, and exempted those within Union lines. This was true, replied abolitionists, but the Proclamation constituted a promise of freedom to all slaves in nonexempt rebel states as soon as the Confederacy was conquered. Edmund Quincy admitted that actual physical emancipation could only be accomplished by the Union army as it advanced southward; but news of the Proclamation would "not only spread with immense rapidity over every portion of the South, but [would] . . . exercise everywhere a moral influence mightily efficacious for the freedmen, and against the slaveholder." William Robinson observed dryly: "That old Declaration of July 4, 1776, remained a ridiculous *brutum fulmen* for seven years. No doubt many a mad wag among the Tories of that day had his jeer at it, comparing it to the Pope's bull against the comet."[61]

+

January 1, 1863, was the climax of the drive for emancipation. But the events of the next two years constituted an important anticlimax. There were still many obstacles to be overcome before the decision to abolish slavery was secure beyond recall. Thomas Wentworth Higginson, colonel of the first regiment of freed slaves enlisted in the Civil War, feared a reaction from the onsweeping

[60] *Liberator,* Jan. 16, 1863; Tilton to Garrison, Jan. 9, 1863, Garrison Papers, BPL. See also *Principia,* Jan. 8, 1863; J. F. Clarke to N. A. Staples, Jan. 1, 1863, Clarke Papers, HU; Lewis Tappan to Sumner, Jan. 9, 1863, Sumner Papers, HU; and *N.A.S. Standard,* Jan. 10, 1863.

[61] Quincy in *N.A.S. Standard,* Jan. 10, 1863; Robinson in *Springfield Republican,* Jan. 3, 1863.

revolution of emancipation. "Sometimes I feel anxious about the ultimate fate of these poor [Negro] people," he confided to his journal a week after Lincoln had issued the Emancipation Proclamation. "After Hungary, one sees that the right may not triumph, & revolutions may go backward, & the habit of inhumanity in regard to them seems so deeply impressed upon our people, that it is hard to believe in the possibility of anything better. I dare not yet hope that the promise of the President's proclamation will be kept."[62]

Higginson had good reason for his fears. Since the summer of 1862 the antiemancipation "Copperhead" movement had grown alarmingly. Capitalizing on northern war-weariness, "Copperheadism" reached a peak of strength in the winter and spring of 1863 when the Army of the Potomac, decisively defeated at Fredericksburg and Chancellorsville, seemed mired in the incompetency of its generals. In order to counter the Copperhead movement, Republicans organized Union Leagues throughout the North in 1863. These societies were virtual adjuncts of the Republican party, and were formed to promote loyalty to the Republican war policy of emancipation and total victory over the South. Many abolitionists belonged to the Union Leagues, and John Jay helped organize Leagues in New York and other cities; he later served as president of the New York League. New York and Boston Republicans established the Loyal Publication Society and the New England Loyal Publication Society to print and distribute thousands of pamphlets, speeches, and editorials calling for loyalty, emancipation, and a vigorous war policy. Several abolitionist speeches were published by these societies.[63]

The Union capture of Vicksburg and the victory at Gettysburg in July 1863, caused great rejoicing in the North and put a temporary damper on the Copperhead movement. But for abolitionists there was a somber side to Yankee success. Once again northern editors told their readers that the rebellion was on the verge of collapse. There was talk of a peace overture to the Confederacy,

[62] Higginson, Journal, entry of Jan. 8, 1863, Higginson Papers, HU.
[63] John Jay to Charles Sumner, Mar. 18, 1863, Sumner Papers, HU; Jay to S. P. Chase, Sept. 13, Oct. 6, 1863, Chase Papers, LC; Frank Freidel, "The Loyal Publication Society: A Pro-Union Propaganda Agency," *Mississippi Valley Historical Review*, xxvi (1939), 191-210; George W. Smith, "Broadsides for Freedom; Civil War Propaganda in New England," *New England Quarterly*, xxi (Sept. 1948), 291-312.

and abolitionists feared that the price of peace at this time would be compromise on the issue of slavery. "We are too victorious; I fear more from our victories than our defeats," wrote Charles Sumner. "If the rebellion should suddenly collapse, Democrats, copperheads, and Seward would insist upon amnesty and the Union, and 'no question asked about slavery.' God save us from any such calamity!"[64]

Radicals and abolitionists asked each other apprehensively whether Lincoln would bow to conservative pressure and modify his Proclamation. The president relieved their anxiety in a public letter of August 26 to James Conkling of Springfield, Illinois. Echoing the war-power arguments of William Whiting, Lincoln affirmed that he possessed full constitutional power to declare military emancipation. He had done so, and he would not retract his action. He had promised freedom to the slaves, "and the promise being made, must be kept."[65]

Abolitionists praised the letter. "We thank the President for that declaration," wrote William Goodell in the *Principia*. "We thank God, and take courage."[66] Republican victories in the 1863 elections gave proponents of emancipation another injection of hope. Lincoln provided abolitionists with further cause for rejoicing in his annual message to Congress on December 8, 1863, when he firmly declared that "while I remain in my present position I shall not attempt to retract or modify the emancipation proclamation; nor shall I return to slavery any person who is free by the terms of that proclamation, or by any of the acts of Congress." Henry Wright wrote fervently, "God bless thee, Abraham Lincoln! With all my heart I bless thee, in the name of God & Humanity."[67] Lincoln's declaration was an important victory for abolition. The president had refused to succumb to the counter-emancipation pressures exerted during 1863, and had placed himself firmly and irrevocably on the side of freedom.

[64] Sumner to John Bright, July 21, 1863, in E. L. Pierce, *Memoir and Letters of Charles Sumner* (4 vols., Boston, 1877-94), IV, 143. See also Sumner to E. L. Pierce, July 29, 1863, *ibid.*, 142; George Cheever to Elizabeth C. Washburn, July 7, Aug. 5, 1863, Cheever Papers, AAS; Cheever to S. P. Chase, Aug. 7, 1863, Chase Papers, LC.

[65] Basler, ed., *Works of Lincoln*, VI, 406-10.

[66] *Principia*, Sept. 10, 1863.

[67] Basler, ed., *Works of Lincoln*, VII, 51; Henry Wright to Lincoln, Dec. 16, 1863, Lincoln Papers, LC.

In the spring of 1863 Elizabeth Cady Stanton and Susan B. Anthony had organized the Women's Loyal National League to promote loyalty and propagandize for emancipation. Abolitionists had been calling for a congressional emancipation act to reinforce Lincoln's Proclamation, and the Women's League decided that their main function would be to circulate petitions urging passage of such an act.[68]

The women hoped to obtain one million signatures to their petition by the end of the 1863-1864 congressional session. This was a lofty goal, far exceeding the number of signatures ever before secured for a single objective in America, but Mrs. Stanton and Miss Anthony went to work with great energy and optimism. Women abolitionists all over the North rallied to the cause. Senator Sumner cooperated gallantly with the ladies, sending out blank petitions under his frank. The League employed lecturing agents to travel through key areas giving speeches, circulating petitions, and establishing auxiliary societies. By the fall of 1863 the petition campaign was in full swing, but the women were plagued by a shortage of funds. Susan B. Anthony persuaded the executive committee of the American Anti-Slavery Society to lend its resources to the petition campaign. The Society decided to send out an expanded corps of lecturers during the winter of 1863-1864 to supplement the work of the Women's Loyal National League. One of the Society's new lecturers was William Andrew Jackson, Jefferson Davis's former slave and coachman.[69]

Late in 1863 there was a growing conviction that the confiscation acts and the Emancipation Proclamation, although legitimate wartime measures, might become legally inoperative once peace was concluded. To be permanent, therefore, emancipation must be

[68] *N.A.S. Standard*, May 23, 30, June 6, 1863; Elizabeth Cady Stanton, et al., *History of Woman Suffrage* (6 vols., New York, 1881-1922), II, 50-78.

[69] Eleanor Flexner, *Century of Struggle: The Woman's Rights Movement in the United States* (Cambridge, Mass., 1959), 109-10; Lillie B. C. Wyman and Arthur Wyman, *Elizabeth Buffum Chace* (2 vols., Boston, 1914), I, 223-24; Ida Harper, *The Life and Work of Susan B. Anthony* (3 vols., Indianapolis, 1898-1908), I, 232-34; E. C. Stanton to Fanny Garrison, May 25, 1863, Garrison Papers, BPL; Mattie Griffith to Mary Estlin, July 27, 1863, copy in Weston Papers, BPL; S. B. Anthony to E. C. Stanton, Oct. 10, 1863, Gerrit Smith to E. C. Stanton, Oct. 23, 1863, Stanton Papers, LC; Giles Stebbins to Gerrit Smith, Oct. 6, 1863, Mar. 22, 1864, Smith Papers, SU; *Commonwealth*, Oct. 2, 30, 1863; *Liberator*, Oct. 2, 16, Nov. 13, Dec. 11, 25, 1863, Jan. 1, 8, Mar. 4, June 3, 1864; *N.A.S. Standard*, Oct. 31, Nov. 21, Dec. 5, 1863, Apr. 9, 1864.

written into the Constitution. Realizing the force of this argument, abolitionists in December 1863, decided to press for a constitutional amendment to abolish and prohibit forever the institution of slavery in the United States. The request for a constitutional amendment was included in all petitions circulated by the anti-slavery societies after December 1863, and in all petitions circulated by the Women's Loyal National League after February 1864.[70]

By early 1864 2,000 men, women, and children were at work circulating petitions. In February Miss Anthony and Mrs. Stanton sent the first installment of petitions bearing 100 thousand signatures to Senator Sumner.[71] On February 9 two tall Negroes, symbolizing the struggle for freedom, carried the huge bundles of petitions into the Senate and placed them on Sumner's desk. The senator rose to speak. "This petition is signed by one hundred thousand men and women, who unite in this unparalleled manner to support its prayer," he told the Senate. "They are from all parts of the country and every condition of life. . . . Here they are, a mighty army, one hundred thousand strong, without arms or banners, the advanced guard of a yet larger army."[72]

It was clear that the women would come nowhere near their goal of one million signatures. Such a goal was unrealistically high for the resources and womanpower of the League. By the time Congress adjourned in July 1864, the League had sent in petitions bearing nearly 400 thousand signatures. Even though they had not reached their goal of one million, this was an impressive achievement. No other petition for a single objective had ever received so many signatures. Senators Sumner and Henry Wilson assured the League that their petition campaign had been of great assistance in the struggle to secure congressional passage of the Thirteenth Amendment.[73]

The Senate adopted the Thirteenth Amendment on April 8, 1864, but it failed to obtain the necessary two-thirds majority

[70] Samuel May, Jr., to Garrison, Dec. 28, 1863, Garrison Papers, BPL; *Liberator*, Jan. 15, 1864; S. B. Anthony to Charles Sumner, Mar. 1, 1864, Sumner Papers, HU.
[71] Stanton et al., *History of Woman Suffrage*, II, 78-87; S. B. Anthony and E. C. Stanton to Sumner, Feb. 4, 1864, Sumner Papers, HU.
[72] *Cong. Globe*, 38 Cong., 1 Sess., 536.
[73] *Liberator*, Mar. 11, 1864; *Independent*, Apr. 7, 1864; *New York Tribune*, May 17, 1864; *N.A.S. Standard*, May 28, June 4, 1864; Harper, *Anthony*, I, 238.

in the House, which the Republicans controlled by only a bare majority. Most Democrats voted against the Amendment, still hoping to preserve the framework of slavery. Lincoln's victory in the election of 1864, however, convinced many Democrats that public opinion desired emancipation. Emancipationists had gained control of most of the border slave states and were rapidly extinguishing slavery therein. Enough Democrats changed their votes or abstained from voting in the lame duck session of Congress to enable the House to pass the Thirteenth Amendment on January 31, 1865.[74] Ratification by the necessary three-fourths of the states was completed before the end of the year.

✦

Abolitionist influence and prestige continued to climb in the last two years of the war. In January 1863, a friend of General Butler returned from a Wendell Phillips speech and wrote to the general that Phillips had praised Butler's work in New Orleans. This was an important endorsement, for "Phillips, in these winter months, manufactures a vast amount of popular opinion. No man will speak oftener or to larger audiences in America for the next few months. . . . These masses in New England and New York and Ohio are reached by men like Phillips who have the public ear in Lyceum Halls." A Philadelphia abolitionist reported that the antislavery office in that city "has become the resort of a class of men who have hitherto kept from Abolitionists, as dangerous & fanatical, and who now seem surprised to find that the abolitionists have but spoken the words of truth & soberness." Officials of the Pennsylvania Freedmen's Relief Association, including some of the city's leading businessmen, frequently consulted with J. Miller McKim on freedmen's affairs. They "almost sit at his feet and are eager for the information and experience which only an old Abolitionist can give."[75]

In the summer of 1863 James Redpath published a book of Phillips' lectures and speeches. The first printing sold out in four days. The book went through four printings in six months.[76]

[74] *Cong. Globe*, 38 Cong., 1 Sess., 1,490, 2,995, 2 Sess., 531.
[75] J. O. A. Griffin to Butler, Jan. 18, 1863, in Jesse A. Marshall, ed., *Private and Official Correspondence of Gen. Benjamin F. Butler during the Period of the Civil War* (5 vols., Norwood, Mass., 1917), II, 580; Abby Kimber to R. D. Webb, Feb. 22, 1863, Garrison Papers, BPL.
[76] *Liberator*, July 24, 1863; Frank Sanborn to Moncure Conway, Sept. 16,

When the United States acquired Alaska in 1867 the only English-language book in the territory's only public library was a copy of Phillips' speeches.[77] In a review of the book the conservative *New-buryport Herald* (Massachusetts) tried to analyze the reasons for Phillips' wartime popularity. "He was the foreteller of this day which we have lived to see," stated the *Herald*. "Few heard him once; but now many will read him, for his ideas are the popular ones of the day, and he holds the ear of the nation, and his audience embraces continents. Garrison and Phillips have been among the most successful reformers the world has ever known."[78]

One of the more remarkable events of abolitionist history was the rise of young Anna Dickinson from obscurity to fame as an abolitionist orator second in demand only to Wendell Phillips. Anna Dickinson was born in 1842, eleven years after Garrison had launched the *Liberator*. She followed in the footsteps of her father, a zealous Quaker abolitionist of Philadelphia. In 1856, at the age of fourteen, Miss Dickinson penned her first contribution to the *Liberator*. In 1860 she pleasantly surprised the abolitionists by delivering an eloquent speech at a Philadelphia antislavery meeting.[79] In the spring of 1862 Garrison signed her on as a lecturer for the Massachusetts Anti-Slavery Society. She made a speaking tour of Rhode Island, and immediately created a sensation. Her rapid-fire manner of delivery, her simple, direct style, her withering sarcasm, and the novelty of a teen-ager attacking political leaders nearly three times her age left audiences gasping and cheering. "We are at a loss to conceive whence sprung this new champion in petticoats of an antislavery war," wrote a correspondent of the *Providence Press* in April 1862, "but in sending her

---

1863, Conway Papers, cu. In 1863 the enterprising James Redpath formed a publishing company and printed several antislavery books to help promote the cause of emancipation. Books published by him included Phillips' lectures; William Wells Brown's *The Black Man*; a biography of Toussaint L'Ouverture; Augustin Cochin's *Results of Emancipation* and *Results of Slavery*; and Louisa May Alcott's first book, *Hospital Sketches*. See Madeleine B. Sterne, *Imprints on History: Book Publishers and American Frontiers* (Bloomington, Ind., 1956), 76-83.

[77] *N.A.S. Standard*, Feb. 8, 1868.

[78] *Newburyport Herald*, quoted in *Liberator*, Dec. 4, 1863.

[79] Giraud Chester, *Embattled Maiden: The Life of Anna Dickinson* (New York, 1951), 10-25; *Philadelphia Press*, Oct. 27, 1860; *N.A.S. Standard*, Nov. 2, 1860; J. Miller McKim to Samuel May, Jr., Nov. 22, 1860, Garrison to Helen Garrison, Oct. 29, 1861, Garrison Papers, BPL.

forth, her coadjutors have made a wise selection—for, with the tongue of *a dozen women*, she combines the boldness of forty men." On April 20 she climaxed her whirlwind tour with a speech before 4,000 eager listeners in Boston's Music Hall. It was a triumphant success. Afterwards Wendell Phillips told her that he had never been so "gratified and deeply moved by a speech." Anna Dickinson soon acquired a reputation as the Joan of Arc of the abolitionist crusade. At the age of nineteen she suddenly blossomed forth as one of the most sensational public speakers of the day.[80]

In March and April 1863, important state elections were scheduled in New Hampshire and Connecticut. Democrats had hopes of recapturing these states and continuing the reaction against the Republicans begun in the 1862 fall elections. In New Hampshire the Democrats nominated a gubernatorial candidate who favored a compromise peace and opposed emancipation. The eyes of the nation were turned toward the Granite State, for a Republican defeat there would be interpreted as a popular rebuke of Lincoln's emancipation policy. Both parties spent vast amounts of money in the campaign and brought in their best speakers.

The young secretary of the New Hampshire Republican state committee, Benjamin Prescott, had heard Anna Dickinson speak at an antislavery meeting the previous year, and in February 1863, he invited her to speak for the Republicans in the campaign. She accepted, and spoke about twenty times in towns throughout the state. At first the seasoned politicians ridiculed the idea of paying good cash to a twenty-year-old girl stump speaker. But her phenomenal success in the first towns where she spoke soon changed their minds. "We must have Miss Dickinson in our town if possible, for it may be the means of saving us," wrote one local Republican leader late in the campaign. "A few of our Copperheads heard her at Moultonboro and they are completely shelled out. . . . Our people say they must have her, or we are 'stuck in the mud.'" The Republicans triumphed narrowly in the election, and many of the state's Republican newspapers gave Anna chief

[80] Chester, *Embattled Maiden*, 32-38; Anna Dickinson to Garrison, Mar. 16, 1862, Garrison Papers, BPL; Garrison to Anna Dickinson, Mar. 22, 27, 30, Apr. 3, 1862, Charles W. Slack to Anna Dickinson, May 14, 1862, Dickinson Papers, LC; the statement by the *Providence Press* was quoted in the *Liberator*, Apr. 18, 1862; other press comment quoted in the same issue; Wendell Phillips' remark is quoted in Anna Dickinson to Susan Dickinson, Apr. 28, 1862, Dickinson Papers, LC.

credit for the victory. If she had spoken in every town in the state, said one journal, the Republican margin would have been greater. The governor-elect praised her efforts. Though it is probable that federal patronage and the furloughing home of soldiers to vote had at least as much to do with the outcome as Anna Dickinson, her personal triumph and soaring fame were nevertheless very gratifying to abolitionists.[81]

The Connecticut election in April was equally important. The Democrats nominated an antiemancipation peace man for governor and prepared for an all-out effort to elect him. Anna Dickinson entered the campaign on March 25, with only two weeks to go before the election. The Democratic tide was running strongly when she began speaking. After her first speech in Hartford the Connecticut Republican state chairman joyfully wired Prescott: "MISS DICKINSON SPOKE TO A CROWDED HOUSE LAST NIGHT. SHE HAS NO EQUAL IN CONNECTICUT. PEOPLE WILD WITH ENTHUSIASM."[82] She spoke all over the state in the next two weeks, creating a sensation. She was so successful that the Republican committee selected her as the speaker for an election eve rally in Hartford, the most important speech of the campaign. The hall was packed three hours before she spoke. Nearly every sentence she uttered was cheered to the echo. One enthusiastic listener remarked the next day: "I am excited. I admit it, I am; it seems as if I was on fire, and everyone else that heard her are about as bad off. . . . [I] never heard anything that would begin to equal it."[83] The Republican candidate won by 3,000 votes, and both parties gave Anna credit for turning the tide and leading the Republicans to victory. The Republican press was ecstatic in its praise. The state committee paid her $100 for every speech she made, plus $400 for the last speech at Hartford.[84]

Fresh from her triumphs in New Hampshire and Connecticut, Anna Dickinson took New York by storm in early May. Five

[81] Chester, *Embattled Maiden*, 45-49; Prescott to Anna Dickinson, Jan. 2, 28, 29, Feb. 1, 10, 11, 12, 15, 25, 26, 27, 1863, Dickinson Papers, LC. Clippings of press comment in the Dickinson Papers, LC. The statement by the local Republican leader was quoted in Chester, *Embattled Maiden*, 48.

[82] Chester, *Embattled Maiden*, 52.

[83] *ibid.*, 58.

[84] *ibid.*, 49-59, is an excellent account of Miss Dickinson's part in the Connecticut campaign. See also the press clippings in the Dickinson Papers, LC.

thousand people crowded into Cooper Union to hear her speak, and she gratified them with a rousing abolitionist address. "The audience at Cooper Union went crazy," wrote a correspondent of a Connecticut newspaper. "Applause came often and in long-continued storms, hats were swung and handkerchiefs waved and at times the whole house was like a moving, tumultuous sea, flecked with white caps. Never have I seen in New York any speaker achieve such a triumph."[85]

In December 1863, a group of more than one hundred Republican congressmen and senators invited Anna Dickinson to deliver an address in the House Chamber. She accepted, and came before an elite assemblage of Washington dignitaries on the evening of January 16, 1864.[86] President and Mrs. Lincoln were present and joined in a standing ovation accorded the speaker when she had finished. "We have heard wonderful stories of her power to win over seemingly the most confirmed old Hunkers," reported the correspondent of the *Boston Journal* after listening to Anna Dickinson's Washington address, "and can now realize their truth." The *Washington Chronicle* declared, "Joan of Arc never was grander, and could not have been better, in her mail of battle, than was this Philadelphia maid in her statesmanlike demand that this war do not cease till slavery lies dead and buried."[87]

Abolitionists marveled at Anna Dickinson's phenomenal success. She was not an original thinker; her speeches were little more than a hodgepodge of other people's ideas. Wendell Phillips and Frederick Douglass owed their preeminence as orators partly to their original, creative minds; Anna Dickinson owed her success to a staccato-like delivery, a sarcastic wit, a youthful exuberance, the inevitable comparison with Joan of Arc, and the emotional fervor generated by the war itself. Yet her success was not transitory; she remained one of the most popular lecturers in the nation for a decade after the war. She was a valuable asset to the abolitionist movement for many years.

[85] Chester, *Embattled Maiden*, 60-63; *Liberator*, May 8, 1863; *N.A.S. Standard*, May 9, 16, 1863. The statement by the Connecticut newspaper correspondent is quoted in Chester, *Embattled Maiden*, 61.

[86] Susan Dickinson to Anna Dickinson, Dec. 23, 1863, Whitelaw Reid to Anna Dickinson, Dec. 16, 1863, Dickinson to Reid, Jan. 7, 1864, Dickinson Papers, LC.

[87] *Boston Journal*, quoted in *Liberator*, Feb. 19, 1864; *Washington Chronicle*, Jan. 18, 1864.

Abolitionist lecturers were drawing larger crowds than any other speakers in the winter of 1863-1864. In January the *Independent* noted that most lectures had been financial failures in New York during the season, but that the appearances of Phillips, Douglass, and Dickinson had drawn huge crowds and made large profits. Douglass reported in February that "I am, this winter, doing more with my voice than with my pen. I am heard with more than usual attention." The Democratic *Hartford Times* remarked sourly after the annual meeting of the Massachusetts Anti-Slavery Society that "it is deemed a sufficiently important matter, now, to telegraph all over the country the sayings and doings of these chronic fanatics and sworn enemies of the Union, though they and their treasonable opinions were held, four years ago, in silent abhorrence by the very men who now strive to be foremost in the race to do them reverence."[88]

In February 1864, the *New York Times,* spokesman of middle-of-the-road Republicanism, paid an unwitting compliment to the abolitionists. "It is extraordinary how completely the idea of gradual emancipation has been dissipated from the public mind everywhere, by the progress of events," commented the *Times.* "Before the rebellion, it was accounted the very extreme of Anti-Slavery fanaticism to believe in the possibility of immediate emancipation without social ruin. . . . Even when it had become a generally accepted fact that Slavery must come to an end, the idea still adhered that the emancipation must be gradual in order to be safe." But the pressures of war changed all that, and "all these gradual methods are now hardly more thought of than if they had been obsolete a century." The "very extreme of Anti-Slavery fanaticism" had become the accepted policy of the American nation, and as prophets of this policy abolitionists found themselves respected and influential for the first time in their lives. "All true reformers have been ridiculed & despised in their own day," observed Lewis Tappan. "We are coming out of the slanderous valley sooner than most reformers have done, for we have lived to hear old opponents say 'I was wrong.'"[89]

✦

[88] *Independent,* Jan. 21, 1864; Douglass to anonymous, Feb. 17, 1864, in Philip Foner, *The Life and Writings of Frederick Douglass* (4 vols., New York, 1950-55), III, 40; *Hartford Times,* quoted in *Liberator,* Feb. 26, 1864.

[89] *New York Times,* Feb. 25, 1864; Lewis Tappan to Gerrit Smith, Oct. 3, 1864, Smith Papers, su.

Most abolitionists reacted with qualified jubilation to the Emancipation Proclamation and the subsequent events culminating in the Thirteenth Amendment. Emancipation was only the penultimate climax of their crusade for freedom and equality. Freedom had been achieved; but only an incomplete "paper" freedom. Emancipation had proceeded not from an overwhelming conviction on the part of the American people of its justice and humanity, but from "military necessity." The massive job of aiding the transition of 4 million bondsmen to a new life of freedom, and of persuading white America to accept the Negro as an equal, still lay in the future. Abolitionists could not yet retire from the conflict; it was still too early to celebrate the final victory.

VI ✦ THE NEGRO: INNATELY
INFERIOR OR EQUAL?

O NE of the most formidable obstacles to the abolition of slavery and the extension of equal rights to free Negroes was the widespread popular and scientific belief, North as well as South, in the innate inferiority of the Negro race. Most white Americans took it for granted that Negroes were by nature shiftless, slovenly, childlike, savage, and incapable of assimilation as equals into white society. Since the beginning of the antislavery movement abolitionists had been confronted by arguments that Negroes belonged to a separate and inferior species of mankind; that they would work only under compulsion; that they could not take care of themselves in freedom and would revert to barbarism; and that emancipation would bring economic and social ruin to the South and the nation.[1]

For thirty years abolitionists had worked tirelessly but without much success to combat these arguments. When war came in 1861 and emancipation became an imminent possibility, the debate about the Negro's racial character reached new heights of intensity and bitterness. Conservatives urged their thesis of Negro inferiority and unfitness for freedom with desperate energy; abolitionists argued from the pulpit, platform, and press that a hostile environment, not innate inferiority, had created the servile, comic creature that was the American concept of the Negro in 1860. The abolitionists affirmed that if this environment were transformed by the abolition of slavery and of racial discrimination, the Negro would prove himself a constructive, capable, and creative member of society.

[1] The following studies treat this subject in considerable detail: William S. Jenkins, *Pro-Slavery Thought in the Old South* (Chapel Hill, 1935), 242-84; Guion G. Johnson, "A History of Racial Ideologies in the United States with Reference to the Negro," MS in the Schomburg Collection, NYPL; William R. Stanton, *The Leopard's Spots: Scientific Attitudes Toward Race in America, 1815-59* (Chicago, 1960). For a good example of the many pamphlets and books arguing the innate inferiority of the Negro, see J. H. Van Evrie, *Negroes and Negro "Slavery"; The First an Inferior Race—the Latter its Normal Condition* (New York, 1853).

Abolitionists were well aware that the common belief in the Negro's racial inferiority constituted one of the main justifications for slavery. In the final analysis, wrote Sydney Howard Gay in 1860, slavery was based "upon the assumed fact that the negroes are an inferior race, over whom the whites possess not merely an artificial superiority dependent upon the existing circumstances of their mutual position, but a natural superiority, which exists and ever must exist." Frederick Douglass said, "In truth, this question is at the bottom of the whole [slavery] controversy." Until the doctrine of the diversity and inequality of races was discredited, abolitionists reasoned, the theory and practice of slavery would remain strongly entrenched in America. "We cannot expect," said Gilbert Haven, the militant, red-headed Methodist clergyman, "the complete removal of this curse from our land until we stand boldly and heartily upon the divine foundation—the perfect unity of the human race."[2]

With the coming of war in 1861 and the impending prospect of emancipation, proslavery advocates roused themselves to even greater efforts to show that bondage was the normal and only possible condition of the Negro. When the emancipationist drive was gathering momentum at the end of 1861, the *New York Journal of Commerce* published a concise summary of the conservative argument against abolition. "A year ago, no thoroughly sane man in America would have consented to a decree of absolute emancipation," declared the *Journal*, and the war was no reason why the nation should suddenly go insane. "Let no man say this is a base and sordid view of a question of personal freedom." It was a matter of racial common sense. The Negro simply could not take care of himself in freedom. "Unless the reformer can, with his emancipation scheme, introduce new and superhuman industry, economy, thrift and perseverance into the negro, it will result that he will not earn a support for himself alone, much less for his family." The attempt "to make use of the war for the purposes of emancipation," concluded the *Journal*, "is virtually a proposition to plunge the South into the depths of poverty."[3] The northern proslavery press echoed these sentiments throughout the war.

[2] *New York Tribune*, Dec. 1, 1860; Philip S. Foner, *The Life and Writings of Frederick Douglass* (4 vols., New York, 1950-55), II, 294; Gilbert Haven, *National Sermons, Speeches, and Letters on Slavery and Its War* (Boston, 1869), 150.

[3] *New York Journal of Commerce*, quoted in *Liberator*, Jan. 3, 1862.

The abolitionist attack on the concept of racial inequality centered on two fronts: one, an attempt to demonstrate, from the Bible, from science, from history, and from observed facts, the essential unity and equality of races; and two, an attempt to show that the unfavorable environmental conditions of slavery and segregation, rather than natural inferiority, had caused the vices and disabilities of the American Negro.

The antebellum generation was fond of quoting the Bible as a weapon in the slavery controversy, and abolitionists could point to several passages of scripture which "proved" the unity of the human race. The book of Genesis told the story of the creation of *man* (not men) in God's own image. In his famous sermon on Mars Hill, St. Paul told the people of Athens that God "hath made of one blood all nations of men for to dwell on the face of the earth." Gilbert Haven contended that the Bible sanctioned the complete equality and fraternity of the races. Solomon treated the Queen of Sheba, an Ethiopian, "with the utmost respect and cordiality." Moses married an Ethiopian; a Negro was called by God to be one of the prophets and teachers of the Church at Antioch. "More than this," declared Haven, "the Bible constantly proclaims the absolute oneness of the race of man, in Adam, Noah, and Christ."[4]

By 1860, however, the Bible argument was pretty well played out. Thirty years of controversy had only shown that the Bible could be quoted effectively on both sides of the slavery issue. Science, especially ethnology and anthropology, commanded a large and growing influence in the mid-nineteenth century. Ethnology in the hands of Josiah Nott, Louis Agassiz, Samuel G. Morton, and George Gliddon (a group that came to be known as the "American School" of anthropology), who taught that the various races of mankind constituted separate species with the Negro at the bottom of the scale, had become a major weapon in the defense of slavery. Abolitionists realized that to combat these teachings they must themselves use the weapons of ethnology. Few abolitionists had any formal anthropological training, but as a group they were well educated and highly literate; and given the rather crude state of nineteenth-century ethnological knowledge, the industrious

[4] Haven, *National Sermons*, 137.

layman could become almost as well informed as the professional scientist.

Several abolitionists made intensive studies of the question of race. To refute the "American School" of anthropology, abolitionists quoted prominent European naturalists who argued for the unity and equality of races. In 1861, for example, the *Anti-Slavery Standard* published a review of *L'Unité de l'Espèce Humaine*, by M. de Quatrefarges, professor of natural history and ethnology at the Museum of Natural History in Paris. Using the classifications of Linnaeus and Lamarck, M. de Quatrefarges defined mankind as a single species; racial differences were the result of varieties within the species developed by conditions of environment and transmitted by heredity. M. de Quatrefarges used his vast knowledge to deny the existence of any fundamental and immutable differences in the mental capacities of various races.[5]

Abolitionists cited several other outstanding European scientists who maintained the unity and equality of races: Dr. R. G. Latham, the British ethnologist; Dumont d'Urville, the French geographer and navigator; George Louis Leclerc Buffon, the brilliant naturalist; and finally, most important of all, the renowned Alexander von Humboldt, who wrote: "Whilst we maintain the unity of the human species, we at the same time repel the depressing assumption of superior and inferior races of men." Through Humboldt, said Charles Sumner, "Science is enlisted for the Equal Rights of All."[6]

Sumner may have overstated his case, since American science, at least, spoke overwhelmingly for inequality. But the ethnologists of the world spoke with a discordant and divided voice on the subject of race in 1860. Abolitionists argued forcefully and accurately that science had failed to *prove* the racial inferiority of the Negro. "You may read Prichard, and Pinkerton, and Morton, and Pickering, and Latham, and all the rest—the whole library of Ethnology," said Theodore Tilton in 1863, "and in the confusion of knowledge you will find one thing clear—and that is, science has not yet proved, in advance, that the negro race is not to be

[5] *N.A.S. Standard*, Nov. 9, 1861.

[6] Charles Sumner, *Works of Charles Sumner* (15 vols., Boston, 1870-73), XIII, 155-57. Curiously enough, none of the disputants in the racial controversy referred to Darwin before 1866, although *The Origin of Species* was known in America soon after its publication in 1859.

a high-cultured, dominant race—rulers of their own continent, and perhaps dictators to the world."[7]

The endless refinements of the scientific racial arguments probably passed over the heads of the general public. The average man was more interested in concrete examples; and the advocates of Negro inferiority thought they had one incontrovertible example to show him: the supposed barbarous and uncivilized condition of Africa. What contribution to civilization and progress had Africa ever made, asked proslavery writers derisively?

This was a potentially damaging argument, and abolitionists advanced boldly to meet it. Negro abolitionists were in the forefront of the struggle to vindicate Africa. The central theme of their argument was that the inhabitants of ancient Egypt, fountainhead of western civilization, were a Negroid or partially Negroid race. "The ancient Egyptians were not white people," declared Frederick Douglass, "but were, undoubtedly, just about as dark in complexion as many in this country who are considered Negroes." Their hair "was far from being of that graceful lankness which adorns the fair Anglo-Saxon head." William Wells Brown, a prominent Negro abolitionist, lecturer, and author, said in 1862, "I claim that the blacks are the legitimate descendants of the Egyptians." While the ancestors of the proud Anglo-Saxons were roaming the forests of northern Europe as savages, declared Brown, Africa had created the foundations of western civilization and passed on this precious heritage to the Jews, Greeks, Romans, and ultimately to western Europe.[8] Martin Delany, another Negro abolitionist, cited the historians Herodotus and Diodorus Siculus in support of his contention that the world was indebted to ancient Egypt and Ethiopia "for the propagation of that glorious light of progressive civilization—religion, philosophy, arts, science and literature in general, which now illuminate the world." In reply to a derisive reference to Negroes by Senator William L. Yancey of Alabama, William Wells Brown told a group of Boston abolitionists in 1860: "When Mr. Yancey's ancestors were bending their backs to the yoke of William the Conqueror, the ancestors of his

[7] Theodore Tilton, *The Negro* (New York, 1863), 5. This was a speech delivered by Tilton at the annual meeting of the American Anti-Slavery Society in 1863. Several thousand copies were published and distributed by the Society.

[8] Foner, *Douglass*, II, 296; *Liberator*, June 6, 1862, quoting speech by William Wells Brown.

slaves were revelling in the halls of science and learning. If the Hon. Senator from Alabama wants antecedents, he shall have them; and upon such, I claim a superiority for the negro. (Loud applause)"[9]

These arguments were most vigorously advanced by Brown in a book entitled *The Black Man, His Antecedents, His Genius, and His Achievements*, published in 1863. Brown wrote the book for the express purpose of dispelling popular notions about the Negro in order to help mobilize popular support for Lincoln's newly adopted emancipation policy. The book was an immediate success; the first edition was sold out soon after publication, and in the next three years ten printings came off the presses. "Such a rapid sale of a book devoted entirely to an exhibition of the genius, the talent and the heroism of the hated Negro," said the *Anti-Slavery Standard*, "shows that a great change has come over the minds of the American people, and that justice to a long injured race is not far off." Lewis Tappan exclaimed, "This is just the book for the hour. It will do more for the colored man's elevation than any work yet published."[10]

But the glories of ancient Ethiopia were not sufficient to convince many skeptics of the inherent equality of Negroes. Modern Africa stood in the way. Most nineteenth century Americans considered Africa a backward, barbaric continent, devoid of any trace of civilization or culture. Most world travelers who visited the dark continent concurred with Bayard Taylor's opinion that the Negro was "the lowest type of humanity on the face of the earth." Not being world travelers themselves, abolitionists perforce obtained much of their information on Africa from such unflattering sources. Consequently they admitted that contemporary Africa stood low in the scale of civilization, but they advanced a kind of cyclical theory of history, by which nations rose and fell, and would rise again. At one time Africa was the center of learning and culture, said Gerrit Smith, but in the course of events she declined in importance. Africa's "inherent, inborn faculties," however, "are

---

[9] Martin Delany, *Principia of Ethnology: The Origin of Races and Color* (Philadelphia, 1879), 42-48; Brown was quoted in *Liberator*, Oct. 26, 1860.

[10] *N.A.S. Standard*, Aug. 1, 1863; Tappan was quoted in William Wells Brown, *The Rising Son* (Boston, 1874), introduction by Alonzo D. Moore, 24. See also *Commonwealth*, Oct. 30, 1863; and Samuel May, Jr., to Richard Webb, Sept. 19, 1865, Samuel May, Jr., Papers, BPL.

neither multiplied nor diminished because developed in one age, and undeveloped in another. . . . Changes of circumstances, along with other causes, alternately lift up and depress a people." Theodore Tilton asked in 1863:

"Do you call the negro race inferior? No man can yet pronounce that judgment safely. How will you compare races, to give each its due rank? . . . You must compare them in their fulfillments, not in their beginnings. . . . How will you estimate the rank of the Roman people? By its beginnings? By its decline? By neither. You rank it at the height of its civilization. . . . The Germans, to-day, give philosophy to Europe—but you can count the years backward when the Germans, now philosophers, were barbarians. . . . No man can now predict the destiny of the negro race. That race is yet so undeveloped—that destiny is yet so unfulfilled—that no man can say, and no wise man pretends to say, what the negro race shall finally become."[11]

Some abolitionists, moreover, did not entirely accept the dark portrait of modern Africa drawn by most travelers. Several months after the outbreak of the Civil War a remarkable little book, written anonymously and entitled *Record of an Obscure Man*, was published in Boston. It purported to be the memoir of a man who had visited a friend in the South in 1842 and had talked with him about the capabilities of the Negro race. In reality it was a fictional essay by Mrs. Mary Putnam, elder sister of James Russell Lowell and an abolitionist sympathizer. Mary Putnam asserted that most travelers who visited Africa penetrated no farther than the coastal areas, whose inhabitants had been subjected to debasing contact with rapacious slave traders, "to which their degradation is to be attributed, rather than to inherent depravity or stupidity." Travelers who had ventured into the interior of Africa found people of finer appearance, gentler manners, greater industry and honesty. "When Central Africa has been fully laid open to the world," she argued, "we shall be called upon to revise many of our opinions."[12]

Displaying great learning, Mrs. Putnam quoted from world-famous travelers and explorers who had ventured into Central

[11] Gerrit Smith to Montgomery Blair, Apr. 2, 1862, in *Liberator*, Apr. 18; Tilton, *The Negro*, 4-5.
[12] [Mary Putnam], *Record of an Obscure Man* (Boston, 1861), 91-92.

Africa: Hugh Clapperton, Mungo Park, and Dixon Denham. "Read what Denham says of the inhabitants of the interior," she urged; "of their industry, their skill in weaving and dyeing, of their love of music and poetry." Denham described the natives as "hospitable, kind-hearted, honest, and liberal." Anticipating the findings of modern scholars, Mrs. Putnam decried the notion that Negroes had been civilized and uplifted by slavery and Christianity. Slavery, she said, had only suppressed their native virtues and intelligence.[13]

In one of the best expressions of "cultural relativism" to come out of the nineteenth century, Mary Putnam warned against accepting at face value the somber descriptions of Africa by certain westerners. "All men are prone to judge the manners of other countries by the standard of their own," she wrote, "and the civilized world views from its own stand-point that which it calls savage. We find the Africans barbarians, wherever customs differ from ours; but they are on the road to civilization, when their nonsense suits our nonsense."[14]

Abolitionists praised Mary Putnam's little book. "Such a studied tribute to the negro, in this way, we have never had the fortune to see," said Garrison in his review of *Record of an Obscure Man*. "The African is contemplated as a man apart from his accidents, and heavy must be the load of prejudice against color that is not lightened by the spirit and the truthfulness with which his claims are urged."[15] Abolitionists adopted many of Mrs. Putnam's arguments in their crusade for emancipation and equal rights.

The advocates of racial equality did not have to confine their researches to Africa to find persuasive examples of the manhood, ability, and achievements of the Negro race. There were plenty of authentic black heroes in the western hemisphere. By all odds, the greatest of these was Toussaint L'Ouverture, the Haitian

13 *ibid.*, 92-96.
14 *ibid.*, 123.
15 *Liberator*, Nov. 29, 1861. The *Anglo-African*, a weekly newspaper published by Negroes in New York City, pronounced *Record of an Obscure Man* "the fullest and most satisfactory record it has been our fortune to meet with, after reading all we could find in print on the subject. . . . She recognizes in the negro an original, inherent germ force of his own, solemn, grand, endowed with energy and vitality enough to develop civil, social, and intellectual greatness out of his own resources." *Anglo-African*, Feb. 15, 1862.

liberator who led his people out of slavery and defeated the armies of Napoleon when the French tried to reenslave the Caribbean island. One of Wendell Phillips' most powerful and compelling lectures was a biography of Haiti's warrior statesman. In 1862-63 Phillips gave this lecture to dozens of audiences throughout the Northeast as a means of dramatizing the Negro's fitness for freedom. "The negro race, instead of being that object of pity and contempt which we usually consider it, is entitled, judged by the facts of history, to a place close by the side of the Saxon," said Phillips. Did anyone doubt the Negro's courage? "Go to 50,000 graves of the best soldiers France ever had, and ask them what they think of the negro's sword." Could the Negro take care of himself in freedom? "Hayti, from the ruins of her colonial dependence, is become a civilized state, the seventh nation in the catalogue of commerce with this country, inferior in morals and education to none of the West Indian isles. Toussaint made her what she is. Courage, purpose, endurance—they are the tests." The *Semi-Weekly New York Tribune* printed a special edition containing Phillips' speech on March 13, 1863, for circulation among the troops in the Union army.[16]

The Negro had proved his physical courage in Haiti, in the American Revolution and War of 1812, and would soon prove it again in the Civil War; but what about mental ability and intellectual achievement? It was while asking himself this question that Moncure Conway stumbled across the remarkable story of Benjamin Banneker. Conway did some research on Banneker's life and published an article on him in the *Atlantic Monthly* at the end of 1862. A free-born, self-taught Maryland Negro, Banneker had devoted all his spare time to scientific research. He corrected some of the errors of the greatest astronomers of his age; in 1790 he compiled an accurate almanac based on his studies, and continued to publish annual almanacs until shortly before his death in 1804. His work was praised by Jefferson and internationally acclaimed by scientists. "History must record," concluded Conway,

[16] *New York Tribune* (Daily), Mar. 12, 14, 1863; *Semi-Weekly Tribune*, Mar. 13, 1863. In 1863 James Redpath edited and published an old biography of Toussaint by John R. Beard as a part of the effort to win public respect for the courage and resourcefulness of the Negro race. James Redpath, ed., *Toussaint L'Ouverture: a Biography and Autobiography* (Boston, 1863).

"that the most original scientific intellect which the South has yet produced was that of the pure African, Benjamin Banneker."[17]

Abolitionists industriously gathered statistics on the intellectual, professional, and business achievements of free Negroes. The American Anti-Slavery Society's *Annual Report* for 1859 pointed to the Negro actor Ira Aldridge, who was delighting European audiences with his portrayal of Othello; to three young Haitian students who had won highest honors at the concourse of all French colleges in Paris; to the New York Negro, Ditz, who had submitted a plan for a Broadway railroad; and the Philadelphia Negro, Aaron Roberts, who had developed a new and improved fire-extinguishing apparatus. These and many other accomplishments by Negroes demonstrated "the black man's capacity for mental culture and improvement . . . wherever a fair chance to test it has been given." In the business world Negroes boasted George T. Downing of Rhode Island and Stephen Smith of Philadelphia, both of them wealthy men by any standards. Some Negro lawyers of mark were John Mercer Langston of Ohio, and Robert Morris and John Rock of Boston. Frederick Douglass was one of the foremost orators in America, and in the pulpit the Reverend Henry Highland Garnet of New York and the Reverend J. Sella Martin of Boston ranked high. In sum, wrote William Wells Brown, the Negroes of the North, though "shut out, by a cruel prejudice, from nearly all the mechanical branches, and all the professions," had "learned trades, become artists, gone into the professions. . . . If this is not an exhibition of capacity, I don't understand the meaning of the term."[18]

✦

Many abolitionists, while arguing vigorously for the inherent equality of the Negro race, nevertheless believed in racial *differences*. "It is a mistake to speak of the African as an inferior race to the Caucasian," said James Freeman Clarke. "It is doubtless *different* from this, just as this is also different from the Malay, the Indian, the Mongolian. There are many varieties in the human

[17] Moncure D. Conway, "Benjamin Banneker, the Negro Astronomer," *Atlantic Monthly*, xi (Jan. 1863), 79-84.

[18] *Annual Report of the American Anti-Slavery Society for the Year Ending May 1, 1859* (New York, 1860), 77-78; Brown, *Black Man*, 49. This book contains short biographies of 57 eminent Negroes.

family." This was an accurate statement by today's ethnological standards, but Clarke parlayed it into a more questionable thesis: that the Negro was innately inferior to the Caucasian in some respects and superior in others. He stated:

"The colored man has not so much invention as the white, but more imitation. He has not so much of the reflective, but more of the perceptive powers. The black child will learn to read and write as fast or faster than the white child, having equal advantages. The blacks have not the indomitable perseverance and will, which make the Caucasian, at least the Saxon portion of it, *masters* wherever they go—but they have a native courtesy, a civility like that from which the word "gentleman" has its etymological meaning, and a capacity for the highest refinement of character. More than all, they have almost universally, a strong religious tendency, and that strength of attachment which is capable of any kind of self-denial, and self-sacrifice. Is this an inferior race—so inferior as to be only fit for chains?"[19]

Several other abolitionists subscribed to the notion of the Negro's superiority in the realm of manners, religion, and the arts, and inferiority in certain aspects of the hard-headed, practical business world. In an effort to convince readers of the Negro's ability to make positive contributions to American culture, Moncure Conway penned an article for the *Boston Commonwealth* in 1862, signing himself "A Native of the South." Negroes were a graceful people, he said, full of exuberance and picturesque charm. It was the Negro who gave to the South its warmth and radiance. The colored people had fertile, poetic imaginations. They had contributed much to southern culture, and would contribute more in freedom. "In our practical, anxious, unimaginative country, we need an infusion of this fervid African element, so child-like, exuberant, and hopeful," wrote Conway. "We ought to prize it, as we do rare woods and glowing gems imported from the gorgeous tropics." One year later, writing for an English audience, Conway stated that Negroes "seem to me to be weaker in the direction of the understanding, strictly speaking, but to have strength and elegance of imagination and expression. Negro

[19] James Freeman Clarke, *Slavery in the United States: A Sermon Delivered on Thanksgiving Day, 1842* (Boston, 1843), 24.

sermons, fables, and descriptions are in the highest degree pictorial, abounding in mystic interpretations which would delight a German transcendentalist. My belief is, that there is a vast deal of high art yet to come out of that people in America. Their songs and hymns are the only original melodies we have."[20]

In his widely publicized speech on "The Negro," Theodore Tilton proclaimed the Negro "the most religious man among men. Is not the religious nature the highest part of human nature? Strike out the negro then, and you destroy the highest development of the highest part of human nature." It was a mistake, thought Tilton,

"to rank men only by a superiority of intellectual faculties. God has given to man a higher dignity than the reason. It is the moral nature. . . . In all those intellectual activities which take their strange quickening from the moral faculties—processes which we call instincts, or intuitions—the negro is superior to the white man—equal to the white woman. The negro race is the feminine race of the world. . . .

"We have need of the negro for his . . . aesthetic faculties. . . . We have need of the negro for his music. . . . But let us stop questioning whether the negro is a man. In many respects he is a superior man. In a few respects, he is the greatest of men. I think he is certainly greater than those men who clamor against giving him a chance in the world, as if they feared something from the competition."[21]

Among American natural scientists of the mid-nineteenth century, Louis Agassiz was foremost in prestige and authority. His adherence to the "American School" of anthropology gave it an influence it could not otherwise have commanded. As a Harvard Professor, Agassiz had many acquaintances in Boston's intellectual circles; several of these acquaintances were abolitionists, and Agassiz's racial ideas could not help but have some effect on their thinking. Samuel Gridley Howe was one such friend. In 1863-1864 Howe served as a member of the American Freedmen's In-

---

[20] *Commonwealth*, Oct. 18, 1862; Conway, *Testimonies Concerning Slavery*, 71. Conway had gone to England in 1863 as a sort of ambassador of good will from the American abolitionists. He liked London so well that he settled down and lived there for the next 20 years.
[21] Tilton, *The Negro*, 11-13.

quiry Commission (see Chapter VIII). In connection with his research for the Commission, Howe asked Agassiz for his views on the effect of race on the problems of emancipation and reconstruction. Agassiz replied that he welcomed the prospect of emancipation, but warned against granting equal political and social rights to freedmen. He reviewed the history of the Negro in Africa and the western hemisphere, and concluded that Negroes were "indolent, playful, sensual, imitative, subservient, good-natured, versatile, unsteady in their purpose, devoted and affectionate." The Negro had never shown himself qualified for self-government. "I cannot," concluded Agassiz, "think it just or safe to grant at once to the negro all the privileges which we ourselves have acquired by long struggles. . . . Let us beware of granting too much to the negro race in the beginning, lest it become necessary hereafter to deprive them of some of the privileges which they may use to their own and our detriment."[22]

Howe was torn between his respect for Agassiz's learning and his own equalitarian principles. "I would not only advocate entire freedom, equal rights and privileges," he told Agassiz, but "open competition for social distinction." Howe was nevertheless influenced by some of Agassiz's notions regarding the mental inferiority of Negroes. In a book on Canadian Negroes published in 1864, Howe lamented that the younger generation, who had never known slavery and who enjoyed equal civil and political rights in Canada, had failed to produce as many outstanding individuals, in proportion to their numbers, as the white community. Howe took into account the prejudice, discrimination, and lack of opportunity that might account for this failure, but concluded that even with these disabilities the Negro community should have produced more superior men. Teachers to whom he talked testified that Negroes learned just as fast as whites in the lower grades, but fell behind at the higher levels "when they come to studies which tax the higher mental powers, or the reasoning and combining faculties." Colored people, thought Howe, were "quick of perception; very imitative; and they rapidly become intelligent. But they are rather knowing, than thinking people. They occupy

[22] Howe to Agassiz, Aug. 3, 1863; Agassiz to Howe, Aug. 9, 10, 1863, in Elizabeth C. Agassiz, *Louis Agassiz: His Life and Correspondence* (2 vols., Boston, 1885), II, 591-608.

useful stations in life; but such as require quick perceptions, rather than strong sense."[23]

To the modern reader familiar with the view of contemporary anthropology that there is no proof of significant differences in the mental capacities of various races, the opinions of Howe and other abolitionists who thought like him appear to border on racism. Even the belief of Tilton, Conway, and others in the inherent superiority of the Negro in the "feminine" virtues—religion and the arts—imply an assumption of Negro *inferiority* in the "masculine" virtues of reason and enterprise. Thus a case of modified racism could be made out against certain of the abolitionists, but only by ignoring the fact that in the contemporary spectrum of opinion on race, the abolitionists were far in the liberal vanguard. The remarkable fact about the abolitionists was not that as champions of the Negro *some* of them believed in racial differences, but that in a nation where popular belief *and* scientific learning overwhelmingly proclaimed the Negro's absolute inferiority, there were men and women who dared to affirm their faith in the innate equality of all men, regardless of race.

✦

Then as now, one of the most explosive aspects of the race question was the issue of intermarriage. "Would you like your daughter to marry a nigger?" was the derisive question hurled at abolitionists hundreds of times through the years. It is not recorded whether any daughter of a white abolitionist did marry a Negro, but it is known that the abolitionists did not shrink from discussing the issue. In the face of popular odium and violence, abolitionists struggled to remove laws barring intermarriage from the statute books of Massachusetts and other states. Marriage "is a personal and private matter, with which neither Congress nor any other law-makers have aught to do," said Gerrit Smith. "When a man and woman want to be married it is *their* business, not mine, nor anybody's else," declared Theodore Tilton. "But to read what some newspapers say of the 'monstrous doctrine of amalgamation,' one would think it consisted in stationing a provost-marshal at street corners, to seize first a white man and then a black woman,

23 Howe to Agassiz, Aug. 18, 1863, *ibid.*, 614; Samuel G. Howe, *The Refugees from Slavery in Canada West* (Boston, 1864), 81-82.

and to marry them on the spot, against their will, for a testimony to human equality." Tilton pointed out the obvious fact, usually ignored by proslavery partisans, that amalgamation occurred under slavery, not freedom, at the bidding of the white man, not the Negro. Tilton declared that "a slave-woman's master, who makes himself the father of her children, is in honor bound to make himself her husband. So far from denouncing the marriage of blacks and whites, I would be glad if the banns of a hundred thousand such marriages could be published next Sunday."[24]

Abolitionists Louisa May Alcott, Lydia Maria Child, and Anna Dickinson defended intermarriage in short stories and novels. Gilbert Haven frequently vindicated amalgamation from his pulpit.[25] Moncure Conway proclaimed boldly that "I, for one, am firmly persuaded that the mixture of the blacks and whites is good; that the person so produced is, under ordinarily favourable circumstances, healthy, handsome, and intelligent. Under the best circumstances, I believe that such a combination would evolve a more complete character than the unmitigated Anglo-Saxon," because it would combine the best traits of both races. "Amalgamation!" exclaimed Wendell Phillips dramatically. "Remember this, the youngest of you; that, on the 4th of July, 1863, you heard a man say, that in the light of all history, in virtue of every page he ever read, he was an amalgamationist to the utmost extent. (Applause)" Phillips had no hope for the future "but in that sublime mingling of races which is God's own method of civilizing and elevating the world. (Loud applause) Not the amalgamation of licentiousness, born of slavery, . . . but that gradual and harmonizing union, in honorable marriage, which has mingled all other races, and from which springs the present phase of European and Northern civilization."[26]

✦

Most modern sociologists and psychologists agree that discrimination, segregation, and "cultural deprivation" rather than

[24] Gerrit Smith to the Hon. John Gurley, Dec. 16, 1861, in *Liberator*, Jan. 3, 1862; Tilton, *The Negro*, 10.

[25] Louisa May Alcott, "M. L.," a short story published serially in the *Commonwealth*, Jan. 24, 31, Feb. 7, 14, 21, 1863; Lydia M. Child, *A Romance of the Republic* (Boston, 1867); Anna Dickinson, *What Answer?* (Boston, 1868); Haven, *National Sermons*, 146.

[26] Conway, *Testimonies Concerning Slavery*, 76; Phillips' speech quoted in *Commonwealth*, July 17, 1863.

innate inferiority are responsible for the inferior status which the Negro occupies in American society. Abolitionists advanced this argument more than a century ago. Like modern sociologists, they maintained that environment, not racial deficiency, was the cause of the Negro's inferiority.

"I well remember what amazement was excited when Mr. Garrison and his partner first took a black boy as an apprentice in the office of 'The Liberator,' " wrote Oliver Johnson in his memoirs. "It was declared on every side that no 'nigger' could learn the art of printing, and it was held to be evidence of arrant folly to try the experiment. If the negroes, under such circumstances, sometimes seemed dull and even stupid, who can wonder? What race or class of men is strong enough to keep its feet under such a load of prejudice and contumely?" Theodore Tilton agreed that discrimination was responsible for the Negro's disabilities. "We put a stigma upon the black man's color, and then plead that prejudice against the commonest fair dealing," he stated. "We shut him out of schools, and then bitterly inveigh against the ignorance of his kind. We shut up all learned professions from his reach, and withhold the motives for ordinary enterprise, and then declare that he is an inferior being, fitted only for menial services."[27]

Prejudice and discrimination against the free Negro were debilitating enough, but the effects of slavery were worse still. "Take any race you please, French, English, Irish, or Scotch," said Frederick Douglass; "subject them to slavery for ages—regard and treat them every where, every way, as property. . . . Let them be loaded with chains, scarred with the whip, branded with hot irons, sold in the market, kept in ignorance . . . and I venture to say that the same doubt would spring up concerning either of them, which now confronts the negro." It was little wonder that "the colored people in America appear stupid, helpless and degraded. The wonder is that they evince so much spirit and manhood as they do." Theodore Tilton conceded that "slavery has reduced the blacks to the lowest point of ignorance and humiliation of which humanity . . . is capable." The "peculiar institution" had produced some singular effects on the Negro, making him childlike and dependent, lacking in initiative and

---

[27] Oliver Johnson, *William Lloyd Garrison and His Times* (2nd ed., Boston, 1885), 101-02; *Independent*, May 29, 1862.

self-respect. "Man is, to a certain extent, the creature of circumstances," argued Tilton, "and two centuries of slavery must needs have molded the character of the slave. . . . The faults of the slave . . . come of training, rather than of natural endowment."[28]

In the *New York Tribune* of February 5, 1863, Sydney Gay presented a cogent and eloquent summary of the environmentalist argument. "We have never supposed that the liberation of so many human beings, heretofore irresponsible, would be without some embarrassments," he wrote in reply to proslavery arguments that slaves were not fit for freedom. "It is Freedom that fits men for Freedom. . . . The crime of Slavery has been that it has found the incapacity of its victims an argument for the continuation of its emasculating influences, and has continually pointed to the ruin it has wrought as an apology for postponing reparation." Nobody in his right senses, continued Gay,

"has expected to find the Freedman . . . a miracle of virtue, a wonder of wit, a paragon of prudence, and a marvel of industry. In him who was yesterday a Slave, we should expect to find the vices of the Slave—the traces of that falsehood which heretofore had been his sole protection against cruelty—of that thievishness which may have saved him from the pangs of hunger, or guarded him from the inclemency of the elements—of that insubordination of the animal passions which his superiors in society have encouraged for their own profit and by their own example. . . . Emancipation will not remove the scars which Slavery has inflicted. There is many a brow from which the brand can never be erased. . . . So much the sooner should we, with all the courage of a genuine repentance, dock this entail of human misery, and at least turn the faces of future generations toward kindlier opportunities and less discouraging vicissitudes!"[29]

The effects of slavery and racial discrimination on the Negro's character, according to abolitionists, were felt primarily in three areas: intelligence, industry, and morals. The Negro's defects of intelligence, remarked Douglass, could be found among the peasants, laborers, and lower classes of all races. "A man is worked upon

[28] Speech by Douglass in Cooper Union, Feb. 12, 1862, published in *New York Tribune*, Feb. 13; article by Tilton in *Independent*, Aug. 20, 1863.
[29] *New York Tribune*, Feb. 5, 1863. See also J. M. McKim to Gay, Jan. 28, 1863, Gay Papers, cu.

by what *he* works on. He may carve out his circumstances, but his circumstances will carve him out as well." Douglass recalled his trip to Ireland in the 1840's, where he found the population of the poorer districts much like plantation slaves in every respect save color. "The open, uneducated mouth—the long, gaunt arm— the badly formed foot and ankle—the shuffling gait—the retreating forehead and vacant expression—and, their petty quarrels and fights—all reminded me of the plantation, and my own cruelly abused people."[30]

Moncure Conway, born and raised on a Virginia plantation, recounted the story of a companion of his youth, a slave boy who was popular with the white boys of the neighborhood and excelled in telling stories, playing games, and so on. The boy had a great native intelligence. He accompanied young Moncure to school every day, but of course was not allowed in the schoolroom. He wanted to know what happened in there, and when he found out he too wanted to learn to read. He could not understand why he was denied this privilege, and soon grew bewildered, then saddened, and finally rebellious, forcing Moncure's father to sell him South. Conway never forgot the boy. "I have dwelt upon this case," he wrote in his *Testimonies Concerning Slavery*, "because it is that which represents, in my own experience, one of the most tragical forms in which Slavery outrages human nature." On the basis of his experience, Conway also denied the theory that because of some natural disability, Negroes learned quickly until the age of ten or twelve, and then fell behind. "It has been my lot to have much to do with the poor whites of the South, and I have observed precisely the same arrest of development, both physical and mental, in those poor whites. . . . They learn well at first, even with a kind of voracity; but, at about the same age with the Negro child, they become dull." This was the result, not of inherent inferiority, but of the child's sudden realization of the cramped circumstances, limited opportunities, and unhappy future that faced the poor whites, as well as Negroes, of the South.[31]

The lazy, shiftless Negro who would work only under compulsion was a byword among those who defended slavery and ridiculed the idea of emancipation. Of course slaves were lazy, wrote Lydia

[30] Foner, *Douglass*, II, 304–05.
[31] Conway, *Testimonies Concerning Slavery*, 4–7, 65-66.

Maria Child in her study of emancipation in the West Indies. Slavery "takes away the motive power from the laborers, who naturally desire to shirk as much as possible of the work, which brings them no pay. . . . It makes them indifferent to the destruction of property on estates, in whose prosperity they have no interest. . . . It kills their ingenuity and enterprise." She cited the testimony of planters and missionaries in the West Indies, who said that emancipation had "almost wholly put an end to sulking, or pretending to be sick. . . . Planters treat their laborers more like fellow-men, and that leads them to be respectful, in their turn. They have now a growing regard for character; a feeling unknown to them in the days of slavery."[32]

The alleged immorality, dishonesty and untruthfulness of the Negro were cited by proslavery propagandists as additional proofs of his inferiority. Of course the slave was immoral, replied abolitionists. Under slavery promiscuity was encouraged, marriage had no legal validity, and the father had no personal responsibility for his children, who belonged, not to their parents, but to their master. "Being regarded as animals, and treated like live-stock, [slaves] unavoidably lived like animals," wrote Mrs. Child. "Modesty and self-respect were impossible to their brutalized condition." In the West Indies, she contended, there was much less immorality a generation after emancipation than there had been under slavery.[33]

"To tell us that Slavery fosters in the enslaved habits of deception, is not to communicate to us any startling novelty," wrote Sydney Gay in 1862. Gay and Conway admitted that Negroes were prone to petty thievery, "but it should be remembered that the rights of property involve some very refined problems," said Conway. "If the Negro is inclined to sympathize with the views of Rousseau on such questions more than the English schools would approve, it must be admitted that the systematic disregard of his own right to his earnings is scarcely the best method of giving him better views. I have never heard yet of a slave who had managed to filch back so much as had been filched from him." Samuel Gridley Howe declared that "the offences against property, with which by

[32] Lydia Maria Child, *The Right Way the Safe Way* (2d ed., New York, 1862), 5-6, 15-16.
[33] Charles K. Whipple, *The Family Relation, as Affected by Slavery* (Cincinnati, 1858), passim; Child, *Right Way Safe Way*, 6.

public voice the [Negroes] are charged, . . . grow directly out of slavery. . . . The owner, in his daily practice, violates the most sacred right of property, by taking the slave's labor without pay; and the slave imitates him by violating the less sacred right of property, in stealing what he can lay his hands on." Upon the basis of his observations of free Negroes in Canada, Howe concluded that "with freedom and the ownership of property, the instinct of family will be developed, marriages will increase, and promiscuous intercourse decrease. . . . [Canadian Negroes] are, upon the whole, sober, industrious, and thrifty, and have proved themselves to be capable of self-guidance and self-support."[34]

"The difference between the Black and White," thought Sydney Gay, "is no other than the difference between the White and the White—differences occasioned by the accidents of location, and susceptible of removal by the opportunities of culture." Abolitionists realized, however, that these differences would not be wiped out in a year or two. "Men going from slavery to freedom cannot change their habits as they change their garments," wrote Howe. "The effects of Slavery will last more than one generation or even two," predicted Wendell Phillips. "It were a very slight evil if they could be done away sooner." The Negro was potentially the equal of the white man, but he had a long, hard road to travel before he reached that potentiality.[35]

In the final analysis, argued abolitionists, the question was not one of race, but of human rights. "I think races are of secondary importance," said Wendell Phillips in 1863. "I despise an empire resting its claims on the blood of a single race. My pride in the future is in the banner that welcomes every race and every blood, and under whose shelter all races stand up equal. (Applause)" Theodore Tilton proclaimed, "Looked at through the centuries, the question of races sinks into insignificance. The only generalization that will stand is, not that there are five races of men, or seven, or twelve, but only one—the universal human race in which all men are brothers, and God is father over all!"[36]

[34] New York Tribune, Jan. 13, 1862; Conway, Testimonies Concerning Slavery, 70; Howe, Refugees in Canada West, 86-87, 103, 101.
[35] New York Tribune, Sept. 17, 1863; Howe, Refugees in Canada West, 86; speech by Wendell Phillips in Boston Music Hall, Dec. 16, 1860, in New York Tribune, Dec. 18.
[36] Liberator, May 29, 1863; Tilton, The Negro, 8.

Ⅰ N an optimistic mood, Wendell Phillips told an assemblage of
abolitionists on the Fourth of July 1861, that "these days of
anti-slavery gatherings for the purpose of emancipation, I believe, will be soon over." Emancipation was sure to come as a result
of the war, and the duty of abolitionists would then be "to watch
for the welfare of this victim race, guard it during its pupilage,
shelter it by patronage, by protection, by privilege, by recognizing
its claim to an equal manhood." A year later William Goodell
asserted that "as soon as slavery shall be abolished, there will be
an opportunity for Christian philanthropists to commence the
arduous work of educating, enlightening, and guiding the emancipated colored people." In 1863 Whittier thanked God for the
virtual abolition of slavery by the war, but warned his fellow
abolitionists that "we must not for a moment forget that, from this
hour, new and mighty responsibilities devolve upon us to aid,
direct and educate these millions, left free, indeed, but bewildered,
ignorant, naked and foodless in the wild chaos of civil war. We
have to undo the accumulated wrongs of two centuries; to re-
make the manhood that slavery has well-nigh unmade."[1]

During the early war years, northern conservatives conjured up
terrifying visions of servile insurrection and barbarism as consequences of emancipation. Abolition would mean social and economic anarchy in the South, with horrible scenes of bloodshed
and carnage the result of inevitable race war. "The Negro will
not work except under compulsion," they cried. "The two races cannot live side by side in freedom." Slavery was an absolute necessity
to the South's social and economic system. "What will you *do*
with the freed slaves?" they asked the abolitionists. Conservatives
cited the alleged failure of emancipation in the West Indies as an
example of the baneful consequences of letting black men go free.
Abolitionists replied with an outpouring of scholarly and popular
studies, based on official British and French sources, designed to

---

[1] Phillips was quoted in *Liberator*, July 12, 1861; Goodell in *Principia*, Oct. 23,
1862; and Whittier in *Proceedings of the American Anti-Slavery Society at its
Third Decade Anniversary* (New York, 1864), 7.

demonstrate the economic and social *success* of emancipation in the West Indies.[2]

Many conservatives, however, remained unconvinced that large numbers of freed slaves could remain in the United States without causing social upheaval. In 1861-1862 there was widespread support among conservative Republicans and Democrats for the colonization abroad of Negroes emancipated by the war. Abolitionists and northern Negroes, of course, were overwhelmingly opposed to the idea of colonization as a solution of the Negro question. James Redpath promoted the emigration of northern Negroes to Haiti in an effort to help build that island republic into a strong nation and make it a showcase of Negro abilities. But Redpath as well as other abolitionists denounced all wartime colonization plans having the general purpose of getting Negroes out of the United States. Most colored men had little desire to leave their homeland. "Sir," said Robert Purvis to an advocate of Negro colonization, "this is our country as much as it is yours, and we will not leave it."[3]

Nevertheless Lincoln lent his support to several unwise colonization schemes during the war. In 1862 the president actually signed a contract with one Bernard Kock, a fly-by-night promoter, for the colonization of more than 450 freed slaves on the Ile A'Vache, a small island off the southern coast of Haiti. This venture proved a tragic failure. Kock confiscated the American dollars of the colonists and failed to provide them with adequate housing. Smallpox and actual starvation decimated the ranks of the emigrants. Lincoln finally admitted failure and sent a ship to bring the surviving Negroes back to the United States in February 1864. Abolitionists hoped that the government had

[2] The most important wartime writings by abolitionists on emancipation in the West Indies were: Lydia Maria Child, *The Right Way the Safe Way* (1st ed., New York, 1860; 2nd ed., 1862); Lewis Tappan, *Immediate Emancipation: The Only Wise and Safe Mode* (New York, 1861); a series of articles by Richard J. Hinton in *The Pine and Palm*, June 15, 22, 29, July 6, 13, Aug. 10, Sept. 14, 1861; a series of articles by Frank Sanborn in the *Springfield Republican*, Nov. 13, 16, 23, Dec. 7, 1861, Jan. 18, 25, Feb. 1, 8, 1862; Frank Sanborn, *Emancipation in the West Indies*, a pamphlet published by the Emancipation League in Boston in March 1862; a series of articles by Sanborn in the *Commonwealth*, Oct. 25, Nov. 8, 22, Dec. 13, 20, 1862, Jan. 10, 1863; and Mary Louise Booth, translation of Augustin Cochin's *Results of Emancipation* and of the same author's *Results of Slavery* (both books published in Boston, 1863).

[3] Purvis to Samuel C. Pomeroy, Aug. 28, 1862, published in the *New York Tribune*, Sept. 20, 1862.

learned something from the failure of its colonization schemes. Edmund Quincy asserted that the collapse of emigration projects showed colonization to be a "wild, delusive and impractical scheme," while emancipation without expatriation, for which abolitionists had always contended, had been successful. "Thus does the boasted wisdom of 'Conservatism' turn out to be folly, while the 'fanaticism' of the 'crazy Radicals' is proved by experience to be the highest wisdom."[4]

The failure of colonization confronted America with the problem of absorbing 4 million freed slaves into the social structure. Abolitionists were ready for this challenge. Opportunities for abolitionists to demonstrate the Negro's fitness for liberty and to help the freedmen in their difficult transition from slavery to freedom came early in the war. As contrabands began pouring into Union lines at Fortress Monroe near Hampton, Virginia, in the summer of 1861, General Butler assigned Private Edward L. Pierce to the job of ministering to their needs and superintending their labor on Union fortifications. Pierce was picked for this task because of his antislavery background, his administrative ability, and his eagerness to prove the Negro's capacity for freedom. He had studied law in the office of Salmon P. Chase, was a friend of Charles Sumner and Wendell Phillips, and had served as a member of Phillips' bodyguard during the antiabolitionist riots of the secession winter.[5]

Pierce worked with the contrabands only a short time before he was mustered out and returned to private life (he had enlisted for three months). But during that brief period he laid down certain basic principles that governed future contraband policy at Monroe. The contrabands were to work the same number of hours per day as white laborers, and receive the same rations as soldiers. They were to be paid for their labor. Part of their wages was to be deducted for support of sick and aged contrabands.

[4] *N.A.S. Standard*, Mar. 19, 1864. There are several studies of wartime colonization projects. The best of these are: Warren A. Beck, "Lincoln and Negro Colonization in Central America," *Abraham Lincoln Quarterly*, vi (Sept. 1950), 162-83; Willis D. Boyd, "Negro Colonization in the National Crisis, 1860-1870," Ph.D. dissertation, UCLA, 1953; Paul J. Scheips, "Lincoln and the Chiriqui Colonization Project," *Journal of Negro History*, xxxvi (1952), 418-53.

[5] Edward L. Pierce, *Enfranchisement and Citizenship, Addresses and Papers*, ed. by A. W. Stevens (Boston, 1896), 4-5, 19; Edward L. Pierce, "The Contrabands at Fortress Monroe," *Atlantic Monthly*, viii (Nov. 1861), 632-36.

Pierce published an article on "The Contrabands at Fortress Monroe" in the *Atlantic Monthly*. He stated that the Negroes had worked hard in the July heat and had shown little of the indolence of which they were usually accused. Many officers had sneered at Pierce's idea of getting Negroes to work by kind treatment and wage incentives, but Pierce asserted that the result proved him right: the contrabands worked better when treated well than when they were whipped and driven like cattle. Pierce had held long conversations with several contrabands, and when he mentioned that most whites considered their race lazy and shiftless, they replied scornfully: "Who but the darkies cleared all the land round here?" Pierce concluded that there were lazy

Letterhead of the National Freedmen's Relief Association.

157

Negroes, but that there were a great many lazy white men as well. With good wages, promptly paid, the Negro would prove as industrious as the southern white, perhaps more so.[6]

Less than two weeks after the firing on Fort Sumter, *The American Missionary*, organ of the American Missionary Association (A.M.A.) proclaimed that the war would create in the South "one of the grandest fields of missionary labor the world ever furnished." By June 1861, the abolitionist-dominated A.M.A. was making plans to send teachers and books to educate the 700 Negroes within Union lines in Virginia. The Reverend L. C. Lockwood went to Fortress Monroe in early September and opened a Sunday school on September 15. Two days later a day school for freedmen was established near the site where the first shipload of slaves landed in America in 1619. The school was a success, and several more schools and churches were started under A.M.A. auspices in subsequent months. The Association also helped the government provide for the physical needs of the freedmen. The Boston auxiliary alone sent more than one hundred barrels of clothing to the contrabands during the winter of 1861-62.[7]

On the morning of November 7, 1861, a Union fleet steamed into Port Royal Sound with guns ablaze, and by nightfall Port Royal Island and the adjacent South Carolina sea islands 50 miles southwest of Charleston were in Union hands. Most of the islands' white population escaped to the mainland, leaving behind scores of fertile cotton plantations and more than 8,000 confused slaves. Here indeed was a challenge to abolitionists. Because of their physical and cultural isolation, these slaves were among the most ignorant and backward of the entire South. If *they* proved themselves capable of a productive and peaceful life in freedom, antiemancipation arguments based on the alleged barbarism and shiftlessness of the Negro race would crumble to pieces. Abolitionists were quick to grasp the significance of this opportunity. Two weeks after the capture of Port Royal, the *Anti-Slavery Standard*

[6] Pierce, "Contrabands at Fortress Monroe," *op.cit.*, 635-40.
[7] Augustus F. Beard, *A Crusade of Brotherhood, A History of the American Missionary Association* (Boston, 1909), 117-18; Richard B. Drake, "The American Missionary Association and the Southern Negro, 1861-1888," Ph.D. dissertation, Emory University, 1957, 1-31; S. S. Jocelyn to Gerrit Smith, June 17, 1861, Smith Papers, su; Lewis Tappan to Charles Sumner, Jan. 16, 1862, Sumner Papers, hu; L. C. Lockwood to George Cheever, Jan. 29, 1862, Cheever Papers, aas; Gerrit Smith to Lewis Tappan, Nov. 23, 1862, Tappan Papers, lc.

urged the government to grant freedom to the slaves and hire them to harvest the cotton crop. "Here, within the protection of the arms of the United States, might a new experiment of tropical culture by free labor be tried," declared the *Standard*. "Succeeding there, as succeed it must and would, how simple the process by which it might be extended wherever the arms of the nation may be predominant!"[8]

In December the Treasury Department sent special agents to the islands to collect and sell the 1861 cotton crop. The agents were to supervise the labor of contrabands and keep records of their work for future payment of wages. Secretary of the Treasury Chase realized, however, that such an arrangement was not satisfactory on a long-term basis since the cotton agents had no interest in the welfare of the Negroes and would do little or nothing to further the great social experiment of freedom on the islands. On December 20 Chase sent a telegram to Edward L. Pierce asking him to accept a commission to investigate the condition and needs of the freedmen at Port Royal. Pierce accepted, and departed for the sea islands on January 13, 1862.[9] After two weeks of intensive observation Pierce drew up a report to Chase on February 3. He thought that "when properly organized, and with proper motives set before them," the contrabands "will as freemen be as industrious as any race of men are likely to be in this climate." Because of their past dependence the Negroes were not yet self-reliant, but "in spite of their condition, reputed to be worse here than in many other parts of the rebellious region, there are such features in their life and character that the opportunity is now offered to us to make of them, partially in this generation and fully in the next, a happy, industrious, law-abiding, free, and Christian people." Pierce recommended that the government appoint labor superintendents for each plantation or group of smaller plantations, "selected with reference to peculiar qualifications, and as carefully as one would choose a guardian for his children." The contrabands, said Pierce, should be treated "with sole reference" to their preparation for the rights and duties of freedom and citizenship.[10]

[8] *N.A.S. Standard*, Nov. 23, 1861.
[9] Willie L. Rose, "Rehearsal for Reconstruction: The Port Royal Experiment," Ph.D. dissertation, Johns Hopkins University, 1962, 19-32.
[10] Pierce, *Enfranchisement and Citizenship*, 77, 82-85.

Pierce talked with President Lincoln on February 15. Afterwards Lincoln gave Chase *carte blanche* to go ahead with the sea island experiment on the basis of Pierce's recommendations. Chase appointed Pierce a special agent of the Treasury Department with full powers to select superintendents and teachers for the contrabands. The government would supply the superintendents with rations, housing, and transportation, but their salaries would have to be paid by private philanthropic societies.[11]

Shortly after arriving on the sea islands Pierce had written to Jacob Manning, abolitionist pastor of the Old South Church in Boston, describing the "strange and chaotic condition" of the contrabands. They were confused, destitute, and in danger of demoralization by their contact with Union soldiers. "If this critical moment be not availed of and some means not taken to make them industrious, orderly and sober, they will become hopelessly demoralized," Pierce informed Manning. "You must see that the heathen to whom we owe a special duty . . . are nearer to us than the Ganges."[12]

Manning published this letter in the *Boston Transcript*, and called a meeting at his home for the formation of a society to send supplies, teachers, and labor superintendents to the contrabands. At a second meeting on February 7 the "Boston Educational Commission" was organized. Its purpose was "the industrial, social, intellectual, moral and religious elevation of persons released from Slavery in the course of the War for the Union." Governor John Andrew was chosen president of the Commission, whose membership included every shade of antislavery conviction from radical abolitionist to moderate Republican. In New York City the Reverend Mansfield French, an abolitionist and a friend of Chase, took the lead in organizing the National Freedmen's Relief Association. In Philadelphia, abolitionist J. Miller McKim took steps to form a similar society. At a public meeting on March 5 the Philadelphia Port Royal Relief Committee was organized, with McKim as executive secretary.[13]

The inception of the freedmen's aid movement touched off a debate within abolitionist ranks over the purpose and strategy

[11] *ibid.*, 90-91.
[12] *Boston Transcript*, Jan. 27, 1862.
[13] Pierce, *Enfranchisement and Citizenship*, 67-68; Rose, "Rehearsal for Reconstruction," 36-45; *Liberator*, Mar. 7, 1862.

of antislavery societies. Early in 1862 McKim submitted his resignation as corresponding secretary of the Pennsylvania Anti-Slavery Society. Slavery was crumbling under the weight of war, argued McKim, and there was no longer any need for agents, lecturers, and other traditional appurtenances of the abolitionist movement. "In my judgment, the old anti-slavery routine is not what the cause now demands," he wrote. "Iconoclasm has had its day. For the battering-ram we must substitute the hod and trowel. . . . We have passed through the *pulling-down* stage of our movement; the building-up—the constructive part—remains to be accomplished." McKim proposed that abolitionists dissolve their old societies or convert them into freedmen's aid associations.[14]

Most abolitionists disagreed with McKim. The officers of the Pennsylvania Anti-Slavery Society refused to accept his resignation, and McKim consented to stay on as corresponding secretary until a replacement could be found. Pillsbury, Powell, and other abolitionist lecturers maintained that lectures, meetings, and so on, were more important to the antislavery cause than ever. "If emancipation comes as a mere 'necessity of war,' " declared the *Anti-Slavery Standard*, "it will come unsanctioned by any considerations of justice or humanity toward the victims of our oppression, and the strenuous exertion of moral influence in their behalf will still be greatly needed." The end of slavery may be near, wrote Giles Stebbins of Michigan, but there was still grave danger of compromise. "Surely the Abolitionists, with tongue and pen, can help to the right answer. Never were their words so earnestly and widely heard as now. . . . Why seal our lips when, more than ever, the people hear and ponder our words?"[15]

McKim hastened to deny the implication that he favored abandonment of the antislavery crusade. He merely wanted to channel it in a new direction. "This *freedmen* business is an immensely 'big job,' " he explained. "It is abolition already begun. It is all important that the first instalment should be well managed. The experiment of freedom should be initiated with as much care as possible." Abolitionists could not do the whole work, of course, but they should take the lead. "We are to continue to be

---

[14] *N.A.S. Standard*, May 3, 1862.

[15] *N.A.S. Standard*, Feb. 15, 1862; Stebbins to Garrison, May 20, 1862, in *Liberator*, May 30. See also *N.A.S. Standard*, May 3, 1862, and *Liberator*, May 16, 1862.

what we have always been, a wheel within a wheel; an original motive power. . . . Our presence & influence should be seen and felt in this & all other important movements."[16]

Meanwhile the freedmen's aid societies selected 41 men and 12 women as the first group of plantation superintendents and teachers for the sea island freedmen. This contingent sailed from New York early in March 1862. Among these "Gideonites," as they soon called themselves, were many abolitionists. Miss Laura Towne, a Philadelphia abolitionist who was destined to become one of the outstanding personalities on the islands, declared when she arrived there in 1862 that "we have come to do antislavery work, and we think it noble work and mean to do it earnestly." Another antislavery veteran observed in August 1862, that some of the foremost young abolitionists in Philadelphia had left comfortable homes to go to Port Royal and teach the freedmen.[17] Charlotte Forten, a highly cultured young Negro from Salem, Massachusetts, complained on the other hand that some of the plantation superintendents were prejudiced against the Negroes and spoke of them in contemptuous terms. Reuben Tomlinson, another Philadelphia abolitionist who became a prominent figure on the islands, deplored the shortcomings of several of the superintendents. "There is also a lukewarmness among them on the subject of anti-Slavery," he wrote, "which I think interferes very materially with their usefulness." The northern societies were forced to dismiss several of the superintendents who had treated the Negroes badly. The great majority of Gideonites were genuinely concerned for the freedmen's welfare, however, and most of those who were not, were quickly weeded out of the enterprise.[18]

[16] McKim to Samuel May, Jr., May 20, 1862, McKim Papers, Cornell.

[17] Rupert S. Holland, ed., *Letters and Diary of Laura M. Towne, Written from the Sea Islands of South Carolina, 1862-84* (Cambridge, Mass., 1912), 8; Sarah Pugh to Mary Edmundson, Aug. 5, 1862, Garrison Papers, BPL.

[18] Ray Allen Billington, ed., *The Journal of Charlotte Forten* (Collier Books, New York, 1961), 165; Tomlinson to J. M. McKim, Sept. 20, Oct. 17, 1862, Jan. 16, 1863, McKim Papers, Cornell. See also Rose, "Rehearsal for Reconstruction," 54-66; William H. Pease, "Three Years Among the Freedmen: William C. Gannett and the Port Royal Experiment," *Journal of Negro History*, XLII (April 1957), 98-117; Sarah Pugh to Elizabeth Gay, Apr. 6, 1862, Gay Papers, CU; Frank Sanborn to Gerrit Smith, Apr. 13, 1862, Smith Papers, SU; Maria W. Chapman to Anne G. Chapman, July 6, 1862, Weston Papers, BPL; T. W. Higginson to Louisa Higginson, Oct. 24, 1863, Higginson Papers, HU.

The Gideonites encountered many trials and difficulties in their first months on the islands. The sea island Negroes spoke a dialect almost unintelligible to northern ears. Harriet Ware, a Massachusetts abolitionist stationed on St. Helena Island, reported in April 1862, that it required a "great deal of tact and ability" to gain the friendship and confidence of the contrabands. "We are not used to these people—it is even very difficult to understand what they say." After her first day in Beaufort, Laura Towne wrote that "it certainly takes great nerve to walk here among the soldiers and negroes and not be disgusted or shocked or pained so much as to give it all up." Charlotte Forten considered the first Negroes she encountered upon her arrival "certainly the most dismal specimens I ever saw."[19] The teachers faced a herculean task in trying to teach Negro children of all ages to read and write in overcrowded schoolrooms. Laura Towne described one of her early classroom experiences: the pupils "had no idea of sitting still, of giving attention or ceasing to talk aloud. They lay down and went to sleep, they scuffled and struck each other. They got up by the dozen, made their curtsies, and walked off to the neighboring field for blackberries, coming back to their seats with a curtsy when they were ready. They evidently did not understand me, and I could not understand them, and after two hours and a half of effort I was thoroughly exhausted."[20]

In the face of such discouragements a few Gideonites gave up and returned home. Most of them stuck it out, however, and soon sang a happier tune. Laura Towne forgot her early disheartenment, and in June 1862, she wrote to a friend:

"I wish you were as free from every fret as I am, and as happy. We found the people here naked, . . . afraid and discontented about being made to work as slaves, and without assurance of freedom or pay, of clothes or food,—and now they are jolly and happy and decently fed and dressed, and so full of affection and gratitude to the people who are relieving them that it is rather too flattering to be enjoyed. It will not last, I dare say, but it is genuine now and they are working like Trojans. . . . It is such

[19] Harriet Ware to ?, Apr. 21, 1862, in Elizabeth Pearson, ed., *Letters from Port Royal* (Boston, 1906), 20-21; Holland, *Letters and Diary of Laura Towne*, 7; Billington, *Journal of Charlotte Forten*, 142.
[20] Holland, *Letters and Diary of Laura Towne*, xiv-xv.

a satisfaction to an abolitionist to see that they are proving conclusively that they can and will and even *like* to work enough at least to support themselves and give something extra to Government."[21]

After they learned to keep order and communicate with the pupils, teachers found to their delight that the children learned to read rapidly. All of the freedmen showed great eagerness to learn to read and write. Most of the teachers agreed that Negro children were fully equal to whites on the lower levels of learning. At the higher levels, such as mathematics, original composition, grammar, and so on, they did not do as well, but most of the teachers attributed this to lack of background, motivation, and opportunity rather than to any innate inferiority. On the whole, most teachers were satisfied with the progress made by their students during the first year. Pierce wrote after observing the contrabands for several weeks that "I was never so impressed as at this hour with the conviction that the lifting of these people from bondage to freedom . . . is a very easy thing, involving only common humanity, and reasonable patience and faith. If white men only did as well under such adverse circumstances, they would be regarded as prodigies."[22]

The Port Royal experiment received a great deal of national publicity in both the proslavery and antislavery press. Much was at stake on the South Carolina islands. If the contrabands there showed themselves capable of an industrious and productive life in freedom, the main argument against emancipation would dissolve into nothingness. For this reason the Democratic and conservative press in the North tried to discredit the whole enterprise. The attempt by Pierce and his "band of Abolition socialists, free lovers, and disorganizers of society generally" to "put in practice the theory of Abolition at Port Royal, will be the beginning of the downfall of the now rampant and powerful Abolition party in the North," declared the *New York Express*. The *Express* charged that the contrabands had become paupers living on the United States Treasury, revelling in idleness at the expense of the

[21] *ibid.*, 68.
[22] Rose, "Rehearsal for Reconstruction," 300-03; Pease, "Three Years Among the Freedmen," *op.cit.*, 100-01; Pearson, *Letters from Port Royal*, 11, 18, 60, 75; Pierce to Sumner, Mar. 20, 1862, Sumner Papers, HU.

northern taxpayer. "The question now arises, if this is the result of letting loose a few thousand negroes in South Carolina, what will it be when the contrabands shall be counted by hundreds of thousands?" The *New York Journal of Commerce* intoned that "the nonsensical, wild and fanatical plans of irresponsible men and women which are having their trial at Port Royal are a subject of sorrow and disgust to the intelligent world." And the *Louisville Democrat* commented that "the abolitionists propose to elevate the black races. Nothing but hemp could do the same thing properly for them."[23]

The abolitionist and antislavery press countered these aspersions with facts, figures, and opinions based on actual observation and study of the situation on the sea islands. On June 2, 1862, Pierce submitted his final report as special agent of the Treasury Department. Under the supervision of Gideonites the Negroes had planted nearly 15,000 acres of cotton, corn, potatoes, and grain. Despite their initial disinclination to plant cotton (they considered it a badge of slavery), and the six weeks' late start on the growing season, the crops were coming along well. The contrabands worked industriously under the stimulus of wages even though they were frequently not paid on time. Their behavior, said Pierce, gave the lie to the old proslavery assertion that Negroes would work only under compulsion. "It is not pretended that many of these laborers could not have done more than they have done, or that in persistent application they are the equals of races living in colder and more bracing latitudes," he wrote. But they worked hard enough to make themselves self-supporting, and with the additional incentives of complete freedom they would work even harder. Nearly 2,500 children were taught in the day schools during the first two months of the experiment, and almost the whole adult population attended Sunday schools. "The success of the movement, now upon its third month, has exceeded my most sanguine expectations," concluded Pierce. "Industrial results have been reached which put at rest the often reiterated assumption that this territory and its products can be cultivated only by slaves.

[23] *New York Express*, quoted in *N.A.S. Standard*, Apr. 5, 1862; *New York Journal of Commerce*, quoted in *Liberator*, May 9, 1862; *Louisville Democrat*, quoted in the *Columbus Crisis*, Dec. 31, 1862.

A social problem which has vexed the wisest approaches a solution."[24]

In the summer of 1862 J. Miller McKim visited the sea islands as the official representative of the Philadelphia Port Royal Relief Committee. McKim was shocked by what he saw of the lingering effects of slavery. Even in his most radical moments as an abolitionist he had never suspected the depths of the soul-corroding and personality-warping effects of human bondage. Nevertheless, after a two weeks' tour of the islands McKim expressed optimism about the future of the Negroes as free men. Most of the anti-Negro stories circulating in the North, he said, came from reporters of the *New York Herald* and *New York World* stationed on the islands, who moved among "the ribald and unprincipled, picking up their items in bar-rooms, . . . and thus it is that at least half of what they write is absolutely false."[25]

McKim returned to Philadelphia and on July 9 gave a public lecture summarizing his observations on the islands. The lecture was widely published by the antislavery press and printed in pamphlet form for distribution throughout the North. Many people were asking: "Has the negro the spirit—the *pluck*, to do his part in maintaining the status now, or hereafter to be, assigned him?" McKim tried to answer this all-important question as fairly as he could. "Servitude is not a condition favorable to the growth of courage," he said. "Slavery in fact as well as law, unmans its victims." But given the incentives and responsibilities of freedom, the Negroes would develop pluck enough. McKim quoted the testimony of one of the plantation superintendents: The freedmen "have their vices. Deception and petty thieving prevail. They are careless, indolent and improvident. They have a miserable habit of scolding and using authoritative language to one another." But "all these vices are clearly the result of *slave education*, and will gradually disappear under improved conditions." McKim stated his firm conviction that the free-labor experiment at Port Royal had thus far been "entirely successful."[26]

[24] Pierce, *Enfranchisement and Citizenship*, 97-102. Pierce's report was widely publicized by the antislavery press.

[25] McKim to Sarah McKim, June 19, 1862, McKim Papers, NYPL. See also Oliver Johnson to Garrison, June 27, 1862, McKim to Garrison, July 13, 1862, Garrison Papers, BPL.

[26] J. M. McKim, *The Freedmen of South Carolina: an Address Delivered in Sansom Hall, July 9, 1862* (Philadelphia, 1862), 18, 30, and passim.

Many other abolitionists and Gideonites contributed their testimony to the positive results of the first months of the Port Royal experiment. Charles P. Ware, a plantation superintendent from Massachusetts, observed in October 1862 that the enterprise had operated under many handicaps during the preceding summer. "The sudden reaction consequent upon the change from slavery to what they hardly knew as freedom; the confusion incident upon military occupation . . . the lateness of the cotton crop, the poorness of the seed . . . and lastly, the shameful delay in the payments" of wages—with all these hindrances it would not have been surprising if the experiment had failed entirely. But it had not failed. Under such adverse circumstances "it is wonderful how much they have done and in what an excellent state they are." E. S. Philbrick wrote after a year on the islands: "If our Northern croakers could only be made to realize as we do here the ease with which we have reduced a comparative degree of order out of the chaos we found, and see how ready this degraded and half-civilized race are to become an industrious and useful laboring class, there would not be so much gabble about the danger of immediate emancipation."[27]

Evidence of the success of the Port Royal experiment and similar efforts elsewhere did not rest upon the testimony of abolitionists alone. John Murray Forbes, a businessman who visited the sea islands in the spring of 1862, wrote in June of that year: "I used to think emancipation only another name for murder, fire and rape, but mature reflection and considerable personal observation have since convinced me that emancipation may, at any time, be declared without disorder."[28] Many others like Forbes were becoming convinced in 1862 by the pressures of war, the reports of teachers of the freedmen, the statements of impartial observers, and personal observation that immediate emancipation was both safe and practicable.

While the freedmen's aid societies were winning converts among conservatives, a few abolitionists warned against the dangers of paternalism inherent in the very concept of freedmen's aid.

[27] Ware and Philbrick quoted in Pearson, *Letters from Port Royal*, 98-99, 180.
[28] Forbes to Charles Sumner, June 21, 1862, in Sarah Forbes Hughes, ed., *Letters and Recollections of John Murray Forbes* (2 vols., Boston, 1899), I, 317-18.

Lydia Maria Child complained about the practice at Fortress Monroe of withholding a portion of the freedmen's wages for support of the sick and aged. "I wish white people could get rid of the idea that they must manage *for* them," she said. "*White* laborers would not work with much heart under such circumstances. They ought to pay them *wages* in proportion to their *work*, and let *them* form Relief Societies among themselves, so that they might feel that *they* did the benevolent work themselves." Wendell Phillips also believed in a greater degree of laissez-faire for the freedmen. "I ask nothing more for the negro than I ask for the Irishman or the German who comes to our shores," said Phillips in May 1862. "I thank the benevolent men who are laboring at Port Royal—all right!—but the blacks at the South do not need them. They are not objects of charity. They only ask this nation—'Take your yoke off our necks.' "[29]

In one sense this criticism was unfair. There was a very real danger of excessive paternalism, to be sure, but the abolitionist teachers and superintendents in the field were no more in favor of paternalism as a permanent policy than Phillips. They were confronted by a set of circumstances, however, which made a certain amount of paternalism necessary at first. The contrabands were just emerging from slavery, an institution that had deeply implanted in their character the habits of dependence and servility. It would take months and years of patient labor, education, and experience before this attitude of dependence on the one side, and the corresponding necessity of a certain amount of paternalism on the other, ceased to exist. The function of the limited paternalism practiced by Gideonites was to help the Negroes take the first steps to freedom, to set them on the path that led to eventual self-reliance, when paternalism would no longer be necessary.[30]

Most of the Gideonites fully recognized the dangers of falling into an attitude of benevolent condescension toward the contrabands. They were annoyed at first by the servile attitude of the Negroes. "These people show their subserviency in the way they put Marm or Sir into their sentences every other word, . . . and in always agreeing to everything you say," wrote Harriet Ware

[29] L. M. Child to Francis G. Shaw, Jan. 28, 1862, Shaw Correspondence, NYPL; Phillips' statement quoted in *Liberator*, May 16, 1862.
[30] Rose, "Rehearsal for Reconstruction," 205-06.

from St. Helena Island in April 1862. "In school it is rather annoying to have them say, 'Yes Marm,' 'zackly Marm,' before it is possible for an idea to have been reached their brains."[31] In many ways the adult freedmen were like children. They had been treated like children, in a sense, all their lives, and for a time they continued to act toward the northern missionaries as they had acted toward their old masters. "The great mass of these people are to all intents and purposes children," observed Reuben Tomlinson early in 1863, "except that they are children with fixed habits, the growth of years, & are therefore even more difficult to manage than children." In view of this childlike behavior, it is not surprising that some of the Gideonites were unconsciously flattered and wheedled into an overindulgent attitude toward their "people." Tomlinson warned against such overindulgence, declaring that it was the worst way to prepare the Negroes for the responsibilities and duties of freedom.[32]

When the Gideonites first came South the contrabands were destitute, in desperate need of food, clothing, and benevolent assistance. The government distributed rations, and the freedmen's aid societies sent thousands of dollars worth of clothing to the islands. This natural impulse to treat the poverty-stricken freedmen as objects of charity was soon overcome, however. The societies set up stores on the islands where the freedmen could buy clothing and supplies at cost, and in November 1862, the government discontinued the issuance of rations to able-bodied freedmen and their families. Most of the Gideonites made conscious efforts to avoid an excess of paternal benevolence, and as time passed the freedmen themselves began to act more like free men.[33]

✦

Port Royal and Fortress Monroe were not the only places where northern teachers and missionaries worked with the freedmen. As the war progressed the A.M.A. established schools and churches in just about every part of the Confederacy penetrated by Union armies. The Boston and Philadelphia Educational and Relief Societies, organized in February and March 1862, later

[31] Pearson, *Letters from Port Royal*, 25.
[32] Tomlinson to J. M. McKim, Feb. 19, Mar. 16, 1863, McKim Papers, Cornell.
[33] Pearson, *Letters from Port Royal*, 33-34; Francis George Shaw to S. P. Chase, Jan. 13, 1864, Chase Papers, LC.

changed their names to the New England Freedmen's Aid Society and the Pennsylvania Freedmen's Relief Association. These two societies plus the National Freedmen's Relief Association of New York expanded the scope of their activities during 1862-1863, established auxiliary societies, and sent an ever-increasing quota of supplies and teachers to the South.[34]

Abolitionists were prominent in the organization and leadership of freedmen's aid societies. A substantial percentage of the officers of the New England, New York, and Pennsylvania societies were old-line abolitionists. The A.M.A. was dominated by abolitionists.[35] In March 1862, George E. Baker, an old abolitionist, helped to organize the National Freedmen's Relief Association in Washington, which distributed supplies, conducted schools, and provided hospital and medical care for freedmen in the District of Columbia and northern Virginia. Joseph Parker, an abolitionist Baptist minister from Boston, became corresponding secretary of the New England Educational Commission for the Freedmen, an organization which directed the freedmen's aid efforts of New England Baptists during the war. In February 1862, Richard J. Hinton founded the Kansas Emancipation League to provide relief, establish schools, and find jobs for the 4,000 contrabands who escaped into Kansas during the first year of the war.[36] In Syracuse Samuel J. May organized an auxiliary freedmen's relief association and spent much of his time and energy directing the work of the association during the rest of the war. The Rochester Ladies Anti-Slavery Society supported a school in Alexandria, Virginia. As the Union armies in the West advanced southward into Tennessee and Mississippi in 1862, thousands of contrabands crowded into filthy camps set up for them behind Union lines. Levi Coffin, famous Cincinnati abolitionist and legendary "President" of the underground railroad, visited a contraband camp at Cairo, Illinois,

[34] Beard, *Crusade of Brotherhood*, passim; Julius H. Parmelee, "Freedmen's Aid Societies, 1861-1871," in *Negro Education: A Study of the Private and Higher Schools for Colored People in the United States; U.S. Dept. of Interior: Bureau of Education Bulletin*, 1916, no. 38 (Washington, 1917), 269-80.

[35] Henry Lee Swint, *The Northern Teacher in the South, 1862-1870* (Nashville, 1941), 26-28.

[36] George E. Baker to Gerrit Smith, July 25, 1864, Smith Papers, su; Joseph W. Parker, "Memoirs," typescript of MS written by Parker in 1880, supplied to the author by Parker's granddaughter, Mrs. Perce J. Bentley, pp. 105-28; Richard J. Hinton to Charles Sumner, Feb. 27, 1862, enclosing circular of the Kansas Emancipation League, Sumner Papers, HU.

late in 1862 and helped start a school there. He returned to Cincinnati and in January 1863, organized the Western Freedmen's Aid Commission. Coffin served as general agent of the Commission, and spent the rest of the war organizing auxiliary societies, raising money, and overseeing the activities of his organization.[37]

Abolitionists also predominated among the teachers and missionaries who went South to instruct and assist the freedmen in their transition to freedom. Few of the old-line abolitionists actually went into the field to teach: that work was usually left to younger and more adventurous persons of antislavery backgrounds, while the older people remained in the North to serve in administrative capacities. A few of the veteran crusaders, however, went South and served on the firing line of freedom. Frances Dana Gage arrived at Port Royal in 1862. Josephine S. Griffing went to work among the freedmen in Washington in 1863 and stayed there until her death in 1872, devoting herself entirely to the work of caring for sick and aged freedmen and finding jobs for the able-bodied.[38] At the outbreak of the war the sixty-year-old Quaker abolitionist, Abigail Hopper Gibbons, offered her services to the government as a nurse. The government accepted, and assigned her to army camps in northern Virginia in the first year of the war. In 1862 she was put in charge of the army hospital at Point Lookout in southern Maryland. A contraband camp was established next to the army hospital. Mrs. Gibbons took charge of the distribution of supplies from freedmen's aid societies, and found jobs in the North for several of the freedmen. She was disliked by the local white populace, most of whom were Confederate sympathizers. She received several threatening letters from irate Marylanders. The following was a typical example of these missives: "Old Lady you are not needed at this place and you had better leave double quick or else the soldiers [Maryland Unionist soldiers] will give you an introduction to the bay you never came here for any good to soldiers as they have found it out you old nigger lover yea worse an old hypocrit the devil has his

[37] Samuel J. May to Garrison, Sept. 9, 24, 1862, Garrison Papers, BPL; *Thirteenth Annual Report of the Rochester Ladies' Anti-Slavery Society* (Rochester, 1864); Levi Coffin, *Reminiscences* (Cincinnati, 1880), 619-50.

[38] F. D. Gage to S. P. Chase, Mar. 4, 1863, Chase Papers, LC; F. D. Gage to Matilda Joslyn Gage, Nov. 20, 1863, Gage Papers, Radcliffe Women's Archives; Elizabeth Cady Stanton et al., *History of Woman Suffrage* (6 vols., New York, 1881-1922), II, 26-39.

house full of better people than ever you were you old Hell hound you must know that you cant rule this whole point now hum yourself away pretty soon."[39]

At the end of the war the various secular and religious freedmen's aid societies had more than 900 teachers in the South. In August 1865, General O. O. Howard, newly appointed head of the Freedmen's Bureau, said that more than 200,000 freedmen had received instruction during the past four years.[40] In the early postwar years there was a great expansion of freedmen's aid activity, especially among the church-connected societies (see Chapter XVII).

✦

Abolitionists made use of every opportunity to proclaim the success of the Port Royal experiment and other free labor enterprises. Edward Pierce and Charlotte Forten published their observations in the *Atlantic Monthly*. Mansfield French and Frances Gage wrote articles about the sea islands for the *New York Tribune*. Mrs. Gage went on an extensive lecture tour in the winter of 1863-64, giving more than 75 lectures about the Port Royal freedmen.[41]

An ever-increasing number of northern conservatives were becoming convinced by the success of the scattered free labor experiments that immediate emancipation was safe and practicable. But the glowingly optimistic reports written for publication by teachers, labor superintendents, and other freedmen's aid workers contained only part of the truth. For many years abolitionists had argued that the dehumanizing institution of slavery destroyed nearly every vestige of manhood, morality, and intelligence in its victims. When the Gideonites first came South and saw for themselves the abject, servile character of many contrabands, their

[39] Sarah Hopper Emerson, *Life of Abby Hopper Gibbons* (2 vols., New York, 1896-97), I, 248, 296-395, II, 1-42, 70-101, 108-32. The letter to Mrs. Gibbons is quoted from *ibid.*, II, 39.

[40] Parmelee, "Freedmen's Aid Societies," *op. cit.*, 273, 277, 284; *Nineteenth Annual Report of the American Missionary Association* (New York, 1865), 18-29; *Philadelphia Ledger*, Aug. 10, 1865.

[41] Edward L. Pierce, "The Freedmen at Port Royal," *Atlantic Monthly*, XII (Sept. 1863), 302-15; Charlotte Forten, "Life in the Sea Islands," *Atlantic Monthly*, XIII (May 1864), 587-96, and (June 1864), 666-76; Mansfield French to S. H. Gay, Oct. 14, 21, 23, 1862, Gay Papers, CU; Frances D. Gage to Matilda Joslyn Gage, Nov. 20, 1863, Gage Papers, Radcliffe Women's Archives; *N.A.S. Standard*, Dec. 12, 1863, Mar. 26, 1864.

theories about slavery were quickly confirmed. But to report the objective truth about the freedmen would only confirm the stereotype of the servile, shiftless, barbarous Negro. Hence in most of their *published* reports and letters they played down the ignoble qualities of the freedmen and emphasized their rapid progress and remarkable achievements under freedom. The countless trials, heartbreaks, and disillusionments faced by the Gideonites were rarely mentioned in public accounts of their work.

Typical of some of the teachers' published reports was this statement by Linda Slaughter, an Ohio abolitionist and teacher for the A.M.A.: "Already has the Freedman been quickened intellectually. . . . What has not freedom done for him? The brutish mind, the servile demeanor, and the clouded soul have given place to noble impulses. . . . A nation has been born in a day. . . . Steadily are they rising; steadfastly are they progressing. . . . The Freedmen are destined shortly to become the ruling race in the South. Labor and education . . . soon will elevate them above the aristocratic level of their former masters."[42]

Such rosy accounts may have been necessary to convince the North of the success of emancipation, but many abolitionists recognized the dangers inherent in these enthusiastic statements. In the first place they did not accurately reflect the facts of the freedmen's character, the difficulty of the transition to freedom, and the many disappointments experienced by the freedmen's aid workers. Secondly, if the Negro found the transition to freedom as easy as Linda Slaughter and others represented it, slavery could not have been such a bad institution after all—but most abolitionists who went South agreed privately that slavery was even worse than they had suspected. Thirdly, these optimistic and exaggerated reports of progress could only build up such high expectations that disillusionment would be inevitable when the real facts of the freedmen's character, abilities, and status became known.

Many teachers of the freedmen warned against rosy distortion of the condition of affairs in the South. A Massachusetts abolitionist teaching in an A.M.A. school at Norfolk wrote in 1863 that on the whole the Negroes were behaving well in freedom. But "some injudicious letter-writers from the South would make them

[42] Linda Slaughter, *The Freedmen of the South* (Cincinnati, 1869), 177, 179.

out *better* than other men and women, almost angelic. . . . This is as unjust and foolish as to go to the other extreme, like the New York *Herald*. They are human, and then, from their births, outraged and wronged, their ideas of morals are very vague and few. How could they be otherwise? . . . Some are honest, some are not. Some are stupid and dull, some brilliant and learn quick. . . . Well, I think it was just so, up in the Old Bay State . . . and, I presume, it is so still, and ever will be with 'white folks' children."

Another A.M.A. teacher at Norfolk wrote in July 1863: "I have sometimes feared, when reading letters from friends of the negro, south, who naturally enough want to look upon the bright side of the slave's character, that false impressions would be made regarding the capabilities of the negroes. . . . We must stand face to face with stern and revolting facts. The contrabands *are* low and degraded, but is it *their* reproach? They *are* unfit for freedom, but are they any more fit for oppression, or will longer servitude ever better prepare them to receive the glorious heritage of liberty? They are what the accursed system of slavery has made them."[43]

An abolitionist friend of Garrison, serving as a Union army chaplain at New Bern, North Carolina, wrote a letter to the *Liberator* asserting that the condition of some of the freedmen was appalling, their morals low, their minds ignorant. "But when we think of the circumstances under which they have been raised, we cannot wonder at their condition. Herded and worked like cattle, . . . kept in total ignorance, governed through their fears, bought and sold, beaten and bruised at will,—no wonder that they are unloving, suspicious, treacherous, impure, passionate, degraded." Abolitionists and all friends of the freedmen should confront these realities with a clear eye. "There must be nothing sentimental or romantic. They, the freedmen, are not angels, they are not even civilized men. . . . We must begin at the root. We must deal with them as children in intellect, but men in instincts and passions. . . . It is useless, it is folly to disguise the difficulties, or to throw a false halo of romance about the negro. It is the highest proof of a genuine sympathy and interest, to admit all

[43] The two letters were published in the *Principia*, June 25 and July 23, 1863.

the disagreeable features of the work, to realize all the difficulties, and *still to go on*."[44]

William Channing Gannett was one of the most thoughtful and objective participants in the Port Royal experiment. Not yet twenty-two years old when he arrived on the sea islands in the spring of 1862, Gannett was the son of one of New England's foremost Unitarian ministers. While attending Harvard he had become an abolitionist and an admirer of Wendell Phillips. He graduated Phi Beta Kappa from Harvard in 1860, and joined the first shipload of Gideonites to Port Royal in March 1862. Gannett stayed on the islands until 1865. After the war he became a prominent Unitarian clergyman and a leader in the Social Gospel movement.[45]

Gannett was a penetrating and lucid thinker. During the war he commented frequently on the progress of the Port Royal experiment. Taken together, his observations constitute a remarkably objective and valuable analysis of the experiment by a participant in it. Gannett considered the experiment a success. "I feel no doubt," he wrote in 1863, "that under conditions of peace, three years would find these people, with but very few exceptions, a self-respecting, self-supporting population." Their behavior had suggested the capacity and power of development. "Their principal vices—dishonesty, indolence, unchastity, their dislike of responsibility, and unmanly willingness to be dependent on others for what their own effort might bring,—their want of forethought and inability to organize and combine operations for mutual benefit . . . can be traced naturally and directly to slavery."[46]

In 1865 Gannett concluded his tour of duty among the freedmen. He published an important article on the freedmen in the *North American Review* of July 1865; and in the fall of the year he visited England, lecturing frequently to eager British audiences on his experiences at Port Royal. In his article and lectures Gannett constantly reiterated that "the real wrong in slavery did not affect the body, but it was a curse to the soul and mind of the

[44] *Liberator*, Apr. 3, 1863.
[45] William H. Pease, "William Channing Gannett, A Social Biography," Ph.D. dissertation, U. of Rochester, 1955, passim.
[46] Pearson, *Letters from Port Royal*, 177-79.

slave. The aim of the master was to keep down every principle of manhood and growth."[47] As a result the slave became childlike and dependent. "In slavery, not only are natural rights denied, but, what is quite as injurious, necessary wants are supplied; everything contributes to the repression of faculty. The slaveholder's institution is a nursery for perpetuating infancy."[48]

In mental ability, said Gannett, the Negroes showed surprising quickness in the faculties of perception and intuition, but were slow in constructive reasoning. This was a defect of training, not of innate capacity. "They have capacity, but lack ability,—the term properly applicable to the mind which by discipline has control of its powers. That the faculty exists dormantly and awaits its training is indicated by the fact that in many individuals it is already partially developed."[49]

Slavery had also dulled the Negro's sense of conjugal fidelity. Sexual promiscuity was encouraged by the example and regulations of the master race. "On the Sea Islands the plantation is a rare exception on which the white family has not contributed to populate the negro houses." There were no proper marriages among slaves; husbands or wives could be sold away from each other, or from their children. "Thus all the props which society usually affords to chastity are changed under slavery into stumblingblocks."[50] In reply to the charge of dishonesty and mendacity commonly leveled against the Negro race, Gannett pointed out that the slave had virtually no protection under law, so he lied to protect himself from abuse and punishment. A piece of property himself, he could have little appreciation of the sanctity of the rest of his master's property. "Laziness, dishonesty, and licentiousness," wrote Gannett, "are the very habits which it is impossible, even in conception, to dissociate from slavery."[51]

Gannett presented a cautiously optimistic view of the future. "If a people were really unfit for freedom," he declared, "it seems likely that emancipation would render them not only paupers, but a race of beggars." Nothing of the kind had occurred at

[47] Clipping from *Bristol Post* (England), Oct. 23, 1865, in the Gannett Papers, RU.
[48] [William C. Gannett], "The Freedmen at Port Royal," *North American Review*, CI (July 1865), 1.
[49] *ibid.*, 2-3.
[50] *ibid.*, 13.
[51] *ibid.*, 11-13.

Port Royal. But the road to freedom would not be smooth. "Not only do their old habits cling to the freedmen as they rise, but their ignorance will betray them into new and perilous mistakes. We look for slow progress and much disappointment. . . . For a time discouragement and failure await the eager restorer." But Gannett concluded that these disappointments and setbacks should never dissuade America from her goal of equal rights and opportunities, under law, for all men.[52]

[52] *ibid.*, 25-28.

THE abolitionists began urging the government to adopt a uniform administrative policy toward the freedmen as soon as it became clear that some degree of emancipation would result from the Civil War. The administrative situation during most of the war was chaotic. One system of caring for the contrabands and utilizing their labor prevailed in Virginia, another at Port Royal, another in Louisiana, and still another in the Mississippi Valley north of Louisiana. There were frequent conflicts of authority regarding freedmen's affairs between the Army and the Treasury Department. Military officers in command of occupation forces believed that the disposition of the contrabands should be under their authority, while the Treasury Department, which had charge of abandoned lands and estates, tried to control the Negro labor that cultivated these lands. Military commanders often placed the Negroes in unsanitary, overcrowded contraband camps where disease and death were common. Lessees of abandoned estates frequently treated their contraband laborers as if they were still slaves.[1]

Foreseeing this unsatisfactory situation, abolitionists in the early months of the war recommended the creation of a federal bureau of emancipation to coordinate and administer the treatment of freedmen. In a sermon at New Bedford, Massachusetts in July 1861, abolitionist William J. Potter stated that "with an act of emancipation, let there be a new Executive Bureau established . . . to care for and protect, and educate these four millions of new born freemen." In January 1862, John Jay urged upon Senator Sumner the necessity of a bureau "to take charge of the blacks wherever our army lands in the Southern States, under rules & regulations to be prepared by the War Department."[2]

In 1862 the Emancipation League initiated a campaign to

---

[1] George R. Bentley, *A History of the Freedmen's Bureau* (Philadelphia, 1955), 16-29; Bell I. Wiley, *Southern Negroes, 1861-1865* (New Haven, 1938), 175-259.

[2] *N.A.S. Standard*, July 27, 1861; Jay to Sumner, Jan. 4, 1862, Sumner Papers, HU.

persuade the government to create an emancipation bureau.[3] In September, Samuel Gridley Howe visited Washington, talked with Chase and other officials, and reported that he found them friendly to the idea of a bureau.[4] The League sent a memorial to the United States Senate, signed by leading abolitionists and Republicans in Massachusetts, requesting creation of an emancipation bureau. "The exigencies of the hour demand more than aught else a Bureau at Washington which shall be devoted to the emancipation of slaves, and their employment," declared the *Commonwealth* in an editorial supporting the memorial. The cruelty and outrages inflicted upon the freedmen by the Army and by Treasury agents, argued the *Commonwealth*, were the result of administrative anarchy in dealing with the freedmen. Freedmen's aid societies could not help the Negroes unless they were assisted by a sympathetic and powerful government agency. An emancipation bureau was needed "to see that Justice, that the right of fair trial, that a field for his labor, are secured to the Negro."[5]

Garrisonian abolitionists seconded the demand for an emancipation bureau. "Without fitting measures, [the Emancipation Proclamation] is worth little to our generation," said Wendell Phillips in January 1863. "Long before this, there should have been created a 'Bureau of Freedmen,' to guard and aid the advent of these millions into the condition of freedmen." Edmund Quincy wanted an agency "to make provision for the first necessities of the freedmen, to allot them lands out of those forfeited by the rebels, [and] to organize and protect their labor." The Massachusetts and New York Anti-Slavery Societies passed resolutions urging creation of a bureau "for the special purpose of guarding the rights and interests of the liberated bondsmen, providing them with land and labor, and giving them a fair chance to develop their faculties and powers through the necessary educational instrumentalities."[6]

[3] Frank Bird to John Andrew, Nov. 15, 1862, Andrew Papers, MHS; S. G. Howe to S. P. Chase, Nov. 19, 1862, Chase Papers, LC; Frank Bird to Benjamin Butler, Dec. 11, 1862, Butler Papers, LC; Frank Sanborn to S. P. Chase, Dec. 8, 1862, Sanborn to Charles Sumner, Dec. 9, 1862, James Redpath to Sumner, Feb. 7, 1863, Sumner Papers, HU; Sanborn to ?, Dec. 28, 1862, Sanborn Papers, Concord Public Library; *Commonwealth*, Dec. 13, 1862.

[4] S. G. Howe to Frank Bird, Sept. 17, 1862, in Laura E. Richards, *Letters and Journals of Samuel Gridley Howe* (Boston, 1909), 502.

[5] "Memorial of the Emancipation League," *Senate Misc. Docs.*, 37 Cong., 3 Sess., no. 10; *Commonwealth*, Jan. 17, 1863.

[6] Phillips' statement quoted in *Liberator*, Jan. 9, 1863; Quincy's statement

Abolitionists realized that they would have a better case for a freedmen's bureau if they could present reliable facts about the condition of the freedmen. "We must be able to present," wrote Samuel Gridley Howe, "as early as possible, a general and reliable coup d'oeil of the actual condition of those who are actually out of the house of bondage; their wants and their capacities. We must collect facts and use them as ammunition." In pursuance of Howe's suggestion the Emancipation League in December 1862 sent a questionnaire to superintendents and supervisors of freedmen's affairs. They received prompt replies from eight supervisors, which were published by the League in the *Commonwealth* and in pamphlet form.[7]

The questionnaire sought information on the industriousness of the freedmen, their scale of wages, whether white men were paid more than freedmen for the same work, and whether freedmen's wages were promptly paid; the habits of the freedmen with regard to intemperance, chastity, honesty, and religion; and the capacity and desire of the freedmen for education. The purpose of the questionnaire was to bring facts "to bear upon the problem as to what is to be the *status* of the negro after the Rebellion is suppressed." On the basis of this information the League hoped to persuade Congress to establish a freedmen's bureau.

The replies came from the District of Columbia, Virginia, South Carolina, Arkansas, and Missouri. Most of them agreed that with proper incentives the freedmen worked well. Average wages paid by the government varied from $7 to $10 per month, plus rations and clothing. White laborers were usually paid more for the same work. Several of the replies stated that freedmen's wages were usually paid late, sometimes not at all, causing distrust and a tendency to shirk. Most of the replies agreed that the freedmen's sexual morals could stand a great deal of improvement. Some of

---

published in *N.A.S. Standard*, Jan. 24, 1863; resolutions of Massachusetts and New York Anti-Slavery Societies published in *Liberator*, Feb. 6, 1863, and *N.A.S. Standard*, Mar. 7, 1863. The Massachusetts Society sent a copy of its resolution to President Lincoln, Lincoln Papers, LC.

[7] S. G. Howe to F. W. Bird, Sept. 17, 1862, in Richards, *Letters and Journals of S. G. Howe*, 502; *Commonwealth*, Jan. 24, 1863; *Facts Concerning the Freedmen, Their Capacity and Their Destiny, Collected by and Published by the Emancipation League* (Boston, 1863). See also *New York Tribune*, Dec. 26, 1862; and *N.A.S. Standard*, Jan. 17, 1863.

the reports declared that slavery had fostered in the Negroes the vices of lying and stealing, but others emphasized that the freedmen were remarkably honest in view of their past training. All replies agreed that the freedmen showed a strong desire for education and were capable of learning as fast and as well as comparable classes of whites. Most replies stated that the Negroes were a religious people but that their piety seemed to have little relation to morality. Several reports complained of ill treatment and contemptuous conduct toward the freedmen by Union officers and soldiers.

The final series of questions asked by the Emancipation League was: "Are the freedmen in your department fit to take their place in society . . . with a fair prospect of self-support and progress? or do they need any preparatory training and guardianship? . . . And would they need any different training and guard-ianship from what other men, equally ignorant, would need?" Most of the replies stated that a temporary system of government protection would be necessary during the difficult transition period and until some degree of recovery was achieved in the war-torn South. Once peace and order were restored, how-ever, "equal laws *faithfully* administered" would be better than any program of guardianship or apprenticeship. Most of the replies compared the Negroes favorably with southern "poor whites" and asserted that the freedmen, with education and a minimum of guidance, could become capable members of society. Some of the replies emphasized that settlement of the freedmen on land of their own would greatly facilitate the transition from slavery to a prosperous freedom. The Emancipation League pre-sented the questionnaire and replies to the government in the hope that Congress could use them as a guide in framing a freed-men's bureau bill.

After his visit to Port Royal in June 1862, J. Miller McKim began to advocate the creation of a government commission to investigate the condition and needs of the freedmen and make a formal report. McKim visited Washington in December 1862, and urged his idea of a freedmen's inquiry commission upon Senator Sumner, Congressmen Thaddeus Stevens and John Bing-ham, and Secretary of War Stanton. All of these men seemed to favor the project, although Stanton advised caution. McKim thought that a congressional commission would be best, and Stevens agreed with him. Stanton and Sumner, however, favored an executive commission that could be appointed quietly and go to work without the possibly harmful fanfare of a congressional debate. McKim was convinced by their reasoning. Sumner, McKim, and Stanton discussed possible appointees to the commission. Someone suggested McKim himself as a member but he declined, arguing that no old-line Garrisonian should be included on the commission because his presence might prejudice conservatives against its findings. Several names of possible members were mentioned, but McKim left Washington without anything final having been decided. He returned to the capital in January for another discussion, but still nothing was decided. McKim expressed a desire to be secretary of the proposed commission, and he evidently left for Philadelphia with the understanding that he would be appointed secretary.[8]

In March 1863, the War Department announced the formation of the "American Freedmen's Inquiry Commission" (A.F.I.C.) to investigate the condition and needs of the freedmen within Union lines. The Commission consisted of three members: Robert Dale Owen, Samuel Gridley Howe, and James McKaye. All were wartime emancipationists, and Howe was a prewar abolitionist. Instead of a secretary, a stenographer would accompany the commissioners to the South and take down verbatim testimony of military commanders, labor superintendents, teachers, and the freedmen themselves. McKim and his Garrisonian friends were chagrined that McKim was not appointed secretary, but they swallowed their disappointment and praised the membership of the Commission. McKim furnished Owen with memoranda of his visit to the sea islands and copies of the reports of British and French commissions on the results of emancipation in the West Indies. Owen could use these reports as models for the report of the A.F.I.C., of which he was chairman.[9]

[8] McKim to Frank Bird, Dec. 23, 1862, McKim Papers, NYPL; McKim to Sumner, Dec. 24, 1862, Jan. 2, 20, 1863, Sumner Papers, HU; Gerrit Smith to McKim, Dec. 27, 1862, S. H. Gay to McKim, Jan. 15, 1863, Sumner to McKim, Jan. 13, 30, 1863, Thaddeus Stevens to McKim, Nov. 27, 1862, McKim Papers, Cornell; Oliver Johnson to McKim, Dec. 29, 1862, Sumner to McKim, Jan. 18, 1863, McKim Papers, NYPL; McKim to S. H. Gay, Jan. 3, 1863, Gay Papers, CU.

[9] *O.R.*, Ser. 3, vol. III, 73-74; *N.A.S. Standard*, Mar. 28, 1863; *Liberator*, Apr. 17, 1863; *Commonwealth*, Mar. 27, 1863; Sumner to Howe, Mar. 14, 1863, Sumner-

The three commissioners set up headquarters in New York and began to plan their method of procedure. They decided to visit personally as many parts of the Union-occupied South as possible and send questionnaires to areas they were unable to visit. All three commissioners inspected freedmen's camps in Virginia in the spring of 1863, and McKaye went to Port Royal in June. On June 30, 1863, the Commission submitted a brief preliminary report of their activities and conclusions up to that point, written primarily by Owen. Owen had not been a prewar abolitionist, although he was active in other reform movements. He came to Washington at the beginning of the war and soon became an articulate wartime emancipationist. He met and formed friendships with several abolitionists and worked closely with them during the war. Owen had a receptive rather than original mind. His biographer states that he absorbed many abolitionist ideas during the war. This is probably true, because both the preliminary and final reports of the A.F.I.C. contained numerous abolitionist ideas and recommendations.[10]

The preliminary report asserted that freedmen worked well for wages if they were promptly paid. Their vices "are such as appertain to their former social condition." Thievery and lying were common among them, but "men who are allowed no property do not learn to respect the rights of property. Men who are subjected to despotic rule acquire the habit of shielding themselves from arbitrary punishment by subterfuges." The report recommended the establishment of a freedmen's bureau to bring order out of the chaos of freedmen's affairs. The bureau should function at least until the end of the war, should supervise the employment and wage contracts of freedmen, and should establish courts to adjudicate disputes relating to freedmen. The preliminary report

---

Howe Correspondence, HU; Sumner to Frank Bird, Mar. 19, 1863, Bird Papers, HU; McKim to Sumner, Mar. 21, 23, 1863, W. H. Furness to Sumner, Mar. 30, 1863, Sumner Papers, HU; Oliver Johnson to McKim, Mar. 25, 1863, McKim Papers, Cornell; McKim to W. H. Furness, Mar. 28, Apr. 3, 6, 1863, McKim to Caroline Weston, Sept. 14, 1863, McKim to R. D. Owen, Mar. 30, 1863, McKim Papers, NYPL. The stenographer who accompanied the commissioners on their investigations was J. M. W. Yerrington, a Boston abolitionist who usually reported the speeches of Wendell Phillips and the proceedings of antislavery conventions.

[10] Richard W. Leopold, *Robert Dale Owen: A Biography* (Cambridge, Mass., 1940), vii, 350-51.

The Contraband Camp at City Point—an Evening Prayer Meeting.
Joseph Becker in *Leslie's Illustrated Newspaper*

emphasized the need for teaching the Negroes self-reliance. Charity was acceptable as a means of temporary relief, but freedmen should be put to work as soon as possible on abandoned or confiscated plantations. They should be paid regular and adequate wages and should be given the opportunity to purchase or otherwise acquire confiscated land. The report conceded that the transition to freedom would be difficult, but advised against any system of permanent or semipermanent guardianship of the freedmen. The Negroes were hungry for education, and a school system, staffed by teachers of the freedmen's aid societies, should be established under the auspices of the proposed freedmen's bureau.[11]

[11] The preliminary report is most conveniently accessible in *O.R.*, Ser. 3, vol. III, 430-54.

During the summer Howe went to Ontario to investigate conditions among Negroes there, most of whom had escaped from American slavery. Owen remained in New York and spent the summer doing research on Negro history and preparing a questionnaire which was sent in August to officials all over the country who had anything to do with freedmen. It was modeled on the questionnaire sent out by the Emancipation League the previous December, and the replies were similar. At the end of 1863 Owen and Howe made a tour of contraband camps in Kentucky, Tennessee and Missouri. The following February, McKaye went to New Orleans. The main burden of writing the Commission's final report fell to Owen. He completed it and submitted it to the War Department in May 1864. Its conclusions reflected the thinking of all three commissioners.[12] In the final analysis the report embodied the results of thirty years of abolitionist research and reflection. "Extensive experience in the West Indies has proved that emancipation, when it takes place, should be unconditional and absolute," stated the report. "The experiment of a few years' apprenticeship, plausible in theory, proved, in practice, a failure." This was taken directly from abolitionist writings on emancipation in the West Indies.[13] The report repeated its earlier recommenda-

[12] Harold Schwartz, *Samuel Gridley Howe: Social Reformer* (Cambridge, Mass., 1956), 261-66; Leopold, *Owen*, 360-63.

[13] In their studies of emancipation in the British West Indies, abolitionists emphasized the failure of the gradualist approach. In 1833 the British Parliament had enacted a law emancipating the 668,000 slaves in its West Indian colonies on August 1, 1834. Instead of becoming immediately free, however, the slaves were to remain bound to their masters as apprentices until 1840. Anticipating difficulties under the apprenticeship system, the planters on Antigua granted their slaves immediate and unconditional freedom in 1834. The apprenticeship policy was designed to "prepare" the slaves for freedom, but it proved burdensome, expensive, and unsatisfactory to planter and slave alike. Several planters on the other islands followed Antigua's example and freed their slaves unconditionally, and in 1838 all of the colonial assemblies officially recognized the failure of apprenticeship by decreeing the unconditional emancipation of all slaves on August 1 of that year. Abolitionists were fond of emphasizing the contrast between Antigua and Jamaica. Whereas in Antigua emancipation was immediate, in Jamaica the planters vigorously attempted to keep the Negroes in a state of quasi-slavery by means of the apprenticeship system. As a result the transition to freedom in Antigua was quick and relatively painless; in Jamaica it was slow and painful. Antigua became the most prosperous of the islands, with a high percentage of land ownership and a relatively low illiteracy rate. Jamaica became the least prosperous of the islands. The moral? Immediate emancipation was far superior to gradual emancipation. "If the experience of Antigua and Jamaica teaches anything," concluded Frank Sanborn, "it teaches that simultaneous and entire emancipation is the safest, the cheapest, and the wisest course." Frank Sanborn, *Emancipation in the West*

tion of a freedmen's bureau. "For a time we need a freedmen's bureau, but not because these people are negroes, only because they are men who have been, for generations, despoiled of their rights." Such federal guardianship should be replaced as soon as possible by equal laws equally administered. The same civil and political rights enjoyed by whites should be granted to freedmen. "The essential thing is that we secure to them the means of making their own way; that we give them, to use the familiar phrase, 'a fair chance.' If, like whites, they are to be self-supporting, then, like whites, they ought to have those rights, civil and political, without which they are but laboring as a man labors with hands bound."[14]

A recent historian has called the Commission's report a "Blueprint for Radical Reconstruction." Certain it is that the work of Owen, Howe, and McKaye laid the foundations for the Freedmen's Bureau. One of the first results in Congress of the Commission's activities was the creation of a Senate Committee on Emancipation (later renamed the Committee on Slavery and Freedmen), with Sumner as chairman. Immediately after submission of the Commission's final report, Sumner introduced a resolution calling for copies of the two official reports for his Senate Committee. Several days later he offered a motion to publish 3,000 extra copies of the final report, calling it "one of the most able contributions to this question that has ever appeared in this country or any other country." Republicans carried the motion over Democratic opposition. Congressmen debating the Freedmen's Bureau bill had copies of the report on hand at all times.[15]

Owen published separately in book form a slightly modified version of the final report.[16] Howe also published a book setting forth the results of his investigation of Canadian Negroes. He strongly endorsed the equalitarian laissez-faire approach to eman-

---

Indies (Boston, 1862), 15. See also Lydia M. Child, *The Right Way the Safe Way* (2nd ed., New York, 1862), 18, 30-31, 33, 58-60, 67; and an article in the *Pine and Palm*, June 21, 1861, by Richard Hinton.

[14] "Final Report of the American Freedmen's Inquiry Commission," *O.R.*, Ser. 3, vol. IV, 289-382. Quoted passages from 381-82.

[15] John G. Sproat, "Blueprint for Radical Reconstruction," *Journal of Southern History*, XXIII (February 1957), 25-44; *Senate Journal*, 37 Cong., 1 Sess., 649-50; *Cong. Globe*, 38 Cong., 1 Sess., 3,285-87; *Senate Exec. Docs.*, 38 Cong., 1 Sess., no. 53 (ser. no. 1,176).

[16] Robert D. Owen, *The Wrong of Slavery, the Right of Emancipation, and the Future of the African Race in the United States* (New York, 1864).

cipation and the transition to freedom emphasized by the A.F.I.C. reports. "The negro does best when let alone," argued Howe, and "we must beware of all attempts to prolong his servitude, even under pretext of taking care of him. The white man has tried taking care of the negro, by slavery, by apprenticeship, by colonization, and has failed disastrously in all; now let the negro try to take care of himself."[17] At the beginning of 1864, Howe wrote a public letter to Congressman Thomas D. Eliot of Massachusetts, chairman of the House Committee considering a freedmen's bureau bill. Howe warned Eliot that "whatever plan is adopted, should be founded on the principle that the negro, once emancipated, is as free as a white man; free to go or to come; free to accept or reject employment; free to work or to starve." A system of guardianship or apprenticeship would be nothing less than "a prolongation of slavery or servitude disguised under the name of *protection*." What was needed, said Howe, was not guardianship but "some general system for putting the negroes upon their own legs, and defending them against those who will strive to push them down, and keep them down."[18]

Most abolitionists favored this equalitarian laissez-faire approach. Frederick Douglass was one of the strongest proponents of such a policy. In reply to the oft-repeated question, "What shall we do with the Negroes?", Douglass said:

"Our answer is, do nothing with them; mind your business, and let them mind theirs. Your *doing* with them is their greatest misfortune. They have been undone by your doings, and all they now ask and really have need of at your hands, is just to let them alone. . . . If you see [a Negro] on his way to school, with spelling book, geography and arithmetic in his hands—let him alone. Don't shut the door in his face. . . . We would not for one moment check the outgrowth of any benevolent concern for the future welfare of the colored race in America or elsewhere; but in the name of reason and religion, we earnestly plead for justice before all else. Benevolence with justice is harmonious and beautiful; but benevolence without justice is a mockery. Let the American people, who have thus far only kept the colored race staggering between partial

---

[17] Samuel G. Howe, *The Refugees from Slavery in Canada West* (Boston, 1864), 104.

[18] *Commonwealth*, Jan. 8, 1864.

philanthropy and cruel force, be induced to try what virtue there is in justice."[19]

While the A.F.I.C. was doing its work, abolitionists kept up the pressure for a freedmen's bureau. In 1863 abolitionist Josephine S. Griffing came to Washington as an agent of the Western Freedmen's Aid Commission. She was appalled by the destitution and misery of the thousands of freedmen who had flocked to the city. She served also as an agent of the National Freedmen's Relief Association in Washington, and was put in charge of doling out governmental and philanthropic aid to the Negroes. She established sewing schools for the women, some of whom became proficient enough to support themselves by making clothes. She found jobs and homes in the North for hundreds of freedmen and their families. But Mrs. Griffing soon discovered that the task was too big for haphazard government relief and private philanthropy. She began to urge the creation of a freedmen's bureau to dispense emergency relief, foster education, and help settle the freedmen in remunerative occupations. Her winning personality and obvious sincerity made a favorable impression on Lincoln, Stanton, Sumner, and other government officials with whom she discussed the subject of a freedmen's bureau.[20]

On November 9, 1863, officials of the freedmen's aid societies of Boston, New York, and Philadelphia held a rally at Cooper Union to bring pressure on the government in behalf of a freedmen's bureau. These three societies plus the Cincinnati organization sent a delegation to Lincoln. The president expressed

[19] *Douglass' Monthly*, Jan. 1862; speech of Douglass at the annual meeting of the Massachusetts Anti-Slavery Society, Jan. 25, 1865, in *Liberator*, Feb. 10, 1865. The idea of some sort of temporary apprenticeship or guardianship for a people emerging from slavery and woefully ignorant of the responsibilities of freedom has a certain attractiveness, even for the liberal. A wisely administered paternal guardianship might have moderated some of the excesses of Reconstruction and paved the way for ultimately better race relations in the South. But in the context of the 1860's and 1870's a wise paternal guidance was probably impossible. After all, apprenticeship had failed in the British West Indies under better conditions than those which existed in the postwar South. Abolitionist fears that temporary guardianship would become a device for perpetual subordination of the Negro were well founded, for this was pretty much what happened in the South after 1877.

[20] Mrs. Griffing's activities are discussed in Elizabeth Cady Stanton et al., *History of Woman Suffrage* (6 vols., New York, 1881-1922), II, 26-30. See also Mrs. Griffing to Garrison, Aug. 19, 1864, published in *Liberator*, Aug. 26, 1864.

his sympathy with their objective and suggested that they draw up a memorial which he would submit to Congress. A committee drafted the memorial and sent it to Lincoln on December 1, 1863. It urged the president to "interpose" with Congress and recommend "the immediate creation of a bureau of emancipation." The care of the freedmen had become a matter beyond the resources of private benevolent societies. The problem required "the best ability the country offers" and a "regularly constituted government bureau, with all the machinery and civil powers of the government behind it." Congressman Thomas Eliot of Massachusetts had introduced a freedmen's bureau bill at the previous session of Congress, but his measure had died quietly in committee. He reintroduced the bill in the 1863-64 session, and shortly afterwards Lincoln sent the memorial of the freedmen's aid societies to Congress as part of a special message endorsing the idea of a freedmen's bureau. J. Miller McKim, Francis George Shaw, Levi Coffin, and other officials of the freedmen's societies spent several weeks in Washington during the winter lobbying for the bill.[21]

Eliot's bill provided for the establishment of a bureau within the War Department to dispense relief, supervise the labor of freed Negroes, provide them with educational facilities, make rules and regulations for their treatment, establish freedmen's courts, and settle the Negroes on abandoned or confiscated lands. Democrats charged that the bill was unconstitutional and would centralize too much power in the federal government. But it passed the House on March 1, 1864. In the Senate, however, it ran into a roadblock set up by its friends. Sumner reported the bill out of committee with an amendment placing the Bureau under the Treasury instead of the War Department. He believed that the most important part of the bill was the provision for settling freedmen on confiscated land. Such land was under the control of the Treasury Department, and Sumner wanted the Bureau to be in the same Department. Military men, however, argued that the Bureau logically belonged in the War Depart-

---

[21] *Commonwealth*, Dec. 11, 1863; *Senate Exec. Docs.*, 38 Cong., 1 Sess., no. 1 (serial no. 1,176); *New York Tribune*, Dec. 28, 1863; Elizabeth Gay to Sarah Pugh, Feb. 21, 1864, Gay Papers, cu; Levi Coffin, *Reminiscences* (Cincinnati, 1880), 647-48.

ment since the army controlled the occupied South. Abolitionists warned Sumner against pressing his version of the bill: the House had passed the act by such a narrow margin that any Senate changes might jeopardize final passage. Sumner persisted, however, and the Senate passed his version on June 28, 1864.[22]

Consequently no bill at all was enacted in 1864, and the matter carried over to the next session. When Congress met in December it was confronted by several more petitions from freedmen's aid societies and other groups urging creation of a bureau. Abolitionists continued to press Sumner to accept a bureau as an autonomous agency within the War Department. Sumner finally agreed to this proposal provided that control of confiscated lands was also placed in the War Department. This was done and the bill finally passed both Houses and was signed by Lincoln on March 3, 1865.[23]

Some abolitionists hoped that Lincoln would appoint a prominent antislavery man as head of the new Bureau.[24] But the president and his military commanders wanted to keep it under army control. Most of the commissioners and assistant commissioners of the Bureau were generals, and a majority of the subordinate posts were filled by lower-grade army officers. Several abolitionists, however, were appointed to important positions in the Bureau. Josephine Griffing served as sub-assistant commissioner in the District of Columbia. John W. Alvord, one of the earliest abolitionists, was appointed superintendent of schools of the Freedmen's Bureau. Reuben Tomlinson served as superintendent of schools for the Bureau in South Carolina. Several other abolitionists who came South with the freedmen's aid societies held positions in the Bureau. In addition, General O. O. Howard, head of the Bureau, was sympathetic with the antislavery cause. Several

22 Bentley, *Freedmen's Bureau*, 36-43; *Cong. Globe*, 38 Cong., 1 Sess., 566-73, 760-63, 893-95, 908, 2,457, 2,798-2,801, 2,931-35, 3,350, 3,527; *Commonwealth*, Apr. 22, 1864.

23 *Liberator*, Dec. 9, 1864; *Independent*, Feb. 9, 1865; Bentley, *Freedmen's Bureau*, 46-49; *Cong. Globe*, 38 Cong., 2 Sess., 563-66, 766-68, 983-90, 1,348, 1,402; *U.S. Statutes at Large*, XIII, 507-09.

24 Martin Conway to Garrison, Jan. 1, 1864, J. S. Griffing to Garrison, Mar. 24, 1864, Garrison Papers, BPL; James Birney to S. P. Chase, Jan. 25, 1864, Chase Papers, LC; John Andrew to S. H. Gay, Feb. 16, 1864, Gay Papers, CU; *Liberator*, Jan. 29, 1864; *N.A.S. Standard*, Mar. 11, 1865; *Commonwealth*, Mar. 18, 1865.

assistant commissioners had been antislavery sympathizers before the war. General Rufus Saxton, assistant commissioner for South Carolina, had been raised by an abolitionist father and had associated with abolitionists during much of his life.[25]

Abolitionists played a major role in the formation of the Freedmen's Bureau. It is probable that some kind of a bureau would have been established without abolitionist urging, but much of the credit for the liberal features of the Freedmen's Bureau bill must go to the abolitionists. They were the first to call for establishment of a bureau. The Emancipation League exerted great pressure on Congress and laid some of the groundwork for a bureau with its questionnaire of 1862. The abolitionist-dominated freedmen's aid societies paved the way for inclusion of education as one of the main objectives of the Bureau. J. Miller McKim fathered the establishment of the Freedmen's Inquiry Commission which in turn formulated the basic principles of the Freedmen's Bureau bill. Abolitionist Samuel Gridley Howe served on that Commission. The opposition of the Commission and of abolitionists to any sort of apprenticeship or guardianship for the freedmen helped prepare the way for the Bureau's treatment of freedmen as free men. Abolitionists could be justly proud of their part in the creation of the Freedmen's Bureau.

[25] Stanton et al., *History of Woman Suffrage*, II, 33-39; Henry Lee Swint, *The Northern Teacher in the South, 1862-1870* (Nashville, 1941), 6, 143; Reuben Tomlinson to J. M. McKim, May 14, 1869, McKim Papers, Cornell; T. W. Higginson to Louisa Higginson, June 22, 1863, Rufus Saxton to Higginson, Dec. 13, 1905, Higginson Papers, HU.

T HE enlistment of Negro troops in the Union Army beginning in late 1862 was one of the most revolutionary features of the Civil War. Colored men had fought in the American Army during the Revolution, and New Orleans Negroes had helped Andrew Jackson defend the city against the British in 1815, but since 1792 Negroes had been barred by federal law from the state militias and there were no Negroes in the regular United States Army. In 1859 the Massachusetts legislature passed a bill repealing the ban on Negro militia service. But Governor Nathaniel Banks vetoed the measure because it conflicted with the federal law of 1792. Public opinion in 1860, except perhaps in a few of the New England states, was overwhelmingly opposed to allowing Negroes in the militia or the army.[1]

With the outbreak of war in 1861 many Negroes and abolitionists believed the national emergency would compel the North to waive its prejudices and accept regiments of Negro volunteers. Frederick Douglass and other abolitionists urged Negroes in northern cities to form militia companies. Within 36 hours of Lincoln's first call for troops, Boston Negroes met and resolved to organize militia units. Philadelphia Negroes began to recruit two regiments. Colored men in New York began drilling in a privately hired hall. In many parts of the North free Negroes were prepared to join the army if the government would accept them.[2] The Negro knew that if he demonstrated his patriotism, manhood, and courage on the battlefields of the Union, the nation would be morally obligated to grant him citizenship and equal rights. As Frederick Douglass put it: "Once let the black man get upon his person the brass letters, *U.S.*; let him get an eagle on his button, and a musket on his shoulder and bullets in his pocket, and there is no power on earth which can deny that he has earned the right to citizenship in the United States."[3]

[1] Francis W. Bird, *Review of Gov. Banks' Veto of the Revised Code, on Account of its Authorizing the Enrollment of Colored Citizens in the Militia* (Boston, 1860).

[2] Benjamin Quarles, *The Negro in the Civil War* (Boston, 1953), 24–29; Dudley Taylor Cornish, *The Sable Arm: Negro Troops in the Union Army, 1861-65* (New York, 1956), 2-3, 6-7; *Liberator*, May 3, 10, 17, 1861.

[3] *Douglass' Monthly*, Aug. 1863.

But the North was not ready in 1861 to let Negroes help save the nation. "We don't want to fight side and side with the nigger," wrote Corporal Felix Brannigan of the New York 74th. "We think we are a too superior race for that." In April Secretary of War Cameron informed a Negro who had offered 300 colored volunteers to help defend the capital that "this Department has no intention at present to call into the service of the Government any colored soldiers."[4]

Abolitionists reacted with predictable wrath to the government's refusal to employ Negro troops. "What upon earth is the matter with the American Government and people?" asked Frederick Douglass in an angry editorial entitled "Fighting Rebels with only One Hand." The government screamed "Men, men! send us men," but refused to accept the services of Negroes. "Why does the Government reject the negro? Is he not a man? Can he not wield a sword, fire a gun, march and countermarch, and obey orders like any other? . . . This is no time to fight only with your white hand, and allow your black hand to remain tied."[5] Abolitionists extolled the courage of the black man in the war for independence and the War of 1812. They quoted Andrew Jackson's praise of the New Orleans Negroes who had helped defeat the British in 1815.[6] "Colored men were good enough to fight under Washington, but they are not good enough to fight under McClellan," said Douglass sarcastically. "They were good enough to help win American independence, but they are not good enough to help preserve that independence against treason and rebellion."[7]

After the northern defeat at Bull Run many Republicans began to reconsider their belief that white men alone could quickly crush the rebellion. Republican congressmen privately urged the arm-

[4] Brannigan quoted in Quarles, *Negro in the Civil War*, 31; the exchange of letters between the Negro volunteer and Cameron is in *O.R.*, Ser. 3, vol. i, 107, 133.

[5] *Douglass' Monthly*, Sept. 1861.

[6] In the fall of 1861 the American Anti-Slavery Society published a pamphlet entitled *Loyalty and Devotion of Colored Americans* (Boston, 1861), detailing the services of Negro soldiers in the Revolution and the War of 1812 and urging the government once again to call black men to the colors to help preserve freedom and Union. For other examples of abolitionist efforts in behalf of the enrollment of Negro soldiers, see John Jay to Sumner, June 19, July 25, 28, 1861, Sumner Papers, hu; *New York Tribune*, July 7, Aug. 8, 1861; *N.A.S. Standard*, May 25, 1861; *Liberator*, Aug. 9, Oct. 18, Nov. 22, Dec. 13, 20, 1861.

[7] Speech by Douglass in New York, Feb. 12, 1862, in *New York Tribune*, Feb. 13.

ing of freed slaves. Republican newspapers began cautiously to broach the proposition in the fall of 1861.[8] At the outbreak of the war Elizur Wright had written several editorials urging the employment of Negro soldiers and had sent them to the *New York Tribune*. They were not printed. But at the end of 1861 when the *Tribune* committed itself to a policy of Negro troops, Wright's editorials, altered slightly to bring them up to date, began appearing in its columns.[9]

More and more northerners were becoming receptive to the idea of Negro soldiers. In a November speech to Colonel John Cochrane's regiment near Washington, Secretary of War Cameron openly advocated the arming of freed slaves as a military necessity. Colonel Cochrane, a nephew of Gerrit Smith and a War Democrat, made a series of speeches in late 1861 urging the use of Negro troops. Conservatives threw up their hands in horror at these suggestions. "Putting arms into the slaves' hands!" exclaimed the *New York Express*. "If this be attempted to any extent, the whole world will cry out against our inhumanity, our savagery, and the sympathies of all mankind will be turned against us." The *New York Journal of Commerce* charged that Cameron and Cochrane had taken "a desperate plunge into the embrace of the Garrison and Phillips party."[10]

Cameron was not disturbed by these cries of alarm. In his annual report to Congress in December he recommended the freeing and arming of slaves of rebels coming into the Union lines. He released the report to the press before Lincoln had read it. The angry president ordered him to recall the report and delete the offending section, but the press and public had already seen the original report. Abolitionists welcomed Cameron's recommendation as the "straightforward and common sense view of the subject." The government would be foolish not to use every resource at its command to win the war. But Lincoln, ever-solicitous of conservative border-state and northern opinion, refused to take this view of the subject.[11]

[8] T. Harry Williams, *Lincoln and the Radicals* (Madison, Wis., 1941), 33; *New York Evening Post*, quoted by *Liberator*, Nov. 8, 1861; *New York Tribune*, Dec. 4, 13, 1861, Jan. 30, 1862.

[9] Wright to Whitelaw Reid, Jan. 30, 1873, Reid Papers, LC.

[10] Cornish, *Sable Arm*, 22; *New York Express* and *New York Journal of Commerce*, quoted by *N.A.S. Standard*, Nov. 30, 1861.

[11] Williams, *Lincoln and the Radicals*, 59; *Liberator*, Dec. 13, 1861.

General Thomas W. Sherman, commander of the Union forces occupying the South Carolina sea islands, had been authorized by Cameron to arm the slaves there "if special circumstances seem to require it." Sherman was opposed to the idea of Negro soldiers, however, and did nothing in the direction of arming slaves. His successor, General David Hunter, was an antislavery sympathizer and decided in May 1862, to organize a Negro regiment on the islands. Most of the Gideonites on the islands were less convinced than their northern abolitionist brethren of the courage and martial ardor of freed slaves. William Gannett wrote in May 1862, that "Negroes—plantation negroes, at least—will never make soldiers in one generation. Five white men could put a regiment to flight."[12] Events seemed to bear out the Gideonites' skepticism, for few freedmen volunteered and Hunter was compelled to order a draft to fill up his regiment. This was a serious mistake. Squads of white soldiers marched into the cotton fields and dragged freedmen off to headquarters, often without explanation. The Negroes began to fear that their old masters' tales about Yankee plans to sell them to Cuba were true after all. They hid in swamps and woods to escape the draft, but were rounded up and driven to General Hunter's headquarters at bayonet point. Teachers and labor superintendents were appalled by Hunter's brutal and ill-advised tactics. The draft was destroying much of the freedmen's confidence in Yankees which had been laboriously built up by the Gideonites. Edward L. Pierce sent strong protests against the draft to Hunter and Chase. Hunter finally filled up his regiment, the first slave regiment to be recruited in the Civil War, but at the cost of sowing no little distrust among the freedmen.[13]

Hunter faced other difficulties as well. Democrats and conservatives in Congress attacked his efforts to arm the freedmen. The Lincoln administration refused to sustain him. The general's repeated requests for uniforms, pay for the soldiers, and authorization for his regiment went unanswered. The government was not yet prepared to commit itself to the arming of Negroes.

[12] Elizabeth Pearson, ed., *Letters from Port Royal* (Boston, 1906), 43.

[13] Cornish, *Sable Arm*, 33-40; Willie Rose, "Rehearsal for Reconstruction: The Port Royal Experiment," Ph.D. dissertation, Johns Hopkins University, 1962, 186-92; Rupert S. Holland, ed., *Letters and Diary of Laura M. Towne, Written from the Sea Islands of South Carolina, 1862-84* (Cambridge, Mass., 1912), 41-54.

Hunter gave up in August 1862, and disbanded all but one company of his regiment. The first attempt to arm the freedmen was an utter failure.[14]

Antislavery Union generals in Kansas and Louisiana also made limited efforts in 1862 to enroll Negro soldiers, but they were not sustained by the administration. In the summer of 1862, however, McClellan's soldiers were bogged down before Richmond and finally driven back by Lee after severe fighting. The defeat was a sharp blow to northern morale. Early in July Lincoln issued a call for 300,000 volunteers, but war-weariness was beginning to creep over the North and few men came forward to join the colors. Public opinion was becoming more favorable to the use of Negro troops to supplement declining white manpower. On July 17, 1862, Congress passed two acts authorizing the president to enlist Negroes as soldiers. The first was the Confiscation Act, which empowered Lincoln to "employ as many persons of African descent as he may deem necessary and proper for the suppression of this rebellion." The second was a militia act repealing the provisions of the 1792 law barring Negroes, and providing for the employment of free Negroes and freedmen as soldiers. Abolitionists applauded these acts and urged President Lincoln to begin immediately to recruit a Negro army from every section of the nation.[15]

But Lincoln was not yet prepared to arm the black man. On August 4 an Indiana delegation offered the government two regiments of colored men from their state, but the president declined the offer. The nation "could not afford to lose Kentucky at this crisis," said Lincoln. "To arm the negroes would turn 50,000 bayonets from the loyal Border States against us that were for us." In vain did abolitionists point out that arming the Negroes would bring many times 50,000 bayonets to the aid of the Union. Lincoln was still solicitous of conservative opinion, and conservatives applauded his speech to the Indiana delegation.[16]

[14] Cornish, *Sable Arm*, 40-53.

[15] Edward L. Pierce, *Memoir and Letters of Charles Sumner* (4 vols., Boston, 1877-94), IV, 112; *U.S. Statutes at Large*, XII, 589-92; *Liberator*, Aug. 8, Sept. 5, 12, 1862.

[16] Roy P. Basler, ed., *The Collected Works of Abraham Lincoln* (9 vols., New Brunswick, N. J., 1955), V, 356-57; *New York Times*, quoted by *New York Tribune*, Aug. 16, 1862.

Yet in the next three weeks the president's opinion on the issue of Negro troops evidently underwent a change, for on August 25 Secretary of War Stanton authorized General Rufus Saxton, military governor of the South Carolina sea islands, to raise five regiments of black soldiers on the islands. Pressure from Republicans and abolitionists, declining white manpower, continuing lack of success of Union arms, and increasing sentiment in the army itself favoring the use of Negro troops were important factors in Lincoln's change of mind. On the sea islands most of the Gideonites had overcome their earlier skepticism about the possibility of making soldiers out of freedmen. Instead of instituting the hated draft, General Saxton relied on volunteers, using the one remaining company of General Hunter's abortive regiment as a nucleus. The Gideonites cooperated enthusiastically, urging the freedmen to enlist to fight for their own freedom and to prove the manhood of their race. Volunteers came forward slowly at first, but by November 7 the regiment was filling up rapidly and was mustered in as the First South Carolina Volunteers. It was the first Negro regiment of the Civil War officially authorized by Washington.[17]

Saxton began looking for the right man to command the regiment. He knew that the eyes of the nation would be focused on this experiment, and he wanted nothing to go wrong. The colonel of the regiment must be fully sympathetic with the experiment, intelligent and flexible but at the same time a strict disciplinarian. J. H. Fowler, a Massachusetts abolitionist serving as chaplain on the sea islands, recommended Thomas Wentworth Higginson as the best man for the job. Several other Gideonites seconded the recommendation. Saxton knew Higginson by reputation, and on November 5 he sent him an official invitation to become colonel of the First South Carolina Volunteers.[18]

Higginson was a true nineteenth century intellectual, a scholar and author imbued with romantic zeal. A leading contributor to the *Atlantic Monthly*, he was also one of New England's most militant abolitionists. He was excited by the prospect of com-

[17] Cornish, *Sable Arm*, 53-55, 80-84, 92-93; *O.R.*, Ser. 1, vol. xiv, 377-78; Rose, "Rehearsal for Reconstruction," 247-51; Holland, *Letters and Diary of Laura Towne*, 86, 93.

[18] Saxton to Higginson, Nov. 5, 1862, Fowler to Higginson, Nov. 10, 1862, Higginson Papers, HU.

manding the first regiment of black men officially mustered into the Union Army. He told the publisher of the *Atlantic Monthly* that he would rather command such a regiment "than anything else in the world."[19] A trip to the sea islands convinced him that the government intended to carry through the enterprise in good faith, and he accepted the colonelcy of the regiment on the spot. "Will not Uncle Wentworth be in bliss!" exclaimed his young niece. "A thousand men, every one as black as coal."[20]

Higginson fully realized the importance of his undertaking. "The first man who organizes and commands a successful black regiment will perform the most important service in the history of the war," he wrote in his journal the day before he assumed his new duties. Chaplain Fowler had observed that "the success or failure of this reg[iment] is to be a most important fact in the solution of this whole Negro question." In May 1863, after his soldiers had proved themselves in several minor battles, Higginson wrote that "there is no doubt that for many months the fate of the whole movement for colored soldiers rested on the behavior of this one regiment. A mutiny, an extensive desertion, an act of severe discipline, a Bull Run panic, a simple defeat, might have blasted the whole movement for arming the blacks." Higginson reported that he had been informed by Secretary Chase that "the Cabinet at Washington kept their whole action in regard to enlisting colored troops waiting to hear from us in Florida, and when the capture of Jacksonville was known [two Negro regiments under Higginson captured Jacksonville in March 1863], the whole question was regarded as settled, the policy avowed."[21]

The performance of Higginson's men was not quite so crucial to the whole policy of Negro soldiers as he pictured it, but it was nevertheless important. After two months of intensive drilling Higginson took his troops on several minor raids into the interior to capture supplies and lumber and to run off slaves. Whenever his men encountered Confederate soldiers they fought

[19] Higginson to James T. Fields, Nov. 17, 1862, A. W. Anthony autograph MS Collection, NYPL.
[20] Higginson to Louisa Higginson, Nov. 16, 1862, Higginson Papers, HU; Higginson's niece quoted in Mary Higginson, *Thomas Wentworth Higginson* (Boston, 1914), 215.
[21] Higginson, Journal, entry of Nov. 23, 1862, J. H. Fowler to Higginson, Nov. 10, 1862, Higginson to Louisa Higginson, May 18, 1863, Higginson Papers, HU.

well, holding their own or besting the rebels. Higginson sent an enthusiastic report of his first expedition to the secretary of war, which found its way into the newspapers. "Nobody knows anything about these men who has not seen them in battle," wrote Higginson. "There is fiery energy beyond anything of which I have read, unless it be the French Zouaves. . . . It would have been madness to attempt with the bravest white troops what I have accomplished with the black ones. . . . No officer in this regiment now doubts that the key to the successful prosecution of the war lies in the unlimited employment of black troops."[22]

The *New York Tribune* prominently featured this report and commented editorially: "It will not need many such reports as this—and there have been several before it—to shake our inveterate Saxon prejudice against the capacity and courage of negro troops." A *New York Times* reporter on the sea islands was even more exuberant. "Our colored troops are more than a match for any equal number of white rebels which can be brought against them," he wrote to his paper, and the *Times*, which had once opposed the use of Negro troops, printed his dispatch happily.[23]

Higginson insisted that the white officers of his regiment treat the Negro soldiers as men. He prohibited the officers from inflicting "degrading punishments" on the troops and from calling them "insulting epithets." He banned the use of the word "nigger" and threatened severe punishment of any officer who uttered it. He inspired respect in his officers and confidence and self-respect in his men.[24] At first most white soldiers sneered or grumbled at the prospect of freed slaves serving in the same army as they. But by the spring of 1863 Higginson's soldiers had won a grudging if not always generous respect from the white troops. Higginson reported that while reviewing a dress parade of his regiment he overheard a white soldier behind him say: "By——, to think of my living to see a nigger regiment drill better than the 104th Pennsylvania." After Higginson's regiment had relieved the 55th Pennsylvania on picket duty one day, Edward L. Pierce asked a private of the 55th: "Isn't this rather new, to be relieved by a negro regiment?" "All right," answered the white soldier.

22 *O.R.*, Ser. 1, vol. xiv, 194-98.
23 *New York Tribune*, Feb. 11, 1863; *New York Times*, Feb. 10, 1863.
24 Cornish, *Sable Arm*, 88-89; Mary Higginson, *Higginson*, 216-18.

"They've as much right to fight for themselves as I have to fight for them."[25]

While serving as colonel of the First South Carolina Volunteers, Higginson kept a journal in which he recorded his observations and experiences. This journal formed the basis of a subsequent series of articles published from 1864 to 1867 in the *Atlantic Monthly*. These articles in turn formed the basis of a book published in 1869 under the title *Army Life in a Black Regiment*, surely one of the true classics of Civil War literature, and according to Howard Mumford Jones "one of the few classics of military life in the national letters."[26]

Higginson's comments in his journal and in his published writings on the character of the freedmen and their adaptability to military life are especially interesting. He found the freedmen equal in courage and superior in enthusiasm to white troops. They took more readily to drill than whites because their plantation background had made them amenable to discipline. They made better over-all soldiers than whites, thought Higginson, because of their "Indian-like knowledge of the country and its ways" and their grim comprehension that they were fighting for the freedom of themselves and their race.[27]

Higginson described the freedmen on the islands as "a simple and loveable people, whose graces seem to come by nature and whose vices by training." He conceded that "they are not truthful, honest, or chaste," but asked, in view of their past training, "why should they be?"[28] His observations dispelled one stereotype of the Negro. Several of the white officers had their wives in camp, and the white women were never molested or annoyed in any way by the black troops. These women, wrote Higginson, "declared that they would not have moved about with anything like the same freedom in any white camp they had ever entered and it

[25] Higginson to Louisa Higginson, June 20, 1863, Higginson Papers, HU; Edward L. Pierce, "The Freedmen at Port Royal," *Atlantic Monthly*, XII (Sept. 1863), 313.

[26] T. W. Higginson, *Army Life in a Black Regiment*, with an introduction by Howard Mumford Jones (Lansing, Mich., 1960 [1869]), xi.

[27] Higginson, Journal, entries of Nov. 27, Dec. 1, 3, 1862, Jan. 12, 13, 1863, Higginson to Louisa Higginson, Dec. 10, 22, 1862, Feb. 24, June 20, 1863, Higginson Papers, HU; Higginson, *Army Life*, 42, 190-94.

[28] Higginson, Journal, entries of Nov. 27, Dec. 1, 3, 1862, Higginson Papers, HU.

The Battle at Milliken's Bend. T. R. Davis in *Harper's Weekly*

always aroused their indignation to hear the negro race called brutal or depraved."[29]

Higginson tended to fall into the same attitude of benevolent paternalism toward the freedmen which overtook several of the Gideonites. "They seem the world's perpetual children, docile & gay & loveable, in the midst of this war for freedom upon which they have intelligently entered," he wrote. "I think it is partly from my own notorious love of children that I like these people so well."[30] But Higginson realized the dangers inherent in excessive paternalism and consciously strove to avoid them. "It saves a great deal of trouble, while it lasts, this childlike confidence," he wrote of his troops; "nevertheless, it is our business to educate them to manhood, and I see as yet no obstacle." Even so, Higginson viewed the transition of the freedmen from childhood to manhood with mixed emotions. "In every way I see the gradual change in them, sometimes with a sigh as parents watch their children growing up and miss the droll speeches and the confiding ignorance of children," he wrote near the end of his tour of duty on the islands. "Sometimes it comes over me with a pang that they are growing more like white men, less naive and less grotesque."[31]

✦

More than any other northern governor, John Andrew of Massachusetts favored the employment of Negro troops. In January 1863, Andrew finally obtained authorization from Stanton to recruit a Negro regiment in his state. Stanton said, however, that all commissioned officers must be white men. Andrew wanted to grant a few lieutenancies to qualified Negroes and give them opportunities for promotion, but Stanton and Lincoln feared the reaction of the northern people if black men became officers. The enlistment of Negro privates was a great leap forward, they said, and public opinion must be allowed to digest this advance before making a further one. Andrew reluctantly agreed, but obtained a promise from Stanton that in all matters relating to pay, status, and treatment his Negro regiment would be equal to other Union regiments.[32]

[29] Higginson, *Army Life*, 197.

[30] Higginson, Journal, Dec. 16, 26, 1862, Higginson Papers, HU.

[31] Higginson, Journal, entries of Dec. 21, 1862, Feb. 11, 1864, Higginson Papers, HU.

[32] Henry G. Pearson, *The Life of John A. Andrew* (2 vols., Boston, 1904), II, 71-74.

Andrew wanted the new regiment to be the grandest achievement of his governorship, and he took great care in selecting its
officers. "I am desirous to have for its officers, particularly its
field officers, young men of military experience, of firm anti-
Slavery principles," wrote Andrew to his friend, abolitionist
Francis G. Shaw of New York. "I shall look for [such officers]
in those circles of educated Anti-Slavery Society, which next to
the colored race itself have the greatest interest in the success of
this experiment."[33] Andrew invited Shaw's son Robert to become
colonel of the 54th Massachusetts Volunteers. After some initial
hesitation, Robert Gould Shaw accepted. A Harvard graduate,
young Shaw was then a captain in the Second Massachusetts
Infantry with considerable combat experience. For lieutenant
colonel, Andrew selected Norwood P. Hallowell, member of a
well-known abolitionist family. Most of the rest of the officers
were abolitionists, some of them having been frequent visitors at
the Garrison home in prewar days.[34]

The next problem was recruitment of men for the regiment.
Negroes were much less eager to flock to the colors now than they
had been at the outbreak of the war when the North did not want
them. There were several reasons for this. In the first place,
the booming war economy had created full employment and
prosperity for Negroes in many parts of the North. A white
Bostonian wrote in February 1863, that "the blacks here are
too comfortable to do anything more than talk about freedom."[35]
In the second place, despite Stanton's promises to Andrew there
were disturbing rumors that Negro volunteers would receive
less pay than white soldiers. Thirdly, and perhaps most important, intelligent and educated northern Negroes deeply resented the ineligibility of black men to become officers in the new
regiments.

Abolitionists and radical Republicans sympathized with the
complaints of northern Negroes. If the experiment of arming
Negroes was to be "hedged about by every restriction or annoy-

[33] Andrew to Francis G. Shaw, Jan. 30, 1863, in Pearson, *Andrew*, II, 74-76.
[34] Lawrence Lader, *The Bold Brahmins: New England's War Against Slavery,
1831-1863* (New York, 1961), 279-83; Wendell P. Garrison and Francis J. Garrison,
William Lloyd Garrison (4 vols., Boston, 1885-89), IV, 79.
[35] Charles Russell Lowell to his mother, Feb. 4, 1863, in Edward W. Emerson,
Life and Letters of Charles Russell Lowell (Boston, 1907), 233-34.

ance," wrote Sydney Gay in the *New York Tribune*, "if they are to have inferior pay, privileges and consideration, to other soldiers —if they are forewarned that they can never win promotion or commendation, . . . we presume all they will do is of small account. Spartans would not volunteer to fight in defiance of such indignities."[36] Garrisonian abolitionists passed resolutions protesting the exclusion of Negroes from officer's rank, "believing that it serves to retard enlistment, to perpetuate an unnatural caste, and to stifle high and honorable aspiration in the mind of the common soldier." The Church Anti-Slavery Society urged the government to give Negro troops "an open field and a fair chance, and let the colored soldier fight on equal terms with the white soldier."[37]

While striving to remove injustices in the treatment of Negro troops, abolitionists nevertheless urged colored men to join the army no matter what the terms. If they fought well they would win equal rights and promotion for themselves; if they refused to enlist, they would only confirm the stereotype of the cowardly, incompetent Negro. "Every race has fought for Liberty and its own progress," Governor Andrew told Massachusetts Negroes. "If Southern slavery should fall by the crushing of the Rebellion, and colored men should have no hand and play no conspicuous part in the task, the result would leave the colored man a mere helot." Speaking to a group of New York City Negroes, George Stearns said, "This is the time God has given your race to conquer its freedom from Northern prejudice and Southern pride and avarice." "You must fight or be slaves," Stearns told the Negroes. "You must fight . . . to obtain a right to fight on terms of equality. . . . It is the duty as well as the privilege of the black man to fight without standing on terms. . . . If he refuses to fight or turns his back on the enemy his doom is sealed for this generation." In March 1863, Frederick Douglass published a stirring broadside entitled *Men of Color, To Arms!* "Liberty won by white men would lack half its lustre. Who would be free themselves must strike the blow," proclaimed Douglass. "The chance is now

36 *New York Tribune*, Mar. 4, 1863.

37 *N.A.S. Standard*, Mar. 7, 1863; *Liberator*, June 5, 1863; copy of resolutions adopted by the Church Anti-Slavery Society on May 25, 1863, in the Cheever Papers, AAS.

given you to end in a day the bondage of centuries, and to rise in one bound from social degradation to the plane of common equality with all other varieties of men. . . . Action! action! not criticism, is the plain duty of this hour."[38]

Recruiting proceeded slowly at first. Massachusetts' small Negro population filled less than two companies. Governor Andrew called on abolitionist George L. Stearns, a wealthy lead-pipe manufacturer and a leading advocate of Negro troops, to form a committee of "prominent citizens" to recruit soldiers for the Massachusetts 54th from all over the North. The legislature appropriated funds for bounties and transportation of recruits to Massachusetts. Stearns went to Buffalo to organize a central recruiting office. He hired prominent Negro abolitionists such as Douglass, William Wells Brown, Charles L. Remond, John Mercer Langston, Henry Highland Garnet, and Martin Delany as recruiting agents. Whenever the funds subscribed by the committee and the legislature ran short, Stearns dipped into his own pocket. His agents crisscrossed the North, making speeches and urging Negroes to join up. Frederick Douglass was extremely active, and his own sons were the first recruits from New York. By the end of April recruits were coming in at the rate of 30 to 40 per day, and Andrew soon had enough men to form a second Negro regiment, the 55th Massachusetts.[39]

There had been much sneering among conservative Bostonians at the idea of a Negro regiment. But as the men of the 54th began drilling at Readville, near Boston, curiosity gradually overcame prejudice and thousands of Bostonians went out to the camp to watch. Many of them came away with changed opinions after witnessing this fine-looking set of colored men march, drill, and shoot with a skill and élan equal to that of most white regi-

[38] Pearson, *Andrew*, II, 69-70; Stearns quoted in *Commonwealth,* May 22, 1863; Frederick Douglass, *Men of Color, To Arms!*

[39] Frank P. Stearns, *The Life and Public Services of George Luther Stearns* (Philadelphia, 1907), 286-92; Pearson, *Andrew*, II, 81-84; Benjamin Quarles, *Frederick Douglass* (Washington, 1948), 204-08; George Stearns to Gerrit Smith, Feb. 15, Mar. 13, 1863, Smith Papers, su; John Andrew to Gerrit Smith, Feb. 17, 1863, Smith Papers, NYPL; Gerrit Smith to Frederick Douglass, Mar. 10, 1863, Stearns to Douglass, Mar. 24, 1863, Douglass Papers, Anacostia. Garrison's oldest son, George, joined the 55th as a lieutenant, abandoning his father's non-resistance teachings to take an active part in the war. Garrison reluctantly acquiesced in his son's decision. William L. Garrison, Jr., to Ellen Wright, May 26, 1863, Garrison Papers, sc.

ments. Abolitionists visited the camp nearly every day. The New England Freedmen's Aid Society sent tobacco, stoves, and other items to the men and dispatched a corps of teachers to instruct those soldiers who were illiterate. In May Governor Andrew presented the colors to Colonel Shaw in an impressive ceremony at Readville. "I know not, Mr. Commander, when, in all human history, to any given thousand men in arms there has been committed a work at once so proud, so precious, so full of hope and glory as the work committed to you," Andrew told Shaw. "I stand or fall, as a man and a magistrate, with the rise or fall in history of the Fifty-Fourth Massachusetts Regiment."[40]

At the end of May the regiment marched in review through Boston on its way to embark for South Carolina. Twenty thousand eager spectators lined the streets to watch a Negro regiment march along the same route taken by Anthony Burns in his return to bondage nine years earlier. Thousands cheered as the regimental band played the John Brown song and the troops swung smartly through Boston Common. No other Massachusetts regiment had received such a send-off. Abolitionist leaders gathered in Wendell Phillips' house on Essex Street to view the parade. As the troops passed the house Garrison stood on the balcony, his hand resting on a marble bust of John Brown. Colonel Shaw paused briefly as he passed the veteran abolitionist, and several officers lifted their hats as the troops marched by. It was a symbolic and memorable day in the history of the Negro's struggle for freedom, and those abolitionists who watched the parade of the 54th through Boston never forgot the scene.[41]

✦

Andrew's success in raising two regiments of colored troops encouraged other northern governors to take similar steps to help fill their state troop quotas. In 1862 John Mercer Langston, Ohio Negro abolitionist, had suggested to Governor David Tod a project to raise colored volunteers to be credited against Ohio's quota. Langston was coolly shown out of the governor's office with the words, "Do you not know, Mr. Langston, that this is a *white man's* government; that white men are able to defend and

---

[40] Garrison and Garrison, *Garrison*, IV, 79; Ednah Bow Cheney, *Reminiscences* (Boston, 1902), 83-84; Pearson, *Andrew*, II, 87-89.
[41] *Liberator*, June 5, 12, 1863.

protect it? . . . When we want you colored men we will notify you."
By June 1863, Tod had changed his mind. He notified Langston
and gave him authority to enlist Negro soldiers. Using his experience gained as a recruiting agent under Stearns, Langston
completed the enlistment of a regiment of Ohio Negroes by
November. Professor G. W. Shurtliff of Oberlin, an abolitionist,
was selected as colonel of the regiment.[42]

Martin Delany helped recruit colored soldiers for Rhode
Island, Connecticut, and Ohio. In Philadelphia, J. Miller McKim,
a member of the Union League, started a movement within the
League to enlist Negro regiments in Pennsylvania. The committee
formed to raise these troops, according to McKim, was composed
of "the antislavery elite" of the Union League. McKim organized
a huge rally at Philadelphia's National Hall on July 6 to kick off
the drive for enlistment of Pennsylvania colored regiments. Frederick Douglass and Anna Dickinson were featured speakers at
the rally. Their eloquence helped swell the ranks of Pennsylvania's
Negro regiments. Within ten months ten regiments of Negro
troops from Pennsylvania and neighboring states were recruited
and organized.[43]

In New York City a group of abolitionists in George Cheever's
Church of the Puritans asked Lincoln for permission to recruit
10,000 Negro soldiers to march South under General Frémont
as a "Grand Army of Liberation." Many prominent New York
Republicans endorsed their request, and a delegation headed by
Cheever talked with Lincoln at the end of May 1863. The presi-
dent expressed interest in the project and promised to appoint
Frémont to a command if the 10,000 troops could be raised.
Frémont, however, was not interested in such a command.[44] The
New Yorkers went ahead anyway in their efforts to raise the
troops, applying to John Jay and the Union League for as-

[42] John M. Langston, *From the Virginia Plantation to the National Capital*
(Hartford, Conn., 1894), 205-17.

[43] Frank A. Rollin, *Life and Public Services of Martin R. Delany* (Boston,
1883), 145-53; McKim to Charles Gibbons, Feb. 12, 1863, McKim Papers, NYPL;
Charles Follen McKim to Frank Garrison, Sept. 11, 18, 1863, Charles Follen
McKim Papers, NYPL; J. M. McKim to Garrison, July 10, 1863, Sarah Pugh
to R. D. Webb, Aug. 11, 1863, Garrison Papers, BPL; *Commonwealth*, July 31,
1863; *Liberator*, July 31, 1863; *N.A.S. Standard*, June 11, 1864.

[44] *New York Tribune*, June 1, 1863; *Principia*, June 18, 1863; Basler, *Collected
Works of Lincoln*, VI, 239; Frémont to Charles Sumner, June 9, 1863, Sumner
Papers, HU.

sistance. They sought authorization from Governor Horatio Seymour to begin recruiting, but the Democratic Seymour was strongly opposed to Negro soldiers and refused to grant the desired permission. Jay and his Union League committee finally obtained permission from Stanton to recruit New York Negroes directly under national authority. The first regiment marched proudly down Broadway in March 1864, and two more followed soon afterward.[45]

In May 1863, General Banks began to organize Negro regiments in Louisiana into a *Corps d'Afrique.* B. Rush Plumly, a Philadelphia abolitionist serving as general appraiser of the Treasury Department in New Orleans, was put in charge of recruitment in the city. He resigned his position in the Treasury Department and was commissioned a major in the army. Plumly reported great success in gaining the confidence of New Orleans' colored people. "I have helped 'get up' their concerts; attended their meetings; churches, balls, parties, funerals, &c. &c. besides visiting constantly in their houses," he wrote. "A man must go among them; personally, he must *like* them. They must *believe* in him. Their instinct is as subtle as any reasoning. They want to know that their leader is fighting for the principle of Freedom, by which they are to benefit. They don't want him to fight for 'niggers.' " Plumly's son commanded one of the Negro regiments. By the end of August, Plumly had raised five regiments in New Orleans, and in the whole of Union-occupied Louisiana Banks had enrolled 12,000 black soldiers.[46]

Perhaps George Stearns' greatest contribution to the Civil

---

[45] John Jay to Sumner, Mar. 8, 1864, Sumner Papers, HU; John Jay, "The Union League Club of New York, Its Memories of the Past," speech delivered to the Union League Club on Mar. 13, 1868, in John Jay, *Slavery and the War* (New York, 1868), #21.

[46] Cornish, *Sable Arm*, 126-29; Plumly to S. P. Chase, July 4, 10, Aug. 1, 28, 1863, Chase Papers, LC; quotation from letter of July 4. In March 1863, Secretary Stanton had sent Adjutant-General Lorenzo Thomas to the Union-occupied portions of the lower Mississippi Valley to arm and equip as many freedmen as he could. A graduate of West Point and a career army officer, but no abolitionist, Thomas went about his work with an unexpected heartiness and efficiency. By the end of the war he had raised 76,000 black troops, more than 40 per cent of the entire number of Negroes who served in the Union Army. Although Thomas sometimes resorted to impressment to fill up his regiments, abolitionists were happy with the over-all effect of his work, for the large number of troops he raised helped convince the nation of the value and contribution of black soldiers. Cornish, *Sable Arm*, 110-26.

War was his work in recruiting the 54th Massachusetts, the most celebrated Negro regiment in American history. But he did not retire from the recruiting field after organizing the 54th and 55th. In May 1863, Secretary Stanton formed the Bureau of Colored Troops to facilitate the enlistment of black soldiers. At the beginning of June, Stearns went to Washington and offered to put his efficient and far-flung recruiting service at the disposal of the government. "I have heard of your recruiting bureau," Stanton told Stearns, "and I think you would be the best man to run the machine you have constructed. I will make you an Assistant Adjutant-General with the rank of Major, and I will give you authority to recruit colored regiments all over the country." Stearns accepted the job. He could draw upon the secret service funds of the War Department to finance his activities. In addition he raised $50,000 by private subscription in the North.[47]

Stearns went first to Philadelphia to help organize the enlistment of Pennsylvania Negroes. The camp where the troops were trained, located on land donated by abolitionist Edward M. Davis, was named by Stearns "Camp William Penn." "The Quakers wince," Stearns told his wife, "but I tell them it is established on peace principles; that is, to conquer a lasting peace."[48] From Philadelphia Stearns proceeded to Maryland to help General William Birney, son of the renowned abolitionist James G. Birney, recruit colored soldiers in that state. In August Stearns was ordered to Nashville, where a large body of freedmen had congregated in the rear of General William Rosecrans' army. When Stearns arrived he found the brutal practice of impressment in force, producing chaos, confusion, and distrust on the part of the freedmen. Union officers and agents of Military Governor Andrew Johnson were indiscriminately drafting Negroes for heavy labor, placing them in filthy compounds, and neglecting to pay them wages. Stearns was appalled by the situation and immediately sent a protest to Stanton.[49]

Secretary Stanton did not give much support to Stearns' efforts

[47] Stearns, *Stearns*, 295-96; *O.R.*, Ser. 3, vol. III, 374, 676, 682-85.

[48] Stearns, *Stearns*, 301-302; quotation from p. 302. See also Sarah Pugh to R. D. Webb, Aug. 11, 1863, Garrison Papers, BPL.

[49] Stearns, *Stearns*, 307-308; *N.A.S. Standard*, Sept. 5, 1863; *O.R.*, Ser. 3, vol. III, 676-77, 840.

to put an end to such practices. But with his personal tact, charm, good sense, and exceptional administrative talents Stearns set about to bring order out of chaos. His first task was to win suspicious Tennesseans to support a policy of humane treatment, prompt payment, education, and enlistment rather than impressment of the freedmen. Two of his agents spent their full time holding public meetings, explaining Stearns' policy and appealing to loyal Tennesseans for support. These methods were eminently successful. Within a few weeks Major Stearns had won the confidence of important Tennessee Unionists, including Governor Johnson. Stearns put an end to impressment. He sent his recruiting agents among the freedmen to hold meetings in churches, cabins, and camps. Stearns established clean and well-run contraband camps for the wives and children of recruited soldiers. He organized schools among the colored troops and their families, and through his contacts with northern freedmen's aid societies he obtained teachers and supplies for these schools.[50]

Stearns' tenure as recruiting agent in middle Tennessee produced a great change in public opinion there toward slavery and Negro soldiers. His successor wrote in October 1864, that Stearns' wise and firm actions had been primarily responsible for "causing the great revolution in public opinion, patent in the last year. Whereas some then opposed, I know of no prominent loyal Tennessean who does not now believe in, advocate, and encourage the raising of colored troops."[51] Stearns enlisted approximately seven regiments, and his successor, Captain R. D. Massey, who followed Stearns' methods, raised another thirteen. But Stearns' most important contribution was not the number of regiments he enlisted. His activities in Tennessee, according to J. Miller McKim, "augmented the power and helped to lick into shape the antislavery sentiment in that part of the country. His dozen recruiting agencies, scattered through middle Tennessee and extending into Alabama, have been a dozen anti-slavery agencies; a dozen education agencies; a dozen Freedmen's agencies; a dozen agencies for promoting Northern ideas."[52]

✦

[50] *O.R.*, Ser. 3, vol. III, 793, 816, 819-20, 823, vol. IV, 762-63, 770-74, vol. V, 120; Stearns to the Boston Committee for Recruiting Colored Soldiers, Oct. 10, 13, 1863, copies in Charles Sumner Papers, HU. See also Cornish, *Sable Arm*, 236-38.
[51] *O.R.*, Ser. 3, vol. IV, 772.
[52] *N.A.S. Standard*, Mar. 26, 1864.

On May 1, 1863, the *New York Tribune* observed that most northerners now acquiesced in the policy of arming Negroes, but that there was still considerable doubt whether they would make good soldiers. "Loyal whites have generally become willing that they should fight," declared the *Tribune*, "but the great majority have no faith that they will really do so. Many hope they will prove cowards and sneaks—others greatly fear it."[53] Abolitionists confidently predicted that Negroes would prove themselves courageous fighting men, but they nevertheless awaited the first important battle fought by Negroes with some anxiety.

Higginson's soldiers had performed well in skirmishes, but as yet no Negro troops had engaged in a major battle. In the early summer in 1863, however, Negro regiments fought courageously in two major engagements at Port Hudson and Milliken's Bend in the Mississippi Valley. The performance of colored soldiers in these battles converted many skeptics into ardent supporters of the policy of arming Negroes. Even more important was the assault of the 54th Massachusetts regiment on Fort Wagner, a Confederate outpost guarding the entrance to Charleston harbor, in July 1863. The attack was repulsed with heavy loss to the regiment, including the death of Colonel Shaw, but the heroic conduct of the 54th during the battle has become enshrined in the history of the Negro race.[54] Colonel Shaw and the men who fell with him were virtually canonized by the abolitionists and by a large segment of northern public opinion. Fort Wagner was "a holy sepulchre" to the Negro race, declared the *Anti-Slavery Standard*. The battle "made Fort Wagner such a name to the colored race as Bunker Hill had been for ninety years to the white Yankees," observed the *New York Tribune*. "Through the cannon smoke of that black night," said the *Atlantic Monthly*, "the manhood of the colored race shines before many eyes that would not see."[55] Angelina Weld asked Gerrit Smith, "Do you not rejoice & exult in all the praise that is lavished upon our brave colored troops even by Pro-slavery papers? I have no tears to shed over their graves, because I see that their heroism is working a great change in public opinion, forcing all men to see the

---

[53] *New York Tribune*, May 1, 1863.

[54] Cornish, *Sable Arm*, 142-45, 151-56.

[55] *N.A.S. Standard*, Aug. 8, 1863; *New York Tribune*, Sept. 8, 1865; *Atlantic Monthly* quoted in Lader, *Bold Brahmins*, 290.

sin & shame of enslaving such men." Mary Grew wrote, "Who asks now in doubt and derision, 'Will the negro fight?' The answer is spoken from the cannon's mouth; it is written in sunlight on flashing steel; it comes to us from . . . those graves beneath Fort Wagner's walls, which the American people will surely never forget."[56]

Perhaps the greatest tribute to the courage of black soldiers came from President Lincoln in a public letter of August 26, 1863, in which he rebuked the opponents of emancipation. "Some of the commanders of our armies in the field who have given us our most important successes, believe the emancipation policy, and the use of colored troops, constitute the heaviest blow yet dealt to the rebellion," wrote Lincoln. "You say you will not fight to free negroes. Some of them seem willing to fight for you." When the war was won "there will be some black men who can remember that, with silent tongue, and clenched teeth, and steady eye, and well-poised bayonet, they have helped mankind on to this great consummation; while, I fear, there will be some white ones, unable to forget that, with malignant heart, and deceitful speech, they have strove to hinder it."[57]

✦

Words of praise were very pleasant to the ears of Negro soldiers, but many of them would have been happier if the Union had shown its appreciation by paying them the same wages as white troops. Higginson's regiment and the 54th and 55th Massachusetts regiments had enlisted under a specific War Department promise of equal pay. But Stanton in fact had no legal authority to make such a promise. The only law applying specifically to colored soldiers was the militia act of July 17, 1862, which stated that Negroes would be paid $10 per month, $3 of which could be deducted for clothing. White privates received $13 per month *plus* a clothing allowance of $3.50. At the time the law was passed it was envisaged that Negroes in the army would serve primarily as laborers rather than soldiers. When Stanton formed the Bureau

---

[56] Angelina Weld to Gerrit Smith, July 28, 1863, Smith Papers, su; [Mary Grew], *Thirteenth Annual Report of the Philadelphia Female Anti-Slavery Society* (Phila., 1864), 17.

[57] Lincoln to James Conkling, Aug. 26, 1863, in Basler, ed., *Collected Works of Lincoln*, vi, 408-10.

of Colored Troops in May 1863, he asked the legal adviser of the War Department for a ruling on the pay of Negro soldiers. He was informed that under the law their pay would have to be $10 per month. Beginning in June 1863, all Negro soldiers were paid at this rate.[58]

Abolitionists were outraged by this inequality in pay. The Negro soldier fought the same battles, faced the same and even greater dangers than his white comrade-in-arms, but was paid only three-fifths as much as the white soldier. To abolitionists this looked like another three-fifths compromise. On August 1, 1863, Frederick Douglass addressed a public letter to George Stearns declaring his intention to resign from Stearns' recruiting agency. He had been enlisting black soldiers for five months, Douglass explained, but the government had not kept good faith with its Negro troops. "When I plead for recruits," he said, "I want to do it with all my heart, without qualification. I cannot do that now. The impression settles upon me that colored men have much overrated the enlightenment, justice and generosity of our rulers at Washington."[59]

Stearns agreed with Douglass and privately urged him to seek an interview with Lincoln to lay the colored man's grievances before the president. Douglass did so, and was shown into Lincoln's office on August 10, 1863. The president listened quietly and sympathetically to Douglass' protests against the inequality in pay and the lack of opportunity for Negroes to become commissioned officers. Lincoln replied that he appreciated the justice of Douglass' complaints, but that there was still a great deal of popular opposition in the North to the use of Negro soldiers and that discrimination in pay and promotion took the edge off some of this opposition—it was "a necessary concession to smooth the way to their employment at all as soldiers." Ultimately, Lincoln promised, Negro soldiers would receive the same pay and treatment as white troops.[60]

[58] Cornish, *Sable Arm*, 184-87; Quarles, *Negro in the Civil War*, 200; *O.R.*, Ser. 3, vol. III, 252; *U.S. Statutes at Large*, XII, 269, 599; Fred A. Shannon, *The Organization and Administration of the Union Army, 1861-1865* (2 vols., New York, 1928), I, 71-72.

[59] Douglass to Stearns, Aug. 1, 1863, in *Douglass' Monthly*, Aug. 1863.

[60] Stearns to Douglass, Aug. 8, 1863, Douglass Papers, Anacostia; Frederick Douglass, *Life and Times of Frederick Douglass* (Hartford, Conn., 1884), 301-04.

In South Carolina the men of the 54th and 55th Massachusetts regiments were angered by the news that their pay was to be only $10 per month. Deciding to meet the challenge head-on, the two regiments refused on principle to accept any pay at all until they were treated as equals. Governor Andrew sympathized with their stand and hurried to Washington to find out why Stanton's promise to his troops had been broken. He saw Lincoln, Stanton, and several other officials. All agreed that the 54th and 55th had been promised equal pay, but pointed lamely to the law of July 17, 1862, as an excuse for discrimination. Andrew was partially mollified by an administration promise to support legislation to equalize pay at the next session of Congress. He returned to Boston and called a special session of the state legislature to appropriate funds to pay the 54th and 55th the difference between their promised and actual wages. The legislature quickly passed the law, but the regiments refused again to accept any pay until Washington abolished the degrading distinction between white and colored troops. They would prefer, they stated, to serve out their enlistments without pay than to be insulted by the federal government. As Theodore Tilton expressed it, they were unwilling "that the Federal Government should throw mud upon them, even though Massachusetts stands ready to wipe it off."[61]

In his annual report of December 1863, Stanton asked Congress to enact legislation equalizing the pay of white and colored soldiers. Thaddeus Stevens immediately introduced a bill to accomplish this objective. Abolitionists expected quick congressional approval of the bill. But a considerable segment of northern opinion still opposed this elementary measure of justice. Democrats and even some Republicans reasoned that to pay Negro troopers the same wages as white soldiers would degrade the white man. The *New York World* declared that "to claim that the indolent, servile negro is the equal in courage, enterprise and fire of the foremost race in all the world is a libel upon the name of an American citizen. . . . It is unjust in every way to the white soldier to put him on a level with the black."[62]

In the face of this kind of pressure from conservatives, Con-

---

[61] Pearson, *Andrew*, ii, 99-104; Quarles, *Negro in the Civil War*, 201.

[62] *House Exec. Docs.*, no. 1, 38 Cong., 1 Sess., p. 8; *Commonwealth*, Dec. 18, 1863; *New York World*, Dec. 13, 1863.

gress dawdled and hesitated. Abolitionists and Republicans organized counterpressure to convince lawmakers of the need for speedy action. The Middlesex County (Massachusetts) Anti-Slavery Society sent Lincoln a resolution denouncing the government's policy of using Negroes "to fight its battles, die miserably in its ditches, without a dollar of bounty, on only part pay, and always under white officers, and against all hope of preferment or promotion." Antislavery meetings all over the North adopted similar resolutions demanding equal pay.[63]

Congress seemed disposed to act favorably on a bill to equalize the *future* pay of white and colored troops. "The public seems to suppose that all required justice will be done by the passage of a bill equalizing the pay of all soldiers for the future," wrote Higginson in a letter published by Gay in the *Tribune*. But this was only half the question. Several Negro regiments, including Higginson's, had enlisted with the promise of equal pay from the date of enlistment. His men had been nearly sixteen months in the service and for them the issue was not only a question of future pay but of arrears for deficiencies in past wages. Higginson declared that there was "nothing mean or mercenary" about his soldiers. If they were convinced that the government needed the money they "would serve it barefooted and on half-rations, and without a dollar—for a time." But they saw white troops all around them receiving higher pay and huge bounties for re-enlisting, and they questioned the good faith of the government. Washington's delay in rectifying its injustice, said Higginson, "has already inflicted untold suffering, has impaired discipline, has relaxed loyalty, and has begun to implant a feeling of sullen distrust in the very regiments whose early career solved the problem of the nation, created a new army, and made peaceful emancipation possible."[64]

Higginson wrote privately to prominent senators urging them to act promptly or sacrifice the good will of Negro soldiers. At Higginson's behest Sydney Gay lashed out in the *Tribune* against conservative Republican senators who were blocking passage of a

[63] Resolution adopted by the Middlesex County Anti-Slavery Society, Dec. 27, 1863, copy in Lincoln Papers, LC; *Liberator*, Jan. 29, Feb. 5, 1864.

[64] Higginson, *Army Life*, 218-21. This letter was printed in broadside form and sent to every member of Congress and to many northern newspapers.

bill to make equal pay retroactive to the date of enlistment.[65] Senator William Pitt Fessenden of Maine was a leading opponent of retroactive equal pay because he had calculated that it would cost the government an extra million and a half dollars. "Has he 'calculated' how much it will cost the country not to pass it?" asked the *Boston Commonwealth* angrily. "Has he calculated the price in infamy to the Government of this country, and to every man who votes against this bill, of denying to these colored soldiers what nobody pretends to say is not justly their due? . . . Would he dare to treat a single squad of Maine white men in this way?"[66]

Massachusetts' Senators Sumner and Wilson were leading the fight in the Senate for equal pay. Realizing that a majority of the Senate was opposed to the retroactive clause of the bill, Wilson introduced an amendment to make equal pay for all Negro regiments retroactive only to January 1, 1864. Boston abolitionists seethed with anger at Wilson's apparent concession to the forces of evil.[67] Wilson sent an indignant letter to Garrison explaining the reasons for his action. "It is not pleasant to be sharply censured by friends when one does the best he can," wrote Wilson. He stated that three-fourths of the Senate was opposed to full retroactive equal pay, and he had moved to make such pay retroactive to January 1 in order to salvage at least part of the retroactive feature. "I had caucussed the Senate and secured a majority and we all felt here that the friends of the colored soldiers had won a great victory," Wilson told Garrison. "Judge then of my amazement when I learned that our friends at home were censuring me." Abolitionists accepted Wilson's explanation and the *Commonwealth* publicly retracted its criticism of the senator. Abolitionists turned their wrath instead on Fessenden and other conservatives who had forced the compromise. "Our Senators [Wilson and Sumner] managed the case of the wronged soldiers with great ability and tact," declared the *Commonwealth*, "but

[65] Higginson to William P. Fessenden, Feb. 13, 1864, Higginson Papers, NYHS; Higginson to S. H. Gay, Feb. 13, 1864, Gay Papers, CU; *New York Tribune*, Jan. 14, 20, Feb. 5, 11, 1864. See also Higginson to the *New York Times*, Feb. 14, 1864, in the *Times*, Feb. 21, 1864.
[66] *Commonwealth*, Feb. 12, 1864.
[67] *ibid.*, Feb. 19, 1864.

were overborne by bigotry, jealousy and copperheadism. And so, this simple act of justice is postponed."[68]

Discontent and even mutiny were mounting among Negro troops who were becoming impatient with Congress's failure to grant them equal pay. Sergeant William Walker of the Third South Carolina Volunteers marched his company to his captain's tent and ordered them to stack arms and resign from an army that broke its contract with them. Walker was court-martialed and shot for mutiny. Edward N. Hallowell, who had succeeded Robert Shaw as colonel of the 54th Massachusetts, reported a desperate situation in his regiment. "I do not wish to continue to keep the men in a condition worse than slavery," wrote Hallowell angrily. His regiment was in a state of near rebellion because they refused to accept unequal pay and hence had received no pay at all for nearly a year. "I believe them to be entirely right, morally, and yet military necessity has compelled me to shoot two of them," declared Hallowell. "We are willing to give our lives to the country, but it is too much to sacrifice our honor & self respect."[69]

On June 15, 1864, Congress finally enacted legislation granting equal pay to Negro soldiers. The law was made retroactive to January 1, 1864, for all Negro soldiers, and retroactive to the time of enlistment for those Negroes who had been free men on April 19, 1861.[70] Justice had been meted out to colored soldiers—but belated and partial justice. Frank Sanborn denounced the discrimination in retroactive pay between free Negroes and freedmen as a travesty on justice, an admission of the legality of property in man. It "divides the colored soldiers into two grades" and "does honor to injustice with a vengeance." It conceded to the Confederacy much of what it was fighting for. "The Government says to the rebels—'Some of these men are free; some of them were once *your slaves*. *We* discriminate between the two grades; what do you intend to do about it?' Let Fort Pil-

[68] Wilson to Garrison, Feb. 22, 1864, Garrison Papers, BPL; *Commonwealth*, Feb. 26, 1864.
[69] Higginson, *Army Life*, 218; E. N. Hallowell to Sumner, June 30, 1864, Henry I. Bowditch to Sumner, July 1, 1864, Sumner Papers, HU.
[70] *U.S. Statutes at Large*, XIII, 129-30.

low tell of the effect of these bloody instructions of pro-slavery prejudice and meanness."[71]

On August 18, 1864, the adjutant general's office issued an order directing commanders of Negro regiments to determine which of their men had been free on April 19, 1861. These men would be given full pay from the date of their enlistment; all others from January 1, 1864. This posed a serious problem for many regiments. Most northern regiments had both free Negroes and freedmen in their ranks; even the 54th and 55th Massachusetts regiments contained a few men who had escaped from slavery after April 19, 1861. Morale in such regiments might be impaired if some of the men received more back pay than others. Colonel E. N. Hallowell of the 54th worked out an ingenious method to avoid this problem. The fact of freedom before April 19, 1861, was established by the soldier's oath. Hallowell devised the following oath: "You do solemnly swear that you owed no man unrequited labor on or before the 19th day of April, 1861. So help you God." This became known as the "Quaker Oath," and even those men of the 54th who had been slaves took the oath in good conscience "by God's higher law, if not by their country's." Several other northern Negro regiments imitated Hallowell's oath.[72]

This did not solve the problem for regiments recruited solely in the South. Such an oath for them would be too patently transparent and would probably invite rebuke from Washington. Higginson urged Sumner to keep up the fight for full justice to freedmen soldiers. Failure to secure full retroactive pay for them "will be the greatest blow ever struck at successful emancipation in the Department of the South," he wrote, "for it will destroy all confidence in the honesty of the government."[73] Higginson fired off more letters to northern newspapers, conceding that under the new law the Massachusetts regiments "will get their

[71] *Commonwealth*, June 24, 1864. See also *Liberator*, Aug. 19, 1864, and *Commonwealth*, Aug. 12, 1864. On April 12, 1864, Confederate troops under General Nathan Bedford Forrest allegedly slaughtered several score Negro soldiers in cold blood after surrender of the Union garrison at Fort Pillow, Tennessee.

[72] *O.R.*, Ser. 3, vol. IV, 565; Pearson, *Andrew*, II, 120; Luis F. Emilio, *History of the Fifty-Fourth Regiment of Massachusetts Volunteer Infantry, 1863-65* (Boston, 1891), 220-21.

[73] Higginson to Sumner, June 20, 1864, Sumner Papers, HU.

pay at last, and be able to take their wives and children out of the almshouse, to which, as Gov. Andrew informs us, the gracious charity of the nation has consigned so many." But the refusal of full back pay to the First South Carolina Regiment was "a deliberate repudiation of the debt deliberately incurred by the Secretary of War." Higginson concluded in disgust, "If a year's discussion . . . has at length secured the arrears of pay for the Northern colored regiments, possibly two years may secure it for the Southern."[74]

Higginson intended to carry on the fight for the next two years or for the rest of his life, if necessary. When the next session of Congress met he wrote more letters to northern newspapers and sent a memorial to Congress, which was presented to the Senate by Henry Wilson on December 12, 1864. Higginson's persistence finally paid off. Wilson guided to passage on March 3, 1865, a law granting full retroactive equal pay to all Negro regiments that had been promised equal pay when they were enrolled.[75]

In spite of all the delays, vacillations, and injustices, the employment of Negro troops by the North was one of the most revolutionary features of the war. More than any other single factor the performance of Negro soldiers earned their race the respect of the North, made emancipation secure, and helped pave the way for the gains made by the Negro during Reconstruction. Abolitionists played an important part in the conception and execution of the policy of arming Negroes. George L. Stearns, John Andrew, J. Miller McKim, John Jay, Frederick Douglass, John

[74] Letters from Higginson in the *New York Times*, July 3, 1864; *New York Evening Post*, July 10, 1864; and *New York Tribune*, Aug. 12, 1864.

[75] Higginson, *Army Life*, 227-28; *N.A.S. Standard*, Dec. 17, 1864; *U.S. Statutes at Large*, xiii, 488; Henry Wilson to Higginson, March 26, 1865, Higginson Papers, hu. One of the most constant complaints of abolitionists and Negroes regarding the government's policy toward its Negro soldiers, aside from the matter of unequal pay, was the denial of officers' commissions to Negroes. Public prejudice and the inexperience of most Negro soldiers were the main reasons for this policy. As prejudice toward the Negro lessened in the last months of the war, the army promoted several Negroes to the rank of lieutenant. Eight Negro physicians were given major's commissions as surgeons during the war, and in the last weeks of the war Martin Delany was commissioned a major of infantry. Several other colored men were given complimentary commissions before being mustered out of the service in 1865. Of course several thousand colored men served as noncommissioned officers, but fewer than 100 Negroes were actually commissioned during the war. Cornish, *Sable Arm*, 214-17; Quarles, *Negro in the Civil War*, 208.

Mercer Langston, Martin Delany, William Birney, and others recruited dozens of Negro regiments. Colonels Shaw, Higginson, Edward and Norwood Hallowell, and many other abolitionist officers of Negro troops contributed to the success of the policy. Finally, abolitionists played a leading role in the efforts to rectify the discrimination in pay between white and Negro soldiers. The success of Negro soldiers was in part a triumph of abolitionism.

X ✦ THE QUEST FOR EQUAL RIGHTS
IN THE NORTH

BY 1863 the Civil War had become a revolution of freedom for 4 million slaves. The antislavery crusade, however, envisaged not only a negative freedom—the absence of chattelism—but a positive guaranty of equal protection of the laws to all men. Once freedom was won, most abolitionists were ready to proceed with the next step in the revolution—equality.

"This is a war not of geographical sections, nor of political factions, but of principles and systems," declared Theodore Tilton in 1863. "Our war against this rebellion is . . . a war for social equality, for rights, for justice, for freedom." In 1863 Moncure Conway wrote that "the war raging in America must be referred to a higher plane than that of Liberty. It is a war for Equality. It is to decide whether the Liberty which each race claims for itself, and knows to be good, shall be given impartially to all, of whatever colour or degree."[1]

These statements were summaries of an idea expressed many times by abolitionists during the war. The most eloquent and persistent spokesman for this revolution of racial equality was Wendell Phillips. His program of reconstruction, said Phillips early in 1862, was the creation of a nation in which there was "no Yankee, no Buckeye, no Hoosier, no Sucker, no native, no foreigner, no black, no white, no German, no Saxon; . . . only American citizens, with one law impartial over all." Phillips wanted to destroy the aristocratic society of the Old South and replace it with a new social order based on equal rights, universal education, and the dignity of labor. He declared: "I hold that the South is to be annihilated. I do not mean the geographical South. . . . [I] mean the intellectual, social, aristocratic South—the thing that represented itself by slavery and the bowie-knife, by bullying and lynch law, by ignorance and idleness. . . . I mean a

[1] *Independent*, June 25, 1863; Moncure D. Conway, *Testimonies Concerning Slavery* (2nd ed., London, 1865), 131-32. For a brilliant discussion of the evolution of equal rights as a northern war aim, see C. Vann Woodward, "Equality: the Deferred Commitment," in *The Burden of Southern History* (Vintage Books, New York, 1961), 69-87.

society which holds for its cardinal principle of faith, that one-third of the race is born booted and spurred, and the other two-thirds saddled for the first to ride. . . . That South is to be annihilated. (Loud applause)" This social revolution must be accomplished primarily by the freedmen. "I want the blacks as the very basis of the effort to regenerate the South," said Phillips. "We want the four millions of blacks—a people instinctively on our side, ready and skilled to work; the only element the South has that belongs to the nineteenth century."[2]

Most abolitionists realized that free Negroes were treated little better in the North than in the South. The revolution of equality, they knew, must embrace North as well as South. "No Abolitionist condemns our Northern oppression of negroes one whit less than he does Southern Slavery," declared Sydney Gay in 1862. "North as well as South, this outraged people encounter DENIAL everywhere," asserted Gerrit Smith in a ringing denunciation of racial discrimination in the North. "Even the noblest black is denied that which is free to the vilest white. The omnibus, the car, the ballot-box, the jury box, the halls of legislation, the army, the public lands, the school, the church, the lecture-room, the social circle, the table, are all either absolutely or virtually denied to him."[3]

Abolitionists could not hope to revolutionize the southern social order without first improving the status of northern Negroes. Gilbert Haven stated the problem succinctly. When southerners observed "no recognition of the unity of man" in the North, he said, "when they see these, our brethren, set apart in churches and schools, or, if allowed to enter our churches, driven into the lowest seats; when they behold every avenue of honorable effort shut against them,—that no clerk of this complexion is endured in our stores, no apprentice in our workshops, no teacher in our schools, no physician at our sick-beds, no minister in our pulpits, —how can we reproach them for their sins, or urge them to repentance?"[4]

[2] Speeches by Phillips published in *Liberator*, Apr. 25, May 23, Nov. 28, 1862.
[3] *New York Tribune*, Mar. 21, 1862; Gerrit Smith to the editor of the *New York Tribune*, July 1, 1861, published in the *Tribune*, July 7.
[4] Gilbert Haven, *National Sermons, Speeches, and Letters on Slavery and Its War* (Boston, 1869), 139.

When the militant phase of abolitionism began in 1831 the status of northern Negroes was deplorable. Shut out from white schools and churches, forced to live in city slums and ghettos, denied equal civil and political rights, subject to Jim Crow legislation and degrading "black laws" in many states, confined to menial occupations, almost universally despised as members of an inferior race, the northern Negroes' lot in 1830 was a harsh one. In some respects their status actually deteriorated in the next thirty years. The huge influx of immigrants in the 1840's and 1850's drove colored people out of many of their former occupations and subjected them to the mob fury of socially and economically insecure immigrants. Some of the western states made their black laws more severe between 1830 and 1860.

At the same time, however, northern Negroes made significant gains in other areas, especially in New England, the center of abolitionist influence. By a combination of moral suasion and political pressure, abolitionists and free Negroes helped to bring about the desegregation of most public schools in New England and the abolition of Jim Crow on New England stage coaches, horse cars, and railroads. Abolitionist efforts were partly responsible for the defeat of the Rhode Island constitution of 1842, which had established *white* manhood suffrage, and the substitution of a new constitution which granted Negro suffrage. Abolitionists registered their protests against "Negro pews" by withdrawing from churches that practiced this form of segregation and by joining or founding congregations which admitted Negroes on an equal basis. Abolitionist and antislavery lecturers almost singlehandedly ended segregated seating in many lecture halls by refusing to speak before segregated audiences. The Hutchinson family refused to sing before segregated groups. In many ways abolitionists tried to bear witness against the system of racial discrimination which prevailed in the antebellum North.

In 1860 Negroes enjoyed equal political rights in all the New England states except Connecticut. In New York, Negroes possessing property worth $250 could vote. In all other northern states colored men were denied suffrage.[5] All but a handful of

[5] In Ohio, men with a greater visible admixture of Caucasian than Negro genes could vote. In some respects, of course, this was a greater insult to the Negro than the denial of suffrage to all colored men.

public schools in New England were open to both races. Public transportation in most of the North was nonsegregated. But Jim Crow still prevailed on the New York, Philadelphia, Cincinnati, and San Francisco streetcars. Public schools in most of the North outside of New England were segregated, and in some areas no public schools at all were open to Negroes. In several western states Negroes were subjected to severe legal discrimination and denied equal rights in the courts. In many parts of the North, including New England, Negroes were discriminated against in housing, employment, restaurants, hotels, and places of recreation.[6]

NEGRO SUFFRAGE.

"Negro Suffrage." From the *Boston Commonwealth*

[6] For the best discussion of the status of northern Negroes before the Civil War and of the efforts of abolitionists to improve that status, see Leon F. Litwack, *North of Slavery* (Chicago, 1961). Most histories of the abolitionist movement and biographies of abolitionist leaders contain references to the attempts of abolitionists to secure equal civil and political rights for Negroes in the antebellum North. For additional descriptions of the condition of northern Negroes on the eve of the Civil War, see *Anglo-African*, Jan. 7, 1860; and *Liberator*, Oct. 5, 26, Nov. 2, Dec. 7, 1860, Jan. 4, Mar. 15, 1861.

With the outbreak of war, some abolitionists feared that the campaign for equal rights in the North might be buried by the confusion and excitement of armed conflict. "The laws respecting the colored man, in Iowa, Illinois, and other Western States, notwithstanding the predominance of Republican majorities, are disgraceful and proscriptive," wrote a western abolitionist. "It seems to me that the work of the Anti-Slavery Society ought to be carried on unrelaxingly. Legislation of a just character needs to be inaugurated. It will not answer to trust these reforms to this war." The Essex County (Massachusetts) Anti-Slavery Society resolved at the end of 1861 that "we still deem the mission of the Abolitionists *unaccomplished* so long as a . . . nominally free colored man is subjected to any proscription, political, educational, or ecclesiastical."[7] Stephen S. Foster declared in January 1862, that the object of the American Anti-Slavery Society was "not merely to destroy the *form* of slavery, but to destroy the *spirit of oppression*, which shows itself at the South, in the form of slavery, and at the North, in the bitter and relentless prejudice against color." Later in the year a Boston Negro reminded abolitionists that there was still much work for them to do right in Boston, where Negroes suffered discrimination in housing, employment, and some restaurants.[8]

In 1861 Susan B. Anthony pronounced a severe indictment of racial discrimination in the North. The northern people were horrified by tales of southern cruelty to slaves, she said, "and yet, what better do we? While the cruel slave-driver lacerates the black man's mortal body, we, of the North, flay the spirit." Even when the northern Negro obtained an education, he found the doors to many vocations shut in his face. Miss Anthony declared that reconstruction of the nation on the basis of equality for all men must begin in the North. She concluded: "Let us open to the colored man all our schools, from the common District to the College. Let us admit him into all our mechanic shops, stores, offices, and lucrative business avocations, to work side by side with his white brother; let him rent such pew in the church, and occupy such seat in the theatre, and public lecture room, as he pleases; let him be admitted to all our entertainments, both public &

---

7 *N.A.S. Standard*, June 22, 1861; *Liberator*, Dec. 27, 1861.

8 *Liberator*, Jan. 31, 1862, Aug. 15, 1862.

private; let him share all the accommodations of our hotels, stages, railroads and steamboats. . . . Extend to him all the rights of Citizenship. Let him vote and be voted for; let him sit upon the judge's bench, and in the juror's box. . . . Let the North thus prove to the South, by her acts, that she fully recognizes the humanity of the black man."[9]

Individually and in small groups, by private persuasion, precept, or example, abolitionists did what they could during the war to lessen prejudice and mitigate discrimination in the North. A Michigan abolitionist who owned a large farm told Garrison that he employed several Negro farmhands, paying them the same wages, serving them at the same table, and sleeping them in the same bunkhouse as his white laborers. Henry Cheever organized a "Freedom Club" in Worcester, containing men of both races, whose object was to break down the barriers between white and colored workingmen.[10] William H. Channing, abolitionist chaplain of the U.S. House of Representatives, invited Negro minister Henry Highland Garnet to occupy his pulpit in the House chamber one Sunday morning in February, 1865. Channing considered this event an important step in the campaign against discrimination in the nation's capital. At about the same time Charles Sumner presented Boston Negro lawyer John Rock as a candidate to argue cases before the Supreme Court. Chief Justice Chase accepted Rock and swore him in, making him the first Negro ever to be accredited as a Supreme Court lawyer. This affair was regarded by abolitionists as a symbol of the revolution in the Negro's status since 1857, when Chief Justice Taney had denied the citizenship of black men.[11]

Abolitionists tried also to cleanse northern churches of segregation. It was not always an easy task. In 1863 the Reverend Horace Hovey, abolitionist pastor of the Congregational church in Florence, Massachusetts, preached that "the negro has the same right that we have . . . to obtain a first-rate education and to rise in social position according as he rises in worth; the same right to

[9] MS of speech, marked "1861," in S. B. Anthony Papers, LC.
[10] H. Willis to Garrison, June 20, 1861, Garrison Papers, BPL; Henry Cheever to Gerrit Smith, July 20, 1864, Smith Papers, SU.
[11] Octavius B. Frothingham, *Memoir of William Henry Channing* (Boston, 1886), 316; Channing to L. M. Child, Mar. 8, 1865, published in *Commonwealth*, Mar. 25, 1865; *New York Tribune*, Feb. 9, 1865.

vote and to sit in legislative and congressional halls." Fifteen or twenty of his parishioners took offense at these words and walked out of the church. But there were some encouraging signs of progress. Maria Weston Chapman rejoiced in 1863 that the Park Street Church in Boston had reversed its long-standing policy of refusing to rent pews to Negroes.[12] Gilbert Haven succeeded in desegregating many New England Methodist churches, in expunging the word "colored" from the minutes of the New England Methodist Conference, and in securing admission of a Negro minister to the Conference as pastor of an integrated church.[13]

Education was another area in which abolitionists worked to promote desegregation wherever they were in a position to do so. Segregation had been abolished in Boston's public schools in 1855 largely through the efforts of abolitionists and antislavery Republicans. During the war abolitionists extended their school desegregation efforts to New York. In 1863 Andrew D. White, antislavery Republican and future president of Cornell University, was elected to the New York legislature to represent the Syracuse district. Because of his teaching experience, White was appointed chairman of the Education Committee and given the task of codifying New York's education laws. A statute of 1841 had authorized the establishment of segregated schools in any district that wished to maintain them. White wanted to repeal this statute and abolish school segregation in the state. One of his closest friends in Syracuse was Samuel J. May, the veteran abolitionist crusader. White asked May for information and arguments against segregation. May supplied him with abolitionist writings on the inherent equality of the Negro, reports of the success of integration in New England schools, and a long letter outlining the main arguments for desegregation. Separate schools for Negroes, wrote May, were "a perpetual imputation of fault, unworthiness or inferiority, which must tend to discourage and keep them depressed" even if the facilities were equal to those of

[12] Horace C. Hovey to M. W. Chapman, July 15, 1864, Weston Papers, BPL; M. W. Chapman to Mary Estlin, Dec. 29, 1863, Estlin Papers, BPL.

[13] William Haven Daniels, *Memorials of Gilbert Haven* (Boston, 1880), 151, 182; William G. Cochrane, "Freedom without Equality: A Study of Northern Opinion and the Negro Issue, 1861-1870," Ph.D. dissertation, University of Minnesota, 1957, 294-96.

white schools. Colored children should enjoy "not only equal educational privileges, but the same, as the white people enjoy." The common schools were the nursery of the Republic, argued May, and the fostering of caste distinctions in the schools would create class and racial divisions in the nation which could prove fatal to democracy. The mission of America was "to show the world that *all* men, not white men alone, but all, of every complexion, language and lineage have equal rights to life, liberty and the pursuit of happiness. . . . Let then our common schools, from the lowest to the highest grade, be equally open to the children of all the people." The efforts of May and White were unavailing, however, and New York did not prohibit segregation in its public schools until nearly forty years later.[14]

In 1861 there were still five New England cities that maintained segregated public schools: Hartford and New Haven, Connecticut, and Providence, Newport, and Bristol, Rhode Island. Abolitionists and Negroes in Rhode Island kept up a steady antisegregation pressure on school officials, city councilmen, and state legislators. They petitioned these bodies repeatedly, arguing that segregation placed a stigma of inferiority on Negro children and that the colored schools were provided with inferior funds and equipment. In May 1864, abolitionists won a preliminary victory when the General Assembly's committee on education recommended abolition of separate schools in Rhode Island. In 1865 the lower House passed a bill embodying this recommendation. But the Senate defeated the measure by a narrow margin, largely because of the determined opposition of Newport senators. Thomas Wentworth Higginson had moved to Newport after his dis-

---

[14] James M. Smith, "The 'Separate But Equal' Doctrine: An Abolitionist Discusses Racial Segregation and Educational Policy during the Civil War," *Journal of Negro History*, XLI (April 1956), 138-47. This article publishes the letter from May to White, Mar. 11, 1864, which can be found in the Collection of Regional History, Cornell University. The public schools of Syracuse, a center of antislavery activity in upstate New York, had been desegregated for more than twenty years. In his report on the condition of Canadian Negroes, Samuel Gridley Howe observed that "the colored children in the mixed schools do not differ in their general appearance and behavior from their white comrades. They are usually clean and decently clad. They look quite as bright as the whites. . . . The association is manifestly beneficial to the colored children. . . . The appearance, and the acquirements of colored children in the separate schools, are less satisfactory." Howe made a strong plea for school desegregation in the United States. Howe, *The Refugees from Slavery in Canada West* (Boston, 1864), 78-79.

charge from the army in 1864 and was elected to the School Board in 1865. As a result of Higginson's efforts, Newport abolished its separate schools in September 1865. With the opposition of Newport legislators thus removed, the Rhode Island legislature in 1866 outlawed school segregation in the entire state. Abolitionists rejoiced in the removal of "this last relic of slavery" from Rhode Island. The Connecticut legislature followed the example of its neighbor and abolished segregated public education in the Nutmeg State in 1868.[15]

Normal schools in New England were open to both races, but many of the private academies and preparatory schools were not. Abolitionists played an important role in desegrating two prominent New England private schools in 1865. John G. Whittier and Theodore Weld were instrumental in securing the admission of colored girls to Dr. Dio Lewis' girls' school in Lexington, Massachusetts, where Weld and his wife Angelina taught from 1864 to 1867.[16] The energetic Rhode Island Quaker abolitionist, Elizabeth Buffum Chace, decided in 1865 that the refusal of the Friends' school in Providence to admit colored applicants was a disgrace that could no longer be tolerated. Through her friend Dr. Samuel Tobey, a wealthy New England Quaker who was one of the main financial supporters of the school, Mrs. Chace obtained a promise from the trustees to admit henceforth all qualified applicants, regardless of race. The action of these two private schools paved the way for the lowering of the color bar at several other New England academies.[17]

More widely publicized than these school desegregation measures were the efforts to remove discrimination in the courts, trans-

[15] *Liberator*, Sept. 6, 1861, Mar. 11, 18, 1864, Sept. 29, 1865; *Commonwealth*, Mar. 4, 18, 1865; *N.A.S. Standard*, Oct. 7, 1865, May 26, 1866; Higginson to Anna and Louisa Higginson, Apr. 19, 1874, Higginson Papers, HU; Irving H. Bartlett, *From Slave to Citizen: The Story of the Negro in Rhode Island* (Providence, 1954), 52-59; *Special Report of the Commissioner of Education on the Condition and Improvement of Public Schools in the District of Columbia . . .* (Washington, 1871), 328, 334-35.

[16] Dio H. Lewis to Whittier, Sept. 11, 1865, Whittier Papers, Essex Institute; Benjamin Thomas, *Theodore Weld: Crusader for Freedom* (New Brunswick, N.J., 1950), 253-57.

[17] Albert K. Smiley to J. B. Smith, Sept. 5, 1865, E. B. Chace to Samuel Tobey, Sept. 15, 1865, Tobey to Mrs. Chace, Sept. 18, 1865, Smiley to J. B. Smith, Sept. 18, 1865, in Lillie B. C. Wyman and Arthur C. Wyman, *Elizabeth Buffum Chace* (2 vols., Boston, 1914), I, 276-78.

portation, and other areas. Charles Sumner was a leader of anti-discrimination activity at the national level. In 1862 he guided to Senate passage a bill to repeal an 1825 law barring colored persons from carrying the mail. Democrats and conservative Republicans defeated the measure in the House, but it finally passed both Houses and became law on March 3, 1865. In 1862 Massachusetts abolitionists called on Congress to enact legislation granting Negroes equal rights in federal courts. Sumner introduced a bill providing that in all proceedings of District of Columbia courts there would be no exclusion of witnesses because of race. The measure passed both Houses. In 1864 Sumner finally secured enactment of a law prohibiting the exclusion of witnesses from federal courts on grounds of race or color. During the war, Congress admitted Negroes to its visitors' galleries for the first time. Many white persons in Washington complained that it was an insult to every white man in the land to admit "niggers" to the congressional galleries, and called down direful maledictions upon the heads of "Sumner and the nasty abolitionists" for perpetrating this vulgar act, but their complaints were of no avail.[18]

In 1863 Sumner and the abolitionists opened an attack on segregation and exclusion of Negroes from the horsecars and railroads of the District of Columbia. Supported by a series of militant editorials in the *New York Tribune* (probably written by Gay), Sumner introduced amendments to the charter renewal grants of several Washington companies prohibiting them from excluding or segregating passengers on account of race. Finally in 1865 Sumner obtained passage of a bill prohibiting segregation on every streetcar line in the District.[19] Desiring to test the effectiveness of this statute, the venerable Sojourner Truth, ageless Negro abolitionist who was working among the freedmen at Arlington, rode on the horsecars of several Washington lines. One conductor tried to make her ride on the outside platform. She threatened to sue him if he persisted, and he gave in. Another

[18] McPherson, *History of the Rebellion*, 239-40, 242-43, 593; *U.S. Statutes at Large*, XII, 351, 407, XIII, 515; *New York Tribune*, Apr. 12, 1862, June 30, 1864; *Liberator*, June 27, 1862; *Commonwealth*, Sept. 27, 1862; *Boston Advertiser*, quoted in *Liberator*, Jan. 6, 1865; *Anglo-African*, Jan. 4, 1862.

[19] McPherson, *History of the Rebellion*, 241-42, 593-94; *U.S. Statutes at Large*, XII, 805, XIII, 537; *New York Tribune*, Feb. 4, 11, 17, Mar. 1, 18, 1864; *Liberator*, Mar. 20, 1863; *Commonwealth*, Mar. 11, 1864.

conductor pushed her roughly against the door in an effort to eject her from the car, causing a painful injury to her shoulder. She had him arrested and caused him to lose his job. Soon after this a conductor was seen to stop his car unasked and beckon kindly to some colored women standing timidly in the street. The right of Washington Negroes to ride in the horsecars was henceforth unquestioned.[20]

Nowhere in the North were Negroes and abolitionists more hated than in New York City. Irish laborers feared economic and social competition from the black man and had little use for a war fought to free the slave. Sparked by the enforcement of the draft, New York's immigrant and lower-class population rioted during four days of bloody mob violence in July 1863. The mob lynched Negroes in the streets and burned the Colored Orphan Asylum to the ground. The rioters attacked the offices of the *New York Tribune* and ransacked the homes of abolitionists and Republicans. New York police and federal troops finally brought the mobs under control.[21]

Abolitionists went immediately to work to get New York's stricken Negro population back on its feet after the riots. The American Missionary Association disbursed temporary relief and assistance. Gerrit Smith contributed $1,000 to help the work. Abolitionists were unexpectedly aided in their efforts by New York City merchants, who organized a relief society and raised thousands of dollars for assistance and for the rebuilding of the orphan asylum. In fact, despite the murders and suffering, the riots in the long run helped to improve the status of New York Negroes. Angelina Weld reported two weeks after the uprising that a reaction against the Irish and in favor of colored people was setting in among the city's middle and upper classes. Wealthy families discharged Irish servants and hired Negroes. The average

---

20 Lillie B. C. Wyman, *American Chivalry* (Boston, 1913), 110-12.

21 Albon P. Man, Jr., "Labor Competition and the New York Draft Riots of 1863," *Journal of Negro History*, xxxvi (1951), 375-405; *New York Tribune*, July 13-20, 1863; Angelina Weld to Gerrit Smith, July 28, 1863, Smith Papers, su; Oliver Johnson to Garrison, July 16, 1863, Garrison to Johnson, July 25, 1863, Sarah Pugh to R. D. Webb, Aug. 11, 1863, Garrison Papers, bpl. In 1862 and 1863 there were anti-Negro riots in many northern cities, caused by real and potential labor competition between white and Negro workingmen. Williston Lofton, "Northern Labor and the Negro during the Civil War," *Journal of Negro History*, xxxiv (July 1949), 251-73.

middle-class New Yorker began to realize that he had been partly responsible for the murderous outrages against Negroes. All classes of white citizens had held Negroes in contempt, spoken disrespectfully of them, and refused to admit them to streetcars, schools, restaurants and hotels. Little wonder then that the lower classes mobbed and lynched them. A more kindly spirit toward colored people began to manifest itself in New York in the weeks and months after the draft riots.[22]

Taking advantage of this shift in public opinion, the three abolitionist newspapers in New York City (*Independent*, *Anti-Slavery Standard*, and *Principia*) plus the *Tribune* and the *Evening Post* inaugurated a campaign to abolish Jim Crow on all of the city's street railroads. Most streetcar companies allowed Negroes to ride in their cars, but the Fourth Avenue and Eighth Avenue roads permitted their conductors to exclude colored people, and the Sixth Avenue company segregated them in special cars. Abolitionists contended that the railroads were common carriers and were required by law to provide transportation equally to everyone. They threatened to take the matter to court. The Fourth Avenue road finally began admitting Negroes to its cars in February 1864, but the other two companies still refused to change their policy. In June 1864, the controversy came to a head when the conductor of an Eighth Avenue car, aided by an Irish policeman, forcibly ejected the widow of a Negro sergeant who had been recently killed in battle. The *Tribune* exploded in anger: "It is quite time to settle the question whether the wives and children of the men who are laying down their lives for their country . . . are to be treated like dogs." Public opinion was hostile to the railroad. The policeman who had helped eject the woman was reprimanded by his superiors. The city police commissioner prohibited his men from helping conductors eject Negroes from the cars. The Eighth Avenue road capitulated to the surge of public opinion and ended its exclusion of Negroes. A few days later the Sixth

[22] Mattie Griffith to Elizabeth Gay, Aug. 6, 1863, Gay Papers, cu; S. S. Jocelyn to Gerrit Smith, July 22, 1863, Gerrit Smith Papers, su; Jocelyn to Lewis Tappan, July 30, 1863, Tappan Papers, lc; W. E. Whiting to Gerrit Smith, July 20, 1863, Angelina Weld to Smith, July 28, 1863, Smith Papers, su; L. M. Child to Frank Shaw, July 27, 1863, Child Papers, Wayland Historical Society; *Principia*, Jan. 7, 1864.

Avenue road likewise surrendered. All of New York City's public transportation was thenceforth integrated.[23]

Philadelphia in 1860 had a larger Negro population than any other northern city. Several Philadelphia Negroes had amassed considerable wealth and resided in comfortable, even luxurious homes. Most colored residents of the City of Brotherly Love, however, lived in squalor and poverty in unsanitary slums. Philadelphia was a rigidly segregated city. Negro children attended separate schools when they attended any schools at all. Some of the city's nineteen streetcar and suburban railroad companies refused to admit Negroes to their cars; those that did admit colored people forced them to ride on the front platform. Negroes seeking transportation in the city were often compelled to walk or hire an expensive carriage.[24]

This extreme Jim Crowism in transportation came under powerful attack by Philadelphia abolitionists. Garrisonian abolitionism was stronger in Philadelphia than anywhere outside New England. A large number of the city's colored people were Garrisonians. Philadelphia's Negroes also supported thriving organizations of their own, particularly the Social, Civil, and Statistical Association of Colored People, which sponsored lectures, provided legal assistance to Negroes, and served as a pressure group in behalf of the interests of all colored people. William Still, a prominent Philadelphia Negro, was leader of this Association and was also an official in the Pennsylvania Anti-Slavery Society.[25]

[23] George Cheever to Elizabeth Washburn, Aug. 5, 1863, Cheever Papers, AAS; *New York Tribune*, Aug. 4, 5, 7, 1863, June 21, 24, 30, 1864; *Principia*, Aug. 13, 1863; *Independent*, Jan. 21, 1864; *Liberator*, Mar. 4, 1864; *Boston Commonwealth*, June 24, 1864; *N.A.S Standard*, July 2, 9, 16, 1864. Quotation is from *New York Tribune*, June 21, 1864. Segregation on San Francisco's street railroads was abolished by a district court ruling in October 1864. *Liberator*, Nov. 18, 1864, quoting *San Francisco Bulletin*, Oct. 3, 1864. In Cincinnati, however, Jim Crow in public transportation was not ended until after the war.

[24] Ira V. Brown, "Pennsylvania and the Rights of the Negro, 1865-1887," *Pennsylvania History*, XXVIII (Jan. 1961), 45-46; *Liberator*, Sept. 21, 1860; *Twenty-Seventh Annual Report of the Philadelphia Female Anti-Slavery Society* (Phila., 1861), 17.

[25] Brown, "Pennsylvania and the Rights of the Negro," *op.cit.*, 49-50; Alberta S. Norwood, "Negro Welfare Work in Philadelphia, Especially as Illustrated by the Career of William Still, 1775-1930," M.A. thesis, U. of Pennsylvania, 1931, 18-24; Larry Gara, "William Still and the Underground Railroad," *Pennsylvania History*, XXVIII (Jan. 1961), 33-39.

The Colored People's Association, the Pennsylvania Anti-Slavery Society, and the Philadelphia Female Anti-Slavery Society all maintained standing committees to work for the abolition of discrimination in Philadelphia's transportation system. William Still inaugurated the militant phase of the antisegregation campaign in 1859 with a long letter to the press detailing the insults and hardships suffered by Negroes on Philadelphia's street railroads. The letter was widely reprinted and focused national attention on the subject. In 1862 Still obtained the signatures of 360 prominent white Philadelphians, including all of the city's leading abolitionists, to a petition requesting the Board of Presidents of the City Railways to end segregation on their lines. The board took no action on the petition, but from this time forward the anti-Jim Crow campaign grew in scope and intensity. The three abolitionist committees kept up the pressure by means of petitions, speeches, letters to the press, and private interviews with railroad presidents. In 1863 Still wrote an eloquent letter to the city's leading newspapers, the *Philadelphia Press*, describing in detail the humiliation suffered by a Negro who tried to obtain transportation in the City of Brotherly Love. The letter was widely published. It appeared in the *London Times*, and was reported by Moncure Conway to have done more harm to the Union cause in England than a military defeat.[26]

The emergence of a national policy of arming Negroes to fight for the Union gave an important fillip to the antisegregation efforts. The antislavery press began to publish stories of wounded colored soldiers who had been ejected from Philadelphia horsecars. Sensing a change in public opinion, abolitionists and Negroes, now supported by the whole Republican press of Philadelphia, stepped up their struggle against segregation. In October 1864, a National Colored Men's Convention met in Syracuse and urged the formation of state Equal Rights Leagues throughout the North to work for desegregation and Negro suffrage. The first (and strongest) such League was formed in Philadelphia, and its initial target was streetcar segregation. It joined in the growing

[26] Norwood, "William Still and Negro Welfare Work," 52-60; William Still, *A Brief Narrative of the Struggle for the Rights of the Colored People of Philadelphia in the City Railroad Cars* (Phila., 1867), 3-10; *Twenty-Seventh Annual Report of the Philadelphia Female Anti-Slavery Society*, 17; *Thirtieth Annual Report of the Philadelphia Female Anti-Slavery Society* (1864), 23-24.

outcry for an end to discrimination in Philadelphia transportation.[27]

William Still suggested to J. Miller McKim the idea of holding a mass meeting at Philadelphia's Concert Hall to demand the abolition of Jim Crow. McKim used his contacts with leading Philadelphia Republicans and businessmen to arrange a meeting for January 13, 1865, sponsored by prominent white Philadelphians. The meeting adopted resolutions calling on the railroads to end their Jim Crow policy, and appointed a committee to negotiate with the railroad presidents. McKim and James Mott, secretary and president respectively of the Pennsylvania Anti-Slavery Society, were two of the leading members of this committee. Their efforts obtained some immediate results. The Philadelphia and Darby Railroad, a suburban line, put an end to segregation on its trains. A few days later a streetcar company also abolished segregation, and another line began admitting Negroes to *some* of its cars. After a month the first company reported that because of integration it had lost white passengers and its revenue had declined; therefore it would henceforth allow Negroes only in special "Colored" cars. The Board of Railway Presidents took a public "poll" in the streetcars and announced that a majority of white Philadelphians still opposed integration. But McKim's committee did not give up. They made a direct appeal to the mayor, a Democrat, who rebuffed them with the statement that he did not wish "the ladies of his family to ride in the cars with colored people."[28]

Defeated at the city level, advocates of equal rights turned hopefully to the state legislature. There they found a staunch ally, Senator Morrow B. Lowry from northwestern Pennsylvania, who for six years had been urging passage of a state law to prohibit segregation in public transportation. Described by Garrison as "a most radical abolitionist, and reminding me alike of Gerrit

---

[27] *New York Tribune*, Nov. 19, 1864; *N.A.S. Standard*, Oct. 15, Nov. 19, 1864, Jan. 14, 21, 1865; *Liberator*, Dec. 23, 1864, Jan. 6, 27, Mar. 24, 1865; *Thirty-First Annual Report of the Philadelphia Female Anti-Slavery Society* (1865), 17-18.

[28] Still, *Brief Narrative*, 11-13; [Benjamin C. Bacon], *Why Colored People in Philadelphia Are Excluded from the Street-Cars* (Phila., 1866), 3-4; *Thirty-Third Annual Report of the Philadelphia Female Anti-Slavery Society* (1867), 26-27; *Liberator*, Jan. 27, 1865; *Boston Commonwealth*, Jan. 28, 1865; *N.A.S. Standard*, Jan. 28, Feb. 25, 1865; *New York Tribune*, Feb. 10, May 3, 1865; William Still to J. Miller McKim, Nov. 10, 1871, McKim Papers, NYPL.

Smith and Charles Sumner," Lowry was a genuine crusader for equal rights.[29] The State Senate passed Lowry's bill by a close vote, but it was shelved in the House. Lowry persisted, and in March 1867, his bill finally passed both Houses and became law. It prohibited discrimination in every form of public transportation in the entire state of Pennsylvania. It was an impressive victory for equal rights, and to abolitionists and Negroes must go the main credit for the triumph. It was they who initiated the struggle and kept up the pressure; and it was an abolitionist who piloted the bill through the state legislature.[30]

Not content with the policy of arming Negroes in separate regiments, a few enthusiastic integrationists among the abolitionists called for the abolition of colored regiments and the complete integration of the army. "I want to sink the differences of race," wrote Samuel Gridley Howe. "I do not believe in black colonies, or black regiments." Gilbert Haven said, "We must abolish colored regiments. . . . A citizen, if he volunteers, should join what regiment he chooses; if he is drafted, those that most need his musket."[31] Such a policy, however, was too radical for the 1860's. The enlistment of Negroes on any basis was a revolutionary step forward; full-scale integration of the armed forces would not come until nearly a century later.

In addition to the antidiscrimination measures described above, northern Negroes made other advances in civil rights during and immediately after the war. California abolished its laws excluding Negro testimony against whites in the courts in 1863. Illinois did the same in 1865, and repealed all the rest of her infamous "black laws" except the exclusion of Negroes from the polls. Chicago's public schools were desegregated in 1865. In 1866 the Indiana Supreme Court declared unconstitutional the worst of that state's black laws. In 1865 Massachusetts enacted the first comprehensive public accommodations law in American history, forbidding the

[29] Garrison to Helen Garrison, Nov. 5, 1865, Garrison Papers, BPL.

[30] Brown, "Pennsylvania and the Rights of the Negro," op.cit., 48-49; Lewis Tappan to Morrow B. Lowry, Jan. 18, 1865, Tappan letterbook, Tappan Papers, LC; Liberator, Feb. 3, Mar. 3, 1865; N.A.S. Standard, Apr. 1, June 3, 1865, Dec. 1, 1866, Feb. 23, Mar. 30, 1867; Report of the Committee Appointed for the Purpose of Securing to Colored People in Philadelphia the Right to the Street-Cars (Phila., 1867).

[31] Howe to John Andrew, n.d., but sometime in spring of 1863, Andrew Papers, MHS; Haven, National Sermons, 405, 510. The United States Navy had always been integrated.

exclusion of any person because of race or color from restaurants, inns, theaters, and places of amusement. The *New York Tribune* and *Anti-Slavery Standard* called for passage of a federal law to prohibit discrimination in public transportation. Such a law, said Sydney Gay, would be "a fit corollary to the Amendment which abolishes slavery." Senator Henry Wilson introduced a bill in February 1865, providing for a fine of $500 against any railroad or steamship in the United States which discriminated against Negroes.[32]

The time was not yet ripe for such a sweeping national law, and Wilson's bill was buried in committee. But the very fact that such a bill could be introduced in 1865 was an indication of the revolution in the status of colored men since 1861. Under the pressure of military necessity the Negro had been freed and given an opportunity to fight for the Union. He fought courageously and well, winning the grudging respect of millions of northern whites. The Negro's contribution as a soldier combined with the patient, effective work of civil rights advocates won large gains for the northern Negro during the war. Black laws and discrimination in civil rights were slowly crumbling away and Jim Crow was gradually disappearing from many parts of the North. Race prejudice, however, remained powerful and discrimination continued to prevail in many walks of life. Negroes in 1865 could vote on equal terms with whites in only five states, and these states contained only 7 per cent of the *northern* Negro population. Negro suffrage would soon become the main issue of southern reconstruction, and so long as most northern states refused the ballot to black men, the North was in a false and stultifying moral position. Abolitionists appreciated this fact and kept up their agitation for equal suffrage in the North. Despite the preeminence of the southern problem during Reconstruction, the status of the northern Negroes continued to occupy much of the attention of abolitionists.

[32] *Commonwealth*, Apr. 17, 1863, Nov. 10, 1866; Benjamin Quarles, *The Negro in the Civil War* (Boston, 1953), 313; *New York Tribune*, Feb. 6, 10, 1865; *Special Report of the Commissioner of Education . . .* (Washington, 1871), 343; Milton R. Konvitz, *A Century of Civil Rights, with a Study of State Law Against Discrimination*, by Theodore Leskes (New York, 1961), 155; *Independent*, Aug 3, 1865; *N.A.S. Standard*, Feb. 11, 1865. Gay's statement from *New York Tribune*, Feb. 5, 1865.

ECONSTRUCTION emerged as a burning issue even before the
war began. At first the word "reconstruction" was used by
Democrats and conservatives to designate a restoration of the
Union on the basis of compromise with the Confederacy. In this
form radicals and abolitionists shunned the term. By the second
year of the war, however, "reconstruction" was beginning to acquire its later meaning of a genuine *reconstruction* of southern
society and politics. In January 1862, George Cheever published
an article in the *Independent* outlining a theory of reconstruction
very similar to the later "conquered provinces," "state suicide,"
and "forfeited rights" theories of Thaddeus Stevens, Charles
Sumner, and Samuel Shellabarger. Cheever argued that by virtue
of their rebellion the Confederate states had forfeited all rights
and protection under the United States Constitution. They were
out of the Union *de facto*. When finally conquered they should be
administered as territories until they could return to statehood
under conditions imposed by Congress.[1]

This was the essence of reconstruction as conceived by abolitionists and radical Republicans throughout the war. The theories of
Stevens, Sumner, and Shellabarger varied slightly in details,
but at their core was the idea that conquered Confederate states
had no rights under the Constitution. Their social and political
systems lay prostrate and malleable. It was the job of Congress
to remodel southern institutions into a form that would guarantee
liberty and equal rights to all men.[2] In February 1862, Sumner
introduced a series of Senate resolutions embodying these ideas
in his "state suicide" theory of reconstruction. Several abolitionists expressed support for Sumner's resolutions. John Jay succinctly summed up the radical theory of reconstruction as it
emerged in 1862: "The Southern states have ceased to be states
of the Union—their soil has become National territory."[3]

[1] *Independent*, Jan. 16, 1862.
[2] Eric L. McKitrick, *Andrew Johnson and Reconstruction* (Chicago, 1960),
99-101, 110-19; *Liberator*, Mar. 28, July 11, 1862; *Independent*, May 22, 1862;
Principia, Nov. 28, 1862.
[3] *Cong. Globe*, 37 Cong., 1 Sess., 736-37; Elizur Wright to Sumner, Feb. 16,

This theory was certain to come into collision with the presidential plan of reconstruction as developed tentatively and experimentally by Lincoln and hardened into doctrinal rigidity by Andrew Johnson. The presidential theory denied that the Confederate states, *as states*, had ever really left the Union. It was a rebellion of individuals, not states. Therefore the function of reconstruction was to appoint loyal state officials to breathe the spark of loyalty and life back into the states. When certain minimum requirements were met these states would again take their place in the Union, their institutions unimpaired and their rights unchanged except for slavery, which was a casualty of the war.[4] In line with these ideas Lincoln appointed a military governor for Tennessee early in 1862 and for several other Confederate states as they came under partial Union control in subsequent months. Some abolitionists expressed opposition to this policy of establishing provisional governments in rebel states. George Cheever protested that such a procedure usurped Congress's powers of reconstruction and defeated the very purpose of Sumner's "state suicide" resolutions, which had envisaged the administration of conquered states as territories under congressional control. In this argument can be found the germ of the later clash between Congress and the executive over the terms of reconstruction.[5]

From the start of the war abolitionists pondered the conditions of reconstruction that would best secure the permanent freedom of emancipated slaves. As early as 1862 many abolitionists came to the conclusion that there could be no security for freedmen without Negro suffrage. But suffrage for the newly emancipated slaves seemed to be an impractical idea in 1862-1863, and several abolitionists hesitated to demand it as a condition of reconstruction. Samuel Sewall declared that he would be satisfied with a policy that granted equal civil rights and left the question of suffrage in abeyance. Not so Wendell Phillips and Frederick Douglass, who were in the vanguard of the movement to require Negro suffrage as a condition of reconstruction.

1862, Thomas Garrett to Sumner, Feb. 24, 1862, George Cheever to Sumner, Feb. 27, 1862, John Jay to Sumner, Feb. 12, 1862, Sumner Papers, HU.

[4] McKitrick, *Andrew Johnson and Reconstruction,* 101-10.

[5] Cheever to Sumner, Feb. 27, 1862, Sumner Papers, HU; *Principia,* June 19, 1862.

Phillips drew a parallel between the Irish immigrant and the emancipated Negro. When the number of Irishmen in the United States was small and politically insignificant, they were the butt of jokes and derision by politicians. But as soon as they became numerous and acquired political power, the attitude of politicians underwent a miraculous change. Phillips asked: "Do you know a politician who dares to make a speech to-day, without a compliment to green Erin? The moment a man becomes valuable or terrible to the politician, his rights will be respected. Give the negro a vote in his hand, and there is not a politician, from Abraham Lincoln down to the laziest loafer in the lowest ward in this city [New York] who would not do him honor. . . . From the possession of political rights, a man gets means to clutch equal opportunities of education, and a fair space of work. Give a man his vote, and you give him tools to work and arms to protect himself." In May 1863, Douglass stated boldly that he would demand for the emancipated Negro "the most perfect civil and political equality." Negro suffrage was "the *only solid*, and *final solution* of the problem before us."[6]

After the Union victories at Gettysburg and Vicksburg in July 1863, there was a great increase in public discussion of reconstruction. The North believed that these victories heralded the collapse of the Confederacy, and the upsurge in reconstruction debate resulted from the assumption that peace was just around the corner. Northern opinion on the issue of reconstruction ranged from the Democratic demand that emancipation not be made a condition of peace to the call of radical abolitionists for Negro suffrage. The whole country looked to Lincoln for a statement on reconstruction. As a supplement to his annual message on December 8, 1863, the president announced his long-awaited policy of restoration. He offered a full pardon to all Confederates (except a small class of prominent military and civilian leaders) who would take an oath of *future* loyalty to the Constitution and swear to uphold all acts of the executive and Congress relative to slavery. Furthermore, whenever a number of white voters equal to one-tenth of those who had voted in 1860 took the oath, they could proceed to reestablish a state government that

[6] Samuel Sewall to Sumner, Jan. 4, 1863, Sumner Papers, HU; speech of Wendell Phillips at Cooper Union on May 12, 1863, published in *Liberator*, May 29, 1863; *Douglass' Monthly*, June 1863.

would be recognized by the president. Lincoln declared that any provision adopted by reconstructed states with respect to the freedmen, "which shall recognize and declare their permanent freedom, provide for their education, and which may yet be consistent, as a temporary arrangement, with their present condition as a laboring, landless, and homeless class" would be acceptable to him.[7] In other words, southern whites were to be allowed to handle the race problem in their own way, even if they adopted a temporary apprenticeship system and excluded Negroes from equal civil and political rights.

Recognizing that the president's plan was designed more as a measure to weaken the rebellion than as a permanent policy of reconstruction, the *New York Tribune* and several abolitionists approved the message. Even Theodore Tilton, who disliked parts of Lincoln's program, wrote that "the Message is only a suggestion, not a final plan—only a hint for the hour. It will create a good deal of wholesome discussion; and while this discussion goes on, the public sentiment marches steadily forward, & makes the politicians ready for a better plan."[8]

But many abolitionists feared the consequences of Lincoln's conservative policy. Wendell Garrison, son of the pioneer abolitionist, denounced the president's exclusion of freedmen from the suffrage. "To free the slave, and then to abandon him in an anomalous position betwixt bondage and manhood, is not this as cruel as slavery?" asked young Garrison. He called for a total reorganization of southern society and politics. "There is no safety short of absolute justice. The reconstruction of Southern society must be thorough, and affect constitutions, statutes, and customs." The *Anti-Slavery Standard* thought that "the proposition to commit the care and education of the freedmen to those revived States is too much like giving the lambs to the nurture and admonition of wolves. That is a duty which belongs, by eminence, to the Nation, and should be entrusted to none but trustworthy hands."[9]

[7] Roy P. Basler, ed., *The Collected Works of Abraham Lincoln* (9 vols., New Brunswick, N.J., 1955), VII, 53-56.

[8] Tilton to W. P. Garrison, Dec. 16, 1863, Garrison Papers, BU. See also *New York Tribune*, Dec. 10, 11, 1863; John Jay to Sumner, Dec. 10, 1863, Sumner Papers, HU; *Commonwealth*, Dec. 11, 18, 1863; *Independent*, Dec. 17, 1863.

[9] Wendell Garrison, writing under the pen-name, "M. du Pays," in the *Liberator*, Dec. 18, 1863; *N.A.S. Standard*, Dec. 19, 1863.

The *Boston Commonwealth* published a blistering editorial denouncing the concept of states' rights which allowed the individual states to determine and regulate the rights of citizenship. "Are [we] going to slink any longer behind the sham, the miserable evasion, that the protection of personal rights and liberty for every citizen of the United States within the limits of any State belongs entirely to the State and in no case to the United States?" asked the *Commonwealth*. "This deplorable nonsense cost us the war, and the nation's life within an inch." Taking Tennessee as an example, the *Commonwealth* produced figures which showed that under Lincoln's 10 per cent plan, 14,000 voters could establish the government of a state that contained more than one million inhabitants. These figures illustrated "the thoroughly anti-republican, undemocratic character of the President's proposition," asserted the *Commonwealth*. "This insignificant fraction determines who shall govern the State hereafter. They have the power to prevent every colored man from voting, and, in the present state of public opinion in all the slave States, *they will prevent it.* . . . Besides being such a burlesque upon popular sovereignty, the thing is impossible."[10]

During the winter of 1863-1864 more and more abolitionists began to condemn Lincoln's reconstruction policy. In January the *Principia* warned that "there is danger that some scheme of apprenticeship—such as that adopted but repudiated in Jamaica —may defeat, delay, or greatly impede and embarrass the progress of the country toward peace, unity, and freedom." The *Principia* joined the growing list of radicals calling for Negro suffrage to avert this danger.[11] Theodore Weld and Anna Dickinson lectured frequently during the winter, raising their eloquent voices in impassioned pleas for equal justice to the freedmen.[12] The Massachusetts Anti-Slavery Society adopted a resolution written by Wendell Phillips demanding for the Negro "an equal share with the white race in the management of the political institutions for which he is required to fight and bleed, and to

[10] *Commonwealth*, Dec. 25, 1863, Jan. 1, 1864.
[11] *Principia*, Jan. 14, 1864.
[12] *Independent*, Feb. 18, 25, 1864; Theodore Weld to Samuel Johnson, Jan. 23, Feb. 4, 1864, Johnson Papers, Essex Institute.

which he is clearly entitled by every consideration of justice and democratic equality."[13]

Phillips was the most persistent, eloquent, and biting critic of the administration's reconstruction program. He traveled up and down the East Coast in the winter of 1863-1864 giving his lecture on reconstruction to scores of audiences in crowded halls. Phillips called for a constitutional amendment to prohibit every state from passing laws "which make a distinction among her citizens on account of race. (Cheers)" Reconstruction was impossible on any other basis. Phillips declared: "Never will this nation be a unit until every class God has made, from the lakes to the Gulf, has its ballot to protect itself. (Applause) . . . The negro has earned land, education, rights. Before we leave him, we ought to leave him on his own soil, in his own house, with the right to the ballot and the school-house within reach. (Loud applause) Unless we have done it, the North has let the cunning of politics filch the fruits of this war."[14]

Radical censure of Lincoln's reconstruction policy focused on Louisiana in early 1864. The president had ordered General N. P. Banks, commander of the Department of the Gulf, to proceed with the reconstruction of Louisiana under the amnesty and re-construction proclamation of December 8, 1863. The nucleus of a Unionist political force existed in New Orleans in the form of a Free State General Committee, controlled by native radicals. Many members of the Committee supported a moderate degree of suffrage for the free Negroes of the city. The Committee favored the calling of a convention to write a new constitution prior to the election of state officers. With the approval of Lincoln, however, Banks scheduled elections for state officials on February 22, 1864, *under the old Louisiana Constitution.* White men who took the oath of allegiance would be eligible to vote. New Orleans radicals and Negroes were outraged by what they considered Banks' high-handed proceedings. By scheduling state elections *before* the convening of a constitutional convention, Banks had cut the ground from under the radicals. New Orleans' free Negroes sent a delegation to Washington armed with a petition requesting

[13] *Liberator*, Feb. 5, 1864.
[14] *New York Tribune*, Feb. 16, 17, 1864; *Liberator*, Feb. 5, Mar. 25, Apr. 8, May 20, 1864.

the ballot. Abolitionists in the North loosed a barrage of attacks on Banks for restricting the suffrage to whites.[15]

Three parties in Louisiana nominated candidates for governor in the February 22 election: conservative, moderate, and radical. Both the moderate and radical parties were pledged to end slavery, but the moderate candidate, Michael Hahn, attacked the radicals for their support of Negro equality. Banks threw his support to Hahn, and with the backing of the United States Army, Hahn won an easy victory.[16] Abolitionists denounced the whole affair. The exclusion of Negroes from the polls, protested the *Commonwealth*, "has no parallel for meanness." Tilton asserted: "Prejudice, even with Gen. Banks to back it, and President Lincoln to confirm it, is a weak foundation for an enduring State. Official injustice is the very worst disturber of the public peace. . . . Let us establish no skin-deep discrimination among our citizens."[17]

The representatives of New Orleans' free Negroes arrived in Washington in March 1864, bearing their petition for suffrage. They cited the high rate of literacy and the large amount of property owned by free colored men in Louisiana. Their request, added to other radical pressures, prompted Lincoln to write a private letter to Governor Hahn, who was preparing for the Louisiana constitutional convention scheduled for early April. "I barely suggest for your private consideration," wrote the president, "whether some of the colored people may not be let in [to the suffrage]—as, for instance, the very intelligent, and especially those who have fought gallantly in our ranks."[18] This idea of a qualified Negro suffrage was gaining considerable support in the North. But most abolitionists wanted no qualifications which were not applied equally to both races. To give the ballot to only a limited number of Negroes would elevate them "into a caste which is dangerous to its members, humiliating to those of inferior grade, an anomaly in free republican society," argued Til-

15 Fred H. Harrington, *Fighting Politician: Major General N. P. Banks* (Philadelphia, 1948), 140-44; *New York Tribune*, Jan. 18, 1864; *Independent*, Jan. 28, Feb. 18, 1864; *Commonwealth*, Mar. 4, 1864; *N.A.S. Standard*, Jan. 28, 1865.

16 Harrington, *Banks*, 144-46.

17 *Commonwealth*, Mar. 18, 1864; *Independent*, Mar. 10, 1864.

18 *New York Tribune*, Mar. 16, 18, 1864; *Liberator*, Mar. 11, 1864; *N.A.S. Standard*, Mar. 19, 1864; Lincoln to Hahn, Mar. 13, 1864, in Basler, *Collected Works of Lincoln*, VII, 243.

ton. "One rule must be applied to all classes, or no rule must be made."[19]

In Louisiana most of the radicals boycotted the constitutional convention that opened in April, declaring angrily that the whole thing was a farce and that Banks had packed the convention with moderates. Banks responded to northern radical pressure to the extent of forcing the convention to empower the legislature to enfranchise Negroes. The provision was permissive, not mandatory, and the legislature elected under the new constitution did nothing whatever in the direction of Negro suffrage. Tennessee and Arkansas, the other states reconstructed under Lincoln's plan in 1864-1865, also refused to enfranchise colored men. Frustrated radicals and abolitionists turned increasingly to Congress in their efforts to obtain equal civil and political rights for freedmen as a condition of reconstruction.[20]

Congress was in a mood to listen to radical demands. Under the leadership of Henry Winter Davis and Benjamin Wade, congressional Republicans had been slowly maturing their reconstruction policy. On March 22 Davis finally got his bill before the House for its third reading. By implication the Wade-Davis bill endorsed the "state suicide" theory of reconstruction. It asserted that restoration of the Union was a congressional rather than executive function. Whereas Lincoln's policy envisaged the reestablishment of state governments by 10 per cent of those voters who took an oath of future loyalty, the Davis bill stipulated that not until 50 per cent of the white men of voting age took such an oath could a civil government be reestablished. Moreover, no one who had voluntarily participated in or supported the rebellion could vote for delegates to the constitutional convention, and no rebel officeholder could vote or hold office under the new state constitution.[21]

Abolitionists approved many features of this bill, but sharply disapproved of its limitation of the franchise to whites. "And this is called 'guaranteeing to the States a Republican form of Government,' is it?" asked William Goodell sarcastically. "What

[19] *Independent*, Mar. 10, 1864. See also *Commonwealth*, Mar. 18, Apr. 29, 1864.
[20] Harrington, *Banks*, 146-49; J. M. Ashley to Garrison, Mar. 22, 1864, Garrison Papers, BPL; *Liberator*, Apr. 8, 1864; *Independent*, Apr. 14, 1864.
[21] Charles H. McCarthy, *Lincoln's Plan of Reconstruction* (New York, 1901), 224-85; *Cong. Globe*, 38 Cong., 1 Sess., Appendix, 82-85.

shall be said of the folly of excluding the votes of that part of the community that is most decidedly and unquestionably loyal [that is, the freedmen]?"[22] Josiah Grinnell in the House and Charles Sumner in the Senate tried to amend the bill to include Negro suffrage, but their amendments were voted down by large majorities in both Houses. Wade explained that he favored the Negro suffrage amendment in principle, but "I would rather it should not be adopted, because, in my judgment, it will sacrifice the bill."[23] Many proponents of the Wade-Davis bill probably considered it a stopgap measure to mark time until northern public opinion could be educated up to the point of accepting Negro suffrage as a basis of reconstruction.

The Wade-Davis bill was finally passed by Congress on July 2, but Lincoln slapped a pocket veto on the radicals' handiwork. Incensed by the president's action, Davis and Wade issued a blistering manifesto denouncing Lincoln's usurpation of Congress's rightful function of controlling reconstruction.[24] Wendell Garrison sympathized with their anger, but declared that he was just as glad to see the bill vetoed because it had left the Negro entirely out of the reconstruction process. The *Commonwealth* had "no tears to shed over the loss of this bill, which though in the main a good one, was . . . disfigured by a requisition that none but 'white' persons should take part in the work of reconstruction. Until Congress has sense enough and decency enough to pass bills without the color qualification, we care not how quickly they are killed."[25]

✦

Education and the ballot for the Negro were two of the most important abolitionist requirements for a sound reconstruction of the South. But many abolitionists realized that political equality and education would mean little to the freed slave without a solid foundation of economic independence. The freedmen must "be made proprietors of the soil in fee simple, as speedily as pos-

[22] *Principia*, May 12, 1864.

[23] *New York Tribune*, May 5, 1864; *Liberator*, May 13, 1864; Wade quoted in *Cong. Globe*, 38 Cong., 1 Sess., 3,449.

[24] Basler, *Collected Works of Lincoln*, VII, 433-34; Wade-Davis Manifesto published in *New York Tribune*, Aug. 5, 1864.

[25] Wendell Garrison quoted in *Liberator*, Aug. 19, 1864; *Commonwealth*, July 15, 1864.

sible," wrote a correspondent of the *Liberator* in 1864. Otherwise the white planter would keep the Negro in a state of semi-serfdom by paying him low wages and making him economically dependent on the old master class. "It is going to make a mighty difference to the 'landless and homeless,' whether they are to get only the poor pittance of twenty-five or thirty cents per day, and be thus kept dependent, or whether they shall receive four or five times this amount by planting on their own land," asserted the *Liberator* correspondent. "The conflict between capital and labor is as old as the world; but in this case the contest could never be more unequal."[26]

This was not a new idea to abolitionists. From the outset of the war many of them had desired the breakup of large southern plantations and their redistribution among landless farmers, black and white. Such action would accomplish two important objectives: it would promote democracy in the South by destroying the economic basis of the "landed aristocracy"; and it would promote the economic independence of the freedmen. Less than a month after the firing on Fort Sumter, William Goodell called for the confiscation of land belonging to rebels and its redistribution among freed slaves.[27] In subsequent months many other abolitionists repeated and endorsed this proposal. When Congress opened its special session in July 1861, several drastic confiscation bills were introduced. But the bill that finally passed was a very mild measure confiscating only property (including slaves) used in direct support of the Confederate military effort.[28]

Abolitionists continued to press for full-scale expropriation. "By all the laws and usages of civilized nations," declared Charles K. Whipple in the *Liberator* in June 1862, "rebels against a government forfeit their property, as well as their other rights and privileges, under it." He urged the administration to confiscate rebel lands and allot a portion of them to the landless laborers who had worked them under compulsion for generations and had thus earned a clear title to the land. This act of simple

[26] *Liberator*, Feb. 5, 1864.
[27] *Principia*, May 4, 1861.
[28] *N.A.S. Standard*, July 13, 1861; *Liberator*, Oct. 18, 1861; *Anglo-African,* Nov. 23, 1861; *Principia*, Dec. 1, 1861; article by Lewis Tappan in the *New York Evening Post*, Jan. 30, 1862; John Jay to Sumner, Nov. 19, 1861, Sumner Papers, HU; *Cong. Globe*, 37 Cong., 1 Sess., 11, 23, 120, 142, 218-20, 415, 430-31, 434, 454.

justice to the freedmen would build the new South on a foundation of small landowners thoroughly loyal to the government. It would expiate the sin incurred by the nation in allowing men to be kept in slavery for so many generations.[29]

The Confiscation Act of July 1862, as originally passed by Congress, met many of the abolitionists' demands. It provided for the permanent confiscation of all property belonging to traitors. Lincoln objected, however, that this provision violated the constitutional ban on bills of attainder that worked forfeiture of property beyond the life of offenders. Under presidential pressure Congress passed a joint resolution declaring that nothing in the act should be construed to work a forfeiture of real estate beyond the life of the offender. Abolitionists were dismayed. If such an interpretation of the Constitution were sustained, the possibility of confiscation and redistribution of southern lands would disappear. In the third edition of his *War Powers of the President*, William Whiting argued learnedly that the constitutional prohibition of bills of attainder did not debar Congress from confiscating property permanently by separate legislative act as a punishment for treason.[30]

Whiting's legal erudition was widely respected, and his arguments were later utilized by Republican congressmen in their efforts to repeal the joint resolution of 1862. Meanwhile, some abolitionist spokesmen explored other means of accomplishing a revolution in southern land ownership. Even before passage of the 1862 Confiscation Act, Elizur Wright had published anonymously a pamphlet suggesting confiscatory taxation as a method of abolishing the southern landed aristocracy. Wright proposed that a tax of $15 per acre be levied on all Confederates who owned more than 300 acres or who had owned slaves before the war. In nearly all cases this tax would not be paid and the government could seize the land and sell part of it to help defray the cost of war. The remainder could be sold or granted to the freedmen. "If the Federal Government, under its war power, has a right to charge batteries with projectiles that sweep down the active and

---

[29] *Liberator*, June 13, 1862.

[30] Williams, *Lincoln and the Radicals*, 164-66; Basler, *Collected Works of Lincoln*, v, 328-31; William Whiting, *The War Powers of the President, and the Legislative Powers of Congress in Relation to Rebellion, Treason, and Slavery* (Boston, 1862), 95-128.

[passive] rebels alike," declared Wright, "can it not charge a battery with an agrarian law which will only annihilate without killing the real rebels?" In a later article for the *Commonwealth* Wright asserted that "a free Republic is utterly impossible . . . where the soil chiefly belongs to a limited small number of princes, patroons, nabobs or ex-slave-holders." He realized that northern conservatives would throw up their hands in horror and conjure up visions of the Jacobin's excesses in the French Revolution. "But an agrarian law for the South is just the next inevitable question," Wright stated. "Let the programme be, not only liberty to the loyal, but the SOIL TO THE TILLER."[31]

When emancipation became an official northern war aim in 1863, abolitionist demands for agrarian reform in the South became more insistent. In an oft-repeated address entitled "Amen to the Proclamation," Wendell Phillips declared that "the whole social system of the Gulf States is to be taken to pieces; every bit of it." All vestiges of slavery and the old aristocracy must be wiped out, said Phillips, and this could be done only by granting land to the freedman, for to him land was the symbol and substance of freedom.[32] Senator Sumner introduced in February 1863, a bill to grant 10 acres of land to every Negro soldier. The bill did not pass, but it was a sign of the increasing congressional concern over the land question in the South. Early in 1863 Indiana Congressman George Julian, a veteran antislavery crusader and foe of land monopoly, urged Congress to adopt "an equitable homestead policy, parcelling out the plantations of rebels in small farms for . . . the freedmen . . . instead of selling it in large tracts to speculators, and thus laying the foundation for a system of land monopoly in the South scarcely less to be deplored than slavery itself."[33]

Julian's remarks probably referred in part to the land sales about to take place on the South Carolina sea islands. In August 1861, Congress had levied a direct tax on every state to raise revenue for carrying on the war. Of course this tax could not be collected in most parts of the Confederacy, and the 1861 law

---

[31] [Elizur Wright], *The Programme of Peace. By a Democrat of the Old School* (Boston, 1862), 15-22; *Commonwealth*, Nov. 15, 1862.

[32] *New York Tribune*, Jan. 23, 1863.

[33] E. Wright to Sumner, Feb. 1, 1863, Sumner Papers, HU; *New York Tribune*, Feb. 12, 1863; Julian's speech quoted in *Cong. Globe*, 37 Cong., 3 Sess., 1,069.

made no provision for collection in the Union-occupied portions of rebel states. This was rectified by an act of June 7, 1862, authorizing the president to appoint tax commissioners to assess the proportion of taxes owed by occupied areas of the Confederacy and to offer the land of delinquent taxpayers for sale at public auction. In effect this was a confiscation act similar to Elizur Wright's proposal.[34]

The tax commissioners arrived at Port Royal in October 1862. They scheduled a public auction of lands for February 11, 1863. Many of the Gideonites became alarmed, fearing that northern speculators would descend upon the islands and buy up most of the desirable land, leaving the Negro with little or nothing. Led by Mansfield French, some of the Gideonites began putting pressure on their friends in Washington to reserve part of the land for the freedmen. "I am greatly troubled in view of the land sales," wrote French to Secretary Chase. "The sharp-sighted speculators are on hand & with larger purses than those of the friends of humanity. If the plantations fall into their hands, *most* of the colored people will suffer greatly." French proposed that General Rufus Saxton, military governor of the islands, be allowed to purchase some of the land with the proceeds of the cotton fund and resell it in small lots to the freedmen.[35] At the beginning of February 1863, Laura Towne suggested to Saxton that he should request a postponement of the sales on grounds of "military necessity." Saxton, who sympathized entirely with the Gideonites, thought this a good idea and persuaded General Hunter to order a postponement of the auction until the whole question was clarified. News soon reached the Gideonites that their efforts in Washington had paid off. On February 6 Congress amended the tax law to allow the tax commissioners to reserve a certain amount of land for educational and charitable purposes. There was "general jubilation" on the islands. The land sales were rescheduled for March 9 and the tax commission reserved most of the saleable property for the future benefit of the freedmen.[36]

[34] Willie Rose, "Rehearsal for Reconstruction: The Port Royal Experiment," Ph.D. dissertation, Johns Hopkins University, 1962, 260-61; *U.S. Statutes at Large*, XII, 294ff., 422-23.

[35] French to Chase, Jan. 2, 1863, Chase Papers, LC; French to Chase, Jan. 6, 1863, Lincoln Papers LC.

[36] Rupert S. Holland, ed., *Letters and Diary of Laura M. Towne, Written from*

Many of the Gideonites believed with Mansfield French that the freedmen had earned a grant of land by long years of suffering and toil. Another group of northern plantation superintendents, led by Edward S. Philbrick of Boston, disagreed with them. Philbrick was a hard-headed practical businessman with years of experience as a successful civil engineer and entrepreneur. He was inclined at times to regard the philanthropic wing of the Gideonites as naïve do-gooders. Philbrick was alert to the danger of speculators grabbing all the good land. But instead of a direct grant of land to the freedmen or the sale of property to them on special terms, he wanted an opportunity for sympathetic northern capitalists to purchase plantations and continue the free-labor experiment on a private-enterprise basis.[37] William Gannett agreed with Philbrick. He thought the freedmen would learn self-reliance best by being thrust into the labor market just like other men. Special grants of land would only reinforce their lack of initiative and self-reliance bequeathed by slavery. "To receive has been their natural condition," argued Gannett. "Give them land, and a house,—and the ease of gaining as good a livelihood as they have been accustomed to would keep many contented with the smallest exertion."[38]

At the land sales of 1863 on the sea islands, 16,479 acres were put up for general sale (the rest of the land was reserved by the government). About 2,000 acres were purchased by freedmen who had pooled their savings. Most of the rest—nearly 8,000 acres—was bought by Edward Philbrick, representing a group of Boston capitalists, at an average price of less than $1 per acre. Philbrick hired several of the government's plantation superintendents, including Gannett and Charles Ware, to run his plantations in 1863 on the basis of private enterprise. The freedmen raised a large cotton crop on these plantations in 1863, and Philbrick cleared a huge profit. He publicized his successful crop and profits in the northern press as an unanswerable argument for emancipa-

---

the Sea Islands of South Carolina, 1862-84 (Cambridge, Mass., 1912), 100-03; Elizabeth Pearson, ed., Letters from Port Royal (Boston, 1906), 154, 159-60; Rose, "Rehearsal for Reconstruction," 262-65, 276-77; U.S. Statutes at Large, XII, 640.

[37] Rose, "Rehearsal for Reconstruction," 277-80; Pearson, Letters from Port Royal, 117-18, 147-48, 165-67.

[38] William Pease, "Three Years Among the Freedmen: William C. Gannett and the Port Royal Experiment," Journal of Negro History, XLII (Apr. 1957), 106.

tion and free labor. Many of the Gideonites, however, remained unconvinced that Philbrick's motives were entirely unselfish. During 1863 there was an undercurrent of belief among the more philanthropic-minded abolitionists that Philbrick's protestations of concern for the freedmen's welfare were mostly a cover for his own desire to make money.[39]

Most northern abolitionists who gave serious thought to the land question agreed with the "do-gooder" wing of the Gideonites. "The confiscated lands of the Southern Rebels ought to be given in suitable portions to the colored people, who so long have tilled them without wages," wrote Samuel J. May in April 1863. A month later the annual meeting of the American Anti-Slavery Society adopted a sweeping resolution calling for permanent confiscation of property owned by Confederates and the allotment of homesteads from these lands to freedmen, loyal southern whites, and Union soldiers.[40] Wendell P. Garrison attacked Lincoln's pardon and amnesty proclamation because it provided for the restoration of confiscated property to southerners who took a loyalty oath. Wendell Phillips was angry because the president's reconstruction plan "leaves the large landed proprietors of the South still to domineer over its politics, and makes the negro's freedom a mere sham. Until a large share of those estates are divided, the aristocracy is not destroyed, neither is any *fair* chance given for the development of a system of free labor."[41]

During the winter of 1863-1864 the abolitionist-controlled *Boston Commonwealth* published a series of powerful editorials urging agrarian reform as a condition of reconstruction. "What do we gain in point of peace, union, republicanism, or genuine

---

[39] Rose, "Rehearsal for Reconstruction," 280-85; Pearson, *Letters from Port Royal*, 170-72. Despite his good year, Philbrick's cotton crop was not as large as the better crops raised under slavery, and his profits were due mainly to the war-inflated price of cotton.

[40] S. J. May to Garrison, Apr. 16, 1863, Garrison Papers, BPL; *Liberator*, May 29, 1863.

[41] W. P. Garrison, in *Liberator*, Dec. 18, 1863; Phillips to Benjamin Butler, Dec. 13, 1863, Butler Papers, LC. In his lectures on reconstruction during the winter of 1863-64, Phillips called repeatedly for a confiscation policy. See, for example, reports of his speeches in the *New York Tribune*, Dec. 23, 1863, and Feb. 17, 1864. The *New York Herald* predicted that the Republicans would eventually adopt Phillips' radical confiscation proposals. "Emancipation, abolition, confiscation, southern lands for landless negroes! This is the programme," declared the *Herald*. "The *Tribune* will, as usual, wait six months, and then follow Wendell Phillips' lead, face foremost. The *Times* will wait about ten months, and then follow, as usual, back foremost." *New York Herald*, Dec. 23, 1863.

democracy by converting Jeff Davis and his patriarchs into Lord Palmerston and a fox-hunting, rent-roll gentry?" asked the *Commonwealth*. A landless peasant class in the South would be a constant source of social unrest. "To be safe, peaceable and permanent," reconstruction "must be primarily economical and industrial; it must commence by planting a loyal population in the soil of the South, not only as its cultivators but its rightful and actual owners." The *Commonwealth* denounced Lincoln's pardon and amnesty program. "If the President can restore to these traitors all their rights to the land," wrote the editor, "then the Confiscation Act is a farce, and the war will have been a gigantic crime and failure."[42]

In February 1864, a committee of prominent abolitionists and antislavery Republicans representing the secular freedmen's aid societies petitioned Congress "to give to the slaves made free by the power of the government, a legal and quiet possession of adequate land for their residence and support."[43] On the South Carolina sea islands, plans were being carried out for precisely that purpose. In September 1863, Lincoln had ordered the tax commissioners to put up for public sale at auction most of the lands reserved by the government at the previous auction in March 1863. The president specified that certain tracts of this land were to be sold to freedmen in 20-acre lots at the special price of $1.25 per acre. Gideonites and freedmen on the islands were overjoyed by Lincoln's order. General Saxton and the Reverend Mansfield French went even further than the order allowed in their zeal to obtain land for the freedmen. They encouraged the Negroes to preempt not only their allotted 20 acres each, but to build cabins on adjoining lots in the hope that bidders would respect their squatters' rights on these adjoining properties. Saxton and French defended their action on the ground that Lincoln's order reserved only 16,000 of 60,000 government-held acres for the freedmen. This, they argued, was hardly enough to support the 15,000 freedmen on the islands. Preemption would enable the Negroes to acquire much more property at the special price of $1.25 per acre than specified in Lincoln's orders.[44]

[42] *Commonwealth*, Dec. 25, 1863, Jan. 1, 8, 15, 22, Mar. 4, 1864.
[43] *Liberator*, Feb. 12, 1864.
[44] Rose, "Rehearsal for Reconstruction," 355-59; Basler, *Collected Works of Lincoln*, VI, 453-59.

Saxton actually issued instructions of his own on November 3 telling the freedmen to stake their claims wherever they wished. He was supported by most of the Gideonites, by Colonel Higginson, and by the *Free South*, a small Port Royal newspaper edited by Philadelphia abolitionist James Thompson. The tax commissioners, supported by Philbrick, were strongly opposed to the scheme, and put pressure on Washington to stop the activities of Saxton and French. But French went personally to Washington in December 1863, to obtain a new set of instructions to ratify General Saxton's preemption orders. French returned triumphantly to Port Royal in January, bearing a new order dated December 31, 1863, allowing Negro heads of families to preempt any government-owned property on the islands up to 40 acres apiece.[45]

The Gideonites were elated. They immediately informed the freedmen of their rights. The tax commissioners' office was soon swamped with preemption claims. But the commissioners were adamantly opposed to preemption. They carried out passive resistance to the new instructions, ignoring some of the preemption claims, attacking the legality of the instructions, and complaining to Washington. Philbrick was outspoken in his opposition to special privileges for the freedmen. They had not earned the land, he argued, and special consideration would break down their moral fiber and vitiate their self-reliance. The Gideonites counterattacked. French and others denounced Philbrick as a selfish capitalist seeking to build a fortune on the sweat and toil of an "agricultural peasantry." In a milder tone Higginson remarked that few of the men in his regiment agreed with Philbrick's arguments. "Sergeant Rivers . . . summed it up in conversation the other day," Higginson reported. "Every colored man will be a slave, & feel himself a slave until he can raise him own *bale of cotton* & put him own mark upon it & say *dis is mine!*" Philbrick lost some of his allies; Gannett, for example, was converted to the proposition that the freedmen must have land and deserved special opportunities to acquire it because of their lifetime of unrequited toil. Nevertheless the tax commissioners persuaded Washington to reverse its policy and cancel the preemption privileges.[46]

---

[45] Rose, "Rehearsal for Reconstruction," 359-73; *Commonwealth*, Jan. 15, 1864; Higginson to Louisa Higginson, Jan. 14, 1864, Higginson, Journal, entry of Jan. 20, 1864, Higginson Papers, HU.

[46] Rose, "Rehearsal for Reconstruction," 373-80; Pearson, *Letters from Port*

French was dismayed, but he was not through fighting. He asked Chase to allow those claims to stand that had been filed before the preemption instructions were rescinded. Since more than a thousand claims had been filed, this would have accomplished nearly everything French desired. Meanwhile in a series of incendiary speeches he urged the freedmen to take the land they needed and defend it with their hoes if necessary. French received no word from Chase, however, and when the sales took place on February 18 there was the utmost confusion over preemption rights, property claims, and so on. In most cases the tax commissioners ruled against the preemptors and sold large slices of preempted land to the highest bidders at an average price of $11 per acre. The freedmen purchased only 2,276 acres at the special rate of $1.25 per acre. In addition several groups of freedmen pooled their resources and purchased 470 acres at an average price of just over $7.00 per acre in the competitive bidding. The whole affair left a sour taste in everybody's mouth. French and the "do-gooder" Gideonites were furious with Philbrick, the tax commissioners, and the government for what they considered deliberate treachery to the freedmen. Philbrick was irritated by abolitionist attacks on him in the press. The freedmen themselves were angry, resentful, and distrustful toward the Yankees who first promised them land and then withdrew the promise.[47]

Meanwhile there was increasing support in Congress for some degree of confiscation. Early in 1864 George Julian introduced a bill to extend the Homestead Act of 1862 to cover the abandoned and confiscated estates of the South. Under Julian's bill these estates would be carved into 40 and 80 acre tracts and made available to Union soldiers, southern freedmen, and loyal southern whites on the homestead principle of full ownership after five years' residence and cultivation. Lydia Maria Child congratulated Julian for his speech in support of the bill, and proclaimed her opinion that land monopoly was "only another phase of Slavery; another form of the absorption of Labor by Capital,

---

Royal, 247-49, 251, 254-55, 257, 265-66, 276-77; quotation is from Higginson, Journal, entry of Nov. 21, 1863, Higginson Papers, HU.

[47] Rose, "Rehearsal for Reconstruction," 382-88; Holland, Letters and Diary of Laura Towne, 129-30; Pearson, Letters from Port Royal, 251, 254-55, 257, 265-66, 277-78; Higginson to S. H. Gay, Feb. 13, 1864, Gay Papers, CU; Independent, Apr. 21, May 5, 1864, Jan. 26, 1865.

which has tormented and degraded the world from the beginning." The House passed Julian's bill on May 12, 1864, by a vote of 75-64; it was reported from Senate committee, but did not come up for discussion before the end of the session in July.[48]

Julian realized that his confiscation-homestead measure would be of little value unless Congress repealed the joint resolution of 1862 (tacked on to the second Confiscation Act) limiting forfeiture of property to the life of the offender. In February 1864, the House voted to amend the joint resolution to read no forfeiture "contrary to the Constitution," hoping that the Supreme Court would uphold permanent confiscation of rebel property. Julian confidently expected an endorsement of repeal by the Republican National Convention. The National Union League convention meeting the day before the Republican conclave approved repeal, but conservatives on the resolutions committee squelched a similar endorsement by the Republican convention. On June 28, however, the Senate passed an amendment to the Freedmen's Bureau bill repealing the 1862 joint resolution outright. Encouraged, Julian went to see Lincoln on July 2, hoping to convince the president of the constitutionality of permanent confiscation. Lincoln admitted that when he had forced Congress to adopt the joint resolution in 1862 he had not examined the question thoroughly. William Whiting's written and spoken arguments, the president said, had since convinced him of his error, and he was now ready to sign a bill repealing the joint resolution of 1862. The 1864 session of Congress ended, however, without House and Senate agreement on the precise form such a repeal should take. On February 24, 1865, the House repealed the joint resolution outright by the margin of one vote. But in the final conference committee report on the Freedmen's Bureau bill the repeal amendment was dropped in order to win conservative support for the Bureau. Thus, although Congress had voted on three separate occasions to repeal the 1862 joint resolution, failure of both houses to get together on the exact form of repeal had defeated the measure. Nor was Julian's confiscation-homestead

[48] Patrick W. Riddleberger, "George W. Julian: Abolitionist Land Reformer," *Agricultural History*, v (July, 1955), 109-10; L. M. Child to Julian, Mar. 27, 1864, Giddings-Julian Correspondence, LC. For additional expressions of abolitionist support for Julian's bill, see Gerrit Smith to Julian, Mar. 25, 1864, and Lewis Tappan to Julian, Mar. 28, 1864, *ibid.*

measure passed during the 1864-65 session.[49] Abolitionists and radical Republicans were disappointed, but they looked hopefully to the next session of Congress for favorable action on the land question.

One provision of the Freedmen's Bureau bill encouraged this hope. William Whiting had used his influence with members of Congress to get a land proviso inserted in the bill. As finally passed on March 3, 1865, the act contained a section stating that to every male refugee or freedman "shall be assigned not more than forty acres" of abandoned or confiscated land at rental for three years and an option to purchase at the end of that time with "such title thereto as the United States can convey." This was rather vague and indefinite, but it was the best Congress could do at the time. Friends of the freedmen hoped that subsequent legislation would provide the freedmen with clear and definite titles to land of their own in the reconstructed South.[50]

As Sherman marched through Georgia in the last month of 1864, thousands of ragged and destitute freedmen straggled along behind his troops. When the army reached Savannah the problem of providing for the refugees became acute. General Sherman and Secretary of War Stanton, who was visiting Savannah, held a conference on January 12 with twenty Negro leaders of the city. Four days later Sherman issued Special Field Order no. 15, designating the coastline and riverbanks 30 miles inland from Charleston to Jacksonville as an area for exclusive Negro settlement. Freedmen settling in this area could take up not more than 40 acres of land per family, to which they would be given "possessory titles" until Congress "shall regulate the title." No white persons except authorized military personnel were to be allowed in the area. Sherman's order gave General Saxton full power over freedmen's affairs from Charleston to Key West.[51]

Abolitionist reaction to the order was mixed. Sydney Gay commended the provision granting land to the freedmen, but he dis-

---

[49] LaWanda Cox, "The Promise of Land for the Freedmen," *Mississippi Valley Historical Review*, XLV (Dec. 1958), 432-34; George Julian, *Political Recollections, 1840 to 1872* (Chicago, 1884), 242, 245-46; *Cong. Globe*, 38 Cong., 1 Sess., 519, 3,327, 38 Cong., 2 Sess., 1,026, 1,125.

[50] Cox, "Promise of Land for the Freedmen," *op.cit.*, 414-18, 426, 432; *U.S. Statutes at Large*, XIII, 507-09.

[51] *O.R.*, Ser. 1, vol. XLVII, part ii, 60-62.

liked the feature setting the Negroes apart from the white race. This smacked too much of colonization. Sherman was known as a conservative on the Negro question, and Gay distrusted his motives. The *Commonwealth* also criticized the order and asserted that "all this effort at segregating the negroes will fail. If they were good enough to live in the presence of white men as slaves, they are good enough to dwell in their presence as freemen."[52]

On the other hand, Tilton wholeheartedly approved of the measure, considering it a long-overdue effort to settle a large number of freedmen on land of their own. He discounted the colonization fears of other abolitionists, and expressed the belief that white teachers and officials of freedmen's aid societies would be allowed in the area. Secretary Stanton sent a private letter to Garrison seeking to allay the suspicions of abolitionists, pointing out that the Negro leaders themselves had expressed a desire to be set apart from whites. Stanton enclosed the minutes of the conference with Savannah Negroes, which Garrison published in the *Liberator* along with a defense of Sherman's order.[53] Abolitionists received private assurances from General Saxton that white teachers and missionaries would be allowed in the area. In fact, said Saxton, the segregation aspect of the order had been designed to keep out speculators, slick traders, and other whites who might take advantage of the freedmen. Saxton had full power over admission or exclusion of whites, and any who had legitimate business in the area would be admitted.[54]

These assurances mollified suspicious abolitionists and converted them to supporters of Sherman's order. Saxton, however, had been by no means as confident at first of the advantages of the plan as he appeared later in his assurances to abolitionists. He was reluctant to accept the duties of administering the order, fearing that it was just one more promise of land to the freedmen destined to be broken. Stanton, however, assured him that all would be well, and Saxton went vigorously to work to place

[52] *New York Tribune*, Jan. 30, 1865; *Commonwealth*, Feb. 4, 1865. See also W. L. Garrison, Jr. to Ellen Garrison, Feb. 5, 1865, Garrison Papers, sc; and S. B. Anthony to E. C. Stanton, Feb. 14, 1865, Stanton Papers, lc.

[53] *Independent*, Feb. 2, 1865; Edwin M. Stanton to Garrison, Feb. 12, 1865, Garrison Papers, bpl; *Liberator*, Feb. 17, 24, 1865.

[54] T. W. Higginson to Anne and Louisa Higginson, Mar. 6, 1865, Saxton to Higginson, Apr. 4, 1865, Higginson Papers, hu.

thousands of Georgia and South Carolina freedmen on the land. He appointed Reuben Tomlinson inspector general of Freedmen's Affairs. French and Gannett also assisted Saxton in the massive project. By the end of June 1865, they had settled more than 40,000 freedmen on the coastal lands. Many of the Negroes were growing good crops on their new land. The experiment seemed to be a success.[55]

By 1865 abolitionists had achieved partial success in their drive to obtain land for the freedmen. Powerful congressional leaders such as Julian, Sumner, and Thaddeus Stevens were committed to the principle. Congress had gone on record in favor of repealing the joint resolution of 1862 forbidding permanent confiscation. The promise of land for the freedmen was embodied in legislation creating the Freedmen's Bureau. Freedmen on the South Carolina sea islands had purchased several thousand acres of land at tax sales. Freedmen from all over the southeastern United States were being settled with "possessory titles" on thousands of acres in South Carolina, Georgia, and Florida. Abolitionists looked ahead hopefully to action by future Congresses guaranteeing these titles and setting aside more land for the freedmen. During the war abolitionist spokesmen had called for a three-cornered policy to insure the safety and permanence of reconstruction: education, land, and the ballot for the freedmen. At the war's end there were encouraging signs in favor of the realization of all three objectives.

[55] Rose, "Rehearsal for Reconstruction," 428-30; Holland, *Letters and Diary of Laura Towne*, 151, 153; *The Freedmen's Record*, i (August 1865), 128.

THE announcement of Lincoln's reconstruction policy in December 1863, crystallized radical opposition to the president. The resulting Republican intraparty struggle over the 1864 presidential nomination produced a schism in abolitionist ranks. Ever since the issuance of the Emancipation Proclamation, Wendell Phillips had been growing impatient with Lincoln's apparent failure to recognize that the revolutionary character of the war required more than mere freedom for the Negro. Garrison, on the other hand, while critical of many presidential policies, was inclined to approve the growth of Lincoln's antislavery sentiments since 1861 and to trust to the future for further advances. During 1864 Phillips became the leader of an anti-Lincoln faction of abolitionists while Garrison championed the president's renomination and reelection.

An epic debate between Phillips and Garrison at the annual meeting of the Massachusetts Anti-Slavery Society in January 1864, brought their disagreements into sharp focus. Phillips offered a resolution affirming that "the Government, in its haste, is ready to sacrifice the interest and honor of the North to secure a sham peace . . . leaving the freedmen and the Southern States under the control of the late slaveholders." In a speech supporting his resolution Phillips conceded that Lincoln had done a great work in freeing the slaves. "All honor to Abraham Lincoln for so much!" But mere negative freedom would leave the Negro in a condition little better than slavery. "There stands the black man naked, homeless; he does not own a handful of dust; he has no education; he has no roof to shelter him." President Lincoln had "no desire, no purpose, no thought, to lift the freed negro to a higher status, social or political, than that of a mere labourer, superintended by others." This was not the man, said Phillips, to undertake the difficult job of reconstruction.

Garrison moved to amend Phillips' resolution by striking out the words "is ready to sacrifice" and inserting "is in danger of sacrificing." Phillips' wording, argued Garrison, implied an impeachment of the president's motives. Garrison was prepared to criticize certain aspects of Lincoln's policy, but he believed in the president's honesty and good will. "There was a time when I had little confidence in Abraham Lincoln, and very little respect for him," confessed Garrison. His revocation of Frémont's and Hunter's emancipation edicts had drawn Garrison's sharp censure. But then came the Emancipation Proclamation and the enrollment of Negro soldiers. "I have changed my opinion of Abraham Lincoln," said Garrison. "True, he is open to criticism for his slowness, and needs spurring on to yet more decisive action; but I am not willing to believe that he is 'ready to sacrifice the interest and honor of the North to secure a sham peace.'" Lincoln was pledged never to revoke his emancipation policy. He had shown great capacity for moral growth while in office. "In my judgment," concluded Garrison, "the re-election of Abraham Lincoln to the Presidency of the United States would be the safest and wisest course."

Phillips replied that he could not accept Garrison's amendment, for he believed that "the Government was knowingly preparing for a peace in disregard of the negro." The unequal treatment of Negro soldiers "is proof that the Government is *ready* for terms which ignore the rights of the negro." The Emancipation Proclamation, moreover, did not "bestow those rights which this [Anti-Slavery] Society was established to secure. The technical liberty which the black man gets is no better than apprenticeship. Equality is our claim, but it is not within the intention of the Government to grant it to the freedmen. I cannot trust the Government, therefore." Garrison replied briefly, arguing that the president had moved ahead as fast as public opinion would allow. When the vote was taken, Garrison's amendment lost by a narrow margin and Phillips' original resolution was adopted. The Massachusetts Anti-Slavery Society had by implication committed itself against Lincoln's renomination.[1]

The outcome of the Massachusetts meeting caused widespread speculation about an impending schism between Garrison and Phillips. The Associated Press telegraphed an account of their debate to newspapers all over the North. The conservative press chortled gleefully over the prospect of a division in radical ranks, but abolitionists hastened to deny that any such division existed. The disagreement between Phillips and Garrison was a mere dif-

[1] *Liberator*, Feb. 5, 1864.

ference of opinion about men and measures, they said, and did not represent a fundamental break between the two men. Garrison published an editorial defending Phillips' right to express any opinion he wished from the antislavery platform. The *Anti-Slavery Standard* stated flatly that "no schism exists in, or impends over, the Anti-Slavery body."[2] But the clash between Garrison and Phillips was more serious than abolitionists were ready to admit publicly. One young abolitionist who was present at the meeting thought "there was something terrible in . . . Phillips' and Garrison's quarrel."[3] Garrison received several letters from abolitionists supporting his position and criticizing Phillips sharply. Oliver Johnson warned privately that nothing but grief could come of abolitionists injecting themselves into partisan politics.[4]

But his warning went unheeded. It was inevitable that abolitionists should become politically involved in 1864. In 1860 the politicians had shied away from them, but by 1864 the situation was reversed, and some abolitionists had become respected spokesmen of the radical wing of the Republican party. Their advice and support was sought by politicians. Two presidential aspirants had been making use of covert abolitionist support for more than a year in their bids to wrest the Republican nomination from Lincoln in 1864.

Secretary of the Treasury Chase was the abolitionists' strongest ally in the cabinet. Chase was a man of inordinate ambition. He wanted very much to become president. Since early 1862 he had been building an organization of loyal supporters in the patronage-rich Treasury Department. Several abolitionists participated in this activity. B. Rush Plumly, special agent of the Treasury Department in Missouri and New Orleans, was quietly preparing for the 1864 nomination as early as April 1862. "*I am* for you," Plumly told Chase. "I do not avow it, but I prepare for it thro' a thousand channels. While I scrupulously discharge every duty of my Office, I *do* use it, here and all over the country—

[2] *Liberator*, Feb. 26, 1864; *N.A.S. Standard*, Feb. 13, 1864. See also *Independent*, Feb. 4, 1864; *Commonwealth*, Feb. 12, 1864; and *Principia*, Feb. 18, 1864.

[3] Lillie B. Chace to Lucy Lovell, Feb. 7, 1864, in Lillie B. C. Wyman and Arthur C. Wyman, *Elizabeth Buffum Chace* (2 vols., Boston, 1914), I, 258-59.

[4] Henry C. Badger to Garrison, Feb. 3, 1864, J. M. McKim to Garrison, Feb. 9, 1864, Samuel J. May to Garrison, Feb. 10, 1864, Oliver Johnson to Garrison, Feb. 18, 1864, Garrison Papers, BPL.

quietly but effectively, for the *future*!"[5] With the knowledge of
Governor Andrew and other members of the Bird Club in Massachusetts, a strong Chase organization was formed in the Boston
Custom House. Tilton and Joshua Leavitt of the *Independent*
were sympathetic to the Chase movement, and stood ready to give
it their support. James Redpath offered to publish a book of
Chase's writings and speeches to publicize the secretary's fitness
for the presidency.[6]

Many radical Republican leaders, dissatisfied with Lincoln's
moderate war and reconstruction policies and resentful of the
influence of William H. Seward and Montgomery Blair in the
cabinet, supported the Chase movement. Greeley and Gay were
sympathetic and were prepared to swing the *Tribune* to Chase's
support at the proper time.[7] On the day after Lincoln announced
his reconstruction policy in December 1863, Chase's supporters
held a strategy conference in Washington. Activity continued
behind the scenes until February 18, when Tilton published an
editorial in the *Independent* calling for the nomination of a man
committed to equalitarianism and justice in the solution of the
reconstruction problem. Without mentioning any names, Tilton
made it clear that Chase fulfilled these requirements and Lincoln
did not. Two days later came publication of the famous Pomeroy
Circular, a statement issued by the manager of the Chase forces,
Senator S. C. Pomeroy, declaring that the interests of the country
required a change of administration and that Chase was the man
to crush the rebellion and reconstruct the nation in accordance
with the principles of justice. Taking the Circular as a cue, the
New York Tribune came out cautiously for Chase.[8]

The Pomeroy Circular backfired and destroyed Chase's candi-

---

[5] Plumly to Chase, Apr. 21, 1862, Chase Papers, LC. See also Plumly to Chase,
Jan. 2, June 20, Aug. 20, Oct. 3, Dec. 1, 1863, Feb. 26, 1864, *ibid.*

[6] James W. Stone to Chase, Jan. 15, May 5, July 2, 1862, May 29, 1863, Joshua
Leavitt to Chase, Sept. 30, Nov. 12, 1863, Feb. 12, 1864, James Redpath to Chase,
Jan. 15, 1864, Chase Papers, LC; Joshua Leavitt to Charles Sumner, Nov. 18,
1863, Sumner Papers, HU. See also John Jay to Chase, Sept. 25, 1862, Chase
Papers, LC.

[7] Whitelaw Reid to Horace Greeley, Jan. 19, 1864, Gay Papers, CU.

[8] William F. Zornow, *Lincoln and the Party Divided* (Norman, Okla., 1954),
32-36, 41-49; Charles R. Wilson, "The Original Chase Organization Meeting and
The Next Presidential Election," *Mississippi Valley Historical Review*, XXIII
(June 1936), 61-63; *Independent*, Feb. 18, 1864; *New York Tribune*, Feb. 23, 24,
1864. The *Boston Commonwealth* also endorsed the Chase movement. *Commonwealth*, Mar. 4, 1864.

dacy. Angry protests arose from local Republican leaders all over the North. The Republican National Committee endorsed Lincoln for renomination by a margin of four to one. State legislatures voted approval of Lincoln. The legislature of Ohio, Chase's home state, came out for "old Abe." In the light of this overwhelming popular support for Lincoln, the Chase boom collapsed. Chase's friend, James Freeman Clarke, advised him to issue a statement declining to be a presidential candidate. Such a statement, said Clarke, would increase the respect of the country for Chase and preserve his influence in the cabinet. Chase received similar advice from Greeley and James Garfield, and on March 5 he announced that he was not a candidate for the presidency. His statement did not preclude a possible draft if Lincoln's support should suddenly falter, and some of Chase's friends continued to hope for a miracle to catapult the secretary back into the presidential race.[9]

Like Chase, John C. Frémont had a strong desire to be president. Frémont had been a special hero of the abolitionists since his issuance of an emancipation edict in Missouri in 1861. A year later, in August 1862, Moncure Conway attacked Lincoln's conservatism on the slavery issue and nominated Frémont as the next president. Later in the month Frémont spoke to a huge crowd in the Boston Music Hall, flanked on the platform by several abolitionist leaders who were beginning to speak more openly of him as a possible presidential candidate in 1864.[10] In 1863 Frémont bought a summer home in Nahant, Massachusetts, and began to consult frequently with abolitionist leaders in the Old Bay State. His wife, Jessie Benton Frémont, exercised her well-known charm on abolitionists in an effort to secure their support for her husband's candidacy. Frémont himself gained the ear and the friendship of Wendell Phillips, who encouraged his presidential aspirations.[11]

Frémont was popular with German-Americans, who were gen-

[9] Zornow, *Lincoln and the Party Divided*, 49-57; James Freeman Clarke to Chase, Feb. 26, 1864, Chase Papers, LC; *New York Tribune*, Mar. 11, 1864; *Independent*, Mar. 17, 1864.

[10] *Liberator*, Aug. 8, Sept. 5, 12, 1862; W. L. Garrison, Jr., to Fanny Garrison, Aug. 30, 1862, Garrison Papers, SC; B. Rush Plumly to S. H. Gay, Nov. 28, 1862, Gay Papers, CU.

[11] M. W. Chapman to "Lizzy and Anne," May 15, 1863, Weston Papers, BPL; Phillips to Charles Sumner, Nov. 27, 1863, Sumner Papers, HU.

erally radical on the slavery question. Karl Heinzen, a militant abolitionist, was the leader of the German-American community in Boston. In May 1863, Heinzen announced his support for Frémont as the next president and set about to rally German-American support for the "Pathfinder." Early in July the "German National Central Committee" issued an appeal for the organization of German-American voters into political clubs. Such clubs were formed in most of the North's major cities. Heinzen organized the Boston club, which adopted a radical platform and endorsed Frémont for president. Delegates from several German clubs came together in Cleveland on October 20, 1863, for a national convention. Heinzen played a major role at this meeting, which adopted a platform calling for revision of the Constitution to bring it into line with the Declaration of Independence; treatment of the southern states as "territories for the purpose of reconstruction"; and the confiscation and redistribution among freedmen of the estates of slaveholders.[12]

The Frémont movement began to gather momentum. Radical German-Americans in Missouri and Illinois endorsed the "Pathfinder" in March 1864. Frémont and his friends began to woo abolitionist support openly. A few young radicals in New York City formed a "Freedom and Frémont Club" in the office of the Women's Loyal National League. On March 18 a Frémont Club was formally organized in the city. Several abolitionists, including Parker Pillsbury, David Plumb, and George Cheever, took part in the meeting; resolutions were passed denouncing Lincoln's reconstruction policy and calling for the equality of all men before the law. A week later the *Principia* placed the Frémont banner at the head of its editorial columns. All over the North radical Germans and the Phillips wing of the abolitionists organized Frémont clubs.[13]

While remaining hostile toward Lincoln, however, many abolitionists refused to follow Phillips into the Frémont movement.

[12] Carl Wittke, *Against the Current, The Life of Karl Heinzen* (Chicago, 1945), 189-91; Ruhl Jacob Bartlett, *John C. Frémont and the Republican Party* (Columbus, Ohio, 1930), 88-97.

[13] *Ibid.*, 96-100; George Thompson to Garrison, Feb. 29, Mar. 2, 1864, Oliver Johnson to Garrison, Mar. 1, 2, 1864, Frémont to Garrison, Mar. 5, 1864, Garrison Papers, BPL; Susan B. Anthony to Charles Sumner, Mar. 6, 1864, John Jay to Sumner, Mar. 7, 8, 1864, Sumner Papers, HU; *Principia*, Mar. 3, 17, 24, Apr. 14, 21, 1864; *Liberator*, Mar. 25, 1864.

Some of Chase's supporters had not given up hope of overturning the Lincoln bandwagon. Tilton, Greeley, and other Chase men urged postponement of the Republican convention (scheduled for June 7) until the beginning of September, hoping that the tide of war or politics would turn in their favor in the interval. The *Boston Commonwealth* endorsed this suggestion and continued to hammer away at the president in strong language. But Lincoln's popularity with rank and file Republicans was too great for the postponement ruse to succeed. The pro-Lincoln Republican National Committee ignored the pressure for postponement. Chase's abolitionist supporters were left temporarily dangling in mid-air.[14]

While Phillips, Cheever, and Goodell threw themselves into the Frémont movement, and while Tilton, Anna Dickinson, and the *Boston Commonwealth* refused to support either Lincoln or Frémont, several other abolitionists publicly committed themselves to Lincoln's renomination. On February 27 Garrison wrote privately to McKim that Lincoln's renomination was in the best interests of the antislavery cause. "I am not his partisan, nor a member of the Republican party, nor a politician," said Garrison, "but I believe it will be the game of the rebels on the one hand, and of the Copperheads on the other, to urge rival Republican candidates to take the field, and thus to 'divide and conquer.' " McKim sent a copy of this letter to the powerful *Philadelphia Press*, which published it to counteract the widespread belief that Phillips spoke for most abolitionists in opposing Lincoln. "Whatever William Lloyd Garrison says has weight," commented the *Press* editorially. "He is still, as he has been for more than thirty years, the leader of the American Abolitionists. . . . Mr. Garrison, in sustaining Mr. Lincoln, proves conclusively that the President is not the candidate of the weak, semi-pro-slavery conservative faction." The managing editor of the *Press* told McKim privately that "the publication of Mr. Garrison's opinion must do great good. Everything that identifies the Government with Abolitionism is a benefit. . . . If the anti-

[14] Zornow, *Lincoln and the Party Divided*, 57-62; Frank Sanborn to Moncure Conway, Mar. 31, 1864, Conway Papers, cu; Ralph Ray Fahrney, *Horace Greeley and the* Tribune *in the Civil War* (Cedar Rapids, Iowa, 1936), 175, 184-85; *Independent*, Apr. 7, 1864; *Commonwealth*, Apr. 22, 1864.

266

slavery radicals cease to give the government support it must of necessity fall into the hands of the conservatives."[15]

Garrison repeated his warning against Republican factionalism in an important editorial in the March 18th *Liberator*. Lincoln was not perfect, said Garrison, but there was nevertheless "much to rejoice over and to be thankful for; and a thousand incidental errors and blunders are easily to be borne with on the part of him who, at one blow, severed the chains of three millions three hundred thousand slaves." Pro-Frémont abolitionists sharply criticized Garrison's editorial, which was widely reprinted or cited in the Republican press. Noting the influence of the editorial among wavering antislavery men, Phillips remarked sadly that "a million dollars would have been a cheap purchase for the Administration of the *Liberator's* article on the Presidency."[16] But Garrison received many approving letters from fellow abolitionists and Republicans.[17] Some of the veteran crusaders who remembered the days when they had received nothing but abuse from politicians were amused by the Republican lionization of Garrison. "It is vastly entertaining to see how Forney's 'Press' . . . quotes from the Liberator, & extols Mr. Garrison as a man of the soundest judgment, . . . and repeats again & again, that *he* is in favor of Lincoln," wrote Mary Grew. "Verily, the abolitionists have wakened up to find themselves famous."[18]

Meanwhile the preparations for Frémont's nomination went forward. On May 6 a group of German-American radicals and several abolitionists, including Stephen S. Foster, Karl Heinzen, and James Redpath issued a call for a nominating convention to be held in Cleveland on May 31. A few days later the Central Frémont Club of New York City issued a similar call, urging as a platform the principles of Negro suffrage and southern land redistribution. Several abolitionists, including Phillips, Goodell,

[15] Garrison to McKim, Feb. 27, 1864, published with editorial comment in *Philadelphia Press*, Mar. 17, 1864; John S. Stockton to McKim, Mar. 16, 1864, enclosed with letter from McKim to Garrison, Mar. 18, 1864, in Garrison Papers, BPL.

[16] *Philadelphia Press*, Mar. 23, 1864; *N.A.S. Standard*, Mar. 26, 1864; E. M. Davis to Garrison, Mar. 17, 1864, E. C. Stanton to Garrison, Apr. 22, 1864, Garrison Papers, BPL; Phillips' statement quoted in *Liberator*, May 20, 1864.

[17] Alfred Love to Garrison, Mar. 10, 1864, J. S. Griffing to Garrison, Mar. 24, 1864, Isaac W. Arnold to Garrison, Apr. 2, 1864, George W. Curtis to Garrison, May 7, 1864, Garrison Papers, BPL.

[18] Mary Grew to Samuel May, Jr., Mar. 31, 1864, Garrison Papers, BPL.

George and Henry Cheever, Elizabeth Cady Stanton, Susan B. Anthony, and Frederick Douglass signed this call or endorsed the convention.[19]

The atmosphere was electric with tension as abolitionists gathered in New York on May 10 and 11 for the annual meeting of the American Anti-Slavery Society. Everyone expected a sharp debate between the partisans of Lincoln and Frémont. They were not disappointed. At the beginning of the meeting Phillips offered a resolution affirming that abolitionists saw "no evidence of [an administration] purpose to put the freedom of the negro on such a basis as will secure it against every peril." Phillips charged that Lincoln's whole philosophy during the war had been to touch slavery as lightly as possible, and then only to save the Union. His philosophy of reconstruction was similar. "What McClellan was on the battle-field—'Do as little hurt as possible!'—Lincoln is in civil affairs—'Make as little change as possible!' " Phillips would consider Lincoln's election "the end of Union in my day, or its reconstruction on terms worse than Disunion." Phillips was booed and hissed by the nonabolitionist spectators in the galleries at Cooper Union. Garrison's pro-Lincoln speeches were applauded by the same spectators. But the hard-core abolitionists were with Phillips by a small majority and the Society adopted his resolution by a margin of three votes.[20]

With an impressive show of unanimity the Church Anti-Slavery Society on May 25 denounced Lincoln's reconstruction policy and came out against his reelection.[21] But the real fireworks were reserved for the meeting of the New England Anti-Slavery Society at the end of May. The prospect of a lively debate drew the largest crowd in the Society's history. They were treated to a pyrotechnic display of oratory. The best speakers were on the anti-Lincoln side and included Phillips, Pillsbury, and Foster. Garrison, Samuel May, Jr., and Henry Wright led the array of speakers supporting Lincoln. Both sides repeated the same arguments they

[19] *Principia*, May 12, 26, June 2, 1864; *New York Tribune*, May 18, 1864; *Commonwealth*, May 13, 1864.

[20] *Liberator*, May 20, 27, 1864. See also Garrison to Helen Garrison, May 13, 1864, Garrison Papers, BPL; and Parker Pillsbury to Sumner, May 8, 24, 1864, Sumner Papers, HU.

[21] Resolutions of the Church Anti-Slavery Society adopted in annual meeting, May 25, 1864, copy in Cheever Papers, AAS.

had been using for several months. Pillsbury introduced resolutions condemning the Lincoln administration for its reconstruction policy, its refusal to support Negro suffrage, and its slowness to grant equal treatment to Negro soldiers. Garrison offered a series of counterresolutions praising the administration for its antislavery achievements and "respectfully but earnestly" urging Lincoln "to use his utmost constitutional power to secure equal rights for all under the national flag." As the debate became acrimonious Andrew T. Foss, veteran abolitionist lecturer, appealed for compromise and good will between the two sides. "I accept Wendell Phillips' criticism" of the administration, said Foss. "On the other hand, I accept the favorable view taken by Mr. Garrison of the reelection of Abraham Lincoln. I will rather accept him for four years more than run the risk of McClellan, or any Copperhead of that sort." When the vote finally came, Garrison's resolutions lost by a slim margin and Pillsbury's were adopted. Then in a gesture of belated magnanimity, Garrison's resolutions, with slight modifications, were also passed.[22] This effort to smooth over differences went for naught. Witnesses reported privately that the discussion had been even more bitter than appeared from the published accounts. The *Anti-Slavery Standard* admitted editorially that the debates had been "marked . . . by the passionate partisanship of the caucus."[23]

Numerous abolitionists were among the 400 delegates who gathered in Cleveland on May 31 to nominate General Frémont as the presidential candidate of the "Radical Democratic Party." The other two groups represented at the convention were radical German-Americans and dissatisfied War Democrats. Wendell Phillips was unable to attend the convention, but his personality nevertheless dominated the proceedings. A letter from Phillips was read to the cheering delegates. "Mr. Lincoln's model of reconstruction is the experiment in Louisiana, which puts all power into the hands of the unchanged white race," proclaimed the letter. "Such reconstruction makes the freedom of the negro a sham, and perpetuates Slavery under a softer

---

[22] *Liberator*, June 3, 10, 1864.
[23] S. B. Anthony to E. C. Stanton, May 30, 1864, Gerrit Smith Papers, su; Pillsbury to Sumner, May 29, 1864, Sumner Papers, hu; Lillie B. C. Wyman, "Reminiscences of Wendell Phillips," *New England Magazine*, xxvii (Feb. 1903), 725-26; *N.A.S. Standard*, June 4, 1864.

name." Phillips urged the convention to "demand a reconstruction of States as speedily as possible, on the basis of every loyal man, white or black, sharing the land and the ballot."

Several abolitionists served on the convention's resolutions committee, which presented a radical platform to the meeting. This platform called for a constitutional amendment to prohibit slavery and "secure to all men absolute equality before the law"; for control of reconstruction by Congress; and for the distribution of confiscated rebel lands "among the soldiers and settlers." Parker Pillsbury had tried to write into the platform a specific endorsement of Negro suffrage and land for *freedmen*, but the phrases about equality before the law and land for *settlers* were the best he could do. Both points were left deliberately vague because of the presence of War Democrats at the convention. This disturbed some of the abolitionists, and the adoption of another plank denouncing Lincoln's suspension of habeas corpus disturbed them even more, for this was the main objection of "Copperheads" to the Lincoln administration. Coupled with the nomination of Colonel John Cochrane (who had voted for Pierce, Buchanan, and Breckinridge before the war) for vice president, the habeas corpus plank created suspicion that the War Democratic wing of the Frémont movement was bidding for an alliance with the Copperhead Democracy.[24]

Pro-Frémont abolitionists were not entirely satisfied with the outcome of the convention, but publicly they praised its work and stepped up their attacks on Lincoln.[25] Phillips at this time believed that Frémont had a good chance to win the election. If the regular Republican convention in Baltimore nominated Lincoln he thought the radicals should stay with Frémont until the end. Phillips had some illusory hopes that the Republicans would drop Lincoln at the last moment and nominate a more radical candidate—Chase, Butler, Frémont, or Grant—in which case the

[24] The proceedings of the convention were reported in the *New York Tribune*, June 1, 1864; *Liberator*, June 3, 1864; *N.A.S. Standard*, June 4, 1864, and many other newspapers. See also *Commonwealth*, June 10, July 8, 1864; S. B. Anthony to E. C. Stanton, June 12, 1864, Stanton Papers, LC; and William F. Zornow, "The Cleveland Convention, 1864, and the Radical Democrats," *Mid-America*, XXXVI (Jan. 1954), 39-53.

[25] *Principia*, June 9, 1864; Henry Cheever to George Cheever, June 8, 1864, Cheever Papers, AAS; Parker Pillsbury to Sumner, June 18, 1864, Sumner Papers, HU.

Frémont party could dissolve itself and endorse the Republican candidate. In any event Phillips was sure the Frémont movement would scare the Baltimore convention into adopting a more radical platform than they would otherwise have done. Phillips got himself elected as a delegate to the Massachusetts Republican convention and tried there to secure an unpledged delegation to Baltimore. He also used his influence in an effort to elect an anti-Lincoln or unpledged delegation from Vermont. Both efforts failed. Phillips' views of politics at this time were curiously unrealistic. His hopes of defeating Lincoln's renomination had no basis in fact. The Baltimore convention unanimously renominated the president on June 7.[26]

Garrison attended the Baltimore convention in company with Theodore Tilton. Strong emotions overcame the veteran crusader as he sat in the galleries and watched the convention adopt a resolution pledging the Republican party to the extinction of slavery by constitutional amendment. He reported to his *Liberator* readers that when this resolution was read "the whole body of delegates sprang to their feet as by one impulse, giving vent to their feelings in prolonged cheering. . . . Was not a spectacle like that rich compensation for more than thirty years of universal personal opprobrium?" Garrison wrote privately that "even my friend Phillips would have been highly gratified with the tone and spirit of the Convention. In the speeches made, every allusion made to slavery as a curse to be extirpated . . . has been most enthusiastically responded to."[27]

From Baltimore Garrison and Tilton proceeded to Washington for Garrison's first visit to the capital. He was cordially welcomed everywhere. He visited the Senate Chamber and sent in his card to Wilson and Sumner, who immediately came out and escorted him to one of the Senate desks on the floor. There he sat for a time while several Republican senators came over to shake his hand and talk with him. He also visited Secretary of War Stanton. The brusque secretary, who usually dispatched callers with haste, took time for a long private interview with Garrison. The next

[26] Phillips to Moncure Conway, Mar. 16, 1864, Conway Papers, cu; *Liberator*, May 27, 1864; *Commonwealth*, May 27, 1864; Wendell P. Garrison and Francis J. Garrison, *William Lloyd Garrison* (4 vols., Boston, 1885-89), IV, 110.

[27] *Liberator*, June 24, 1864; Garrison to Helen Garrison, June 8, 1864, Garrison Papers, BPL.

day Garrison and Tilton visited Lincoln and talked with him for more than an hour. The president thanked Garrison for his support, and confided that the antislavery plank in the Republican platform had been inserted at presidential request. Garrison found his interview with Lincoln "very satisfactory." "There is no mistake about it in regard to Mr. Lincoln's desire to do all that he can . . . to uproot slavery, and give fair-play to the emancipated. I was much pleased with his spirit."[28]

Many Republican papers printed Garrison's praises of Lincoln after the nomination. "Our papers are publishing all of Garrison's eulogies on Lincoln and calling the attention of all abolitionists and radical republicans to them," noted Susan B. Anthony, a Frémont supporter, with disgust. "In their eyes, Mr. Garrison is now a sound philosopher and wise statesman."[29] Several abolitionists who had previously opposed Lincoln's renomination now came out in his favor, arguing that anything which split the Republican party created a danger of Democratic victory.[30]

The *Liberator* and the Republican press began to excoriate the Frémont movement. Frémont's supporters struck back hard. General G. P. Cluseret, French-born radical and former officer on Frémont's staff, had established a Frémont organ in New York City called the *New Nation*. After Lincoln's nomination Cluseret published a bitter criticism of Garrison, calling him "a lost leader . . . drunk with the wine of political expediency." Garrison the reformer had descended to the level of a conservative politician. "Mr. Garrison is in his dotage," charged the *New Nation*. "The old man is no longer the prophet whom we revered. . . . Either Garrison has been wrong for a quarter of a century; or he is wrong now."[31] Several pro-Frémont abolitionists canceled their subscriptions to the *Liberator*. The Hovey trust fund committee, dominated by anti-Lincoln abolitionists, cut off its subsidy to the *Liberator*. For a time it appeared that Garrison might have to suspend publication of the paper. But abolitionist friends who agreed with his political views came to the rescue. Gerrit

[28] Garrison to Helen Garrison, June 9, 11, 1864, Garrison Papers, BPL.

[29] S. B. Anthony to E. C. Stanton, June 12, 1864, Stanton Papers, LC.

[30] C. A. Stackpole to Garrison, June 6, 1864, M. W. Chapman to Elizabeth Pease Nichols, July 18, 1864, Francis George Shaw to Garrison, Aug. 12, 1864, Garrison Papers, BPL; Wm. Channing to W. L. Garrison, Jr., Aug. 20, 1864, Garrison Papers, SC.

[31] Reprinted in *Liberator*, June 24, 1864.

Smith sent a check for $200. E. D. Draper and Samuel Sewall raised enough money to replace the Hovey fund subsidy. Scores of abolitionists all over the North sent small contributions, and the *Liberator* was saved.[32]

In June, Oliver Johnson published in the *Anti-Slavery Standard* a sharp editorial attack on the Frémont movement. This editorial set the tone for pro-Lincoln abolitionists during the rest of the campaign. Johnson asserted that the habeas corpus plank in the Cleveland platform and the acceptance letters of Frémont and Cochrane, both of which passed lightly over the slavery question and dwelt on points calculated to appeal to Democrats, proved that Frémont's political managers were bidding for an alliance with the Copperhead Democracy. Johnson called Cochrane an "unscrupulous and slippery politician" who had been proslavery before the war and now posed as an antislavery radical. "And this man, without a drop of anti-slavery blood in his veins, and whose life has been one long chapter of intrigue, is led in triumph to the chair of a Political Anti-Slavery Convention by a non-voting Abolitionist [Pillsbury] who can find no ground for confidence in President Lincoln, the emancipator of 3,000,000 slaves!" Johnson believed that there was Copperhead money behind the *New Nation*. The Frémont party was "an ally of Jeff Davis," he told George Cheever. "Frémont I believe is a scoundrel, in alliance with the corrupt leaders of the Copperhead Democracy to divide the loyal voters of the country in the Presidential election. The Anti-Slavery of the Cleveland platform is Homeopathic, its Copperheadism conspicuous and emphatic; and so . . . [are] the letters of its candidates."[33]

And indeed there appeared to be much truth in Johnson's statements. The editorial policy of the *New Nation* seemed to be "anything to beat Lincoln." Cluseret actively sought an alliance with the Democrats. "There is so little difference between this party and the Democratic party," said the *New Nation*, "that it would be easy to adopt a common ticket, which would sweep every thing before it." The *New York World* and other Demo-

---

[32] Gerrit Smith to Garrison, Aug. 1, 1864, Tilton to Garrison, Sept. 6, 1864, Garrison Papers, BPL; *Liberator*, July 8, 15, 22, 29, Aug. 19, 26, Sept. 2, 16, Oct. 7, 14, Dec. 30, 1864.

[33] *N.A.S. Standard*, June 18, 1864; Oliver Johnson to George Cheever, June 16, 1864, Cheever Papers, AAS.

cratic papers praised the Frémont movement and publicly chortled over the prospect of facing a divided Republican party at the polls.[34] In the light of these facts many abolitionists who opposed Lincoln were forced to repudiate Frémont also. "Applying the same rule of judgment to that political movement that we habitually apply to all others," wrote Aaron M. Powell, "I cannot see how Mr. Phillips, or any other truly conscientious Abolitionist can give it support." Yet Powell could not bring himself to support Lincoln either, and thought that abolitionists should remain completely independent of politics in this campaign as they had done in the past. Lydia Maria Child had disliked the Frémont movement from the beginning, and after the developments of June 1864, she liked it even less. "I am exceedingly sorry for the course Wendell Phillips is pursuing," she wrote. "Since Frémont has written a letter so obviously courting the Copperheads, I don't see how he *can* stand by him."[35]

Even Frank Sanborn, who had little use for Lincoln, turned against the Frémont movement. If there was a prospect of the success of any other Republican, said Sanborn, "we would denounce Lincoln tomorrow. But bad as Lincoln is, he is better than Wood and Vallandigham. . . . Of all evils we wish to avoid throwing power into the hands of the peace Democrats." Frémont had destroyed himself by his behavior since his nomination. "His *New Nation* has been wretchedly edited and his strength since the Cleveland letter has fallen off two thirds. So much for dallying with Copperheads. . . . Except Phillips, who is not very confidently for Frémont, there is not a leading man in N[ew] E[ngland] who favors him. . . . It is a great pity—for Frémont had good stuff in him."[36]

But Frémont's abolitionist backers were not yet ready to give up on the general. On July 11 George Cheever delivered a power-

---

[34] Statements by the *New Nation* and Democratic papers quoted in *N.A.S. Standard*, June 18, July 2, 1864; and *Liberator*, June 24, July 1, 1864.

[35] Powell to Samuel May, Jr., June 25, 1864, Samuel May, Jr., Papers, BPL; L. M. Child to Whittier, June 19, 1864, in John Albree, ed., *Whittier Correspondence from Oakknoll* (Salem, Mass., 1911), 147-48. See also Sarah Shaw to Elizabeth Gay, June 25, 1864, Gay Papers, CU; and H. C. Neall to Whittier, June 20, 1864, Whittier Papers, Essex Institute.

[36] Sanborn to Moncure Conway, July 10, 1864, Conway Papers, CU. See also *Commonwealth*, July 8, 22, 1864. Fernando Wood and Clement Vallandigham were prominent Copperheads.

ful attack on Lincoln which was later published in pamphlet form. He reviewed Lincoln's slowness to act against slavery, his revocation of emancipation edicts issued by his generals, his efforts to delay emancipation thirty-seven years and colonize the Negroes abroad, his unequal treatment of Negro troops, and his reconstruction policy which would restore the slaveholding element to power and leave the freedman little more than a serf on the soil of his former master. Contrast this man, said Cheever, with John C. Frémont, who throughout the war had been in the forefront of the revolution of freedom and equality. How could any abolitionist hesitate to choose between these two men?[37] William Goodell, Parker Pillsbury, Phillips, and several other abolitionists continued their active support of Frémont.

In June, however, Theodore Tilton came out flatly against the Frémont movement. The Republican platform, he said, was better than the platform of the "Radical Democratic Party" despite the radicalism of the latter, because the *real* purpose of the Frémont movement was an alliance with the Democratic forces. "Our chief regret in view of the Cleveland Convention is, that it has unhappily led a number of excellent friends of the Good Cause into a snare," wrote Tilton. "Those well-known Abolitionists identified with the Cleveland movement—and whose sincerity and uprightness we do not for a moment question—have unwittingly placed themselves in a false position, where their influence is working against the best interests of the country, and is bringing a lamentable discredit upon themselves." Tilton admired Phillips and agreed with most of his criticisms of Lincoln, but he could see no reason to support a party which, in the end, would turn out far worse than the Lincoln party.[38]

Phillips replied in the next issue of the *Independent*. He denounced the conservatism of the Republican party and stated that he preferred the whole loaf of the Cleveland platform to the half-loaf of Baltimore. The Cleveland platform called for a constitutional amendment not only to abolish slavery, but to guarantee to all men equality before the law. "To me this is the chief gem of its crown," said Phillips. "There can be no possible

---

[37] George B. Cheever, *A Change of Administration, for the Security of the Government, a Christian Duty and a National Necessity* (New York, 1864).

[38] *Independent*, June 23, 1864.

salvation for the Union, and no safety for the negro in his freedom, except on the basis of every man of every race equal in privilege, right, and franchise before the law. This idea, again, owes its birth to the Cleveland Movement, and is, as yet, the high-water mark of American politics." Phillips would welcome an alliance between Frémont and the Democrats if it came on the basis of the Cleveland platform. Even if unsuccessful at the ballot box, the Frémont movement would have served its purpose if it forced the Republican party to adopt a more radical policy.

Tilton answered Phillips' arguments in the same issue of the *Independent*. Preserving a tone of respect and admiration for the great orator, Tilton nevertheless accused him of political naiveté for believing that any alliance could be forged between the Frémont party and the Peace Democracy on terms favorable to the former. Tilton recounted his experience at the Frémont ratification meeting in New York on June 27. Nearly all the speakers were Peace Democrats! The loudest cheers were for McClellan! The chief speaker, Colonel Cochrane, alluded to Frémont and McClellan as "twin cherries on one stalk!" It should have been obvious, said Tilton, that the Democrats were using the Frémont movement as a weapon to wound the Republican party. The "equality before the law" plank of the Cleveland platform, he declared, was a sham. "Now, we would be glad if a great political party could go before the country on the high issue of giving every black man a vote," wrote Tilton. "But the country is not ready for such an issue. . . . If the next election were to turn upon the question of giving every black man a vote, the Copperheads would achieve the next administration. If the country were ready for such an issue, the Baltimore Convention would have made it. . . . Any man who knows the meaning of the Cleveland movement laughs at the idea that Frémont and Cochrane are fighting a battle for the sake of the negro's right to vote. Neither of these men, in their letters of acceptance, said a word about the rights of the negro." Tilton was not happy with the Republican nomination either. "If the great Union party represented at Baltimore had chosen some other candidate, we would have had no regrets. If, before November, some strange change in events should put another name at the head of this great party, we would cheerfully acquiesce. But we shall not join the Copperheads in a coalition to make bad worse."[39]

Phillips restated his position in the next issue of the *Independent*, chiding Tilton for his declaration that the country was not ready for Negro suffrage. That may be true, said Phillips, but since when did radicals wait until the country was ready for a reform before advocating it? Phillips avowed himself an agitator, not a politician. He had taken an advanced position in the Frémont movement not for political reasons, but for purposes of reform. He criticized Tilton for rejecting his abolitionist training and supporting Lincoln on grounds of expediency. In a brief reply, Tilton repeated his earlier arguments and asserted that he was as much in favor of Negro equality as Phillips. But before that measure became acceptable to public opinion there would have to be a great deal more discussion and agitation of the issue than there had been. "We are in for the agitation, heart and soul —as zealously as Mr. Phillips. But it is simply unwise to push a great question to an untimely defeat at the ballot-box." Phillips was foolish if he really believed that the Cleveland movement was genuinely in favor of Negro suffrage. "Let Mr. Phillips go to a Frémont ratification meeting, and speak on the 'absolute equality' of negroes and Irishmen, and he will be rioted out of the house," wrote Tilton. "We are willing to join Mr. Phillips in any new and needful labors to make the country ready for the negroes' fullest rights; but the Frémont meetings are just the places where such ideas are not welcome."[40]

This exchange between two of the foremost radicals in the country was widely reprinted and commented on by the northern press. Tilton conceded privately that his set-to with Phillips had been the most unpleasant experience of his editorial career. He was worried that his friend Phillips would take it personally. That worry was erased when Phillips sent him a cordial note

[39] *ibid.*, June 30, 1864. Tilton informed a friend privately that "the Frémont meeting at Cooper Institute was the most complete and disastrous Copperhead display that could possibly have happened. The genuine antislavery men who have joined this company are in great sorrow and confusion." Tilton to Hugh Bond, June 30, 1864, Tilton Papers, NYHS.

[40] *Independent*, July 7, 1864.

declaring that their difference of opinion in no way impaired their friendship.[41]

But if the exchange between Phillips and Tilton was conducted in a spirit of cordiality, the same could not be said of the dispute within the American Anti-Slavery Society itself. Phillips was incensed by the *Anti-Slavery Standard's* criticisms of the Frémont movement. He accused Oliver Johnson of making the *Standard* a partisan Lincoln sheet. Phillips maintained that the anti-Lincoln resolutions adopted in 1864 by the Massachusetts, American, and New England Anti-Slavery Societies bound the *Standard*, as official organ of the American Society, to pursue an anti-Lincoln course. He called a meeting of the Society's executive committee and demanded suspension of the *Standard* unless it changed its policy.[42] Oliver Johnson was just as adamant. "If I am required either to set the Standard in opposition to Lincoln's election," he told the executive committee, "or to suppress my honest convictions in regard to the Frémont movement, its candidates and platform, I shall resign the editorial chair."[43] Despite Phillips' fulminations, a majority of the executive committee, led by Garrison, supported Johnson and passed a vote of confidence in his editorial policy. The committee told Johnson only to avoid "undue partiality" toward Lincoln. The *Standard* subsequently followed a course of "non-partisan" support of the president. Its position was the same as in 1860, explained Johnson, when the *Standard* was not a partisan proponent of Lincoln but nevertheless hoped for his victory.[44] This did not satisfy Phillips and his adherents, who denounced the *Standard* as "a disgrace to the Society & a fraud upon it," and withdrew their financial support from the paper. The schism in the Society grew so bitter that the executive committee canceled the usual Fourth of July and August First (anniversary of West Indian emancipa-

[41] Tilton to Garrison, June 30, 1864, Garrison Papers, BPL; Tilton to Anna Dickinson, July 13, 1864, Dickinson Papers, LC.

[42] Garrison to Samuel May, Jr., June 17, 1864, Garrison to Oliver Johnson, June 17, 20, 1864, George Thompson to Garrison, June 18, 1864, Garrison Papers, BPL.

[43] Johnson to Garrison, June 20, 1864, Garrison Papers, BPL.

[44] Samuel May, Jr., to S. J. May, June 22, 1864, S. J. May Papers, BPL; Oliver Johnson to Samuel May, Jr., June 23, 30, 1864, Samuel May, Jr., Papers, BPL; Johnson to Garrison, June 23, 1864, Johnson to Phillips, June 22, 1864, Garrison Papers, BPL; *N.A.S. Standard*, Aug. 6, 1864.

tion) celebrations in order to prevent additional public quarrels.[45]

The *Standard, Liberator,* and *Independent* continued to hammer away at the theme that pro-Frémont abolitionists were playing into the hands of Copperheads. Some radical Republicans who disliked Lincoln warned the Frémont abolitionists that their activities endangered the Republican party.[46] Late in July, Phillips and Karl Heinzen, sensitive to Republican criticism of their course and of Frémont's alleged dalliance with Copperheads, had a long talk with the "Pathfinder" and published the results. Frémont reaffirmed his support of the radical planks in the Cleveland platform. "The negroes ought to have all the rights of whites," he said. "The word white must disappear from the laws and Constitutions." Frémont indignantly denied the rumors that he would throw over the radical planks in the Cleveland platform in return for the regular Democratic nomination. He would like to make an alliance with the War Democrats to beat Lincoln, Frémont said, but he would accept such an alliance on none but his own terms. Phillips, Heinzen, and other abolitionist backers of Frémont were satisfied with the interview. If the Democratic convention in Chicago at the end of August nominated McClellan and repudiated the antislavery portion of the Cleveland platform, said Goodell, the Frémont ticket would go its own way and have nothing to do with the Democrats. If, on the other hand, the Democratic party split apart at Chicago, the Frémont party would be glad to absorb the War Democrats on the basis of the Cleveland platform.[47]

The Boston Emancipation League and its organ, the *Commonwealth,* represented those abolitionists who were opposed to Lincoln but who were suspicious of the Frémont movement. George Stearns, chief backer of the *Commonwealth,* invited a group of abolitionists to meet with Frémont at Stearns' home on August 9 to discuss the political situation. Present at the meeting besides Stearns and Frémont were Phillips, Frank Bird, Elizur Wright, Bronson Alcott, and two lesser-known officials of the Emancipa-

[45] Oliver Johnson to Samuel May, Jr., Oct. 15, 1864, Garrison Papers, BPL; Johnson to Samuel May, Jr., Sept. 22, 1864, Samuel May, Jr., Papers, BPL; W. L. Garrison, Jr., to Martha Wright, Oct. 6, 1864, Garrison Papers, SC; *Liberator,* June 24, July 22, 1864.

[46] *N.A.S. Standard,* July 16, 1864; *Liberator,* July 29, 1864; *Principia,* July 21, 1864; Henry Wilson to George Cheever, July 27, 1864, Cheever Papers, AAS.

[47] *Principia,* Aug. 4, 1864; *Commonwealth,* Aug. 5, 1864.

tion League. They questioned Frémont closely. The general stated that he expected a contest between the War Democrats and the Copperheads at the Chicago convention. The former would prevail, he believed, and nominate him on a radical platform. Frémont thought that with the support of the War Democrats and radical Republicans he had a good chance of beating Lincoln. Stearns and some of the others were skeptical, but Phillips came away from the meeting with renewed enthusiasm for the Frémont cause. He wanted to call an immediate convention of New England radical Republicans to endorse Frémont.[48]

But two weeks later Phillips' optimism had vanished and he told Elizabeth Cady Stanton that McClellan would be nominated at Chicago on a peace platform.[49] What had happened to dull Phillips' hopefulness? Northern morale dropped to its lowest point in August 1864. Grant was stalemated in Virginia and casualty lists were mounting. Sherman was stymied before Atlanta. Frustration, despair, and defeatism overcame the northern people in July and August. Early in August Sydney Gay reported that things were "never so gloomy." "The people would vote today for any compromise that would bring peace without sacrifice of the Union," and there was "a growing party for peace at any price, even disunion." Lincoln's "chances of reelection grow daily less & less, & the chances of any Copperhead traitor better and better." Many other abolitionists echoed Gay's somber observations. Henry Raymond, chairman of the Republican National Committee, received letters from dozens of Republican politicians reporting defeatism and an alarming growth of anti-Lincoln sentiment around the country. On August 23 Lincoln wrote his famous memorandum stating that he would probably not be reelected and that it would be his duty to cooperate with the president-elect to save the Union before the next inauguration.[50]

The North's defeatism, plus the growing exasperation of radical Republicans with the president after his pocket veto of the

[48] George Stearns to Bronson Alcott, Aug. 8, 1864, Alcott Papers, Concord Public Library; Alcott, Diary, entries of August 9 and 10, ibid.

[49] Phillips to E. C. Stanton, Aug. 22, 1864, in Theodore Stanton and Harriot Stanton Blatch, Elizabeth Cady Stanton (2 vols., New York, 1922), ii, 98.

[50] Gay to Elizabeth Gay, Aug. 6, 1864, Gay Papers, cu; Francis Brown, Raymond of the Times (New York, 1951), 259-60; Roy P. Basler, ed., The Collected Works of Abraham Lincoln (9 vols., New Brunswick, 1955), vii, 514.

Wade-Davis bill, combined to produce a movement to replace Lincoln on the Republican ticket with someone more likely to unite the party and win the election—such as Chase, Butler, or Grant. Several abolitionists were active in this movement. On July 21 Henry Winter Davis, one of the radical congressional leaders, got in touch with George Cheever and suggested the possibility of persuading both Lincoln and Frémont to withdraw in favor of a new candidate. Cheever wrote to several abolitionist friends to ask them what they thought of this idea. He received favorable replies from Tilton and from the leaders of the Emancipation League. At the end of July Cheever drew up a list of men to consult about the project. Davis approved the list and on August 14 and 18 a group of abolitionists and radicals, including Cheever, Tilton, Greeley, and Parke Godwin (managing editor of the *New York Evening Post*) met at the homes of David Dudley Field and George Opdyke in New York to formulate plans. Senators Chandler, Wade, and Sumner, ex-Secretary Chase, and Governor Andrew gave cautious and qualified support to the project.[51]

The radicals tentatively scheduled a new Republican convention for September 28 in Cincinnati.[52] Meanwhile on August 21 a group of Boston abolitionists headed by Stearns apprised Frémont in a public letter of the movement for a new convention and "emphatically advise[d]" both Frémont and Lincoln to withdraw their candidacies. They asked Frémont to state definitely whether he would withdraw if Lincoln agreed to do so. Frémont replied four days later that he would pull out of the race if Lincoln did the same and if the new convention nominated a candidate pledged to total victory over the Confederacy and a complete abolition of slavery.[53]

The radical leaders of this movement met again in New York

[51] Zornow, *Lincoln and the Party Divided*, 108-16; Henry Winter Davis to George Cheever, July 21, 31, 1864, Smith Regnas to George Cheever, July 25, 1864, Cheever Papers, AAS; George Cheever to Tilton, July ?, 1864, Amasa Walker to Tilton, July 22, 1864, Tilton Papers, NYHS; Elizur Wright to Gerrit Smith, Aug. 13, 19, 1864, Smith Papers, SU; Sumner to Whittier, Sept. 1, 1864, Whittier Papers, Essex Institute; Henry G. Pearson, *The Life of John Andrew* (2 vols., Boston, 1904), II, 156-63; Fahrney, *Greeley and the* Tribune *in the Civil War*, 198-200.

[52] John A. Stevens to Henry Cheever, Aug. 25, 1864, Amasa Walker to Henry Cheever, Aug. 26, 31, 1864, Cheever Papers, AAS.

[53] *Commonwealth*, Aug. 26, 1864; *Liberator*, Sept. 9, 16, 1864.

at the end of August and decided to sound out northern Republican governors on the plan to replace Lincoln. On September 2, letters written by Tilton and signed by Tilton, Greeley, and Godwin went out to all Republican governors asking them three questions: Can Lincoln be elected? Can he carry your state? Should another candidate be substituted for him? Before these letters were sent, the Democrats had nominated McClellan for president on a virtual peace-at-any-price platform. This was expected, but somehow its actual accomplishment tended to unite Republicans behind Lincoln as the only alternative to McClellan and disaster. Suddenly on September 3 the news flashed across the country that Sherman had taken Atlanta. The North went wild with joy. The long summer of discontent was over. The long-awaited victory was here at last. In this new mood of exhilaration and enthusiasm northern war-weariness and defeatism dissolved like a fog at sunrise. Republican governors received Tilton's inquiry at just the time when this mood was manifesting itself. Consequently the replies were overwhelmingly opposed to the replacement of Lincoln by another candidate. Before the capture of Atlanta a majority of Republican governors might have favored a new convention. But military victory transformed the situation overnight. Lincoln was no longer the discredited leader of a lost cause; he was the mighty captain of a victorious nation, confident of vindication at the polls in November. The plans for a Cincinnati convention were quietly abandoned.[54]

Even before he received the replies of northern governors, Tilton had concluded that unqualified support of Lincoln's candidacy was the only sensible course. "I was opposed to Mr. Lincoln's nomination; but now it becomes the duty of all Unionists to present a united front," he wrote to Anna Dickinson on September 3. "The Baltimore platform is the best in American history—we can pardon something to a second-rate candidate." In an *Independent* editorial Tilton wholeheartedly endorsed the

[54] The replies of the governors to Tilton's letters are in the Tilton Papers, NYHS. See also Sydney Gay to Elizabeth Gay, Sept. 3, 1864, Gay Papers, CU; *New York Tribune*, Sept. 3, 1864; *Liberator*, Sept. 9, 1864; Fahrney, *Greeley and the* Tribune *in the Civil War*, 202; John Nicolay to Tilton, Sept. 6, 1864, and Tilton to Nicolay, Sept. 6, 1864, Lincoln Papers, LC; George Cheever to Elizabeth Washburn, Sept. 10, 1864, and John Austin Stevens to Henry Cheever, Sept. 14, 1864, Cheever Papers, AAS.

Republican party and repeated his lukewarm endorsement of Lincoln. He privately advised Miss Dickinson to come out in favor of Lincoln. She did so in a letter to the *Independent* which attracted wide attention. "This is no personal contest," she declared; "I shall not work for Abraham Lincoln; I shall work for the salvation of my country's life, . . . for the defeat of this disloyal peace party, that will bring ruin and death if it comes into power." In the weeks after the capture of Atlanta many other abolitionists who had previously withheld support from Lincoln followed Tilton's and Dickinson's lead.[55]

On September 6 the *New York Tribune* unequivocally endorsed Lincoln's reelection in an editorial universally attributed to Greeley, but actually written by Sydney Gay.[56] Despite its faults the Lincoln administration, said Gay, was ten thousand times better than the Copperhead Democracy. "Henceforth we fly the banner of ABRAHAM LINCOLN for the next Presidency, choosing that far rather than the Disunion and a quarter of century of wars, or the Union and political servitude which our opponents would give us." Gay agreed with much of the radicals' criticism of Lincoln, but the president "has done seven-eighths of the work after his fashion; there must be vigor and virtue enough left in him to do the other fraction. . . . We MUST re-elect him, and, God helping us, we WILL."

McClellan partly repudiated the Democratic peace platform, but his letter of acceptance stated that peace should be concluded solely on the basis of Union and the southern states readmitted with all their rights unimpaired. This seemed to mean that if elected, McClellan would seek to preserve slavery in a restored Union. Since all abolitionists and most Republicans by this time linked Union with emancipation as inseparable war aims, McClellan's position was as abhorrent to them as Vallandigham's.[57]

Several abolitionists took the stump for Lincoln. Anna Dickinson made numerous well-publicized speeches. Tilton threw himself into the campaign with such abandon that he fainted from ex-

[55] Tilton to Anna Dickinson, Sept. 3, 5, 1864, Dickinson Papers, LC; Tilton's and Miss Dickinson's public endorsements of the Republican party published in *Independent*, Sept. 8, 1864. In a letter to the *Liberator* of Sept. 23, 1864, Frederick Douglass retracted his earlier opposition to Lincoln and declared that every friend of the slave should now rally to the president's support.
[56] S. H. Gay to Elizabeth Gay, Sept. 9, 1864, Gay Papers, cu.
[57] *Liberator*, Sept. 16, 1864.

haustion on the speaker's platform at a rally three days before the election. Henry Wright stumped for Lincoln in Illinois and Michigan. William Burleigh spoke frequently in and around New York City. Andrew T. Foss gave forty speeches for Lincoln during the campaign. Gerrit Smith spoke nearly every day for five weeks in upstate New York. Worthy of note is the fact that many of these speeches, especially those by Anna Dickinson, consisted mainly of attacks on McClellan and contained little praise of Lincoln or his administration.[58]

After the capture of Atlanta, Republicans generally were confident of victory. But Frémont was still in the race, and there was a danger that he would take away enough votes from Lincoln to put McClellan in the White House. Republican Senator Zachariah Chandler journeyed to New York in an effort to persuade Frémont to withdraw from the race. Chandler may have been authorized by Lincoln to promise that in return for Frémont's withdrawal, Montgomery Blair, the *bête noire* of the radicals, would be dropped from the cabinet.[59] Meanwhile a number of Boston abolitionists, headed by George Stearns, put pressure on Frémont to pull out of the race. Frémont consulted several abolitionist friends. Whittier advised him to withdraw for the good of the country. Wendell Phillips, implacable to the end, urged Frémont to stay in the race as a symbol of radical ideas. But Phillips was the only prominent figure to give Frémont this advice, and on September 17 the "Pathfinder" decided to withdraw. In a letter on that day to Stearns and his associates, Frémont grudgingly urged his backers to support Lincoln for reelection. The letter was published on September 22, and the next day Lincoln accepted Montgomery Blair's resignation. Frémont's

[58] Tilton to Anna Dickinson, Sept. 14, Oct. 4, 1864, Dickinson Papers, LC; Tilton to John Nicolay, Nov. 12, 1864, Lincoln Papers, LC; *Liberator*, Sept. 16, Oct. 7, 28, Nov. 4, 1864, Feb. 3, 17, 1865; William H. Burleigh, *Poems by W. H. Burleigh, With a Sketch of His Life by Celia Burleigh* (New York, 1871), xxv-xxvi; Gerrit Smith to Garrison, Oct. 10, 1864, Garrison Papers, BPL; *Commonwealth*, Sept. 16, 1864; *N.A.S. Standard*, Sept. 24, 1864.

[59] For a discussion of the Chandler mission, see Winfred A. Harbison, "Zachariah Chandler's Part in the Re-election of Abraham Lincoln," *Mississippi Valley Historical Review*, XXII (Sept. 1936), 267-76; and Charles R. Wilson, "New Light on the Lincoln-Blair-Frémont 'Bargain' of 1864," *American Historical Review*, XLII (Oct. 1936), 71-78.

withdrawal united the Republican party once more. Republicans now looked forward confidently to victory in November.[60]

Some of Frémont's supporters were angered by his withdrawal. Elizabeth Cady Stanton, Susan B. Anthony, and George Cheever refused to follow the general into the Lincoln camp.[61] There were rumors that Phillips would take the stump for Lincoln, but Phillips himself squelched these with the statement that he would "cut off both hands before doing anything to aid Abraham Lincoln's election."[62] Phillips tried to make his position clear in speeches to hostile Boston and New York audiences in October. He avowed himself a reformer, not a politician. He judged Lincoln by the reform standards of equality and justice for the freedmen. The president had fallen short of these standards, said Phillips, and hence he could not support him for reelection. Most of Phillips' fellow abolitionists regretted these speeches, for by giving them Phillips had sacrificed some of the influence and prestige he had gained since the outbreak of the war.[63] Phillips' stand in 1864 revealed a lack of political realism. If all antislavery sympathizers had followed his advice and refused to support Lincoln, the abolitionist cause would have suffered a disastrous defeat. Fortunately for the cause and for the nation, all but a handful of antislavery men followed Garrison rather than Phillips in 1864.

All abolitionists, even Phillips, hailed the Republican triumph in November as a great victory for freedom. "The people pronounced for the prosecution of the war in the first place, and in the next for the abolition of slavery," said the *Commonwealth*.

[60] George Stearns to Bronson Alcott, Sept. 11, 1864, Alcott Papers, Concord Public Library; George Stearns, S. R. Urbino, James Stone, Frank Bird, Samuel G. Howe, and Elizur Wright to Frémont, Sept. 9, 1864, and Frémont to Stearns et al., Sept. 17, 1864, published in the Boston papers, Sept. 22, 1864, and the rest of the northern press, Sept. 23, 1864. Jessie Benton Frémont later recalled that Whittier's advice had been decisive in her husband's decision to withdraw. Allan Nevins, *Frémont: Pathmaker of the West* (2nd ed., New York, 1955), 582. See also *ibid.*, 579-82; and *Commonwealth*, Oct. 8, 1864.

[61] Stanton and Blatch, *Elizabeth Cady Stanton*, II, 100-01; George Cheever to Elizabeth Washburn, Nov. 1, 1864, Cheever Papers, AAS; Oliver Johnson to Gerrit Smith, Nov. 23, 1864, Smith Papers, SU.

[62] Stanton and Blatch, *Elizabeth Cady Stanton*, II, 100-01n.

[63] *Liberator*, Oct. 28, 1864; *Commonwealth*, Oct. 29, 1864; W. L. Garrison, Jr., to Martha Wright, Oct. 23, Nov. 13, 1864, Samuel J. May to W. L. Garrison, Jr., Oct. 26, 1864, Garrison Papers, SC; W. P. Garrison to W. L. Garrison, Oct. 27, 1864, W. P. Garrison Papers, HU.

"With a logic which never fails them, they linked together these two things and made them one and inseparable." Phillips urged all abolitionists to forget past differences and work together for the common cause. "Now our common duty is to throw all personal matters behind us and rally together to claim of the Republican party the performance of their pledge [the Thirteenth Amendment]," he told Elizabeth Cady Stanton. "On that issue the canvass was conducted, and now we have a right to demand the 'bond,' and they a right to demand that we shall help them attain the capability of granting it." Universal freedom for the Negro was assured by Lincoln's reelection; abolitionists must work to persuade the people and their government to take the next step forward—universal equality.[64]

[64] *Commonwealth*, Nov. 19, 1864; Wendell Phillips to E. C. Stanton, Nov. 20, 1864, Stanton Papers, LC. See also *Liberator*, Nov. 18, 1864; and a speech by Phillips published in the *Philadelphia Press*, Dec. 19, 1864.

XIII ✦ SCHISM IN THE RANKS:

1864-1865

IN 1865 there occurred a schism in the Garrisonian abolitionist movement comparable in importance to the division of 1840. One of the main causes of the schism of 1865 was the sharp clash between the followers of Garrison and Phillips over the presidential election of 1864, but there were other causes, dating back many years. The controversy between Pillsbury and Foster, on the one hand, and Garrison on the other regarding the attitude of abolitionists toward the Republican party was long-standing and foreshadowed the conflict of 1864. During the early war years Wendell Phillips exercised a mediating influence between the two factions, but as the war progressed his increasingly revolutionary concept of reconstruction drove him closer to the Pillsbury-Foster camp.

Disputes among Garrisonians over the future of their antislavery societies broke out in the first year of the war. McKim's attempt to resign from the Pennsylvania Anti-Slavery Society and devote himself full-time to freedmen's aid work sparked the controversy. After Lincoln made emancipation an official war aim, the discussion of the fate of organized abolitionism became more heated. At the annual meeting of the Massachusetts Anti-Slavery Society in 1863, Garrison hinted that before another year went by abolitionists might be able to proclaim the jubilee and disband their societies. Stephen S. Foster and Charles Remond, a fiery New England Negro abolitionist, were angered by this kind of talk. After all, they argued, malignant prejudice and discrimination against the Negro would still exist after slavery was gone. One of the declared purposes of the antislavery societies was to end this discrimination. The societies could not consider their work done when slavery was abolished. Garrison agreed that abolitionists were pledged to remove racial discrimination, but maintained that "as Abolitionists, distinctively, our special work is . . . the utter annihilation of slavery." The work of educating, uplifting, and securing equal rights for the freedmen should be done through other organizations or through the established social and political institutions of the nation. The historic mission of antislavery societies, he asserted, would be fulfilled when slavery disappeared from the nation.[1]

Many abolitionists could not see it this way. America's hostility to emancipation had compelled them to organize separately, and they anticipated as much opposition to their drive for equality as they had encountered in the struggle for liberty. Pillsbury and Phillips registered their protest against what they considered Garrison's conservatism by staying away from the Third Decade Anniversary Celebration of the founding of the American Anti-Slavery Society at Philadelphia in December 1863. This meeting was planned partly as a joyous jubilee anticipating the end of the antislavery crusade. Pillsbury and Phillips, ever-mindful of the dangers of a conservative reconstruction, could see little to be thankful for and hence stayed away.[2] Aware of the reasons for their absence, Garrison tried to assuage the apprehensions of the Pillsbury-Phillips faction in his opening speech to the Philadelphia meeting. "We may now confidently hope that our labors are drawing near to an end, so far as the abolition of slavery is concerned," he said. "But our labors in the field of a common humanity, and in the cause of reform, are never to terminate here, except with our mortal lives." Emancipation would confront the nation with the task of lifting generations of enforced ignorance from the minds of the freedmen. "This is a work of mercy and benevolence, in the doing of which we believe the great mass of the people of all denominations, and parties, and sects will flow together."[3]

Frederick Douglass was not entirely satisfied with Garrison's statement. "A mightier work than the abolition of slavery now looms up before the Abolitionist," he told the veteran crusaders at Philadelphia. "The work of the American Anti-Slavery Society will not have been completed until the black men of the South, and the black men of the North, shall have been admitted, fully and completely, into the body politic of America." A month later

[1] *Liberator,* Feb. 6, 1863.
[2] W. L. Garrison, Jr., to Ellen Wright, Dec. 11, 1863, Garrison Papers, sc.
[3] *Proceedings of the American Anti-Slavery Society at its Third Decade Anniversary* (New York, 1864), 5.

Douglass warned a New York audience of the reaction that usually followed revolutions. When the Confederacy was conquered and slavery abolished, there would be danger of a reaction that could rob the black man of his rights. "There never was a time when Anti-Slavery work was more needed than right now. The day that shall see the Rebels at our feet, their weapons flung away, will be the day of trial."[4]

The controversy over presidential politics in 1864 intensified abolitionist differences, but other issues were also driving a wedge between the two wings of the Garrisonian movement. One of these issues was General N. P. Banks' freedmen's labor system in Louisiana. Many Louisiana planters within Banks' department had taken the oath of allegiance and were allowed to continue working their plantations with Negro labor. The Negroes were now free, but Banks had established a system of regulations to govern their conduct that, according to some abolitionists, left the planter-laborer relationship very little different from what it had been under slavery.

When he arrived in New Orleans in December 1862, Banks had found the contrabands in a pitiable condition, crowded into filthy camps and huts, living on half-rations handed out by the army. In an effort to get them back to work on the plantations, Banks issued a general order establishing rules and regulations for a system of labor on January 29, 1863, supplemented by an additional order of February 3, 1864. These orders were designed to put every able-bodied male Negro to work. All freedmen not assigned to plantations were required to labor on public works without wages. The Negro could choose his own employer, but once having chosen he must remain with him for one year. Banks' officers encouraged the Negroes to go to work for their old masters. The order regulated the wage scale by ability up to $10 a month, and stipulated that payment of half the wages would be reserved until the end of the year. Workers were promised "just treatment, healthy rations, comfortable clothing, quarters, fuel, medical attendance, and instruction for children." But plantation hands would not be allowed to leave the plantation without a pass, and provost marshals were ordered to enforce the "continuous and

4 *ibid.*, 111; *New York Tribune*, Jan. 14, 1864.

faithful service, respectful deportment, correct discipline and perfect subordination" of the freedmen.[5]

Abolitionists denounced Banks' order of 1863 as an "execrable proclamation" and called Banks a "born slave-driver." A Massachusetts abolitionist stationed with the army in Louisiana declared that the Banks system was tantamount to a "reestablishment of slavery." Some of Banks' officers, he declared, were Negrophobes and treated the freedmen with cruelty and contempt.[6] Charles K. Whipple asserted that Banks' system "substitutes serfdom for slavery, and seems merely a modification of that intermediate state which Great Britain found to work so ill." A British abolitionist agreed that Banks' policy was similar to the West Indian apprenticeship system which had worked so badly "that it was obliged to be thrown to the dogs."[7]

"It is not easy," wrote Theodore Tilton, "to conceive all the injustice, the oppression, the wrong to inalienable rights, the insult to men keenly capable of feeling it, the misery inflicted on those without redress or opportunity to appeal, [and] the general degradation of a race struggling up toward freedom" produced by Banks' system. Sydney Gay asserted in a *New York Tribune* editorial that Banks' labor system was little better than serfdom. "The negro bound to the soil for a year, compelled to work for wages two-thirds less than he could command in open market, not permitted . . . to have a voice in the contract by which he becomes bound, exposed to the tyrannous caprices of lifelong slaveholders. . . . Such is the serfage which predominates on the soil of Louisiana," wrote Gay angrily.[8]

Abolitionist attacks on Banks found a sympathetic hearing among radical Republicans, but Lincoln supported the general's policy, and it was not substantially changed until after the end of the war. Banks defended himself publicly against radical attacks, and even persuaded some abolitionists, including Garri-

[5] Fred. H. Harrington, *Fighting Politician: Major General N. P. Banks* (Philadelphia, 1948), 104-05; Banks' orders were published in *O.R.*, Ser. 1, vol. xv, 666-67, vol. xxxiv, pt. ii, 227-31.

[6] *Commonwealth*, Feb. 14, 1863; Daniel Mann to S. H. Gay, Feb. 11, 1864, Gay Papers, cu.

[7] *Liberator*, Mar. 11, 1864; J. Perronet Thompson to George Cheever, Mar. 22, 1864, Cheever Papers, aas.

[8] *Independent*, May 5, 1864; *New York Tribune*, July 16, 1864. See also *Independent*, Apr. 7, 1864; and *N.A.S. Standard*, Apr. 23, 1864.

son, that his policy was humanely conceived and wisely carried out for the good of the freedmen. Garrison had never criticized Banks very sharply, and during 1864 he began to reexamine the Banks system more sympathetically. A major reason for this reexamination, of course, was Garrison's support of Lincoln. The president had authorized Banks' policy, and Garrison soon began to defend Banks as part of his effort to vindicate Lincoln. This angered the Phillips wing of the American Anti-Slavery Society and confirmed their belief that Garrison had unaccountably become conservative.

Garrison had several friends stationed with the Union forces in Louisiana who assured him of the essential benevolence of the Banks system. Two men in particular played an important role in shaping Garrison's thinking on this question: Major B. Rush Plumly and the Reverend Edwin Wheelock. Both were veteran abolitionists. Plumly served as special treasury agent in New Orleans and later as a major in the *Corps d'Afrique*. Wheelock had come South as chaplain of a New Hampshire regiment and on February 20, 1863, was appointed deputy superintendent of labor in Louisiana.[9]

Plumly stated that he had been consulted by Banks before issuance of the labor orders, which were drafted primarily with an eye to the best interests of the freedmen. Before Banks came, said Wheelock, the freedmen had been huddled together in filthy camps, and some policy such as that initiated by Banks was absolutely necessary to save them from disease or starvation. Under the Banks system the planter had to provide his laborers with food, clothing, housing, and medical care plus a small plot of land on which the Negroes could grow some of their own food. As a deputy superintendent of labor, Wheelock was assigned to inspect conditions on the plantations. At first there was much disorder. The planters were wedded to their old ways and did not comprehend the revolution going on around them. They did their best to obstruct Banks' policy and make it fail. Wheelock reported planter abuses and obstructionism to Banks, who took

[9] Charles Kassel, "Edwin Miller Wheelock," *Open Court*, xxxiv (Sept. 1920), 564-69, "A Knight-Errant in the Department of the Gulf: Episode in the Life of Edwin Miller Wheelock," *Open Court*, xxxix (Sept. 1925), 563-76, "The Labor System of General Banks—A Lost Episode of Civil War History," *Open Court*, xliii (Jan. 1929), 35-50.

prompt corrective action. Undesirable overseers and provost marshals were removed; some planters were fined or deprived of their plantations. Order gradually emerged from chaos, and by the end of 1863, Wheelock reported, the system had proved a success.[10]

One abolitionist criticism of Banks' labor policy was its fixed rate of low wages. But Garrison pointed out that the provision of food, clothing, housing, and medical care must be added to the wage rate to form a true picture. When this was done, he said, the Louisiana freedmen's standard of living compared favorably with other parts of the South. In the fall of 1864 General Banks spoke in vindication of his policy to a crowded audience in Boston's Tremont Temple. Garrison published the entire speech in the *Liberator* and editorially praised Banks for his successful efforts "to deliver the oppressed from the yoke of bondage, give vitality and success to paralyzed industry, . . . reconcile employers and the employed, . . . [and] establish and multiply schools for those hitherto forbidden to learn the alphabet." Louisiana Negroes were guaranteed equal rights in the courts under the new state constitution, a provision which, said Garrison, some northern states would do well to emulate. Several other abolitionists joined Garrison in approving Banks' policy.[11]

These champions of the Banks system were especially impressed by its provision for education of the freedmen. Banks' labor order of 1863 envisioned creation of a public school system for freedmen financed by property taxes. Under the leadership of Major Plumly a few schools were opened in October 1863. In March 1864, Banks issued a general order creating a "Board of Education for the Department of the Gulf" with power to levy and collect the school tax, establish common schools, employ teachers, and erect schoolhouses. Plumly served as chairman and Wheelock as secretary of the Board. These veteran abolitionists virtually ran the public school system of Louisiana for more

[10] Plumly to Garrison, Sept. 6, Oct. 20, 1864, in *Liberator*, Sept. 23, Nov. 11, 1864; Wheelock to Garrison, Feb. 8, 1865, in *Liberator*, Mar. 3. See also *Liberator*, Apr. 8, July 29, Nov. 11, 1864; and George Hepworth to Garrison, July ?, 1864, Garrison Papers, BPL.

[11] *Liberator*, July 29, Nov. 11, 1864; *N.A.S. Standard*, Nov. 19, 1864; Oliver Johnson to Garrison, July 16, 1864, Garrison Papers, BPL.; Gerrit Smith to Gen. Banks, Nov. 21, 1864, in *Liberator*, Dec. 16. Statement by Garrison quoted from *Liberator*, Nov. 11, 1864.

than a year. By May 1864, they had established 49 schools with an average daily attendance of 5,200 pupils. By the end of July 1865, Plumly and Wheelock had organized 126 schools for the freedmen with 230 teachers giving instruction to 15,000 children in day classes and 5,000 adult freedmen in night and Sunday schools. Garrison pointed to these accomplishments as evidence of the benevolent operation of General Banks' policy.[12]

In spite of these educational achievements, most abolitionists were, in the words of Elizabeth Cady Stanton, astonished that "Garrison should defend the proposed apprenticeship system for the emancipated negroes [in Louisiana]. We say now, as ever, Give us immediately unconditional emancipation, and let there be no reconstruction except on the broadest basis of justice and equality." James McCune Smith, a Negro abolitionist in New York City, was profoundly sorry that his friend Gerrit Smith had expressed approval of the Banks system. "If I had a century of life secured to me," said McCune Smith, "I would not hope to live to see the day of Negro Emancipation, while serfdom of Banks' kind is endorsed by progressive friends of freedom to-day." The *Boston Commonwealth* lamented that Garrison's endorsement of Banks had convinced many Republicans of the safety of reconstruction on the basis of the Banks-Lincoln policy. The *Commonwealth* asserted: "No middle course between acknowledgement and denial of the negro's manhood is possible. If abolition is to be held to mean simply that the negro shall no longer be sold at the auction-block; no longer separated from his wife and children; no longer denied the alphabet; but that he may be put under guardianship; bound out to long terms of service; compelled to work for inadequate wages; made subject to all the old policy regulations . . . of chattelhood; . . . if this is the definition which the administration and the people prefer, we have got to go through a longer and severer struggle than ever."[13]

---

[12] Charles Kassel, "Educating the Slave—A Forgotten Chapter of Civil War History," *Open Court*, xli (Apr. 1927), 239-56; "Education of the Freedmen," *North American Review*, ci (Oct. 1865), 531; *Liberator*, Apr. 15, Sept. 30, 1864, Feb. 24, 1865.

[13] E. C. Stanton to S. B. Anthony, Dec. 29, 1864, in Theodore Stanton and Harriot Stanton Blatch, *Elizabeth Cady Stanton* (2 vols., New York, 1922), ii, 104; James McCune Smith to Gerrit Smith, Feb. 17, 1865, Smith Papers, su; *Commonwealth*, Nov. 19, 1864.

Another issue dividing abolitionists in 1864 was the question of Negro suffrage as a condition of reconstruction. Theoretically all abolitionists were pledged to secure equal civil and political rights for Negroes. Under the leadership of Wendell Phillips a majority of abolitionists had committed themselves to impartial or universal manhood suffrage in the South as a practical condition of reconstruction. But some abolitionists maintained that the American Anti-Slavery Society *as an organization* had nothing to do with the suffrage issue. "I am in favor of universal suffrage, without regard to color," said J. Miller McKim, "but as a member of the American Anti-Slavery Society my work will be accomplished when the slave shall be emancipated." Garrison asserted that the antislavery societies were "not organized specifically to determine" the question of Negro suffrage. "It is a new issue, and one to be settled upon a new basis, as much as the voting of women."[14]

Thus far the abolitionist discussion of Negro suffrage had been confined to procedural problems. But in July 1864, Garrison injected a substantive flavor to the debate in a public letter to Professor Francis W. Newman, an English abolitionist who had criticized Lincoln's failure to include Negro suffrage as part of his reconstruction policy. "The elective franchise is a conventional, not a natural right," said Garrison. Lincoln should not be censured for his refusal to require Negro suffrage, for in the United States the right of suffrage was granted by the states rather than the federal government. Moreover, asked Garrison, "when was it ever known that liberation from bondage was accompanied by a recognition of political equality? Chattels personal may be instantly translated from the auction block into freemen; but when were they ever taken at the same time to the ballot-box, and invested with all political rights and immunities?" Garrison believed that even if Lincoln had the power to enfranchise the freedmen, such action might backfire. "Submitted to as a necessity at the outset, as soon as the [reconstructed] State was organized and left to manage its own affairs, the white population, with their superior intelligence, wealth and power, would unquestionably alter the franchise in accordance with their prejudices." Universal

[14] McKim to Garrison, Mar. 17, 1864, Garrison to Oliver Johnson, May 5, 1864, Garrison Papers, BPL.

suffrage in the South, said Garrison, would come slowly only "by a struggle on the part of the disfranchised, and a growing conviction of its justice."[15]

Garrison's statement shocked many of his fellow abolitionists. "Often during the last thirty years, Anti-Slavery men have denounced the black laws of some of the States which disfranchise citizens on account of color, as part and parcel of Slavery, the work of doughface politicians," declared the *Commonwealth.* "When before now did Mr. Garrison aid and comfort these doughfaces, by saying that 'the elective franchise is a conventional not a natural right?' When did he petrify his zealous friends by telling them majestically that 'according to the laws of development and progress it is not practicable' to extend the right of suffrage to colored men?" Liberty included the right of self-government, said the *Commonwealth,* and without the ballot the Negro's freedom would be a mere sham. "O Garrison, this is not abolitionism," proclaimed the *Commonwealth.* "Black men may well enough rejoice that they have got, out of our military necessity, a certain instalment of liberty. . . . But for a prophet to say they may well be contented with this . . . is of the madness which goes before ruin."[16]

The *Commonwealth's* strictures probably represented the opinion of most abolitionists. But no matter how much they might publicly deprecate Garrison's course, several abolitionists privately conceded some of his points. After all, they had been arguing for thirty years that slavery deadened the intellect and dulled the moral sense of the Negro. How then could they ask immediate suffrage for this creature degraded by generations of slavery? This question posed a serious dilemma for many abolitionists. "Suffrage to me, is a difficult problem of solution," said Parker Pillsbury. "I cannot believe it should be enjoyed by those who cannot both write and read their ballots."[17] Some abolitionists thought the solution lay in a literacy test applied impartially to both races. Others admitted the injustice of the North trying to impose Negro suffrage on a reconstructed South while most northern states barred black men from the polls.

15 *Liberator,* July 22, 1864.
16 *Commonwealth,* Aug. 5, 1864. See also *ibid.,* Sept. 9, 1864; and Lillie B. Chace to Anna Dickinson, Aug. 21, 1864, Dickinson Papers, LC.
17 Pillsbury to Sumner, July 3, 1864, Sumner Papers, HU.

For most abolitionists, however, these considerations gave way to their belief in the overwhelming practical necessity of Negro suffrage in the postwar South. Professor Newman stated the case succinctly: "In all history I know not where to find so senseless an infatuation as that of putting power into the hands of your disloyal conquered enemies, and casting your loyal friends under their feet." Thomas Wentworth Higginson declared that "if under any other circumstances we might excuse ourselves for delaying the recognition of the freedmen's right to suffrage, yet it would be utterly disastrous to do so now, when two-thirds of the white population will remain disloyal, even when conquered." Charles K. Whipple affirmed that Negro suffrage was necessary for two reasons: to give the freedmen the means to protect their freedom; and to "secure an immediate loyal population to transact political affairs and uphold the United States government in the Southern States." Whipple was not much impressed by the argument that the southern Negro was too ignorant to vote. Since the nation had "refused to make ignorance a bar in the case of Irish immigrants, it would not be fair to set up the plea of similar ignorance against these other new comers. Let us stick by the principle stated in the Declaration of Independence, that the right of the governing power depends on the consent of the governed."[18]

Wendell Phillips proclaimed that universal suffrage was a vital requisite of genuine democracy. "I do not believe in an English freedom," said Phillips, "that trusts the welfare of the dependent class to the good will and moral sense of the upper class. This is aristocracy. . . . Our philosophy of government, since the 4th day of July, 1776, is that no class is safe, no freedom is real, . . . which does not place in the hands of the man himself the power to protect his own rights." Benevolent enterprises to educate the freedmen were not sufficient. "Gen. Banks says that he has set up schools for the blacks. . . . I have no doubt there are some hundreds of scholars in those schools; but I undertake to say that Gen. Banks cannot educate a mass of men by any system of benevolence." Only when the state feared the power of the ballot in

[18] Newman quoted in *Liberator*, July 1, 1864; Higginson quoted in *Atlantic Monthly*, xiv (Oct. 1864), 517-18; Whipple's statements published in *N.A.S. Standard*, June 11, Dec. 17, 1864.

the hands of ignorant men did it take steps to provide universal education in order to insure social stability. Universal suffrage, therefore, was a prerequisite to universal education in the South.[19]

Negro suffrage was rapidly becoming the central issue of reconstruction, and Garrison came under increasing pressure to make his position on this issue clear. In January 1865, he published an editorial reaffirming his belief in equal rights for all men. But the national government, said Garrison, had no more right to require Negro suffrage in Louisiana than in Connecticut. Moreover, so long as most northern states denied the ballot to Negroes the North had no *moral* right to impose equal suffrage on the South. Abolitionists should rejoice in the great revolution of opinion that had made emancipation possible instead of grumbling that liberty was worthless without the ballot. Garrison believed that emancipation "would open the way for ultimate social, civil and political equality; but this through industrial and educational development, and not by any arbitrary mandate."[20]

Most abolitionists were far from satisfied with this explanation of Garrison's position. Even his allies in the contest with the Phillips-Pillsbury wing of the antislavery society urged him to make his endorsement of equal suffrage more emphatic. "As abolitionists, we are the friends and *advocates* of Negro suffrage," McKim told Garrison. "For there is not, and in the nature of things cannot be, any difference of opinion among abolitionists on any essential point connected with this subject." McKim urged Garrison "to say, in terms not to be mistaken—'The right to vote for the negro on the same terms that it is given to the white man.'" The *Anti-Slavery Standard* stated flatly that "the black men must have their political rights asserted and maintained, or they cannot long retain their personal rights. . . . These are questions which naturally grow out of such a revolution as we are now enacting, and now is the time to settle them in the right way forever." Oliver Johnson, editor of the *Standard*, urged Garrison to take a clear stand in favor of impartial suffrage at the forthcoming meeting of the Massachusetts Anti-Slavery Society. "Don't let Phillips & Co. drive you too far by their attempts to put you in a

---

[19] *Liberator*, Feb. 10, 1865. See also speeches of Phillips published by *Liberator*, Dec. 16, 1864, and *Commonwealth*, Dec. 31, 1864.
[20] *Liberator*, Jan. 13, 1865.

false position," wrote Johnson. "Obliged as we are to defend the Administration from their unjust assaults, we must still stand firmly for the equal rights of the colored race."[21]

At the Massachusetts meeting Phillips introduced a series of resolutions affirming that "no emancipation can be effectual and no freedom real, unless the negro has the ballot." Garrison offered a counterresolution asserting that "if, as reconstructed, Louisiana ought not to be admitted to the Union because she excludes her colored population from the polls, then Connecticut, New Jersey, Pennsylvania, and all the Western States ought not to be in the Union for the same reason." Garrison agreed with Phillips that racial discrimination would be intolerable in the reconstructed Union, and he therefore proposed that "Congress should lose no time in submitting to the people an amendment of the Constitution, making the electoral law uniform in all the States, without regard to complexional distinctions." The suggestion of a constitutional amendment prohibiting racial discrimination was not new, for Phillips had broached the idea nearly a year before. But it was an important statement coming from Garrison, since it represented his first firm declaration in favor of equal suffrage as a condition of reconstruction. But the Phillips wing of the Society now regarded the method of constitutional amendment inadequate. If the southern states were once readmitted without Negro suffrage they could form a bloc large enough to defeat ratification of such an amendment. Negro suffrage must be secured by congressional act *prior* to the readmission of southern states as a *fundamental condition* of readmission. The time to strike for equal rights was *now*, while the national government wielded absolute power over the rebel states. After reconstruction was completed on the basis of Negro suffrage, said Phillips, the principle of equal suffrage could be nailed down permanently by a constitutional amendment.[22]

[21] McKim to Garrison, Jan. 17, 1865, in *Liberator*, Jan. 27, 1865; *N.A.S. Standard*, Jan. 21, 1865; Oliver Johnson to Garrison, Jan. 24, 1865, Garrison Papers, BPL.

[22] A year later Garrison had come around to Phillips' point of view on the suffrage question. In February 1866, Garrison wrote that "the ballot must be insisted on at least as strenuously for the loyal blacks as for the pseudo-loyal whites, and as a *sine qua non* to the recognition of State independence." Garrison to George Julian, Feb. 11, 1866, Giddings-Julian Correspondence, LC.

There was a great deal of acrimonious discussion of this and other issues at the Massachusetts meeting. Stephen S. Foster denounced Garrison's support of Banks and accused Garrison of making "a compromise with the devil." Garrison's partisans rushed to his defense and excoriated Foster in harsh language. The meeting threatened to erupt into an orgy of name-calling. Cooler heads finally prevailed and the vote was taken on Phillips' and Garrison's resolutions. The former were adopted overwhelmingly and the latter laid on the table. The Massachusetts Anti-Slavery Society had rejected Garrison's leadership and raised the standard of Phillips.[23]

Ironically, at the same time that Garrison's influence was declining among his fellow abolitionists, it was rising among the people at large. Because of his support of Lincoln in 1864 and his defense of the administration against the attacks of other abolitionists, Garrison had acquired great prestige among moderate Republicans.[24] He reciprocated their praise by trusting them with the future of the Negro. So many of his old enemies had come to believe in his doctrine of immediate emancipation, Garrison reasoned, that there was no reason to doubt the eventual triumph of equality as well. It was a time to sing praises and thanksgiving. Garrison seemed to have reached the pinnacle of success in 1865, and the protests of Phillips, Foster, and others that the success was not yet complete rankled his nerves. He considered the Thirteenth Amendment the crowning victory of the antislavery crusade. He was not indifferent to the problem of the freedmen's future; far from it. But he wanted nothing to mar his sense of triumph in the Thirteenth Amendment.[25]

[23] *Liberator*, Feb. 3, 10, 17, 1865. See also Samuel May, Jr., to Richard Webb, Feb. 14, 1865, S. May, Jr., Papers, BPL; and Oliver Johnson to Samuel May, Jr., Feb. 9, 1865, Johnson Papers, VHS.

[24] Charles Eliot Norton, editor of the *North American Review*, told Garrison in January 1865: "You are teaching the nation a most important lesson by your present course, in showing them that it is possible to unite common sense & moderation . . . with the most uncompromising fidelity to principles,—and by convincing them that the leader of the Abolition movement is not, as he has been esteemed, a fanatic but a calm and wise man." Norton to Garrison, Jan. 14, 1865, Garrison Papers, BPL.

[25] For evidence of Garrison's new popularity among Republicans and moderates generally, see George Putnam to Garrison, Nov. 24, 1864, John Murray Forbes to Garrison, Jan. 18, 1865, Garrison to Forbes, Jan. 21, 1865, Garrison to Helen Garrison, July 23, 1865, Edwin M. Stanton to Garrison, Sept. 18, 1865, Garrison Papers, BPL; Edmund Quincy to Richard Webb, Oct. 16, 1865,

One of the high points of Garrison's career was an invitation from the United States government to attend as a guest of honor the ceremonial raising of the flag over Fort Sumter on April 14, 1865, exactly four years after the surrender of the fort to the Confederacy. Along with George Thompson (the noted British abolitionist) and Henry Ward Beecher, who was to deliver the main address at the celebration, Garrison traveled to Charleston in a government steamship. Several New York abolitionists and members of Beecher's church chartered another ship and came South to help liven the festivities. Left behind to edit the *Liberator*, Samuel May, Jr., commented that the honor done to Garrison and Thompson was a just recognition of their great services to the cause of freedom. "Mr. Garrison is no longer a proscribed, but an honored man—in the land of his birth. . . . He bears a name and has acquired a reputation,—to be enjoyed while yet he lives—which the most greedy of fame might covet."[26]

While in Charleston Garrison experienced some of the most gratifying moments of his life. He was lionized by a throng of 3,000 freedmen, several of whom lifted him to their shoulders and bore him triumphantly to the speakers' stand in Citadel Square. He visited Calhoun's tomb in the cemetery of St. Phillip's Church and solemnly intoned, "Down in a deeper grave than this slavery has gone, and for it there is no resurrection." He visited the offices of the *Charleston Courier*, now in Yankee hands, and set in type a paragraph of Beecher's oration. Everywhere he went in Charleston, Garrison was the center of attention. A week after his return to Boston one of Garrison's sons reported that "father has [not] quite 'come to himself' yet, his trip was so crowded with delightful wonders. It was like dreamland."[27] The prophet scorned and ridiculed for thirty years had lived to receive a king's homage in the city of his bitterest enemies. Little wonder that Garrison was elated by the strong wine of success. Little wonder

---

Quincy-Webb Correspondence, BPL; *Commonwealth*, Feb. 11, 1865; *Boston Traveller*, quoted in *Liberator*, Mar. 24, 1865; *Boston Transcript*, quoted in *N.A.S. Standard*, Apr. 8, 1865.

[26] Wendell P. Garrison and Francis J. Garrison, *William Lloyd Garrison* (4 vols., Boston, 1885-89), IV, 136-39; May's statement published in *Liberator*, Apr. 14, 1865.

[27] Garrison and Garrison, *Garrison*, IV, 139-52; W. L. Garrison, Jr., to Martha Wright, Apr. 25, 1865, Garrison Papers, SC.

that for a time he considered his crusade gloriously consummated and could not comprehend the jeremiads of men like Phillips.

During the interval between the meeting of the Massachusetts Anti-Slavery Society in January and the annual convention of the American Anti-Slavery Society in May, the infighting among abolitionists intensified. Roughly speaking, there were two main factions among Garrisonians regarding the future of their societies. One group, led by Garrison and Edmund Quincy, favored a formal dissolution of the American Anti-Slavery Society in May 1865. Phillips, Pillsbury, and Foster led the other faction that believed the Society should continue the battle until equal civil and political rights were granted to all Negroes.[28] By making it clear that he would resign as president of the Society whether it disbanded or not, Garrison rallied a majority of the executive committee to his side. On March 16 the committee voted to recommend disbandment of the Society at the annual meeting.[29] Oliver Johnson warned that on the issue of immediate dissolution Phillips would probably defeat Garrison, and urged that the whole question be postponed until after ratification of the Thirteenth Amendment. Garrison remained firm in his intention to retire, however, and Johnson reluctantly decided to vote for dissolution at the May meeting.[30]

In *Anti-Slavery Standard* editorials, Johnson and Edmund Quincy urged abolitionists to devote themselves to the work of the freedmen's aid societies as a logical continuation of their anti-slavery crusade. "The work of the *Anti-Slavery* Societies will obviously be done when slavery is abolished," said Johnson, "but the work of the friends of Liberty and Equality will not be done so long as any form of injustice or oppression exists in the world." Johnson also expressed approval of the idea of forming a new society to agitate the question of Negro suffrage. "There is not

[28] Samuel May, Jr., to Richard Webb, Feb. 14, 1865, Oliver Johnson to May, Mar. 2, 13, 1865, Mary Grew to May, Mar. 7, 1865, Samuel J. May to May, Mar. 10, 1865, S. H. Gay to May, Mar. 12, 27, 1865, Samuel May, Jr., Papers, BPL; Samuel May, Jr., to S. J. May, Mar. 5, 1865, S. J. May Papers, BPL.

[29] Henry Wright to Garrison, Mar. 13, 15, 1865, Garrison Papers, BPL; Oliver Johnson to Samuel May, Jr., Mar. 17, 31, Apr. 6, 24, 1865, Johnson Papers, VHS; Samuel May, Jr., to S. H. Gay, Mar. 22, 1865, Elizabeth Gay to Sarah Pugh, Apr. 3, 1865, Gay Papers, CU.

[30] Oliver Johnson to Samuel May, Jr., Mar. 17, 31, Apr. 6, 1865, Johnson Papers, VHS.

an Abolitionist in all the land," he declared, who would not "heartily cooperate" with such an organization. "But to keep an *Anti-Slavery* Society alive after slavery is abolished would seem, in our judgment, to be folly."[31]

Phillips protested against this reasoning. In a letter to the *Standard* he pointedly quoted the clauses of the American Anti-Slavery Society's constitution relating to the attainment of equal rights for free Negroes. A man was still a slave, argued Phillips, until he enjoyed all the rights of free men, including the ballot. Therefore it was entirely appropriate for an *antislavery* society to continue its work after the technical abolition of chattelism. Phillips depreciated the value of freedmen's aid associations. "Alms giving to the Negro is very well, highly honorable to the newly-converted givers, very useful to the Negro, and may be necessary for a little while," he said. "But I protest against its continuance for any length of time. I am still an Abolitionist, still a believer in the 'Negro's ability to take care of himself,' and do not intend to insult him by holding him up before the country as a chronic pauper. Let us . . . stand claiming for the Negro JUSTICE, not privileges; RIGHTS, not alms." In a reply to Phillips, Johnson asserted that the freedmen's aid societies went far beyond mere alms-giving. They were as resolute in their determination to secure equal suffrage for the Negro as Phillips himself. "But in order that there may be Negro Suffrage, there must be Negroes, and self-supporting and intelligent ones," wrote Johnson. "That there may be Negroes, they must be fed during the transition stage; . . . they must be furnished with . . . protection against extortion and oppression; that they may be intelligent, they must have school teachers."[32]

In February Phillips had feared that Garrison might carry the Society with him for dissolution at the May convention.[33] But as the meeting drew near, Phillips acquired important allies. His friends Elizabeth Cady Stanton and Susan B. Anthony rallied many of the women abolitionists to his side. Robert Purvis and Charles Remond assured him of the support of Philadelphia and Boston Negroes. On May 1 a group of New York Negroes passed

[31] *N.A.S. Standard*, Feb. 11, Mar. 18, Apr. 8, 1865.
[32] *N.A.S. Standard*, Apr. 22, 1865.
[33] Frank Sanborn to Moncure Conway, Feb. 17, 1865, Conway Papers, cu.

a resolution affirming that the American Anti-Slavery Society "cannot, in good faith, without violation of assumed honorable trust, at present dissolve." The executive committees of the Pennsylvania and the Philadelphia Female Anti-Slavery Societies voted to oppose dissolution. The *Boston Commonwealth* published an editorial urging the Society to keep itself intact for the upcoming struggle for equal rights. George Stearns and other backers of the *Commonwealth* made plans to go to New York City and help Phillips defeat Garrison's bid to dissolve the Society.[34]

An unusually large crowd filled the hall of Cooper Union for the public meetings of the Society, anticipating a sharp debate. They were not disappointed. Before the convention met, Johnson had urged Garrison to prepare careful resolutions explaining his motives for wishing to dissolve the Society. "Set the question of Negro Suffrage in such a light as to destroy the advantage which Phillips seeks to gain over us by his vehement partizan talk on that subject," Johnson advised Garrison. "Make it clear that in dissolving we do not withdraw ourselves from any work that needs to be done for the protection of the rights of the colored people. The strength of our opponents lies in cunningly making a false issue at this point." Garrison accepted the advice. In his opening speech to the convention he stated flatly that "there is no difference among Abolitionists . . . in regard to this matter of giving the ballot to those who have been so long disfranchised. We are one in this measure, and we must endeavor to see that it is carried without delay."[35]

[34] S. B. Anthony to E. C. Stanton, Apr. 19, 1865, Stanton Papers, LC; S. B. Anthony, Diary, entry of Apr. 27, 1865, Anthony Papers, LC; Oliver Johnson to Garrison, May 1, 3, 1865, Garrison Papers, BPL; Mary Grew to Samuel May, Jr., Apr. 28, 1865, Garrison Papers, SC; Oliver Johnson to M. W. Chapman, May 4, 1865, Weston Papers, BPL; *Commonwealth*, Apr. 29, 1865; Frank P. Stearns, *The Life and Public Services of George Luther Stearns* (Phila., 1907), 352-53. Resolution passed by New York Negroes published in *New York Times*, May 3, 1865. The interest of New York Negroes, the *Boston Commonwealth*, George Stearns, and other non-Garrisonian abolitionists in the fate of the Garrisonian societies may seem strange until it is recalled that the war had put an end to most of the old constitutional and methodological disputes among abolitionists. The distinctions between Garrisonians and non-Garrisonians were now little more than academic, and many former non-Garrisonians, such as Gerrit Smith, Frederick Douglass, Theodore Weld, and George Stearns, had begun to take part in the activities of the American Anti-Slavery Society. (See Chapter V of this study.)

[35] Johnson to Garrison, Apr. 24, May 3, 1865, Garrison Papers, BPL; *Liberator*,

Garrison introduced a resolution affirming that slavery was virtually abolished and that the American Anti-Slavery Society could therefore dissolve itself amid a chorus of thanksgiving and hallelujahs. "We organized expressly for the abolition of slavery," he said. "We called our Society an *Anti-Slavery* Society." It would be "an anomaly, a solecism, an absurdity to maintain an anti-slavery society after slavery is dead." Garrison repudiated the intimation that he meant to abandon the cause of the Negro. "Of course, we are not to cease laboring in regard to whatever remains to be done; but let us work with the millions, and not exclusively as the American Anti-Slavery Society." Edmund Quincy, Samuel May, Jr., and a few other speakers supported Garrison's resolution. May thought that abolitionists could do more good now for the Negro outside the antislavery societies than in them. "Take the leaven of this Society," he said, "and infuse it into every Freedmen's Aid Society in the land, and every other society, and my word for it, that leaven will leaven the entire mass, and its power will be multiplied a thousand-fold."[36]

Phillips introduced a counterresolution calling for the continuation of the Society until "the liberty of the negro" was placed "beyond peril." "Now, friends," said Phillips, "my abolitionism, when I pledged my faith to that Declaration of Sentiments and Constitution of the American Anti-Slavery Society, was, 'Absolute equality before the law; absolute civil equality'; (Loud applause) and I shall never leave the negro until, so far as God gives me the power, I achieve it." A whole array of eloquent speakers supported Phillips' resolution. Anna Dickinson spoke for continuation of the Society. Senator Henry Wilson expressed the hope of radical Republicans that the Society would remain in existence. Negro abolitionists especially insisted on the need for keeping up the antislavery organizations. Charles L. Remond asserted that despite the great wartime revolution in the Negro's status, there

---

May 19, 1865. Garrison's statement represented a departure from his earlier opposition to immediate enfranchisement of the freedmen (see discussion earlier in this chapter). What had caused his change of mind? There is no definite evidence on this point, but abolitionist criticism of his earlier position probably had something to do with it.

[36] *Liberator*, May 26, 1865.

was still a crushing load of prejudice bearing down the colored man in America. Frederick Douglass recalled the earlier struggles against Jim Crow in the North and the victories for equal rights in New England. "That was good anti-slavery work twenty years ago; I do not see why it is not good anti-slavery work now," said Douglass. "Slavery is not abolished until the black man has the ballot. While the Legislatures of the South retain the right to pass laws making any discrimination between black and white, slavery still lives there. (Applause)"[37]

After two days of debate the vote was finally taken on Garrison's dissolution resolution. It was rejected by a vote of 118-48. As a gesture of harmony the Society then reelected Garrison as its president for the ensuing year. But the pioneer abolitionist had already announced his intention to withdraw from the Society, and he refused the presidency. Phillips was thereupon elected as the new president. Samuel May, Jr., Edmund Quincy, Anne Warren Weston, and several other allies of Garrison also resigned from the Society. Oliver Johnson and Edmund Quincy resigned as editors of the *Anti-Slavery Standard*. Though the over-all strength of the Society was undoubtedly weakened by these resignations, there was an infusion of new abolitionists—men who had stood aloof from the Garrisonians before the war—that helped offset the absence of those who withdrew. Gerrit Smith, George Cheever, and John G. Whittier were elected vice presidents of the reorganized Society; George L. Stearns was appointed to the executive committee; Parker Pillsbury took over as editor of the *Standard*, assisted by Phillips' son-in-law, George W. Smalley. Phillips henceforth wrote many of the *Standard*'s lead editorials.[38]

The schism in the Garrisonian antislavery societies left a legacy of bitterness. Phillips and Garrison remained friends, but relations between them were strained. Phillips was alienated from his old friends Quincy and Johnson. The hostility that had been building for years between Pillsbury and Foster on the one hand, and Garrison, McKim, and Johnson on the other erupted into an open

[37] *ibid.*, May 26, June 2, 1865.

[38] *ibid.*, June 2, 1865; *N.A.S. Standard*, May 27, 1865. After resigning as editor of the *Anti-Slavery Standard*, Oliver Johnson became managing editor of the *Independent*, a post he held for five years. Garrison published the final issue of the *Liberator* on December 29, 1865, eleven days after the Thirteenth Amendment was declared ratified.

break after the events of 1865. Both sides blamed the other for the schism. Garrison and his friends ascribed motives of "personal pique and an ulterior purpose" to Pillsbury and Foster.[39] Johnson considered Phillips' course "disgraceful." "What a shame that he should put himself at the head of this clique that has so long waged an insidious and venomous war upon you!" Johnson told Garrison. Samuel May, Jr., thought Phillips "*mainly* to blame—because the sympathy & countenance he has given this set [Pillsbury and Foster] has magnified their self-importance & encouraged their petty plots."[40]

Those who advocated continuation of the antislavery societies, on the other hand, disclaimed personal motives for their action. They emphasized the need to continue active work on behalf of equal rights and intimated that Garrison and his allies had abandoned the cause. Pillsbury was sorry that he had alienated Garrison and others, "but it was Mr. Garrison who taught me to be true to myself." In Pillsbury's opinion "suffrage for the negro is now what immediate emancipation was thirty years ago. If we emancipate from slavery and leave the European doctrine of serfdom extant, even in the mildest form, then the colored race, or we, or perhaps both, have another war in store." One of the younger followers of Phillips sadly accused Garrison of "deserting the true banner."[41]

The truth, as usual, probably lay somewhere between the claims of either side. The schism of 1865 resulted partly from an honest difference of opinion over substantive and procedural issues. It was also caused partly by a power struggle between the Pillsbury and Garrison factions that had been going on for at least ten years. So long as Phillips took no sides or stood with Garrison, the Pillsbury faction was an insignificant minority. But when Phillips sided with the Pillsbury-Foster group because of his distrust of Lincoln and his concern for the freedmen's future, he took a majority of the American Anti-Slavery Society with him and displaced Garrison as leader of the abolitionist move-

[39] Garrison to Helen Garrison, May 10, 1865, Garrison Papers, BPL.
[40] Johnson to Garrison, May 18, 1865, Garrison Papers, BPL; Samuel May, Jr., to Richard Webb, May 29, 1865, S. May, Jr., Papers, BPL.
[41] Pillsbury to S. B. Anthony, May ?, 1865, in Ida Harper, *The Life and Work of Susan B. Anthony* (3 vols., Indianapolis, 1898-1908), I, 246; Lillie B. Chace to Anna Dickinson, May 22, 1865, Dickinson Papers, LC.

ment. Garrison's assertion that his opponents were actuated only by spite and personal enmity was unfair, although there was a germ of truth in the accusation. Pillsbury's charge that Garrison had forsaken the Negro was equally unfair. Garrison and his allies were subsequently active in the freedmen's aid movement and availed themselves of every opportunity to speak out for civil rights and Negro suffrage. Yet there *was* an element of ideological conflict between some of the participants in the 1865 schism. Garrison, Quincy, Johnson, McKim, and May were essentially moderates in their social and political ideas. They had joined the antislavery movement because they saw in slavery an enormous injustice demanding cauterization. Phillips, Pillsbury, and Foster were motivated by the same belief in the injustice of slavery, but in addition they were genuine, thoroughgoing radicals in their social philosophy. It was no mere coincidence that Phillips, Pillsbury, and Foster were active in the labor reform movements of the 1870's while Garrison opposed militant labor agitation. These ideological and temperamental differences played a significant part in the schism of 1865.

HE problem of reconstruction occupied the mind of every
politician and reformer in the winter of 1864-1865. Abolitionists applauded an intimation by Lincoln in his annual message
of a willingness to compromise with congressional radicals on the
issue.[1] The thorny problem of the readmission of Louisiana under
the Banks-Hahn Constitution of 1864 was dumped into the House
Committee on Rebellious States in December. The chairman of
this committee was James Ashley of Ohio, a radical antislavery
man and a friend of several leading abolitionists. Ashley and
Thomas Eliot, a radical Republican from Massachusetts, evidently negotiated a compromise with Lincoln whereby Ashley
promised to accept the admission of Louisiana, Tennessee, and
Arkansas under Lincoln's 10 per cent plan in return for the
administration's acceptance of the right of Congress to prescribe
the terms of reconstruction in the other Confederate states.
Charles Sumner participated in the negotiation of this compromise and reluctantly approved its terms.[2]

Phillips and most other abolitionists denounced the compromise.
Phillips argued that no matter what conditions Congress laid down
for other states, the readmission of Louisiana would create a
dangerous precedent for presidential reconstruction of the rest
of rebeldom.[3] "If Congress allows the President to determine the
conditions on which Louisiana shall return to the Union," asked
the *Commonwealth*, "what resistance can it make when he brings
Florida and Alabama along?"[4] Phillips and George Stearns hurried to Washington for consultation with radical leaders. Henry
Winter Davis and William D. Kelley told Phillips that most radicals favored Negro suffrage but that they were powerless in the

[1] Roy P. Basler, ed., *The Collected Works of Abraham Lincoln* (9 vols., New
Brunswick, N.J., 1955), VIII, 152; *Independent*, Dec. 8, 1864; *Liberator*, Dec. 9,
1864; *Commonwealth*, Dec. 10, 1864.
[2] Charles H. McCarthy, *Lincoln's Plan of Reconstruction* (New York, 1901),
286-91; *N.A.S. Standard*, Dec. 24, 31, 1864; Edward L. Pierce, *Memoir and
Letters of Charles Sumner* (4 vols., Boston, 1877-94), IV, 221.
[3] Phillips to Moncure Conway, Jan. 8, 1865, McKim-Maloney-Garrison Papers,
NYPL.
[4] *Commonwealth*, Dec. 24, 1864.

face of Lincoln's control of a majority of the party. The only hope was in an aroused public opinion that would convince the president that the North wanted equal suffrage as a condition of reconstruction. They urged Phillips and the abolitionists to keep up the demand for Negro suffrage. Meanwhile the radical leaders promised to do all they could to defeat the admission of Louisiana.[5]

Ashley drafted a proposal for equal suffrage in the eight nonreconstructed Confederate states, but a coalition of Democrats and moderate Republicans voted down his plan in committee. Instead, Ashley was forced to report to the House a bill to admit Louisiana, Arkansas, and Tennessee under Lincoln's reconstruction plan and to admit the rest under conditions similar to those of the Wade-Davis bill vetoed by Lincoln the previous summer. By prior arrangement with Ashley, Congressman William D. Kelley introduced an amendment on the House floor enacting impartial suffrage. Kelley was a prominent radical from Pennsylvania, allied to Philadelphia's abolitionist circles by friendship and marriage. He pleaded for his amendment in a speech that became a classic in the struggle for equal suffrage. The House was impervious to his eloquence, however, and refused to pass the amendment.[6]

Ashley was criticized by abolitionists who were not aware of his backstage maneuvers in the House and thus did not understand why he had reported out his reconstruction bill without Negro suffrage. He explained in a House speech of February 22 that he had no choice; an adverse committee majority had compelled him to report the emasculated bill. He frankly expressed the hope that the House would pass no reconstruction measure at all this session. He wanted the question to go over to the next Congress in which the radicals would be stronger. Ashley also sent a private note to Tilton and to Charles Slack, editor of the *Commonwealth*, explaining the complex maneuvers in Congress. The *Independent*

[5] Phillips to Moncure Conway, n.d., but sometime in January or February, 1865, Conway Papers, cu.

[6] McCarthy, *Lincoln's Plan of Reconstruction*, 291-313; Ira V. Brown, "William D. Kelley and Radical Reconstruction," *The Pennsylvania Magazine of History and Biography*, LXXXV (July 1961), 317, 321; *Commonwealth*, Jan. 28, 1865; *Independent*, Mar. 16, 1865.

and *Commonwealth* published these letters in order to vindicate Ashley's fidelity to the cause.[7]

As Ashley had hoped, the House laid all reconstruction proposals on the table. The real battle, however, was shaping up in the Senate where moderate Republicans were trying to force passage of a resolution recognizing Louisiana as a legitimate state "entitled to the guaranties and all other rights of a State government." Abolitionists feared that adoption of this resolution would establish a precedent against the requirement of equal suffrage as a condition of reconstruction. Garrison was silent on the issue, but Phillips and the *Commonwealth* frantically urged antislavery Republicans to defeat "this suicidal act."[8] Sumner and a small band of radical associates were equal to the occasion. They introduced dilatory motions and filibustered against the resolution, preventing it from coming to a vote before Congress adjourned on March 4.[9] Sumner received the fervent thanks of abolitionists for his decisive role in defeating the admission of "the sham state of Louisiana." The Bird Club in Boston unanimously approved Sumner's course and praised him as the savior of Negro suffrage.[10]

The defeat of Louisiana's bid for readmission buoyed up the spirits of abolitionists. During the winter they professed to discern a favorable movement of northern public opinion toward Negro suffrage. Phillips reported that his audiences cheered his most radical utterances. Henry Ward Beecher came out strongly for Negro suffrage, and several northern Protestant denominations followed suit. Prominent public figures such as Salmon P. Chase and important Republican newspapers such as the *New York Tribune* and the *Boston Journal* endorsed the principle of equal suffrage.[11] Charles Slack informed Sumner at the end of February

[7] *Cong. Globe*, 38 Cong., 2 Sess., 968-69, 1,002; Ashley to editor of the *Commonwealth*, Feb. 27, 1865, published in *Commonwealth*, Mar. 4; Ashley to Tilton, Feb. 27, 1865, Garrison Papers, BPL; *Independent*, Mar. 2, 1865.

[8] *Commonwealth*, Feb. 25, Mar. 4, 1865.

[9] *Cong. Globe*, 38 Cong., 2 Sess., 903, 1,011-12, 1,091-99, 1,101-11; Edward McPherson, *The Political History of the United States of America during the Great Rebellion* (Washington, 1865), 579-81.

[10] Sumner received nearly a dozen letters from abolitionists thanking him for his stand against the admission of Louisiana. The quotation is from Elizur Wright to Sumner, Mar. 6, 1865; the information on the action of the Bird Club is from E. L. Pierce to Sumner, Mar. 4, 1865, Sumner Papers, HU.

[11] O. B. Frothingham to Moncure Conway, Jan. 2, 1865, Conway Papers, CU;

that "the idea of negro suffrage in the disloyal states grows daily in favor and advocacy among [Boston] business men." Lydia Maria Child believed that many northerners had been converted to equal suffrage by the performance of Negro troops in the war. In early April Frank Sanborn observed that "the question of Reconstruction on the basis of negro suffrage is coming up for discussion everywhere, and the converts to Phillips' view are increasing fast."[12]

But a new danger to abolitionist hopes appeared as the war drew to a close. With victory assured there was a noticeable softening of the northern attitude toward rebels. Lincoln's inaugural plea for malice toward none and charity for all appealed to a growing number of Yankees. The fall of Richmond and Lee's surrender sent the North into paroxysms of joy. The war was virtually over, and many Americans stood ready to forgive their enemies. Abolitionists feared that this mood boded ill for the freedmen. A soft attitude toward southern whites might be translated into a reconstruction policy that failed to secure the rights of Negroes. Abolitionists warned against sentimentality in dealing with the South. "I am astonished at the gammon still prevailing at the North about our Southern brethren, and their softened feelings and longings to come back, etc., etc.," wrote Laura Towne from the South Carolina sea islands. "They are hungry, and long for loaves and fishes, but . . . they are bitter and spiteful and 'cantankerous' as ever, and show extreme contempt for Northerners while they are accepting their benefactions." Sanborn rejoiced in Lee's surrender at Appomattox but lamented that "the danger of neglecting the colored men in our plans of Reconstruction is still great."[13]

M. W. Chapman to Mary Estlin, Feb. 5, 1865, Estlin Papers, BPL; Phillips to E. C. Stanton, Feb. 8, 1865, Stanton Papers, LC; *Liberator*, Feb. 10, Mar. 3, 1865; *N.A.S. Standard*, Feb. 4, 18, 1865; *New York Tribune*, Feb. 22, 1865; *Commonwealth*, Mar. 4, 11, 18, 1865.

[12] Slack to Sumner, Feb. 28, 1865, Sumner Papers, HU; L. M. Child to George W. Julian, Apr. 1, 1865, Giddings-Julian Correspondence, LC; Frank Sanborn to Moncure Conway, Apr. 6, 1865, Conway Papers, CU.

[13] Rupert S. Holland, ed., *Letters and Diary of Laura M. Towne, Written from the Sea Islands of South Carolina, 1862-84* (Cambridge, Mass., 1912), 155-56; Sanborn to Gerrit Smith, Apr. 10, 1865, Smith Papers, SU. See also Sumner to Garrison, Mar. 29, 1865, Garrison Papers, BPL; Amasa Walker to Sumner, Apr. 5, 1865, Sumner Papers, HU.

"PARDON. Columbia—'Shall I Trust These Men'?" Nast
in *Harper's Weekly*

"FRANCHISE. 'And Not This Man'?" Nast in *Harper's Weekly*

In a speech to a group of happy White House serenaders on the evening of April 11, Lincoln appealed for public acceptance of the reconstructed government of Louisiana. He wished that suffrage could have been extended to black soldiers and literate Negroes, but he felt that colored men would get the ballot sooner by working through the established Louisiana government than by tearing it down and starting anew. Lincoln regarded his reconstruction policy as a promise to Louisiana to be broken only if it proved a bad promise.[14]

Some abolitionists were discouraged by the president's renewed commitment to the Louisiana policy, but others found grounds for hope in Lincoln's willingness to break a "bad promise." It would be the task of radicals to convince the president that reconstruction, Louisiana-style, was a "bad promise." Many abolitionists, remembering Lincoln's step-by-step progress from a war policy of noninterference with slavery to one of universal emancipation looked forward hopefully to his conversion to Negro suffrage.

Less than four days after his speech of April 11, the president was dead. Abolitionist reaction to his assassination was mixed. All, of course, were shocked and appalled by the enormity of the crime. Nonetheless some abolitionists interpreted Lincoln's murder as a warning against leniency in the reconstruction of the South. It was widely believed that Andrew Johnson held more radical ideas on reconstruction than Lincoln. Johnson seemingly confirmed this belief by his thundering denunciations of traitors during the week after the assassination. "Mr. Lincoln's too great kindness of heart led him to a mistaken leniency," wrote William Lloyd Garrison, Jr., "but Andy Johnson has fought the beasts of Ephesus on their own soil and has learned by bitter experience their implacable nature. 'Thorough' will be the word now. . . . The nation sails into new waters now and it may be providential that a new hand grasps the rudder." But here and there arose a dissent. William Robinson recorded in his diary that the Bird Club had great confidence in Johnson, but that he personally thought Lincoln's death "an unmixed evil." Lincoln had possessed the confidence of the country as had no other man since Washington, but Johnson was a relatively unknown quantity. "Lincoln had no adequate idea of what ought to be done," wrote Robinson, "but

[14] Basler, *Collected Works of Lincoln*, VIII, 399-405.

I fear Johnson has still less. Lincoln was, at least, master of himself, and master of the situation: Johnson *may* be the tool of anybody and everybody. Lincoln we have summered and wintered for four years, and knew exactly what he was: Johnson is wholly untried."[15]

Abolitionists welcomed the hardening of northern opinion toward the South produced by Lincoln's assassination. In the weeks before that tragic event, wrote Higginson, the North seemed to be "swiftly sliding back" into "a mush of concession." But Booth's bullet "restored us to our senses" and united the North as it had not been united since the firing on Fort Sumter. The chances for a reconstruction based on justice, he thought, were far better now than before the assassination.[16]

One manifestation of the post-assassination reaction of the North, however, was unwelcome to abolitionists. A cry for bloody vengeance against traitors rent the air. A few abolitionists echoed this demand for blood, but most of them were opposed to execution as a punishment for rebellion. They feared that the cries for vengeance would distract attention from the real issues of reconstruction. "We [don't] want a reign of blood and terror," wrote William Robinson; "we should have, instead, a settled and firm policy of reconstruction on the basis of *justice to the negro*." Tilton argued that *slavery*, not individual rebels, was the real criminal. The rebellion should be punished not by hanging traitors but by exterminating slavery and by putting the Negro's freedom on an indestructible foundation. Phillips declared that executions would only create martyrs. Confiscation of rebel lands and the grant of suffrage to freedmen, not mass hangings, were the proper punishments for rebellion. "What, cover the continent with gibbets!" exclaimed Phillips. "We cannot sicken the nineteenth century with such a sight. . . . [This country] needs for its safety

[15] W. L. Garrison, Jr., to Martha Wright, Apr. 16, 1865, Garrison Papers, sc; Wm. S. Robinson, Diary, entry of Apr. 16, 1865, in Mrs. Wm. S. Robinson, ed., *"Warrington" Pen-Portraits: A Collection of Personal and Political Reminiscences from 1848 to 1876, from the Writings of William S. Robinson* (Boston, 1877), 304-05. See also S. B. Anthony to E. C. Stanton, Apr. 19, 1865, Stanton Papers, lc; *Liberator*, Apr. 21, 1865; and *N.A.S. Standard*, Apr. 22, 1865.

[16] *Commonwealth*, Apr. 29, 1865. See also Caroline Weston to Mary Estlin, Apr. 18, 1865, Estlin Papers, bpl; *Independent*, Apr. 20, 27, 1865; and Vincent Y. Bowditch, *Life and Correspondence of Henry Ingersoll Bowditch* (2 vols., Boston, 1902), ii, 48-52.

no such policy of vengeance; its serene strength needs to use only so much severity as will fully guarantee security for the future."[17]

Abolitionists had another reason for opposing the popular clamor for bloody revenge. Many of them were opposed to capital punishment and were active in the movement to outlaw it. Gerrit Smith, John G. Whittier, and the *New York Tribune* took the lead in calling for clemency to traitors. Smith sent personal letters to President Johnson pleading for leniency, and published two broadsides, a speech, and a sermon urging clemency. Whittier publicly deplored the cries for vengeance. Almost alone among leading Republican newspapers, the *New York Tribune* pleaded for sanity and mercy toward rebel leaders. In a pointed editorial the *Tribune* noted that more than any other single group in the North the abolitionists desired clemency for rebels. They had the good sense, said the *Tribune*, to see that the real enemy was not Jefferson Davis but the spirit of slavery and aristocracy which had spawned the rebellion.[18]

The desire for wholesale executions soon passed away, but the problem of reconstruction remained. Despite William Robinson's prescient fears, most abolitionists had great confidence in Andrew Johnson in April 1865. This confidence was based partly on Johnson's stern denunciations of rebels and partly on his record as wartime military governor of Tennessee. Abolitionists had been impressed by Johnson's vigorous efforts to make Tennessee a free state in 1864-1865 and especially by his famous "Moses" speech to the Negroes of Nashville in October 1864, in which he promised to be their Moses and lead them out of bondage. George L. Stearns had known Johnson during his tenure as recruiting agent of Negro troops in Tennessee. Stearns had been sufficiently convinced of Johnson's radicalism to invite him to join a Negro suffrage association that Stearns was organizing in the fall of 1864.[19]

[17] Robinson, *"Warrington" Pen-Portraits*, 305; *Independent*, Apr. 20, 27, 1865; Wendell Phillips, *Speeches, Lectures and Letters*, 2nd Series (Boston, 1900), 449-50.

[18] Gerrit Smith to Andrew Johnson, Apr. 19, 24, 1865, Johnson Papers, LC; *Gerrit Smith to President Johnson*, April 24, 1865, published letter (Peterboro, 1865); Gerrit Smith, *No Treason in Civil War* (New York, 1865); O. B. Frothingham, *Gerrit Smith* (New York, 1879), 294-95; Whittier to the editor of the Amesbury (Mass.) *Villager*, reprinted in *Liberator*, May 26, 1865; *New York Tribune*, Apr. 20, May 5, 8, 1865.

[19] Stearns to Johnson, Sept. 26, 1864, Johnson Papers, LC. See also L. M. Child to Whittier, Nov. 8, 1864, Child-Whittier Correspondence, LC; W. L. Gar-

Abolitionists did not realize that Johnson's opposition to slavery, like that of Hinton Rowan Helper, sprang not from sympathy for the Negro but from the yeoman farmer's traditional hatred of large slaveowners. Johnson had despised abolitionists before the war. He identified himself with the white yeoman class which disliked both the Negroes and the large planters. His private secretary once wrote in his diary that Johnson "exhibited a morbid distress and feeling against the negroes." During the war a friend in Tennessee reminded Johnson that the abolitionists hoped to make free citizens out of the slaves. "Damn the negroes," replied Johnson. "I am fighting these traitorous aristocrats, their masters."[20]

In the weeks after Lincoln's assassination abolitionists were unaware of the new president's feelings toward Negroes. Stearns assured friends that Johnson would do the right things in reconstructing the South. John M. Langston led a delegation of Negroes to see the president, who told them that he was a firm friend of their race. Wendell Phillips declared that Johnson's whole life was pledged to the extirpation of caste and aristocracy in the South. "I believe in him," said Phillips, "I believe he means suffrage." Abolitionists applauded every reference to Johnson at the annual meeting of the American Anti-Slavery Society on May 9-10.[21]

There was one report from Washington, however, that disturbed some radicals. Johnson told a visiting Indiana delegation that he agreed with Lincoln's theory of the legal indestructibility of the states. Radicals were startled, for logically pursued this theory denied the right of Congress to establish suffrage require-

---

rison, Jr., to Martha Wright, Nov. 13, 1864, Garrison Papers, sc; John Pierpont to L. M. Child, Nov. 20, 1864, Pierpont Papers, pml; and *N.A.S. Standard*, May 6, 1865.

[20] Benjamin Thomas and Harold Hyman, *Stanton: The Life and Times of Lincoln's Secretary of War* (New York, 1962), 440; Clifton Hall, *Andrew Johnson, Military Governor of Tennessee* (Princeton, 1916), 221.

[21] George Stearns to Gerrit Smith, Apr. 21, 1865, Smith Papers, su; Stearns to Sumner, Apr. 30, 1865, Sumner Papers, hu; *Commonwealth*, Apr. 22, 1865; *N.A.S. Standard*, Apr. 29, May 6, 13, 1865; *Liberator*, Apr. 28, May 12, June 2, 1865. Phillips' statement quoted from *ibid.*, June 2, 1865. Lewis Tappan wrote in his journal on April 23, 1865, "we have the encouragement to believe that [Johnson] will prove an able & faithful magistrate." A year later, however, Tappan made a note in the margin next to this entry: "This prophecy falsified by his *treachery!*" Tappan Papers, lc.

ments as a condition of readmission because the states were already *in* the Union and hence possessed the right to regulate their own suffrage qualifications. There were also rumors from Washington that Montgomery Blair was cultivating a close relationship with the new president. Worried Boston abolitionists urged Sumner to establish contact with Johnson and make sure that he was influenced in the right direction. "Save him from the Blairs," Frank Bird told Sumner.[22] The Massachusetts senator needed little urging. Along with Senators Wade and Chandler and Chief Justice Chase, Sumner paid several visits to the White House in the last two weeks of April "with the view of conversing on negro suffrage." The senators seemed to be satisfied with Johnson's views on this question. "He is as radical as I am and as fully up to the work," Chandler wrote to his wife. Sumner informed friends that Johnson was "well-disposed, & sees the right and necessities of the case. . . . Our new President accepts the principle and application" of Negro suffrage. Phillips thanked Sumner for his assurances of Johnson's fidelity to equal rights. "I am glad & *strengthened* by the knowledge," said Phillips.[23]

In letters to George Stearns, however, Sumner expressed less confidence. The president had declared himself in favor of a broadened franchise, said Sumner, but Johnson thought that Negro suffrage should be granted by the states *after* reconstruction rather than imposed by Congress on the states as a condition of restoration. Sumner was worried, because he believed that once readmitted to the Union, southern states would never voluntarily adopt Negro suffrage. He therefore hoped that a decision on reconstruction could be postponed until the next session of Congress. Meanwhile radicals should try to educate public opinion up to the level of demanding Negro suffrage as a condition of readmission. If public opinion supported such a policy, Sumner was sure that Johnson, like Lincoln, would acquiesce in the will of the majority. Stearns agreed, and promised to do everything possible to help mature a correct public opinion.[24]

[22] *Commonwealth*, Apr. 29, 1865; Frank Bird to Sumner, Apr. 15, 1865, Sumner Papers, HU.
[23] Sumner to Bird, Apr. 25, 1865, Bird Papers, HU; Chandler quoted in Joseph B. James, *The Framing of the Fourteenth Amendment* (Urbana, Ill., 1956), 5-6; Sumner to R. Schleiden, May 1, 1865, in Pierce, *Sumner*, IV, 242; Wendell Phillips to Sumner, May 5, 1865, Sumner Papers, HU.
[24] Sumner to Stearns, May 4, 11, and May ?, 1865, quoted in Frank P. Stearns,

Radicals began their intensified campaign for equal suffrage in May 1865. The *Commonwealth* published trumpet blasts warning the nation of the injustice and danger of reconstruction without Negro suffrage. "Refuse this, and the Southern States will make such laws as will allow the freedmen only to be 'hewers of wood and drawers of water,' and, uniting with Northern copperheads, will control the legislation of the country." Phillips promised that the slogan of the American Anti-Slavery Society under his leadership would be "No Reconstruction without Negro Suffrage." "No matter what else we yield, here our demand is to be inexorable," said Phillips. "Abolitionists are to be educated to see that, without this, freedom, so called, is a sham."[25] George L. Stearns published at his own expense in April 1865, a pamphlet entitled *The Equality of All Men before the Law*, containing speeches in behalf of Negro suffrage by Phillips, Douglass, and William D. Kelley. Stearns printed 50,000 copies for distribution throughout the North in April; he prepared another edition of 40,000 in May, and told Sumner that he had enough money on hand or pledged by interested parties to finance the eventual printing of 500,000 copies.[26]

During his trip to South Carolina for the flag-raising ceremonies at Fort Sumter, Theodore Tilton had come to the conclusion that "if the whip-using gentry who formerly held sway in those regions are to return to their former crown and kingdom, the North will have won only half a victory over the rebellion." In a series of militant editorials Tilton argued that the Negro must be granted land and the ballot as inexorable conditions of reconstruction. He admitted that many well-intentioned men had doubts about the constitutional right of the federal government to impose such conditions. But "he is the statesman of a great occasion who is not hampered by mere usage, bigotry, or narrow technicality. It is criminal to let a nation die while hunting after a precedent by which to save it." Whether the rebel states were

---

The Life and Public Services of George Luther Stearns (Phila., 1907), 343-44; Stearns to Sumner, May 8, 1865, Sumner Papers, HU.

[25] *Commonwealth*, May 6, 1865; *N.A.S. Standard*, May 27, June 3, 1865.

[26] Stearns to William Still, Apr. 29, 30, 1865, quoted in Alberta S. Norwood, "Negro Welfare Work in Philadelphia, Especially as Illustrated by the Career of William Still," M.A. thesis, U. of Pennsylvania, 1931, 136-37; Stearns to Sumner, Apr. 30, 1865, Sumner Papers, HU.

theoretically in or out of the Union was a moot question, said Tilton, but no one could deny that legitimate governments did not exist in those states. There was no prescription in the Constitution for the problem of reconstruction. Whatever action was taken by the federal government on this question would be extraconstitutional, not unconstitutional. "The people of the rebel states, having been conquered in war, are at the mercy of the conqueror, and have no other recourse but in his clemency," declared Tilton. "The restoration of the states to their rank in the Union, is an act of pure clemency; of course the entire details as to the manner and form rest in the discretion and judgment of the conquering power."[27]

The radicals were alarmed by continuing rumors that Johnson would soon announce a reconstruction policy without Negro suffrage. On May 17 Stearns sent a personal entreaty to the president recalling their friendship in wartime Nashville and appealing to Johnson's well-known hatred of aristocracy. The rebellion was more than a slaveholder's war against Union and liberty, said Stearns. "It was the deadly strife of the Aristocratic Principle against the Democratic, of the Capital of the country against its Labor." Negroes constituted a majority of the southern laboring class, and without guaranties for their future security and equal rights, aristocracy would continue to rule the South. Would Andrew Johnson "be true to the Democratic principle of Government," asked Stearns, "or will he like all his predecessors ally himself with Capital and continue the war against labor?" Frank Sanborn reported on May 26 that Phillips and Stearns were afraid Johnson would go wrong on the suffrage question unless pressure was brought to bear upon him. An imposing array of radicals gathered in Boston on May 29 for the annual meeting of the Emancipation League. Hoping to impress Johnson with the strength of radicalism in New England, several abolitionists and Republican speakers made eloquent appeals for Negro suffrage.[28]

But it was too late. On that very day the president issued an amnesty proclamation and a reconstruction proclamation for

[27] *Independent*, May 4, 11, 25, 1865.

[28] Stearns to Johnson, May 17, 1865, Johnson Papers, LC; Sanborn to Moncure Conway, May 26, 1865, Conway Papers, CU; *Commonwealth*, June 3, 1865.

North Carolina. The latter named William Holden as provisional governor and stipulated that when a majority of the state's qualified white voters had taken an oath of future loyalty they could form a new constitution and bring the state back into the Union.[29] The reaction of abolitionists was swift and angry. Meeting in Boston on May 31, the New England Anti-Slavery Society unanimously passed a resolution condemning the North Carolina proclamation. "The reconstruction of rebel states without Negro suffrage is a practical surrender to the Confederacy," said Phillips. "Better, far better, would it have been for Grant to have surrendered to Lee than for Johnson to have surrendered to North Carolina." Phillips feared that reconstruction on the basis of white suffrage would doom the freedmen to "a century of serfdom." He pointed to the black code already passed by one house of the Tennessee legislature and predicted that all the reconstructed states would enact such codes unless the black man was enfranchised. Charles C. Burleigh charged Johnson with inconsistency in his reconstruction theory. If the rebel states were actually in the Union, as Johnson claimed, the president had no right to create the extraconstitutional office of provisional governor. But if he *did* have the right to create such an office, he had the same right to require Negro suffrage.[30]

On June 13 the president issued a reconstruction proclamation for Mississippi identical to the North Carolina edict. Even moderate abolitionists who wanted to believe in Johnson's good intentions were depressed by this sign that the president had drawn up the North Carolina proclamation as a pattern for the rest of the South. "If reconstruction is to go on as in North Carolina and Mississippi the slave is not yet free nor is the Union secure," wrote Edgar Ketchum. "People inquire with amazement, believing fully in the patriotism and integrity of President Johnson, whether he can persevere in the exclusion of the freedmen from the suffrage in view of what is now going on in the South. It is a great mystery." Just one small glimmer of light penetrated Phillips' gloomy appraisal of Johnson's actions. "We can only hope the North Carolina policy is adopted

[29] James D. Richardson, ed., *The Messages and Papers of the Presidents* (20 vols., Washington, 1897-1913), VIII, 3508-12.

[30] *N.A.S. Standard*, June 3, 10, 1865. See also *Independent*, June 8, 1865; *Commonwealth*, June 3, 1865; and *New York Tribune*, May 31, June 1, 1865.

as an experiment, not as a finality," said Phillips. "The government, let us trust, is only feeling its way, and has no purpose to plunge headlong into such a vortex as reconstruction on the present theory would set whirling."[31]

Only an experiment! This was the straw of hope grasped by many abolitionists and Republicans in the summer of 1865. Alarmed by the efforts of Democrats and conservative Republicans to drive a wedge between the president and radicals, the *Commonwealth* hastily reaffirmed its support of Johnson as head of the Republican party. "We expect him to see, before long if he does not now see, that the spirit of the Rebellion, and the spirit which denies the loyal black man the suffrage, are one and the same," declared the *Commonwealth*. Despite the unfortunate North Carolina reconstruction proclamation, "it is not yet too late to modify or wholly change that plan of reorganization." Samuel May, Jr., expressed willingness to accept Johnson's policy as an experiment. If the southern states demonstrated their good faith by granting equal rights to the freedmen, abolitionists would applaud Johnson's policy as a success. But if the new constitutions of former rebel states showed a continuing devotion to the spirit of slavery and oppression, "let such States remain under Provisional or Military Governorship, until the true light dawns upon them." "I cannot doubt," concluded May, "that such essentially will be the reply of Congress to any State presenting a Constitution excluding the freed people from citizenship and suffrage."[32]

In the summer of 1865 George L. Stearns, chief executive of the abolitionist campaign for Negro suffrage, had three separate but interrelated projects on hand. The first of these was an organization to distribute throughout the nation pamphlets, speeches, and newspapers favoring Negro suffrage. In the fall of 1864 Stearns had decided to organize a league of antislavery men to finance the dissemination of radical material. He collected a list of 2,000 sympathizers who could be called upon for contribu-

[31] Ketchum to Sumner, June 17, 1865, Sumner Papers, HU; *N.A.S. Standard*, June 3, 1865. See also *Liberator*, June 9, 1865; *Principia*, June 29, July 6, 1865; *N.A.S. Standard*, June 24, July 1, 1865; and George Cheever to Elizabeth Washburn, June 14, 1865, Cheever Papers, AAS.

[32] *Commonwealth*, June 10, 17, 1865; May's statement published in *Liberator*, June 23, 1865.

322

tions and for service as local agents to distribute pamphlets. Using mainly his own money, Stearns had printed nearly 90,000 pamphlets by June 1, 1865. The initiation of Johnson's reconstruction policy and the consequent need for stepped-up radical activity brought the Emancipation League and interested Massachusetts Republicans into Stearns' network. In June he sent out a circular proposing the formation of a "Universal and Equal Suffrage Association." The response was favorable, and within three months Stearns had compiled a list of 20,000 "members" of this association. By July 1 he was employing between six and ten clerks to send out 10,000 newspapers and 3,000 pamphlets per week. The pamphlets contained speeches by Phillips, Douglass, William D. Kelley, Sumner, Henry Ward Beecher, Benjamin Butler, Richard Henry Dana, and other prominent figures. At the end of July Stearns began mailing 12,000 copies of the *Commonwealth* each week to selected subscribers, trebling the circulation of that radical journal. By September he was sending out 20,000 newspapers and 5,000 pamphlets per week, and looking forward to a weekly total of 100,000 newspapers and 50,000 pamphlets if he could raise enough money. He had already distributed a total of 230,000 newspapers and 3 million pages of pamphlets.[33]

Stearns' second project was the founding of a weekly newspaper to represent the interests of the freedmen. J. Miller McKim and the freedmen's aid societies were also laying plans for a weekly. Each group had raised several thousand dollars by the spring of 1865, when they decided to pool their resources and put the proposed paper on a sound financial basis. Wendell P. Garrison, soon to marry McKim's daughter, was appointed associate editor of the new paper. Stearns and McKim cast about for an experienced journalist to serve as editor-in-chief. After George William Curtis and Whitelaw Reid had turned them down, they approached Edwin L. Godkin, a young British-born journalist who had been recommended to Stearns by friends in Boston.

[33] Stearns, *Stearns,* 351-52; Stearns to Gerrit Smith, Sept. 20, 1864, Smith Papers, su; Stearns to Benjamin Butler, June 10, Sept. 16, 1865, enclosing circulars of the "Universal and Equal Suffrage Association," Butler Papers, lc; Stearns to Sumner, Apr. 30, Oct. 4, 1865, Sumner Papers, hu; *N.A.S. Standard,* June 10, Aug. 19, 1865; *Commonwealth,* June 10, July 29, Aug. 5, Sept. 30, 1865.

Stearns and Wendell Phillips interviewed Godkin for four hours, discussing the questions of reconstruction, Negro suffrage, the freedmen, and so on. Godkin gave them the impression that he agreed with their views on all important aspects of reconstruction. They approved of him as editor with the understanding that he was to have complete independence in editorial matters but that the paper was to represent primarily the interests of the freedmen.[34] The stockholders sent out circulars to announce the publication of the first issue of the *Nation* in July 1865. All abolitionist papers gave generous publicity to the new enterprise, and Garrison gave his blessing to the *Nation* as the logical successor of the *Liberator*. Several abolitionists were listed among the contributors to the *Nation*.[35]

With a capitalization of $100,000 and the backing of prominent abolitionists and Republicans, the *Nation* appeared headed for top rank among radical journals. But difficulties plagued the undertaking from the outset. In the first place the *Nation* was caught in the middle of the schism in the American Anti-Slavery Society. McKim had supported Garrison's effort to dissolve the Society and was bitter toward the Phillips faction that now controlled the organization. Stearns, on the other hand, had sustained Phillips in his successful effort to preserve the Society. Godkin disliked the radical crusading fervor of the Phillips wing, and sided with McKim. The early issues of the *Nation* contained oblique disparagements of Phillips and Stearns. Godkin also made a derisive remark about Stearns in a private letter, a report of which came to Stearns' ears. Stearns and Phillips were outraged by these insults. Stearns had contributed and raised more money for the *Nation* than any other person, and he felt that at the very least he deserved respect from its editor. Secondly, Godkin hoped to make the *Nation* into an outstanding

---

[34] Stearns, *Stearns*, 332-35; Rollo Ogden, ed., *Life and Letters of Edwin Lawrence Godkin* (2 vols., New York, 1907), I, 223-41; W. P. Garrison to W. L. Garrison, Dec. 11, 1864, Apr. 3, May 5, 1865, W. P. Garrison Papers, HU; Lucretia Mott to Martha Wright, Apr. 17, 1865, Mott Papers, SC; Stearns to Sumner, Apr. 30, 1865, Sumner Papers, HU; McKim to Gerrit Smith, May 18, 1865, Smith Papers, SU; Frank Sanborn to Moncure Conway, May 26, 1865, Conway Papers, CU; McKim to M. W. Chapman, June 6, 1865, Weston Papers, BPL.

[35] *N.A.S. Standard*, May 6, 1865; *Commonwealth*, May 13, June 17, 1865; *Liberator*, June 30, 1865.

political and literary review, modeled on English weekly reviews. Its abolitionist backers had conceived of it primarily as a radical freedmen's paper. Thirdly, Phillips and Stearns desired a hard-hitting, no-holds-barred radical journal that would sound the trumpet call of equality in stentorian tones. Instead the *Nation* offered long and scholarly editorials designed to appeal to the intellectual elite rather than to the masses. The editorials of the early months of the *Nation* favored Negro suffrage and equal justice to the freedmen, but they were characterized by a conservative restraint and impartial flavor which rendered them totally inadequate in the eyes of many radicals.[36]

Even Garrison and McKim were slightly unhappy with the first issues of the *Nation*, and Godkin adopted some of their friendly suggestions for improvement. But Phillips, Stearns, and other Boston radicals were entirely dissatisfied. They tried to force Godkin to change the style and spirit of the paper, and failing that, to force him out of the editor's chair. Charging bad faith on the part of Godkin, Stearns and most of the Boston stockholders withdrew their capital from the *Nation* in May 1866. Godkin reorganized the paper and became its proprietor as well as editor. Thenceforth the *Nation* turned gradually more conservative on the reconstruction question. What Stearns had originally conceived of as a large-circulation radical journal crusading for social reform and racial equality became under Godkin a genteel political-literary review of limited circulation but of considerable influence among the patrician class of intellectuals and businessmen in America.[37]

[36] Stearns, *Stearns*, 336-37, 351n.; Ogden, *Godkin*, I, 241-48; *Nation*, I (July 6, 1865), 1, 4-5 (July 13, 1865), 40 (July 20, 1865), 69, 73-74 (Sept. 21, 1865), 357, 359; *Liberator*, July 7, 1865; *Commonwealth*, July 15, 1865; *Independent*, July 13, 1865; McKim to E. L. Pierce, July 10, 1865, Godkin to McKim, July 10, 1865, Pierce to Benjamin Butler, July 11, 1865, in Jesse Marshall, ed., *Private and Official Correspondence of Gen. Benjamin F. Butler during the Period of the Civil War* (5 vols., Norwood, Mass., 1917), v, 491; Mary Stearns to A. Bronson Alcott, July 25, 1865, Alcott Papers, Concord Public Library.

[37] Stearns, *Stearns*, 337-38, 366; Ogden, *Godkin*, I, 242, 246-48; Alan P. Grimes, *The Political Liberalism of the New York Nation, 1865-1932* (Chapel Hill, 1953), 5-12; McKim to Samuel May, Jr., July 19, 1865, Quincy to May, Aug. 16, 1865, McKim to Richard Webb, Aug. 31, 1865, Garrison Papers, BPL; McKim to M. W. Chapman, Aug. 26, 1865, Weston Papers, BPL; Quincy to Webb, Oct. 21, 1865, Quincy-Webb Correspondence, BPL; Samuel May, Jr., to Webb, Sept. 19, 1865, Samuel May, Jr., Papers, BPL; *Nation*, I (Oct. 26, 1865), 520-21; *Liberator*, Sept. 22, Dec. 8, 1865; *Commonwealth*, Feb. 17, 1866, May 30, Nov. 14, 1868;

Made wiser by his experience with the *Nation*, Stearns kept control in his own hands of the next newspaper he founded (see discussion near the end of this chapter). Before the collapse of his hopes for the *Nation*, however, he set on foot his third major project to win public support for Negro suffrage: a mass meeting of the leading men of New England in Boston's Faneuil Hall on June 21, 1865. In an effort to portray this convention as an assemblage of moderates, Stearns engineered the selection of his friend Theophilus Parsons, Harvard law professor and nationally known jurist, as chairman and keynote speaker of the occasion. Richard Henry Dana, a respected lawyer and conservative anti-slavery veteran gave the main address. Although Stearns organized the convention and several abolitionists served as vice presidents and secretaries, radicals generally remained in the background and allowed the solid, substantial men of New England to take the lead. Parsons and Dana both emphasized the need of Negro suffrage to insure the success of reconstruction. Dana frankly admitted that "to introduce to the voting franchise four millions of slaves is a revolution. If we do not secure that now in the time of revolution, it can never be secured except by a new revolution. (Loud applause)"[38]

Stearns considered the Faneuil Hall meeting a great success. It attracted nationwide attention and inspired similar meetings in other cities. All over the North the subject of reconstruction and Negro suffrage was a vital topic of political discussion in the summer of 1865. Abolitionists held several meetings to promote the cause of equal suffrage. Northern Negroes organized rallies and demanded the franchise for themselves and their southern brethren. Radical Republican leaders spoke out for Negro suffrage. Southern freedmen held meetings and asked for the ballot to guarantee their freedom and security. Abolitionists spared no effort to bear witness for equal rights. "I have again and again, in sermon, speech and conversation urged the necessity of universal suffrage and emphatically of black suffrage—on grounds of humanity, justice, equity, reason and safety," re-

---

McKim to William Still, May 26, 1866, quoted in Norwood, "Negro Welfare Work in Philadelphia," 145; Sarah Pugh to McKim, Dec. 20, 1866, McKim Papers, NYPL. Garrison later became critical of the *Nation's* conservative course.
[38] Stearns, *Stearns*, 346-50; *Commonwealth*, June 24, 1865.

ported O. B. Frothingham in August 1865. "And I shall continue to do so as long as I have breath."[39]

The Democratic and conservative Republican press was annoyed by the outburst of Negro suffrage propaganda in the summer of 1865. The *Chicago Times* lamented: "This is an afflicted nation. To-day the negro is the one thing in every man's mouth from the Gulf to the St. Lawrence. The entire press of the country is wrangling over the negro; Boston philanthropists are holding secret meetings and arranging plans with reference to the negro. . . . Orators are shouting about the negro; preachers are advocating higher law for the benefit of the negro; and, in short, the whole country is . . . 'going it' exclusively on account of the negro." The *New York Times* was tired of the Negro question but was resigned to a continuation of the agitation. "It is evident," said the *Times*, "that this whole negro question can only be got rid of by getting rid of the negroes; and as this is impossible, we must rest content with our lot."[40]

In the discussion of Negro suffrage several phrases were bandied about, often indiscriminately. The four phrases most frequently used were "Negro suffrage," "impartial suffrage," "equal suffrage," and "universal suffrage." There were real differences in the meanings of these phrases, but as time went on the differences tended to disappear. "Impartial suffrage" and "equal suffrage" meant that whether the franchise was unrestricted or qualified it would be open equally to both races. Any qualifications, such as a literacy test or property ownership, must be applied impartially to both races. "Universal suffrage" meant universal manhood suffrage for both races, unrestricted except for age and residence requirements. "Negro suffrage," the phrase most often used, could mean either universal or impartial suffrage. Sometimes it was also used (but seldom by abolitionists) to mean a limited grant of suffrage to Negroes who met special requirements not applicable to whites.

At first several abolitionists, including Theodore Tilton, Gerrit Smith, and Lydia Maria Child, were willing to accept impartial

[39] O. B. Frothingham to Charles Sumner, Aug. 3, 1865, Sumner Papers, HU. Antislavery newspapers were filled with details of speeches, meetings, etc. on behalf of Negro suffrage in the summer of 1865.

[40] *Chicago Times*, July 7, 1865; *New York Times*, quoted by *N.A.S. Standard*, July 1, 1865.

suffrage. Conceding the argument that the freedmen were ignorant and lacked political experience, they endorsed a literacy qualification applied equally to both races. They hoped that the rapid spread of education in the South would soon enable most of the freedmen to qualify for the franchise.[41]

Most abolitionists, however, called for universal rather than impartial suffrage. It was unfair, they argued, to impose a literacy qualification on the franchise when the southern Negro for generations had been denied educational opportunities.[42] As time passed the distinction between impartial and universal suffrage became less important. By the end of 1865 nearly all those who advocated Negro suffrage meant, in effect, universal suffrage. There were two reasons for this. In the first place the creation of impartial literacy and/or property qualifications would have disfranchised many white men who already enjoyed suffrage. The principle of universal (white) manhood suffrage was deeply rooted in America, and it was a rare politician who would vote to disfranchise any man except for treason. Secondly, abolitionists and Republicans soon realized that impartial suffrage would give the freedmen negligible political power at first. There would not be a literate colored electorate large enough to counterbalance the white voters or to build the foundations of a strong Republican party in the South. "All my first impressions were for the writing and reading qualification; but on reflection it seemed to me impracticable," wrote Charles Sumner in August 1865. "You cannot get votes of Congress to disfranchise, which you must do in imposing this qualification. . . . Besides, there are very intelligent persons, especially among the freedmen, who cannot read or write. But we need the votes of all, and cannot afford to wait."[43]

✦

[41] Tilton to Garrison, Jan. 11, 1865, Garrison Papers, BPL; Lydia M. Child to Tilton, Mar. 7, 1865, in *Independent,* Mar. 16; *Independent,* July 20, Nov. 9, 1865; *Liberator,* Apr. 21, June 16, 1865; *N.A.S. Standard,* Apr. 8, 1865; Gerrit Smith, *Thoughts for the People,* broadside published April 14, 1865 (Peterboro, 1865).

[42] See, for example, *Commonwealth,* Mar. 11, June 3, 17, 24, Oct. 14, 1865; Wendell Phillips, *Lectures, Speeches, and Letters* (2nd Series; Boston, 1900), 451-52; *Liberator,* May 19, 1865; *N.A.S. Standard,* Sept. 30, 1865, Feb. 17, 1866; Parker Pillsbury to Charles Sumner, Sept. 16, 1865, Sumner Papers, HU.

[43] Sumner to Francis Lieber, Aug. 14, 1865, in Pierce, *Sumner,* IV, 256.

Despite the criticisms of radical abolitionists, most Republican leaders reserved judgment on President Johnson's reconstruction policy in 1865. The desire to regard that policy as an "experiment" which Johnson would abandon if it proved a failure was all-powerful. Moderate Republicans were unwilling to risk a party split over Negro suffrage.[44] Disgusted with the pusillanimity of politicians, Wendell Phillips decided to launch a full-scale attack on Johnson in a deliberate attempt to alienate him from the Republican party and to force the party to repudiate his policy. Phillips was the first prominent figure to come out squarely against the president, blazing a trail followed by thousands of abolitionists and Republicans in the next twelve months.

In powerful editorials in the *Anti-Slavery Standard* of June 24 and July 1, Phillips declared that Johnson's reconstruction program could no longer be considered an experiment. His extension of it to all Confederate states indicated a settled purpose. "We must make up our minds that we have to deal henceforth with a President implacably hostile to the only method of reorganization which is safe, peaceful, and permanent," wrote Phillips. Johnson had surrounded himself with conservative advisers and had rejected the counsels of true Republicans. Like President Tyler before him, he was in the process of abandoning the party that had elected him. Phillips was not deaf to the pleas of Republicans to avoid splitting the party. But Johnson had already gone over to the enemy, and "in these circumstances, he is manifestly a force to be resisted, not one to be counted on our side; a power to be subdued, not one to be waited on and conciliated." Most of the speakers at the abolitionist Fourth of July picnic in Framingham, Massachusetts, echoed Phillips' sentiments. The picnickers resolved unanimously that any reconstruction policy that failed to recognize "the absolute equality of every man before the Law" would be "a practical surrender of the North to the South" and "the essential triumph of the Slave Power."[45]

Theodore Tilton was also apprehensive about Johnson's course, but in midsummer of 1865 he was not yet prepared to declare a

[44] Eric McKitrick, *Andrew Johnson and Reconstruction* (Chicago, 1960), 42-84.

[45] *Liberator*, July 14, 1865. See also Parker Pillsbury to Samuel Johnson, Aug. 3, 1865, Johnson Papers, Essex Institute.

total break with the president. Instead he implored Johnson to reject the counsels of Democrats and remember that he had been elected by a party that meant to safeguard the Negro's freedom won at so dear a cost in war. Charles Slack, editor of the *Commonwealth* and spokesman for the old John Brown wing of Massachusetts abolitionists, expressed confidence that Johnson would soon recognize the failure of his "experiment" and move closer to the radical idea of reconstruction. "Andrew Johnson still stands before the tribunal," wrote Slack on July 22. "Press and people as yet only cry, 'He is going wrong, but he is honest and will come right.' So be it then. We will wait. But . . . if he wants the outspoken, unflinching support . . . of just men everywhere, he must bid for it soon."[46]

"I feel anxious at Pres. Johnson's course & think he mistakes it lamentably by his method of reconstruction, but am not ready to join in the hasty impeachment of him which is getting so popular," wrote William Lloyd Garrison, Jr., on July 9. "I prefer to believe in his good intentions & integrity till otherwise convinced." His father shared these sentiments. The elder Garrison censured Phillips and other abolitionists who had openly declared war on the president. There was "no ground for discouragement or alarm," said Garrison. "There is positive growth and constant progress." Garrison's continued faith in Johnson was echoed by many abolitionists in the summer of 1865. William H. Channing asserted that the president had not "a shade of a purpose to betray the cause of freedom. Let us stand by him and uphold his hand & so at once impel & guide him onward." An abolitionist friend of Frederick Douglass urged the Negro leader to be more charitable in his judgment of the president. "Did you not once have as little faith in Pres. Lincoln when you said he was 'wrong from choice, & right from necessity,' as you have now in Johnson?" she asked. "Does the past justify the present?"[47]

Wendell Phillips did more than denounce Johnson in the summer of 1865. In a July 4th speech he made a positive suggestion

---

[46] *Independent*, July 6, 13, 1865; *Commonwealth*, July 8, 22, 1865.

[47] W. L. Garrison, Jr., to Martha Wright, July 9, 1865, Garrison Papers, SC; *Liberator*, July 14, 1865; Wm. H. Channing to R. H. Dana, July 13, 1865, quoted by McKitrick, *Andrew Johnson and Reconstruction*, 63n.; Martha Greene to Douglass, Aug. 2, 1865, Douglass Papers, Anacostia. Charles Sumner was disturbed by Garrison's endorsement of Johnson. "Has not the time come for

that became the keystone of Republican strategy at the next session of Congress. If Clerk of the House Edward McPherson called the names of southern congressmen elected under Johnson's plan when Congress convened in December, warned Phillips, the game would be up, for the southerners would vote with the Democrats, organize Congress, and enact a reconstruction policy of their own. In a letter to the *Anti-Slavery Standard* of July 8 Phillips amplified his discussion of this question. Under House rules the clerk called the role before organization of the House or choice of a speaker. If the clerk called the names of southern representatives these former rebels would be in a position to control legislation. Phillips urged Clerk McPherson and the Republicans to make sure that this did not happen.[48] Phillips' speech and letter were the first public references to this problem, and they were widely reprinted and discussed in both the northern and southern press. Democrats denounced Phillips' proposal for the omission of southern names from the clerk's roll as "revolutionary" and "fanatical." But many Republicans were jarred into an awareness of the danger by Phillips' warning. McPherson privately assured Phillips in September that he would not call the names of southerners, and a month later the clerk publicly announced his position. When Congress met in December the members from former rebel states were automatically excluded by McPherson's omission of them from the roll, allowing the Republicans to proceed freely with their discussion of the proper method of reconstruction.[49]

In an effort to gather information on southern conditions for use as a weapon against Johnson's policy, Boston abolitionists and radicals helped finance Carl Schurz's southern tour in the summer of 1865 and arranged for publication of Schurz's letters in the *Boston Advertiser*. J. M. W. Yerrington, the abolitionist stenographer, accompanied Schurz and took down the testimony

---

your voice?" Sumner asked the veteran abolitionist on July 22. "This unwise and evil experiment of the Prest. must be exposed. I would not break with him, but let him know frankly the opportunity he has lost, & the mischief he has caused." Sumner to Garrison, July 22, 1865, Garrison Papers, BPL.

[48] *Liberator*, July 14, 1865; *N.A.S. Standard*, July 8, 1865.

[49] *N.A.S. Standard*, July 15, Aug. 26, Sept. 2, 1865; *New York Times*, July 9, 1865; *New York Herald*, July 15, 1865; *Richmond Commercial Bulletin*, July 19, 1865; LaWanda Cox and John H. Cox, *Politics, Principle, and Prejudice, 1865-1866* (New York, 1963), 140-41.

of all classes of southerners.[50] But radicals did not have to await Schurz's report for evidence of southern oppression of the freedmen. The lower house of the Tennessee legislature had already passed a black code barring Negroes from juries, inflicting more severe punishments on Negroes than whites for the same crime, subjecting Negroes to sale into temporary bondage for vagrancy, and giving the courts power to bind out colored children to white men as apprentices. Reports by military personnel, newspaper correspondents, and teachers in the South of whippings, shootings, and lynchings began to make their way into the northern press. Antislavery and Republican papers ran daily and weekly columns filled with stories of southern outrages against Negroes. The chaotic condition of affairs in the South had its bright side for abolitionists, because it convinced many northerners of the dangers of Johnson's program. Tilton recalled that Lincoln had advanced from a proslavery to an antislavery policy under the pressure of events and of public opinion, "So we believe will President Johnson yet [advance] if the press and the people persist in their just demands."[51]

In Mississippi, Provisional Governor William Sharkey began reorganizing the state militia in August 1865, using Confederate veterans as a nucleus. Union General Henry W. Slocum issued an order prohibiting the formation of militia units, but upon appeal from Sharkey the president overruled his general and allowed the organization of state troops to proceed. More than almost anything Johnson had done thus far, this action aroused the suspicion and distrust of the North.[52] Abolitionists who had not already done so began to turn against the president. "What can be hatched from such an egg but another rebellion?" asked the *Commonwealth*. "If rebels in Mississippi are to be thus armed, then also will they be in every rebel State. Can there be but one end to such a beginning?" Still protesting that he was not a member of the Phillips-Pillsbury party of "doubt, distrust, and denunciation," Samuel May, Jr., nevertheless feared that "if the coming Congress does not present itself, like an immovable wall

[50] F. W. Bird to Garrison, July 5, 1865, Garrison Papers, BPL; Howard K. Beale, *The Critical Year: A Study of Andrew Johnson and Reconstruction* (2nd ed., New York, 1958), 70-71.

[51] *Independent*, Aug. 10, 1865.

[52] McKitrick, *Andrew Johnson and Reconstruction*, 163-64, 193-94.

of adamant, to the encroachments of the Southern managers & their friends, . . . we shall be left in a most singular position, and the culmination of our terrible struggle . . . will be a most absurd, a most lamentable, & at the same time a most farcical one." Even Garrison, who had managed to preserve his jaunty optimism all through the summer, confessed at the beginning of October that "the aspect of things at the South is somewhat portentous. I begin to feel more uneasy about the President."[53]

Radicals realized that to impose Negro suffrage on the South while ignoring the same issue at home would leave them open to charges of hypocrisy. Only five northern states allowed Negroes to vote on equal terms with whites in 1865. Since "we of the North have a great battle to fight in order to secure suffrage to the negro at the South," wrote Sydney Gay in May 1865, "it behooves us to clear our own skirts from stain as rapidly as possible."[54] Republican legislatures in Connecticut, Wisconsin, and Minnesota put Negro suffrage constitutional amendments on their ballots for the fall elections. As the elections approached, however, abolitionists detected a tendency among Republican politicians to hedge on the question of Negro suffrage in their own states. The Minnesota Republican convention endorsed equal suffrage, but the conventions of Wisconsin, New York, Pennsylvania, Ohio, and New Jersey evaded the issue. Connecticut Republicans issued a broadside urging voters to approve the amendment, but the state committee showed a notable lack of enthusiasm for the measure. In truth, Negro suffrage *in the North* was by no means popular among northern voters, and Republican politicians knew it.[55]

[53] *Commonwealth*, Sept. 30, 1865; Samuel May, Jr., to S. J. May, Sept. 17, 1865, S. J. May Papers, BPL; Garrison to Henry Wright, Oct. 2, 1865, Garrison Papers, BPL. Lydia Maria Child commented in October that "I feel more uneasy about public affairs than I care to say. . . . I have called to mind my impatience with Lincoln, and I have tried to think the best of Andy Johnson, and to hope for the best; but I confess faith and hope are dying out." L. M. Child to Elisa Scudder, Oct. 22, 1865, Child Papers, Cornell.

[54] *New York Tribune*, May 27, 1865.

[55] *ibid.*, Sept. 12, 26, 1865; *N.A.S. Standard*, Aug. 19, Sept. 30, 1865; *Independent*, Aug. 24, Sept. 28, 1865; G. W. Curtis to S. H. Gay, Aug. 23, 1865, Gay Papers, CU; Henry Stanton to Gerrit Smith, Sept. 22, 1865, Smith Papers, SU; Leslie H. Fishel, Jr., "Northern Prejudice and Negro Suffrage, 1865-1870," *Journal of Negro History*, XXXIX (Jan. 1954), 12-15.

A great deal was at stake in the Connecticut election early in October. A victory for Negro suffrage in the pivotal Nutmeg State would imply a repudiation of Johnson's reconstruction policy and an endorsement of the radicals. A defeat, on the other hand, would be interpreted as a victory for Johnson. The administration and the Democrats did their best to defeat the amendment, using appeals to race prejudice as their main weapon. Republicans failed to make similar efforts on the other side, and the amendment lost by 6,000 votes. A month later Minnesota and Wisconsin voters also turned down Negro suffrage. Abolitionists and radicals were inconsolable. The Connecticut vote was "the most disastrous event since the death of Mr. Lincoln and the inauguration of the present policy of his successor," wrote Wendell P. Garrison in the *Liberator*. "We feel humiliated and ashamed of this ingratitude and shortsightedness," declared the *Boston Commonwealth* a few days after the Connecticut vote. "It was an unworthy, unmanly and discreditable act, and will cover the New England name with shame the world over." The *Commonwealth* frankly conceded that the defeat of Negro suffrage in Connecticut "jeopardizes—at least, delays—the permanent settlement of the questions in dispute in the rebellious States." Tilton was disenchanted with moderate Republican leadership after the Connecticut election, and abandoned all efforts to promote reconciliation between moderates and radicals. "The Republican party must stand either *for* or *against* Equal Suffrage," announced Tilton. "If this party refuses to fulfill its moral mission, it will go to pieces. . . . We shall be glad to stand with the great body of the Republican party in so far as that body shall stand inflexibly for Freedom and Justice; but we have no intention of abandoning moral principles for the sake of keeping company with political friends."[56]

Abolitionists were discouraged by the entire course of events in the autumn of 1865. A reaction in favor of Johnson and of reconstruction without Negro suffrage seemed to have set in. Southern constitutional conventions were refusing to grant even equal *civil* rights to the freedmen. Unless something intervened

[56] *Liberator*, Oct. 13, 1865; *Commonwealth*, Oct. 7, 1865; *Independent*, Oct. 12, 1865. See also George Cheever to Elizabeth C. Washburn, Oct. 3, 1865, Cheever Papers, AAS; *New York Tribune*, Oct. 3, 7, 1865; and *N.A.S. Standard*, Oct. 14, 1865.

it appeared that these states would be readmitted to the Union with constitutions and "Black Codes" relegating the Negroes to a permanent subordinate status. Hoping against hope, abolitionists looked forward to the meeting of Congress to remedy the situation. Meanwhile they did not sit back and wring their hands in despair. Anna Dickinson, Tilton, Phillips, Douglass, and several lesser abolitionists embarked on lecture tours that would take them before hundreds of audiences during the winter. Reconstruction was virtually the sole topic of their lectures. Nearly every abolitionist speaker kept up a relentless fire against President Johnson's policy throughout the winter.[57]

The title of Phillips' most oft-repeated lecture was "The South Victorious." This jarring title brought thousands who had thought the North victorious to hear Phillips in Boston and New York in October. Judging by the present hour, Phillips told skeptical listeners, the South was indeed victorious. Beaten on the field of battle, she had a good prospect of winning the political game of reconstruction. Phillips reminded his audiences of the revolution of 1848 in France, when the people deposed a king only to install an emperor in his place. "Now, we stand exactly as France stood," said Phillips. The North had overthrown slavery but was in danger of installing a new version of the aristocratic slave power in its place. Under Johnson's plan, said Phillips, the South would return to the Union "with the same theories, with the same men to work them, and the same element to work them with. . . . It must be evident to any reasoning man that the single advantage the North has gained in changing the political and social condition of the Southern States was the elimination, possibly, of this single element of chattelhood." Phillips denounced the Republican party for its timid failure to take a stand against Johnson's policy. "There is really no political force in existence worthy the name of the Republican party," he declared. "We

[57] For examples of abolitionist discouragement, see *Commonwealth*, Oct. 14, 21, 1865; Wendell Phillips to Benjamin Butler, Oct. 24, 1865, Butler Papers, LC; Tilton to Sumner, Nov. 11, 1865, Sumner Papers, HU; *N.A.S. Standard*, Sept. 16, 23, Oct. 21, 1865. Phillips wrote privately in October 1865, that "we have no hope but in such utterly abominable conduct on the part of [Johnson's] protégés at the South as will cause the North & Congress to checkmate his plan." Phillips to Moncure Conway, Oct. ?, 1865, Conway Papers, CU.

335

can trust neither Congress, nor Andrew Johnson, nor the Republican party. The only hope remaining is in the People."[58]

Charles Sumner had remained in Washington during the summer of 1865 in a futile effort to hold Johnson to the radical line. He returned to Boston at the end of August and confessed his failure to Phillips, Howe, and Stearns. Sumner was prepared to follow Phillips into open opposition to the president. Stearns, however, was not yet ready to give up. He had known Johnson well in Tennessee, and he believed that he could accomplish more in a single conversation with the plebeian president than the scholarly, polished Sumner had achieved all summer. Stearns journeyed to Washington early in October and spent a pleasant hour chatting with Johnson. The president denied that he was going over to the Democrats. On the burning question of Negro suffrage Johnson restated his belief that the federal government had no more right to prescribe suffrage conditions for Alabama than for Pennsylvania. If he were back in Tennessee, said Johnson, he would favor a gradual extension of suffrage to Negroes who had served in the army or could meet a property or literacy qualification. He was opposed to an immediate grant of universal suffrage, fearing that it would cause a war of races in the South.[59]

Stearns returned to his hotel and immediately wrote down the substance of the president's remarks. He requested Johnson's permission to publish the interview, believing that "it will go far to promote a good understanding between you and our leading men."[60] Johnson acquiesced, and Stearns returned to Boston for consultation with his colleagues before publishing the interview. Sumner and Boston's leading abolitionists attended a meeting to discuss the question. Stearns argued that publication would cut the ground from under Democrats who were claiming Johnson as one of themselves, repair the widening breach in the Republican party, and insert an opening wedge for Negro suffrage. The interview put Johnson on record as favoring qualified suffrage, said Stearns, and after six months an improved public opinion would make it possible to get a stronger presidential endorsement of Negro suffrage. Johnson would move, like Lincoln, with the

[58] *N.A.S. Standard*, Oct. 21, Nov. 4, 1865.
[59] Stearns, *Stearns*, 358-60; *New York Tribune*, Oct. 23, 1865.
[60] Stearns to Johnson, Oct. 8, 1865, Johnson Papers, LC.

advancing tide of public opinion. "All my former intercourse with the President taught me to respect his honesty, sincerity and ability," said Stearns, "and I shall trust him until he for the *first time* deceives me." Sumner, Phillips, and others were opposed to publication of the interview. They believed Johnson to be an implacable foe of radical reconstruction, and did not favor anything that would increase the president's stature in the eyes of the Republican party. They considered Johnson less dangerous as an avowed enemy than as a false friend. Stearns nevertheless published the interview in the Boston and New York papers on October 23, and it was reprinted or summarized by nearly every newspaper in the North.[61]

Most of the Republican press reacted precisely as Stearns desired, hailing the interview as evidence that Johnson was still a loyal Republican and a friend of the Negro.[62] But most abolitionists failed to find any reason for encouragement in the interview. Johnson's assertion that universal suffrage would breed a war of races reminded Tilton of the old conservative argument that *emancipation* would spark a race war. The *Anti-Slavery Standard* ridiculed Johnson's statement that he could no more interfere with suffrage requirements in Alabama than in Pennsylvania. Had he appointed a provisional governor for Pennsylvania? Had he ordered Pennsylvania to repudiate her state debt? He had taken such steps in the former rebel states, proving by his own actions that the government possessed the power of a conqueror over the southern states and could mold their institutions into any shape it desired. The *Standard* was opposed to any efforts to reconcile Johnson and the radicals, for it believed Johnson irrevocably hostile to nearly everything the radicals stood for. "We assure Mr. Stearns that the Radicals mean to *smash* the reconstruction policy of the President," declared the *Standard*, "and believe they can do it if their friends and the true friends of the Negro will stand by them."[63]

By the end of October 1865, many abolitionists had come to agree with Higginson that "what most men mean to-day by the

---

[61] Stearns, *Stearns*, 360-61; quotation from Stearns to Moncure Conway, Oct. 23, 1865, Conway Papers, cu.

[62] *New York Tribune*, Oct. 23, 1865; *Right Way*, Nov. 18, 1865; Stearns to Andrew Johnson, Nov. 13, 1865, Johnson Papers, lc; Stearns, *Stearns*, 361-62.

[63] *Independent*, Oct. 26, Nov. 9, 1865; *N.A.S. Standard*, Oct. 28, 1865.

'President's plan of reconstruction' is the pardon of every rebel for the crime of rebellion, and the utter refusal to pardon a single black loyalist for the crime of being black. . . . The truth is that we are causing quite as much suffering as a conqueror usually does. It is simply that we are forgiving our enemies and torturing only our friends." The Garrison family was finally becoming convinced of Johnson's bad faith. "Notwithstanding Stearns' interview which amounts to nothing," wrote William Lloyd Garrison, Jr., "it will take a different course of action on the President's part to inspire much trust in his administration."[64]

But there were some abolitionists not yet ready to give up on Johnson. J. Miller McKim told a fellow abolitionist that "I share your fears in regard to President Johnson, and yet my hopes exceed my fears."[65] George Stearns still had faith in the president. In November 1865, Stearns began publishing a weekly radical newspaper called the *Right Way*. The purpose of this journal was to win public support for Negro suffrage as the right way to accomplish a successful reconstruction. Stearns employed Alpheus Crosby, an abolitionist and the leading American authority on ancient Greece, as editor of the *Right Way*. William W. Thayer, a John Brown abolitionist, served as business manager of the paper and wrote many of its shorter editorials. The *Right Way* was published in the *Liberator* office, and every week 60,000 copies were sent to members of Stearns' Universal and Equal Suffrage Association. Negroes in the South formed clubs to distribute the *Right Way* among the freedmen. In its early issues the paper advocated Stearns' policy of reconciliation between the radicals and President Johnson. It praised Johnson as a "patriotic President" who needed the support of all "faithful men" in the difficult task of reconstruction. The *Right Way* was convinced that Negro suffrage was necessary for reconstruction and equally convinced that Johnson would soon realize this fact.[66]

As the important 1865-66 session of Congress approached, abolitionists' spirits revived somewhat from the doldrums of

[64] Higginson's statement published in *Independent*, Oct. 26, 1865; W. L. Garrison, Jr., to Martha Wright, Nov. 5, 1865, Garrison Papers, sc.

[65] McKim to S. J. May, Nov. 7, 1865, McKim letterbook, I, 55, McKim Papers, Cornell.

[66] Stearns, *Stearns*, 357; W. W. Thayer, ms. autobiography, fragment in the MS Division, lc; *Right Way*, Nov. 18, 25, Dec. 9, 23, 1865.

October. Leading Republicans were giving signs of opposition to Johnson's policy. Phillips and some of the other ultraradical abolitionists believed congressional Republicans to be almost as culpable as Johnson because of their indecisive stand on Negro suffrage. But most abolitionists expressed confidence in Congress. In November Garrison embarked on a lecture tour that took him as far west as Springfield, Illinois. The veteran abolitionist was heartily welcomed and loudly cheered wherever he appeared. His lectures urged the exclusion of southern representatives from Congress until the freedmen were granted equal rights.[67] Garrison returned to the East on the same train with several Republican congressmen on their way to Washington. Most of them agreed, reported Garrison, that the South should not be readmitted without further examination of the problem and greater safeguards for the freedmen.[68] As the senators and representatives gathered in Washington, John G. Whittier published an Ode to the Thirty-Ninth Congress:

> Make all men peers before the law,
> Take hands from off the negro's throat,
> Give black and white an equal vote.[69]

At the end of 1865, abolitionists were divided roughly into four groups in their opinion of President Johnson. Some abolitionists, including Stearns and McKim, still believed that Johnson would prove faithful to his trust. Others such as Garrison, Lydia Maria Child, and Samuel May, Jr., were disappointed with the president but still possessed a glimmer of hope that he would change his policy under the pressure of congressional action and public opinion. A third group of abolitionists, including Tilton, Higginson, and Charles Slack, had preserved a precarious trust in the president until October, when it became obvious to them that Johnson considered his policy a finality rather than an experiment. They had turned against him and now reposed their confidence solely in Congress, still hoping against hope, however, that the president could somehow be persuaded to abandon his disastrous policy. Finally, the abolitionists led by

---

[67] *Liberator,* Nov. 10, Dec. 8, 15, 1865; *Cleveland Leader,* Nov. 9, 1865; *Chicago Tribune,* Nov. 17, 1865.

[68] Garrison to Helen Garrison, Nov. 27, 29, 1865, Garrison Papers, BPL.

[69] The *Nation,* I (Dec. 7, 1865), 714.

Phillips had long since relegated Johnson to the status of an enemy who must be overcome before the Negro could obtain equal justice. As the representatives of the people gathered in Washington for their weighty deliberations, Phillips and his followers openly challenged President Johnson and dared him to do his worst.

Iɴ his first annual message to Congress on December 2, 1865, President Johnson restated his belief that he had no right to prescribe suffrage qualifications in the southern states and declared that the reconstructed state governments provided ample protection and security for all citizens. Radical abolitionists derided the message. They noted again the president's inconsistency in appointing provisional governors and prescribing certain conditions for reconstruction but denying the right to fix suffrage requirements. As for the protection and security of citizens, one needed only to read the black codes or scan the daily reports of atrocities against freedmen to perceive the falsity of Johnson's assertion.[1] A good example of the southern attitude, said abolitionists, was a box received by Charles Sumner in the mail containing the severed finger of a Negro and a note: "You old son of a bitch, I send you a piece of one of your friends, and if that bill of yours passes I will have a piece of you."[2]

Abolitionists were gratified when Congress, in effect, repudiated Johnson's annual message by refusing to admit southern congressmen and by creating the Joint Committee of Fifteen to formulate a reconstruction policy.[3] A few days later the American Freedmen's Aid Commission, a union of the secular freedmen's aid societies, memorialized Congress for a continuation and enlargement of the Freedmen's Bureau. In an address written by McKim, the societies noted that freedmen could not get justice in the civil courts of the South, where they were excluded as jurors and sometimes as witnesses. McKim urged Congress to create military courts for the Negroes under the auspices of the Freedmen's Bureau.[4] Soon after this Senator Lyman Trumbull introduced two bills intended to clarify and protect the status of

[1] James D. Richardson, ed., *Messages and Papers of the Presidents* (20 vols., Washington, 1897-1913), vɪɪɪ, 3551-60; *N.A.S. Standard*, Dec. 9, 30, 1865, Jan. 6, 27, 1866; *Commonwealth*, Dec. 9, 23, 30, 1865, Jan. 20, 1866; *Liberator*, Dec. 15, 1865; *Independent*, Jan. 4, Feb. 8, 1866.
[2] *Right Way*, Jan. 27, 1866.
[3] Tilton to Thaddeus Stevens, Dec. 6, 1865, Stevens Papers, ʟᴄ.
[4] *Liberator*, Dec. 22, 1865.

southern freedmen. One bill enlarged the scope of the Freedmen's Bureau; the second defined the civil rights of freedmen and empowered federal district courts to enforce these rights.[5]

While Congress debated these measures, abolitionists continued to urge Negro suffrage as a minimum condition of restoration. The first test of the suffrage question came on a bill to grant the ballot to colored men in the District of Columbia. Petitions for enactment of this bill poured in from abolitionists and Negroes all over the North. The House passed the bill on January 18, 1866, to the thundering applause of 300 Negroes in the galleries. Abolitionists hailed the event as the greatest victory for the Negro since the Thirteenth Amendment.[6]

While the District of Columbia suffrage bill rested in Senate committee, the full Senate took up an enabling act to admit Colorado as the newest state of the Union. Republicans backed the Colorado bill in order to gain two additional Republican senators to help override Johnson's vetoes. But Sumner and the abolitionists opposed admission because Colorado's constitution limited the franchise to white men. They appreciated the partisan advantages of two more Republican senators, but they were trying to make Negro suffrage the main issue of reconstruction, and admission of a new northern state without equal suffrage would stultify their efforts and create a disastrous precedent. Senator Henry Wilson took the lead in urging Colorado's admission, and abolitionists denounced him unmercifully for his action. Despite the efforts of Sumner and the abolitionists, Congress passed the enabling act. But Johnson vetoed it on the ground that Colorado's population was insufficient for statehood, and Congress could not muster enough votes to override the veto. It was the only Johnson veto of which abolitionists ever approved.[7]

Meanwhile the tension between President Johnson and the Republican congressional majority was mounting. At the be-

[5] Eric McKitrick, *Andrew Johnson and Reconstruction* (Chicago, 1960), 277-79.

[6] *Liberator*, Dec. 15, 1865; *N.A.S. Standard*, Dec. 16, 30, 1865, Jan. 27, Feb. 3, 1866; *Commonwealth*, Jan. 20, 1866; *Right Way*, Dec. 23, 1865, Jan. 20, 27, 1866; *Independent*, Jan. 25, 1866.

[7] Edward McPherson, *Political History of the United States of America during the Period of Reconstruction* (Washington, 1871), 81-83; Edward L. Pierce, *Memoir and Letters of Charles Sumner* (4 vols., Boston, 1877-94), IV, 284-86; *Independent*, Feb. 8, Mar. 15, May 3, 1866; *N.A.S. Standard*, May 12, 19, 1866; *Right Way*, Apr. 28, 1866; *Commonwealth*, Jan. 27, Apr. 21, 28, May 5, 19, 1866.

ginning of the session Horace Greeley, George Stearns, and John Andrew made several attempts to preserve harmony between the president and Congress. Greeley journeyed to Washington in an effort to prevent a breach between Johnson and Republican leaders. Stearns made a personal appeal to his old friend Johnson for reconstruction on the basis of equal rights. In his valedictory address to the Massachusetts legislature on January 5, 1866, Andrew pleaded for the good will and cooperation of all classes, North and South, in solving the complex problem of reconstruction.[8]

Many abolitionists disapproved of these efforts to reconcile President Johnson and the Congress. Phillips thought that Republicans had carried conciliation far enough and that it was time for them to strike boldly against Johnson's policy. In reply to the moderate Republican argument that precipitate action would drive the president into the Democratic party, Phillips said: "If he is capable of being there, he ought to be. If he means to betray his party, the sooner the better." In January Senator Fessenden, chairman of the Joint Committee of Fifteen, publicly stated that there was no breach between the president and the Republican congressional majority. A special meeting of the American Anti-Slavery Society in Boston on January 24, denounced Fessenden's attempt to harmonize Johnson and Congress. "Those who bestow general approval of the President take off the edge of public vigilance," said Phillips. If Fessenden and his associates really thought there was no major difference of opinion between themselves and Johnson, "the leaders of the Republican party are to be watched, not trusted. . . . We need outside pressure and remorseless criticism upon Congress and the President."[9]

During the congressional session a delegation of Negro abolitionists, headed by George Downing, came to Washington to lobby for Negro suffrage. On February 7 Downing, Frederick Douglass, and three other Negroes held an important interview

[8] Glyndon G. Van Deusen, *Horace Greeley, Nineteenth Century Crusader* (Phila., 1953), 342-43; *Right Way*, Dec. 16, 1865; Stearns to Johnson, Dec. 14, 1865, Johnson Papers, LC; Henry G. Pearson, *The Life of John A. Andrew* (2 vols., Boston, 1904), II, 276-87.

[9] *N.A.S. Standard*, Jan. 20, Feb. 3, 1866. See also Phillips to Sumner, Dec. 25, 1865, Sumner Papers, HU; *Principia*, Jan. 11, 1866; and *Commonwealth*, Jan. 27, 1866.

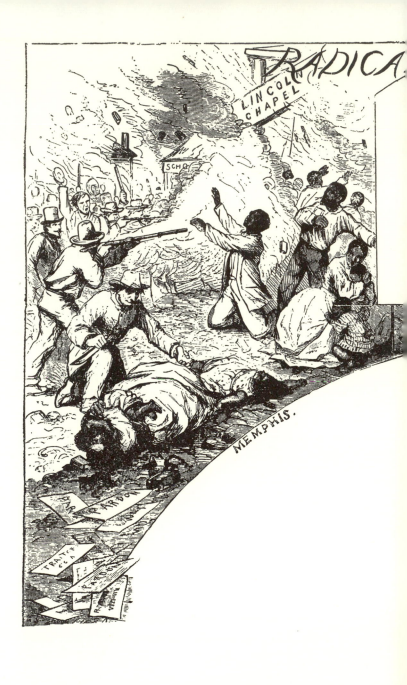

"Andrew Johnson's Reconstruction and How It Works."
Nast in *Harper's Weekly*

with President Johnson. In short introductory speeches Downing and Douglass assured the president that they came in a spirit of respect and friendship. They urged Johnson to enfranchise the Negro as a measure of justice and necessity. In his reply the president declared that he had always been a friend of the colored race. "If I know myself, and the feelings of my own heart, they have been for the colored man. I have owned slaves and bought slaves, but I never sold one." Warming to his subject, Johnson declared that Negro suffrage in the South would cause a war of races. If enfranchised the freedmen would become mere political pawns of the planter class, who would use them to grind down further the small white farmers. The president could see no solution of the race problem except emigration of the Negroes from the South. Stunned by Johnson's remarks, Douglass tried to reply, but was cut off by the president before he could utter more than a few sentences. The delegation was ushered out of Johnson's office.[10]

After consultation with radical congressional leaders, Douglass penned a reply to the president's statement and published it in the *Washington Chronicle*. Douglass denied that Negro suffrage would create a race war or that the Negro voter would become the pawn of the planter class. Enmity between Negro and poor white grew out of slavery. In freedom the Negroes and the small white farmers would have similar interests and would vote accordingly. Even if hostility between poor white and Negro did continue in freedom, said Douglass, how was the freedman to protect himself without equal rights? Experience proved that "Men are whipped oftenest who are whipped easiest." To keep the Negro politically powerless would only invite abuse and oppression of the defenseless freedmen. "Peace between races is not to be secured by degrading one race and exalting another," concluded Douglass, "but by maintaining a state of equal justice between all classes."[11]

[10] *Washington Chronicle*, Feb. 8, 1866. One of Johnson's private secretaries reported to a friend that after the "darkey delegation" had left his office, the president "uttered the following terse Saxon: 'Those d----d sons of b----s thought they had me in a trap! I know that d----d Douglass; he's just like any nigger, and he would sooner cut a white man's throat than not.'" P. Ripley to Manton Marble, Feb. 8, 1866, quoted by LaWanda Cox and John H. Cox, *Politics, Principle, and Prejudice, 1865-1866: Dilemma of Reconstruction America* (New York, 1963), 163.

[11] *Washington Chronicle*, Feb. 8, 1866. An account of the interview and a copy

The interview and Douglass' reply attracted widespread attention. The Republican press was almost unanimously critical of Johnson's behavior toward the Negroes. Abolitionists exploded in anger at this new evidence of Johnson's race prejudice. In an editorial entitled "Our Poor White President" the *Anti-Slavery Standard* assailed Johnson's address to the colored delegation as "one of the most brutal and insolent speeches anywhere on record." Elizabeth Cady Stanton commented that the interview showed "how much better Douglass understands the philosophy of social life and republican institutions than the President." The Worcester Freedom Club resolved that the interview had revealed the real attitude of the president toward the Negro: there was no longer any doubt that Johnson's policy was based on the belief that the country belonged to white men alone.[12]

Most abolitionists had given up hope of securing Johnson's cooperation for a just reconstruction program, but there were still many Republicans seeking a basis of accommodation with the president. In mid-February their hopes centered on Trumbull's Freedmen's Bureau bill, recently passed by large majorities in both houses of Congress. Senators Trumbull and Fessenden fully expected Johnson to approve the act. Speaker of the House Schuyler Colfax wagered a box of Havana cigars that the president would sign. J. Miller McKim scouted Democratic rumors that the president would veto the bill. "I can hardly think he will be so unwise as to do so," wrote McKim. "That bill . . . is a growth of the loyal and virtuous public sentiment of the land. To veto it . . . would be to fly in the face of the whole people."[13]

But on February 19 Johnson shocked Republicans by vetoing the act. The *Anti-Slavery Standard* was not surprised. Phillips tossed an "I told you so" editorial at Republicans who had labored to reconcile President Johnson and the Congress. Two days after the veto Theodore Tilton told his friend Greeley that "it is a crime henceforth to deceive the Nation by the pretence

---

of Douglass' reply are in McPherson, *History of Reconstruction*, 52-56. See also *New York Tribune*, Feb. 12, 1866.

[12] *N.A.S. Standard*, Feb. 17, 1866. See also *ibid.*, Feb. 24, 1866; *Commonwealth*, Feb. 17, 1866; *Independent*, Feb. 15, Mar. 1, 1866; *Right Way*, Feb. 24, Mar. 3, 1866.

[13] McKitrick, *Andrew Johnson and Reconstruction*, 284; *New York Tribune*, Feb. 14, 15, 1864; *N.A.S. Standard*, Feb. 24, 1866; McKim to Joseph Simpson, Feb. 16, 1866, McKim letterbook, I, 273, McKim Papers, Cornell.

that Andrew Johnson is the head of the Republican Party. . . . All disguise is now taken off. The way to victory is no longer by going *with* him but *against* him." Greeley was stunned by the veto and expressed his grief in a series of *Tribune* editorials. He did not yet take Tilton's advice to break completely with the president, but his editorials were henceforth much more critical of the administration.[14]

Among abolitionists there was hardly one who ever again said a good word for Johnson. Stearns, Oliver Johnson, McKim, Garrison, and others who had been hoping against hope that the president could be dissuaded from his wrongheaded course were completely disillusioned by the veto. "What is to be done with Andrew Johnson?" asked Samuel May, Jr., dejectedly. "It looks to me now that he has *betrayed his friends*, when he might have easily prevented any rupture if he chose." General Howard, head of the Freedmen's Bureau, told McKim that the veto had emboldened white southerners to increase their attacks on the Bureau and had made freedmen's aid efforts in the South more difficult. "I have talked hopefully of the President," reported McKim from Washington. "We have kept our fears to ourselves. But it is no use. Loyal and virtuous men here, who are well informed, as a general thing have no confidence in & no sanguine hope of much good from President Johnson."[15]

Johnson followed his veto with one of the most remarkable public speeches ever uttered by an American president. On February 22 a group of Democrats held a Washington's birthday celebration at Grover's Theatre in the capital. They adopted resolutions endorsing Johnson's reconstruction policy and affirming that "the grand old declaration that 'all men are created equal' was never intended by its authors . . . [to place] the African race in this country on a civil, social, or political level with the Caucasian."[16] In a festive mood the revelers trooped to the White

[14] *N.A.S. Standard,* Feb. 24, 1866; Tilton to Greeley, Feb. 21, 1866, Tilton Papers, Misc. Mss, NYPL; *New York Tribune,* Feb. 20, 21, 23, 1866.

[15] Samuel May, Jr., to McKim, Feb. 20, 1866, McKim Papers, NYPL; McKim to Joseph Simpson, Feb. 28, 1866, McKim letterbook, I, 398-400, McKim Papers, Cornell. See also *Right Way,* Mar. 3, 1866; Oliver Johnson to Garrison, Feb. 20, 1866, Garrison Papers, BPL; George Thompson to Oliver Johnson, Feb. 22, 1866, Dickinson Papers, LC.

[16] Garrison to W. P. Garrison, Feb. 22, 1866, Garrison Papers, BPL; *Independent,* Mar. 1, 1866.

House to serenade President Johnson, who responded with a long speech full of diatribes against radical leaders. Johnson compared himself to Christ; he denounced the radicals as traitors and disunionists, and when asked to name his tormentors, he called out the names of Thaddeus Stevens, Charles Sumner, and Wendell Phillips. These plotters were planning to assassinate him, charged Johnson. "If my blood is to be shed because I vindicate the Union and the preservation of this government in its original purity and character," he proclaimed, "let it be shed; let an altar to the Union be erected, and then, if it is necessary, take me and lay me upon it, and the blood that now warms and animates my existence shall be poured out as a fit libation to the Union of these States."[17]

The nation was mortified by the president's speech. Some of his best friends were appalled. Even abolitionists who believed Johnson capable of any villainy were taken aback. "Has the [presidential] office *ever* been so degraded before?" asked Samuel May, Jr. J. Miller McKim, usually restrained of speech, was moved by Johnson's behavior to call the president "an obstinate, pigheaded, ill-conditioned, border-state, 'poor white,' and locofoco Democrat." Garrison delivered a few well-publicized speeches and wrote several articles for the *Independent* denouncing Johnson and calling for his impeachment.[18]

Radical abolitionists who had long urged an unremitting war against the president were delighted by the public reaction to his Freedmen's Bureau veto and his February 22 speech. Many moderate Republicans turned against the president. Eight state legislatures passed resolutions rebuking Johnson.[19] The disillusionment with the president raised the stock of abolitionists who had been declaiming against him for months. Republican newspapers that had previously criticized the abolitionists for inciting ill will between President Johnson and the Congress now printed their speeches with editorial endorsement. Abolitionists

[17] The speech is reprinted in McPherson, *History of Reconstruction*, 58-63.

[18] Samuel May, Jr., to McKim, Mar. 5, 1866, McKim Papers, NYPL; McKim to Arthur Albright, Mar. 23, 1866, McKim Papers, BPL; *New York Tribune*, Feb. 28, 1866; *N.A.S. Standard*, Mar. 10, 1866; *Independent*, Mar. 29, April 26, 1866. See also McKitrick, *Andrew Johnson and Reconstruction*, 295.

[19] *Commonwealth*, Feb. 24, 1866; *New York Tribune*, Mar. 5, 1866; *N.A.S. Standard*, Mar. 3, 10, 24, 1866; *Philadelphia Press*, Feb. 27, 1866; *Right Way*, Mar. 17, 1866.

spoke to cheering crowds on the lecture circuit. Radical congressional leaders encouraged their work of agitation. "Every school district in the country should be canvassed in the cause of justice and equality," Congressman William D. Kelley told Phillips. In March 1866, Sumner urged Phillips to hold the antislavery societies together. "You and they are doing indispensable work; in this I express the conviction of every Senator and every Representative on our side of the pending questions."[20]

One of the pending questions was Trumbull's Civil Rights bill. This measure was passed by Congress in March. Again there was much speculation about whether Johnson would veto or sign it. Recovered somewhat from the debacle of February, moderate Republicans were negotiating for a reconciliation with Johnson on the basis of the Civil Rights bill. But again the president spurned their overtures and vetoed the bill. For most Republicans this was the last straw. From that time forward there was a virtually irreparable breach between the president and the party that had elected him. On April 9 Congress passed the Civil Rights bill over Johnson's veto. Abolitionists were overjoyed. At last the Republicans had shown a bold and united front against the perfidious president. "Things begin to look a little brighter," commented young Frank Garrison, "and if we can only keep the two-thirds majority obtained for the bill, we can snap our fingers at the wretched occupant of the White House." Abolitionist David Plumb praised Congress for its defiance of the executive. "Now for the *'Main Question'*—the Suffrage of the Negro," wrote Plumb. "I do not expect great things from the 'Civil Rights Bill,' unless backed by Negro Suffrage. . . . Since half-measures cannot win the President, now, why not go for a whole one?"[21]

Plumb expressed the sentiments of many abolitionists. Despite their happiness with the passage of the Civil Rights bill, they were far from satisfied. The Civil Rights bill, said Tilton, was

[20] Kelley quoted in *N.A.S. Standard*, May 12, 1866; Sumner to Phillips, Mar. 17, 1866, quoted by Carlos Martyn, *Wendell Phillips: The Agitator* (New York, 1890), 353. See also *N.A.S Standard*, Mar. 10, 17, 1866.
[21] McKitrick, *Andrew Johnson and Reconstruction*, 298-324; *Independent*, Mar. 22, 29, Apr. 5, 12, 1866; *New York Tribune*, Mar. 28, Apr. 9, 10, 1866; Francis Jackson Garrison to Fanny Garrison Villard, Apr. 8, 1866, F. G. Villard Papers, HU; David Plumb to Sumner, Apr. 12, 1866, Sumner Papers, HU.

all right as far as it went, but "the negro will never be thoroughly protected, even in person and property, until he has the ballot." Gerrit Smith wrote an open letter to Senator Henry Wilson declaring that "the Civil Rights Bill cannot serve the black man in place of the ballot." "What is suffrage, if it be not a civil right?" asked the *Anti-Slavery Standard*. "What are civil rights worth that do not include suffrage?" The *Standard* welcomed Congress's display of backbone in passing the bill over Johnson's veto, but nevertheless considered the measure only "half the loaf. And if this be, as many fear, *the substitute for suffrage*, it may prove far worse than no bread."[22]

Abolitionists looked hopefully but not confidently to the Joint Committee of Fifteen for favorable action on the suffrage question. Since the beginning of January the Committee had been deliberating the problem of reconstruction. One of the first questions to come before it was the increase in southern representation occasioned by the abolition of slavery. Before emancipation the slave had counted as three-fifths of a man in determining congressional representation; the freed Negro now counted as a whole man. Without a constitutional amendment the South could return to the Union stronger than ever in Congress, her Negro population disfranchised but counted for representation purposes. In January the Joint Committee sent to Congress a constitutional amendment which would reduce the size of a state's congressional delegation if that state denied or abridged the franchise on account of race or color. Believing that northern public opinion would not sanction a direct grant of Negro suffrage, moderate Republicans rallied behind the apportionment amendment as the best attainable substitute.[23]

Abolitionists denounced the amendment. In a public letter Gerrit Smith asserted that if the South were readmitted under such a plan she would gladly accept reduced representation in order to keep her Negro population disfranchised. Tilton assailed the proposed amendment because it "puts the Negro into the hands of the Rebel. . . . It proves that a Republic is ungrateful." The

22 *Independent*, Feb. 8, 1866; *Gerrit Smith's Reply to Henry Wilson*, Mar. 26, 1866, broadside (Peterboro, 1866); *N.A.S. Standard*, Apr. 7, 14, 1866.

23 Joseph James, *The Framing of the Fourteenth Amendment* (Urbana, Ill., 1956), 55-56; McKitrick, *Andrew Johnson and Reconstruction*, 336-37.

American Anti-Slavery Society resolved that the amendment was "only fitted to protect the North and the white race, while it leaves the Negro to his fate. . . . In times of revolution the decisions, the mistakes, of a single hour may settle the opinions of a nation and its forms of civil life for centuries." Therefore it would be better to defeat this half measure than to accept it and run the risk of it becoming the final basis of settlement.[24]

Sumner was in complete accord with abolitionists on this question. The amendment was passed by the House at the end of January, but in the Senate it ran into the opposition of the powerful senator from Massachusetts. In a marathon Senate speech occupying two days (February 5 and 6), Sumner uttered an exhaustive excoriation of the Amendment and pleaded for congressional enactment of Negro suffrage. Abolitionists and northern Negroes praised Sumner's speech as the greatest effort of his life. They moved quickly to back up his efforts with petitions and memorials against the proposed Amendment.[25] Democrats as well as radical Republicans opposed the Amendment, and by the middle of February Sumner claimed to have enough Senate votes to defeat it. When the vote was taken on March 9 it fell short of the two-thirds majority necessary for passage. Abolitionists rejoiced in its failure and heaped renewed praise on Sumner.[26]

Victory in the battle of the ballot, however, still seemed remote. Convinced that northern public opinion opposed Negro suffrage, moderate Republican leaders continued to seek a less radical solution to the reconstruction puzzle. Abolitionists denounced these Republicans for their willingness to sacrifice the Negro on the altar of political expediency. "They have sought only to tinker, not to *change* 'the President's plans'; to merely prune,

[24] *Gerrit Smith to Senator Sumner*, Feb. 5, 1866, published letter (Peterboro, 1866); Tilton to Sumner, Feb. 2, 1866, Sumner Papers, HU; *N.A.S. Standard*, Feb. 3, 1866. See also *Commonwealth*, Jan. 27, 1866; *Principia*, Feb. 8, 1866; *Independent*, Feb. 1, 8, 15, 1866.

[25] Pierce, *Sumner*, IV, 277-81; "Memorial of a Delegation Representing the Colored People," *House Misc. Docs.*, #109, 39 Cong., 1 Sess.; *Commonwealth*, Feb. 10, 17, 1866; *N.A.S. Standard*, Feb. 17, Mar. 24, Apr. 21, 1866. There are nearly a dozen letters from abolitionists to Sumner praising his speech against the proposed Fourteenth Amendment in the Sumner Papers, HU.

[26] *Cong. Globe*, 39 Cong., 1 Sess., 1,224-35, 1,275-89; *Commonwealth*, Mar. 17, 1866; *N.A.S. Standard*, Mar. 17, 1866.

not to uproot and destroy," charged the *Anti-Slavery Standard* in April. "Were the Democrats in power, they could not possibly be worse."[27] In an effort to improve the climate of public opinion and exert pressure on Congress, the Boston Emancipation League reorganized in March 1866, as the Impartial Suffrage Association. The Association sponsored lectures and aided George Stearns in the circulation of newspapers and pamphlets throughout the nation.[28]

Disturbed by Congress's failure to propose an effective reconstruction program, Robert Dale Owen came to Washington at the end of March and laid before Thaddeus Stevens a comprehensive plan. Owen proposed a constitutional amendment that would prohibit discrimination in civil rights, enact impartial suffrage in every state after July 4, 1876, and provide for proportional reduction of the representation of any states that denied Negro suffrage before that date. Stevens professed enthusiasm for the plan, but Sumner and the abolitionists disliked the postponement of equal suffrage until 1876. Even this modest Negro suffrage proposal, however, was too strong for the Joint Committee. With the congressional elections of 1866 looming on the horizon, they were extremely sensitive to political considerations. The Committee rewrote Owen's amendment. On April 30 Fessenden and Stevens reported to Congress a constitutional amendment that prohibited states from abridging the civil rights of citizens or denying any person the equal protection of the laws; provided for the proportional reduction of the congressional representation of any state that abridged or denied suffrage to any of its male citizens; disfranchised until 1870 all persons who had voluntarily supported the rebellion; and forbade payment of the Confederate debt. Congress struck out the section disfranchising all rebels and substituted a provision to disqualify from political office certain classes of leading Confederates. Otherwise the proposal submitted on April 30 was substantially the same as the measure eventually adopted as the Fourteenth Amendment.[29]

27 *N.A.S. Standard*, Apr. 14, 1866. See also *ibid.*, Apr. 21, June 23, 1866; *Independent*, Apr. 19, 1866.
28 Loring Moody to Gerrit Smith, Mar. 20, 1866, Smith Papers, su; *Right Way*, Mar. 17, 31, Apr. 14, May 5, 1866.
29 James, *Framing of Fourteenth Amendment*, 100-02, 109-16; McKitrick, *Andrew Johnson and Reconstruction*, 343-49.

The *Anti-Slavery Standard* denounced the Joint Committee's proposed Amendment as a "fraud." On the central issue of Negro suffrage it was no better than the Amendment defeated in March. "It is a substitute for suffrage and citizenship," said the *Standard*. "It is the blighted harvest of the bloodiest sowing the fields of the world ever saw." Phillips told Thaddeus Stevens that the report of the Joint Committee was "a fatal & total surrender. The South carries off enough of the victory to enable her to control the Nation, mould its policy & shape its legislation for a dozen years to come." Tilton vigorously criticized the Amendment in the columns of the *Independent*.[30]

Not all abolitionists reacted so sharply to the action of the Joint Committee. George Stearns expressed unwillingness "to accept as a finality any thing less than Impartial Suffrage," but thought that Congress should pass the Amendment "rather than have 'no policy.' " Adoption of the Amendment would not preclude radicals "from asking all we need at a future time. . . . Our support of Congress would be more efficient and direct, if, without denouncing this scheme we claim all we ought to have." The *Boston Commonwealth* regretted that Negro suffrage had not been incorporated into the proposed Fourteenth Amendment. But with an eye to the 1866 elections, the editor commended the Amendment as the best that could be obtained at this time. The *Right Way* considered it "criminal and idiotic" to enfranchise rebels and withhold the ballot from black loyalists. Nevertheless adoption of the Fourteenth Amendment would be "of great value for national security and national justice." Meanwhile, declared the *Right Way*, abolitionists should urge the inclusion of Negro suffrage in the enabling acts admitting southern states and the adoption of a Fifteenth Amendment incorporating equal manhood suffrage into the Constitution.[31]

Abolitionists therefore were divided into two camps in their attitudes toward the proposed Fourteenth Amendment. Neither group approved the measure as the final condition of reconstruction. One faction, led by Phillips, condemned the Amendment un-

[30] *N.A.S. Standard*, May 5, 1866; Phillips to Stevens, Apr. 30, 1866, Stevens Papers, LC; *Independent*, May 3, June 14, 1866.

[31] Stearns to Sumner, May 1, 1866, Sumner Papers, HU; *Commonwealth*, May 5, 19, 26, June 2, 1866; *Right Way*, May 12, June 9, 1866.

equivocally and hoped for its defeat, fearing that adoption would lead to the admission of southern states when they had ratified the Amendment. The other faction, led by George Stearns, approved the Amendment as far as it went, urged its passage, and hoped by an enabling act or a Fifteenth Amendment to secure Negro suffrage.

The House passed the Fourteenth Amendment in its original form on May 10. While the Senate deliberated, Phillips and his followers stepped up their attacks. In *Anti-Slavery Standard* editorials Phillips charged that by failing to enact Negro suffrage Congress had, in effect, surrendered to President Johnson and the South. The vaunted "practical statesmanship" of Fessenden, Trumbull, and other Republican leaders who had formulated the Fourteenth Amendment was nothing but "hypocrisy, fear, and a compromise." In a series of powerful sermons and discourses, several of which were published in pamphlet form, George Cheever excoriated the Amendment as a fraud, a sham, a political trick, and a "robbery of the colored race." Frederick Douglass considered the measure a personal insult to every Negro. "For to tell me that I am an equal American citizen, and, in the same breath, tell me that my right to vote may be constitutionally taken from me by some other equal citizen or citizens, is to tell me that my citizenship is but an empty name," declared Douglass. "To say that I am a citizen to pay taxes . . . obey the laws, support the government, and fight the battles of the country, but, in all that respects voting and representation, I am but as so much inert matter, is to insult my manhood."[32] The New England Anti-Slavery Society resolved that admission of rebel states under the proposed Fourteenth Amendment would be "total surrender" and "an unworthy trick to mislead the nation." In a speech at the Society's annual convention Phillips expressed hope for defeat of the Republican party if it fought the 1866 elections on the basis of the Fourteenth Amendment. "The Re-

[32] *N.A.S. Standard*, May 27, June 2, June 30, 1866; George B. Cheever, *Impartial Suffrage a Right; and the Infamy of the Revolution Against It in the Proposed Amendment of the Constitution* (New York, 1866), *Protest Against the Robbery of the Colored Race by the Proposed Amendment of the Constitution* (New York, 1866), *The Republic or the Oligarchy? Which? An Appeal Against the Proposed Transfer of the Right to Vote from the People to the State* (New York, 1866); Douglass' statement quoted in *N.A.S. Standard*, July 7, 1866.

publicans are occupied chiefly in keeping up their own organization," charged Phillips. "Let that party be broken that sacrifices principle to preserve its own existence."[33]

Garrison, Oliver Johnson, and McKim condemned Phillips' anti-Republican speeches and called for support of Congress and the Fourteenth Amendment. They professed to be no less ardent in their desire for Negro suffrage than Phillips, but declared that this objective would sooner be reached by cooperating with the Republican majority than by defying it. Stearns organized a mass meeting at Faneuil Hall on May 31 under the auspices of the Impartial Suffrage Association. The meeting adopted resolutions endorsing the Fourteenth Amendment and urging Congress to pass enabling acts requiring southern states to enact impartial suffrage before returning to the Union.[34]

Meanwhile a Senate Republican caucus bound all Republicans to vote for the Fourteenth Amendment on the Senate floor. Sumner and a few other radicals were opposed to the Amendment. But they were bound by the caucus decision and voted for the measure when it passed the Senate on June 8. The battle line for radicals now became the enabling act setting forth the conditions under which former Confederate states would be readmitted. Sumner introduced a bill drafted by abolitionist lawyer Samuel Sewall requiring equal suffrage as a condition of readmission. Congressional radicals rallied behind this measure, and Tilton gave it the support of the powerful *Independent*. But moderate Republicans considered Negro suffrage in an enabling act just as much a political liability as in a constitutional amendment. A majority of Republicans were reluctant to commit themselves to any final conditions of readmission. They preferred to go to the country on the basis of the Fourteenth Amendment as it stood, leaving the final terms of reconstruction to the next session of Congress after the 1866 elections. Congress adjourned in July without passing any enabling legislation.[35]

---

[33] *N.A.S. Standard*, June 9, 1866.

[34] Oliver Johnson to Garrison, June 16, 1866, Garrison Papers, BPL; McKim to John Bingham, July 20, 1866, McKim letterbook, II, 144, McKim Papers, Cornell; *N.A.S. Standard*, June 23, 1866; *Commonwealth*, June 2, 1866; *Right Way*, June 9, 1866.

[35] James, *Framing of Fourteenth Amendment*, 142-52, 169-70; S. E. Sewall to Sumner, June 1, 1866, Sumner Papers, HU; Sumner to Tilton, June 27, 1866, Tilton Papers, NYHS; *Independent*, June 7, 21, 1866; *Commonwealth*, June 16,

Most abolitionists were not reluctant to see this issue postponed until the next session, hoping that time, circumstances, and an improved state of public opinion would make Congress more radical in December. But in the last weeks of the 1865-66 session Tennessee, having ratified the Fourteenth Amendment, knocked on the congressional door for readmission. Moderate Republicans seized upon Tennessee's application as an opportunity to display the good faith of Congress and the success of its reconstruction policy by admitting the state with no other conditions than those contained in the Fourteenth Amendment. Sumner in the Senate and Boutwell in the House tried to incorporate an equal suffrage provision in the act of admission, but their motions were defeated. Tennessee was restored to the Union by joint resolution on July 23. Sumner was deeply discouraged and many abolitionists were sullen. Tilton feared that Tennessee's restoration would create a precedent for the admission of other southern states without Negro suffrage. "Tennessee is permitted to deny to her blacks a voice in the state, while she herself is permitted to resume her voice in the nation," he wrote in the *Independent*. "The spectacle is a national humiliation."[36]

Meanwhile Phillips had been thinking over his statement of May 31 that a Republican defeat in the 1866 elections would be better than a victory on the platform of the Fourteenth Amendment. Phillips' radical friends warned him that expression of such opinions could destroy his influence in the Republican party. At a Fourth of July celebration in Framingham, Massachusetts, Phillips renewed his attacks on the Fourteenth Amendment. But this time instead of calling for the defeat of the Republican party, he proclaimed his belief that the Amendment would not be ratified. He predicted that the South would reject it. Phillips announced that his radical Republican friends did not want the Amendment

---

July 14, 1866. In line with the decision of the Republican majority to play down the suffrage issue, the Senate quietly shelved the House bill granting the ballot to colored men in the District of Columbia. The *Anti-Slavery Standard* could hardly find words to express its disgust with Republicans for this new act of cowardice. *N.A.S. Standard*, June 23, July 28, 1866.

[36] James, *Framing of Fourteenth Amendment*, 171-72; Pierce, *Sumner*, IV, 286-87; Sumner to Moncure Conway, July 30, 1866, Conway Papers, CU; *Right Way*, July 28, 1866; *N.A.S. Standard*, July 28, Aug. 11, 1866; *Commonwealth*, July 28, 1866; *Independent*, July 26, 1866.

ratified; they considered it nothing more than a platform for the fall elections, and hoped to enact a more thorough reconstruction program at the next session of Congress. Phillips therefore hoped the Republican party would succeed. "I know no other channel, this summer, in which to work. I cannot tell you to desert the Republican party; I know nowhere else for you to go."

This advice was not entirely welcome to some abolitionists. Gerrit Smith said that he could never support a party that campaigned on the basis of the infamous Fourteenth Amendment. Stephen S. Foster introduced a resolution declaring that abolitionists would support no party that did not recognize the absolute equality of all men before the law. Phillips hastily replied that he had not meant that abolitionists should give unqualified support to the party. They should condemn Republican shortcomings, as they had always done, but "let us support any one in that organization who does maintain, and promises to support, the true ideas of freedom." In the end Foster's resolution was adopted unanimously, with the understanding that it did not preclude abolitionist support of individual radical Republicans who were true to the idea of equality.[37]

As election day approached, abolitionists toned down their criticism of Republicans and concentrated their fire on President Johnson and his supporters, who were making a determined bid for electoral endorsement of Johnson's reconstruction policy. In June, conservatives issued a call for a National Union convention on August 14 in Philadelphia to rally all of Johnson's supporters in a new party. Republicans and abolitionists directed their main attacks on this new conservative threat. The *Anti-Slavery Standard* described the National Union movement as a bid for power by those who "agree that this is a white man's government. . . . It is virtually a movement for the re-establishment of slavery."[38]

One of the major issues of the 1866 campaign was the increasing oppression of freedmen in the South. In May a mob of white men in Memphis, aided by part of the police force, went on

[37] *N.A.S. Standard*, July 14, 1866. See also *New York Tribune*, July 6, 1866; *Commonwealth*, July 7, 14, 1866; and *N.A.S. Standard*, July 28, Aug. 4, 11, 18, 1866.

[38] *New York Tribune*, July 6, 1866; *Independent*, July 12, 19, 1866; *Commonwealth*, July 7, 1866; *N.A.S. Standard*, July 7, 1866.

a drunken, murderous rampage against the city's Negro population, burning, raping, and pillaging in the colored section of town and killing 46 Negroes. Northerners were appalled. Republicans charged that the riot was the inevitable result of Johnson's reconstruction policy. With Memphis as an example, observed the *New York Tribune* sarcastically, "who doubts that the Freedmen's Bureau ought to be abolished forthwith, and the blacks remitted to the paternal care of their old masters, who 'understand the nigger, you know, a great deal better than the Yankees can?' "[39] The Republican and abolitionist press continued to publish reports of outrages against freedmen all through the summer. Despite conservative charges that the Republican press exaggerated these reports for political purposes, the atrocity stories had some basis in fact. In September 1866, the assistant commissioner of the Freedmen's Bureau in Arkansas reported officially that crimes against freedmen had increased sharply since March. He stated that southern whites felt that "any effort to secure justice for the Freedmen is simply the work of 'abolitionists' . . . and [was] in direct opposition to the wishes of the President of the United States."[40]

The most spectacular anti-Negro violence occurred in New Orleans on July 30. A convention of radical whites and Negroes which had been called to consider a Negro suffrage amendment to Louisiana's Constitution was attacked by a mob of New Orleans whites containing many policemen and former Confederate soldiers. Scores of Negroes and their white allies were killed or wounded by the cold-blooded assault. In the North the affair redounded with great discredit to President Johnson and his policy. Republicans were quick to depict the riot as the inevitable consequence of Johnson's reconstruction program. Some abolitionists went even further and blamed the affray partly on the conservative policy of Congress. Gerrit Smith hoped that the New Orleans murders had "opened the eyes of Congress to its folly in restoring Tennessee, & to the folly of restoring any other Rebel State whilst such State was continuing to oppress the negro." Most radicals joined Elizur Wright in hoping that the

[39] *Independent*, May 17, 1866; *New York Tribune*, May 22, 1866.
[40] Quoted in George R. Bentley, *A History of the Freedmen's Bureau* (Phila., 1955), 158.

riots would prove a blessing in disguise by rousing the people to the necessity of a thorough reconstruction.[41]

Abolitionists unleashed a volley of ridicule and denunciation of the National Union convention when it met in Philadelphia on August 14. The convention adopted a resolution stating that "there is no section of the country where the Constitution and the laws of the United States find more prompt and entire obedience than in [the former Confederate] States." Gerrit Smith was appalled by the mendacious effrontery of this resolution. "This is said of that half of our country in every part of which it is unsafe to be a black man or the friend of a black man," wrote Smith. "Can the people respect the men who so trifle with truth?" Another radical described the Philadelphia convention as "a meeting of marvelous odds and ends, the reconstructed shreds and patches of rebellion; cunning men from down East, . . . gangs of rough and ready men from New York, freebooters in politics; several solemn old men from Pennsylvania, who will stand by the Constitution as it ought to have been two thousand years ago; . . . old pro-Slavery fossils from North Carolina; South Carolina implacables, with the whip-hand itching; . . . Mississippi gentlemen, who are determined to reconstruct by burying the negro." These men had come together "to stand by the Union, and the Constitution, and Andrew Johnson, to defend the New-Orleans massacre, and indorse the policy which gave us the murders at Memphis."[42]

To counter the National Union movement, a convention of Southern Loyalists met in Philadelphia in early September. Hundreds of northern Republicans attended as observers and as "honorary" delegates. The issues of Negro suffrage and the Republican party's relation to the Negro nearly broke up the convention. Trouble began when Rochester Republicans elected Frederick Douglass as a delegate. Many Republicans feared that Douglass' attendance would hurt the party in parts of the North where "social equality" was anathema. One Republican

[41] Gerrit Smith to Garrison, Aug. 5, 1866, Garrison Papers, BPL; article by Wright in *Independent*, Aug. 16, 1866. McKitrick, *Andrew Johnson and Reconstruction*, 422-27, is the best brief discussion of the New Orleans riot and its political consequences.

[42] Article by Gerrit Smith in *N.A.S. Standard*, Sept. 1, 1866; *New York Tribune*, Aug. 14, 1866. See also *Independent*, Aug. 23, 30, 1866.

urged Thaddeus Stevens to use his influence to keep Douglass away from Philadelphia. "If he goes it will certainly injure our cause and we may lose some Congressmen in doubtful districts."[43]

Douglass was not deterred by the fears of white Republicans. He told Governor Oliver Morton of Indiana that if he was prevented from attending the convention the Republican party would gain a reputation for "hypocrisy and cowardice." Failing to persuade Douglass to stay away from Philadelphia, Republican leaders decided to ignore him as much as possible at the convention. When the delegates assembled at Independence Hall for a grand procession to National Hall where the convention was to be held, all Republicans but General Butler shied away from Douglass. The delegates were supposed to march two abreast, but it appeared that Douglass would have to walk alone until Theodore Tilton came up, locked arms with Douglass, and marched proudly with him down streets lined with cheering onlookers.[44] Despite the cheers, many Republicans were alarmed by the incident. "A good many people here are disturbed by the practical exhibition of racial equality in the arm-in-arm performance of Douglass and Tilton," wrote Thaddeus Stevens to Congressman William D. Kelley. "It does not become radicals like us particularly to object, but it was certainly unfortunate at this time. The old prejudice, now revived, will lose us some votes."[45]

At the convention itself there was some reluctance to seat Douglass as a delegate, and a motion to invite him to sit on the platform was ignored. But Douglass and a Negro delegate from Louisiana were finally seated. The significance of their presence, however, was soon overshadowed by the mighty struggle over Negro suffrage. Without Negro votes, Republicans from the deep South would be politically powerless. Most of the delegates from former Confederate states, therefore, wanted a declaration by the convention in favor of Negro suffrage. They were encouraged in this direction by a number of abolitionists at the convention. Under the leadership of Tilton the New York delega-

[43] Samuel Shock to Thaddeus Stevens, Aug. 27, 1866, Stevens Papers, LC.
[44] Philip S. Foner, *The Life and Writings of Frederick Douglass* (4 vols., New York, 1950-55), IV, 25-26; Benjamin Quarles, *Frederick Douglass* (Washington, 1948), 229-31.
[45] Stevens to Kelley, Sept. 6, 1866, Stevens Papers, LC.

tion passed a Negro suffrage resolution. But the "practical politicians" of the Republican party exerted all their influence to prevent any statement on the suffrage question. A caucus of northern Republican governors resolved that the question of Negro suffrage must be kept out of the campaign. Governor Samuel Cony of Maine said that he favored equal suffrage as much as any man in the country, "but I don't believe in making negro suffrage an issue now. Our great object now is to secure the next Congress. If we don't get that, then all is lost; if we do get it, then all is safe."[46]

In this temper the convention spent three days attacking Andrew Johnson and the Democrats. But on the fourth day the Committee on Unreconstructed States submitted a report that included an endorsement of Negro suffrage. Border-state delegates tried to force an adjournment, and failing that, most of them withdrew, leaving an unorganized and confused mass of delegates from former Confederate states. Seizing the opportunity, Theodore Tilton, Frederick Douglass, and Anna Dickinson marched to the platform and proposed a reorganization of the convention into a popular mass meeting. The enthusiastic southerners agreed, and selected Tilton as chairman. Douglass, Dickinson, and Tilton made rousing speeches that evoked thunderous cheers from the crowd. The southerners, most of whom had never before heard a woman speak in public, were absolutely entranced by Anna Dickinson. After several hours of oratory the meeting broke up in high spirits. The next morning the Southern Loyalists met again formally and the Committee on Unreconstructed States again submitted its Negro suffrage resolutions. At the climax of the debate which followed, reported Tilton, Dr. Randolph, the Negro delegate from New Orleans, "leaped to the stage, and made an electric speech, picturing the wrongs of his race, demanding redress, claiming the ballot, and, suddenly turning to a colossal portrait of Mr. Lincoln behind the platform, exclaimed, 'We are coming, Father Abraham, three hundred thousand more!' The effect was irresistible. The house sprang to its feet, and gave cheer after cheer." The Negro

[46] *New York Herald*, Sept. 5, 6, 1866; *Independent*, Sept. 13, 1866; Foner, *Douglass*, IV, 26-27; Howard K. Beale, *The Critical Year: A Study of Andrew Johnson and Reconstruction* (2nd ed., New York, 1958), 185-86.

suffrage resolution was adopted by an overwhelming majority. Moderate northern Republicans were chagrined, but abolitionists were jubilant. The endorsement of Negro suffrage by southern Republicans was an important victory for the radical cause. Many observers agreed that had it not been for the prompt action and persuasive eloquence of Tilton, Douglass, and Dickinson the Southern Loyalists would have adjourned in confusion without declaring for Negro suffrage.[47]

In a campaign speech at Cleveland on September 3, President Johnson repeated his familiar argument that northern radicals who opposed restoration of the Union under his reconstruction policy were traitors. "He who is opposed to the restoration of this Government and the reunion of the States is as great a traitor as Jeff Davis or Wendell Phillips," shouted Johnson. "I would ask you, Why not hang Thad Stevens and Wendell Phillips?"[48] Phillips laughed off the president's bloodthirsty question. But Johnson's designation of Phillips and Stevens as his greatest enemies pointed up an important fact: despite his strictures of the Republican party, Phillips was an influential leader of the party's radical wing. It was an era highly charged with excitement; Phillips was a bold, exciting, uncompromising spokesman for radicalism, and every word he uttered attracted attention. He might have been elected to Congress in 1866. He was nominated for Congress by a workingmen's party in Boston, and a word from Phillips probably would have given him the Republican nomination also. But the great orator declined, believing that he could be more influential as an independent, unfettered spokesman of radicalism than as a member of Congress where he would be hampered by party responsibilities and the exigencies of party politics.[49]

[47] *Independent*, Sept. 13, 1866. See also *New York Herald*, Sept. 7, 8, 1866; *N.A.S. Standard*, Sept. 15, 22, 1866; *Commonwealth*, Sept. 15, 1866; Frederick Douglass to E. C. Stanton, Feb. 6, 1882, Douglass Papers, Anacostia; Douglass to Anna Dickinson, Sept. 10, 1866, Ben Butler to Anna Dickinson, Sept. 8, 1866, Whitelaw Reid to Anna Dickinson, Nov. 11, 1866, Dickinson Papers, LC. Miss Dickinson received many letters of praise and thanks from Southern Loyalists for her part in the convention.

[48] McPherson, *History of Reconstruction*, 135.

[49] *Commonwealth*, Aug. 18, 1866; *Independent*, Sept. 13, Oct. 4, 1866; *New York Times*, Aug. 28, 1866; *N.A.S. Standard*, Sept. 15, 29, Oct. 6, 1866; *New York Herald*, quoted in *N.A.S. Standard*, Oct. 6, 1866.

Phillips was not the only abolitionist held in high regard by radical Republicans. The party recruited an army of abolitionist speakers for the 1866 campaign, headed by Anna Dickinson. But despite the participation of abolitionists in the campaign, Republican strategy in most parts of the North was to avoid the Negro question and concentrate on excoriating Johnson and extolling the Fourteenth Amendment. The Amendment was praised not so much as a benefit to the Negro but as a defense of the North from the renewed ascendancy of the South in national politics. The *Anti-Slavery Standard* complained in September that "most Republicans on the stump, and most Republicans in the press, are alike in this: they denounce the President unsparingly, praise the Congress and its proposed Amendment unmeasuredly, and threaten the rebels unfearingly. But *the negro* is, with them, nowhere remembered: 'The South Carolina rebel shall not have two votes to the New York loyalist's one;' but whether the loyalist of South Carolina shall have one or not, our halting Republican friends do not say. Northern Unionists —being all white—are to be protected; Southern Unionists— being nineteen-twentieths black—are to be left to rebel discretion."[50]

The question whether the Fourteenth Amendment constituted Congress's final terms of reconstruction emerged as a major campaign issue. Moderate Republicans insisted in stump speeches and newspaper editorials that Congress would readmit southern states when they had ratified the Amendment. They pointed to Tennessee as an example. "There can be no question that the amendment was proposed with the distinct intention of submitting it as the final condition of restoration," declared the influential *Boston Advertiser*. The *Nation* stated that enough Republican candidates had committed themselves on the issue to insure southern readmission in return for ratification. Even the *New*

[50] *N.A.S. Standard*, Sept. 8, 1866. Republican speakers tailored their remarks to the temper of the area in which they were speaking. In the middle states and the Old Northwest they carefully avoided any mention of Negro suffrage. In New England and parts of upstate New York, northern Ohio, etc., where antislavery sentiment had always been strong, Republican orators frequently advocated equal suffrage. As one Ohio correspondent of Chief Justice Chase explained: "In the Reserve counties, some of our speakers have openly advocated impartial suffrage, while in other places it was thought necessary, not only to repudiate it but to oppose it." B. R. Cowan to Chase, Oct. 12, 1866, Chase Papers, LC.

York Tribune, while continuing to plead for impartial suffrage and universal amnesty, conceded that readmission on the basis of the Fourteenth Amendment was favored by a majority of the party. In September the Republican National Committee issued an official address which proclaimed the Amendment to be "a just and safe plan of reconstruction" upon acceptance of which the southern states would be readmitted.[51]

Abolitionists and radical Republicans were alarmed by this renewed evidence of Republican perfidy to the Negro. They hastened to denounce the moderates and to deny that the Fourteenth Amendment constituted the final terms of reconstruction. Congress had made no formal commitment, argued the *Right Way,* and the admission of Tennessee was in no way a binding precedent. "We know personally every prominent member of Congress, and we know that the leaders do not mean to admit the unadmitted States on the mere adoption of the amendment," asserted Theodore Tilton emphatically. "In the name of the radical party, whose heart we know, and whose voice we speak, we repudiate the Committee's pledge to the rebels as wholly unauthorized, invalid, and void. . . . The radical party . . . can assent to no reconstruction short of Impartial Suffrage."[52]

In a rousing New York speech on October 25, Phillips unleashed another broadside against the Fourteenth Amendment. "The Constitutional amendment, so far as the negro is concerned, is a swindle," he said. "The absent, the unheard, the disfranchised race is sacrificed between the upper and nether millstones of Rebeldom, while the Republican party knowingly, systematically and persistently sacrifice it to preserve their political supremacy."[53] But despite their anger with the Republicans, abolitionists were gratified by the overwhelming Republican victory in the 1866 congressional elections. "The House of Representatives can send a dozen members off to a picnic," exulted Tilton, "and yet leave a majority large enough to pass a radical measure over the

[51] *Boston Advertiser,* Sept. 29, 1866; *Nation,* iii (Oct. 4, 1866), 270; *New York Tribune,* Sept. 26, 1866; address of the Republican National Committee reprinted in *Right Way,* Sept. 29, 1866. For a discussion of the part this issue played in the 1866 election, see James, *Framing of Fourteenth Amendment,* 169-73.

[52] *Right Way,* Sept. 29, 1866; *Independent,* Sept. 27, 1866. See also *Commonwealth,* Sept. 29, Oct. 6, 13, 1866; *N.A.S. Standard,* Sept. 22, Oct. 6, 13, 1866.

[53] *New York Tribune,* Oct. 26, 1866.

President's veto." Both Tilton and Phillips interpreted the election results as a thumping repudiation of Johnson but not necessarily a popular endorsement of the Fourteenth Amendment as the final condition of reconstruction. "The Radical men of the North are neither to be conquered by the Democratic, nor trifled with by the Republican, party," wrote Tilton. Phillips declared that Congress, "which abdicated leadership and postponed action till they were 'certain sure' what the elections would be, can now resume their places. Let them go back and, throwing this chaff of Reconstruction out of one window and swindling amendments out of the other," enact a thorough reconstruction program granting the ballot to the freedmen.[54]

The *New York Daily News* affirmed that "where Mr. Phillips stood a few months ago the Radicals stand to-day; where he stands to-day they will doubtless be a few months hence." But despite this comment, most of the evidence in November 1866, indicated that if southern states ratified the Amendment, the moderate Republican majority would admit them to the Union with few if any additional conditions. If this happened the future of Negro suffrage would be dark. Abolitionists and radicals looked hopefully to the South for negative action on the Fourteenth Amendment and girded themselves for a sharp struggle in Congress.[55]

[54] *Independent*, Nov. 15, 1866; *N.A.S. Standard*, Nov. 17, 1866.
[55] *New York Daily News*, quoted in *N.A.S. Standard*, Nov. 24, 1866; James, *Framing of Fourteenth Amendment*, 174-77; McKitrick, *Andrew Johnson and Reconstruction*, 449-54.

THE prestige and influence of the abolitionists climbed to new heights after the 1866 elections. The mood of the North reached a postwar peak of radicalism in the winter of 1866-1867, and as the chief exponents of this mood the abolitionists saw their popularity increase correspondingly. Abolitionist lecturers reaped a rich harvest. Phillips, Anna Dickinson, Tilton, and Frederick Douglass embarked on ambitious tours of the Middle West, delivering an average of nearly one hundred political lectures apiece during the season. Everywhere they went these orators enriched the treasuries of local lecture bureaus. During the winter of 1866-67 the small town of Mount Pleasant in southeastern Iowa enjoyed a rare treat. No less than five prominent abolitionist lecturers spoke there: Anna Dickinson, C. C. Burleigh, Tilton, Douglass, and Phillips. Joseph Dugdale, a local abolitionist, reported that the words of these speakers had made such an impression in the small Iowa town that the people abandoned their policy of school segregation and allowed the community's Negro children to attend the new school on the same basis as whites.[1]

Phillips was by far the most popular and influential abolitionist lecturer. By 1867 he had become practically a national institution. On his tour of the Middle West he lectured in many towns where he had never before appeared, and delighted the audiences with his quiet but penetrating voice, his magnetic personality, his sharp thrusts at prominent politicians, and his bold ideas. Thousands of St. Louis' leading citizens came to hear him speak in that city, where he put on one of his best performances. Afterwards even the hostile *St. Louis Dispatch* remarked that Phillips was "a man who, as a private citizen, has exercised a greater influence upon the destinies of this country than any public man or men of his age." After listening to a Phillips lecture the editor of the *Keokuk* (Iowa) *Gate City* wrote: "It is

[1] *Independent*, Mar. 14, May 2, 1867; *New York Tribune*, Feb. 22, 1867; *N.A.S. Standard*, Dec. 29, 1866, Mar. 30, June 15, 1867. The Mt. Pleasant incident was recounted in *ibid.*, Mar. 30, 1867.

easy to understand why Wendell Phillips had so large a share in abolitionizing New England. His arguments grow upon you. . . . Impracticable? Fanatical? Why, he is one of the most entirely plain, common-sense, practical and practicable men we ever heard. . . . He gives you clear-impressed, new-minted, intellectual coin. . . . The difference between Wendell Phillips and other men, on the score of character, is his boldness. He speaks what other men think."[2]

Phillips' weekly editorials in the *Anti-Slavery Standard* also reached a wide audience. His terse, trenchant prose, so different from the ornate style of many editorial writers of the day, made Phillips' written words almost as popular as his lectures. The *New York Times*, the *New York Herald*, and dozens of smaller papers frequently reprinted Phillips' editorials. Senator Sumner testified to the good effect of the *Standard* among radical congressmen, to whom it was sent gratis every week. The moderate *Times* commented in May 1867, that "the political history of the past two years has been little more than a record of the triumphs of what was originally the abolition party, and which has since become the ultra absolutist element in the Republican party." Thus "it becomes a matter of considerable importance to watch carefully all indications as to what this restless, insatiate and potent element of the dominant party proposes to do next. What they *propose* today may be *law* tomorrow." The Democratic *New York World* observed ruefully that radicalism was like a marching army: "Mr. Weed lags in the rear; Mr. Raymond is only six months behind Mr. Greeley, and Mr. Greeley is only six weeks behind Thad Stevens, and Thad Stevens is only six days behind Wendell Phillips, and Wendell Phillips is not more than six inches from the tail and the shining pitchfork of the master of them all."[3]

Phillips was not the only abolitionist who commanded respect among the politicians. Early in the 1866-67 session of Congress, Speaker of the House Schuyler Colfax wrote to John G. Whittier:

[2] *St. Louis Dispatch* and *Keokuk Gate City*, quoted in *N.A.S. Standard*, Apr. 27, 1867; see also the issues of Mar. 2, Apr. 6, May 18, June 15, 1867.

[3] *N.A.S. Standard*, Dec. 8, 1866; *New York Times*, quoted in *N.A.S. Standard*, May 11, 1867; *New York World*, quoted in *N.A.S. Standard*, May 25, 1867. See also Phillips to Gerrit Smith, Jan. 19, 1867, Smith Papers, su. The circulation of the *Standard* was less than 3,000, but its influence reached far beyond its circulation.

"I respect your good opinion so highly that I take the liberty of enclosing you the last speech made by me on political questions, to be certain that it shall fall under your eye." Phillips modestly told the Pennsylvania Anti-Slavery Society that his wide influence was not due so much to personal qualities as to the fact that he was a spokesman for organized abolitionism. "What do you suppose ever entitled me to the distinction of having the President wish I were hung?" asked Phillips. "I was not a Senator, like Charles Sumner. . . . I did not have the Republican party behind me. I had nothing but the Anti-Slavery Society behind me; but as long as I had that, the President knew it weighed as heavy as the Commonwealth of Pennsylvania, because the people had learned to look at it and give it respect, and heed its teachings."[4]

✦

By the fall of 1866 several abolitionists were calling for the impeachment of President Johnson. In a speech at Cooper Union on October 25, Phillips declared that it was necessary to go one step beyond the defeat of the president's policy: the author of that policy must be removed from office. A thorough reconstruction program enacted by Congress would be worth little if its enforcement was left in the hands of an executive wholly unsympathetic to it. "The very first task I would set before the reassembled Congress," said Phillips, "is to impeach the Rebel at the White House. (Loud Cheers) . . .What is the advantage? Then *we* run the machine. (Laughter)" Phillips branded as irrelevant the argument that President Johnson had committed no specific impeachable act. An ordinary citizen could be indicted only for a specific crime, he said, "but an officer may be impeached for any grave misuse of his powers, or any mischievous nonuse of them —for any conduct which harms the public or perils its welfare."[5]

Most abolitionists fell into line with Phillips' demand for impeachment. The Pennsylvania Anti-Slavery Society unanimously adopted an impeachment resolution. The *Commonwealth* began urging Congress to depose Johnson. The *Right Way* deprecated the impeachment agitation at first, fearing that it might weaken

4 Colfax to Whittier, Dec. 13, 1866, Whittier Papers, Essex Institute; *N.A.S. Standard*, Dec. 8, 1866.

5 *New York Tribune*, Oct. 27, 1866. There is a copy of Phillips' Cooper Union address in the Andrew Johnson Papers, LC.

the Republicans by making a martyr of Johnson, but in January 1867, that journal also committed itself to impeachment. Garrison came out strongly for the deposition of Johnson, declaring that while the president remained in office "neither Union men nor negroes will possess any rights on Southern soil that rebels will be bound to respect."[6] There was a certain amount of popular support for the removal of Johnson. Phillips' audiences cheered his references to impeachment. But the *New York Tribune* and other Republican journals approached the question with caution. The House of Representatives directed the Judiciary Committee to investigate Johnson's conduct and determine whether he had done anything impeachable. The Committee undertook its task, but nothing came of the matter at the 1866-67 session of Congress.[7]

Phillips' suggestions to Congress went far beyond impeachment. In 1865 he had thought that when Negro suffrage was enacted, the southern states could be safely readmitted. But by November 1866, he had modified his ideas on this point. Even with Negro suffrage, he said, "you cannot govern the South against its educated classes. . . . Four millions of uneducated negroes, with none of that character which results from position, with none of that weight that comes from one or two generations of recognized manhood, cannot outweigh that element at the South." Through no fault of their own the freedmen were illiterate, landless, penniless. It would be criminal of the North, Phillips now thought, to turn them over to their former masters with nothing more than the ballot to protect them. "This is primarily a social revolution," he said. "You must plant at the South the elements which make a different society. You cannot enact four millions of slaves, ignorant, down-trodden, and despised, into personal equals of the old leaders of the South." The nation must hold the former Confederate states as national territory for several years. During that time the federal government should enact measures to provide the freedmen with education, land, and economic independence. "We do not mean to leave the negro at

[6] *N.A.S. Standard*, Dec. 1, 1866; *Commonwealth*, Nov. 10, 1866; *Right Way*, Oct. 27, Nov. 24, 1866, Jan. 12, 19, 1867; Garrison's statement published in *Independent*, Jan. 10, 1867.

[7] *New York Tribune*, Jan. 8, 1867; Eric McKitrick, *Andrew Johnson and Reconstruction* (Chicago, 1960), 491-93.

The First Vote. A. R. Waud in *Harper's Weekly*

the bottom of the ladder," proclaimed Phillips. "We mean to make a thoroughly developed reconstruction. We mean that Northern brains and ideas and capital shall go down there, and help him . . . until he actually gets education and wealth; until he actually stands on his feet in comparative equality with the white race. We mean to hold [those states] in some shape, until that is done."[8]

Phillips' speeches and editorials on this subject attracted widespread attention and condemnation. His policy of indefinite territorialization of the South was too radical for most antislavery men. But a few abolitionists endorsed portions of Phillips' program. The *Boston Commonwealth*, for example, urged legislation "to secure *education and land*" as well as the ballot "to the poor and ignorant masses at the South. For without education and land even suffrage would be found, for the immediate future, a somewhat illusory boon. . . . We have no doubt of the power of Congress to do whatever is best for the welfare of the South and the country—to cut up and divide among the poor and loyal the great plantations of the rebels . . . to enforce, if need be, universal education under loyal auspices . . . in short, to do everything to civilize and assimilate the South."[9]

At the end of 1866, however, the Fourteenth Amendment was still at the center of the reconstruction controversy. Moderate Republicans urged southern legislatures to ratify the Amendment. "There is no one thing so much dreaded to-day by Wendell Phillips, Sumner, Boutwell, Stevens, and the rest of that school," declared the *New York Times*, "as the acceptance of the Constitutional Amendment by the Southern States—followed, as they know it would be, in spite of their opposition, by the admission of the Southern members into Congress."[10] When Congress convened in December, three southern states had already rejected the Amendment. Prospects appeared bright for the radical cause. But moderate Republican leaders were still committed to the Amendment as the final condition of readmission. Senator Sherman, Congressman Bingham, and many other moderates reaffirmed their belief that Congress would admit southern states if

[8] *N.A.S. Standard*, Nov. 17, 24, Dec. 1, 8, 1866.
[9] *Commonwealth*, Dec. 15, 1866.
[10] *New York Times*, quoted in *N.A.S. Standard*, Nov. 10, 1866.

and when they ratified the Amendment. *Harper's Weekly* anticipated no other conditions of reconstruction than adoption of the Amendment. The *Nation* stated flatly that most of the party considered the Fourteenth Amendment the final condition of restoration. This opinion was not confined to moderates, for on December 14, in reply to a direct question by Sumner, Senator Benjamin Wade stated his intention to vote for readmission when the South accepted the Amendment.[11]

Abolitionists and radical leaders were alarmed by these developments. They feared that the moderate Republican assurances might induce southern states to reconsider their actions, ratify the Amendment, and apply successfully for readmission to Congress. Phillips warned of dire consequences for the Negro if this should happen, and urged Congress "to give the negroes land, ballot and education and to hold the arm of the Federal government over the whole Southern Territory until these seeds have begun to bear fruit beyond any possibility of blighting."[12]

Abolitionists took direct action to counter the apparent Republican willingness to reconstruct on the basis of the Fourteenth Amendment. Henry Cheever in Massachusetts and George Cheever in New York circulated petitions to their respective state legislatures urging them not to ratify the Amendment. The Equal Rights Association led by Elizabeth Cady Stanton and Susan B. Anthony memorialized the New York legislature to reject the Amendment on the grounds that it would permit the continued disfranchisement of both Negroes and women. On January 24 Wendell Phillips appeared before a Massachusetts legislative committee and uttered an eloquent protest against ratification of the Amendment by the Old Bay State. Behind the scenes, Massachusetts radicals and abolitionists were struggling successfully to postpone the state's ratification.[13] By this

11 *Cong. Globe*, 39 Cong., 2 Sess., 124-28, 500, 1,104; *Harper's Weekly*, x (Nov. 17, 1866), 722; *Nation*, iii (Dec. 20, 1866), 485. For a discussion of this issue, see Joseph James, *The Framing of the Fourteenth Amendment* (Urbana, Ill., 1956), 164-77, and McKitrick, *Andrew Johnson and Reconstruction*, 450-55.

12 *N.A.S. Standard*, Jan. 5, 1867. See also Phillips to Sumner, Dec. 27, 1866, Sumner Papers, hu; *Commonwealth*, Dec. 22, 1866; *Right Way*, Dec. 22, 29, 1866; *Independent*, Jan. 17, 1867.

13 Henry Cheever to Gerrit Smith, Dec. 22, 1866, Smith Papers, su; James L. Child to Henry Cheever, Dec. 26, 1866, Henry Cheever to Elizabeth C. Washburn, Dec. 27, 1866, Cheever Papers, aas; S. B. Anthony to Frederick Douglass,

time, however, the question had become academic. With the exception of Massachusetts, every northern state had ratified the Amendment by February 7, 1867, and every former Confederate state (except Tennessee) had refused to ratify it. With the encouragement of President Johnson the South had rejected the Amendment. They had cut the ground from under congressional moderates and had given radicals and abolitionists a new lease on life.[14]

As it became clear that southern states were unconditionally rejecting the Fourteenth Amendment, Congress settled down to formulate a comprehensive reconstruction policy.[15] After a bewildering series of amendments and counteramendments, the House on February 13 finally passed a bill sponsored by George Julian and Thaddeus Stevens providing for the simple territorialization and indefinite military administration of the unreconstructed South. The measure contained no provision for the readmission of southern states to the Union. Phillips was delighted with the bill. It was similar to the program he had been advocating since November. "We consider Stevens's bill the best thing yet offered," he wrote on February 16.[16]

Several abolitionists and radicals agreed with Phillips, but political exigencies dictated some provision for the readmssion of southern states when they had fulfilled certain requirements. Moderate Republicans in the Senate passed on February 17 the Sherman substitute for the Julian-Stevens bill. The Sherman substitute would have readmitted southern states when they had

Dec. 15, 1866, Douglass Papers, Anacostia; Alma Lutz, *Susan B. Anthony, Rebel, Crusader, Humanitarian* (Boston, 1959), 125; *N.A.S. Standard*, Feb. 2, 1867; Sumner to Frank Bird, Jan. 10, 1867, Bird Papers, HU; Phillips to Sumner, Feb. 1, 1867, Frank Bird to Sumner, Mar. 7, 8, 1867, Sumner Papers, HU; *Boston Commonwealth*, Mar. 9, 16, 1867. Massachusetts finally ratified the Fourteenth Amendment after the Reconstruction Act of March 2 had made Negro suffrage the basis of reconstruction.

[14] McKitrick, *Andrew Johnson and Reconstruction*, 469-72.

[15] During the session Congress passed over Johnson's veto two bills enacting Negro suffrage in the District of Columbia and admitting Nebraska as a state with a provision for equal suffrage. President Johnson allowed another bill forbidding the denial of suffrage on grounds of race or color in all the territories to become law without his signature. Edward McPherson, *The Political History of the United States of America during the Period of Reconstruction* (Washington, 1871), 154-66, 184.

[16] McKitrick, *Andrew Johnson and Reconstruction*, 474-81; *N.A.S. Standard*, Feb. 16, 1867.

ratified the Fourteenth Amendment and adopted new constitutions guaranteeing Negro suffrage. Radicals and abolitionists were opposed to the Sherman bill for two reasons: it did not disfranchise any former rebel leaders, who would take the lead in the reconstruction process and perhaps nullify the effects of Negro suffrage unless they were disfranchised; and it made the reorganization of civil government permissive instead of mandatory, thus allowing the Johnson governments in southern states to continue in power indefinitely if they so wished. Under Stevens' leadership the House refused to concur in the Senate bill. The deadlock was finally broken on February 20 by passage in both Houses of the Wilson and Shellabarger amendments disfranchising all persons disqualified from officeholding under the Fourteenth Amendment and declaring the existing southern state governments "provisional only, and in all respects subject to the paramount authority of the United States." Johnson vetoed this Reconstruction Act on March 2, but it was immediately passed over his veto. The reconstruction process was still permissive, and to remedy this defect the Fortieth Congress on March 23 passed over Johnson's veto an act making civil reorganization mandatory and authorizing military commanders to register voters and set the machinery in motion for the convening of constitutional conventions.[17]

There was some abolitionist dissatisfaction with the Reconstruction Acts as finally passed. Phillips would have been happier with the Julian-Stevens bill. Several abolitionists pointed out that once those southern states with white majorities were readmitted to the Union, there would be nothing to stop them from disfranchising their Negroes. Others urged Congress to enact legislation to guarantee universal public education in the South and to help the freedmen obtain land of their own. Numerous abolitionists denounced Congress for failing to impeach Johnson. They affirmed that the Reconstruction Acts would be little more than a dead letter with an unsympathetic president to administer them. These com-

[17] McKitrick, *Andrew Johnson and Reconstruction*, 481-85; George Julian, *Political Recollections* (Chicago, 1884), 306-08. See also Lewis Tappan to Julian, Feb. 19, 1867, Giddings-Julian Correspondence, LC; Whittier to Sumner, Feb. 27, 1867, Sumner Papers, HU; *Commonwealth*, Feb. 9, 23, Mar. 2, 16, 23, 1867; *Right Way*, Feb. 16, 1867; *New York Tribune*, Feb. 18, 21, 25, 1867; *Independent*, Feb. 21, 28, Mar. 14, 1867; *N.A.S. Standard*, Feb. 23, Mar. 2, 9, 1867.

plaints were outweighed, however, by abolitionist jubilation over the adoption of Negro suffrage and the belief that additional measures necessary to safeguard the Negro's freedom would be enacted in the future. It was reported on good authority from Washington that Johnson would faithfully administer the Reconstruction Acts as the law of the land, and radicals temporarily dropped their cry of impeachment and settled back to await events. There was a general mood of confidence among abolitionists in the spring of 1867. At the annual meeting of the American Anti-Slavery Society in May, Phillips addressed his auditors in an unwonted tone of optimism. "We seem to be on the very eve," he said, "of the accomplishment of all that the friends of freedom have ever asked of the nation; . . . that is, the absolute civil and political equality of the colored man under our institutions of government."[18]

But abolitionists did not rest on their oars. The greatest single shortcoming of the Reconstruction Acts, in their eyes, was the fact that the question of Negro suffrage still rested with the individual states. Abolitionists renewed their demand for a Fifteenth Amendment. "The friends of the negro will never rest satisfied with any scheme that does not place that right [suffrage] beyond contingency," proclaimed the *Independent*. "They demand that it be incorporated into the Federal Constitution." The Philadelphia Female Anti-Slavery Society affirmed that it would accept "no schemes of reconstruction which will leave [the Negro's] highest right of citizenship at the mercy of State legislation or action, after the Southern States shall be restored to sovereignty."[19]

[18] *Independent*, Feb. 28, Mar. 7, 14, Apr. 4, 1867; *Commonwealth*, Mar. 9, 16, 23, 1867; Samuel May, Jr., to Richard Webb, Apr. 2, 1867, Samuel May, Jr., Papers, BPL; E. L. Pierce to McKim, Apr. 20, 1867, McKim Papers, Cornell; *N.A.S. Standard*, Mar. 2, 9, 23, 30, 1867. Statement by Phillips published in *ibid.*, May 18, 1867. The *Right Way*, founded as a spokesman for equal suffrage, ceased publication after passage of the Reconstruction Acts. A shortage of funds was the main reason for the paper's demise, but the achievement of Negro suffrage in the South was also an important factor in the decision to cease publication. *Right Way*, Mar. 2, 1867; Frank P. Stearns, *The Life and Public Services of George Luther Stearns* (Phila., 1907), 377-78. George Stearns, main financial backer of the *Right Way* and one of the most respected abolitionists during the early years of Reconstruction, died suddenly of pneumonia in April 1867.

[19] *Independent*, Feb. 21, 1867; *Thirty-Third Annual Report of the Philadelphia*

Before a Fifteenth Amendment could be passed, however, the majority of northern people who opposed Negro suffrage in their own states must be persuaded to overcome their prejudices. "The states that now need reconstruction are the Northern," declared Tilton in an *Independent* editorial entitled "A Beam to be Plucked from Our Own Eyes." The *Commonwealth* denounced northern Republicans who had voted for Negro suffrage in the South but refused to support it in their own states as "hypocrites and cowards."[20] Abolitionists launched a drive to convince northern voters of the moral and political necessity of equal suffrage in *every* state. New York held a state constitutional convention in the summer of 1867, and abolitionists mobilized their resources to put equal suffrage into the new constitution. They had a staunch ally in Horace Greeley, who served as chairman of the convention's suffrage committee. Although Greeley refused to heed the pleas of Elizabeth Cady Stanton and Susan B. Anthony for woman suffrage, he persuaded the committee to report in favor of universal manhood suffrage (at this time New York Negroes had to meet a $250 property qualification in order to vote). The full convention accepted the committee's report, but over Greeley's protest the convention voted to submit the suffrage article to the voters separately from the rest of the constitution, thereby virtually assuring its defeat.[21]

The question of the Negro's status in the North was important for the future of reconstruction, but in 1867 it was overshadowed by events in the South. In the wake of the Reconstruction Acts, conservative southern leaders, following the example of Wade Hampton, began urging the enfranchised freedmen to vote in harmony with their old masters. Hampton told South Carolina Negroes that the planter class was in the best position to help them achieve stability and prosperity in freedom. Northern Republicans viewed this development with ill-concealed alarm. Some abolitionists declared that the Negro's right to vote was the

---

Female Anti-Slavery Society (Phila., 1867), 22. See also *N.A.S. Standard*, Mar. 9, 16, 23, Apr. 6, 27, May 11, 1867.

[20] *Independent*, Apr. 18, 1867; *Commonwealth*, Mar. 2, 1867.

[21] Van Deusen, *Greeley*, 361-64. See also *Independent*, Apr. 11, Aug. 1, 1867; *N.A.S. Standard*, May 25, July 6, Sept. 28, 1867; *New York Tribune*, Apr. 3, 4, June 20, 26, 28, July 10, 13, 17, 19, 26, 31, Aug. 6, 9, Sept. 27, Oct. 12, 1867.

important thing, and professed unconcern whether he voted Republican or not. But one of the political reasons for the enactment of Negro suffrage had been the hope of extending Republican power into the South. Abolitionist Reuben Tomlinson, serving as superintendent of education for the Freedmen's Bureau in South Carolina, wrote that "I am a universal suffrage man, but I do not care a cent for it unless we can keep Northern influence here along with it." A Democratic victory in the Connecticut state election in April 1867, startled Republicans out of their lethargy and convinced them of the need to organize and control the southern Negro vote.[22]

Radical leaders Henry Wilson and William D. Kelley immediately started on a southern speaking tour to explain the virtues of Republicanism to the freedmen. Republican officials urged Phillips, Tilton, and Anna Dickinson to speak in the South also. Despite considerable Republican pressure, they refused. They valued their position as radical spokesmen independent of partisan politics. Tilton stated privately that the massive Republican effort in the South was nothing more than "a crusade of politicians—a stumping tour of the old stagers" looking toward the 1868 presidential election. This was important work, but it was not the work of reformers.[23]

Many other abolitionists, however, did not recognize the fine line between reform and politics drawn by Tilton, and proceeded to make their influence felt in southern affairs. Frederick Douglass and Frances E. W. Harper (a Negro abolitionist and poet) undertook speaking tours of the South in the summer of 1867, urging the freedmen to vote for the party that had emancipated and enfranchised them. In April 1867, John Mercer Langston, prominent Negro abolitionist from Ohio, was appointed inspector of schools of the Freedmen's Bureau. For more

[22] Francis Butler Simkins and Robert H. Woody, *South Carolina during Reconstruction* (Chapel Hill, 1932), 85-86; Reuben Tomlinson to J. M. McKim, Dec. 4, 1866, McKim Papers, Cornell. See also *New York Tribune*, Mar. 27, 29, Apr. 3, 4, 12, 22, 1867; *Independent*, Mar. 14, 1867; *New York World*, Apr. 19, 1867; *Commonwealth*, Apr. 13, 1867; *N.A.S. Standard*, Apr. 20, May 11, 1867; Henry Wilson to Angelina G. Weld, Apr. 12, 1867, Weld Papers, LC.

[23] *New York Tribune*, Apr. 22, 1867; L. Edwin Dudley, secretary of the Union Republican Congressional Executive Committee, to Anna Dickinson, May 7, June 15, 26, 1867; S. B. Anthony to Anna Dickinson, May 15, 1867, Dickinson Papers, LC; the quotation is from Tilton to Anna Dickinson, May 16, 1867.

than two years he traveled through the South inspecting the facilities of the Bureau and helping to organize the freedmen into the Republican party and the Republican-sponsored Union Leagues. In the spring of 1867 Loring Moody of Boston, a one-time Garrisonian who later became a political abolitionist, was appointed general agent of the National Union League. He was put in charge of organizing Union Leagues throughout the South to marshal votes for the Republican party. In the summer of 1867 a delegation of northern Republicans, including abolitionists John Jay and Charles W. Slack, intervened to quell a factional struggle in the Virginia Republican party.[24]

Uncounted dozens of abolitionists residing in the South were also active in politics. Nearly every official and teacher of the freedmen's aid societies was to some degree a Republican organizer. Edwin M. Wheelock, one of the creators of the Louisiana public school system (see Chapter XIII), moved to Texas after the war where he served successively as the state superintendent of education, reporter of the state supreme court, and superintendent of the state Institute for the Blind. Reuben Tomlinson was elected state auditor of South Carolina in 1868 and was politically prominent in the state until the end of Reconstruction. Gilbert Pillsbury, the abolitionist brother of Parker Pillsbury, came to South Carolina in 1863. In 1867 he was one of the architects of the new South Carolina Constitution, and was later elected mayor of Charleston. Henry Purvis, son of the wealthy Philadelphia Negro abolitionist Robert Purvis, was a member of the South Carolina legislature during Reconstruction. These are only a few examples of the activities of the many abolitionists who became permanent or semipermanent residents of the South after the war.[25]

[24] Rosetta Douglass Sprague to Frederick Douglass, Apr. 24, 1867, Douglass Papers, Anacostia; Douglass to Anna Dickinson, May 21, 1867, Dickinson Papers, LC; John M. Langston, *From the Virginia Plantation to the National Capital* (Hartford, Conn., 1894), 258-95; George Bentley, *A History of the Freedmen's Bureau* (Phila., 1955), 187-89; information on the activities of Loring Moody obtained from the Loring Moody Papers, BPL, which include several dozen letters relating to his activities as an organizer for the National Union League in 1867; Union League Club of New York, *Report of the Proceedings of the Conference at Richmond, June 11 and 12, 1867* (New York, 1867), in John Jay, *Slavery and the War*, #18.

[25] Charles Kassel, "Edwin Miller Wheelock," *Open Court*, XXXIV (Sept. 1920), 569; Simkins and Woody, *South Carolina during Reconstruction*, 125-26, 204,

Southern whites soon realized that an overwhelming majority of the freedmen would vote Republican. Most whites ceased their abortive attempt of 1867 to persuade the freedmen to cooperate with the Democratic party. They began to stage anti-Republican riots and to break up Republican meetings with increasing frequency in the spring and summer of 1867. The Democratic party reverted to its old belief that, in the words of the *New York Express*, "this is a Democratic government of white men, made for white men, and exclusively for white men."[26]

In Washington, meanwhile, the Johnson administration was taking steps to curtail the effectiveness of the Reconstruction Acts. Military commanders enforcing these Acts in the South had overruled the provisional state governments on many points and had issued orders to prevent the swearing of false oaths by former Confederates who hoped to qualify for voting. On June 20, 1867, Johnson issued a set of counter-orders prohibiting boards of registry from challenging a man's oath and directing military commanders to cooperate with existing state governments. If carried out these orders would have given the Johnson governments in the South a large measure of control over the reconstruction process. General Philip Sheridan declared that Johnson's orders opened "a broad macadamized road for perjury and fraud to travel on." Abolitionists praised Sheridan and renewed their demand for Johnson's impeachment. Republicans who had expected President Johnson to carry out the Reconstruction Acts in good faith were startled into convening Congress in July to pass a third Reconstruction Act to nullify the effect of the president's orders. Radicals urged Congress to impeach Johnson, but moderate counsels prevailed and the legislators confined themselves to passing a bill declaring that the existing state governments in the South were subject to the absolute authority of Congress and the military commanders.[27]

449, 464-68; Reuben Tomlinson to Ellen Collins, May 14, 1869, McKim Papers, Cornell; Tomlinson to E. D. Cheney, July 27, 1868, Cheney Papers, BPL; Gilbert Pillsbury to S. P. Chase, Sept. 24, 1867, Chase Papers, LC; *Liberator*, July 21, 1865; *N.A.S. Standard*, Aug. 29, Sept. 19, 1868; *Freedmen's Record*, IV (May 1868), 73.

[26] *New York Express*, quoted in *N.A.S. Standard*, July 6, 1867. See also the *Jackson* (Miss.) *Democrat*, quoted in *N.A.S. Standard*, Aug. 17, 1867; *New York Tribune*, May 18, June 20, 1867; and *Independent*, May 30, 1867.

[27] McKitrick, *Andrew Johnson and Reconstruction*, 493-94; *New York Tribune*, July 7, 11, 1867; *N.A.S. Standard*, June 29, Aug. 17, 24, 1867; *Independent*, June 27, July 4, 11, 1867.

In July 1867, President Johnson offered the post of commissioner of the Freedmen's Bureau to Frederick Douglass. One can only guess at the president's motives in making this offer. Perhaps he hoped to stifle the radical cry of impeachment by appointing a Negro to a prominent government position. He may have planned to wreck the Bureau by placing a Negro in charge of its operations, hoping that this would provoke many white officials to resign. At any rate Douglass, after pondering the offer, rejected it. He explained to friends that he was unwilling to "facilitate the removal of a man as just and good as General Howard and especially to place myself under any obligation to keep the peace with Andrew Johnson." Abolitionists applauded Douglass' decision. "The greatest black man in the nation," said Theodore Tilton, "did not consent to become the tool of the meanest white."[28] When Douglass refused, Johnson offered the job to John Mercer Langston, who also turned him down. Finally the president approached Robert Purvis. Purvis sought the advice of Wendell Phillips, who urged him to reject the offer. Nothing could make him happier than to see a Negro in such a high position, said Phillips, but he thought the president's offer "only a cunning trick. Johnson wishes just now to confuse & divide the loyal sentiment." Purvis accepted Phillips' advice and turned down the proposal. General Howard remained at the head of the Bureau.[29]

In August the president moved against the most important administrators of the Republican reconstruction policy. On August 12 he suspended Stanton and appointed General Grant as *ad interim* secretary of war. He followed this act by removing Generals Sheridan and Sickles from their commands of southern military districts and replacing them with conservative generals. Johnson's action gave a strong fillip to the impeachment drive. "It is now universally recognized that there will be no peace, no restoration, no business stability, till something is done to prevent Andrew Johnson from enthroning perpetual turmoil," declared the *Com-*

---

[28] Benjamin Quarles, *Frederick Douglass* (Washington, 1948), 237-40; Wm. Slade to Douglass, July 29, Aug. 18, 1867, Douglass to Slade, Aug. 12, 1867, Douglass Papers, Anacostia; Douglass' statement quoted from Douglass to Tilton, Sept. 2, 1867, Tilton Papers, NYHS; Tilton's statement quoted in Quarles, *Douglass*, 239.

[29] Bentley, *Freedmen's Bureau*, 196; Phillips to Purvis, Sept. 13, 1867, Weston Papers, BPL.

monwealth. Impeachment sentiment increased sharply among all segments of the Republican party in August and September.[30]

The approach of the important 1867 state elections temporarily eclipsed the drive for impeachment. Negro suffrage amendments were on the ballots in Ohio, Kansas, and Minnesota. Abolitionist lecturers canvassed Ohio and Kansas on behalf of the amendments, and the Republican parties in all three states officially endorsed Negro suffrage. But the voters rejected the amendments in every state. The issue of Negro suffrage also played an important part in the Pennsylvania and New York elections, both of which were won by the Democrats.[31] Abolitionists were dismayed by this renewed demonstration of northern race prejudice. "Deep & malignant & murderous is the hatred of the Negro" in Ohio, reported Henry Wright. Parker Pillsbury could hardly find words strong enough to express his disgust with northern people who supported Negro suffrage in the South but rejected it at home. "Our whole demeanor toward the southern states," he wrote, "is like that of the Pharisee toward the Publican."[32]

"I almost pity the Radicals," wrote one of President Johnson's supporters after the elections of 1867. "After giving ten states to the negroes, to keep the Democrats from getting them, they will have lost the rest. . . . Any party with an abolition head and a nigger tail will soon find itself with nothing left but the head and tail."[33] Moderate Republicans began whispering that the party must hold back on the Negro question, especially in the North, if it wished to remain in power. Abolitionists denounced this tendency toward conservatism. "The cowardly friends of a political party are more to be dreaded by it than its bravest foes," de-

. [30] McKitrick, *Andrew Johnson and Reconstruction*, 494-98; *Commonwealth*, Aug. 17, 1867. See also Senator Richard Yates of Illinois to Anna Dickinson, Aug. 21, 1867, Dickinson Papers, LC; George Cheever to Henry Cheever, Aug. 28, 1867, Cheever Papers, AAS; *N.A.S. Standard*, Aug. 17, 1867; *New York Tribune*, Aug. 28, 1867; *Independent*, Sept. 19, 1867.

[31] *N.A.S. Standard*, Sept. 14, Oct. 12, Nov. 9, 1867; *New York Tribune*, Oct. 12, 1867; *Independent*, Oct. 17, 31, 1867; *Thirty-Fourth Annual Report of the Philadelphia Female Anti-Slavery Society* (Phila., 1868), 15-16.

[32] Wright to Garrison, Nov. 23, 1867, Garrison Papers, BPL; Pillsbury to Gerrit Smith, Nov. 27, 1867, Gerrit Smith Papers, SU. See also W. H. Furness to Sumner, Nov. 24, 1867, Sumner Papers, HU; and Parker Pillsbury, *Letter to a Radical Member of Congress*, Oct. 20, 1867, published letter, copy in Gerrit Smith Papers, SU.

[33] Quoted in Ira Brown, "Pennsylvania and the Rights of the Negro, 1865-1887," *Pennsylvania History*, XXVIII (Jan. 1961), 51.

clared Theodore Tilton in the *Independent*. "If the Republican party is not to stand for the negro's rights, then it has no better mission than the Democratic." Phillips maintained that the party's failure to take a bold, uncompromising stand on the questions of a national Negro suffrage amendment and impeachment was the reason for its electoral losses in 1867. The remedy for Republican weaknesses, according to Phillips, was more radicalism, not less. He urged adoption of three constitutional amendments to enfranchise the Negro in every state, guarantee a public school system in every state, and make national and state citizenship synonymous under the aegis of the federal government.[34]

Impeachment emerged as the main political issue during the 1867-68 session of Congress. Abolitionists circulated petitions demanding the removal of Johnson. On November 20 the House Judiciary Committee voted to recommend impeachment. Abolitionists hailed this action and urged Congress to do its duty. But Democratic gains in the 1867 elections had made Republican politicians wary. "We shall have burdens enough to carry in the next campaign," said Horace Greeley, "without making Mr. Johnson a martyr and carrying him also." The full House defeated the impeachment resolution on December 7.[35]

The impeachment question would have disappeared from politics after this vote had Johnson not chosen to make fresh assaults on Congress and its reconstruction policy. In his annual message the president excoriated the Reconstruction Acts and launched into a racist diatribe on the evils of Negro rule. On December 18 he publicly endorsed the actions of Winfield Hancock, a Democratic general who had replaced Sheridan and had issued orders asserting the supremacy of civil over military government in direct defiance of the Third Reconstruction Act. A few days later Johnson removed Generals Pope and Ord from command of southern military districts and replaced them with more conservative officers. Radicals writhed in anger as Johnson committed these provocative acts with impunity. "It is pitiful," wrote Frank

[34] *Independent*, Nov. 14, Dec. 5, 1867; *N.A.S. Standard*, Sept. 21, Nov. 30, 1867.
[35] *New York Tribune*, Dec. 9, 1867. See also McKitrick, *Andrew Johnson and Reconstruction*, 498-99; *N.A.S. Standard*, Sept. 28, Oct. 5, 26, Nov. 30, Dec. 7, 14, 21, 1867; *Independent*, Dec. 19, 1867.

Bird, "to see Congress floundering along, from one expedient to another, vainly endeavoring to tie the hands which they should have chopped off a year ago."[36]

On February 21 Johnson committed the act that finally caused his impeachment. Defying the Senate vote restoring Stanton to the War Department, the president dismissed Stanton and appointed Lorenzo Thomas secretary of war *ad interim.* Nearly the whole of the Republican party now clamored for impeachment. Construing the removal of Stanton as a breach of the Tenure of Office Act, the House on February 24 impeached Johnson. Abolitionists hailed the House vote with joy. Conviction of Johnson by the Senate, said the *Anti-Slavery Standard,* would mean "the emancipation of the Northern mind from the dominion of Southern, pro-slavery influence. It will end the 'Border State' policy in politics."[37]

National attention focused on the Senate, where for more than two months the trial of President Johnson proceeded amidst mounting drama and tension. Theodore Tilton, Gilbert Haven, Richard Hinton, Edmund Quincy, and other abolitionists descended on the capital to cover the trial for abolitionist and Republican newspapers. All of them served as lobbyists in behalf of impeachment. Tilton was especially active, flitting here and there, buttonholing senators in corridors and cloakrooms, urging upon them the necessity for the president's removal.[38] In reply to the skillful defense of Johnson by his lawyers, abolitionists and radicals asserted that impeachment should be construed as a *political* rather than as a narrowly legal process. Johnson should be removed, said Phillips, because of his persistent efforts to restore the rebel South to power, his attempts to frustrate the congressional plan of reconstruction, and his sanction of the murder and oppression of southern freedmen. "If the executive will not execute," wrote Elizur Wright, "there is no possible

[36] James D. Richardson, *Messages and Papers of the Presidents* (20 vols., Washington, 1897-1913), IX, 3762-63; McKitrick, *Andrew Johnson and Reconstruction,* 499-500; *N.A.S. Standard,* Jan. 11, 1868; *Commonwealth,* Jan. 11, 1868; Frank Bird to Sumner, Jan. 11, 1868, Sumner Papers, HU.

[37] McKitrick, *Andrew Johnson and Reconstruction,* 501-05; *N.A.S. Standard,* Feb. 29, 1868.

[38] *Zion's Herald,* Mar. 5, 26, Apr. 9, 1868; *New York Herald,* May 13, 1868; *Independent,* May 7, 1868; Howard K. Beale, ed., *The Diary of Gideon Welles* (3 vols., New York, 1960), III, 357.

reasonable remedy but to have the law-making power replace him with something that will execute."[39]

In March and April abolitionists expressed confidence that Johnson would be convicted. But as the date for the Senate vote approached, it became clear that several Republican senators considered impeachment a legal process and were unconvinced that Johnson had committed any impeachable acts. When the decisive vote was taken on May 16, seven Republicans voted with the Democrats and President Johnson was acquitted. Abolitionists were enraged. They excoriated the recalcitrant senators in bitter language. The New England Anti-Slavery Society resolved that in failing to convict Johnson "the Republican party records judgment against its own capacity, and justifies the Nation for distrusting its leadership." Wendell Phillips regarded the failure of impeachment as a sign of conservative resurgence. He urged radicals to gird themselves for a renewed struggle on behalf of justice and equality for the freedmen.[40]

In many ways the end of the impeachment struggle cleared the air. The Republican party began to close ranks in preparation for the presidential election of 1868. This election was crucial for the cause of Negro suffrage, but before turning to the campaign of 1868, it is necessary to consider two other measures that abolitionists deemed essential: education and land for the freedmen.

[39] *N.A.S. Standard,* Mar. 14, 1868; Wright's statement published in *Commonwealth,* Mar. 14, 1868.
[40] Resolution of New England Anti-Slavery Society published in *N.A.S. Standard,* June 6, 1868; Phillips' statement published in issue of May 23, 1868. See also *Independent,* May 21, 1868; *Commonwealth,* May 23, 1868; and Tilton to E. C. Stanton, May 28, 1868, Stanton Papers, LC.

Abolitionists played an important part in the efforts to bring education and land to the freedmen. Garrison noted at the end of 1864 that emancipation would meet the southern Negroes "just where slavery leaves them—in need of everything that pertains to their physical, intellectual, and moral condition." Here was a vast field for philanthropic effort, and Garrison urged his fellow abolitionists to fulfill their obligations to the freed slaves. The *Anti-Slavery Standard* asserted that reconstruction of the South "must be social as well as political. . . . It must reach to the very groundwork of social order." The freedmen would have to be prepared for their new rights and responsibilities as citizens. "The duty of abolitionists to their clients will not cease with the technical abolition of slavery," said the *Standard*. "These [Freedmen's] Relief Associations prefigure the work that will remain to be done—the finishing of Emancipation and the perfecting of Reconstruction through Education."[1]

In 1864 an abolitionist army officer stationed in Louisiana issued an appeal for northern teachers to instruct the freedmen. He wanted "ABOLITIONISTS! dyed with the pure dye—men who dare face this *miserable, wheedling conservatism*, and *do* something to merit at least the prevalent epithet '*nigger on the brain.*' "[2] Of the several thousand northerners who went South to teach the freedmen during the war and reconstruction, a majority were probably abolitionists. Some teachers, of course, were motivated primarily by a desire for a change of climate, adventure, or by religious zeal, but most of them hoped to bear witness to their abolitionist faith by aiding the Negro in his transition to freedom. The correspondence of teachers was filled with references to their antislavery backgrounds. Several abolitionists devoted the rest of their lives to the southern Negro. Laura Towne, for example, founded the Penn School on St. Helena Island, South Carolina, in 1862 and remained there until

---

[1] *Liberator*, Dec. 30, 1864; *N.A.S. Standard*, Jan. 7, 1865.
[2] *American Missionary*, VIII (June 1864), 150.

her death in 1901. Sallie Holley and Caroline Putnam, old-line Garrisonian abolitionists from upstate New York, started a school for the freedmen at Lottsburgh, Virginia, in 1868. Miss Holley remained there until her death in 1893, and Miss Putnam was still instructing the Negroes of Lottsburgh in 1907. These examples of philanthropic longevity could be multiplied many times.[3]

Abolitionists predominated not only among the teachers of the freedmen but among the officers of the freedmen's aid societies as well. Professor Henry Swint found that of the 135 leading officials of the freedmen's societies, nearly half had been abolitionists, and many of the remainder had been active to a lesser degree in the antislavery movement. A few prominent abolitionists formed the backbone of the whole freedmen's aid movement. J. Miller McKim served as the corresponding secretary (chief executive officer) of the American Freedmen's Union Commission, which comprised all the secular freedmen's societies from 1866 to 1869. George Whipple and Lewis Tappan, secretary and treasurer respectively of the American Missionary Association, were the chief officials of this largest of the evangelical freedmen's aid societies. Levi Coffin was general agent of the Western Freedmen's Aid Commission. John W. Alvord was superintendent of education for the Freedmen's Bureau from 1865 to 1870. Reuben Tomlinson, H. R. Pease, and Edwin Wheelock served as state superintendents of education in South Carolina, Mississippi, and Texas during Reconstruction.[4]

[3] Rupert S. Holland, ed., *Letters and Diary of Laura M. Towne, Written from the Sea Islands of South Carolina, 1862-84* (Cambridge, Mass., 1912), xvi-xvii and passim; John White Chadwick, *Sallie Holley, A Life for Liberty* (New York, 1899); Caroline Putnam to William L. Garrison, Jr., May 23, 1907, Garrison Papers, sc. See also Henry Lee Swint, *The Northern Teacher in the South, 1862-1870* (Nashville, 1941), 35-56. The private correspondence of leading abolitionists, the antislavery newspapers, and the monthly journals of the various freedmen's aid societies contain uncounted hundreds of letters from abolitionists who had gone South to teach the freedmen.

[4] Swint, *Northern Teacher*, 26-32, 51n., 143-74; for McKim's activities, see his letterbooks as corresponding secretary of the American Freedmen's Aid Commission and the American Freedmen's Union Commission in the McKim Papers, Cornell; for the personnel of the A.M.A., see Richard B. Drake, "The American Missionary Association and the Southern Negro, 1861-1888," Ph.D. dissertation, Emory University, 1957, 78-98; Levi Coffin, *Reminiscences* (Cincinnati, 1880), 651-712; Charles Kassel, "Edwin Miller Wheelock," *Open Court*, xxxiv (Sept. 1920), 569.

Abolitionists were active at every level of the drive for education of the freedmen: organizing auxiliary societies, soliciting
funds, lecturing, recruiting teachers, writing textbooks, and
founding schools in the South. Samuel J. May devoted much of
his time between 1863 and 1869 to organizing and administering
the Syracuse Freedmen's Aid Society, an auxiliary of the New
York association. His cousin Samuel May, Jr., formed an auxiliary of the New England Freedmen's Aid Society in Leicester,
Massachusetts. Lydia Maria Child wrote a brief history of the
Negro, entitled *The Freedmen's Book*, to dramatize the heroes of
the race and inculcate honesty, courage, and morality in Negro
children; this book was used as a primer and textbook in freedmen's schools. John G. Fee, one of the founders of Berea College,
organized several schools, hospitals, and churches for the freedmen in his native Kentucky. As corresponding secretary of the
New England Educational Commission for the Freedmen, a Baptist society, abolitionist Joseph Parker made several trips to the
South and organized many freedmen's schools. Elected a bishop
of the Methodist Episcopal Church in 1872, abolitionist Gilbert
Haven was stationed in Atlanta for eight years, where he brought
new energy to the work of the Methodist Freedmen's Aid Society
and helped found Clark University. These are only a few examples
of the activities of abolitionists at every level of the freedmen's aid
movement.[5]

One instance of abolitionist organization of southern schools
deserves special mention. In February 1865, Union troops
marched into Charleston, accompanied by James Redpath, reporter for the *New York Tribune*. Colonel Woodford seized all
school buildings and appointed Redpath superintendent of public

[5] G. B. Emerson, S. May, Jr., and T. J. Mumford, *Memoir of Samuel Joseph
May* (New York, 1871), 229-30; Samuel J. May to J. Miller McKim, Jan. 28,
31, Feb. 1, 16, May 13, July 9, 20, 26, Aug. 15, 1866, July 18, Oct. 21, 1867,
McKim Papers, Cornell; L. M. Child to James T. Fields, Aug. 23, 28, Sept. 3,
1865, Child Papers, Radcliffe Women's Archives; L. M. Child to Lewis Tappan,
Jan. 1, 30, 1869, Tappan Papers, LC; John G. Fee, *Autobiography* (Chicago, 1891),
173-80; Joseph W. Parker, "Memoirs," typescript of MS supplied by Mrs.
Perce J. Bentley, 106-10, 121-22, 128-34, 143-46; William H. Daniels, *Memorials
of Gilbert Haven* (Boston, 1880), 183-84, 202-05. The Pennsylvania Society for
the Abolition of Slavery, founded in 1775 by antislavery Quakers of Philadelphia, contributed money to 61 schools and colleges for the freedmen
during Reconstruction. *Centennial Anniversary of the Pennsylvania Society for
Promoting the Abolition of Slavery . . . April 14, 1875* (Philadelphia, 1875), 40.

instruction. Within ten days Redpath had secured teachers, text-books, and students. On March 4 he formally opened the schools to 1,200 freedmen and 300 white children. Negroes and whites were taught in the same building but segregated by classroom. Teachers were paid and textbooks supplied by northern freed-men's aid societies. Within a few weeks the children of Charleston were off the streets and in school. By the end of March there were 3,114 children of both races in the schools. Most of the teachers were natives of Charleston: 74 of the 83 teachers, including 25 Negroes. By the end of May there were more than 4,000 pupils studying under 34 northern and 68 native southern teachers in 9 day schools and 5 night schools. Redpath returned North in June, followed by the praises of Charlestonians, army officers, and abolitionists for his efficient reorganization of Charleston schools.[6]

Another abolitionist who accomplished a great deal as an educator and social worker among the freedmen was Josephine Griffing. During the war thousands of freedmen flocked into Washington. Appalled by the miserable living conditions of these people in disease-ridden slums, Mrs. Griffing became general agent of the National Freedmen's Relief Association of the District of Columbia in 1863. She distributed food and clothing and established vocational schools to teach new skills to freed men and women. In a period of two years—1865 to 1867—she found homes and employment in the North for more than 7,000 Washington Negroes. Thereafter she continued to send three or four hundred freedmen North every year for several years.[7]

[6] *Freedmen's Record*, I (April 1865), 61-64 (May 1865), 73 (July 1865), 110-11, 120; *Commonwealth*, Apr. 15, July 1, 1865; *N.A.S. Standard*, July 22, 29, 1865; *Liberator*, July 21, 1865; Luther P. Jackson, "The Educational Efforts of the Freedmen's Bureau and Freedmen's Aid Societies in South Carolina, 1862-1872," *Journal of Negro History*, VIII (Jan. 1923), 19-20; Alrutheus A. Taylor, *The Negro in South Carolina during Reconstruction* (Washington, 1924), 85-86. With the opening of the fall term in 1865 the public school system in Charleston again came under the control of native white officials, who assigned all Negro children to the Morris Street School, where they were taught by southern whites. One of the best Negro schools in the city, however, was the Shaw Memorial Institute, named in honor of Colonel Robert Shaw, and sustained primarily by the Shaw family and their abolitionist friends until 1874, when it was incorporated into the public school system of the city. Taylor, *The Negro in South Carolina Reconstruction*, 86-89.

[7] E. C. Stanton et al., *History of Woman Suffrage* (6 vols., New York, 1881-1922), II, 28-33; Josephine Griffing to Sumner, Nov. ?, 1864, Sumner Papers,

Primary School for Freedmen A. R. Waud in *Harper's Weekly*

Despite her efforts the freedmen continued to pour into the District faster than she could find homes for them in the North. Unskilled and unemployed, these people became a grave social problem and their miserable hovels an eyesore and a danger to public health. Especially serious was the problem of aged or crippled freedmen, who had almost no hope of future rehabilitation. The task seemed hopeless, but Mrs. Griffing continued to work undauntedly: she distributed private and public relief, and visited Negroes in their homes. In 1865 she was appointed sub-assistant commissioner of the Freedmen's Bureau in the District of Columbia. When the Bureau proposed to reduce rations at the end of 1865 to avoid encouraging pauperism and idleness, she protested vigorously and gave several lectures publicizing the destitute condition of many freedmen in the capital. The aged and crippled Negroes could not support themselves, she declared, and the able-bodied men could not find work. Her lectures aroused considerable attention and controversy. Democrats cited the poverty and disease of Washington Negroes as proof that they had been better off in slavery. Some abolitionists were unhappy with Mrs. Griffing's disclosures, fearing that they would only confirm the popular image of the shiftless, helpless Negro. General Howard dismissed her from the Freedmen's Bureau because of her protests against Bureau policy. Yet Mrs. Griffing's portrayal of conditions in the District was essentially accurate, and the Bureau was compelled to renew the distribution of rations to needy freedmen.[8]

Mrs. Griffing continued to serve as a one-woman welfare agency for Washington Negroes until her death in 1872. She was on good terms with radical Republican leaders in Congress. Every year she appeared before congressional committees and tried to wheedle more money out of them for relief. She urged the creation of public works programs in Washington to alleviate unemploy-

---

HU; Memo. of Governor Buckingham of Connecticut, in Griffing Papers, cu; *N.A.S. Standard*, Sept. 1, 1866.

[8] George Bentley, *A History of the Freedmen's Bureau* (Phila., 1955), 77-78; Stanton et al., *History of Woman Suffrage*, II, 29, 33; Mrs. Griffing to E. B. Chace, Dec. 26, 1865, in Lillie B. C. Wyman and Arthur C. Wyman, *Elizabeth Buffum Chace* (2 vols., Boston, 1914), I, 285-86; Levi Coffin to McKim, Jan. 2, 1866, McKim to Coffin, Jan. 6, 1866, McKim Papers, Cornell; *Freedmen's Record*, I (Feb. 1865), 17-18; *N.A.S. Standard*, Jan. 27, 1866.

ment.[9] Mrs. Griffing remained a target of criticism from certain Republican quarters. In 1870 Horace Greeley charged that her activities among the freedmen had done them great injury. "They are an easy, worthless race, taking no thought for the morrow, and liking to lean on those who befriend them," Greeley told Mrs. Griffing. "Your course aggravates their weaknesses, when you should raise their ambition and stimulate them to self-reliance." In an angry reply, Mrs. Griffing pointed out that she helped only those who could not help themselves. She had found work for many of the able-bodied, and her relief efforts were directed toward "those broken-down aged slaves whom we have liberated in their declining years, when all their strength is gone, and for whom no home, family, friendship, or subsistence is furnished." If it was a "great injury" to help these people, then "there is no call for alms-house, hospital, home, or asylum in human society." Criticism such as Greeley's was exceptional, however. Most observers praised Mrs. Griffing for her herculean labors and steadfast humanitarianism. Senator Benjamin Wade told her in 1869, "I know of no person in America who has done so much for the cause of humanity for the last four years as you have done. Your disinterested labors have saved hundreds of poor human beings, not only [from] the greatest destitution and misery, but from actual starvation and death."[10]

Whether serving as organizers, administrators, teachers, or social workers, abolitionists were in the forefront of efforts to educate and rehabilitate the freedmen. Their contribution was recognized by a speaker at the National Education Association meeting in 1884: "Those very men, extremists, enthusiasts, 'fanatics,' who had formed the backbone of the abolition movement . . . became the dauntless leaders of an educational movement which was the natural sequel and supplement of their first crusade."[11]

✦

9 Mrs. Griffing to Sumner, Feb. 12, 1867, Mar. 30, Apr. 10, 1869, Sumner Papers, HU; Mrs. Griffing to Gerrit Smith, Aug. 5, 12, 1869, Aug. 26, 1870, Mar. 13, 1871, Catharine Stebbins to Gerrit Smith, Aug. 17, 1870, Smith Papers, SU; Sumner to Mrs. Griffing, Apr. 2, 1868, July 27, Dec. 7, 1869, Mrs. Griffing to Lucretia Mott, Apr. 22, 1870, Griffing Papers, CU; *New York World*, Feb. 25, 1870; *National Standard*, Apr. 1, 1871.

10 Horace Greeley to Griffing, Sept. 7, 1870, Griffing to Greeley, Sept. 12, 1870, Wade to Griffing, Nov. 12, 1869, Griffing Papers, CU.

11 Quoted in Swint, *Northern Teacher*, 27.

The main purpose of freedmen's aid was to bring the rudiments of education to illiterate Negroes. "If the blacks are kept in ignorance they can be subjected to a system of serfdom," wrote J. Miller McKim. "If we enlighten them they are secure against the machinations of their old enemies—to which they will always be subject until educated." McKim proclaimed repeatedly that education was necessary to equip the freedmen for the rights and responsibilities of citizenship. "Democracy without the schoolmaster is an impossibility," he said. "Universal suffrage without universal education would be universal anarchy."[12] An element of cultural imperialism also entered into the thinking of some educators. The New England Freedmen's Aid Society announced in 1865 that "New England can furnish teachers enough . . . to make a New England of the whole South; God helping, we will not pause in our work until the free school system . . . has been established from Maryland to Florida, and all along the shores of the Gulf."[13]

The Freedmen's Bureau was an important partner of the freedmen's aid societies in the work of educating southern Negroes. The Bureau extended its benevolent protection over all educational activities in the South. It provided school buildings for the societies and transportation allowances for teachers. It systematized the record-keeping and reports of the societies. The state superintendents of education of the Bureau worked closely with officials and teachers of the freedmen's societies. General Oliver O. Howard, head of the Bureau, was in complete sympathy with the purposes of the aid societies and established cordial relations with their leaders. As a devoted Congregationalist Howard was particularly close to the leaders of the American Missionary Association. The A.M.A. also enjoyed the special friendship of John W. Alvord, superintendent of education of the Freedmen's Bureau, who had been associated with the evangelical wing of the abolitionist movement before the war.[14]

---

[12] McKim to Arthur Albright, Oct. 19, 1866, McKim Papers, BPL; McKim to S. P. Chase, Oct. 15, 1866, Chase Papers, LC.

[13] *Freedmen's Journal*, I (Jan. 1865), 3.

[14] Bentley, *Freedmen's Bureau*, 172-76; Luther Jackson, "The Educational Efforts of the Freedmen's Bureau and Freedmen's Aid Societies in South Carolina," *op.cit.*, 13-15; McKim to Joseph Simpson, Feb. 28, 1866, McKim letterbooks, I, 400, McKim Papers, Cornell; McKim to Arthur Albright, Mar. 23, 1866, McKim Papers, BPL; Drake, "American Missionary Association," 37-43.

Under the leadership of J. Miller McKim, the regional secular freedmen's societies were merged into a loose national federation in the fall of 1865, known as the American Freedmen's Aid Commission (A.F.A.C.). Officials of the freedmen's associations were happy with the progress of their work in 1865-1866. Excluding night schools and Sunday schools, the societies operated a total of 975 schools with 1,405 teachers and 90,778 pupils during the school year of 1865-66. Of this total the A.F.A.C. supplied 760 teachers and instructed approximately 50,000 pupils. The A.M.A. sent 353 missionaries and teachers into the field who had more than 20,000 students under their charge. The remainder of the schools were operated by independent evangelical associations.[15]

Teachers of the freedmen were confronted by many difficulties. In the early years of freedom the Negroes moved about a great deal and the school population was highly transient. Attendance was irregular and seasonal because so many Negro children had to work in the fields at planting and harvest time. The children came from a cultural environment almost entirely devoid of intellectual stimulus. Many of them had never heard of the alphabet, geography, or arithmetic when they first came to school. Few of them knew their right hand from their left, or could tell the date of their birth. Most of them realized only vaguely that there was a world outside their own plantation or town. The only contact they had with such mysteries was during their few hours in school a few months of the year. Progress was slow under such circumstances, but there were compensating factors. The freedmen had an almost passionate desire to learn to read and write, and children laboriously taught their parents the alphabet and multiplication tables during their spare time. Teachers invariably testified that despite their disadvantages in background, training, and environment, Negro children learned to read almost as well and as rapidly as white children.[16]

[15] The story of the merger of the secular freedmen's aid societies can be traced in the correspondence of J. Miller McKim in his papers at Cornell; Julius H. Parmelee, "Freedmen's Aid Societies, 1861-1871," *Negro Education: A Study of the Private and Higher Schools for Colored People in the United States, U.S. Dept. of Interior; Bureau of Education Bulletin*, 1916, no. 38, pp. 269-71, 275, 289; and *American Freedman*, I (May 1866), 25-31 (Sept. 1866), 82 (Oct. 1866), 99.

[16] The statements in this paragraph are based upon a reading of hundreds of letters from teachers printed in the *American Freedman* and *Freedmen's Record* from 1865 to 1869.

The problems faced by the teacher in the classroom were often less severe than those confronting her in the community. Many southern whites did not take kindly to the idea of Yankee "school-marms" instructing their former slaves. Some southern communities accepted the inevitability of Negro education and cooperated with the northern teachers. In most places, however, the white people regarded the Yankee teachers as aliens come to instill ideas of political and social equality into the heads of Negroes. Some southerners considered education of the Negro a harmful waste of time. "To talk about educating this drudge is to talk without thinking," asserted the *Paducah* (Kentucky) *Herald*. "Either to 'educate,' or to teach him merely to read and write, is to ruin him as a laborer. Thousands of them have already been ruined by it."[17] Where the whites felt this way the teachers were sometimes insulted, beaten, and their schoolhouses burned. Southern contempt for the "nigger teacher," however, usually took the milder form of social ostracism. White teachers frequently found it impossible to get room and board in white southern homes, and native whites would deliberately snub the teachers socially.

Even in southern communities that favored Negro education the Yankee teachers were regarded with a certain amount of suspicion. In the spring of 1867 Anna Gardner, teacher of a freed-men's school in Charlottesville, Virginia, asked J. C. Southall, local newspaper editor and friend of Negro education, if he would print some diplomas for her school without charge. Southall replied that he would print them if he could be satisfied that the school confined itself to the ordinary rudiments of education. But he suspected that "you instruct them in politics and sociology; that you come among us not merely as an ordinary school teacher, but as a political missionary; that you communicate to the colored people ideas of social equality." Even if she did not actually teach these things in the classroom, "you may, by precept and example, inculcate ideas of social equality with the whites among the pupils of your school and the colored people generally." Such ideas were "mischievous, . . . tending to disturb the good feeling between the two races." Therefore Southall refused to print the diplomas. Anna Gardner sent him a blunt reply: "I teach *in school* and *out*, so far as my influence extends, the funda-

[17] *Paducah Herald*, quoted in *Right Way*, June 23, 1866.

mental principles of 'politics' and 'sociology,' viz.:—'Whatsoever ye would that men should do to you, do ye even so unto them.' " Anna Gardner's statement typified the attitude of many teachers, who did indeed practice "social equality"; and after the passage of Negro suffrage most of them taught Republican politics as well. Consequently relations between the Yankee teachers and a majority of southern whites remained somewhat strained as long as the schools existed.[18]

Another difficulty confronting the freedmen's aid enterprise was descriptions by newspaper correspondents, travelers, and so on, of the degraded, ignorant, and destitute condition of many freedmen. Such reports were gleefully picked up by the Democratic press and cited as proof of the Negro's worthlessness. In 1866 an official of the Freedmen's Bureau made a speech describing the freedmen as "ignorant, degraded, indolent, sensual, false, far below what I had supposed." The *London Times* published the speech. English friends of the freedmen wrote in alarm to J. Miller McKim telling him that such stories had a tendency in England to discourage contributions to freedmen's aid. McKim replied that the freedmen were indeed degraded. That was why they needed assistance and education. McKim told the British friends of the freedmen: "Of course the blacks are *to a degree* just what Major Lawrence represents them; and just what anyone of common sense must *a priori* know them to be. Among the *least* of slavery's evils are the manacles which it fastens on the limbs and the stripes which it inflicts on the backs of its victims. Our 'zeal' against it & in behalf of its injured subjects is kindled by the fact that its iron enters the soul—darkens the mind—dulls the intellect—perverts the affections—chokes the aspirations— and does every thing it can toward making the black man in fact what it has made him in law: a chattel. . . . The victims of the slave-system *are* 'degraded'; therefore it is that we labor to lift them up." The freedmen were actually less degraded than abolitionists had expected, said McKim. They had shown marked progress and gave every sign of susceptibility to improvement and education. The present backward condition of the freedmen,

[18] *Freedmen's Record*, iii (Apr. 1867), 54. For a general discussion of the tensions between northern teachers and southern whites, see Swint, *Northern Teacher*, 77-142.

he concluded, should stimulate their friends to greater effort rather than cause them to despair for the future of the race.[19]

The freedmen's aid enterprise encountered hostility not only from its enemies but from those who should have been its friends. During the war Phillips and other abolitionists had criticized the aid societies for their paternalism (see Chapter VII). When at the end of the war the Garrison wing of the American Anti-Slavery Society suggested that abolitionists should dissolve their organizations and continue their work for the Negro in the freedmen's societies, Phillips renewed his criticism. He conceded that the freedmen's associations were "doing a good work," but it was a work of charity, an "old clothes movement" and "not the work of an Abolitionist." Frederick Douglass told J. Miller McKim:

"I have my doubts about these Freedmen's Societies. They may be a necessity of the hour and as such may be commended; but I fear everything looking to their permanence. The negro needs justice more than pity; liberty more than old clothes; rights more than training to enjoy them. Once give him equality before the law and special associations for his benefit may cease. He will then be comprehended as he ought to be, in all those schemes of benevolence, education and progress which apply to the masses of our Countrymen every where. In so far as these special efforts shall furnish an apology for excluding us from the general schemes of civilization so multitudinous in our country they will be an injury to the colored race. They will serve to keep up the very prejudices, which it is so desirable to banish from the country."[20]

McKim and other proponents of freedmen's aid resented these disparagements. McKim thought it more important to prepare the freedmen for the rights and duties of citizenship than to agitate for those rights in the abstract. "The Freedmen's movement . . . is not an eleemosynary movement; not an *old clothes* movement; not a movement merely to relieve physical want & teach little negroes to read," he declared. "It is a re-

[19] Arthur Albright to McKim, Feb. 16, 1866, McKim to Albright, Mar. 6, 1866, McKim letterbook, I, 445-49, McKim Papers, Cornell.

[20] *N.A.S. Standard*, May 6, 1865; *Liberator*, May 26, 1865; Douglass to McKim, May 2, 1865, McKim Papers, Cornell.

constructive movement. It is to reorganize Southern Society on a basis of impartial liberty. It is to remodel public opinion in regard to the black man by fitting him for [the responsible exercise of equal rights]. . . . It is a movement established and conducted in the interests of civilization."[21]

While the intramural abolitionist debate over the merits of freedmen's aid societies continued, an important development was taking place within the secular freedmen's associations. In November 1865, representatives of the A.F.A.C. and the American Union Commission met to discuss the possibility of merging the two organizations. The American Union Commission had been formed in 1864 to give aid to Unionist refugees, mostly whites, in the South. The leaders of this Commission and of the A.F.A.C. believed that they could prosecute their work more efficiently if their organizations were united. The merger was approved on January 31, 1866. The name of the new association was the American Freedmen's and Union Commission (the "and" was dropped in May 1866). The objectives of the new Commission were relief and education of blacks and whites alike in the wartorn South.[22]

Some of the auxiliary societies of the A.F.A.C. were opposed to the merger on the ground that it would divert too large a share of their limited resources to the education of southern whites. McKim worked hard to overcome this opposition. To a Pittsburgh abolitionist he wrote that "we can do more for the freedmen on the broad basis of man than of *freed* man or *black* man. We who go against class legislation & color distinctions—shall we legislate for a class—give preference to a color?" Was not the poor white southerner also a victim of slavery, McKim asked a Philadelphia abolitionist who opposed merger? "Shall we denounce President Johnson & his Congressional confreres for not legislating and administering the Government without respect to color, and yet ourselves . . . minister *with* regard to color?" McKim's arguments finally prevailed, and by May 1866, all the auxiliary societies had ratified the new constitution of the American Freedmen's Union Commission (A.F.U.C.). McKim became correspond-

[21] McKim to Richard Webb, Mar. 27, 1865, Garrison Papers, BPL.
[22] Ira Brown, "Lyman Abbot and Freedmen's Aid, 1865-1869," *Journal of Southern History*, xv (Feb. 1949), 23-28.

ing secretary of the new Commission, and Lyman Abbott, former secretary of the American Union Commission, became recording secretary of the merged organization. Abbott also edited the Commission's monthly journal, the *American Freedman*.[23]

The issue of school desegregation soon confronted the A.F.U.C. The Commission made its position on this question perfectly clear in the first issue of its monthly journal. "[We] insist . . . that both races shall enjoy the same rights, immunities, and opportunities," declared the *American Freedman*. "Our Commission is pledged to the maintenance of the doctrine of equal rights. . . . It took America three-quarters of a century of agitation and four years of war to learn the meaning of the word 'Liberty.' God grant to teach us by easier lessons the meaning of the words 'equal rights.' " The constitution of the A.F.U.C. declared that no person would be excluded from the Commission's schools because of race or color. The executive committee conceded that this integration policy "will produce difficulties in the South." Nevertheless integration was "inherently right" and the Commission would never "shut out a child from our schools because of his color."[24]

The constituent societies faithfully carried out the policy of desegregation. The New England Society, for example, instructed its teachers to admit white children "on precisely the same footing, and no other, with blacks; that is to say, they are to occupy the same rooms, recite in the same classes, and receive the same attention as the blacks. You cannot control public opinion outside of the school but, within its limits, you must secure entire respect from every pupil to every other."[25] The A.M.A. had always adhered to a desegregation policy, and most of the other evangelical societies did the same. In practice, however, few whites attended the freedmen's schools. Elizabeth Botume, a teacher in South Carolina, told of two white girls who came to her school

[23] McKim to E. H. Irish, Feb. 8, 1866; McKim to Wm. H. Furness, Mar. 30, 1866; Samuel May, Jr., to McKim, Feb. 20, Mar. 5, 1866; Garrison to McKim, Mar. 31, 1866; McKim to F. J. Child, Dec. 9, 1865, McKim to Joseph Simpson, Feb. 16, 1866, McKim to Laura Towne, Feb. 21, Apr. 4, 1866, McKim to Reuben Tomlinson, Apr. 4, 1866, McKim letterbooks, i, 170-71, 328-29, 381, 458-60, 535-36, McKim Papers, Cornell; *American Freedman*, i (May 1866), 19-20.
[24] *American Freedman*, i (April 1866), 2-3, 5-6.
[25] *Freedmen's Record*, ii (Mar. 1866), 37-38.

because there was no other school within a reasonable distance of their home. The children were happy, but after two months they suddenly stopped coming. Miss Botume visited their mother to learn the reason for their withdrawal. The mother "confessed the Southern white people had 'made so much fuss' because she allowed the children to go to a *'nigger school*,'" reported Miss Botume, that "she felt obliged to take them away." The mother told Miss Botume, "I would not care myself but the young men laugh at my husband. They tell him he must be pretty far gone and low down when he sends his children to a *'nigger school.'* That makes him mad, and he is vexed with me." To avoid family quarrels she withdrew the children. In the term ending June 30, 1867, there were 111,442 pupils in schools operated by the freedmen's societies, of whom only 1,348 were white.[26]

Abolitionists were delighted by the strong equal rights and integrationist position of the A.F.U.C. There was a noticeable decline in radical abolitionist criticism of the freedmen's aid movement in 1866. Several speakers at the annual meeting of the American Anti-Slavery Society praised the good work of the freedmen's associations, and the Society adopted a resolution expressing its gratitude to "the devoted, most efficient, and inexpressibly important labors" of the freedmen's teachers.[27]

But there was still some friction between the Phillips wing of abolitionism and the freedmen's aid societies. Both groups were competing for financial support from the same class of northern people. The competition for funds erupted into a major quarrel in 1867 over the issue of the Jackson bequest. When Francis Jackson died in 1861 he left a trust fund of $10,000 to the antislavery cause. The money did not become available until 1867, two years after the abolition of slavery. Both Garrison and Phillips were on the board of trustees of the Jackson fund, and a dispute arose between them over the disposition of the legacy. Phillips claimed the money for the American Anti-Slavery Society on the ground that the Society's campaign for Negro suffrage was a

[26] Elizabeth Botume, *First Days Amongst the Contrabands* (Boston, 1893), 257-58; *Freedmen's Record*, III (Oct. 1867), 154.

[27] *N.A.S. Standard*, May 12, 19, 1866. For several letters from abolitionists praising the stand of the freedmen's societies on school integration, see *American Freedman*, I (May 1866), 23-24.

direct continuation of the antislavery movement. Garrison wanted the $10,000 for the New England branch of the A.F.U.C., arguing with equal assurance that freedmen's aid was the logical heir of the abolitionist crusade. The two sides compromised in January 1867, and assigned half the legacy to freedmen's aid and half to the American Anti-Slavery Society. But when Congress passed the Reconstruction Acts two months later, Garrison changed his mind and claimed all the money for the freedmen again. The enactment of Negro suffrage, he maintained, completely obviated the need for an antislavery society. Phillips disagreed, and the board of trustees was unable to reach agreement on the disposition of the legacy. The matter went to the Massachusetts Supreme Court, which decided in Garrison's favor. Phillips was deeply angered by the decision and attacked Garrison and his supporters sharply in a series of *Standard* editorials. Garrison replied in kind. Abolitionists ranged themselves on either side of the quarrel and the whole affair became intensely bitter. Garrison and Phillips broke off personal and social relations for two years, and for a long time several of Phillips' old abolitionist friends passed him on the street without speaking. The upshot was a partial revival of the hostility of Phillips and some of his associates toward the freedmen's aid societies.[28]

✦

The A.F.U.C. began to break up almost as soon as it was formed. Religious factionalism was the main cause of its downfall. The American Missionary Association and other evangelical freedmen's aid societies required their teachers to be Christian missionaries as well as instructors. The evangelical associations believed that purification of the soul was as important as enlightenment of the mind. There was a sharp cleavage between the secular educational philosophy of the A.F.U.C. and the evangelical zeal of the A.M.A. This cleavage was essentially a continuation of the prewar rift between Garrisonian and evangelical abolitionists.

[28] The Garrison Papers and the Samuel May, Jr., Papers, BPL, contain a great deal of correspondence relating to this issue. See also *N.A.S. Standard*, July 20, Aug. 10, 24, 1867, Feb. 15, Mar. 14, June 13, 1868. Garrison and Phillips effected a personal reconciliation in the early 1870's, and the bitterness between other abolitionists gradually dissolved during the decade.

Garrisonians predominated among the abolitionist element in the A.F.U.C., and the leadership of the A.M.A. was the same as the leadership of the prewar evangelical abolitionists.

From the outset of the freedmen's aid movement there was competition between the secular societies and the A.M.A., especially in the matter of raising money in the North. In 1866-1867 the differences between the two groups came to a head. The A.M.A. declared that a freedman's education would not be complete unless he was "imbued with the principles of evangelical religion." Teachers of the A.F.U.C., on the other hand, were told that they were not "missionaries, nor preachers, nor exhorters" and instructed "not to inculcate doctrinal opinions or take part in sectarian propagandism of any kind." The A.F.U.C. accused the A.M.A. of conducting "parochial schools" and of placing proselytism above education. Such statements by leaders of the eastern wing of the A.F.U.C. precipitated a crisis in the organization. The western branches of the A.F.U.C. had always required their teachers to be practicing Christians. Angered by the aggressive secularism of the eastern leaders, the Cincinnati branch withdrew from the A.F.U.C. in 1866 and was absorbed by the A.M.A. It was followed by the Cleveland branch in 1867 and the Chicago branch in 1868.[29]

The result of these withdrawals was a sharp decrease in the strength of the A.F.U.C. The A.M.A. had several advantages in its competition with the secular societies. In the first place it was an older organization with well-established sources of income. As a missionary society it could rely on consistent church support while the A.F.U.C. was forced to depend on the North's short-lived philanthropic enthusiasm for education of the freedmen. Secondly, the A.M.A. enjoyed a greater degree of cooperation from the Freedmen's Bureau than did the secular societies. General Howard and the Reverend Alvord were devoted Congrega-

[29] The dispute between the secular and evangelical societies can be traced in *American Missionary*, x (Sept. 1866), 193-94 (Oct. 1866), 226-28, xi (Sept. 1867), 205; *Freedmen's Record*, iii (Jan. 1867), 1-2; *American Freedman*, i (Dec. 1866), 130-31 (Jan. 1867), 146-47, ii (April 1867), 194; Lewis Tappan to J. Sella Martin, July 3, 1865, Tappan to Levi Coffin, Jan. 30, 1865, Tappan letterbook, Tappan Papers, lc; McKim to Garrison, Mar. 29, 1866, McKim to Arthur Albright, Mar. 15, 1867, McKim to J. W. Alvord, Jan. 23, 1868, McKim Papers, Cornell; Swint, *Northern Teacher*, 37-40; and Drake, "American Missionary Association," 18-26.

tionalists. They sympathized with the A.M.A.'s philosophy of religious education. In many small ways the Freedmen's Bureau extended more assistance to the A.M.A. than to the secular societies, causing anger and frustration among some officials of the A.F.U.C. Lastly, A.M.A. teachers were often able to establish a closer rapport with the freedmen because their evangelical piety was more akin to the Negro's own religious experience than was the secularism of A.F.U.C. teachers.[30] The declining strength of the A.F.U.C. in relation to that of the A.M.A. is revealed by a glance at the statistics:

1865-66		1866-67	
A.F.U.C.			
Cash expended	$318,670.08	Cash and supplies:	$250,662.52
Supplies shipped	$90,755.27		
Teachers in the field	760	Teachers in the field	494
A.M.A			
Cash expended	$271,586.78	Cash expended	$334,500.00
Supplies shipped	$105,441.00	Supplies shipped	$90,000.00
Teachers in the field	353	Teachers in the field	528

The expenditures and number of teachers of the A.F.U.C. continued to decline in subsequent years while those of the A.M.A. remained steady for the rest of the decade.[31]

The competition of evangelical associations was not the only reason for the decline of the A.F.U.C. From 1864-1866 a great many people contributed to freedmen's aid who were not deeply concerned about uplifting the Negro but who gave because it was the most "deserving" charity of those years. But in 1866 there was a slackening of popular interest in the movement. As early as 1865 one Gideonite commented on "the lethargy creeping over our community on this subject. . . . The feeling is somewhat general that the negro must make the most of his chances and pick up his a, b, c's as he can." All of the secular societies were forced to retrench during 1866-1867. The *American Freedman* noted in April 1867, that "the enthusiasm which accompanies a new movement, one especially which appealed so strongly to

[30] Drake, "American Missionary Association," 37-75; O. O. Howard to McKim, June 6, 1867, Samuel May, Jr., to McKim, July 22, 1870, McKim Papers, Cornell.

[31] *American Freedman*, I (Jan. 1867), 147, II (April 1867), 196; Parmelee, "Freedmen's Aid Societies," *op.cit.*, 275.

philanthropic and humane considerations as did this during the desolations of war, has somewhat passed away and left as its supporters only those who are attached to it by cardinal and well-considered principles."[32]

In 1868 the executive committee decided to dissolve the A.F.-U.C. The activities of the Commission had decreased to the point where the constituent societies could carry on the work more efficiently by themselves. Dissolution of the A.F.U.C. was accomplished in 1869. The New York and Pennsylvania societies disbanded in the same year. The only secular societies remaining in existence after 1869 were the Baltimore and New England associations. The Baltimore society was absorbed by the city's public school system in 1871. The New England society continued to support a few normal schools in the South until 1874, when it finally disbanded. The A.F.U.C. never fulfilled the grand hopes of its founders, but it accomplished a great deal for the education of southern freedmen. During their existence the secular freedmen's aid societies spent nearly $3,000,000 on southern education and brought the rudiments of learning to more than 150,000 freedmen.[33]

Most important of all, however, the freedmen's societies helped to lay the foundations of public education in the South. When the reconstructed state governments established their public school systems in the years 1868 to 1870, several of the freedmen's schools were taken over directly by the state boards of education. Many of the teachers of the South's new public schools had been educated by the northern freedmen's associations. In several southern states, officials of freedmen's aid societies drafted the public school legislation and served as the first superintendents of education. The public school system in the South was hardly

---

[32] E. S. Philbrick to Wm. C. Gannett, Oct. 15, 1865, in Elizabeth Pearson, ed., *Letters from Port Royal* (Boston, 1906), 317-18; *American Freedman*, ii (Apr. 1867), 195. See also *Freedmen's Record*, ii (Sept. 1866), 157-59, iii (April 1867), 52 (May 1867), 69, iv (April 1868), 51; and Reuben Tomlinson to McKim, Sept. 24, 1866, McKim Papers, Cornell.

[33] Parmelee, "Freedmen's Aid Societies," *op.cit.*, 271-75, 292-96; Drake, "American Missionary Association," 275-76; McKim to Garrison, Dec. 2, 15, 1867, Feb. 1, 1868, Gerrit Smith to J. Miller McKim, Nov. 1, 1868, S. P. Chase to McKim, Nov. 6, 1868, Garrison Papers, BPL; McKim to Gerrit Smith, Nov. 6, 18, 1868, Smith Papers, SU; *Freedmen's Record*, iv (July 1868), 106-08 (Nov. 1868), 169; *American Freedman*, iii (April 1869), 1-2.

in a flourishing condition when the A.F.U.C. disbanded in 1869, but the secular societies had run out of money, and making a virtue of necessity they proclaimed that the spread of public education in the South had ended the need for a northern freedmen's commission.[34]

The financial inability of the South to support an efficient public school system, however, and the takeover of several state governments by conservatives unfriendly to public education sparked a movement for federal aid to education in the early 1870's. In 1869 the new conservative government of Tennessee repealed the statewide compulsory school law, leaving the question of public education to the option of individual counties. All the state's public schools for Negroes except those in Memphis and Nashville soon closed down. Caroline Putnam, a veteran abolitionist teaching the freedmen in Lottsburgh, Virginia, reported in 1870 that Virginia's property tax for schools was unpopular with landowners. The new conservative governor had promised that the tax law would not be enforced. Caroline Putnam urged federal action to compel southern states to maintain a system of universal public education open to both races.[35] In 1870 Congressman George F. Hoar of Massachusetts introduced a bill to establish public schools by national authority in states that failed to do it themselves. Senator W. T. Willey of West Virginia sponsored a bill for the distribution of the proceeds of public land sales among the states to help finance public schools. Abolitionists gave their support to these measures, and both Houses at different times passed different versions of them, but the bills never came to final passage. Abolitionist hopes for an efficient public school system for both races in the South were doomed to disappointment.[36]

✦

During the war and early reconstruction years the freedmen's aid societies concentrated almost entirely on elementary educa-

[34] *Freedmen's Record*, IV (Oct. 1868), 155-56; *American Freedman*, III (April 1869), 2.

[35] Alrutheus A. Taylor, *The Negro in Tennessee, 1865-1880* (Washington, 1941), 182; *National Standard*, I (July 1870), 146-51.

[36] *National Standard*, Oct. 22, Nov. 19, Dec. 17, 1870, Jan. 7, Feb. 11, Mar. 11, Apr. 15, Oct. 28, 1871; George F. Hoar, *Autobiography of Seventy Years* (2 vols., New York, 1903), I, 265.

tion. This emphasis was designed to make literate a large body of people recently emancipated and soon to be enfranchised. But this policy proved very expensive, and did little more than dent the crust of southern illiteracy. At no time were more than 10 per cent of the freedmen of school age attending the societies' schools. Officials of the freedmen's associations realized by 1866 that the establishment of normal schools and colleges to train Negro teachers would be a more effective use of their limited resources. The movement toward normal schools came after the decline of the A.F.U.C. had set in, and the secular societies never supported more than six or eight small normal schools in the South. But the A.M.A. and other evangelical societies established a large number of normal schools and colleges. The A.M.A. was the pioneer in Negro higher education in the South. Between 1866 and 1869 the Association founded seven chartered institutions, all of which were called colleges, although they were at first little more than high schools: Berea College (founded in 1855 and reopened in 1866), Fisk University, Atlanta University, Hampton Institute, Talladega College, Tougaloo College, and Straight University. The A.M.A. also aided in the establishment of Howard University. Some of these schools are today among the best southern universities for Negroes. By 1876 the A.M.A. was also operating 14 nonchartered normal and high schools in the South. As early as 1869 there were 314 teachers trained in A.M.A. institutions teaching in southern schools. It was estimated in 1873 that graduates of A.M.A. normal schools and colleges were teaching 64,000 pupils in southern schools; by 1879 this number had risen to 150,000.[37]

The other denominational societies were not far behind the A.M.A. in founding institutions of higher learning for Negroes in the South. In 1879 there were 39 normal schools, colleges, and theological seminaries and 69 schools of lower grade supported by northern churches and missionary societies in the South. The various northern freedmen's aid and missionary societies and the Freedmen's Bureau spent more than $31,000,000 on southern edu-

[37] *Freedmen's Record*, iii (Jan. 1867), 2 (Oct. 1867), 143, iv (April 1868), 50-51; Augustus F. Beard, *Crusade of Brotherhood, A History of the American Missionary Association* (Boston, 1909), 100-04, 147-89; Drake, "American Missionary Association," 159-85.

cation from 1861 to 1893. This was nearly 30 per cent of the total amount expended for all Negro education in the South during those years. In 1888 of a total of 15,000 Negro teachers instructing more than 800,000 pupils in the South, 13,500 had been trained in schools supported by northern benevolence. The A.M.A. institutions alone had educated 7,000 teachers.[38] The freedmen's societies helped decrease the Negro illiteracy rate in the South from more than 90 per cent in 1861 to 81.1 per cent in 1870 and 70 per cent in 1880. Statistics do not tell the entire story of the contribution of freedmen's associations. Their influence penetrated every southern state, awakening the freedmen to the need for education and proving that the Negro was capable of higher learning. The southern Negro colleges founded by these societies have helped to produce the present generation of Negro leaders who are gradually changing the pattern of race relations in the South. Truly the abolitionist impulse, which motivated the original freedman's aid movement, has had a deep and lasting impact upon the southern Negro.

✦

Abolitionist efforts to win suffrage and education for the freedmen were partially successful. The same cannot be said of their attempts to obtain land for the emancipated Negroes. After the war many abolitionists stepped up their agitation for the confiscation and redistribution of large plantations. "The nominal freedom of the slaves . . . must be actually secured by the possession of land," wrote Edmund Quincy in April 1865. "If the monopoly of land be permitted to remain in the hands of the present rebel proprietors . . . the monopoly of labor might almost as well be given them, too."[39] Wendell Phillips, Anna Dickinson, Gerrit Smith, Lydia Maria Child, James Freeman Clarke, Thomas Wentworth Higginson, and many other abolitionists echoed these sentiments.

President Johnson's amnesty proclamation of May 29, 1865, dealt a sharp blow to radicals who hoped for wholesale confiscation. The proclamation restored political and property rights to most

[38] Harriet Beecher Stowe, "The Education of Freedmen," *North American Review*, cxxviii (June 1879), 605-15, and cxxix (July 1879), 81-94; Drake, "American Missionary Association," 185-205.

[39] *N.A.S. Standard*, Apr. 1, 1865.

rebels who would take an oath of allegiance. In subsequent months Johnson issued a large number of special pardons to men who had been exempted from the May 29 proclamation. Despite this setback, abolitionists continued to work for governmental action to secure land for the freedmen. They hoped for congressional reversal of Johnson's policy of property restoration, just as they hoped for congressional reversal of the rest of his reconstruction program. Several radical Republican leaders agreed with the abolitionists on this question. "We must see that the freedmen are established on the soil, and that they may become proprietors," wrote Charles Sumner. "From the beginning I have regarded confiscation only as ancillary to emancipation." In his famous speech at Lancaster, Pennsylvania, on September 6, 1865, Thaddeus Stevens advocated confiscation of the property of large southern landholders and the grant of 40 acres to each adult freedman. But most Republicans shied away from the radicalism of wholesale confiscation. Prospects for the adoption of Stevens' proposal or anything like it appeared dim in 1865.[40]

One of the anticipated functions of the Freedmen's Bureau was resettlement of freedmen on abandoned and confiscated land. Johnson's pardon and amnesty program, however, threatened to leave the Bureau with very little land for this purpose. In August 1865, Johnson issued a series of executive orders to General Howard instructing him to restore all confiscated property to former rebel owners except that which had already been sold under court decrees. These orders affected nearly all lands under Bureau control. The status of property along the South Atlantic coast assigned to the freedmen by Sherman's Order no. 15 (see Chapter XI) became a burning issue during the winter of 1865-1866. More than 40,000 freedmen lived on 485,000 acres with the "possessory titles" granted by Sherman's Order. In October 1865, Johnson sent General Howard to the sea islands to persuade the freedmen to return their farms to the pardoned owners. Howard had no taste for his mission, but like a good soldier he

[40] Sumner to John Bright, Mar. 13, 1865, in Edward L. Pierce, *Memoir and Letters of Charles Sumner* (4 vols., Boston, 1877-94), IV, 229; Fawn M. Brodie, *Thaddeus Stevens: Scourge of the South* (New York, 1959), 231-33. See also *Commonwealth*, June 10, 17, 1865; *Independent*, June 22, 1865; *Liberator*, June 23, Aug. 11, 1865; *N.A.S. Standard*, May 26, 1866; *New York Tribune*, Apr. 11, Sept. 11, 12, 1865.

carried out his superior's orders. He urged the freedmen quietly to abandon their farms and go back to work for their former masters.[41]

Freedmen on the sea islands could hardly believe their ears. "To turn us off from the land that the Government has allowed us to occupy, is nothing less than returning us to involuntary servitude," said one of them. "They will make freedom a curse to us, for we have no home, no land, no oath, no vote, and consequently no country."[42] Some of the Negroes vowed to defend their farms by force if necessary. Abolitionists summoned all their eloquence to denounce the government's action. "This villainous effort to rob loyal men for the benefit of ruffianly rebels whose hands are red with the blood of Northern soldiers, can succeed only through a breach of faith on the part of our government such as would be without parallel in history," declared the *Commonwealth*. The *Right Way* asked: "Shall our own, and all coming ages, brand us for the treachery of sacrificing our faithful friends to our and their enemies? GOD IN HIS MERCY SAVE US FROM SUCH PERFIDY AND SUCH IDIOCY." General Rufus Saxton, commissioner of the Freedmen's Bureau in South Carolina, refused to carry out the order dispossessing the Negroes of their land, and Johnson removed Saxton from office on January 15, 1866. Even after Saxton's removal the Freedmen's Bureau moved slowly, hoping that Congress would enact legislation nullifying the president's orders.[43]

In the end most of the freedmen were dispossessed. But the Freedmen's Bureau bill passed over Johnson's veto in July 1866, contained a provision for the lease of 20 acres of government-owned land on the sea islands to each dispossessed freedman with a six-year option to buy at $1.50 per acre. At the same time Congress passed the Southern Homestead Act, extending the principle of the homestead law of 1862 to the public lands of Alabama, Arkansas, Florida, Louisiana, and Mississippi. The

[41] Bentley, *Freedmen's Bureau*, 87-98; Edwin D. Hoffman, "From Slavery to Self-Reliance," *Journal of Negro History*, XLI (January 1956), 20-24; *N.A.S. Standard*, Oct. 7, 1865.

[42] Quoted in *N.A.S. Standard*, Oct. 7, 1865.

[43] *Commonwealth*, Nov. 4, 1865; *Right Way*, Dec. 30, 1865; Bentley, *Freedmen's Bureau*, 98-101. See also *Liberator*, Nov. 17, Dec. 1, 15, 22, 1865; *Independent*, Dec. 7, 1865.

bill stipulated that until January 1, 1867, no one who had supported the Confederacy would be eligible for a homestead. This provision was intended to give the freedmen and Unionist whites first chance at the land. Abolitionists hoped for good results from the Southern Homestead Act, but their hopes were doomed to disappointment. Most of the lands opened for settlement were of inferior quality, and few freedmen had the necessary capital to buy tools and farm implements or to support themselves while they were trying to coax the first crop from the sandy soil. As a means of placing the freedmen on fertile land of their own, the Southern Homestead Act was a failure.[44]

Abolitionists soon discerned the inadequacy of the Homestead Act and renewed their demands for a program of confiscation and redistribution of southern plantations. An abolitionist traveler in the South reported in the fall of 1866 that the destitution of landless freedmen was appalling. He was alarmed by the nascent share-cropping and crop-lien systems that were taking root in the South. The Negroes "appear to have neither mind nor hope above their present condition, and will continue to work on from day to day, and from year to year, without more than enough to keep soul and body together," wrote the traveler. "When addressing their masters, they take off their hats, and speak in a hesitating, trembling manner, as though they were in the presence of a Superior Being." The freedman could never improve his status as long as he remained landless and penniless. "No other government ever ended a great rebellion before without confiscating the estates of principal rebels, and placing that mighty power, the landed interest, on its side."[45]

In the spring of 1867 abolitionists stepped up their agitation for confiscation, hoping to win public support for such a policy before the next session of Congress. The *Boston Commonwealth* published a series of militant editorials, some of them by Elizur

[44] Bentley, *Freedmen's Bureau*, 134, 144-46; Patrick W. Riddleberger, "George W. Julian: Abolitionist Land Reformer," *Agricultural History*, v (July 1955), 110; *Independent*, July 5, 1866; *Commonwealth*, July 14, 1866; *Right Way*, July 14, 1866; *N.A.S. Standard*, Dec. 18, 1869. See also Paul W. Gates, "Federal Land Policy in the South, 1866-1888," *Journal of Southern History*, vi (Aug. 1940), 304-10.

[45] Article by the Rev. John Savary in *N.A.S. Standard*, Nov. 3, 1866.

Wright, calling for expropriation. Wright chided "practical" Republican politicians who shrank from the radicalism of confiscation: "O ye mighty 'practical' men! don't you know—are you not sensible—does it not ever enter your noddles to suspect—that if you have thirty thousand disloyal nabobs to own more than half the land of the South, they, and nobody else, will *be* the South? That they laugh, now in their sleeves, and by-and-bye will laugh out of their sleeves, at your schoolma'ams and ballot-boxes? *They who own the real estate of a country control its vote*."[46]

At the annual meeting of the American Anti-Slavery Society in May 1867, Phillips introduced a resolution urging agrarian reform in the South as "an act of justice" to the Negro. Several speakers supported the resolution. Higginson said that confiscation "is an essential part of abolition. To give to these people only freedom, without the land, is to give them only the mockery of freedom which the English or the Irish peasant has." Without land the Negro voter would be at the mercy of the planter, who could use economic coercion to dictate his vote. "The time will come," said Higginson, "when the nation must recognize that even political power does not confer safety upon a race of landless men." Phillips' resolution was adopted almost unanimously by the Society.[47] The New England Anti-Slavery Society passed a similar resolution three weeks later. In the following months Phillips hammered away relentlessly at the confiscation theme. "What we want to give the negro is what the masses must have or they are practically serfs, the world over," he declared. Confiscation during the French Revolution crippled the aristocracy; confiscation uprooted Toryism in the American Revolution. "Land is the usual basis of government," said Phillips; "the class that hold it must, in the long run, give tone and character to the Administration. It is manifestly suicidal, therefore, to leave it in the hands of the hostile party."[48]

But abolitionists were fighting a losing battle on the confiscation front. A majority of the Republican party was opposed to the measure. The *New York Times* thought that "the colored race is likely to be injured, rather than aided, by this sycophantic and

[46] *Commonwealth*, Mar. 23, 1867. See also *ibid.*, Mar. 30, Apr. 6, 1867.
[47] *N.A.S. Standard*, May 18, 25, 1867.
[48] *ibid.*, June 8, 15, 1867.

extravagant crusade on its behalf." The *Times* urged friends of the freedmen to teach the lessons of labor, patience, frugality, and virtue to the Negro rather than demand special favors for him. Horace Greeley thought the agitation for confiscation was "either knavery or madness. People who want farms work for them. The only class we know that takes other people's property because they want it is largely represented in Sing Sing."[49] The Democratic gains in the 1867 elections put a virtual end to the drive for confiscation. The mood of radicalism which might have sustained confiscation in 1866 or 1867 had passed away. There was no longer any chance (if indeed there ever had been) that Congress would pass a confiscation bill or any other wholesale measure to provide farms for the freedmen.

In 1869 abolitionists set forth a new plan to obtain land for the freedmen. Aaron M. Powell, editor of the *Anti-Slavery Standard*, drew up a petition urging Congress to create a federal land commission, to be composed of "well-known, disinterested friends of the freed people." The commission would be capitalized at $2,000,000 by the U.S. Treasury and empowered to buy up large tracts of available southern land for resale in small lots to the freedmen at low cost and on easy terms. The commission would also be authorized to make loans to the freedmen for transportation, tools, implements, building materials, and seed. Abolitionists circulated the petition widely in 1869-1870, obtaining thousands of signatures from southern freedmen as well as their northern sympathizers. A Tennessee congressman introduced a bill to create such a land commission, but it died in committee, the last monument to Congress's failure to place the freedmen in a position of economic viability.[50]

Abolitionists backed several private schemes to settle the freedmen on farms of their own. In 1865 a group of Boston and New York capitalists incorporated the "American Land Company and Agency," with Governor John Andrew as president. George L. Stearns was one of the largest stockholders in this company, whose purpose was to channel northern investment into the South to help rebuild the section's economy and settle as many freedmen as possible on land of their own. Andrew and Stearns rea-

---

[49] *New York Times*, June 1, Oct. 26, 1867; *New York Tribune*, June 20, 1867.
[50] *N.A.S. Standard*, Dec. 18, 25, 1869, Jan. 29, Feb. 5, 12, 26, Mar. 12, 1870.

soned that the war had left southern planters poor in everything except land. They planned to buy part of this land in order to provide the planters with enough capital to farm the remainder. The company could then resell some of its purchased property to the freedmen. Things went badly from the beginning, however. The company invested heavily in Tennessee cotton plantations, but crop failures in 1866 ate up most of the capital. Stearns' death in the spring of 1867 brought the enterprise to bankruptcy and failure.[51]

Not all of the private efforts to provide freedmen with land were failures. In 1865 John G. Fee, a Kentucky-born abolitionist and cofounder of Berea College, purchased 130 acres in central Kentucky and resold the land in small tracts to freedmen, who established a village on the property. In 1891 there were 42 families living in this village. Fee urged the American Missionary Association to go into the business of selling land to the freedmen. In 1868 the A.M.A. began purchasing plantations for resale to Negroes. On each tract of land the A.M.A. established a church and school, and several small agricultural villages grew up in the South around these A.M.A. centers. The A.F.U.C. also had a small fund for the purchase and resale of farms to the freedmen. In 1869 a group of Boston abolitionists and philanthropists purchased a plantation in Georgia and started a "Southern Industrial School and Labor Enterprise." William and Ellen Craft, a couple who had escaped from slavery before the war, went to Georgia to manage the enterprise. They were accompanied by Yankee farmers who taught the freedmen the latest methods of planting, seeding, plowing, and so on. The freedmen attended the vocational and agricultural school part of the day and worked in the fields the rest of the time. They were encouraged to save their wages to buy land for themselves. The Ku Klux Klan burned the crop and buildings of the plantation in 1871, but the Crafts rebuilt the school and carried on in Georgia until 1878, when they sold the plantation in small tracts to the freedmen and returned to Boston.[52]

---

[51] Henry G. Pearson, *The Life of John A. Andrew* (2 vols., Boston, 1904), II, 267-69; Frank P. Stearns, *The Life and Public Services of George Luther Stearns* (Phila., 1907), 352.

[52] John G. Fee, *Autobiography* (Chicago, 1891), 182-83; Drake, "American Missionary Association," 115-19; McKim to O. O. Howard, Nov. 27, 1866, Howard to McKim, Dec. 1, 1866, McKim Papers, Cornell; *N.A.S. Standard*, Nov. 6,

One of the most ambitious abolitionist efforts to secure land for the freedmen by private investment was a plan developed by Charles Stearns, an old-line Garrisonian from Springfield, Massachusetts. In 1854 Stearns had gone to Kansas to fight for freedom, and in 1860 he drifted west to Colorado Territory. He went to Georgia in May 1866, and purchased a 1,500-acre plantation near Augusta. He hoped to run the plantation for a few years on the cooperative principle and then sell it in small tracts to the freedmen who had worked for him.[53]

Stearns was filled with enthusiasm for his project when he first came South. He established night and Sunday schools to teach his laborers to read and write. Southern neighbors told him that he could never "manage the niggers" with kindness, but would be compelled to use force and punishment if he wanted to get any work out of them. Stearns hoped to prove his neighbors wrong. He substituted kindness, incentive bonuses, and moral suasion for insults and punishment. In a summary of his experiences written several lears later, Stearns admitted that the practical realities of the situation had soon modified his enthusiasm. The freedmen were inefficient workers and destroyed tools and implements by their carelessness. Stearns almost succumbed to disillusionment and despair several times. But he always rallied himself with the thought that slavery was a poor school for efficiency, honesty, or skill, and returned to work with renewed dedication. He later evaluated his experiment as a success. After six years the Negroes on his plantation were better educated, more honest, and more industrious than when he first came.[54]

Inability to pay off the mortgage on his plantation forced Stearns to postpone his plans to sell the land to his employees. In 1869 his creditors threatened to foreclose, and Stearns hurried to Boston to raise $6,000 to pay the mortgage. Samuel Sewall and Wendell Phillips listened sympathetically to Stearns' proposition. Sewall gave him a $1,000 loan, and Phillips and Sewall

---

20, 1869; L. M. Child to Elisa Scudder, Feb. 6, 1870, Child to Lucy Osgood, Feb. 14, 1870, Child Papers, Cornell; *Commonwealth*, Aug. 16, 1873; Garrison to Fanny Garrison Villard, June 14, 1878, Garrison Papers, BPL.

[53] Charles Stearns to Garrison, Jan. 21, 1863, in *Liberator*, Mar. 20, 1863; Stearns to Garrison, Mar. 27, 1865, in *Liberator*, Apr. 21, 1865; Charles Stearns, *The Black Man of the South, and the Rebels* (New York, 1872), 20-39.

[54] *ibid.*, 28, 49-54, 59-71, 115-16, 164, and passim.

helped him raise the remaining $5,000. He returned to Georgia and inaugurated his plan to sell the plantation in 25-acre lots to the Negroes. Only 20 freedmen were able to buy during the first year, and some of them soon fell behind on their payments. By the end of 1870 Stearns was in debt again and about ready to give up in despair. "I am certain I can never cultivate a farm successfully with the blacks as laborers," he wrote in his diary. "Nothing can be done without incessant and minute supervision of them, such as I am not able to give." He almost sold the plantation to one of his white neighbors, but his mother, who had come South to teach the freedmen, convinced him that to do so would be a breach of faith with the Negroes he had worked so hard to help. Stearns heeded her pleas. He stayed on for another year and began writing a book about his experiences in an effort to promote northern interest in the needs of the freedmen.[55]

In 1872 Stearns brought a group of 50 Massachusetts farmers and missionaries to his plantation to establish an agricultural and industrial colony. The Yankee farmers soon transformed the establishment into a model of efficiency and neatness. Most of the Negroes stayed on the plantation and tried to learn better methods of farming from the Yankees. Stearns returned to Boston to finish his book and to set on foot a project for northern purchase and resale of southern plantations to freedmen. In 1873 he organized a "Laborers' Homestead and Southern Emigration Society" with a planned capitalization of $50,000. Samuel Gridley Howe served as president, and Stearns, Phillips, and James Buffum (an abolitionist) acted as a three-man board of trustees. The Society purchased some property in Virginia to start their experiment. Stearns sent out hundreds of circulars urging capitalists to invest in his Society. Lands purchased by the trustees would be resold in 25-acre tracts on easy terms to freedmen and northern settlers. The Society planned also to make loans to the purchasers to enable them to buy tools, seed, and implements. Stearns had grandiose plans for his Society. He urged Congress to lend it $1,000,000 per year for ten years. Congress took no note of his appeal, however, and the panic of 1873 soon dried up Stearns'

[55] Stearns to Gerrit Smith, June 26, 1869, Smith Papers, su; *Commonwealth*, July 24, 1869; *N.A.S. Standard*, Sept. 25, Nov. 20, 1869; Stearns, *The Black Man of the South*, 154-55, 170, 258-75, 278-319; quotation from *ibid.*, p. 279.

meager sources of private capital. Apart from the Georgia plantation and the property in Virginia he had little to show for his efforts. He had established one agricultural colony and sold land to several dozen freedmen. It was a rather small ending to an ambitious beginning.[56]

In 1880 Frederick Douglass attributed the failure of Reconstruction to the refusal of Congress to provide the freedmen with an opportunity to obtain good land of their own. "Could the nation have been induced to listen to those stalwart Republicans, Thaddeus Stevens and Charles Sumner, some of the evils which we now suffer would have been averted," declared Douglass. "The negro would not today be on his knees, as he is, supplicating the old master class to give him leave to toil. . . . He would not now be swindled out of his hard earnings by money orders for wages with no money in them."[57] Many abolitionists still alive in 1880 would have agreed with Douglass. They had done their best to call attention to the necessity of land for the freedmen, but the nation was not sympathetic enough toward the plight of the Negro to provide any adequate means by which he could obtain land. As a result the Negroes remained economically a subordinate class, dependent upon white landowners or employers for their livelihood. The South was not "reconstructed" economically, and consequently the other measures of reconstruction rested upon an unstable foundation.

[56] *ibid.*, 319-25, 512-42; Stearns to Gerrit Smith, Feb. 17, 1873, Feb. 4, 11, 1874, Smith Papers, su; *Commonwealth*, June 27, Sept. 19, 1874; Stearns to Garrison, Dec. 12, 1876, Garrison Papers, bpl.

[57] Speech of Douglass at Elmira, New York, Aug. 1, 1880, copy in Douglass Papers, Anacostia.

XVIII ✦ THE CLIMAX OF THE CRU-
SADE: THE FIFTEENTH
AMENDMENT

THE presidential election of 1868 was crucial for the cause of Negro suffrage: a Republican victory would insure continuation of the congressional reconstruction program; a Democratic triumph would probably foreshadow the overthrow of radical reconstruction and the readmission of southern states without Negro suffrage. It was almost inevitable that General Grant, the nation's foremost military hero, would be the leading contender for the presidency. Both the Republicans and the Democrats realized that Grant would probably be the next president, and from 1865 to 1868 they jockeyed to win his political affections.

As early as 1866 Wendell Phillips began trying to stop the Republican swing toward Grant. Grant's Democratic affiliations before the war, his conservative report on southern conditions in 1865, and his accompaniment of President Johnson on the famous Swing Around the Circle campaign in 1866 caused radicals to distrust him. As general of the army, Grant was gravitating toward a radical concept of reconstruction in 1866-1867, but his public silence left most observers uncertain of his views on politics. During his lecture tour of 1866-67 Phillips repeatedly disparaged Grant as a political leader. In these days of crisis, said Phillips, the country could not afford an inarticulate president who probably lacked the brains to form his own political opinions. But Phillips' unfavorable references to Grant were poorly received by his audiences—an indication of the widespread popular support for the taciturn general.[1]

Most abolitionists in 1867 concurred with Phillips' appraisal of Grant. Many of them, like Phillips, had no particular alternative candidate in mind. But one group of radicals, led by Tilton and Greeley, was definitely backing Chase for the Republican nomination. The next president "ought to be a man with whom the

---

[1] *N.A.S. Standard*, Nov. 3, 1866, May 18, 25, June 15, 1867.

love of Liberty has been a life-long passion; with whom Political
Equality is a cherished idea," declared Tilton. "He ought to be
a man whose life has been identified with the great controversy of
principles which ended in the overthrow of American Slavery; not
a man who has been indifferent all his life long to the greatest
moral movement of modern times." The *Independent* and the
New York Tribune published frequent editorials favoring Chase
in 1867.[2]

But political availability, not principle, was uppermost in the
minds of most Republican leaders. By the summer of 1867 it was
clear that Grant would be the Republican nominee unless some
unforeseen event intervened. Radical leaders tried to quiet abolitionist fears of Grant's conservatism. "It looks now as if Gen.
Grant would inevitably be the next President," Oliver Johnson
informed Garrison in July 1867. "Such being the fact I am
happy in being assured by Senator Wilson and others that he is
in thorough sympathy with Congress in all that pertains to reconstruction and that he loathes and hates the whole Copperhead
party."[3] But disturbing signs continued to disquiet the abolitionists. When Grant accepted the office of secretary of war *ad interim* after Johnson's ouster of Stanton in August 1867, the
shock was felt all through the Republican party. Although Grant
had advised against the suspension of Stanton and had protested
the removal of General Sheridan from command of the South-
western military district, many radicals believed that by accepting office under Johnson, Grant had made himself a tool of the
president's attempt to overturn congressional reconstruction.
"If Grant is a Republican, by what rule of party fidelity does
he accept the office out of which Stanton has been turned simply
for being a Republican?" asked Phillips. "To-day Grant is the
staff which holds up the traitor President. Without him Johnson
could neither stand nor walk."[4]

But Grant was still the Republican party's best hope to win
the presidency. Republican leaders pointed out (truthfully) that
Grant continued to enforce congressional reconstruction and that

[2] *Independent*, May 30, July 11, Oct. 24, 1867; *New York Tribune*, Apr. 12,
15, Nov. 7, 13, 22, Dec. 30, 1867. Quotation from *Independent*, May 30, 1867.
[3] Johnson to Garrison, July 29, 1867, Garrison Papers, BPL.
[4] *Independent*, Aug. 15, 29, Sept. 5, 1867; *N.A.S. Standard*, Aug. 3, 24, Sept.
7, 1867. Quotation from *ibid.*, Aug. 24, 1867.

his presence in the War Office probably prevented Johnson from further obstructionism. The *New York Tribune* and *Independent* were still backing Chase, and it was rumored that such radical leaders as Sumner and Julian were opposed to Grant's nomination. But a majority of the Republican party remained pledged to the general.[5]

Wendell Phillips, Anna Dickinson, and other abolitionists continued to criticize Grant during the winter of 1867-1868. He was "the great American riddle!" said Phillips. "Out of twenty millions of people who have watched him for six years, there is not one who knows his opinions."[6] But most abolitionists by this time realized that the general's nomination was inevitable. Grant's prompt relinquishment of the War Office when the Senate refused to concur in Stanton's suspension and the subsequent controversy between Johnson and Grant raised the latter's prestige in the eyes of many radicals. Chase's flirtation with the Democrats and his handling of Johnson's impeachment trial caused a collapse of the faltering Chase movement. Grant was nominated unanimously at the Republican convention in Chicago on May 21.[7]

Abolitionists hoped for endorsement by the Republican platform of a constitutional amendment to enact Negro suffrage. As early as December 1867, the Boston correspondent of the *New York Tribune* reported that Republicans in New England were determined "to see that the General shall be put upon a sound Republican platform. . . . Wendell Phillips, who has as great an influence on political affairs as any man can have who is outside of political organizations, is doing something by lectures to stimulate this feeling." Tilton wrote in April 1868, "Our demand, in case of General Grant's nomination, is, that as he is not popularly known to hold any political opinions, the platform on which he is to stand shall be unequivocally for Impartial Suffrage, North and South."[8]

[5] *Commonwealth*, Aug. 31, Sept. 7, Nov. 16, 1867; *Independent*, Oct. 24, 1867; *New York Tribune*, Nov. 7, 13, 22, 1867; Edward L. Pierce, *Memoir and Letters of Charles Sumner* (4 vols., Boston, 1877-94), IV, 358; George Julian, *Political Recollections* (Chicago, 1884), 319.

[6] *Commonwealth*, Nov. 9, 1867. See also *N.A.S. Standard*, Jan. 18, Feb. 1, 15, 29, 1868; *Independent*, Jan. 2, 16, 1868.

[7] *Commonwealth*, Feb. 1, 8, 15, 1868; *Independent*, Mar. 12, 19, Apr. 16, May 28, 1868; *N.A.S. Standard*, Mar. 21, 1868.

[8] *New York Tribune*, quoted in *N.A.S. Standard*, Dec. 7, 1867; *Independent*, Apr. 9, 1868. See also *N.A.S. Standard*, Jan. 25, Feb. 1, 1868.

In the spring of 1868, however, the voters of Michigan turned down a new constitution that contained Negro suffrage. At the same time the Democrats were victorious in Connecticut for the second straight year. Moderate Republicans interpreted these defeats as a popular repudiation of Negro suffrage in the North. "Discreditable as the fact may be, it is pretty evident that the enfranchisement of the colored race in the Northern States will have to wait," stated the *Springfield Republican*. "The more immediate interests of reconstruction might be jeopardized by forcing the issue at this juncture." The *New York Times* predicted that moderate Republicans would defeat radical attempts to insert a national Negro suffrage plank into the Republican platform. "Even Wendell Phillips will stand an excellent chance of being unceremoniously thrown overboard," said the *Times*, "when the Convention undertakes to construct a platform for States, not one of which has committed itself to the negro suffrage principle."[9]

Despite these signs of conservative opposition, radicals and abolitionists mounted an all-out drive for Republican commitment to national Negro suffrage. "No reconstruction at the South will be safe and enduring which does not give the negro a national guarantee that he shall not be deprived of the ballot under the shield of 'State Sovereignty,'" declared the *Anti-Slavery Standard*. "Nor should the invidious distinctions now made against the blacks in the North be long allowed to continue." Thomas Wentworth Higginson chided northerners for their hypocritical willingness "that the negro should be a man at the South, to spite the white man, but not . . . that he should be a man at the North, when it offends their prejudices." Tilton considered it "a mockery of justice to ordain negro suffrage in one-half the states and to forbid it in the other." The Republicans would not deserve to win if they refused justice to the northern Negro. "To dodge the issue, or to cover it out of sight under some meaningless generality, would be moral depravity and political folly."[10]

[9] *Springfield Republican*, quoted in *The Revolution*, Apr. 23, 1868; *New York Times*, quoted in *N.A.S. Standard*, Apr. 25, 1868.
[10] *N.A.S. Standard*, Apr. 18, 1868; Higginson quoted in *ibid.*, May 30, 1868; *Independent*, May 14, 1868.

Conservatism triumphed at Chicago in spite of the radicals' best efforts. The Republican platform proclaimed that Negro suffrage in the South "was demanded by every consideration of public safety, of gratitude, and of justice," while "the question of suffrage in all the loyal States properly belongs to the people of those States." Sumner considered this suffrage plank "foolish & contemptible. The Democrats will have a great opportunity in exposing its Janus-faced character." The *Anti-Slavery Standard* denounced the failure of the platform to endorse national Negro suffrage as a "criminal blunder," and the New England Anti-Slavery Society declared it "a practical surrender of the whole question." But Senator Henry Wilson told Aaron Powell, editor of the *Anti-Slavery Standard*, that the weak suffrage plank was necessary if the Republicans were to carry doubtful northern states. Wilson assured Powell that once the election was over, Congress would adopt a Fifteenth Amendment. Theodore Tilton denounced the "mean-spirited" suffrage resolution. But he did not despair. He recalled that in 1860 the Republican party had promised not to interfere with slavery in the states, but four years later the party pledged itself to universal emancipation. "In like manner," said Tilton, "the Republican platform of 1868 may hint or imply that the Federal Government has no right to interfere with suffrage in the Northern States," but after the election this plank would "fall to pieces by its own rottenness."[11]

In June 1868, Congress readmitted seven southern states to the Union upon the "fundamental condition" that their constitutional provisions for equal suffrage would never be repealed. Most abolitionists opposed readmission of the former Confederate states at this time. The New England Anti-Slavery Society predicted that the "fundamental condition" would prove unenforceable, and urged the delay of readmission until a Fifteenth Amendment guaranteeing equal suffrage and public schools in every state had been ratified. The *Anti-Slavery Standard* considered readmission "premature." "The conditions of self-government," said the *Standard*, "do not yet exist at the South. To at once readmit

[11] *New York Tribune*, May 22, 1868, published the Republican platform; Sumner to Frank Bird, May 28, 1868, Bird Papers, HU; *N.A.S. Standard*, May 30, 1868; resolution of the New England Anti-Slavery Society published in *ibid.*, June 6, 1868; Henry Wilson's statement cited in *ibid.*, June 13, 1868; *Independent*, May 28, June 18, 1868.

the reconstructed States and withdraw direct Federal control, is to expose the South unnecessarily to renewed strife, violence and bloodshed." Phillips charged that the Republicans were restoring the southern states for the sole purpose of gaining their votes in the presidential election. "No one claims that they are ready or fit for places in Congress," declared Phillips. "But the Grant party needs them. We sink principle and risk the negro in order to elect Mr. Grant."[12]

Phillips continued to hammer away at the Republicans during the summer of 1868 until it appeared to some observers that he was absolutely opposed to Grant's election. "Its faults are legion," said Phillips of the Republican party. "Its defects glaring. It has never been loyal to a single principle." Grant was wholly inadequate. "Of the half dozen catch-words that the Nation has extorted from his lips, not one has any relation to Liberty. The mottoes he has lent to politics, or history, are such as a bull-dog might have growled forth."[13] But in *Standard* editorials of August 29 and September 26 Phillips made it clear that he desired Republican victory. He described the Republican party as "shuffling, evasive, unprincipled, corrupt, cowardly and mean, almost beyond the power of words to describe. Still a vote for Grant means the negro's suffrage recognized; a vote for Seymour [the Democratic candidate] means the negro disfranchised and another war." Bad as the Republican party was, it contained the only radical elements in the country and gave promise of future improvement. Some of Phillips' more radical followers criticized his support of the "shuffling, evasive, corrupt" Republican party. But the Republican press hailed Phillips' endorsement, and most abolitionists pitched in to help elect Grant.[14]

Phillips' aversion to the Democrats was not unfounded. That party nominated Horatio Seymour and Frank Blair on a platform that denounced the Reconstruction Acts as "usurpations, and unconstitutional, revolutionary, and void," and called for the readmission of southern states without Negro suffrage. The

[12] *U.S. Statutes at Large*, xv, 72-74; *N.A.S. Standard*, May 23, June 13, June 20, 1868.
[13] *N.A.S. Standard*, Aug. 29, Sept. 26, 1868.
[14] *Revolution*, Sept. 10, Oct. 8, 1868; S. B. Anthony to Anna Dickinson, Oct. 27, 1868, Dickinson Papers, LC; *Commonwealth*, Oct. 3, 1868; *Boston Advertiser*, Oct. 28, 1868.

Democrats pitched their campaign on a key of racism and violence. Frank Blair, the party's vice-presidential candidate, declared that "there is but one way to restore the Government and the Constitution, and that is for the President-elect to declare these acts null and void, compel the army to undo its usurpations at the South, disperse the carpet-bag State Governments, [and] allow the White people to reorganize their own governments."[15] Blair repeatedly referred to Negroes as "semi-barbarous blacks," "idle vagabonds," and "degraded men." One of Seymour's supporters, Brick Pomeroy of the *La Crosse Democrat*, declared that if the Democrats received a majority of *white* votes in the election they should "march to Washington . . . and take their seats, and reinaugurate the white men's government, in spite of man or devils. . . . If this brings bloodshed, then let blood flow!"[16]

One southern white man entered the campaign proclaiming his belief that "the noble Gothic race is the one that should inhabit this continent, and the only one. It is the kind of beings that must rule America; and not only America, but the whole earth."[17] Southern whites backed their words with action. The Ku Klux Klan and similar organizations stepped up their activities during the campaign. The Republican and abolitionist press publicized (and probably exaggerated) southern violence against the freedmen as examples of what the Negro's "best friends" would do if the Democrats won the election. Garrison in particular waved the bloody shirt. The purpose of the Democratic party, he wrote, was "to disfranchise the entire colored population and give them over to the tender mercies of their former owners, . . . who are never so jubilant as when burning negroes alive by a slow fire." In September the conservative majority of the Georgia legislature expelled its 32 Negro members and replaced them with whites, many of whom could not even qualify for office under the terms of the Fourteenth Amendment. Here was a concrete example, said abolitionists, of what would happen all over the South if the Democrats won in November.[18]

[15] *New York Tribune*, July 10, 1868; *Independent*, July 16, 1868.

[16] *La Crosse Democrat*, quoted in *N.A.S. Standard*, Mar. 7, 1868. See also *N.A.S. Standard*, July 11, 18, 25, Aug. 1, 29, 1868.

[17] *Norfolk Journal*, quoted in *N.A.S. Standard*, Nov. 7, 1868.

[18] Statement by Garrison published in *Independent*, Aug. 13, 1868. Garrison also wrote articles for *ibid.*, Oct. 1, 15, 22, 29, 1868. For a discussion of the

Abolitionists welcomed Grant's election as a triumph of liberty and equal rights. But they did not rest content with electoral victory. In the winter of 1868-1869 radicals opened an intensive drive for a constitutional amendment to enact Negro suffrage nationally. The adoption of Negro suffrage by substantial majorities in Iowa and Minnesota in November 1868, gave an important fillip to the movement for a Fifteenth Amendment. Gilbert Haven expressed the prevailing feeling among abolitionists when he declared that the North could no longer deny justice to its own colored citizens while compelling the South to maintain equal rights. "It is the worst sore in the Southern heart to-day that they are required to receive what the North will not give itself," said Haven. "We have no moral right to impose an obligation on one part of the land which the rest will not accept. We can have no peace till this right is made national."[19]

Prominent Republican newspapers backed the drive for a Fifteenth Amendment. Several equal suffrage amendments were introduced in both Houses when Congress met in December 1868. These amendments fell into three general categories. The first type would have simply prohibited the states from denying the ballot on grounds of race, color, or previous condition. The second type of amendment would also have forbidden states to impose literacy, property, or nativity qualifications upon suffrage. The third class of amendment would have nationalized suffrage by giving the federal government complete control over voting rights in every state.[20]

Abolitionists favored, at least in theory, a broad amendment that would prohibit the imposition of literacy or property as well as racial qualifications upon the franchise. Richard Hinton declared that the form of amendment that forbade only racial disfranchisement "will not prevent any State adopting a property qualification, one of education, or any similar dodge."[21] But on

---

expulsion of Negro members from the Georgia legislature, see C. Mildred Thompson, *Reconstruction in Georgia* (New York, 1915), 211-16.

[19] *Zion's Herald*, Dec. 10, 1868. See also *Independent*, Nov. 5, 12, 19, 1868; *N.A.S. Standard*, Nov. 14, 21, Dec. 12, 1868.

[20] John M. Mathews, *Legislative and Judicial History of the Fifteenth Amendment* (Baltimore, 1909), 21-32.

[21] *N.A.S. Standard*, Dec. 12, 1868. See also *ibid.*, Nov. 21, 1868, Jan. 23, Feb. 6, 1869.

January 30, 1869, the House passed an amendment stipulating that "the right of any citizen of the United States to vote shall not be denied or abridged by the United States or any State by reason of race, color, or previous condition of servitude." The *Anti-Slavery Standard* protested that there was nothing in this amendment to prevent "future State application of unequal tests of education or property. Landless and almost without schools, [the freedmen] are at a great disadvantage, and there will be no stone left unturned by which to compass their political subjugation by the old ruling white class." Tilton also demanded protection of the freedmen against disfranchisement by literacy or property qualifications. Under the House-passed amendment, he wrote, "the Southern States may invent a dozen cunning schemes to defraud the negro of his franchise."[22]

Several senators agreed with Tilton, and on February 9 the Senate passed an amendment forbidding the denial of suffrage on grounds of "race, color, nativity, property, education, or creed." A storm of protest immediately arose from many Republicans who favored Negro suffrage. They argued that such a comprehensive amendment could never be ratified by the requisite number of states. Massachusetts and Connecticut required a literacy test, Rhode Island imposed a property qualification upon naturalized citizens, and the "nativity" provision would almost certainly run afoul of the anti-Chinese sentiment in California, Oregon, and Nevada. The *Boston Commonwealth* preferred "as an abstract proposition" the Senate version "because it makes suffrage less restricted than might possibly result from the House's limitation." But as a practical matter the *Commonwealth* favored the House amendment, for it seemed certain that the Senate version could not be ratified. The House-passed amendment was sufficient for present purposes, said the *Commonwealth*, "and if any one State, upon the adoption of the amendment, shall make invidious and unjust discriminations against any class of citizens, both Congress by appropriate legislation, and the Supreme Court by decisions in the spirit of the amendment, will remedy the wrong."[23]

22 *Cong. Globe*, 40 Cong., 3 Sess., 286, 742-45; *N.A.S. Standard*, Feb. 6, 1869; *Independent*, Feb. 11, 1869.

23 *Cong. Globe*, 40 Cong., 3 Sess., 1,044; Mathews, *Fifteenth Amendment*, 33-35; *Commonwealth*, Feb. 6, 13, 20, 1869.

The House refused to concur in the Senate amendment, and a deadlock ensued between the two Houses that threatened to prevent passage of any amendment at all before Congress adjourned on March 4. At this critical juncture Wendell Phillips published an important editorial in the *Anti-Slavery Standard*. In a statement that must have surprised nearly every reader, Phillips chastised the Senate for being too radical. The Fifteenth Amendment was confronted by "an emergency which calls for the most delicate handling," he wrote. The amendment passed by the House covered "all the ground that the people are ready to occupy." The Senate's attempt to prohibit educational, property, and nativity qualifications, said Phillips, "is utter lack of common sense, . . . a total forgetfulness of the commonest political prudence." Phillips urged Senate concurrence in the House amendment. "For the first time in our lives we beseech them to be a little more *politicians*—and a little less reformers." The editor of the *New York Times* blinked his eyes in amazement at Phillips' editorial. "The event is notable," said the *Times*. "That must have been rashness which elicits from the champion of all innovations a protest against its folly."[24]

Phillips' statement helped break the congressional deadlock and pave the way for Senate concurrence in the House version of the amendment. Congressman George Boutwell of Massachusetts, leader of the House forces supporting a Fifteenth Amendment, wrote Phillips a letter thanking him for his timely editorial. "That article saved the amendment," said Boutwell. "Its influence was immediate and potential. Men thought that if you, the extremest radical, could accept the House proposition they might safely do the same." Boutwell later told friends that without Phillips' editorial "the Fifteenth Amendment to the Constitution would have been lost in the Senate." Boutwell wrote in his memoirs that Phillips' "name and opinion settled the controversy."[25] It was one of the ironies of Reconstruction that the nation's greatest radical and equalitarian was partly responsible for adoption of a Fifteenth Amendment whose loopholes later allowed southern

24 *N.A.S. Standard*, Feb. 20, 1869; *New York Times*, Feb. 19, 1869.
25 Boutwell to Phillips, Mar. 13, 1870, printed in George S. Boutwell, *Reminiscences of Sixty Years in Public Affairs* (2 vols., New York, 1902), II, 48-50; *Commonwealth*, Apr. 30, 1870; Oliver Johnson, *William Lloyd Garrison and His Times* (2nd ed., Boston, 1885), 41; Boutwell, *Reminiscences*, II, 46.

states to disfranchise their Negroes. But Phillips and Boutwell were probably right in 1869. The Senate version could not have been ratified, and if Congress had not passed the simpler House amendment at that time there may not have been another opportunity for a Negro suffrage amendment for several decades. Phillips' editorial, therefore, was instrumental in creating a constitutional framework for Negro suffrage that might not have otherwise existed.

"What shall be said at the annual meeting of the American An[ti]-Slavery Society?" asked Frederick Douglass in April 1869. "There really seems not much to be said. Fifteenth amendment is on its [way to] passage, and is in a fair way to become a part of the organic law of the land." Many other people shared this belief that the antislavery movement no longer had any causes to agitate. Phillips and Tilton publicly declared that ratification of the Fifteenth Amendment would take the Negro question out of politics. Most abolitionists seemed to agree with this view, for the American Anti-Slavery Society resolved at its annual convention in May 1869, that the Fifteenth Amendment was "the capstone and completion of our movement; the fulfillment of our pledge to the Negro race; since it secures to them equal political rights with the white race, or, if any single right be still doubtful, places them in such circumstances that they can easily achieve it."[26]

But several delegates cautioned that the work of the abolitionists was not yet finished. Henry Wilson told the assembled crusaders that their mission would not be accomplished until the Negro was equal in fact as well as law. The convention resolved that social discrimination against Negroes "fully justifies the continued and earnest remonstrance of this Society." In one of his speeches to the meeting Phillips stated that "even with the ratification of the Fifteenth Amendment, our work is not done." As an organization the antislavery society could dissolve, but as individuals abolitionists must continue to work against segregation, discrimination, and inequality with every means at their command. There was a "continued obligation resting upon Abolitionists,

[26] Frederick Douglass to Tilton, Apr. 24, 1869, autograph MS, PML; *N.A.S. Standard*, Mar. 27, 1869; *Independent*, Apr. 8, 1869; resolution of the American Anti-Slavery Society published in *N.A.S. Standard*, May 15, 1869.

individually, never to cease their individual and collateral work, in all the various forms in which a man can influence his times, to blot out the idea of race in the minds of the American people," said Phillips. "In regard to those great social forces which still continue in their influence to shape the future, our work is not done; we probably never shall live to see it done."[27]

By the end of 1869 the Fifteenth Amendment, capstone of the abolitionist crusade, appeared certain of ratification. Even in their rejoicing, however, abolitionists once again warned each other that they must not let down their guard. Despite the advances made since 1861, said John Sargent, the Negro did not yet enjoy "the fulness of those social rights, relations, and privileges . . . without which all this pretence of his freedom is but an idle sham and a tantalizing mockery." Lydia Maria Child said, "The passage of the Fifteenth Amendment will give a legal finish to the Anti-Slavery work," but the Amendment might "yet be so evaded, by some contrivance, that the colored population will in reality have no civil rights allowed them."[28] Wendell Phillips promised that dissolution of the antislavery societies would not be a signal for abolitionists to retire from their life's work. On the contrary, said Phillips, the *Anti-Slavery Standard* would be continued under the title *The Standard*. It would crusade for labor reform, women's rights, temperance, and racial equality. Aaron Powell called for renewed abolitionist dedication to equal social and economic rights for all men. Powell promised that "if not in the name of the *Anti-Slavery* Societies, then under some other —if not in the ANTI-SLAVERY STANDARD, then in a journal to be known simply as THE STANDARD, we shall press our demand earnestly and conscientiously until FREEDOM shall mean as much for the colored, as for the white people of America."[29]

The Fifteenth Amendment became part of the Constitution on March 30, 1870. This event touched off a general chorus of praise and tribute to the old abolitionists, especially Phillips. A correspondent of the *Troy* (New York) *Whig* wrote that "all the old epithets that used to defile [the abolitionists'] reputation have

---

[27] *N.A.S. Standard*, May 15, 22, 29, June 5, 1869.

[28] Sargent quoted in *N.A.S. Standard*, Nov. 27, 1869; Child quoted in *ibid.*, Dec. 25, 1869.

[29] *ibid.*, Feb. 5, 12, Mar. 12, 1870; Powell's statement quoted from *ibid.*, Feb. 5, 1870.

turned into trophies of their march, and are worn as wreaths of laurel. Yes, to have been an abolitionist is simply an honor now." Speaking for his race, Frederick Douglass praised Phillips as the foremost architect of the Fifteenth Amendment. "None have been more vigilant, clear-sighted, earnest, true and eloquent. Without office, without party, only a handful at his back, he has done more to lead and mould public opinion in favor of equal suffrage than any man I know of." And in a private letter Senator Henry Wilson declared: "More than to any other, more than to all others, the colored people owe it that they were not cheated out of their citizenship after emancipation, to Wendell Phillips."[30]

The executive committee of the American Anti-Slavery Society met and decided to dissolve the organization. The Society's constitution pledged its members to work for equal civil and political rights for Negroes. These rights had been attained, and the Society no longer had a formal reason for existence. Abolitionists gathered in New York on April 9, 1870, to disband their societies and commemorate the final victory of their organized crusade. The veteran agitators met in a festive mood. Congratulatory letters from dozens of politicians, journalists, and fellow reformers were read to the assemblage. Several abolitionists urged that the Society remain in existence to combat race prejudice, help the freedmen obtain land of their own, and agitate for strict enforcement of equal rights in the South. But Phillips, Douglass, and others maintained that these activities were outside the formal sphere of the Society. Abolitionists should remain vigilant, however, and carry on individually or in new organizations their work for the Negro. "Our long crusade for him is not therefore really and fully ended," said Phillips. "We may break up our ranks, but we may not yet dismiss our care nor lessen our interest. While this generation lasts it is probable the negro will need the special sympathy of his friends. The victim of cruel prejudice, of long disfranchisement, of accumulated wrongs, . . . he must long struggle under heavy disadvantages."[31]

[30] *Troy Whig*, quoted in *Commonwealth*, Apr. 30, 1870; *New National Era*, May 5, 1870; Wilson to Sumner, Apr. 19, 1870, quoted in Carlos Martyn, *Wendell Phillips: The Agitator* (New York, 1890), 374.
[31] *N.A.S. Standard*, Apr. 16, 1870.

On the day after the commemorative meeting, Aaron Powell and several other abolitionists organized the "National Reform League" as a successor of the American Anti-Slavery Society. The purpose of the League was to achieve desegregation of schools and public accommodations in the North, agitate for enforcement of equal rights in the South, and in general to watch over the welfare of the Negro.[32] Never very strong, the Reform League faded out of existence by 1872. For all practical purposes the *organizational* history of American abolitionism came to an end in 1870. As individuals most abolitionists remained active and vigilant in the cause of the Negro for the rest of their lives. But the militant antislavery crusade reached its climax and consummation in 1870, the year the Fifteenth Amendment was adopted.

✦

The abolitionists could look back with considerable satisfaction in 1870 upon the achievements of the past decade. Most of the measures they had originally advocated had been adopted: the immediate and universal abolition of slavery, the enlistment of Negro soldiers, government assistance for the education of freedmen, the creation of a Freedmen's Bureau, and the incorporation of the Negro's civil and political equality into the law of the land. Abolitionists themselves had been transformed by the crucible of war from troublesome fanatics to prophets honored in their own country.

But the next decade was to prove that many of the equalitarian achievements of the Civil War and Reconstruction were built on a foundation of sand. The freedom and equality of the Negro were based in part on the idealistic traditions of the abolitionist movement, but in greater part on the military and political exigencies of war and reconstruction. The North's conversion to emancipation and equal rights was primarily a conversion of expediency rather than one of conviction. The South was converted only by force. A policy based on "military necessity" may be abandoned when the necessity disappears, and this is what happened in the 1870's. It became expedient for northern

---

[32] *National Standard*, I (May 1870), 46-48, Apr. 29, May 13, 1871; Aaron Powell to George Julian, Feb. 24, 1871, Giddings-Julian Correspondence, LC; John K. Wildman to Sumner, Mar. 14, 1871, Sumner Papers, HU.

political and business interests to conciliate southern whites, and an end to federal enforcement of Negro equality in the South was the price of conciliation. The mass of northern people had never loved the Negro, were tired of the "everlasting negro question," and were glad to see the end of it.

A few abolitionists acquiesced in the northern abandonment of Reconstruction, but most of them protested strongly against it. Not many northerners, however, listened to their protests after 1875. Abolitionists were not slow to discern and deplore the North's return to apathy. It was startling "to realize how completely the antislavery struggle is forgotten by the people, and how even the terrible expenditure of blood and treasure, which followed it, is fast sinking into oblivion," wrote Lydia Maria Child in 1878. "The lamentable misfortune is that emancipation was not the result of a popular *moral sentiment*, but of a miserable 'military necessity.' It was not the 'fruit of righteousness,' and therefore it is not 'peace.' " Five years later Frederick Douglass declared that "as the war for the Union recedes into the misty shadows of the past, and the Negro is no longer needed to assault forts and stop rebel bullets, he is . . . of less importance. Peace with the old master class has been war to the Negro. As the one has risen, the other has fallen."[33]

Abolitionists had done their best to rally the conscience of the nation, but in the final analysis the nation refused to follow their leadership. Was this a "failure of the American abolitionists," as one historian has called it?[34] Perhaps. Such abolitionist techniques as incisive criticism, harsh language, and moral absolutism may have been ill-suited to the conversion of conscience. But in a larger sense, their failure was the failure of the American people, and the United States has yet to measure up to the ideals of the abolitionist crusade. The civil rights movement of today has a greater chance of permanent success than did its counterpart in the 1860's. But whatever success the contemporary movement finally does achieve will be built partly on the foundations laid down more than a century ago by the abolitionists. They

[33] Lydia Maria Child to George Julian, Sept. 28, 1878, Giddings-Julian Correspondence, LC; Philip S. Foner, ed., *The Life and Writings of Frederick Douglass* (4 vols., New York, 1950-55), IV, 355.
[34] Merton L. Dillon, "The Failure of the American Abolitionists," *Journal of Southern History*, XXV (May 1959), 159-77.

were the first "freedom riders," and their spirit still pervades the struggle for racial justice. The victories of Martin Luther King and his followers are, in a very real sense, victories of the abolitionist crusade.

BIBLIOGRAPHICAL ESSAY*

MANUSCRIPTS

The manuscript collections of individual abolitionists yielded rich results. The William Lloyd Garrison Papers, BPL, the largest and best organized collection of abolitionist letters in existence, contain the correspondence of a great many abolitionists besides Garrison's. The Garrison Family Papers, SC, include a large number of letters, clippings, and scrapbooks relating to the Garrison family. The William Lloyd Garrison Papers, NYHS, the Wendell Phillips Garrison Papers, HU, the Garrison Family Papers, RU, and the Fanny Garrison Villard Papers, HU, contain additional material of value.

The papers of many other Garrisonian abolitionists have been preserved. There are small collections of Susan B. Anthony's letters in the LC, NYHS, and SC. The Lydia Maria Child Papers, Cornell, contain many important letters from Mrs. Child to personal friends. Additional letters can be found in the Child-Whittier Correspondence, LC, the Child-Shaw Correspondence, NYPL, the Lydia and David Child Papers, BPL, the Child Papers, Radcliffe Women's Archives, and the Child Papers, Wayland (Mass.) Historical Society. The large collections of Moncure Conway Papers, CU, Anna Dickinson Papers, LC, and Sydney Howard Gay Papers, CU, are indispensable for an understanding of these three important Civil War figures. The J. Miller McKim Papers, Cornell, include letters from several abolitionists to McKim and letterbook copies of McKim's correspondence as secretary of the American Freedmen's Aid Commission and of the American Freedmen's Union Commission, 1865-68. The J. Miller McKim Papers, BPL, the J. Miller McKim Papers, NYPL, the McKim-Maloney-Garrison Papers, NYPL, and the Charles Follen McKim Papers, NYPL, contain additional material on the activities of McKim and his fellow abolitionists. The Samuel May, Jr., Papers, BPL, include a great deal of correspondence relating to the organizational aspects of the Garrisonian movement. The Samuel J. May Papers, BPL,

* For the sake of brevity the following abbreviations are used to designate the repositories of manuscript collections: AAS (The American Antiquarian Society, Worcester, Mass.); BPL (The Boston Public Library); CU (Columbia University Library); Cornell (Cornell University Library); HU (Houghton Library, Harvard University); LC (Library of Congress); MHS (Massachusetts Historical Society); NYHS (New York Historical Society); NYPL (New York Public Library); RU (Rochester University Library); SC (Smith College Library); SU (Syracuse University Library); VHS (Vermont Historical Society). The following abbreviations are used to designate periodicals: JNH (*Journal of Negro History*); JSH (*Journal of Southern History*); MVHR (*Mississippi Valley Historical Review*).

consist of letters from Samuel May, Jr., to his elder cousin, Samuel J. May. The Mary E. Estlin Papers, BPL, contain many letters from Garrisonian abolitionists to Mary Estlin, an English abolitionist. There are collections of the letters of Stephen S. Foster and Abby Kelley Foster in the AAS and the Worcester Historical Society. The Josephine S. Griffing Papers, CU, contain a small number of valuable letters relating to Mrs. Griffing's social welfare work among the freedmen of Washington. The small collections of Oliver Johnson Papers, VHS, Lucretia Mott Papers, SC, Wendell Phillips Papers, LC, Parker Pillsbury Papers, SC, the Quincy-Webb Correspondence, BPL, and the Edmund Quincy Papers, MHS, yielded some relevant information. The Elizabeth Cady Stanton Papers, LC, the Theodore Tilton Papers, NYHS, and the Weston Papers, BPL, include many important letters. The Records of the Board of Managers of the Massachusetts and New England Anti-Slavery Societies, bound MS volume, BPL, contain the minutes of the executive committee meetings of these two societies.

Non-Garrisonian abolitionists also diligently preserved their papers. The small collection of Francis W. Bird Papers, HU, contains several letters from Charles Sumner. The extensive Cheever Papers, AAS, include the letters and diaries of George and Henry Cheever, and many of the records of the Church Anti-Slavery Society. The James Freeman Clarke Papers, HU, and the Frederick Douglass Papers, Douglass Memorial Home, Anacostia Heights, Washington, D.C., were of limited value. The William Channing Gannett Papers, RU, include diaries, letters, and memoranda concerning Gannett's work among the Port Royal freedmen. The Thomas Wentworth Higginson Papers, HU, consist of diaries, journals, and scrapbooks as well as letters. The large collection of Samuel Gridley Howe Family Papers, HU, is restricted, and the author was able to consult only those letters to Howe from persons outside his family. The Sumner-Howe Correspondence, HU, contains letters from Charles Sumner to Samuel Gridley Howe. The Samuel Johnson Papers, Essex Institute, Salem, Mass., the Joshua Leavitt Papers, LC, the Loring Moody Papers, BPL, the John Pierpont Papers, Pierpont Morgan Library, the Franklin Sanborn Papers, Concord (Mass.) Public Library, and the Sanborn Papers, LC, were of minor value. The huge and well-indexed collection of Gerrit Smith Papers, SU, contains hundreds of letters from abolitionists during the 1860's. Two smaller collections of Gerrit Smith Papers are housed in the NYHS and the NYPL. The Lewis Tappan Papers, LC, contain letters to Tappan, journals, and letterbook copies of letters from Tappan. The William W. Thayer MS autobiography, LC, contains some interesting information on George L.

Stearns and the *Right Way*. The John G. Whittier Papers, Essex Institute, and the Whittier Papers, NYPL, were of limited importance. The Elizur Wright Papers, LC, include many relevant letters. The Miscellaneous Manuscript Collections of the LC, NYHS, and NYPL, and the Alfred Williams Anthony Autograph Collection, NYPL, contain several letters of abolitionists.

The papers of leading Republican politicians yielded considerable material relating to the abolitionists. The John A. Andrew Papers, MHS, and the large but unindexed collection of Benjamin Butler Papers, LC, were of limited importance. The Salmon P. Chase Papers, LC, on the other hand, are completely indexed, easy to use, and proved fruitful. The Joshua Giddings-George Julian Correspondence, LC, includes many letters from abolitionists to Julian. The Horace Greeley Papers, NYPL, and the Andrew Johnson Papers, LC, contain only a small number of abolitionist letters, but the Abraham Lincoln Papers (Robert Todd Lincoln Collection), LC, were unexpectedly rich in abolitionist materials. The Charles Sumner Papers, HU, include a very large number of important letters from abolitionists. The Thaddeus Stevens Papers, LC, and the Henry Wilson Papers, LC, were of limited value.

PUBLISHED CORRESPONDENCE, COLLECTED WRITINGS AND SPEECHES

Herbert Aptheker, ed., *Documentary History of the Negro People in the United States* (New York, 1951) contains many valuable items on the activities of Negro leaders during the 1860's. William H. Burleigh, *Poems by W. H. Burleigh. With a Sketch of His Life by Celia Burleigh* (New York, 1871) is useful for biographical information about this abolitionist poet. Jesse A. Marshall, ed., *The Private and Official Correspondence of Gen. Benjamin F. Butler during the Period of the Civil War* (5 vols., Norwood, Mass., 1917) includes several abolitionist letters. Lillie B. C. Wyman and Arthur Crawford Wyman, *Elizabeth Buffum Chace, 1806-1899* (2 vols., Boston, 1914) is especially valuable for its large number of letters from various abolitionists to Mrs. Chace. Harriet W. Sewall, ed., *Letters of Lydia Maria Child* (Boston, 1883) is poorly edited but helpful. Edward Everett Hale, ed., *James Freeman Clarke: Autobiography, Diary, and Correspondence* (Boston, 1891) is useful and informative. Philip S. Foner, *The Life and Writings of Frederick Douglass* (4 vols., New York, 1950-55) is invaluable. Vols. III and IV cover the period of the Civil War and Reconstruction. They contain private correspondence, speeches, and published writings. Ray Allen Billington, ed., *The Journal of Charlotte Forten* (New York, 1961 [1953]) is a superbly edited journal of a young northern Negro who came to the South Carolina sea islands to teach the freedmen. Sarah Hopper Emerson, *Life of Abby Hopper Gibbons, Told Chiefly Through Her Correspondence* (2 vols., New York, 1896-97) is a poorly organized but nevertheless valuable compilation. Gilbert Haven, *National Sermons, Speeches, and Letters on Slavery and Its War . . .* (Boston, 1869) sets forth the views of this radical, red-headed abolitionist clergyman. Laura E. Richards, ed., *Letters and Journals of Samuel Gridley Howe: The Servant of Humanity* (Boston, 1909) contains helpful information on the founding of the Emancipation League and the work of the American Freedmen's Inquiry Commission. John Jay, *Slavery and the War* (New York, 1868) is a collection of twenty-one pamphlets, speeches, and public letters by Jay during the war and early reconstruction years. Roy P. Basler, ed., *The Collected Works of Abraham Lincoln* (9 vols., New Brunswick, N.J.) contains information on Lincoln's relations with certain abolitionists. Elizabeth W. Pearson, ed., *Letters from Port Royal, Written at the Time of the Civil War* (Boston, 1906) is an indispensable source of information on the activities of the Gideonites. Wendell Phillips, *Speeches, Lectures, and Letters,* 1st Series (Boston, 1863) contains addresses by Phillips from 1837 to 1863. His *Speeches, Lectures, and Letters,* 2nd Series (Boston, 1891) includes speeches made from 1865 to 1881. By far the greater portion of Phillips' utterances on the Negro question, especially after 1863, are not published in these volumes. A. W. Stevens, ed., *Enfranchisement and Citizenship, Addresses and Papers of Edward L. Pierce* (Boston, 1896) includes several articles and reports by Pierce on freedmen's education. Mrs. William S. Robinson, ed., *"Warrington" Pen-Portraits: A Collection of . . . the Writings of William S. Robinson* (Boston, 1877) contains important excerpts from the diaries, letters, and articles of this Massachusetts free-soiler and abolitionist. Theodore Stanton and Harriot Stanton Blatch, *Elizabeth Cady Stanton, as Revealed in Her Letters, Diary, and Reminiscences* (2 vols., New York, 1922) includes many letters unavailable elsewhere. Gerrit Smith, *Speeches and Letters of Gerrit Smith . . . on the Rebellion* (2 vols. in 1, New York, 1864-65) contains Smith's wartime published letters and speeches from 1863-65. Charles Sumner, *The Works of Charles Sumner* (15 vols., Boston, 1870-73) include a considerable amount of material on Sumner's relations with abolitionists. Rupert S. Holland, ed., *Letters and Diary of Laura M. Towne, Written from the Sea Islands of South Carolina, 1862-84* (Cambridge, Mass., 1912) is useful for a portrayal of everyday life on the South Carolina sea islands. John Albree, ed., *Whittier Correspondence from Oakknoll* (Salem, Mass., 1911) contains several Whittier letters dealing with the issues of war and reconstruction.

John G. Whittier, *Anti-Slavery Poems: Songs of Labor and Reform* (vol. III of his *Poetical Works*, Riverside ed., Boston, 1888), and Whittier, *The Conflict with Slavery* (vol. III of his *Prose Works*, Riverside ed., Boston, 1889) contain Whittier's antislavery poems and prose writings from this period.

GOVERNMENT PUBLICATIONS AND ARCHIVES

The various issues of the *Congressional Globe, House Miscellaneous Documents, House Executive Documents, House Reports,* and the corresponding documents of the Senate were consulted where relevant. Edward McPherson, *The Political History of the United States of America during the Great Rebellion* (Washington, 1865), and *The Political History of the United States of America during the Period of Reconstruction* (Washington, 1871) contain reports, letters, orders, messages, public statements, and summaries of congressional action that are invaluable guides to the activities of the government. McPherson was clerk of the House of Representatives and had access to all government publications in the preparation of these volumes. James D. Richardson, ed., *The Messages and Papers of the Presidents* (20 vols., Washington, 1897-1913), and *The United States Statutes at Large* were also consulted. *War of the Rebellion: . . . Official Records of the Union and Confederate Armies* (128 vols., Washington, 1880-1901) contain a great deal of information on Negro soldiers and military administration of freedmen's affairs. *Special Report of the Commissioner of Education on the Condition and Improvement of Public Schools in the District of Columbia . . .* (Washington, D.C., 1871) is useful as a source of information about public education for Negroes in all the states as well as in the District of Columbia. Government publications and records concerning freedmen's education are overwhelming. They include several hundred linear feet of Freedmen's Bureau records in the National Archives, the annual reports of the commissioners and the superintendents of education of the Freedmen's Bureau, and various congressional and Treasury Department reports.

NEWSPAPERS

A. Abolitionist Newspapers

The *National Anti-Slavery Standard*, published weekly in New York, was the most important single source for this study. Oliver Johnson was editor-in-chief of the *Standard* until May 1865. Edmund Quincy was associate editor during the same period, and wrote most of the leading editorials. Parker Pillsbury and George W. Smalley took over as editors in May 1865. Smalley resigned early in 1866, and Pillsbury stepped down as editor soon afterward because of a disagreement with Phillips on the woman suffrage question. Aaron M. Powell succeeded Pillsbury as editor, and Phillips served as associate editor. Phillips wrote most of the leading editorials, and the paper was entirely under his influence after 1865. The *Standard's* circulation was never very large—it averaged less than 3,000 during the 1860's—but its influence was much greater than its circulation would indicate, especially after Phillips became associate editor. After the adoption of the Fifteenth Amendment in 1870 the *Standard* changed its name to *The National Standard*. At the beginning of 1872 it became a monthly instead of a weekly. The *National Standard* was merged with the *National Temperance Advocate* in 1873.

The *Liberator* was the most famous of all abolitionist newspapers. During the war Garrison wrote only about half of the weekly editorials. Charles K. Whipple and Samuel May, Jr., wrote most of the others and supervised much of the makeup work on the paper. Its circulation fluctuated between 2,500 and 3,000 during the war, but like the *Standard* its influence reached far beyond its circulation. Garrison terminated the *Liberator* at the end of 1865, exactly 35 years after he had begun publishing it.

For the early years of an important antislavery newspaper, see Louis Filler, "Liberalism, Anti-Slavery, and the Founders of the *Independent*," *New England Quarterly*, XXVII (Sept. 1954) 291-306. Under Theodore Tilton's editorship the *Independent*, published weekly in New York, was almost as much an abolitionist paper as the *Standard* or the *Liberator*. From the spring of 1863, when Tilton took over as editor, until the early 1870's the circulation of the *Independent* hovered around the 70,000 mark. In 1864-65 Wendell P. Garrison served as assistant editor of the *Independent*. Oliver Johnson was managing editor from 1865 through 1870. In addition, several abolitionists contributed regular or occasional columns to the *Independent*. Tilton resigned from the editorship at the end of 1870, winding up a brilliant eight-year career as editor of one of the most influential radical journals in the land.

The weekly *Boston Commonwealth* was founded in August 1862, as the semiofficial organ of the Emancipation League. It was financed at first primarily by George Stearns. Moncure Conway and Frank Sanborn served as dual editors of the *Commonwealth* until April 1863, when Conway went to England and Sanborn took over as editor-in-chief. The *Commonwealth* became the spokesman for the old John Brown abolitionists and radical Republicans of Massachusetts. Charles W. Slack became editor in October 1864, and continued in that position until his death in 1885. The circulation of the *Commonwealth* seldom rose higher than 5,000. Most of the time during Reconstruction the paper was less radical than the *Standard* or the *Independent*. Slack held several political offices in Massachusetts after the war, and he could not afford to be too far in advance of his party.

The *Principia* was a weekly paper edited in New York by William Goodell. It served as the semiofficial organ of the Radical Abolitionist party and the Church Anti-Slavery Society. Goodell was an uninspiring writer and the *Principia* a rather dull paper. Its circulation was small, and Goodell was forced to suspend publication temporarily several times during the war and scrape up more money to keep his paper going. The *Principia* was suspended permanently in 1866.

In Rochester Frederick Douglass published his own newspaper, *Douglass' Monthly*, until August 1863. The paper was the spokesman for northern Negroes and for the Douglass wing of the abolitionist movement. Another Negro newspaper was the *Anglo-African*, edited in New York by Robert Hamilton and James McCune Smith. The *Anglo-African* represented more narrowly than *Douglass' Monthly* the interests of northern Negroes, especially of New York City Negroes, and was a little bit out of the main current of abolitionism. The paper was suspended in 1865 after the death of Smith. I. Garland Penn, *The Afro-American Press and Its Editors* (Springfield, Mass., 1891) supplies background information on the personalities of the Negro press during the Civil War era.

In May 1861, James Redpath began publishing in Boston a weekly newspaper called *The Pine and Palm*, organ of Redpath's Haitian Emigration Bureau. The paper advocated traditional abolitionist doctrines plus voluntary emigration of American Negroes to Haiti. The *Pine and Palm* folded in October 1862, when the Haitian Emigration Bureau was dissolved.

In November 1865, George Stearns published the first issue of a Negro suffrage weekly newspaper called the *Right Way*, edited by Alpheus Crosby and William W. Thayer. Stearns financed the free distribution of 60,000 copies weekly until May 1866, when he began charging a subscription fee of $1 per year. Circulation promptly dropped to 30,000, where it remained until the paper was terminated after the passage of the first Reconstruction Act in March 1867.

The Revolution, a weekly newspaper published in New York, 1868-1870, and edited by E. C. Stanton and Parker Pillsbury, was the militant organ of the woman suffrage wing of the abolitionists.

Two religious journals edited by abolitionists during the 1860's were the *American Baptist*, a small Baptist weekly edited in New York by

Nathan Brown; and *Zion's Herald,* published in Boston as the official organ of the New England Methodist Conference. Gilbert Haven became editor of *Zion's Herald* in 1867, and continued in that post until 1872; this journal had a circulation of 16,000.

Most of the larger freedmen's aid societies published monthly or quarterly journals recording their activities and exhorting the faithful to contribute more money. The three most important such journals were the *American Missionary Magazine,* organ of the A.M.A., published monthly throughout the Civil War and Reconstruction; the *American Freedman,* monthly organ of the American Freedmen's Union Commission during its three-year existence, 1866-69; and *The Freedmen's Record,* organ of the New England Freedmen's Aid Society, published monthly from 1865-1868 and quarterly thereafter until it ceased publication in 1874.

B. Nonabolitionist Newspapers

The daily issues of the *New York Tribune* constituted one of the more important sources for this book. The *Tribune* published many speeches, letters, and articles by abolitionists, and occasionally printed news stories and editorials about antislavery leaders. From 1862 to 1866 the *Tribune* was, in part, an extension of the personality and ideas of its managing editor, Sydney Howard Gay. Gay resigned in 1866, but the *Tribune* continued to be a valuable source of information and opinion about radical activities after that time. Ralph Ray Fahrney, *Horace Greeley and the* Tribune *in the Civil War* (Cedar Rapids, Iowa, 1936), Harry W. Baehr, *The New York* Tribune *since the Civil War* (New York, 1936), and Glyndon G. Van Deusen, *Horace Greeley, Nineteenth Century Crusader* (Phila., 1953) furnish useful background information about the *Tribune.* Louis M. Starr, *Bohemian Brigade: Civil War Newsmen in Action* (New York, 1954) includes an excellent discussion of Gay's connection with the *Tribune.*

The *New York Times* was the most important single source for the opinions of moderate Republicans about the abolitionists and their ideas. The excellent index of the *Times* from 1863 onward made it possible to find many valuable editorial comments and news stories about the abolitionists and the radicals. Although generally aligning itself with moderate Republicans, the *Springfield Republican* carried a weekly column by William S. Robinson ("Warrington") throughout the entire Civil War and Reconstruction period, and Franklin Sanborn was a member of the *Republican's* editorial staff from 1868 to 1872.

Scattered issues of the following newspapers and periodicals were also consulted for information relating to the abolitionists: the *Boston Advertiser* (moderate Republican); the *Boston Courier* (Whiggish); the

Boston Herald (Democratic); the *Boston Journal* (Republican); the *Chicago Times* (Copperhead Democratic); the *Chicago Tribune* (Republican, tending to radicalism); the *Cincinnati Gazette* (Republican, leaning toward radicalism); the *Cleveland Leader* (Republican); the *Columbus Crisis* (Copperhead Democratic); the *Continental Monthly* (emancipationist); *Harper's Weekly* (Republican); the *Nation* (Republican); the *New York Evening Post* (moderate Republican); the *New York Herald* (maverick Democratic and independent); the *New York World* (Democratic); the *Philadelphia Press* (Republican); the *Washington Chronicle* (Republican); and the *Worcester Spy* (radical Republican).

PAMPHLETS, BROADSIDES, SPEECHES, BOOKS, AND OTHER ABOLITIONIST PUBLICATIONS

The *Annual Reports* of the American Anti-Slavery Society for 1860 and 1861 (they were discontinued after 1861) contain information on the abolitionists' attitude toward the Republican party, the election of 1860, and the secession crisis. The *Proceedings of the American Anti-Slavery Society at Its Third Decade Anniversary Meeting in Philadelphia, December 3 and 4, 1863* (New York, 1864), includes much useful material on the abolitionists during the war. William Lloyd Garrison, *The Abolitionists, and Their Relation to the War* (*Pulpit and Rostrum*, nos. 26 and 27, New York, 1862), pp. 31-54; Wendell Phillips, *The Philosophy of the Abolition Movement* (New York, 1860); and Phillips, *The War for the Union* (New York, 1862) set forth the Garrisonian position toward the Republican party and the war. The *Annual Reports* of the Philadelphia Female Anti-Slavery Society, 1860-1869, provide a useful compendium of the year-by-year reaction of abolitionists to the events of the Civil War and Reconstruction.

Abolitionists' wartime pamphlets and books about West Indian emancipation are listed in footnote 2, Chapter VII of this book. The *Annual Reports* of the American Missionary Association, the New England Freedmen's Aid Society, the National Freedmen's Relief Association, and other freedmen's aid societies document the yearly activities in the field of freedmen's education.

The number of pamphlets, broadsides, printed letters and other published material produced by individual abolitionists during the Civil War and Reconstruction is immense. Gerrit Smith alone was the author of more than 40 broadsides and printed letters in the 1860's, which have been bound and deposited with the Gerrit Smith Papers, su. Speeches or sermons by such men as Wendell Phillips and George Cheever were frequently published in pamphlet form. For a useful although primitive bibliography of pamphlet material the reader is referred to John Russell Bartlett, *The Literature of the Rebellion* (Boston, 1866), which lists more than 6,000 titles, including hundreds of abolitionist items.

No effort will be made here to list every pamphlet or broadside consulted in the research for this book. Many of these items are cited in the footnotes. The following discussion will be confined to items of particular importance, interest, or relevance. John W. Alvord, *Letters from the South, Relating to the Condition of the Freedmen, addressed to Major General O. O. Howard* (Washington, 1870) were written while Alvord, superintendent of education for the Freedmen's Bureau, was on a tour of the South in 1869-1870. Two books by the Negro abolitionist, William Wells Brown—*The Black Man, His Antecedents, His Genius, and His Achievements* (Boston, 1863), and *The Rising Son* (Boston, 1874)—argue the case for the Negro's innate equality with the white man. David Lee Child, *Rights and Duties of the United States Relative to Slavery under the Laws of War* . . . (Boston, 1861) was an important exposition of the government's power over slavery in wartime. Three books by Moncure Conway presented moving pleas for emancipation and equal rights: *The Rejected Stone: or Insurrection vs. Resurrection in America* (Boston, 1861); *The Golden Hour* (Boston, 1862); and *Testimonies Concerning Slavery* (2nd ed., London, 1865). The Emancipation League published the replies to its questionnaire on the condition and needs of freedmen within Union lines in a pamphlet entitled *Facts Concerning the Freedmen, Their Capacity and Their Destiny* (Boston, 1863). William Channing Gannett, "The Freedmen at Port Royal," *North American Review*, ci (July 1865), 1-28 is an excellent article by a participant in the Port Royal experiment, setting forth soberly and incisively the difficulties and achievements of the freedmen's aid enterprise. Most of the chapters in Thomas Wentworth Higginson's classic *Army Life in a Black Regiment* (East Lansing, 1960, with an introduction by Howard Mumford Jones [1st ed., Boston, 1869]) had appeared as articles in the *Atlantic Monthly* from 1864 to 1867. Samuel Gridley Howe, *The Refugees from Slavery in Canada West* (Boston, 1864) is an interesting book growing out of Howe's research among Canadian Negroes for the Freedmen's Inquiry Commission. James Miller McKim, *The Freedmen of South Carolina* . . . (Phila., 1862) is a brief but shrewd appraisal of the possibilities of freedmen's education by one of the leading abolitionist workers in the cause. Mary Traill Spence Putnam, *Record of an Obscure Man* (Boston, 1861) argues eloquently for the nobility of the African race. Linda W. Slaughter, *The Freedmen of the South* (Cincinnati, 1869), by a teacher of the A.M.A., is polemical, zealous, but nevertheless useful.

Charles Stearns, *The Black Man of the South, and the Rebels* (New York, 1872), a very revealing book, recounts the experiences of an abolitionist who went South after the war with the intention of buying and reselling land to the freedmen. George L. Stearns published two pamphlets in 1865 containing speeches by Phillips, Douglass, William D. Kelley, Henry Ward Beecher, and others urging Negro suffrage and equal rights: *The Equality of All Men before the Law* (Boston, 1865); and *Universal Suffrage, and Complete Equality in Citizenship, The Safeguards of Democratic Institutions* (Boston, 1865). Harriet Beecher Stowe, "The Education of Freedmen," *North American Review*, cxxviii (June 1879), 605-15, cxxix (July 1879), 81-94 is a convenient and able summary of the record of the freedmen's aid societies. Theodore Tilton, *The Negro* (New York, 1863) is a poetic and moving statement of the essential equality of the Negro race. William Whiting, *The War Powers of the President, and the Legislative Powers of Congress in Relation to Rebellion, Treason, and Slavery* (1st ed., Boston, 1862), the foremost statement of the war power argument, went through 42 subsequent editions, with additions, revisions, and changes in title.

MEMOIRS, AUTOBIOGRAPHIES, AND REMINISCENCES

There is a plethora of memoirs by abolitionists and antislavery leaders. Most of them conceal more than they reveal. Only those that were helpful in the preparation of this study will be listed here.

Elizabeth Botume, *First Days Amongst the Contrabands* (Boston, 1893) is an excellent book of reminiscences written by one of the best teachers at Port Royal. William Wells Brown, *My Southern Home* (Boston, 1880) is the somewhat episodical and sensationalist autobiography of an ex-slave who became a leader in the abolitionist movement. James Freeman Clarke, *Anti-Slavery Days* (New York, 1884) is anecdotal in nature, but supplies an occasional insight of value. Levi Coffin, *Reminiscences* (Cincinnati, 1880) includes much useful information on Coffin's wartime efforts in behalf of freedmen's relief in the West. Moncure D. Conway, *Autobiography, Memoirs and Experiences* (2 vols., Boston, 1904) is important for an understanding of this southern-born abolitionist. Frederick Douglass, *Life and Times of Frederick Douglass* (Hartford, 1884) is somewhat disorganized, and less helpful than had been anticipated. James R. Gilmore, *Personal Recollections of Abraham Lincoln and the Civil War* (Boston, 1898) contains useful information on the *New York Tribune*, Sydney Gay, and the *Continental Monthly* during the war. Two books of autobiographical and biographical sketches by Thomas Wentworth Higginson—*Cheerful Yesterdays* (Boston, 1898) and *Contem-*

poraries (Boston, 1899)—include several chapters about the abolitionist movement and the Civil War. Oliver Johnson, *William Lloyd Garrison and His Times* (2nd ed., Boston, 1885) is a valuable account of the Garrisonians by one of Garrison's closest associates. George W. Julian, *Political Recollections, 1840 to 1872* (Chicago, 1884) provided some insights on the relation of abolitionists to radical Republicans. John Mercer Langston, *From the Virginia Plantation to the National Capital* (Hartford, 1894) is long-winded but useful. Samuel J. May, *Some Recollections of Our Anti-Slavery Conflict* (Boston, 1869) is a carefully written and important book, of limited value for the period after 1861. Joseph Whiting Parker, "Memoirs," typescript of MS written in 1880, supplied to the author by Parker's granddaughter, Mrs. Perce J. Bentley, is rambling and frequently inaccurate, but is nonetheless a valuable account of a Boston abolitionist who had lived in the South briefly before the war, and returned there after the war as a representative of New England Baptist freedmen's aid societies. George W. Smalley, *Anglo-American Memories*, 1st Series (London, 1911) contains a few anecdotes about Wendell Phillips. Lillie B. C. Wyman, *American Chivalry* (Boston, 1913) is also valuable for personal anecdotes about Phillips and other abolitionists.

BIOGRAPHIES

Henry Greenleaf Pearson, *The Life of John A. Andrew* (2 vols., Boston, 1904) is a comprehensive and valuable work containing much information about Andrew's antislavery career and his relations with the abolitionists. Ida H. Harper, *The Life and Work of Susan B. Anthony* (3 vols., Indianapolis, 1898-1908) prints several letters which are unavailable elsewhere. Alma Lutz, *Susan B. Anthony, Rebel, Crusader, Humanitarian* (Boston, 1959) is an accurate and readable biography, although sometimes overly sympathetic to Miss Anthony. Octavius B. Frothingham, *Memoir of William Henry Channing* (Boston, 1886) quotes liberally from Channing's diaries and letters. Robert M. York, *George B. Cheever, Religious and Social Reformer, 1807-1890* (Orono, Me., 1955) is informative and accurate. Mary Elizabeth Burtis, *Moncure Conway* (New Brunswick, N.J., 1952) is a readable but sometimes inaccurate biography. Frank A. Rollin, *Life and Public Services of Martin R. Delany* (Boston, 1868) is a eulogistic but useful study of a Negro abolitionist. Giraud Chester, *Embattled Maiden: The Life of Anna Dickinson* (New York, 1951) is well written and informative, although undocumented. It should be supplemented for the Civil War years by James Harvey Young, "Anna Elizabeth Dickinson and the Civil War: For and

Against Lincoln," MVHR, XXI (June 1944), 59-80. Benjamin Quarles, *Frederick Douglass* (Washington, 1948) is a sound and valuable biography. William H. Pease, "William Channing Gannett, A Social Biography," Ph.D. dissertation, University of Rochester, 1955 is a good study of one of the younger abolitionists who went to Port Royal in 1862.

Wendell P. Garrison and Francis J. Garrison, *William Lloyd Garrison* (4 vols., Boston, 1885-89), though marked by filial piety, is the basic source for an understanding of the Garrisonian abolitionist movement. The authors not only traced Garrison's life in great detail, but brought together and published excerpts from hundreds of his letters and editorials. Two recent biographies, Walter M. Merrill, *Against Wind and Tide: A Biography of William Lloyd Garrison* (Cambridge, Mass., 1963), and John L. Thomas, *The Liberator: William Lloyd Garrison* (Boston, 1963) supersede earlier studies of Garrison.

Catherine H. Birney, *The Grimké Sisters: Sarah and Angelina Grimké* . . . (Boston, 1885) is old but serviceable. William Haven Daniels, *Memorials of Gilbert Haven* (Boston, 1880) is eulogistic, but valuable because of the many letters which it publishes. Carl Wittke, *Against the Current, The Life of Karl Heinzen* (Chicago, 1945) is an important study of this little-known German-American abolitionist. Mary Thacher Higginson, *Thomas Wentworth Higginson* (Boston, 1914) is better than the usual family biography. It should be supplemented by Tilden Edelstein, "Strange Enthusiasm: Thomas Wentworth Higginson, 1823-1877," Ph.D. dissertation, Johns Hopkins University, 1961, and Anna Mary Wells, *Dear Preceptor, The Life and Times of Thomas Wentworth Higginson* (Boston, 1963). C. Carroll Hollis, "R. J. Hinton, Lincoln's Reluctant Biographer," *The Centennial Review of Arts & Sciences*, V (Winter 1961), 65-84 is an excellent biographical article, although unfortunately it is undocumented. John White Chadwick, *Sallie Holley, A Life for Liberty* (New York, 1899) is valuable for the many letters it prints. Harold Schwartz, *Samuel Gridley Howe: Social Reformer* (Cambridge, Mass., 1956) is accurate and helpful, but thin. Carol Brink, *Harps in the Wind: The Story of the Singing Hutchinsons* (New York, 1947) is an excellent biography of a family of musical abolitionists. Ira V. Brown, "Miller McKim and Pennsylvania Abolitionism," *Pennsylvania History*, XXX (January 1963), 56-72, presents a skeletal outline of McKim's career.

Irving H. Bartlett, *Wendell Phillips: Brahmin Radical* (Boston, 1961) is a first-rate piece of work and supersedes all earlier biographies of Phillips, including Oscar Sherwin's *Prophet of Liberty: The Life and Times of Wendell Phillips* (New York, 1958) which is poorly written, uncritical, and unoriginal. Richard Hofstadter, "Wendell Phillips: The Patrician as Agitator," in *The American Political Tradition and the*

Men Who Made It (Vintage ed., New York, 1958), 137-63 is a stimulating and suggestive essay.

Abe C. Ravitz, "John Pierpont: Portrait of a Nineteenth Century Reformer," Ph.D. dissertation, NYU, 1955, was moderately useful. Benjamin B. Hickok, "The Political and Literary Career of F. B. Sanborn," Ph.D. dissertation, Michigan State University, 1953, is disappointing on the Civil War and Reconstruction years. Octavius B. Frothingham, *Gerrit Smith* (New York, 1879) is valuable chiefly for the letters and writings of Smith which it publishes. A more complete study of Smith is Ralph Volney Harlow, *Gerrit Smith: Philanthropist and Reformer* (New York, 1939). Alma Lutz, *Created Equal: A Biography of Elizabeth Cady Stanton* (New York, 1940) is less satisfactory than the same author's study of Susan B. Anthony. Frank P. Stearns, *The Life and Public Services of George Luther Stearns* (Phila., 1907) is uncritical, but constitutes a vital source for an understanding of this important abolitionist, and prints many letters unavailable elsewhere. Larry Gara, "William Still and the Underground Railroad," *Pennsylvania History,* XXVIII (Jan. 1961), 33-44 and Alberta S. Norwood, "Negro Welfare Work in Philadelphia, Especially as Illustrated by the Career of William Still," M.A. thesis, University of Pennsylvania, 1931, provide helpful information on this Philadelphia Negro abolitionist. Edward L. Pierce, *Memoir and Letters of Charles Sumner* (4 vols., Boston, 1877-94) is a detailed and eulogistic study, containing many Sumner letters. It has been largely superseded for the pre-Civil War period by David Donald, *Charles Sumner and the Coming of the Civil War* (New York, 1960). Benjamin Thomas, *Theodore Weld: Crusader for Freedom* (New Brunswick, N.J., 1950) is an excellent biography, treating fully Weld's return to the platform during the Civil War. A series of articles by Charles Kassel in *Open Court,* XXXIV (Sept. 1920), 564-69, XXXVII (Mar. 1923), 167-75, XXXVIII (July 1924), 406-18, XXXIX (Sept. 1925), 563-76, XLI (Apr. 1927), 239-56, and XLIII (Jan. 1929), 35-50 (Feb. 1929), 94-106 constitute the basic biographical sources for Edwin M. Wheelock, a New Hampshire abolitionist who lived in the South during and after the war. Samuel T. Pickard, *Life and Letters of John Greenleaf Whittier* (2 vols., New York, 1894) includes information on Whittier's wartime activities. Phillip Wright and Elizabeth Wright, *Elizur Wright: The Father of Life Insurance* (Chicago, 1937) is a rather disappointing study of this interesting abolitionist.

MONOGRAPHS, ARTICLES, AND OTHER WORKS

Several studies touch lightly upon the subject of the abolitionists and the Negro in the 1860's. William G. Cochrane, "Freedom without Equal-

ity: A Study of Northern Opinion and the Negro Issue, 1861-1870,"
Ph.D. dissertation, University of Minnesota, 1957, is superficial and thin,
but not without value. Two histories of the antislavery movement which
deal briefly with abolitionism in the early war years are Dwight L. Dumond, *Antislavery: The Crusade for Freedom in America* (Ann Arbor,
1961), a polemical and uncritical work; and Lawrence Lader, *The Bold
Brahmins: New England's War against Slavery, 1831-1863* (New York,
1961), which deals only with New England abolitionists and is inade-
quately researched. Benjamin Quarles, *The Negro in the Civil War* (Boston, 1953) is a readable and worthwhile study. The same author's *Lincoln
and the Negro* (New York, 1962) glosses over some of the anti-Lincoln
sentiment among radical Negroes, while William O. Douglas, *Mr. Lincoln and the Negroes: The Long Road to Equality* (New York, 1963)
is thin and not profound. Margaret Shortreed, "The Anti-Slavery Radicals, 1840-1868," *Past and Present*, no. 16 (Nov. 1959), 67-87 is a
Marxist interpretation of the revolutionary aspects of the antislavery
movement. Elizabeth Cady Stanton, Susan B. Anthony, and Matilda
Joslyn Gage, *History of Woman Suffrage* (6 vols., New York, 1881-1922),
vol. II, contains information on the activities of women abolitionists during the war and Reconstruction. Edith Ellen Ware, *Political Opinion in
Massachusetts during the Civil War and Reconstruction* (New York,
1916) and T. Harry Williams, *Lincoln and the Radicals* (Madison, Wis.,
1941) are important for an understanding of the political milieu in
which the abolitionists operated.

Most of the northern Protestant denominations included a number
of abolitionists among their leaders. The activities of these evangelicals
are touched upon in Chester F. Dunham, *The Attitude of the Northern
Clergy toward the South, 1860-1865* (Toledo, 1942); Ralph E. Morrow,
Northern Methodism and Reconstruction (East Lansing, 1956); William
Warren Sweet, *The Methodist Episcopal Church and the Civil War* (Cincinnati, 1912); and Lewis G. Vander Velde, *The Presbyterian Church
and the Federal Union, 1861-1869* (Cambridge, Mass., 1932).

The basic studies of the 1860 election are Emerson D. Fite, *The Presidential Campaign of 1860* (New York, 1911), which surveys all parties,
and Reinhard H. Luthin, *The First Lincoln Campaign* (Cambridge, Mass.,
1944), which concentrates primarily on the Republicans. Two excellent
studies of the North during the secession winter are David M. Potter,
Lincoln and His Party in the Secession Crisis (New Haven, 1942), and
Kenneth M. Stampp, *And the War Came: The North and the Secession
Crisis, 1860-61* (Baton Rouge, 1950), both of which mention briefly the
role of the abolitionists. Dwight L. Dumond, ed., *Southern Editorials on
Secession* (New York, 1931) and Howard C. Perkins, ed., *Northern*

Editorials on Secession (2 vols., New York, 1942) are valuable compilations of editorial opinion on the crisis. The Perkins volumes contain a great deal of material on the antiabolitionist attitudes of the northern conservative and Democratic press.

On the question of the Negro's racial potential, William S. Jenkins, *Pro-Slavery Thought in the Old South* (Chapel Hill, 1935), Guion G. Johnson, "A History of Racial Ideologies in the United States with Reference to the Negro," MS in the Schomburg Collection of the NYPL, Arthur Young Lloyd, *The Slavery Controversy, 1831-1860* (Chapel Hill, 1939), and William R. Stanton, *The Leopard's Spots: Scientific Attitudes Toward Race in America, 1815-59* (Chicago, 1960), provide the necessary background for an understanding of the abolitionists' attitude toward this issue. The anti-Negro, antiabolitionist sentiments of the northern workingman and Democrat are ably discussed in Williston Lofton, "Northern Labor and the Negro during the Civil War," JNH, XXXIV (July 1949), 251-73; Albon P. Man, Jr., "Labor Competition and the New York Draft Riots of 1863," JNH, XXXVI (1951), 375-405; and Emma L. Thornbrough, "The Race Issue in Indiana Politics during the Civil War," *Indiana Magazine of History*, XLVII (June 1951), 165-88. For a sample of the many studies of wartime efforts to colonize the Negro abroad, see footnote 4, Chapter VII of this book.

There are several able monographs and articles which deal with the freedmen's aid enterprise. Augustus F. Beard, *A Crusade of Brotherhood, A History of the American Missionary Association* (Boston, 1909), although old and eulogistic, is nevertheless valuable for an understanding of the A.M.A.'s work. George R. Bentley, *A History of the Freedmen's Bureau* (Phila., 1955) supersedes earlier studies of the Bureau, and contains helpful information on the relation of the Bureau to the freedmen's aid societies. Ira V. Brown, "Lyman Abbott and Freedmen's Aid, 1865-1869," JSH, XV (Feb. 1949) provides useful insights into the postwar activities of the freedmen's associations. Richard Bryant Drake, "The American Missionary Association and the Southern Negro, 1861-1888," Ph.D. dissertation, Emory University, 1957, is an excellent study, indispensable for an understanding of the A.M.A. Luther P. Jackson, "The Educational Efforts of the Freedmen's Bureau and Freedmen's Aid Societies in South Carolina, 1862-1872," JNH, VIII (Jan. 1923), 1-40, is a thorough study, written from the Negro's point of view. Julius H. Parmelee, "Freedmen's Aid Societies, 1861-1871," in *Negro Education: A Study of the Private and Higher Schools for Colored People in the United States; U.S. Department of Interior, Bureau of Education Bulletin*, 1916, no. 38, pp. 268-95 (Washington, 1917), is crammed full of facts, and supplies a framework for the study of freedmen's education. William H. Pease, "Three Years Among the Freedmen: William C. Gannett and the Port Royal Experiment," JNH, XLII (Apr. 1957), 98-117 discusses the experiences of a young Gideonite. Willie L. Rose, "Rehearsal for Reconstruction: The Port Royal Experiment," Ph.D. dissertation, Johns Hopkins University, 1962, is an outstanding piece of work, indispensable for anyone interested in the Port Royal enterprise. This dissertation has recently been published by the Bobbs-Merrill Co. Henry Lee Swint, *The Northern Teacher in the South, 1862-1870* (Nashville, 1941), although marred by a slight pro-southern bias and a certain superficiality, remains required reading for anyone working in this field. Bell Wiley, *Southern Negroes, 1861-1865* (New Haven, 1938) contains a section on the transition of the Negro to freedom, written from the point of view of the southern white.

John Hope Franklin, *The Emancipation Proclamation* (New York, 1963) provides a detailed story of the formulation and execution of that historic edict. On the Negro as a soldier the standard work is Dudley T. Cornish, *The Sable Arm: Negro Troops in the Union Army, 1861-1865.* Cornish's excellent bibliography lists additional secondary material on Negro troops. Ira V. Brown, "Pennsylvania and the Rights of the Negro, 1865-1887," *Pennsylvania History*, XXVIII (Jan. 1961), 45-57, ably describes the efforts of abolitionists and Negroes to desegregate transportation facilities in Pennsylvania. Leon F. Litwack, *North of Slavery* (Chicago, 1961) is an excellent study of northern discrimination against the free Negro before the Civil War. John G. Sproat, "Blueprint for Radical Reconstruction," JSH, XXIII (Feb. 1957), 25-44, is an able article discussing the work of the American Freedmen's Inquiry Commission. Martin Abbott, "Free Land, Free Labor, and the Freedmen's Bureau," *Agricultural History*, XXX (1956), 150-56, portrays the efforts of the Bureau to settle freedmen upon land of their own. LaWanda Cox, "The Promise of Land for the Freedmen," MVHR, XLV (Dec. 1958), 413-40, is a very good article discussing the various wartime proposals for providing the freedmen with land. Edwin D. Hoffman, "From Slavery to Self-Reliance," JNH, XLI (Jan. 1956) recounts the fate of the freedmen who were assigned lands along the South Carolina, Georgia, and Florida coast under Sherman's Order no. 15. Patrick W. Riddleberger, "George W. Julian: Abolitionist Land Reformer," *Agricultural History*, V (July 1955), 108-15, summarizes Julian's efforts to obtain confiscation-homestead legislation for the freedmen.

Ruhl Jacob Bartlett, *John C. Frémont and the Republican Party* (Columbus, 1930) includes a helpful account of Frémont's candidacy for the presidency in 1864. William F. Zornow, *Lincoln and the Party Divided* (Norman, Okla., 1954) is the best general account of the election of 1864. Important works on Reconstruction include Howard K. Beale, *The Critical Year: A Study of Andrew Johnson and Reconstruction* (2nd ed., New York, 1958); LaWanda Cox and John H. Cox, *Politics, Principle, and Prejudice, 1865-1866* (New York, 1963); Leslie H. Fishel, Jr., "Northern Prejudice and Negro Suffrage, 1865-1870," JNH, XXXIX (Jan. 1954), 8-26; William B. Hesseltine, *Lincoln's Plan of Reconstruction* (Tuscaloosa, Ala., 1960); Joseph B. James, *The Framing of the Fourteenth Amendment* (Urbana, Ill., 1956); Charles H. McCarthy, *Lincoln's Plan of Reconstruction* (New York, 1901); and Eric L. McKitrick, *Andrew Johnson and Reconstruction* (Chicago, 1960). John G. Sproat, "Party of the Center: The Politics of Liberal Reform in Post-Civil War America," Ph.D. dissertation, U. of Cal., 1959, portrays the growing dissatisfaction of several liberals with Reconstruction after 1867. Jacobus Ten-Broek, *The Antislavery Origins of the Fourteenth Amendment* (Berkeley, 1951) gives the legal and legislative background of the equal protection and other important clauses of the Fourteenth Amendment. The standard work on the 1868 election is Charles H. Coleman, *The Election of 1868: the Democratic Effort to Regain Control* (New York, 1933), which deals primarily with the Democratic party. Republican activities are treated in William B. Hesseltine, *Ulysses S. Grant, Politician* (New York, 1935). John M. Mathews, *Legislative and Judicial History of the Fifteenth Amendment* (Baltimore, 1909) is old and inadequate. It should be supplemented by William Gillette, "The Power of the Ballot: the Politics of the Passage and Ratification of the Fifteenth Amendment," Ph.D. dissertation, Princeton University, 1963.

INDEX

Abbott, Lyman, 399

Abolition of Slavery the Right of the Government under the War Power, The, 67

abolitionist, definition of, 3

abolitionist organizations, description of, in 1860, 3-8; bury differences during war, 7-8, 104-06, 303n

abolitionists, growth of prestige and influence of, 81-90, 127-32, 262, 267, 299-300 and 299n, 363-64, 366, 367-69, 428-29; prominent as organizers and teachers of freedmen's aid societies, 170-72, 386-88; oppose execution of rebels, 315-16; achievements of, 430-32

Adams, Charles Francis, Jr., 71

Adams, John Quincy, on war power over slavery, 50, 67

Africa, believed to be barbarous, 138-39; abolitionists challenge view, 138-41

Agassiz, Louis, and "American School" of anthropology, 136; on Negro inferiority, 145-46

Alcott, A. Bronson, 279

Alcott, Louisa May, 148

Aldridge, Ira, Negro actor, 143

Alvord, John W., supt. of schools of Freedmen's Bureau, 190, 387; and freedmen's education, 393; and American Missionary Association, 402-03

American and Foreign Anti-Slavery Society, 5

American Anti-Slavery Society, 14, 21, 22, 34; composition of, in 1860, 3-4; on Lincoln and the Republican party in 1860, 11-12, 15; annual convention canceled in 1861, 55; urges emancipation under war power, 67; on Lincoln and Emancipation Proclamation, 122; emancipation petitions, 125-26; on Negro achievement, 143; urges arming of Negroes, 193n; equal rights a vital aim of, 225; urges confiscation and reallocation of southern land, 252, 411; criticizes Lincoln in 1864, 268; and election of 1864, 268, 278-79; growing schism in, 102-04, 106, 287-300; schism of 1865, 301-07, 324; and Negro suffrage, 294, 319; early con-

fidence in Andrew Johnson, 317; opposes efforts to reconcile A. J. and Congress, 343; assails 14th Amendment, 352; and freedmen's aid societies, 397, 400; and Jackson bequest controversy, 400-01; on 15th Amendment, 427; dissolution of in 1870, 429. *See also* Garrisonian abolitionists

American Freedman, on school integration, 399; on declining support for freedmen's education, 403-04

American Freedmen's Aid Commission, petitions for continuation of Freedmen's Bureau, 341; organization and work of, 394; merges with American Union Commission, 398

American Freedman's Inquiry Commission, 145-46; formation of, 181-82; preliminary report, 183-84; urges creation of freedmen's bureau, 184-86; final report, 185-86; advocates equal rights for freedmen, 186; influence of, 186, 191

American Freedmen's Union Commission, 387, 401; organized, 398-99; operates desegregated schools, 399-400; normal schools of, 406; competition with A.M.A., 401-03; decline and dissolution of, 401-05; helps freedmen obtain land, 413

American Land Company and Agency, 412-13

American Missionary, 158

American Missionary Association, 387, 393; activities of before 1861, 5-6; establishes schools for freedmen, 158, 169, 173-74; dominated by abolitionists, 170; aids victims of N.Y. draft riot, 231; competition with A.F.U.C., 401-03; founds normal schools and colleges for Negroes, 406-07; helps freedmen obtain land, 413

American Peace Society, 53-54 and 54n

"American School" of anthropology, and diversity of races, 136-37, 145

American Union Commission, 398

Andrew, John A., 3, 7, 58; elected governor of Mass., 14-15 and 15n; rebukes Butler, 69; praises Frémont's emancipation edict, 73; on Emancipation Proclamation, 119; president of

Boston Educational Commission, 160; and 54th Mass. Volunteers, 202-06, 219; urges equal pay for Negro troops, 214; and Chase's presidential ambitions, 263; and movement to oust Lincoln as Republican candidate in 1864, 281; effort to reconcile Andrew Johnson and Congress, 343; and land for freedmen, 412-13

Anglo-African, Negro newspaper, 51, 60; on African heritage of Negro, 141n

Anthony, Susan B., 4, 110; threatened by mob violence, 44; protests suspension of abolitionist meetings in 1861, 56; arranges lecture series, 80; organizes Women's Loyal National League, 125; and petition campaign of W.L.N.L., 125-26; denounces racial discrimination in North, 225-26; supports Frémont for president in 1864, 268, 272; refuses to support Lincoln, 285; opposes dissolution of Am. A.S. Soc., 302; opposes 14th Amendment, 373; urges woman suffrage in N.Y., 377

Anti-Slavery Bugle, 4; on Republican party, 25

Army Life in a Black Regiment, 200

Ashley, James, and reconstruction, 308-10

Atlanta, Sherman's capture of, and election of 1864, 282-84

Atlanta University, founded by A.M.A., 406

Atlantic Monthly, 142, 157, 172, 197, 198, 200; on assault of 54th Mass. on Fort Wagner, 211

atrocities against freedmen, 332, 341, 358-59

Bacon, Leonard, 88

Baker, George E., 170

Bancroft, George, 78

Banks, Nathaniel P., vetoes Mass. militia law enrolling Negroes, 192; organizes *Corps d'Afrique*, 208; and reconstruction of La., 243-45; labor system of, in La., abolitionists on, 289-93, 296, 299

Banneker, Benjamin, 142-43

Bassett, George, welcomes secession, 38n; opposes war, 57

Beecher, Henry Ward, opposes emancipation as war aim, 58; as ed. of *Inde-pendent*, 88; on Garrison's popularity, 90; urges emancipation, 110; at Fort Sumter flag-raising ceremony, 300; favors Negro suffrage, 310, 323

Bennett, James Gordon, 89

Berea College (Ky.), 413; founded by A.M.A., 5, 406

Bingham, John A., 181, 372

Bird, Francis W., 75, 318; head of Bird Club, 7; presides over disunion convention in 1857, 7; and Frémont's presidential candidacy in 1864, 279; urges impeachment of Andrew Johnson, 383-84

Bird Club, stronghold of antislavery politics in Mass., 6-7; and nomination of Andrew for governor, 14; and Chase's presidential hopes in 1864, 263; praises Sumner for defeating readmission of La., 310; early confidence in Andrew Johnson, 314

Birney, Gen. William, 209, 220

"black codes," in southern states, 321, 332, 335, 341

"black laws," in northern states, 223, repealed, 236-37

Black Man, His Antecedents, His Genius, and His Achievements, The, 139

Blair, Francis P., Jr., 422-23

Blair, Montgomery, 58; disliked by radicals, 263, 284, 318; resigns from Cabinet, 284

Boston, antiabolitionist riots in, 41-44

Boston Advertiser, 331; suggests compensated emancipation 40; on emancipation pressure, 111; on 14th Amendment, 364

Boston Commonwealth, 120, 144, 266, 279, 323; founded by Emancipation League, 79; urges creation of freedmen's bureau, 179-80; urges equal pay for Negro soldiers, 216-17; denounces Lincoln's plan of reconstruction, 242, 253; on reconstruction policy in La., 244; on Wade-Davis bill, 246; urges confiscation and reallocation of southern land, 249, 252-53, 372, 410-11; on Sherman's Order no. 15, 258; supports Chase candidacy in 1864, 263n, 266; on Lincoln's reelection, 285-86; criticizes Garrison's defense of Banks' labor system in La., 293; on Garrison and Negro suffrage, 295; opposes dissolution of Am. A.S. Soc., 303; opposes readmission of La.,

308-10; urges Negro suffrage as condition of reconstruction, 319; reaffirms support of Andrew Johnson, 322; on Johnson's policy, 330; on defeat of Negro suffrage in Conn., 334; on 14th Amendment, 354; urges impeachment of A.J., 369, 381-82; on Negro suffrage in North, 377; on restoration of land to pardoned rebels, 409; on proposed 15th Amendment, 425

Boston Courier, 114; on Wendell Phillips' influence, 89

Boston Educational Commission, 160, 169. *See also* New England Freedmen's Aid Society

Boston Herald, 79

Boston Journal, on W. Phillips' reception in Washington, 85n; on Anna Dickinson, 131; favors equal suffrage, 310

Boston Transcript, 160

Botume, Elizabeth, on school desegregation, 399-400

Boutwell, George S., 79, 372; supports bill for equal suffrage, 357; on W. Phillips and 15th Amendment, 426-27

Bowditch, Henry I., 7; response to war, 47

Bowen, Henry C., 87-88

Bowles, Samuel, 14, 36

Brannigan, Felix, 193

Brown, John, 6, 14, 15, 36, 41, 44, 48, 206

Brown, William Wells, on African heritage of Negro, 138-39; on Negro achievement, 143; recruits Negro soldiers, 205

Brownson, Orestes, 67

Buffon, George Louis Leclerc, 137

Buffum, James, 415

Bull Run, 1st battle of, 64; northern and abolitionist reaction to, 70-72, 193-94

Bull Run, 2nd battle of, northern and abolitionist reaction to, 117

Bunker, William, 51

Burleigh, Charles C., 21, 367; attacked by mob, 44-45; critical of Andrew Johnson's reconstruction theory, 321

Burleigh, William H., campaigns for Lincoln in 1860, 20-23; in 1864, 284

Burritt, Elihu, opposes war, 54

Butler, Benjamin, 323, 361; offers to suppress slave insurrection, 56, 69; rebuked by Andrew, 69; devises "contraband" policy, 69-70, 101; praised by Phillips, 127; and contrabands at Fortress Monroe, 156; presidential possibility in 1864, 270, 281

Calhoun, John C., 300

Cameron, Simon, favors emancipation, 78; refuses to enroll Negro volunteers, 193; advocates arming of Negroes, 194, 195

Chace, Elizabeth Buffum, 229

Chandler, Zachariah, and election of 1864, 281, 284; on Andrew Johnson and Negro suffrage, 318

Channing, William H., 75; interview with Lincoln, 84; chaplain of House of Reps., 226; confidence in Andrew Johnson, 330

Chapman, Maria Weston, on abolitionist wartime tactics, 78; on Lincoln's gradual emancipation message, 96; on Confiscation Act of 1862, 112; on Emancipation Proclamation, 121; on church desegregation, 227

Charleston, S.C., Garrison's visit to, 300; freedmen's schools in, 388-89

Charleston Courier, 300

Chase, Salmon P., 74, 156, 250, 255; supports Hunter's emancipation edict, 108; and free labor experiment on S.C. sea islands, 159-60; on Negro soldiers, 198; as chief justice, accepts John Rock as Supreme Court lawyer, 226; hopes for presidency in 1864, 262-64, 266; abolitionist support of in 1864, 262-64, 266, 270, 281; and movement to oust Lincoln as Repub. candidate, 281; favors Negro suffrage, 310; interviews with Andrew Johnson on Negro suffrage, 318; presidential aspirations in 1868, 417-19

Cheever, George B., 5, 78, 207, 273; urges emancipation, 64; sermon in House of Reps., 83-84; in demand as speaker, 84; criticizes Lincoln's gradual emancipation message, 97; works with Garrisonians during war, 106; on northern military victories, 107; on defeat of confiscation bill, 109; on Emancipation Proclamation, 118; reconstruction theory of, 238-39; supports Frémont's presidential candidacy in 1864, 265-66, 268, 274-75; attacks Lincoln, 274-75; and movement to oust Lincoln as Repub. candidate, 281; refuses to support Lincoln, 285; elected v.p. of Am. A.S. Soc., 305; opposes 14th Amendment, 355, 373

Cheever, Henry, 5; votes for Gerrit Smith in 1860, 19n; on Lincoln's election in 1860, 26; on 1st battle of Bull Run, 71; desires national abolitionist convention, 75; organizes "Freedom Club," 226; supports Frémont's candidacy in 1864, 268; opposes 14th Amendment, 373

Chicago Times, denounces abolitionists, 41; laments outburst of Negro suffrage propaganda, 327

Chicago Times and Herald, denounces abolitionists, 41

Child, David Lee, supports Lincoln in 1860, 14; almost mobbed at war meeting, 48; on war power of govt. over slavery, 67-68; welcomes Bull Run defeat, 71

Child, Lydia Maria, 4, 14, 43, 75-76; on Republicans and secession, 30-31; prefers civil war to compromise, 46; response to outbreak of war, 48; on return of fugitive slaves, 58; discouraged by "military necessity" argument, 91; criticizes Lincoln, 95; on emancipation in District of Columbia, 97; on racial intermarriage, 148; on alleged Negro inferiority, 151-52; dislikes paternalism toward freedmen, 168; favors measures to obtain land for freedmen, 255-56, 407; opposes Frémont candidacy in 1864, 274; on northern support for Negro suffrage, 311; on "impartial suffrage," 327-28; uneasy about Andrew Johnson, 333n; fading confidence in A.J., 339; writes *The Freedmen's Book*, 388; on 15th Amendment, 428; on North's abandonment of Reconstruction, 431

Church Anti-Slavery Society, 19; description of, in 1860, 5; urges emancipation under war power, 39; works with Garrisonians during war, 106; urges equal treatment for Negro soldiers, 204; opposes Lincoln's reelection, 268

Cincinnati, streetcar segregation ended in, 233n

Cincinnati Daily Enquirer, denounces abolitionists, 41

civil rights, *see* equal rights; Negro suffrage; segregation

Civil Rights bill of 1866, 342, 350

Civil War, few abolitionists foresee, 45-46; most abolitionists support Union cause, 47-55; abolitionists see as "Second American Revolution" of freedom, 65-66

Clapperton, Hugh, 141

Clark University, 388

Clarke, James Freeman, 7; approves disunion, 38n; urges emancipation, 77; on racial differences, 143-44; advises Chase to withdraw pres. candidacy in 1864, 264; urges land for freedmen, 407

Cluseret, G. P. 272-73

Cochrane, John, makes emancipation speeches, 78; advocates Negro troops, 194; v.p. candidate of Radical Democratic Party in 1864, 270, 276; acceptance letter of, 273

Coffin, Levi, 7; organizes Western Freedmen's Aid Commission, 170-71; lobbies for Freedmen's Bureau bill, 189; general agent of Western F. A. Comm., 387

Colfax, Schuyler, 347, 368-69

Collyer, Robert, 117

colonization, of Negroes, advocated by Lincoln, 94, 155; opposed by abolitionists, 155-56; failure of, 155-56

Colorado, issue of equal suffrage in, 342

Concord Anti-Slavery Society, 68

confiscation, *see* land for freedmen

Confiscation Act of 1861, 72, 73, 94, 101, 247

Confiscation Act of 1862, 111-12, 196, 248, 256

Congdon, Charles, 87

Conkling, James, 124

Connecticut, ends school segregation, 229; defeats Negro suffrage, 333-34

Continental Monthly, emancipationist journal, 91-92

"contraband," term coined by Butler, 69-70

Conway, Moncure D., 234; supports Lincoln in 1860, 14; supports war, 55; urges emancipation, 63-64; desires war to be revolution of freedom, 66; welcomes Bull Run defeat, 71; denounces Lincoln's revocation of Frémont edict, 73-74; interview with Lincoln, 84-85; on Lincoln's gradual emancipation proposals, 96, 120; on Emancipation Proclamation, 118; article on Benjamin Banneker, 142-43; on racial differences, 144-45, 147; on racial intermarriage, 148; on alleged Negro inferiority, 151, 152; wants Civil War to be war for racial equality, 221; nominates Frémont for pres., 264

Cony, Samuel, 362

"Copperheads," growth of movement, 123; and Frémont candidacy in 1864, 270, 273, 274-77, 277n, 279-80

Corps d'Afrique, 208, 291

Craft, Ellen, 413

Craft, William, 413

Crittenden, John J., 30

Crittenden Compromise, denounced by abolitionists, 30

Crittenden resolution on slavery and the war, 70; fails of repassage, 95

Crosby, Alpheus, 338

Curtis, George W., 323

Dana, Charles A., 86, 87n

Dana, Richard Henry, 323, 326

Davis, Edward M., 209; fears war won't abolish slavery, 58; and Frémont's emancipation edict, 72

Davis, Garrett, 81, 89

Davis, Henry Winter, 245; and movement to oust Lincoln as Repub. candidate in 1864, 281; on Negro suffrage, 308-09

Davis, Jefferson, 59, 103, 113, 125, 273, 316, 363

Delany, Martin R., on African heritage of Negro, 138; recruits Negro soldiers, 205, 207, 220; commissioned as major, 219n.

Democratic party, and elections of 1862, 119; and Frémont candidacy in 1864, 273-74, 275-76, 279-80; nominates McClellan on peace platform, 282, 283; and election of 1868, 422-23. *See also* elections

Denham, Dixon, 141

desegregation, *see* equal rights, segregation

Dicey, Edward, 87

Dickinson, Anna E., 266, 367; denounces Lincoln, 108; blossoms into prominent orator, 128-32; and 1863 elections in N.H. and Conn., 129-30; on racial intermarriage, 148; recruits Negro soldiers, 207; urges equal justice for freedmen, 242; campaigns for Lincoln in 1864, 282-84; opposes dissolution of American A.S. Soc., 304; speeches opposing Johnson's reconstruction policy, 335; and issue of Negro suffrage at Southern Loyalist convention, 362-63; campaigns for Repubs. in 1866, 364; refuses to stump the South, 378; urges land for freedmen, 407; criticizes Grant, 419

Dickinson, Daniel S., 78, 99

discrimination, *see* equal rights, segregation

District of Columbia, emancipation in, 97; abolitionist response, 97-98, 101-02, 107; fugitive slave law enforced in, 102-03, 108-09; streetcar segregation ended in, 230-31; Negro suffrage bill, passed by House, 342; shelved by Senate, 357n; becomes law, 374n

disunion, urged by Garrisonian abolitionists before 1860, 31-32; most abolitionists welcome in 1860-61, 33-38; non-Garrisonian abolitionists on, 36-39; repudiated by most Garrisonians after outbreak of war, 47-51, 55-60, 99-102

Douglas, Stephen A., 23, 61

Douglass, Frederick, 5, 13, 121, 131, 132, 143, 330, 367, 427; supports Frémont in 1856, 16; on Republicans in 1860, 17-19; supports Radical Abolitionist party in 1860, 18-19; on Republican party and Negro suffrage, 25-26; on Lincoln's election in 1860, 26-27; approves disunion, 37; urges emancipation during secession crisis, 39; believes North won't fight, 46; on northern war fever, 47; urges emancipation as military necessity, 62-63; on northern response to Bull Run defeat, 71; on Lincoln's deference to border-state slaveowners, 73; wartime increase of prestige, 82; on nature of northern opposition to slavery, 92-93; on progress of abolitionist cause, 98; cooperates with Garrisonians during war, 104-06; disgust with Lincoln, 117; on Emancipation Proclamation, 118; on alleged inferiority of Negro, 135, 149, 150-51; on African heritage of Negro, 138; on transition of slave to freedman, 187-88; advocates arming of Negroes, 192-93, recruits Negro soldiers, 204-05, 207, 219; on govt.'s refusal of equal pay to Negro soldiers, 213; interview with Lincoln, 213; urges Negro suffrage as condition of reconstruction, 239-40, 319, 323; supports Frémont's candidacy in 1864, 268; comes out for Lincoln, 283n; speeches opposing Johnson's reconstruction policy, 335; opposes dissolution of a.s. societies, 288-89, 305; interview with Johnson, 343, 346-47; urges Johnson to support Negro suffrage, 343, 346; denounces 14th Amendment, 355; delegate to Southern Loyalist convention, 360-61; speaking tour of South, 378; turns down commissionership of Freedmen's Bureau, 381; criticizes paternalism freedmen's aid societies, 397; on failure to provide freedmen with land, 416; on Phillips and the Am. A.S. Soc., 429; on North's abandonment of Reconstruction, 431

Douglass, H. Ford, 25, 32n

Douglass' Monthly, 104

Downing, George T., 143; interview with Andrew Johnson, 343, 346

draft riots, in New York City, 231-32

Dugdale, Joseph, 367

d'Urville, Dumont, 137

Duvall, W. O., 99

Eastman, Zebina, 64

education of freedmen, by freedmen's aid societies, abolitionists and, 154, 158, 160-77, 386-407; purpose of, 392-93, 405-06; problems of, 394-400; southern opposition to, 395-96; in La., 292-93; and the founding of public schools in South, 404-05; abolitionists urge federal aid to education, 370, 372-73, 375, 383, 405; founding of normal schools and colleges, 406-07; achievements of f.a. societies, 404, 406-07

elections, of 1856: 9, 16; of 1860: 9-28; of 1862: and Democratic gains, 119; of 1863: and Republican victories, 124, 129-30; of 1864: abolitionists and, 260-86, 287, 289, 299; of 1866: 358-66; of 1867: Democratic gains in, 378, 382, 383, 412; and Negro suffrage, 382; of 1868: 385; abolitionists and, 417-24, issue of Negro suffrage in, 417, 419-23

Eliot, Thomas, 308; and formation of Freedmen's Bureau, 187, 189

emancipation, abolitionists urge during secession crisis, 39-40; abolitionists anticipate as consequence of war, 47-51; urged by abolitionists as "military necessity," 61-63, 65; dangers of military necessity argument, 90-93; advocated by abolitionists as act of justice, 63-65; and "war power" argument, 66-69; increased northern opinion favoring, 81-82, 84n, 90, 93-98, 110-12; conversion of north to immediate emancipation, 132; in District of Columbia, 97; abolitionist response, 97-98, 101-02, 107. *See also* Emancipation Proclamation; Thirteenth Amendment

Emancipation League, 77, 323; formation and activities of, 75-76, 79; Garrisonian abolitionists support, 106; urges creation of freedmen's bureau, 178-79, 180-81, 191; questionnaire on freedmen, 180-81; and Frémont's candidacy in 1864, 279-80; and movement to oust Lincoln as Repub. candidate, 281; urges Negro suffrage, 320; reorganized as Impartial Suffrage Assoc., 353

Emancipation Proclamation, of Sept. 22, 1862, 1st draft of, 111; issuance of, 117-118; abolitionist response, 117-19; Democratic attacks on, 119

Emancipation Proclamation, of Jan. 1, 1863, abolitionists anticipate, 120-21; issuance of, 121-22; abolitionist response, 121-22, 133

"emancipationist," term coined, 92

equal pay, for Negro soldiers, abolitionists work for, 213-20; achieved, 217-19

equal rights, for Negroes, supported by abolitionists, 23-26; fundamental aim of abolitionist movement, 221, 225, 261; abolitionists work for in North, 222-37. *See also* Negro suffrage; segregation

Equal Rights Association, opposes 14th Amendment, 373

Equal Rights Leagues, organized, 234-35

equal suffrage, definition of, 327. *See also* Negro suffrage

Equality of All Men before the Law, The, 319

Essex County Anti-Slavery Society, on Lincoln, 24; on equal rights as aim of abolitionist movement, 225

Everett, Edward, 99

Fairbanks, Dexter, 78

Fee, John G., 388, 413

Fessenden, William Pitt, 343; opposes retroactive equal pay for Negro troops, 216; expects Andrew Johnson to sign Freedmen's Bureau bill, 347; and 14th Amendment, 353, 355

Field, David Dudley, 281

Fifteenth Amendment, 421, 429, 430; abolitionists urge passage of, 354-55, 376-77, 383, 424-25; passed by Congress, 425-27; ratified, 428. *See also* Negro suffrage

Fifty-Fifth Massachusetts Volunteers, Negro regiment, recruited, 205, 209; and struggle for equal pay, 212, 214, 218

Fifty-Fourth Massachusetts Volunteers, Negro regiment, recruited, 202-05, 209; parade through Boston, 205-06; assault on Fort Wagner, 211-12; and struggle for equal pay, 212, 214, 217, 218

First South Carolina Volunteers, Negro regiment, recruited, 197; commanded by T. W. Higginson, 197-202; fights well, 198-99, 211; struggle for equal pay, 212, 215-16, 218-19

Fish, William, 33

Fisk University, founded by A.M.A., 406

Forbes, John Murray, on success of emancipation, 167

Forrest, Nathan Bedford, and Fort Pillow massacre, 218n

Fort Pillow, "massacre," 217-18 and 218n

Fort Sumter, reaction of abolitionists to bombardment of, 46-51; flag-raising ceremony in 1865, abolitionists attend, 300

Fort Wagner, assault on, of 54th Massachusetts Volunteers, 211-12

Forten, Charlotte, teacher of freedmen in S.C., 162-63; publicizes Port Royal experiment, 172

Foss, Andrew T., 269, 284

Foster, Abby Kelly, 4, 10

Foster, Stephen S., 4, 14, 16, 307; denounces Repub. party, 10; organizes

"Union Democratic party," 13; opposes disunion, 38-39; on abolitionist support of Union war effort, 58-59, 101, 103-04; denounces Union government, 99, 100, 102-03; on equal rights as aim of abolitionist movement, 225; opposes Lincoln in 1864, 268; supports Frémont's candidacy, 267; criticizes Garrison's support of Banks' labor system in La., 299; opposes dissolution of Am. A.S. Society, 287, 301, 305-07; on Republican shortcomings, 358

Fourteenth Amendment, 423; first proposed, 351; revised, 353; shortcomings of, criticized by abolitionists, 351-58, 364-66, 372-74; passed by Congress, 355-56; seen by Repubs. as final terms of reconstruction, 364-65, 372-74; rejected by southern states, 374; and Reconstruction Acts, 374-75

Fowler, J. H., 197-98

Franklin, Benjamin, 388n

Free Soil party, 20, 22; not an abolitionist party, 3, 5, 6, 18; cooperates with abolitionists in Massachusetts, 6-7; attitude of Garrisonians toward, 9

Free South, 254

freedmen's aid societies, *see* education of freedmen; and the names of individual societies (e.g., New England Freedmen's Aid Society)

Freedmen's Book, The, 388

Freedmen's Bureau, 172, 378-79, 381, 387, 391, 396; creation of, urged by abolitionists, 178-91; passage of bill establishing, 189-90; abolitionist personnel of, 190-91; and land for freedmen, 256-57; and crimes against freedmen, 359; assists freedmen's aid societies, 393, 406; favors A.M.A., 402; and Andrew Johnson's restoration of land to pardoned rebels, 408-09

Freedmen's Bureau bill, of 1866, introduced, 341-42; passed by Congress, vetoed by Johnson, 347-49; passed over veto, 409

Freedom Club, in Worcester, aims of, 226; on Andrew Johnson, 347

French, Mansfield, organizes Natl. Freedmen's Relief Assoc., 160; publicizes Port Royal experiment, 172;

efforts to obtain land for freedmen, 250-51, 253-55, 259

Frémont, Jessie Benton, 264, 285n

Frémont, John C., 9, 16, 95, 98, 207; emancipation edict in Mo., 72; abolitionists applaud, 72-73; Lincoln modifies, 73, 76, 77; abolitionists support for president in 1864, 264-71, 272-77, 279-81, 284; nominated for president, 269-70; acceptance letter of, 273, 274; candidacy opposed by abolitionists, 272-79, 281, 284; abolitionists try to persuade to withdraw from race, 281, 284; withdraws, 284

Frothingham, Octavius B., 7, 78; speaks out for Negro suffrage, 326-27

fugitive slaves, returned to masters by Union officers, 48, 58; declared "contraband of war" by Butler, 69-70; no national policy on in 1861, 70n; Congress forbids army officers to return, 97; captured in District of Columbia, 102-03, 108-09

Furness, William H., 44, 52

Gage, Frances D., 171, 172

Gannett, William C., participant in Port Royal experiment, 175; evaluates experiment, 175-77; opposes grants of land to freedmen, 251; supports measures to assure land for freedmen, 254, 259

Gardner, Anna, philosophy of teaching freedmen, 395-96

Garfield, James, 264

Garnet, Henry Highland, 143; recruits Negro soldiers, 205; invited to preach in House chamber, 226

Garrison, Francis J., 350

Garrison, George T., 205n

Garrison, Wendell P., on Lincoln's plan of reconstruction, 241, 252; on Wade-Davis bill, 246; associate ed. of *Nation*, 323; on defeat of Negro suffrage in Conn., 334

Garrison, William Lloyd, 3, 4, 13, 14, 22, 26, 68, 86, 92, 98, 106, 128, 174, 194, 216, 235, 310, 418; on Free Soil and Repub. parties before 1860, 9; on Repub. party and Lincoln in 1860, 12-13, 15; praises John Andrew, 15; on Radical Abolitionist party, 18; praises Lincoln's refusal to compromise on slavery in territories, 31; favors disunion, 33-34; condones slave

insurrections, 34-35; discouraged by antiabolitionist mobs, 45; supports war effort despite pacifism, 52-54; urges support of Lincoln's war policy, 55; repudiates disunion and supports war for Union, 57-59, 100 and n, 101-02; support of Union criticized, 58-60; denounces Lincoln's modification of Frémont's emancipation edict, 73; opposes holding of national abolitionist convention, 75; consulted on *Independent* editorial policy, 88; wartime growth of prestige and influence of, 90, 299-300, 299n; writes emancipation petitions, 93, 110; denounces Lincoln's conservatism, 94, 108, 112, 117; on Lincoln's gradual emancipation proposals, 96-97, 120; on emancipation in District of Columbia, 97; on Emancipation Proclamation, 118-19, 120, 121; on African heritage of Negro, 141; reviews parade of 54th Mass. Volunteers, 206; on Sherman's Order no. 15, 258; defends Lincoln, supports his reelection, 260-62, 266-67, 268-69, 272, 285, 291, 299; dispute with Phillips over election of 1864, 260-62, 268-69, 278, 287; attends Repub. convention in 1864, 271; interview with E. M. Stanton, 271; interview with Lincoln, 272; denounced by Frémont supporters, 272; favors dissolution of Am. A.S. Soc., 287-88, 301-07; resigns as president of Am. A.S. Soc., 305; defends Banks' labor system in La., 291-93, 299; defense criticized by other abolitionists, 291, 293, 299; ambiguous position on Negro suffrage, 294-95, 297-98, 298n; position criticized by other abolitionists, 295, 297-99; visit to Charleston in 1865, 300; favors Negro suffrage, 303-04, 304n; and last issue of *Liberator*, 305n; and founding of *Nation*, 324-25; confidence in Andrew Johnson, 330 and n; fading confidence in A.J., 333, 339; urges impeachment of A.J., 349, 370; on 14th Amendment, 356; on abolitionists' obligation to freedmen, 386; clash with Phillips over Jackson bequest, 400-01, 401n; in election of 1868, 423

Garrison, William Lloyd, Jr., 45; welcomes secession, 36; supports war despite pacifism, 52-53; early confidence in Andrew Johnson, 314; on A.J.'s policy, 330; critical of A.J., 338

Garrisonian abolitionists, 78; description of, 3-4; disunion convention of 1857, 7; on antislavery political parties before 1860, 9-10; and election of 1860, 9-16, 27-28; support Andrew in 1860, 14-15; advocate disunion, before 1860, 31-32, during secession crisis, 33-36; suspend meetings at start of war, 55-56; repudiate disunionism, support war for Union, 55-60; growing schism in ranks, 99-104, 106, 287-300; schism of 1865, 301-07; work with non-Garrisonians during war, 104-06; urge creation of freedmen's bureau, 179; urge appointment of Negro army officers, 204; work to end streetcar segregation in Philadelphia, 233-34. *See also* American Anti-Slavery Society; New England Anti-Slavery Society; Massachusetts Anti-Slavery Society

Gay, Sydney Howard, 4; supports Lincoln in 1860, 14; publishes Frémont's emancipation edict, 72; becomes managing ed. of *New York Tribune*, 86-87 and 87n; urges emancipation, 96; interview with Lincoln, 114-15; on Lincoln and slavery, 116; on alleged inferiority of Negro, 135, 150, 152-53; on impediments to Negro soldier recruitment, 203-04; urges equal pay for Negro troops, 215-16; denounces racial discrimination in North, 222; urges streetcar desegregation in Washington, 230; advocates federal law against segregation in transportation, 237; on Sherman's Order no. 15, 257-58; sympathetic to Chase candidacy in 1864, 263; on northern war-weariness in 1864, 280; comes out for Lincoln's reelection, 283; on Banks' labor system in La., 290; urges Negro suffrage in North, 333

Georgia, legislature expels Negro members, 423

Gettysburg, battle of, abolitionist and northern reaction to, 123-24, 240

Gibbons, Abigail Hopper, 171-72

Giddings, Joshua, 67

"Gideonites," missionaries to freedmen in S.C., 162-69, 172-73, 175; skeptical about arming of freedmen, 195; support the arming of freedmen, 197; efforts to obtain land for freedmen, 250-52, 253-55, 259

Gilbert, Edward, 78; supports Lincoln in 1860, 19; hails disunion, 37

Gilmore, James R., on Gay and Greeley, 87n; founds *Continental Monthly*, 91; on Greeley and Lincoln, 115-16

Gliddon, George, 136

Godkin, Edwin L., and founding of *Nation*, 323-25

Godwin, Parke, 281-82

Goodell, William, 22, 93; editor of *Principia*, 5; in election of 1860, 17-18; opposes disunion, urges emancipation under war power, 39; response to outbreak of war, 48; urges emancipation as military and political necessity, 63; desires "Second American Revolution" of freedom, 65; on growing emancipation sentiment in North, 78-79; organizes National Emancipation Association, 80; on wartime increase of abolitionist prestige, 81; welcomed in capital, 84; interview with Lincoln, 84; on Lincoln's revocation of Hunter's emancipation edict, 108; praises Lincoln's pledge to sustain Emancipation Proclamation, 124; on freedmen's education, 154; on Wade-Davis bill, 245; urges confiscation and reallocation of southern plantations, 247; supports Frémont's presidential candidacy in 1864, 267-68, 275, 279

Grant, Ulysses S., 321; presidential possibility in 1864, 270, 281; probable Repub. presidential nominee in 1868, 417-19; nominated, 419; abolitionists on, 417-19, 422; election of, 424

Greeley, Horace, 81, 283, 368; on Repub. party and slavery in 1860, 12; and S. H. Gay, 86-87, 87n; critical of Lincoln, 115; "Prayer of Twenty Millions," 116; supports Chase candidacy in 1864, 263, 266; advises Chase to withdraw from race, 264; and movement to oust Lincoln as Republican nominee, 281-82; efforts to reconcile Johnson and Congress, 343; stunned by Johnson's veto of Freedmen's Bureau bill, 347-48; works for Negro suffrage in N.Y., 377; opposes impeachment in 1867, 383; on charity to freedmen, 392; on abolitionist efforts to obtain land for freedmen,

412; supports Chase for presidential nomination in 1868, 417-18

Grew, Mary, 4; opposes concessions to save Union, 30; on increased prestige of abolitionists, 89, 267; on progress of abolitionist cause, 98; on assault of 54th Mass. Volunteers on Fort Wagner, 212

Griffing, Josephine S., 4; on Republican party in 1860, 13; and antiabolitionist mob violence, 45; social worker among Washington freedmen, 171, 188, 389, 391-92; official of Freedmen's Bureau, 190, 391

Griffith, Mattie, approves disunion, 33

Grinnell, Josiah, 246

Grow, Galusha, 85

Hahn, Michael, 244

Haiti, Negro emigration to, 155-56

Halleck, Gen. Henry, 112

Hallett, Benjamin, 78

Hallowell, Edward N., officer in Negro regiment, 217, 220; devises "Quaker Oath," 218

Hallowell, Norwood P., officer in Negro regiment, 203, 220

Hamlin, Hannibal, 25

Hampton, Wade, 377

Hampton Institute, founded by A.M.A., 406

Hancock, Gen. Winfield, 383

Harper, Frances E. W., 378

Harper's Weekly, 373

Hartford Times, on wartime growth of abolitionist influence, 132

Haven, Gilbert, 7; on equality of races, 135, 136; on racial intermarriage, 148; on racial discrimination in North, 222; works for church desegregation, 227; opposes segregation in army, 236; at impeachment trial, 384; and Methodist Freedmen's Aid Society, 388; urges 15th Amendment, 424

Heinzen, Karl, 265, 267, 279

Helper, Hinton Rowan, 317

Herndon, William H., 31, 35-36

Hicks, Thomas, governor of Maryland, 69

Higginson, Thomas Wentworth, 6; supports Lincoln in 1860, 23; on secession, 37; on northern war fever, 47; says that slavery is root of rebellion, urges emancipation, 62, 72; on northern military victories, 107; fears

reaction against Emancipation Proclamation, 122-23; colonel of 1st S.C. Volunteers (Negro regiment, 197-202, 211, 220; *Army Life in a Black Regiment*, 200; works for equal pay for Negro soldiers, 212, 215, 218-19; opposes school segregation in Newport, 228-29; urges Negro suffrage as condition of reconstruction, 296; favors land for freedmen, 254, 407, 411; on northern reaction to Lincoln's assassination, 315; on Johnson's reconstruction policy, 337-38; turns against Johnson, 339; on Negro suffrage in North, 420

Hinton, Richard J., 6, 51; writes campaign biographies of Seward and Lincoln, 20; organizes Kansas Emancipation League, 170; at impeachment trial, 384; on proposed 15th Amendment, 424

Hoar, George F., 405

Holden, William, 321

Holley, Sallie, on Emancipation Proclamation, 118; long service as teacher of freedmen, 387

Hovey, Horace, 226-27

Howard, Gen. Oliver Otis, commissioner of Freedmen's Bureau, 381; on achievements of freedmen's aid societies, 172; antislavery sympathizer, 190; aids freedmen's education, 393; favors A.M.A., 402-03; and restoration of land to pardoned rebels, 408-09

Howard University, founded, 406

Howe, Samuel Gridley, 6, 336; member of Bird Club, 7; opposes Union-saving efforts, 37; response to outbreak of war, 47-48; and Emancipation League, 75, 76, 79; on racial differences, 145-47; on alleged Negro inferiority, 152-53; urges creation of freedmen's bureau, 179, 180; member of American Freedmen's Inquiry Commission, 182-86, 191; book on Canadian Negroes, 186-87; on transition of slave to freedman, 187; opposes school segregation, 228n; opposes segregation in army, 236; and efforts to obtain land for freedmen, 415

Humboldt, Alexander von, 137

Hunter, Gen. David, 250; emancipation edict, revoked by Lincoln, 102-03,

107-08, 111; abolitionist response, 107-08; tries to recruit Negro regiment on S.C. sea islands, 195-96, 197

Hutchinson, John Wallace, 20-21

Hutchinson family, singing group, support Lincoln in 1860, 20-21, 23; refuse to sing before segregated audiences, 223

Illinois, denies equal rights to Negroes, 25

impartial suffrage, definition of, 327; abolitionists on, 327-28. *See also* Negro suffrage

Impartial Suffrage Association, 353, 356

impeachment, *see* Johnson, Andrew

intermarriage, *see* racial intermarriage

Independent, 14, 238, 309-10, 349, 383; change in editorship of, 87-88; circulation of, 88, 89n; emancipation editorials of, 110; opposes streetcar segregation in New York, 232; supports Chase candidacy in 1864, 263; opposes Frémont candidacy, 275-78; comes out for Lincoln, 282-83; supports Negro suffrage enabling act, 356; opposes Tennessee's readmission, 357; urges adoption of 15th Amendment, 376; favors Negro suffrage in North, 377; supports Chase for Repub. presidential nomination in 1868, 418, 419. *See also* Tilton, Theodore

Iowa, adopts Negro suffrage in 1868, 424

Jackson, Francis, antislavery bequest, dispute over, 400-01 and 401n

Jackson, William Andrew, 125

Jay, John, 7, 90; supports Lincoln in 1860, 22-23; approves disunion, 37; on slavery and the war, 61; discourages distinct abolitionist organizations, 77-78; bases emancipation plea on military necessity, 91n; organizes emancipation meeting in New York, 110; regrets Phillips' attacks on Lincoln, 113; president of New York Union League, 123; urges creation of freedmen's bureau, 178; recruits Negro troops, 207-08, 219; theory of reconstruction, 238; and southern Republicans, 379

Jay, William, 23

Jocelyn, Simeon S., 5, 19n

Johnson, Andrew, 316, 366, 417; military governor of Tenn., 209-10; theory of reconstruction, 239, 317-18; theory criticized by abolitionists, 321, 337, 341; denounces traitors, 314, 316; early abolitionist and radical confidence in, 314, 316-18; prejudice against Negroes, 317, 346n, 347; interviews with Negroes, 317, 343, 346 and n; on Negro suffrage, 318, 320, 334, 336, 341, 346; position on N. suffrage denounced by abolitionists, 346-47; interview with Stearns, 336-37; reconstruction policy, 320-21; policy criticized by abolitionists, 321-22, 329-33, 335-36, 336-40; increasing tension with Congress, 342; efforts to reconcile Congress and A.J., 342-43; efforts opposed by abolitionists, 343; vetoes Freedmen's Bureau bill, 347-48; Washington's Birthday speech, 348-49; vetoes Civil Rights bill and breaks with Republicans, 350; and National Union movement, 358; and New Orleans riot, 359; denounces Phillips and T. Stevens as traitors, 363; advises South to reject 14th Amendment, 374; and Reconstruction Acts, 375-76, 380, 383; offers commissionership of Freedmen's Bureau to Negroes, 381; abolitionists urge impeachment of, 349, 369-70, 375, 381-82, 383-85; suspends Stanton, 381, 418; controversy with Grant, 419; dismisses Stanton, 384; impeached by House, 384; acquitted by Senate, 385; abolitionist reaction to acquittal, 385; restores land to pardoned rebels, 407-08; abolitionists denounce, 409

Johnson, Oliver, 23, 78, 79, 95, 307; ed. of *National Anti-Slavery Standard*, 4; on Repub. party in 1860, 16; on northern war fever, 47; anticipates emancipation as result of war, 48; hopes Phillips will support Union War effort, 49; praises Phillips' war speech, 51; on Gay's accession as managing ed. of *New York Tribune*, 86-87; consulted on. *Independent* editorial policy, 88; on Parker Pillsbury's antigovernment stand, 101-02; tries to promote harmony in Am. A.S. Soc., 102; urges Lincoln to proclaim emancipation, 110; on growing emancipation pressure, 111; on Lincoln's dismissal of McClellan, 119; on Emancipation Proclamation, 120; on alleged Negro inferiority, 149; warns abolitionists against political activity, 262; attacks Frémont candidacy in 1864, 273; supports Lincoln, 278; urges Garrison to support Negro suffrage, 297-98; on Negro suffrage, 301-02, 303; favors dissolution of Am. A.S. Society, 300-03, 305-07; resigns as ed. of *Standard*, 305; urges abolitionists to join freedmen's aid societies, 301-02; becomes managing ed. of *Independent*, 305n; disillusioned by Andrew Johnson's veto of Freedmen's Bureau bill, 348; on 14th Amendment, 356; on probable nomination of Grant in 1868, 418

Johnson, Samuel, 7

Joint Committee of Fifteen, 343; formation of, 341; and 14th Amendment, 351-54

Jones, Howard Mumford, 200

Julian, George W., 3, 419; on emancipation in District of Columbia, 97; favors land for freedmen, 249; bill to provide land for freedmen, 255-57, 259; urges Lincoln to approve permanent confiscation, 256; and Reconstruction Acts, 374-75

Kansas, Negro suffrage defeated in, 382

Kansas Emancipation League, 170

Kelley, William D., 361; favors Negro suffrage, 308-09, 319, 323; urges abolitionists to keep up fight for Negro suffrage, 350; southern tour of, 378

Keokuk Gate City, on Phillips' influence, 367-68

Ketchum, Edgar, 78, 321

King, Martin Luther, 432

Kock, Bernard, 155

Ku Klux Klan, 413, 423

Laborers' Homestead and Southern Emigration Society, 415-16

La Crosse Democrat, 423

land for freedmen, abolitionists urge measures to provide, 179, 246-59, 319, 370, 372-73, 375, 407-12; and Confiscation Acts, 247-48; on S.C. sea islands, 249-51, 253-55; government measures for, 253-57; Sherman's Order no. 15, 257-59; and Frémont's presidential candidacy in 1864, 267, 270; abolitionist efforts to help freedmen obtain land, 386, 412-16

Langston, John Mercer, 143; recruits Negro soldiers, 205, 206-07, 219-20; interview with Andrew Johnson, 317; appointed inspector of schools of Freedmen's Bureau, 378; organizes Negro Republicans in South, 378-79; turns down commissionership of Freedmen's Bureau, 381

Latham, R. G., 137

Leavitt, Joshua, 6, 106; on Lincoln's election in 1860, 26; sympathetic to Chase's presidential ambitions in 1864, 263

Lee, Robert E., 321

Leland, Charles G., 91

Lewis, Dio, 229

Liberator, 4, 15, 51, 92, 94, 100n, 120, 128, 174, 300, 324, 334, 338; and land for freedmen, 246-47; on Sherman's Order no. 15, 258; supports Lincoln's reelection, 267; opposes Frémont's candidacy, 272, 279; pro-Frémont abolitionists cancel subscriptions to, 272-73; defends Banks' labor system in La., 292; last issue of, 305n

Liberty party, 5, 6, 7, 17-18, 22 104

Lincoln, Abraham, 9, 55, 98, 192, 215, 240, 287, 299, 318, 334, 362; attitude of abolitionists toward, in election of 1860, 11-28; on slavery before Civil War, 11; opposed to social and political equality of races, 11, 23-25; refuses to compromise on slavery in territories, 31; promises to avoid interference with slavery, 56, 70; Lincoln administration, Garrisonian abolitionists on, 59-60; abolitionists begin to criticize L.'s leadership, 60-61, 74; abolitionists urge L. to proclaim emancipation under war power, 66-67; modifies Frémont's emancipation edict, 73, 76, 77; abolitionists denounce, 73-74; attends abolitionist lectures, 81, 131; interviews with abolitionists, 84-85, 115, 213, 272; and colonization of freedmen, 94, 155; colonization criticized by abolitionists, 94-95, 156; recommends gradual, compensated emancipation, 96, 119-20; conservatism criticized by abolitionists, 102, 109-13, 116-17; by Republicans, 114-15; revokes Hunter's emancipation edict, 102-03, 107-08, 111; recommends border-state emancipation, 111; drafts Emancipation Proclamation, 111; reply to Greeley's "Prayer of Twenty Millions," 116; issues preliminary Emancipation Proclamation, 117-18; dismisses McClellan, 119; issues final Emancipation Proclamation, 120-22; pledges to sustain Proclamation, 124; and contrabands on S.C. sea islands, 160; recommends creation of Freedmen's Bureau, 188-89; signs bill creating Bureau, 190; opposes arming of Negroes, 194-96; authorizes enlistment of Negro soldiers, 197, 202, 207; praises courage and contribution of Negro troops, 212; promises equal pay for Negro soldiers, 213-14; and Confiscation Act of 1862, 248; and land for freedmen, 253, 256; reconstruction theory of, 239, 317; reconstruction policy, 239, 240-41, 308-09; criticized by abolitionists, 241-43, 252-53, 260-61, 268, 269-70; and reconstruction of La., 243-45, 314; pocket veto of Wade-Davis bill, 246, 280-81; and Negro suffrage, 294; favors qualified Negro suffrage, 244, 314; election of 1864, abolitionists and, 260-86; strong support of in 1864, by rank and file Republicans, 264, 266; renominated, 271; anticipates defeat at polls, 280; movement to oust L. as Republican candidate in 1864, abolitionists and, 280-82; most abolitionists support L. in election of 1864, 285; sustains Banks' labor system in La., 290-91; 2nd inaugural address, 311; assassination of, abolitionist reaction, 314-16; compared to Andrew Johnson, 314-15, 330, 332, 336. *See also* elections; Republican party

Livermore, George, denounces Phillips, 113

Lockwood, Lewis C., missionary to freedmen, 158

London Times, 234, 396

Louisiana, reconstruction of, under Lincoln's policy, 243-45, 269; Gen. Banks' labor system in, abolitionists on, 289-93, 296, 299; education of freedmen in, 292-93; abolitionists and radicals oppose readmission of, 1865, 308-10

Louisville Democrat, 165

Lovejoy, Owen, 3; opposes return of fugitive slaves, 70; resolution forbidding return of fugitive slaves, 95

Lowell, James Russell, 140

Lowry, Morrow B., bill to abolish segregation in public transportation in Pa., 235-36

Loyal Publication Society, 123

L'Unite de l'Espece Humaine, 137

McClellan, George B., 110, 268, 269, 276, 280; denounced by abolitionists, 113; and battle of Antietam, 117; dismissed by Lincoln, 119; failure of peninsula campaign, 196; Democratic candidate for president in 1865, 282, 283, 284

McKaye, James, member of A.F.I.C., 182-86

McKim, James Miller, 4, 76, 210, 307; anticipates emancipation as result of war, 48-49; wartime growth of influence, 127; organizes Philadelphia Port Royal Relief Committee, 160; resigns as secretary of Pa. A.S. Soc., 161, 287; urges abolitionists to go into freedmen's aid work, 161-62; on Port Royal experiment, 166; and formation of A.F.I.C., 181-82, 191; lobbies for Freedmen's Bureau bill, 189; recruits Negro troops, 207, 219; works to end streetcar segregation in Philadelphia, 235; and election of 1864, 266; on Negro suffrage, 294, 297; and schism in Am. A.S. Soc., 305; and founding of *Nation,* 323-25; continued confidence in Andrew Johnson, 338, 339; urges enlargement of Freedmen's Bureau, 341; expects A.J. to sign Freedmen's Bureau bill, 347; disillusioned by A.J.'s veto, 348; denounces A.J., 349; on 14th Amendment, 356; corresponding secretary of A.F.U.C., 387, 398-99; organizes A.F.A.C., 394; organizes A.F.U.C., 398; on purpose of freedmen's education, 393, 397-98; on degradation of Negro by slavery, 396-97

McPherson, Edward, 331

Manning, Jacob, 160

Martin, J. Sella, 143

Massachusetts, center of antislavery strength, 6-7; enacts public accommodations law, 236-37

Massachusetts Anti-Slavery Society, 4, 68, 128, 132, 287; convention disrupted by mob, 43; wartime influence of, 83; supports Union government, 100; urges creation of freedmen's bureau, 179; urges Negro suffrage, 242-43; criticizes Lincoln in 1864, 260-61, 278; convention of 1865, and Negro suffrage, 297-99, 301

Massey, R. D., 210

May, Samuel, Jr., 307; and election of Andrew in 1860, 15; on election of Lincoln, 27; welcomes secession, 33; on northern war fever, 47; supports Union govt. and war, 54, 60, 103; on northern opinion of slavery, 95; on emancipation in District of Columbia, 97; on Pillsbury's antigovernment stand, 102; on Lincoln's revocation of Hunter's emancipation edict, 108; on Emancipation Proclamation, 119; supports Lincoln's reelection, 268; on increase of Garrison's prestige, 300; favors dissolution of Am. A.S. Society, 304-06; resigns from Society, 305; urges abolitionists to join freedmen's societies, 304; on Andrew Johnson's reconstruction policy, 322; fears consequences of A.J.'s policy, 332-33; fading confidence in A.J., 339; organizes freedmen's aid society, 388

May, Samuel J., 4; urges compensated emancipation, 40; threatened by mob violence, 44; belief in pacifism shaken by war, 52; organizes Syracuse Freedmen's Aid Society, 170, 388; argument against school segregation, 227-28; urges confiscation and reallocation of southern land, 252

Memphis riot of 1866, 358-59

Methodist Freedmen's Aid Society, 388

Michigan, antiabolitionist mobs in, 45; defeat of Negro suffrage in, 420

Middlesex County (Mass.) Anti-Slavery Society, urges equal pay for Negro troops, 215

Milliken's Bend, battle of, and Negro soldiers, 211

Minnesota, Negro suffrage defeated, in 1865, 333-34; in 1867, 382; Negro suffrage adopted in 1868, 424

miscegenation, see racial intermarriage

Mississippi, militia in, 332

mob violence, against abolitionists, 40-45, 85-86

Montgomery Advertiser, 62

Moody, Loring, 379

Morris, Robert, 143

Morton, Oliver P., 361

Morton, Samuel G., 136

Mott, James, 4, 235

Mott, Lucretia, 4

Nation, founding of, abolitionists and, 323-26; on 14th Amendment, 364; sees 14th Amendment as final terms of readmission, 373

National Anti-Slavery Standard, 16, 27, 51, 86, 137, 301-02, 412, 421-22; organ of Am. A.S. Society, 4; critical of all parties in 1860, 12; on Repub. party and Negro suffrage, 26n; opposes concessions to save Union, 29; welcomes secession, 36; expects emancipation to result from war, 49; urges suspension of abolitionist criticism of govt., 55-56; urges emancipation as military and political necessity, 63; wartime increase in prestige of, 82; on emancipation in District of Columbia, 98; on alleged inferiority of Negro, 139; urges free labor experiment on S.C. sea islands, 158-59; on need for continued antislavery work, 161; on assault of 54th Mass. Volunteers on Fort Wagner, 211; opposes streetcar segregation in New York, 232; urges federal law against segregation in transportation, 237; on Lincoln's reconstruction plan, 241; denies schism in abolitionist ranks, 262; on partisanship of abolitionists in 1864, 269; opposes Frémont candidacy in 1864, 273, 278-79; supports Lincoln, 278; denounced by Phillips, 278; on Negro suffrage, 279; change in editorship of, 305; attacks Andrew Johnson, 329; implacably hostile to A.J., 337; denounces A.J.'s race prejudice, 347; on A.J.'s veto of Freedmen's Bureau bill, 347; urges Negro suffrage as condition of reconstruction, 351; criticizes shortcomings of Repub. party, 352-53, 354, 355, 357n; on National Union movement, 358; denounces 14th Amendment, 364; influence of Phillips' editorials in, 368; circulation of, 368n; urges impeachment of A.J., 384; on duty of abolitionists to educate freedmen, 386;

and Jackson bequest dispute, 401; urges Negro suffrage in North as well as South, 420; on Negro suffrage plank in 1868 Repub. platform, 421; on proposed 15th Amendment, 425; continued after 1870 as *The Standard*, 428

National Colored Men's Convention, 234

National Education Association, 392

National Emancipation Association, 80, 93

National Freedmen's Relief Association (New York), organized, 160; sends teachers to freedmen, 170; urges creation of freedmen's bureau, 188-89; dissolution of, 404

National Freedmen's Relief Association (Washington, D.C.), 170, 188, 389

National Reform League, 430

National Union League, 256

National Union movement, abolitionists denounce, 358-60

Nebraska, Negro suffrage in, 374n

Negro, innate inferiority of, most Americans believe in, 134-35; belief challenged by abolitionists, 134-53

Negro soldiers, abolitionists urge enlistment of, 192-94, 196; northern Negroes volunteer services as, 192-93; opposed by Lincoln administration, 193-96; enlistment of, authorized by Congress, 196; enlistment begun, 197ff; recruited by abolitionists, 204-10, 219-20; few Negroes become officers, 202-04, 219n; abolitionist officers of, 197, 203, 205n, 207, 208, 217, 220; prove fighting ability, 211-12; praised by Lincoln, 212; denied equal pay, 212-17; granted equal pay, 217-20

Negro suffrage, principle of, advocated by abolitionists, 24; denial of, in most northern states, 223-24, 237; defeat of, in northern states during the war and Reconstruction, 25-26, 333-34, 377, 382; advocated by abolitionists as a condition of reconstruction, 239-43, 294-99, 301-29, 333-34, 336-39, 342-46, 350-58, 360-63, 365-66, 376, 378; as issue in reconstruction of La., 243-45, 308-10; abolitionists criticize absence of from Wade-Davis bill, 245-46; as issue in election of 1864, 267, 269, 270, 275-77, 279; northern discussion of in 1865, 310-11, 326-27; Andrew Johnson on, 318, 320-21, 334, 336, 341,

346; Republicans and, 329, 333-34; in District of Columbia, 342, 357n, 374n; in Colorado, 342; issue at Southern Loyalist Convention, 360-63; as issue in 1866 elections, 364n; in Nebraska, 374n; in the territories, 374n; in Reconstruction Acts, 375; abolitionists urge North to adopt, 377, 382-83; as issue in election of 1868, 385, 417, 419-23; and Republican platform of 1868, 419-21; adopted in Minnesota and Iowa, 1868, 424. *See also* Fifteenth Amendment; Fourteenth Amendment

New England, center of Garrisonian abolitionism, 4

New England Anti-Slavery Society, annual convention of 1861 canceled, 55; grudging support of Lincoln administration, 102-03; denounces enforcement of fugitive slavery law in District of Columbia, 109; on defeat of confiscation bill, 109; and election of 1864, 268-69, 278; condemns Johnson's reconstruction policy, 321; denounces 14th Amendment, 355; on failure of impeachment, 385; urges agrarian reform in South, 411; on Negro suffrage plank in 1868 Republican platform, 421

Newburyport Herald, on increase of abolitionist influence, 128

New England Educational Commission for the Freedmen, 170, 388

New England Freedmen's Aid Society, 388; sends teachers to freedmen, 170; urges creation of freedmen's bureau, 188-89; instructs Negro soldiers, 206; cultural imperialism of, 393; operates desegregated schools, 399; dissolution of, 404

New England Loyal Publication Society, 123

Newman, Francis W., 294, 296

New Nation, Frémont organ in 1864, 272-74

New Orleans, Negroes of, petition for suffrage, 243-44; riot of 1866, 359-60

New York, state of, equal suffrage in defeated, 25-26, 377; antiabolitionist riots in, 44; school segregation in, opposed by abolitionists, 227-28

New York Anti-Slavery Society, 4, 100-01; urges creation of freedmen's bureau, 179

New York City, Emancipation League

formed in, 80; draft riots in, 231-32; streetcar segregation ended in, 232-33

New York City and County Suffrage Committee of Colored Citizens, 25

New York City Anti-Slavery Society, 14

New York Daily News, on Phillips' influence, 366

New York Evening Post, 281; opposes streetcar segregation in New York, 232

New York Express, 380; on Port Royal experiment, 164-65; on proposal to arm Negroes, 194

New York Herald, 45, 120, 166; on abolitionists, 89; denounces Phillips, 113; on Phillips' confiscation proposals, 252n; reprints Phillips' editorials, 368

New York Journal of Commerce, calls Negro race inferior, 135; on Port Royal experiment, 165; on proposal to arm Negroes, 194

New York Times, on slavery and the war, 56; on the Negro as an issue in the war, 71-72; on abolitionist prestige and influence, 83, 368; on northern acceptance of immediate emancipation, 132; on success of Negro soldier policy, 199; on discussion of Negro question, 327; urges South to ratify 14th Amendment, 372; on abolitionist efforts to obtain land for freedmen, 411-12; on Negro suffrage in the North, 420; on Phillips' support of "conservative" 15th Amendment, 426

New York Tribune, 14, 45, 78, 113, 142, 388, 419; ridicules Radical Abolitionist party, 18-19; supports Negro suffrage in New York, 25; suggests compensated emancipation, 40; says war will not destroy slavery, 56; begins to urge emancipation as war measure, 71; publishes Frémont's emancipation edict, 72; prints Sumner's emancipation speech, 77; on W. Phillips' reception in Washington, 85; on influence of Phillips' speeches, 86; S. H. Gay becomes managing ed. of, 86-87; Gay's influence on Greeley, 87n; advocates emancipation, 86, 95-96; on emancipation petitions, 93-94; on alleged Negro inferiority, 150;

publicizes Port Royal experiment, 172; on enrollment of Negro troops, 194; on success of Negro soldier policy, 199; on impediments to Negro soldier recruitment, 203-04; on courage of Negro soldiers, 211; urges equal pay for Negro troops, 215-16; urges end of streetcar segregation in Washington, 230; in New York, 232; office of, attacked by draft rioters, 231; advocates federal law against segregation in transportation, 237; on Lincoln's plan of reconstruction, 241; supports Chase candidacy in 1864, 263; comes out for Lincoln, 283; on Banks' labor system in La., 290; favors equal suffrage, 310; opposed to execution of rebels, 316; on Johnson's veto of Freedmen's Bureau bill, 348; on Memphis riot, 359; on 14th Amendment, 364-65; on impeachment, 370; supports Chase for Repub. presidential nomination in 1868, 418, 419. *See also* Gay, Sydney Howard; and Greeley, Horace

New York World, 120, 166; opposes equal pay for Negro Soldiers, 214; on Frémont candidacy, 273-74; on Phillips' influence, 368

North American Review, 175, 299n

Norton, Charles Eliot, 299n

Nott, Josiah, 136

Ohio, denies equal rights to Negroes, 24; antiabolitionist mobs in, 45; Negro suffrage defeated in (1867), 382

Opdyke, George, 281

Ord, Gen. E.O.C., 383

Owen, Robert Dale, chairman of A.F. I.C., 182-86; relations with abolitionists, 183; and drafting of 14th Amendment, 353

pacifism, abolitionists support war despite belief in, 52-55

Paducah Herald, on freedmen's education, 395

Park, Mungo, 141

Parker, Joseph, secretary of New Eng. Educational Comm. for the Freedmen, 170; organizes freedmen's schools, 388

Parker, Theodore, 6, 80

Parsons, Theophilus, 326

Pease, Henry R., 387

Pennsylvania, segregation in public transportation abolished in, 236

Pennsylvania Anti-Slavery Society, 4, 235; McKim resigns as secretary of, 161, 287; works to end streetcar segregation in Philadelphia, 233-34; opposes dissolution of Am. A.S. Society, 303; urges impeachment of Johnson, 369

Pennsylvania Freedmen's Relief Association, 127; sends teachers to freedmen, 170; urges creation of freedmen's bureau, 188-89; dissolution of, 404

Pennsylvania Society for Promoting the Abolition of Slavery, assists Negro schools, 388n

petitions, urging emancipation, abolitionists circulate, 93-95, 96-97, 110-11, 125-26

Philadelphia, streetcar segregation in, ended, 233-36

Philadelphia Female Anti-Slavery Society, works to end streetcar segregation in Philadelphia, 234; opposes dissolution of Am. A.S. Soc., 303; urges adoption of 15th Amendment, 376

Philadelphia Port Royal Relief Committee, 160, 166, 169. *See also* Pennsylvania Freedmen's Relief Association

Philadelphia Press, 234; denounces Phillips, 113; prints Garrison's letter supporting Lincoln's reelection, 266-67

Philbrick, Edward S., on success of Port Royal experiment, 167; opposes grants of land or special favors to freedmen, 251-52, 254-55

Phillips, Wendell, 3, 13, 45, 75, 131, 132, 156, 175, 194, 206, 297, 307, 332, 381, 383; on Free Soil party, 9; favors Seward's nomination in 1860, 10; on Lincoln, 12; on Lincoln's election in 1860, 27-28; welcomes secession, 34, 35-36; condones slave insurrections, 35; threatened by mobs, 42-44, 85-86; opposes war, 46; repudiates disunion, supports war for Union, 49-51, 55, 58-59, 99-100; support of Union criticized, 58-60; anticipates emancipation as result of war, 50-51, 59, 98; welcomes Bull Run defeat, 71; growth in prestige and influence of, 82, 89,

90, 127-28, 367-69; triumphant welcome in capital, 85; speaks to millions in 1862, 86; on Lincoln's gradual emancipation message, 96; grudging support of Lincoln administration, 103; denounces Lincoln's conservatism, 109-10, 112-14, 116-17; attacks McClellan, 113; is denounced by northern press, 113; on Greeley's "Prayer of Twenty Millions," 116; on Lincoln and Emancipation Proclamation, 118; on Anna Dickinson, 129; lecture on Toussaint L'Ouverture, 142; on racial amalgamation, 148; on racial differences, 153; on duty of abolitionists to freedmen, 154; criticizes paternalism of freedmen's aid, 168, 397; urges creation of freedmen's bureau, 179; foremost spokesman for racial equality, 221-22; urges Negro suffrage as condition of reconstruction, 239-40, 242-43, 294, 296-99, 310, 311, 319, 321, 323; advocates confiscation and reallocation of southern land, 249, 252 and n, 407, 411; efforts to help freedmen obtain land, 414-15; dispute with Garrison over election of 1864, 260-62, 268-69, 287; criticizes Lincoln, opposes his reelection, 260-62, 266, 268-70, 285; supports Frémont's candidacy, 264-66, 267, 269-71, 274-78, 279-80, 284; denounces *N.A.S. Standard* for supporting Lincoln, 278; expects nomination of McClellan by Democrats, 280; urges Frémont to stay in race, 284; urges abolitionist unity, 286; on Garrison's conservatism, 288, 291; opposes dissolution of Am. A.S. Soc., 301-07; wants Society to work for Negro suffrage, 302-04; elected president of Society, 305; opposes readmission of La., 308-10; opposes execution of rebels, 315-16; early confidence in Andrew Johnson, 317, 318; on Johnson and Negro suffrage, 320; condemns Johnson's reconstruction policy, 321; hopes it is only an experiment, 321-22; and founding of *Nation*, 324-25; launches attack on Johnson, 329; on House roll call, 330-31; denounces Johnson and the Republicans, 335-36, 339-40; and Stearns' interview with Johnson, 336-37; opposes efforts to reconcile Johnson and Congress, 343; denounced as traitor by Johnson, 349, 363; assails 14th Amendment, 354-57, 365-66, 372-73; denounces Republican party, 355-.56; supports party in election of 1866, 357-58; refuses nomination to Congress, 363; *Daily News* on influence of, 366; urges impeachment of Johnson, 369-70, 384; on failure of impeachment, 385; urges massive federal aid to freedmen, 370-72, 373; on Reconstruction Acts, 374-75; refuses to stump the South, 378; clash with Garrison on Jackson bequest, 400-01, 401n; opposes Grant's nomination in 1868, 417-19; on Grant, 422; and Republican party, in election of 1868, 422; urges national Negro suffrage plank in Repub. platform, 419-20; and Congressional passage of 15th Amendment, 426-27; on continuing responsibilities of abolitionists to Negro, 427-29; praise of, for role in winning equal rights for Negroes, 428-29

Pierce, Edward L., 199; supt. of contrabands at Fortress Monroe, 156-58; and Port Royal experiment, 159-60, 164-66; publicizes experiment, 172; protests Hunter's draft of Negro soldiers, 195

Pierpont, John, organizes Union Democratic Party, 13; welcomes secession, 37; president of Washington Lecture Association, 80-81

Pillsbury, Gilbert, 379

Pillsbury, Parker, 4, 16, 161, 287, 297, 332, 379; denounces Republican party, 10, 13; attacked by mob, 45; protests cancellation of abolitionist meetings in 1861, 56; denounces Lincoln administration, 59-60, 100-02; dislikes "military necessity" argument, 91; criticizes Garrisonian support of Union, 103-04; opposes Lincoln in 1864, 268-69; supports Frémont, 265, 273, 275; on Garrison's conservatism, 288, 306; on Negro suffrage, 270, 295, 306; opposes dissolution of Am. A.S. Society, 301, 305-07; becomes ed. of *N.A.S. Standard*, 305; denounces northern race prejudice, 382

Plumb, David, 265, 350

Plumly, B. Rush, denounces Lincoln's modification of Frémont's emancipation edict, 74; recruits Negro troops, 208; supports Chase's presidential ambitions, 262-63; and Banks' labor system in La., 291; and education of freedmen in La., 292-93

Pomeroy, Brick, 423

Pomeroy, Samuel C., and Pomeroy Circular, 263

Pope, Gen. John, 383

Port Hudson, battle of, and Negro soldiers, 211

Port Royal experiment, *see* sea islands, South Carolina

Potter, William J., 178

Powell, Aaron M., 4, 101, 103, 161, 421, 428; protests cancellation of abolitionist meetings in 1861, 56; opposes political activity by abolitionists, 274; urges creation of land commission for freedmen, 412; founds National Reform League, 430

Prescott, Benjamin, 129-30

Principia, 124; organ of Radical Abolitionist party, 5; opposes streetcar segregation in New York, 232; urges Negro suffrage as condition of reconstruction, 242; supports Frémont's presidential candidacy in 1864, 265

Providence Press, on Anna Dickinson, 128-29

Pugh, Sarah, 4

Purvis, Henry, 379

Purvis, Robert, 4, 379; denounces Union, 32n; opposes colonization of freedmen, 155; opposes dissolution of Am. A.S. Soc., 302; turns down commissionership of Freedmen's Bureau, 381

Putnam, Caroline, long service as teacher of freedmen, 387; urges federal aid to southern education, 405

Putnam, Mary, vindicates African civilization, 140-41

Quatrefarges, M. de, 137

Quincy, Edmund, 4, 75, 307; on politics in 1860, 12; on Lincoln's election in 1860, 27; on secession, 29; approves disunion, 33; on Lincoln's modification of Frémont's emancipation edict, 73; on Lincoln's reply to Greeley, 116; on Emancipation Proclamation, 122; on colonization, 156; urges creation of freedmen's bureau, 179; favors dissolution of Am. A.S. Soc., 301,

304; resigns as associate ed. of *N.A.S.
Standard*, 305; at impeachment trial,
384; urges measures to provide freedmen with land, 407

racial discrimination, *see* equal rights;
segregation
racial intermarriage, abolitionists de-
fend, 147-48
Radical Abolitionist party, description
of, in 1860, 5; nominates Gerrit Smith
for president, 13; in election of 1860,
16-20
Radical Democratic party, nominates
Frémont for president in 1864, 269,
275
Rathbun, George, 114-15
Raymond, Henry, 280, 368
Reconstruction, abolitionist theory of,
238-39; abandonment of, by the
North, 430-31. *See also* Fifteenth
Amendment; Fourteenth Amendment; Johnson, Andrew; Lincoln,
Abraham; Louisiana; Negro suffrage
Reconstruction Acts, 374-75, 377, 378,
383
Record of an Obscure Man, 140-41
Redpath, James, 6; chairman of abolition meeting, 42; rebukes British
pacifists, 54; on wartime reconciliation of abolitionist groups, 104; publishes abolitionist books, 127, 128n,
142n; and Negro emigration to Haiti,
155; supports Chase candidacy in
1864, 263; supports Frémont's candidacy, 267; organizes freedmen's
schools in Charleston, 388-89
Reid, Whitelaw, 323
Rejected Stone, The, 63; complimented
by Lincoln, 84-85
Remond, Charles L., recruits Negro soldiers, 205; opposes dissolution of Am.
A.S. Society, 287, 302, 304-05
Republican Campaign Songster, The,
21
Republican party, not an abolitionist
party, 3, 5, 6; controlled by Bird
Club in Mass., 7; repudiates abolitionist label, 13; stands for white
supremacy in 1860, 23-26; on secession, 29, 31; timidity on Negro suffrage issue, 329, 333-34, 364n; timidity criticized by abolitionists, 329,
334-36, 355-58, 360-64, 377, 382-83,

420-22; growing opposition of, to
Andrew Johnson, 339; breaks with
Johnson, 349-50; sees 14th Amendment as final terms of readmission,
364-65, 372-74; Negro suffrage plank
in 1868, 421. See also elections; Johnson, Andrew; Lincoln, Abraham
Republican Pocket Pistol, The, 21
Rhode Island, school segregation in,
ended by abolitionist efforts, 228-29
Right Way, founded, 338; on 14th
Amendment, 354, 365; urges passage
of a 15th Amendment, 354; urges impeachment of Johnson, 369-70; denounces restoration of freedmen's
land to pardoned rebels, 409; ceases
publication, 376n
*Rights and Duties of the United States
Relative to Slavery under the Laws
of War, The*, 67
Roberts, Aaron, 143
Robinson, Marius, 4, 33
Robinson, William S., opposes concessions to save Union, 29-30; on Emancipation Proclamation, 122; skeptical
about Andrew Johnson, 314-15, 316;
opposed to execution of rebels, 315
Rochester Ladies Anti-Slavery Society,
170
Rock, John, 143, 226
Rosecrans, Gen. William, 209

St. Louis Dispatch, on Phillips' influence, 367
Sanborn, Franklin B., 6, 75; member of
Bird Club, 7; welcomes secession, 37;
on emancipation in West Indies,
185n; on denial of equal pay to
Negro soldiers, 217-18; opposes Frémont in 1864, 274; on northern attitude toward Negro suffrage issue,
311; on Andrew Johnson and Negro
suffrage, 320
San Francisco, streetcar segregation
ended in, 233n
Sargent, John, 428
Savannah Republican, 62
Saxton, Gen. Rufus, asst. commissioner
of Freedmen's Bureau for S.C., 191;
recruits 1st S.C. Volunteers, 197; efforts to obtain land for freedmen,
250, 253-54, 257-59; dismissed from
Freedmen's Bureau, 409

Schurz, Carl, 331-32

sea islands, South Carolina, 101; labor and education of freedmen on, 158-60, 162-69, 172-73, 175-77; recruitment of Negro soldiers on, 195-202; efforts to obtain land for freedmen on, 249-51, 253-55, 259

secession, most abolitionists welcome in 1860-61, 33-38. *See also* disunion

segregation, and discrimination against Negroes, in North, abolitionists work to abolish, 222-37, 367; banned in schools of freedmen's aid societies, 399-400. *See also* equal rights

Sewall, Samuel, 7, 239; president of Emancipation League, 79; drafts Negro suffrage bill, 356; efforts to obtain land for freedmen, 414-15

Seward, William H., 10, 11, 20, 27, 124; on Republicans and white supremacy, 24; on slavery and the war, 56; and Emancipation Proclamation, 111; disliked by radicals, 263

Seymour, Horatio, 208, 422

Sharkey, William, and Mississippi militia, 332

Shaw, Francis G., 203; on Hunter's emancipation edict, 107; lobbies for Freedmen's Bureau bill, 189

Shaw, Robert G., 389n; colonel of 54th Mass. Volunteers, 203, 206, 217, 220; killed, 211

Shaw Memorial Institute, Charleston, 389n

Shellabarger, Samuel, 238, 375

Sheridan, Gen. Philip, 380, 381, 418

Sherman, John, on growing emancipation pressure, 111; sees 14th Amendment as final terms of reconstruction, 372-73; and Reconstruction Acts, 374-75

Sherman, Gen. Thomas W., 195

Sherman, Gen. William Tecumseh, 111; land "grant" to freedmen, 257-59, 408

Shurtliff, G. W., 207

Sickles, Gen. Daniel, 381

Slack, Charles W., 309; member of Bird Club, 7; organizes Emancipation lectures, 80; reads Emancipation Proclamation, 121; on support for Negro suffrage in Boston, 310-11; on Johnson's reconstruction policy, 330; turns against Johnson, 339; and southern Republicans, 379

Slaughter, Linda, 173

slavery, abolitionists contend is the root of rebellion, 61-63

Slocum, Gen. Henry W., and Mississippi militia, 332

Smalley, George W., 49, 305

Smith, Gerrit, 5, 6, 78, 95, 194, 211, 235-36; presidential candidate of Radical Abolitionist party in 1856, 16; in 1860, 13, 18-20, 22; on Republican party and abolitionists, 17-18; on Lincoln's opposition to equal rights, 24-25; on Lincoln's election, 26; approves disunion, 37; supports war despite membership in Peace Society, 53; hopes war will abolish slavery, 60; urges emancipation under war power, 66-67; praises Frémont's emancipation edict, 72-73; desires national abolitionist convention, 75; applauded in capital, 84; criticizes Lincoln's conservatism, 94; support of Union criticized, 99; wartime cooperation with Garrisonians, 104; despair at state of nation, 117; on Emancipation Proclamation, 118; on African heritage of Negro, 139-40; on racial intermarriage, 147; denounces northern racial discrimination, 222; aids victims of New York draft riots, 231; aids *Liberator*, 272-73; campaigns for Lincoln in 1864, 284; approves Banks' labor system in La., 293; elected v.p. of Am. A.S. Soc., 305; opposes execution of rebels, 316; on "impartial suffrage," 327-28; urges Negro suffrage as condition of reconstruction, 351; criticizes 14th Amendment and Republican party, 351-358; on New Orleans riot, 359; on National Union convention, 360; urges measures to provide freedmen with land, 407

Smith, James McCune, 60, 293

Smith, Stephen, 143

Social, Civil, and Statistical Association of Colored People, 233-34

Society of Progressive Friends, 110

South Carolina, secession of, 28, 29, 33, 37

Southall, J. C., on Yankee teachers of freedmen, 395

Southern Homestead Act, 409-10

Southern Industrial School and Labor Enterprise, 413

Southern Loyalist Convention, abolitionists and, 360-63

Springfield Republican, 14, 30; predicts war will not destroy slavery, 57-58; on W. Phillips' reception in Washington, 85n; on Negro suffrage in North, 420

Stanton, Edwin M. 69, 188; supports Hunter's emancipation edict, 108; and formation of A.F.I.C., 181-82; authorizes enlistment of Negro soldiers, 197, 202, 208n, 209; and equal pay for Negro troops, 212-13, 214; and land for freedmen, 257-58; interview with Garrison, 271; suspended as sec. of war, 381; dismissed, 384

Stanton, Elizabeth Cady, 4, 280, 286; organizes Women's Loyal National League, 125; and petition campaign of W.L.N.L., 125-26; supports Frémont for president in 1864, 268; refuses to support Lincoln, 285; criticizes Garrison's defense of Banks' labor system in La., 293; opposes dissolution of Am. A.S. Soc., 302; on Andrew Johnson's interview with Negro delegation, 347; opposes 14th Amendment, 373; urges woman suffrage in N.Y., 377

Stanton, Henry B., 6, 78; supports Lincoln in 1860, 22, 23; foresees civil war, 46; anticipates emancipation as result of war, 48

Stearns, Charles, efforts to obtain land for freedmen, 414-16

Stearns, George L., 6, 75, 76; member of Bird Club, 7; supports Lincoln in 1860, 23; welcomes Bull Run defeat, 71; treasurer of Emancipation League, 79; urges Negroes to enlist in army, 204; recruits Negro regiments, 205, 208-10, 219; on denial of equal pay to Negro soldiers, 213; and Frémont's candidacy in 1864, 279-80; and movement to persuade Lincoln and Frémont to withdraw as candidates, 281, 284; opposes dissolution of Am. A.S. Soc., 303; appointed to exec. comm. of Soc., 305; opposes readmission of La., 308-09; early confidence in Andrew Johnson, 316-17; activities on behalf of Negro

suffrage, 319, 322-26, 336-38, 353; personally urges A.J. to support Negro suffrage, 320; organizes Universal and Equal Suffrage Association, 322-23; and the founding of the *Nation*, 323-26; continued confidence in A.J., 337-39; interview with A.J., 336; publishes interview, 336-37; founds *Right Way*, 338; effort to reconcile A.J. and Congress, 343; disillusioned by A.J.'s veto of Freedmen's Bureau bill, 348; on 14th Amendment, 354-55, 356; efforts to obtain land for freedmen, 412-13; death of, 376n, 413

Stebbins, Giles B., 4, 161; and antiabolitionist mobs, 45

Stephens, Alexander, 61

Stevens, Thaddeus, 3, 181, 368, 372; urges emancipation under war power, 95; bill for equal pay to Negro soldiers, 214; reconstruction theory of, 238; favors confiscation and reallocation of southern land, 259, 408, 410; denounced as traitor by Andrew Johnson, 349, 363; and 14th Amendment, 353-54; on Frederick Douglass' presence at Southern Loyalist Convention, 361; and Reconstruction Acts, 374-75

Still, William, campaign against streetcar segregation in Philadelphia, 233-35

Storrs, Richard S., 88

Straight University, founded by A.M.A., 406

suffrage, *see* Negro suffrage

Sumner, Charles, 3, 6, 7, 16, 110, 113, 115, 156, 178, 236, 271, 319, 341, 369, 419; speeches urging emancipation, 76-77, 78; bases emancipation plea on "military necessity," 90-91; on northern military victories, 107, 124; on Lincoln and Emancipation Proclamation, 120-21; and Women's Loyal National League, 125-26; on equality of races, 137; and formation of A.F.I.C., 181-82; and creation of Freedmen's Bureau, 186, 188, 189-90; works for equal pay to Negro troops, 216, 218; presents John Rock to Supreme Court, 226; promotes desegregation in federal govt. and of Washington streetcars, 230; "state suicide" theory of reconstruction, 238-39; bill for Negro suffrage, 246; urges measures to provide land for freedmen, 249, 259, 408, 416; and movement to oust Lincoln as Repub. candidate in 1864, 281; on reconstruction, 308; prevents readmission of La., 310; on Andrew Johnson and Negro suffrage, 318; speech urging Negro suffrage, 323; on "impartial" vs. universal suffrage, 328; on Garrison's support of Andrew Johnson, 330-31n; fails to persuade A.J. to radical viewpoint, 336; and Stearns' interview with A.J., 337; opposes admission of Colorado without Negro suffrage, 342; denounced as traitor by A.J., 349; urges abolitionists to keep up fight for equal rights, 350; opposes 14th Amendment, 352, 372-73; votes for 14th Amendment, 356; introduces equal suffrage enabling act, 356-57; on influence of *N.A.S. Standard*, 368

Swint, Henry, 387

Syracuse Freedmen's Aid Society, 388

Talladega College, founded by A.M.A., 406

Taney, Roger B., 226

Tappan, Lewis, 5, 77, 106, 139; votes for Gerrit Smith in 1860, 19n; and change in editorship of *Independent*, 88; on wartime revolution in abolitionists' status, 132; early confidence in Andrew Johnson, later destroyed, 317n; treasurer of A.M.A., 387

Taylor, Bayard, 139

Tennessee, readmission of, 357

Testimonies Concerning Slavery, 151

Thayer, William W., 338

Thirteenth Amendment, 286, 342; adopted and ratified, 126-27, 305n; abolitionist response, 133; Garrison considers crowning victory of anti-slavery crusade, 299

Thomas, Gen. Lorenzo, 208n, 384

Thompson, George, 26, 300

Thompson, James, 254

Thompson, Joseph, 88

Tilton, Theodore, 4, 78, 266, 309, 367, 381; supports Lincoln in 1860, 14; becomes ed. of *Independent*, 88; on progress of abolitionist cause, 98; denounces enforcement of fugitive slave law in Washington, 109; urges emancipation, 110; on Emancipation Proclamation, 118, 122; on alleged inferiority of Negro, 137-38, 140, 149-50; on racial differences, 145, 147, 153; on racial intermarriage, 147-48; on denial of equal pay to Negro soldiers, 214; sees Civil War as war for racial equality, 221; on Lincoln's plan of reconstruction, 241; opposes reconstruction policy in La., urges Negro suffrage, 244-45; on Sherman's Order no. 15, 258; sympathetic to Chase's presidential hopes in 1864, 263, 266; attends Repub. convention, 271; interview with Lincoln, 272; opposes Frémont candidacy, 275-78, 277n; and movement to oust Lincoln as Republican candidate, 281-82; comes out for Lincoln, 282-83; campaigns for Lincoln, 283-84; on Banks' labor system in La., 290; opposes execution of rebels, 315; urges land for freedmen, 319; urges Negro suffrage as condition of reconstruction, 319, 350-51, 356, 361-63; theory of reconstruction, 319-20; on "impartial suffrage," 327-28; apprehensive about Andrew Johnson's policy, 329-30; hopes for best from A.J., 332; criticizes timidity of Repubs. on Negro suffrage issue, 334, 382-83; speeches opposing A.J.'s policy, 335; on Stearns' interview with A.J., 337; turns against A.J., 339; urges Greeley to break with A.J., 347-48; opposes 14th Amendment, 351, 354, 365; opposes Tennessee's readmission, 357; at Southern Loyalist convention, 361-63; on Republican victory in 1866, 365-66; urges Negro suffrage in North, 377; refuses to stump South, 378; at impeachment trial, 384; supports Chase for Republican nomination in 1868, 417-18; urges national Negro suffrage plank in Repub. platform, 419-20; on platform, 421; on proposed 15th Amendment, 425; on consequences of 15th Amendment, 427. *See also Independent*

Tobey, Samuel, 229

Tod, David, and recruitment of Negro soldiers, 206-07

Tomlinson, Reuben, supt. of freedmen in S.C., 162; on childlikeness of freedmen, 169; supt. of schools of Freedmen's Bureau in S.C., 190; works to provide freedmen with land, 259; on Negro suffrage, 378; in southern politics, 379; st. supt. of education in S.C., 387

Tougaloo College, founded by A.M.A., 406

Toussaint L'Ouverture, 141-42

Towne, Laura, teacher of freedmen in S.C., 162-64, 386-87; on recalcitrance of defeated rebels, 311

Troy Whig, 428-29

Trumbull, Lyman, 95, 355; sponsors Freedmen's Bureau and Civil Rights bills, 341-42, 350; expects Andrew Johnson to sign Freedmen's Bureau bill, 347

Truth, Sojourner, 230-31

Union Democratic party, 13

Union Leagues, abolitionists help form, 123; recruit Negro troops, 207-08; organized in South, 379

Universal and Equal Suffrage Association, 323

Vallandigham, Clement L., 274, 283

Vicksburg, capture of, abolitionist and northern reaction to, 123-24, 240

Wade, Benjamin, 392; and Wade-Davis bill, 245-46; and Wade-Davis Manifesto, 246; and movement to oust Lincoln as Repub. candidate, 281; interviews with Andrew Johnson, 318; favors 14th Amendment as final terms of reconstruction, 373

Wade-Davis bill, 309; abolitionists criticize for failure to include Negro suffrage, 245-46; political consequences of veto of, 280-81

Wade-Davis Manifesto, 246

Walden, J., 80

Walker, Amasa, 71

Walker, Robert J., 91

Walker, William, 217

War Powers of the President, 248

Ware, Charles P., 167, 251

Ware, Harriet, 163, 168-69

Washington City, *see* District of Columbia

Washington Chronicle, 131, 346

Washington Lecture Association, 80-81

Waterston, R. C., 30, 121

Weed, Thurlow, 368

Weld, Angelina Grimke, 229; emancipation petition of, 110-11; on assault of 54th Mass. on Fort Wagner, 211-12; on aftermath of N.Y. draft riots, 231-32

Weld, Theodore, returns to lecture platform during war, 106; and private school desegregation, 229; urges equal justice for freedmen, 242

West Indies, emancipation in, 154-55; abolitionist studies of, 182, 185, 185n

Western Anti-Slavery Society, 4, 16; attacks Repubs. in 1860, 13; denounces racism of Republican party, 24

Western Freedmen's Aid Commission, 171, 387; urges creation of Freedmen's Bureau, 188-89

Weston, Anne Warren, 305

Wheelock, Edwin M., and Banks' labor system in La., 291-92; and education of freedmen in La., 292-93; in Texas politics, 379; st. supt. of education in Texas, 387

Whipple, Charles K., criticizes motives of "emancipationists," 92; urges confiscation and reallocation of southern land, 247-48; on Banks' labor system in La., 290; urges Negro suffrage as condition of reconstruction, 296

Whipple, George, 5, 387

White, Andrew D., 227-28

Whiting, William, on war power of govt. over slavery, 68-69; appointed solicitor of War Dept., 69; on legality of confiscation, 248; and land for freedmen, 256-57

Whittier, John G., 7, 75; on Lincoln's election in 1860, 26; welcomes secession, 37-38; poem urging emancipation, 64-65; on duty of abolitionists to freedmen, 154; and private school desegregation, 229; advises Frémont to withdraw candidacy in 1864, 284, 285n; elected v.p. of Am. A.S. Soc., 305; opposes execution of rebels, 316; poem urging Negro suffrage, 339; influence of, 368-69

Willey, W. T., 405

Wilson, Henry, 6, 7, 126, 271; works for equal pay to Negro troops, 216, 219; bill to prohibit segregation in transportation, 237; opposes dissolution of Am. A.S. Soc., 304; support for admission of Colorado without

equal suffrage denounced by abolitionists, 342; southern tour of, 378; and 15th Amendment, 421; urges abolitionists to continue their work, 427; praises Phillips' role in winning equal rights for Negro, 429
Wilson, James F., 375
Wisconsin, defeat of Negro suffrage in, 333-34
woman suffrage, 377
Women's Loyal National League, organized, 125; emancipation petition of, 125-26; and Frémont's presidential candidacy, 265
Wood, Fernando, 274
Wright, Elizur, 6; member of Bird Club, 7; supports Lincoln in 1860, 22, 23; on slavery and the war, 61; urges arming of Negroes, 194; advocates confiscation and reallocation of southern land, 248-49, 250, 410-11; and Frémont's candidacy in 1864, 279; on New Orleans riot, 359-60; urges impeachment of Johnson, 384-85
Wright, Henry, praises Lincoln's pledge to sustain Emancipation Proclamation, 124; supports Lincoln reelection, 268; campaigns for Lincoln, 284; on race prejudice in Ohio, 382

Yancey, William L., 138-39
Yerrington, J. M. W., 183n, 331-32